I0539136

A House Needs to Breathe...
Or **Does It?**

ALLISON A. BAILES III, PhD

A House Needs to Breathe...
Or *Does It?*

An Introduction to Building Science

©2022 by Allison A. Bailes III, PhD
All rights reserved. No part of this publication may be reproduced or transmitted in any form or by any means, electronic or mechanical, including photocopying, recording, or any other information storage and retrieval system, without the written permission of the publisher.
Internet addresses given in this book were accurate at the time it went to press.
Printed in the United States of America
Published in Hellertown, PA
Cover design by 100 Covers
Interior design and layout by Dina Hall and Jennifer Giandomenico
Cover and part opener photos courtesy of Richard Pedranti Architect
ISBN Hardcover 978-1-958711-12-5
ISBN Paperback 979-8-89420-032-3
Library of Congress Control Number 2022915202
2 4 6 8 10 9 7 5 3 1

Although every effort has been made to ensure this book is free from errors, this publication is sold with the understanding that the author, editors, and publisher, are not responsible for the results of any action taken on the basis of information in this work, nor for any errors or omissions. The author, editors, and publisher expressly disclaim all and any liability to a person, whether a purchaser of this publication or not, in respect of anything and of the consequences of anything done or omitted to be done by any such person in reliance, whether whole or partial, upon the whole or any part of the contents of this publication. If expert advice is required, services of a competent professional person should be sought.
For more information or to place bulk orders,
contact the publisher at Jennifer@BrightCommunications.net.

BrightCommunications.net

To Hazel Green Bailes and Allison Arthur Bailes Sr.
(Mam-maw and Pap-paw)
For their love and patience.
For teaching me how to use tools.
For having a home filled with fascinating stuff,
great fort-building locations, and a million ways
to stimulate my curiosity

Contents

Preface

In 2001, I embarked on my building science career when I bought land in rural Georgia and began the process of building a house. I took a three-day homebuilding class at Southface in Atlanta to kick off my building science education, and I had many questions. One of them was about vapor barriers, because my initial reading on that topic had me confused.

During introductions, the instructor asked us to tell about ourselves and also throw out a question we'd like to get answered. Mine was: Should the vapor barrier go on the inside or the outside of the wall? (The answer is that you don't need a vapor barrier in above-grade walls in our mixed-humid climate zone. See Chapter 9.)

As I spent two years building that house—always thinking I was only two months away from moving in—I kept running into questions like that. You know what I'm talking about. The kind of questions that seem like they should have clear-cut answers. But the more you read or talk to people, the more confused you get. When I finished building the house, I took another class at Southface, this one a weeklong class on home energy ratings. Even that didn't answer all my questions, though.

So, I left my job as a professor and started a business. I offered energy modeling services, home performance assessments, and heating and cooling load calculations. The questions only multiplied. Around every corner, in every attic, and with every client, I ran into more questions. To find the answers, I kept reading and talking to people and I started going to conferences. Gradually I began to make sense of the details and see the big picture. But it wasn't quick. Nor was it easy. It takes time and effort for this stuff to sink in.

After working at Southface and then teaching with my co-worker Mike Barcik for a couple of years, I felt confident enough in my knowledge to start writing about building science in the Energy Vanguard Blog. That was 2010. Holy moly! I had no idea then how much I still needed to learn.

This book is the culmination of my 20 years of learning building science. It's the book I wished I'd had when I started out in 2001. Even at 350-plus pages, though, this book won't answer all your questions. I've covered a lot of ground and gone into some depth. But there's just so much to know. By necessity, I've had to simplify some topics and leave out details and alternatives that would make this book more complete. But the resources and the book's website can help you go deeper.

Is this book for you? Maybe. It's not a book for absolute beginners in building science, although you can still get a lot out of it if you are. And it's not an engineering textbook, although engineers will use it. The kind of person who will get the most from this book is a residential building professional (architect, engineer, home builder, trade contractor, real estate agent, home inspector, etc.), an owner-builder, a do-it-yourselfer, or a motivated homeowner. It will help to have some kind of technical background or aptitude.

Having said that, I've tried to write in plain language and explain terms as they appear. If you run across one that doesn't seem clear from the context, use the index or the appendices to find the definition. I've avoided acronyms, abbreviations, and initials as much as possible. Occasionally, I do use them but have tried to keep the full explanation near to their use. There's also an appendix with a list of a bunch of acronyms, abbreviations, and initials.

Another language issue is that I've used the word "house" throughout the book. Don't automatically assume, however, that the material applies only to single-family detached houses. Most of the information in this book applies to duplexes, townhomes, condominiums, and apartments, too.

My final word here is that you'll get the most benefit from this book by using it as a reference work. More power to you if you can sit down and read it cover-to-cover and feel like you have a good understanding of the material. My 20-year-younger self definitely would have needed to read parts of it over and over for them to sink in properly. The list of resources at the end of the book will provide much more building science education for you. And you also can go to the website for the book for even more information, including online courses and videos as we develop them.

Now let's cut to the BS! Building science, that is.

Part 1
Start at the End

CHAPTER 1
What's the Purpose of a House?

A medical doctor would never tell a smoker, "Oh, don't worry about your lungs being caked with gunk. That's normal." Yet people are sometimes asked to believe the equivalent about their homes. Case in point: I once gave a proposal to a medical doctor to clean up, seal, and condition his vented crawl space in the humid climate of Georgia. The insulation was falling down. The humidity was high. And the air conditioner was rusty and mildewed (Figure 1.1). When I followed up with him later, he told me he didn't think he needed to do anything about it. Why, I asked? His answer was that his air-conditioning contractor told him it was normal.

Cognitive dissonance is the best term to describe what happens to many homeowners. After a while of living in the house, the ugly reality of what they have clashes with the beautiful visions of what they thought they were building or buying. Eventually, trying to believe two contrary things forces a choice. Some homeowners acknowledge the deficiencies of the house. Others continue believing the beautiful visions, repeating what the builder, contractor, or real estate agent told them. "Don't worry. That's normal."

There's a whole lot going on in houses. Trying to understand it all can be overwhelming, but we'll break it down into pieces and take it a step at a time. And our first step is to start at the end. To do so, we need to answer this fundamental question: What do the people who live in a house expect from it? It's not as simple as it was for our ancestors.

Needless to say, we want shelter from the elements and a place to eat, sleep, and raise our families. But we also want more comfort than even our more recent ancestors enjoyed. We want running water and electricity. Let's throw in some entertainment and connectivity to the Internet. Then we want a house that will hold all

> *"There is nothing like staying at home for real comfort."*
> *–Jane Austen*

our stuff and keep it in good condition. And we want all this to be affordable and easy on the planet, right?

Figure 1.1. *A contractor told a homeowner that it's normal for an air conditioner in a crawl space to look this bad. (This is not the doctor's air conditioner, but a similarly decrepit one.)*

More important, though, we want a house that brings us joy. A house should nourish our spirit. In addition to being just a place to raise a family, it should nurture those within, from infants to the elderly. To accomplish both the mundane and the loftier goals, a house shouldn't be a burden on comfort, health, or bank accounts. How much joy can you feel when the air conditioner is so loud you have to turn up the television whenever the unit runs? How nourishing is it to keep finding—and fixing—water spots on the ceiling? How nurturing can a house be when low levels of carbon monoxide make the kids have headaches and nausea every summer?

Figure 1.2. *For a house to bring us joy, it shouldn't be a burden on our comfort, health, or bank account.*

These goals are inextricably tied to building science. Whether your interest in this topic is professional or personal, learning how comfort and health are connected to windows and heating systems, for example, can lead you to designing, building, improving, and living in better houses.

Stewart Brand's Shearing Layers of Change

As we get further into the book, we'll look closely at the two main parts of a house from a building science perspective: the building enclosure and the mechanical systems. But it will help if we first organize a house around what Stewart Brand called "shearing layers of change" in his brilliant book, *How Buildings Learn*.

"The fundamental problem of buildings is that they're always trying to tear themselves apart," Brand wrote. One way to understand that problem is by seeing the building as a set of layers that change at different rates. The inner layers—stuff and space plan—change most quickly. The site and the structure change most slowly. The skin and services are somewhere in between. Figure 1.3 shows the layers, with thicker lines representing longer time scales.

> *"The fundamental problem of buildings is that they're always trying to tear themselves apart."*
> *—Stewart Brand*

The reason they're called "shearing" layers stems from the fundamental problem of buildings. But first, let's talk about scissors. The two blades move parallel to each other in opposite directions, creating a shearing force. When the blades are sharp enough, that shearing force results in cutting a material placed between the blades.[1] Shearing forces don't have to come from two layers moving in opposite directions, though. They can come

1. Although all scissors could be called shears because they create a shearing force, the two are usually distinguished by blade length and angle.

from the layers moving in the same direction at different rates. That's what Figure 1.3 shows for some of the layers. The directions and thicknesses of the layers may be different than shown for different buildings, but the result is the same. The parts change at different rates, and the building tears itself apart.

Now let's take a closer look at the individual layers. First, there is the site. You've got to have a place for the house. That place will have a particular climate based on its general location and may also be subject to microclimates. It will have a particular orientation and interact with infrastructure at the site. The site, naturally, has a large impact on the performance of the house. And yes, even if you have a tiny house on wheels, it will always be interacting with the site, whether it's the lot where you've had it for the past three years or the open road. The site changes slowly.

When you look at a building, you usually see the site and the skin together. Houses that win awards for their architects do an excellent job of integrating site and skin. The skin can be made of just about anything, as long as it can stand up to the local conditions. But the skin changes more quickly than the site.

Beneath the skin is the structure. Sometimes the structure and the skin are the same. Think of a log cabin or an adobe house in the American Southwest. Most North American homes, though, have one set of materials for the skin and another for the structure, like a wood-framed

home with clapboard siding. The structure layer moves slowly, and replacing it usually means you have a new building.

The next layer is the services. The electrical wiring, plumbing pipes, and Internet cables are in this group. This layer is where Brand puts windows because they change at about the same time scale as electrical, plumbing, and communications.

The space plan is how the space inside the house is subdivided–or not. This includes the interior walls separating bedrooms from bathrooms and floor/ceiling structures separating the various levels. This is the second fastest layer.

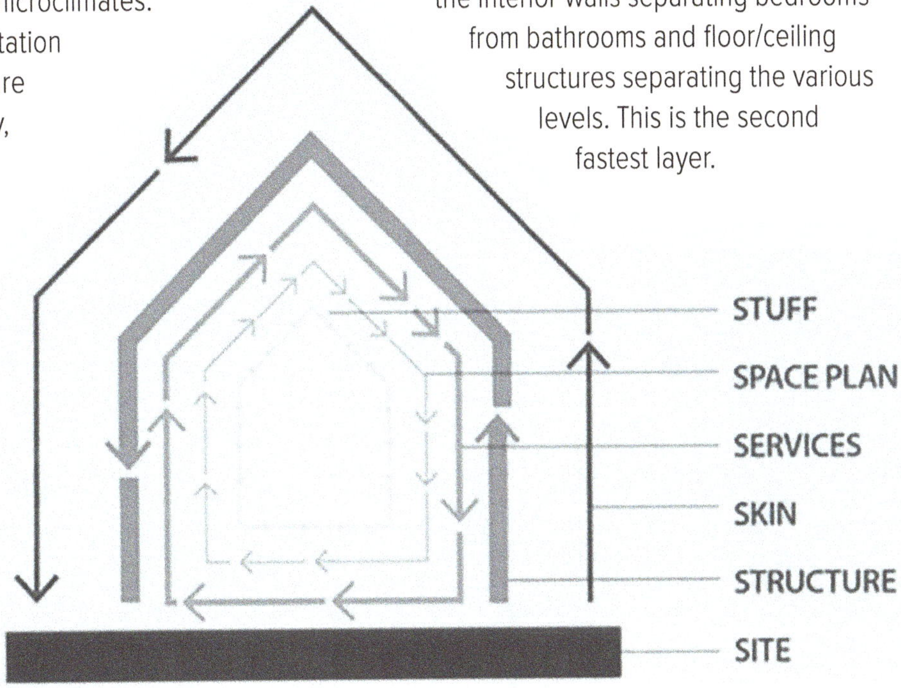

Figure 1.3. *Stewart Brand's shearing layers of change [Adapted from* How Buildings Learn, *by Stewart Brand]*

Finally, there is the stuff, all the things you bring into the house when you move in and that you take with you when you move out. In a time-lapse video of the life of a house, the stuff would be moving so quickly you'd just see a blur.

All of these layers have some bearing on the performance of the house, and we'll be touching on each one in different contexts. In Chapter 11, I'll add a seventh layer. First, though, let's take a look at this most important property of homes called indoor environmental quality.

Indoor Environmental Quality

You probably have heard the term indoor air quality (IAQ), but have you heard of indoor environmental quality (IEQ)? This includes indoor air quality and several other qualities of indoor environments. It's the sum of all the environmental factors that affect the quality of life for the people who spend time in the home. When the IEQ of a house is high, the people who live there will be more satisfied with the house. High IEQ also may raise the value of a home.

In the beginning of this chapter, I listed a number of things people expect from their homes. We can assign several of those to this group called IEQ. Here's a list of six important IEQ factors:

- Indoor air quality (IAQ)
- Thermal comfort
- Light
- Sound
- Vibrations
- Odor

Figure 1.4. *Six components of indoor environmental quality*

Indoor Air Quality (IAQ)

Your indoor air can be filled with a wide variety of pollutants. Some of them originate from the materials used in building the house. Some are drawn in from spaces around your house: the garage, crawl space, outdoor air, or ground. And some come from things you do in the house, like bringing in new furniture or cooking a meal.

The key property of indoor air pollutants is that they're not good for you. Some can make you sick or even kill you in a short time. Carbon monoxide, a colorless, odorless gas, is in that category. Pollutants like radon, another colorless, odorless gas, may give you cancer years after your exposure to them. Many of the indoor air pollutants are respiratory irritants or even toxins,

like the fine particles emitted by cooking. (We'll look at those pollutants in more detail in the next chapter.)

Indoor air pollutants have negative effects on the human body. From coughing and sneezing to creating scar tissue in the lungs to getting into the bloodstream and causing cancer of an organ, these microscopic invaders kick our bodies' self-protection mechanisms into action. Because each human body has a different capacity for fighting disease, some people suffer serious consequences of indoor air pollution, whereas others show no effects. Also, the time scale of some diseases is long enough that you may miss the connection between the pollutant and the illness.

Indoor air quality is just one element of indoor environmental quality, but because of its link to our health, it's a really important one. If you follow the recommendations in this book, you can have excellent indoor air quality.

Thermal Comfort

The term "thermal comfort" automatically makes a person think of temperature, as in the temperature of the air, which you set at the thermostat. But thermal comfort is so much more than that single quantity. If pressed, most people probably would include humidity as another factor that affects their thermal comfort. Air movement, as in cold drafts or cool breezes, are easy to identify, too. But can you name the other factors that affect thermal comfort?

We'll cover those factors in more depth in Chapter 3, but briefly, they are:

1. Metabolic rate
2. Clothing insulation
3. Air temperature
4. Radiant temperature
5. Air speed
6. Humidity

The first two of these factors are related only to the person. The other four factors are mostly designed into the building and are there for a long time. Yes, you can exert some control by turning the air conditioner up or down, using a ceiling fan, or closing the window shades. But the mechanical equipment and operable parts of the building enclosure can do only so much. The air barrier, insulation, windows, vent placement, and other building components are pretty much fixed parts of the comfort experience. And they're often in the house for 20 years or longer.

There's a lot more to being comfortable in a home than most people think.

There's a lot more to being comfortable in a home than most people think. The six layers in Stewart Brand's breakdown of a house all contribute to the thermal comfort felt by the people inside. Orient a house poorly on a site and a family room with big west-facing windows may keep the family away because of overheating in the afternoon. Structure and skin are where the insulation and air barrier are, potentially affecting the last four thermal comfort factors listed above. The services layer includes the heating, air-conditioning, and ventilation systems. The space plan can affect the balance of temperatures and air pressures in different parts of the house. Even the stuff in the house can make the difference between comfort and discomfort. For example, putting your dog's bed right on top of a floor vent can make a significant change in the temperature in a room.

Even understanding those factors, we still haven't directly mentioned the most important part of thermal comfort. Reading the above paragraphs may give you the impression that it's all about the house. The reality, however, is that it's about the human body and the human mind. Here's the definition from the international standard (ASHRAE Standard 55). Thermal comfort is:

> *That condition of mind that expresses satisfaction with the thermal environment and is assessed by subjective evaluation.*

That "condition of mind" is the result of signals to the brain from the many sensors throughout the human body. More on that in Chapter 3.

Odor

The smell of things is an interesting aspect of indoor environmental quality. The first thing to note is that a house won't get high marks for IEQ if it always smells like someone just warmed up leftover fish in the microwave oven. Unpleasant smells are bad for IEQ. If you store pesticides in your garage and that smell is in your house, too, it's an indication that you should change something.

Pleasant smells, however, don't necessarily mean good indoor environmental quality. The mind and the body can be at odds with each other here. We may have come to associate a particular odor with a pleasant experience, yet the chemicals responsible for the odor may have long-term damaging effects on the body. That new car smell, for example, is a mixture of hundreds of different chemicals (volatile organic compounds), some of which can lead to birth defects, liver damage, and cancer. The same can be true for the new house smell.

So, for odors, the core truth is that unpleasant smells are bad for IEQ, and pleasant smells are not a sufficient condition for good IEQ because indoor air quality is also a critical factor. Also, the sense of smell saturates in a short time. You can fill your house with fresh-cut gardenias, but you won't smell them all day long. When you leave and come back, though, you will notice the smell again. A consequence of the fading sense of smell is that you can spend a long time breathing in bad stuff that you might otherwise avoid.

The keys to controlling odors (i.e., controlling pollutants) are largely the same as those for creating good indoor air quality, as we will discuss in Chapter 2.

Sound

As with thermal comfort and odor, sound has both physical and mental components. We can measure the loudness and frequency of sounds, but the effect on indoor environmental quality in a house depends on how the occupants perceive the sounds, too. And the same sound can have different effects in different circumstances. A person using the bathroom may appreciate a noisy bath fan, while a person in the nearby family room watching TV may be annoyed by it.

Two important kinds of sound quality are room acoustics and building acoustics. If a room has unpleasant noises that prevent a person from doing something like reading a book or talking on the phone, the IEQ is lower. Likewise, if noise from another room in the house or from outdoors carries through walls, floors, or ceilings, that's bad for IEQ.

> **Pleasant smells don't necessarily mean good indoor environmental quality.**

We can solve the problem of noise from outdoors by paying attention to air sealing, insulation, and windows. I recall visiting a home that had a noise problem in Seattle back in the 1980s. The owner took me to a window that looked out over Interstate 5, and I was there close to rush hour. Very little traffic noise came through the window. Then he showed me why. The original single-pane window had a storm window . . . and another storm window beyond that. When the homeowner opened the interior window, the noise became a distraction. When he opened the first storm window, the roar of traffic became annoying. Those two extra panes of glass made a dramatic difference.

Even if you don't live right next to a noisy freeway, you can benefit from this principle. Many neighborhoods are afflicted with the noise of lawn mowers, leaf blowers, and the occasional chipper truck when a neighbor is having tree work done.

Again, all six of Brand's layers can have an effect on this IEQ factor.

Light

As with the other factors on this list, the lighting quality in a house can be pleasant or unpleasant. An adequate amount of natural light is important for health and well-being, but you'll still need artificial lights. The key is proper integration so you can use natural light as much as possible and turn on artificial light when you need it for task lighting any time of day and general lighting in darker parts of the home on dark, cloudy days and at night.

It's tempting to put in floor-to-ceiling windows to bring in natural light and take advantage of views, but you have to be careful not to put in too many windows or you may create a host of new problems. Large expanses of windows can result in a lot of glare in the home, which can be irritating. They can create comfort problems because even the best windows transfer a lot more heat than the surrounding walls. That results in lower surface temperatures in winter, which can create drafts. Those cold windows can also condense moisture out of the air. And the excess heat flow through the glass will mean higher energy bills. The key is finding the right balance of window area to get natural light, views, and escape routes with minimal heat transfer.

Vibrations

This is another sensation where small changes in amplitude can turn something from unnoticeable to constant irritant. Houses have motors and pumps that vibrate. Nearby vibrations from outdoors sometimes transmit through the ground and into the house. And the stuff people do in the home can create vibrations.

The main ways to control vibrations are to choose the right equipment, isolate the building from outdoor vibrations, isolate the home's mechanical equipment from the structure, and create a structure that is good at damping out vibrations from indoor activities. A variety of products exist to provide vibration isolation and damping. One of the biggest vibration sources in homes is the blower in a forced-air heating and cooling system. Special fabric isolators can prevent those vibrations from traveling through the duct system.

A more recent source of vibrations has arrived with the growing popularity of mini-split heat pumps. Some installers attach them to an exterior wall to keep them off the ground. The compressor in those units then can transmit vibrations into the walls. Sometimes it's not a problem. Other times it is. It depends on the frequency of vibration and the particular frequencies that the wall resonates at. Vibration isolators can help. Sometimes moving the unit helps.

Figure 1.5. *The outdoor unit of a heat pump or air conditioner attached to the house can transmit vibrations and reduce IEQ.*

Integrating Sustainability with Indoor Environmental Quality

Everyone has different expectations for their homes. Naturally, we all want our house to suit our needs and be a nice place to live. Some people go the extra step to make sure they also have good indoor environmental quality. Others see the house itself as only part of the picture. They're interested in how it fits into its community. Beyond the local community is the global environment, and that's an important issue to many.

Climate change is a huge, global issue, and buildings account for nearly 40 percent of all greenhouse gas emissions in the United States.[2] Most of the emissions are from the energy used in the buildings (operational carbon), but some emissions are from the manufacturing of materials used in buildings, (upfront carbon, also called embodied carbon). So, if you want to lower your carbon footprint, the most important thing you can do is to reduce your energy use. If you're building a new house or remodeling your existing home, you can also look at what you might do to reduce your upfront carbon emissions.

I'm not going deeper on this topic because it's covered in so many other places. But I'll give you just a bit of advice:

- In a more normal world, operational carbon would be more important than upfront carbon.
- Because the climate crisis is accelerating so rapidly, upfront carbon is now a huge issue.
- Upgrading an existing home and keeping the same foundation results in huge carbon savings compared to tearing the whole thing down and rebuilding new.
- Reducing the energy used by homes is more important than adding photovoltaic modules to generate electricity, especially if you can do so with less embodied carbon.
- Reducing carbon emissions can be done without hurting indoor environmental quality.

The good news on that last point is that when you build, remodel, or improve a house the right way, you get energy savings and indoor environmental quality. Yes, some of the IEQ measures may use a little more energy, but a house is a system. Keep your focus on the bigger picture.

Saving Energy

Whether you save energy to reduce your carbon emissions or because you just don't like to waste anything, it is a goal for many people. The positive consequences of reducing energy consumption go beyond those two things, though. When you make your home more efficient, you may be increasing its value. You also make it less expensive to install solar electric modules to provide enough power to cover your consumption in a net zero energy home. And you save money, which helps to pay for the work you do to save energy.

Reducing energy consumption and cutting your energy bills is easy . . . and it doesn't mean being less comfortable. You do it by making

---

2. From Architecture 2030, based on US EIA data. https://architecture2030.org/why-the-building-sector.

the house airtight and well-insulated, putting in good windows, using high-efficiency heating and cooling systems (including distribution!), and just not doing stupid stuff. You don't need the latest smart gizmos. You just need a solid understanding of how energy is used in the house.

As I mentioned above, however, reducing energy consumption should never be done without paying attention to what the consequences might be for the home's indoor environmental quality and building enclosure durability. Airtightness saves energy, but

Reducing energy consumption and cutting your energy bills is easy . . . and it doesn't mean being less comfortable.

you'll need to give some of that back to run your mechanical ventilation system. Indoor environmental quality should always come before energy savings.

Design for People

Robert Bean, RET, PL (Eng), is a retired engineering technology professional who specialized in high-performance building design. He has had a large impact on many professionals in the industry, me among them, through his tireless work on ASHRAE committees, conference presentations, and his website, healthyheating.com. I mention him here because my decision to "start at the end" is largely due to him. Rather than laying out a path to high-performance homes based on programs and best practices,

I'm starting with the end because it's hard to achieve your goals if you don't even know what you're aiming for.

Bean's motto, which he uses every chance he gets, is: "Design for people, and good buildings will follow." That's the approach I'm taking in this book, and it applies whether you're designing and building new homes or improving existing homes. Put the focus on what people need. That is, pay attention to indoor environmental quality first.

Chapter Takeaways

- The parts of a house—from the stuff inside to the site it sits on—can be thought of as a set of layers, as described in Stewart Brand's *How Buildings Learn*. These layers change at different rates, which can result in the decay of the house.
- When you design, build, maintain, and improve a house by focusing on the needs of the people who live in it, you'll achieve superior results.
- Designing for people provides the additional benefits of energy savings and sustainability.

CHAPTER 2

Creating a Healthy Home

A healthy home should be your highest priority. What good is it to be featured in a flashy architectural magazine or to have the lowest energy bills in the city if your house is slowly killing you? You already know that means good indoor air quality (IAQ), but there's more to healthy homes than just what's in the air. The Building Performance Institute provides some guidance in this regard. Their *Healthy Housing Principles Reference Guide* covers what to do to have a healthy home, and they put it in the form of "Keep it . . . " commands, including:

- Keep it dry
- Keep it clean
- Keep it pest-free
- Keep it safe
- Keep it contaminant-free
- Keep it ventilated
- Keep it maintained

Many of these commands impact indoor air quality, and IAQ is arguably the biggest factor.

> *"Poison is in everything, and no thing is without poison. The dosage makes it either a poison or a remedy."*
>
> *–Paracelsus, the father of toxicology*

But if you think through the implications of each one of those seven steps, you'll see that the requirements for a truly healthy home are indeed broader. For example, keeping a home safe means eliminating fall hazards, having smoke alarms, and taking similar precautions. Also, not all contaminants are in the air. The lead found in the paint in older homes is an example.

The *Healthy Housing Principles* list is useful, and I'll come back to some of the commands later in this chapter. First, let's start with indoor air quality and then look at healthy home requirements that stem from other components of the indoor environment.

The Keys to Good Indoor Air Quality

Indoor air quality is sometimes boiled down to a simple statement: Build tight; ventilate right.[3] That dictum is appealing for its simplicity but deceiving for a couple of reasons. First, there's ambiguity within the statement itself. How airtight is tight? And what's the right way to ventilate? The more you know about both airtightness and ventilation, the more you understand how complex that statement really is. The other reason the statement is deceiving is that airtightness and ventilation are only two ingredients in the recipe for good indoor air quality.

Here's a more complete list:
- Airtightness
- Moisture control
- Source control
- Filtration
- Mechanical ventilation
- Pressure balancing

We know these things work. Indoor air quality researchers have proved it in many studies. Unfortunately, the occasional news story comes out to scare people, claiming, for example, that

---

3. Jim White of the Canada Mortgage and Housing Corporation gets credit for that statement. He and Joseph Lstiburek, PhD, PE, were working together on mold, rot, and combustion safety problems when he came up with that general solution that fixed a lot of problems.

energy-efficient homes can cause asthma. (See "Myth: Energy-Efficient Homes Cause Asthma" on page 35.) The problem is not energy efficiency or airtightness or even lack of ventilation. It's a lack of understanding that a house is a system. In fact, airtight, energy-efficient houses can be much more healthful than inefficient, leaky houses.

Airtightness

The first step in achieving a healthy indoor environment is airtightness. An airtight home will be less likely to bring in bad air from a smelly garage, moldy crawl space, dirty attic, or smoke-filled outdoor air. It also will limit the infiltration of humid air, which can find places to accumulate, grow mold, and rot your home. And it makes your ventilation and filtration more effective by not overwhelming those systems with pollutants and humidity.

Figure 2.1. *Air sealing gives you more bang for the buck than just about anything else you can do to a home.*

Airtightness is critical. If you can't control the flow of air into and out of your home, you have little hope of controlling the quality of the indoor air. Yes, outdoor air is often cleaner than indoor air, but random leaks in the building enclosure won't guarantee you'll get the right amount of outdoor air coming in and indoor air going out. And what about those days when the outdoor air is not cleaner than the indoor air? You can always turn off a mechanical ventilation system or filter the air coming in through it—and you should—but random leaks can't be turned off and don't get filtered enough.

One of the most significant indoor air pollutants is fine particles, usually called $PM_{2.5}$, for particulate matter whose size is 2.5 µm (called microns) or smaller. In many homes, the largest source of $PM_{2.5}$ is the outdoor air. Relying on random, unsealed air leaks rather than controlled ventilation makes it worse.

Also, outdoor air isn't the only kind of air that comes in through those leaks. Homes with attached garages usually have higher levels of carbon monoxide in the indoor air than homes without attached garages. Then there are the fumes from gasoline-powered lawn mowers, paint, pesticides, and all the other stuff we keep in our garages. Crawl spaces and unconditioned basements tend to be damp and moldy and sometimes filled with the same kind of stuff kept in garages, and random leaks bring that air into the house as well. Vented attics may have asbestos, dead animals, dust, and other nasties that are best kept out of your indoor air.

A house does **not** need to breathe. It needs to have good indoor air quality so the people can breathe. Your first step in creating good indoor air quality is a robust air barrier that separates the conditioned space containing the indoor air you breathe from pollutants on the other side of your air barrier. We'll discuss airtightness in greater detail in Chapter 9.

A house does NOT need to breathe.

Moisture Control

Excessive moisture in a home can lead to health problems, for you and your home. When parts of a building get wet and stay wet, microbial growth of mold, dust mites, bacteria, and viruses can take off. That in turn puts allergens into the indoor air, setting off respiratory problems with symptoms of coughing, wheezing, sneezing, rhinitis, conjunctivitis, and more. If someone is exposed for just a short time, they may not have any further problems afterward. Prolonged exposure, however, can lead to chronic problems, like asthma.

So, we need our homes to stay dry. We can accomplish that by following these two simple rules:

- Keep water out.
- Use materials and building assemblies that dry easily if they do get wet.

Keeping the house dry means keeping liquid water away from places where it can do damage. Groundwater or rainwater (including snow) that leaks into the home can accumulate in hidden places and grow mold. It also invites moisture-loving insects like termites and carpenter ants, which can do structural damage to your home as well as put allergens into the air.

To control liquid water on the outside of a house, you need good water management details that keep rainwater flowing down and away from the house. Having a sloped roof with gutters that send the water into a yard that slopes away from the house is probably the most important step. Flashing details around windows and doors, the most vulnerable parts of walls, are critical.

Keeping the house dry also means maintaining the relative humidity in the home within the range of about 30 to 60 percent. The classic chart demonstrating the importance of keeping to the middle is from a 1986 paper titled *Indirect Health Effects of Relative Humidity in Indoor Environments* and is shown in Figure 2.2. The authors of that paper recommended the narrower range of 40 to 60 percent relative humidity, but trying to stay above 40 percent can lead to moisture accumulation and mold growth in cold-climate homes with weak building enclosures.

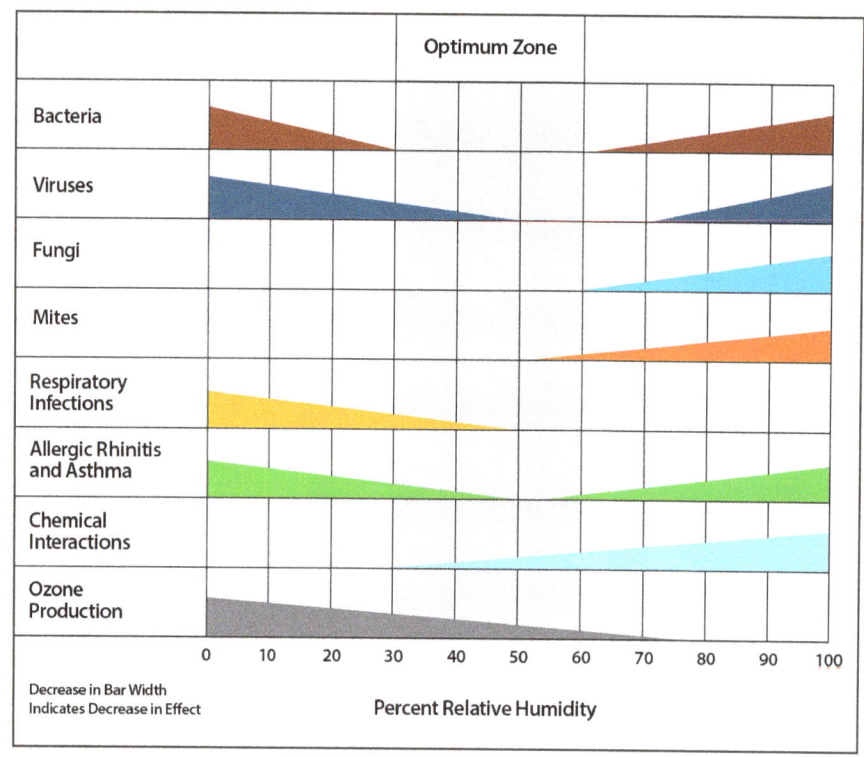

Figure 2.2. *Sterling chart [Adapted from Sterling paper]*

In cold weather, the first step to keeping the indoor relative humidity above 30 percent is by making the house airtight and then adding sufficient outdoor air through mechanical ventilation. As you'll see later, ventilating with cold air dries out a house (Chapter 9), but ventilating with an energy recovery ventilator (ERV) keeps it from drying out too much (Chapter 17). If the humidity is still too low, you may need to add moisture with a humidifier. Or just cook a lot of pasta! Be careful of increasing the indoor humidity beyond what the building enclosure can handle. We'll talk about that more in Chapter 9.

If your humidity goes above 60 percent in cold weather, you might want to see if there's an uncontrolled moisture source that needs attention. If not, it's easy to bring the humidity down in cold weather. Since the maximum amount of water vapor in cold air is lower than in warm air, all you need to do is bring in more cold, outdoor air to mix with your too-humid indoor air. The smaller the home and the higher the occupancy, the more this tactic might be needed. Condensation on windows because of 60 percent or higher relative humidity isn't uncommon in some cold-climate homes, even with double-pane windows that meet building code requirements.

We'll get into the details of how to control liquid water (Chapter 7) and water vapor (Chapter 9) later. For now, just remember the two rules: Keep things dry and let them dry out when they do get wet. Following that guidance will prevent the kind of moisture problems that turn into indoor air quality and health problems.

Source Control

Have you ever gotten new carpet and your house stank for a couple of weeks afterward? Maybe you're old enough to have painted with oil-based paints that made you dizzy. Or perhaps you've lived in a house with someone who smoked indoors. Those are examples of how we can affect the indoor air quality by the things we do and the materials we bring into our homes. A lot of things, like carpet, paint, cigarettes, and household cleaners, release indoor air pollutants.

One of the biggest improvements in indoor air quality over the past three decades has been not allowing people to smoke indoors. It has been banned from most public places, but it's voluntary in homes. Even so, the smoking ban in public buildings has affected how people behave at home, especially since the percent of people who smoke is dwindling. According to the Centers for Disease Control (CDC), only 14 percent of adults in the US were smokers in 2019, whereas three decades earlier, the rate was 30 percent.

Cooking is one of the largest sources of indoor air pollutants. Concentrations of fine particles, nitrogen dioxide, acrolein, and other pollutants increase in your home's air when you cook. The kind of pollutants you get depends on the type of burners you use. Gas cooktops can put a lot more pollutants into the indoor air, so switching to an electric cooktop can clean up your indoor air. An electric induction cooktop is even better than electric resistance burners because it transfers heat to the pan much more efficiently.

Then there's the issue of how you cook. Doing a lot of frying is less healthy from a nutrition standpoint and also because of what goes into the air you breathe. But, hey, we all love food that's been fried, sautéed, or seared, right? So, make sure you run the range hood whenever you do that kind of cooking to remove pollutants from the house right at the source of their creation.

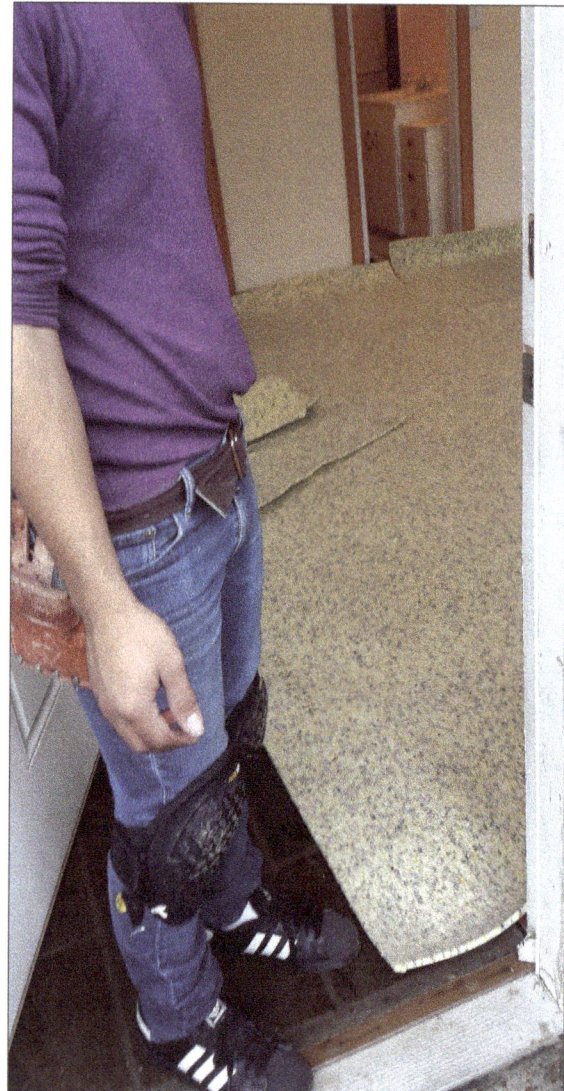

Figure 2.3. *Getting new carpet can load a house with a lot of volatile organic compounds. [Credit: Wonderlane, flickr.com, CC]*

One class of chemicals to look out for is called volatile organic compounds (VOCs). In the past 20 years, there's been a revolution in paint, furniture, and other VOC-emitting materials. It began with low-VOC materials. Now some products even come in zero-VOC lines. That doesn't mean they don't affect the air, though, because they still could contain another class of materials called semi-volatile organic compounds (SVOCs). They include things like polybrominated flame retardants and phthalates, which are part of a class of substances called

endocrine-disrupting chemicals. So, look for low- and zero-VOC as much as possible, but pay attention to the SVOCs, too.

The truth is that unless you have a lot of money and a lot of time, you're not going to be able to eliminate all sources of indoor air pollutants. Sometimes there are just no acceptable alternative products available. That doesn't mean there's nothing you can do, though. ASHRAE's *Indoor Air Quality Guide* lists several actions you can take to minimize the pollutants in your indoor air:

- **VOC barriers.** Drywall over spray foam insulation in the walls is one example, but you can also use a variety of coatings to cover the surfaces of any materials that might emit pollutants.
- **Material conditioning.** Store new materials outside the house for a while before using them, especially if they come in packaging that doesn't allow them to air out.
- **Local exhaust of unavoidable emissions.** This works primarily when the unavoidable emissions come from a specific part of the house.
- **Staged entry of materials.** Don't load the house all at once with a lot of off-gassing materials.
- **Delayed occupancy.** The emissions from new products decay with time, often rapidly, so the longer you wait to move in, the cleaner the air will be when you do.
- **Building flush-out.** Again, because emissions (and material wetness) are highest early on, flushing out the building will get rid of most of those initial pollutants. Pay attention to the humidity levels when flushing out the building with outdoor air, though, especially in humid climates.
- **Higher ventilation rates early on.** Same reason as the previous two items: The emissions are higher at first, so you'll need to do more to get rid of them.

- **Filtration.** Make sure your HVAC system is designed to handle high-efficiency filters. (See Chapter 15 for details.)

Another way to control the sources of indoor air pollutants is to consider how you might change pollutant-generating activities you normally do inside your home. If you're cleaning, painting, or engaging in hobbies that could be done outdoors, in the garage, or somewhere other than inside the house, do them in the other place. You could also do some time-shifting to minimize the impact on indoor air quality by doing the pollutant-generating activity right before you leave the house for a while or when other people who live there are gone. Naturally, you also need to make sure the ventilation and filtration systems are operating.

> *Relying on filters and ventilation instead of controlling the sources of indoor air pollutants is like throwing a bucket of mud in the washer when doing a load of laundry.*

Source control is one of the most important steps you can take to improve your indoor air quality. Relying on filters and ventilation instead of controlling the sources of indoor air pollutants is like throwing a bucket of mud in the washer when doing a load of laundry. With extra cycles, your clothes will eventually get clean, but it'll take more water, detergent, and time.

Filtration

The previous measures give you a great start on achieving good indoor air quality. You'll find, however, that they won't get you all the way to the IAQ promised land. Even with an airtight house, no moisture problems, and all the best materials, you'll still have dust and other small particles in your indoor air. This is where filtration can help.

In terms of indoor air quality, the stuff you really want to filter out of the air is the small particles, especially the ones that are 2.5 microns and smaller in size, the dreaded $PM_{2.5}$.

To do that, you need to up your game and use a high-efficiency filter. The Minimum Efficiency Report Value (MERV) rating system classifies filters based on what percent of particles they remove. A standard one-inch fiberglass filter is typically MERV-2. A high-efficiency filter removes a minimum of 85 percent of the $PM_{2.5}$ from the air and is MERV-13 or higher.

There are good ways and bad ways to use high-efficiency filters, though, and you'll find much more detail on all of that in Chapter 15.

Mechanical Ventilation

Another way to reduce the indoor air pollutant level in the house is to ventilate. Some may think that just means running exhaust fans in the bathroom and the range hood in the kitchen, but there's more to it than that. Those are local ventilation methods, and they definitely need to be part of your overall ventilation strategy. Their purpose is to remove pollutants, odors, and moisture at the source.

The larger-scale ventilation method you need in an airtight home is whole-house ventilation. You can do that with just your bath fans and range hood if you have controllers to operate them at lower rates for longer times (usually

Why You Need a Low-Level Carbon Monoxide Monitor

One of the most common ways people die of carbon monoxide poisoning is by running a gasoline-powered generator or kerosene space heater inside their home after the power goes off. Standard UL-listed carbon monoxide detectors can help in those cases.

It's more common, however, for people to experience levels of carbon monoxide high enough to cause problems but too low to trip the standard CO detectors. Low levels of carbon monoxide can cause fatigue, headaches, chest pain, shortness of breath, and other symptoms. The effects of carbon monoxide are cumulative. If low levels of CO weren't risky, would the literature from UL-listed detectors say things like this:

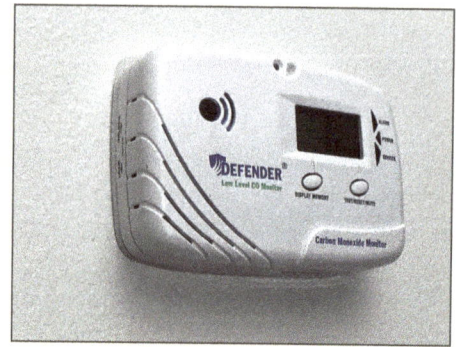

Figure 2.9. The Defender™ low-level carbon monoxide monitor is essential in a house with combustion appliances or an attached garage. [Courtesy of Bill Spohn]

"Pregnant women should be aware that their unborn fetus could be harmed by exposure to carbon monoxide, even when the mother suffers no ill effect herself."

"Is there anyone in the household who is elderly, or who has anemia, heart disease or respiratory problems, emphysema or chronic bronchitis? These individuals are at higher risk for CO poisoning and for health problems from exposure to low levels of carbon monoxide."

According to the UL standard, a CO detector is not supposed to sound an audible alarm unless the CO level in the house is:

> 30 parts per million (ppm) for 30 days
> 70 ppm for 60 minutes
> 150 ppm for 10 minutes

In other words, you could inhale 29 ppm every minute of every day in your house, and your CO detector would never sound an alarm. And as noted above, that can be really bad for people more at risk.

The solution is to keep your regular CO detectors but get a low-level CO monitor in addition. Two models available in North America are made by CO Experts and Defender, and they provide a digital readout of the CO level starting at 5 ppm and audible alarms at 10 ppm or 15 ppm.

continuously). That's called the exhaust-only ventilation strategy. You also can bring outdoor air directly into your forced-air heating and cooling system and have that distributed throughout the house in a supply-only ventilation strategy.

The third type is where you do both—exhaust stale air from the house at the same time you're bringing outdoor air in. That's a balanced ventilation strategy. When you allow heat to move between incoming and outgoing airstreams, you'll use a device called a heat recovery ventilator (HRV). When you allow both heat and moisture to move between the airstreams, you'll use an energy recovery ventilator (ERV).

Ventilation is a big topic, which is why there's a whole chapter on it. We'll look at the three ventilation strategies, how to do them properly, and which one is best for different situations in Chapter 17.

Pressure Balancing

Pressure imbalances among different zones inside a house can lead to indoor air quality problems, dry out the air, make the air too humid, create discomfort, and even become serious safety hazards. Let's say your home has a central heating and air-conditioning system that doesn't pull air directly from each of the bedrooms. When the bedroom doors are closed, the system is pushing air into the bedrooms but not pulling any out. If the return air pathways are insufficient for the amount of air delivered to the bedrooms, the pressure in the rooms will be higher than the pressure in the part of the house where the central return vent is. We say the bedrooms have positive pressure, and the main part of the house is under negative pressure.

Pressure imbalances can develop in other ways, too. Exhaust fans, the clothes dryer, unbalanced duct leakage, and wind all can cause negative pressure in one part of the house while another part is running positive. The areas with positive pressure generally don't result in indoor air quality problems, although they can lead to enclosure durability problems when humid air gets pushed into wall cavities. (See Chapter 8.) Negative pressure certainly can hurt your indoor air quality. If the negative pressure is connected to a garage or a moldy crawl space, for example, it's going to bring pollutants in from those places. Even if it just pulls in air from outdoors, that air could bring pollen, wildfire smoke, and PM$_{2.5}$ with it.

But probably the worst thing negative pressure can do inside your house is to cause backdrafting of a natural draft combustion appliance. Figure 2.4 shows the top of a natural draft water heater. Notice the gap between the conical draft hood and the opening at the top of the water heater. That's where air from the space around the water heater is supposed to be pulled in to aid the draft of exhaust gases as they move up and out of the house.

Figure 2.4. *A natural draft water heater has a gap between the flue carrying exhaust gases out of the house and the flue inside the water heater (arrow). It also has a metal flue.*

Unfortunately, air doesn't always follow the arrows someone draws on the plans. Say the water heater is in the laundry room, near the clothes dryer and maybe a furnace, too. When the dryer, furnace, or both are running, the room likely is under negative pressure. That may cause air to come down the flue instead of going up. As a result, the exhaust gases that were supposed to go up and out of the house are now staying in the house. If those exhaust gases include a lot of carbon monoxide, usually caused by faulty or dirty equipment, that toxic gas stays in the house. If the negative pressure is great enough, flames can come out of the bottom of the water heater, which could start a fire in the house. Figure 2.5 shows a gas water heater with evidence of what may have been flame roll-out.

In short, it's important to pay attention to the pressures in various parts of the house under various operating conditions. What you especially want to know is what happens with the bedroom doors closed and the exhaust fans, air handler, and clothes dryer all operating. That's called a worst-case depressurization test. The idea is to see how negative you can make the pressure in the house and compare that to the limits of negative pressure recommended for the type of combustion appliances in your home. Although it's not a guarantee you'll backdraft a gas water heater, you ought to be worried if your house fails the test.

Figure 2.5. *The discoloration near the opening at the bottom of this gas water heater may be evidence of flame roll-out.*

If you think you might have one, you can look for the openings that bring combustion air into the lower part of the furnace and bring in draft air higher up. Figure 2.6 shows what this looks like on a horizontal natural draft furnace.

Here's the short answer of what to do for these two types of problems. If you don't have any combustion appliances that might backdraft, to avoid pressure imbalances, make sure you have adequate return air pathways for rooms to which you'll supply conditioned air. If you have combustion appliances that might backdraft inside the living space, get rid of them. If your house isn't all-electric, choose sealed combustion, power-vented, or direct-vent appliances.

So, for which combustion appliances do you need to worry about the possibility of backdrafting? That's easy. First is the natural draft water heater. They're still made today and common in a lot of houses. But if you have an old house with a furnace made before 1992, it, too, may be of the natural draft type.

Figure 2.6. *A natural draft gas furnace with intakes for combustion air and draft air.*

Indoor Air Pollutants

The indoor air in your home may be filled with a lot of different pollutants. Here's a partial list of some of the baddies:

- Particulate matter
- Secondhand smoke from cigarettes (SHS)
- Nitrogen dioxide (NO_2)
- Carbon monoxide (CO)
- Ozone (O_3)
- Gas-phase organics (a.k.a. volatile organic compounds [VOCs])
- Mold
- Allergens
- Bioeffluents (including carbon dioxide)
- Radon
- Viruses
- Dust mite carcasses and fecal matter

Of course, if we wanted to include every possible indoor pollutant, we'd have to expand this list quite a bit. VOCs, for example, include a wide range of different chemicals: formaldehyde, benzene, acrolein, and more. And, according to the Centers for Disease Control (CDC), "Tobacco smoke contains more than 7,000 chemicals, including hundreds that are toxic and about 70 that can cause cancer."

Measures for Specific Indoor Air Pollutants

Thinking about improving your indoor air quality in the abstract is all well and good, but what specific steps can you take to improve your home's IAQ? Here's my short list of recommendations:

1. **$PM_{2.5}$.** Always run your kitchen range hood, especially if you have a gas stove or oven. Cook on the back burners, where the hood better captures the pollutants created. Use bath fans whenever you're doing anything that might generate particulate matter. And because the outdoor air is often the largest source of fine particles, make sure to filter the air that comes in through a mechanical ventilation system and use high-efficiency filtration for the indoor air.

2. **Secondhand smoke.** Don't allow smoking in the house. Simple, right?

3. **Mold and moisture.** Address any moisture problems in the house to make sure things stay dry and that they can dry out when they get wet. This is one of the biggest issues in building science because moisture causes a lot of problems. See the section on moisture control earlier in this chapter and Chapter 8, which is all about this topic.

4. **Radon.** Get a radon test. Get your home remediated for radon if the results show too high a radon level. Radon is the second-leading cause of lung cancer.

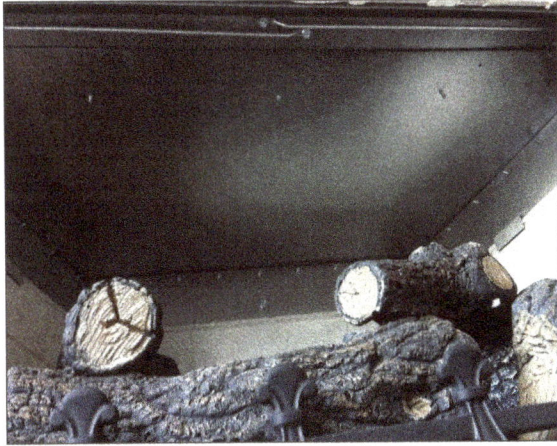

Figure 2.7. *The venting of a gas fireplace is easy to identify by looking up into the fireplace. If there's no hole to carry the exhaust gases away, as is the case here, it's unvented.*

5. Nitrogen dioxide. Never use unvented combustion appliances inside the house. That nice-looking ventless gas log fireplace could be making you sick.

6. Carbon monoxide. Get a low-level CO monitor. The standard UL-rated CO detectors won't give you an alert until the level is dangerously high, like 70 parts per million (ppm) for a couple of hours. But you could have 60 ppm for days on end with no idea that you're slowly being poisoned. Knowledge is power. (See sidebar on page 28.)

7. VOCs and other chemicals. Source control: As much as possible, pay attention to the materials you bring into the home. Don't know enough? Go to Six Classes.org, which offers a lot of great information on chemicals of concern. Then use mechanical ventilation to dilute what you do get.

There's nothing inherently difficult about changing an existing home to improve the indoor air quality or building a new home that will have good IAQ from the beginning. The devil, as always, is in the details.

Now that you know which indoor air pollutants might have the biggest impact on your health, you can craft a strategy to reduce their concentrations from the poison level to something more benign. I don't recommend trying to turn $PM_{2.5}$ or radon into a remedy, though, the way Paracelsus used that word. But I'm not the alchemist he was.

Figure 2.8. *An indoor air quality monitor can give you an idea of how good your IAQ is. The Awair Element© shown here is displaying the carbon dioxide level, but it also monitors temperature, relative humidity, chemicals, and particulate matter.*

Non-IAQ Measures for Healthy Homes

As mentioned at the beginning of this chapter, a healthy home is more than just having good indoor air quality. In that list of seven "Keep it" commands, the four with healthy home requirements that go beyond indoor air quality are the ones about keeping it clean, pest-free, safe, and contaminant-free.

The National Healthy Housing Standard from the National Center for Healthy Housing has a thorough list of requirements for healthy homes, and that would be a good resource for anyone looking for guidance on the broader scope of healthy homes. Some of their requirements overlap with indoor environmental quality factors, such as noise and thermal comfort. Many are related to indoor air quality, of course, but a significant portion of the standard covers items not related to IAQ. Let's take a look at some of this guidance, under the headings of the "Keep it" commands earlier in this chapter.

Keep It Clean

Hygiene can have a big effect on health, especially in the kitchen. Preparing food on surfaces that haven't been cleaned properly can contaminate the food with bacteria or toxic chemicals. Materials that are impervious to water (e.g., laminate or tile instead of wood) make cleaning easier. Keeping it clean also reduces the chances of getting pests.

Keep It Pest-Free

Rodents can carry disease. Roaches, in great enough numbers, can generate allergens

Can't I Just Use an Electronic Air Cleaner?

The COVID-19 pandemic has been a boon for companies in the indoor air quality business. That includes some with products that may not actually improve IAQ and may even make things worse. The problem is that most lay people don't understand how to discern what's good and what's bad. An electronic air cleaner that promises to get rid of 99.99 percent of all bacteria and viruses sounds good, right? But does it really do what they claim?

Here's the indoor air quality technology that we know works:

- Filtration
- Ventilation
- Electrostatic precipitator. This is a device that takes the place of a regular filter in a duct system. It works by putting an electrical charge on particles in the air stream, which makes them easy to remove.
- Ultraviolet germicidal irradiation (UVGI). Just as ultraviolet light can give us skin cancer, it can zap bacteria and viruses with high energy.

For most homes, stick with filtration and ventilation. An electrostatic precipitator is another way to do filtration, but it doesn't have a minimum efficiency report value (MERV) rating. Yes, UVGI works, but it needs to be engineered to a higher degree than usually happens in the residential world. It works great in hospitals, though.

Here's the technology that may or may not help:

- Ionization
- Photocatalytic oxidation
- Ozone generators
- Hydrogen peroxide

This class of device is additive, meaning that it adds something to the air. Those additives then are supposed to react chemically with the bad stuff in your air to clean it up. Some may work, but since there are no standards to judge them by, manufacturers often devise and run their own tests. One thing we can say for sure is that you should avoid any device that puts ozone into your indoor air. Here's what the US EPA has written:

When inhaled, ozone can damage the lungs. Relatively low amounts can cause chest pain, coughing, shortness of breath and throat irritation. Ozone may also worsen chronic respiratory diseases such as asthma and compromise the ability of the body to fight respiratory infections.

that cause dermatitis, asthma, and other problems. They also can carry salmonella. And on the microscopic level, dust mites can trigger reactions in people with allergies and asthma.

Keep It Safe

Falls are one of the biggest sources of injury in homes, so this is a biggie. This category covers much more than falls, though. No one wants to imagine their home on fire, of course, but having smoke alarms, fire extinguishers, and plans for leaving the house in a fire are critical. Keeping it safe also means preventing children from getting

access to medications, toxic chemicals, and swimming pools or hot tubs.

Keep It Contaminant-Free

Lead-based paint and asbestos are two of the concerns here. Children up to 5 years old and pregnant women are most at risk. Lead was banned from paint in 1977, so if your home is newer than that, you probably don't have any lead-based paint. Asbestos has been used in tape on duct systems, insulation for older heating systems, tile flooring, some vermiculite insulation, drywall joint compound, and plaster. If you suspect asbestos is in your home, have it tested. And then there are the various chemicals often kept in and around houses, such as gasoline, antifreeze, and pesticides. Find substitutes (like electric-powered lawn equipment) or keep them secure from children and pets.

Building healthy homes is a big topic, and some of it is beyond the scope of this book. If you want more information, see the list of resources at the end of this book.

Figure 2.10. *Vermiculite attic insulation, the shiny stuff, can contain asbestos.*

Protecting Your Home from the Spread of Infectious Diseases Like COVID-19

Before 2020, probably few people could list even five things they could do to keep themselves from getting a cold or the flu from someone in their house who had it. Stay away. Don't kiss them. Don't drink from their glass or eat from their plate. That may be about it. Oh, how much difference a pandemic can make. In the early months of COVID, we were taught to:

- Sneeze and cough into your elbow.
- Wash your hands.
- Disinfect doorknobs and other often-touched surfaces.
- Avoid touching your face.
- Wear a mask.
- Stay at least six feet away from someone who may be infected.

Those early recommendations turned out not to be the best advice, however. As the pandemic developed, we learned that COVID was airborne. It was rarely spread by droplets going straight from one person to another or onto a surface later touched by another. Instead, tiny aerosols with bits of virus on them were doing most of the spreading. They could float around in the air for hours, whereas droplets would fall quickly and be out of circulation. In a poorly ventilated room, one infected person exhaling viral particles could increase the concentration enough to infect people sitting on the other side of the room.

Keeping droplets to yourself, wearing a mask, and staying away from others were good measures. Also, keeping the concentration of viral or bacterial particles low works to prevent the spread of airborne contagions. For homes, in addition to keeping sick people out or separated, the two best ways to do that are filtration and ventilation.

Filter Out the Small Particles

If you have or are installing a forced air heating and air-conditioning system, upgrade your return air so you can filter out the small particles. ASHRAE recommends a minimum of MERV-13. Be careful, though. This requires enough filter area to prevent air flow problems. Another great way to do this is with a do-it-yourself portable air cleaner that has come to be known as a Corsi-Rosenthal box, named after the two people who came up with the idea.[4] You can make one in about 30 minutes for less than $100. See the resource list at the end of the book for details and the sidebar in Chapter 15.

Ventilate with Outdoor Air

If you know or suspect that someone in your home is sick with an infectious disease that can spread

4. Richard Corsi, PhD, PE, an indoor air quality researcher at the University of California, Davis, and Jim Rosenthal, owner of Tex-Air Filters.

through the air, filtration should be the primary way to clean the air of infectious particles, but you also can use your home ventilation more. Run the bath fans and the kitchen range hood. If you have a whole-house ventilation system, make sure it's on and consider increasing the rate if that's possible. That will remove some of the potentially contaminated aerosols and dilute the rest.

Myth: Energy-Efficient Homes Cause Asthma

A few years ago, a newspaper article claimed that reducing energy use in homes can hurt indoor air quality (IAQ) and worsen the asthma epidemic in particular. And the article went further, claiming that asthma may not be the only thing to fear with energy-efficient homes. A researcher whose report was cited in the article said that poor IAQ also can lead to "lung cancer, chronic obstructive pulmonary disease, airborne respiratory infections, and cardiovascular disease." Should you be worried? Is your energy-efficient house going to kill you?

The subtitle of the article, which called out lack of ventilation, hinted at one part of the real problem. The truth is: More people get sick because of poor indoor air quality in homes that are not energy efficient. Here are a few possible culprits:

- Leaky homes over moldy crawl spaces or basements allow musty air into the house.
- Leaky ducts bring bad air into the house, sometimes by sucking in effluents from that dead possum in the crawl space. (Yes, this really has happened. See Figure 2.11.)
- Moisture problems from inadequate water management details cause mold to grow in walls.
- Unvented space heaters add lots of water vapor to the indoors, causing mold to grow on the walls.

According to a 2007 study on asthma and mold, "Of the 21.8 million people reported to have asthma in the U.S., approximately 4.6 million cases are estimated to be attributable to dampness and mold exposure in the home." In other words, fix the moisture problems.

So, no, the real problem isn't energy efficiency. The real problem is lack of understanding that a house is a system. When you make a house more airtight and energy efficient, you need to consider how that affects other properties of the house, like the indoor air quality.

Figure 2.11. *This disconnected return duct lying next to a dead possum in a crawl space provides an extra dose of nasty air to the living space above.* [Courtesy of E3 Innovate]

Chapter Takeaways

- Indoor air quality is one of the biggest factors in determining whether you have a healthy home.
- Many factors contribute to good indoor air quality, but source control is one of the most important.
- Following the seven "Keep it" commands is a good way to have a healthy home.

CHAPTER 3
Getting Comfortable

Until 2003, I lived in standard American housing. Mostly it was single-family detached homes, but I've also lived in dorm rooms, apartments, and a condominium. Some homes were insulated; others weren't. One of the most uncomfortable places I lived at was an apartment on Capitol Hill in Seattle. Seattle doesn't get very cold, but this apartment had large single-pane windows with metal frames. It was on the end of the building, with a nice view of the Space Needle. I often felt cold there. The other places I've lived had their problems, too, but when that's all you know, you think it's normal.

In 2003, I moved into a house I built in Georgia. The building enclosure was made of structural insulated panels. We had double-pane windows with low-e coatings. All the ducts were inside the conditioned space. Even though I had never seen or done a blower door test before I embarked on this project, I air-sealed the house so well that the airtightness was one-third of what the current Georgia energy code requires in 2021. (For those interested in the number, it was 1.7 air changes per hour at 50 Pascals. See Chapter 8.) That was when I found out how comfortable a house really could be. I was shocked that I could feel warm enough in winter with the thermostat at 65 °F. That was my first real lesson in thermal comfort.

The association for heating, air-conditioning, and ventilation professionals (ASHRAE) defines thermal comfort[5] as, "that condition of mind that expresses satisfaction with the thermal environment and is assessed by subjective evaluation." As indicated, this is a subjective measure because each person answering such questions has to search their mind for the answer. The mind gets its sensory input from the 166,000 sensors spread across the 16 to 22 square feet of skin on the human body. The nervous system then carries those signals to the brain, which interprets the data and decides: Comfortable or uncomfortable?

> **"Design for people. Good buildings will follow."**
> —Robert Bean

Two similar people might have different reactions to the same conditions. Perhaps the conditions are right on the edge of comfort for the two of them, with one falling on the comfortable side and the other uncomfortable. Or maybe one of them has trained their mind to accept a wider range of conditions as comfortable. Or some of the multitudinous sensors are getting different readings because the people are standing in different locations.

> **The mind gets its sensory input from the 166,000 sensors spread across the 16 to 22 square feet of skin on the human body.**

You might be thinking that we have no hope of getting a handle on comfort if it is indeed just a state of mind. I have good news for you. Even though your mind plays a big role, we know a lot about the range of conditions that lead to comfort. Researchers have looked deeply into this topic over the past century. They've put people into hot, cold, or humid rooms, had them wear various levels of clothing, used different levels of air movement over the subjects' bodies, and more. By polling the subjects, they've discovered what sets of conditions make people comfortable. And it's not just the temperature of the air.

The ASHRAE thermal comfort standard has identified six factors that affect comfort, and you can find them later in this chapter. First, let's see if we can strip down this topic to its bare essence.

---

5. ANSI/ASHRAE Standard 55: Thermal Environmental Conditions for Human Occupancy

Naked People Need Building Science

Don't you love to strip down to your socks and jump on the bed? As a kid, you may not get away with it, but you're a grownup now, so who's to stop you? And then, once you've exhausted yourself, you can walk naked to the kitchen to get a glass of water. You can sit down *au naturel* and check your email or post an update on LinkedIn, maybe even write a blog article.

but that's not the operative factor for unclad folks in homes with weak building enclosures. Convection could be one because drafts cause air to move over bare skin, making it feel cool. Even without drafts, though, the disrobed may be cold. The naked truth is that this thing called radiant temperature is to blame. Here's how it works.

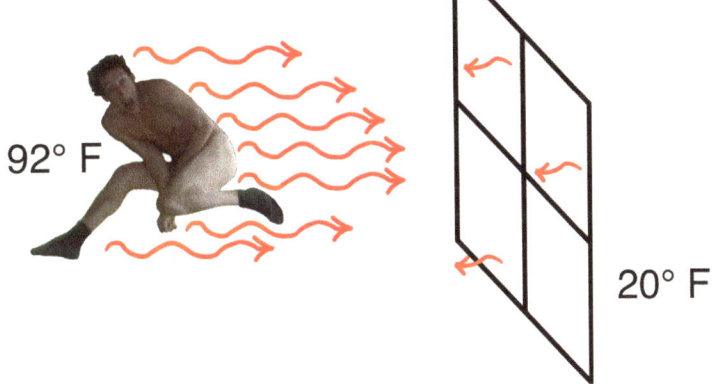

Figure 3.2. *A naked man jumping on a bed on a cold morning radiates more heat to his surroundings than the surroundings radiate back to him. [Credit: Graphic by author using naked man photo by Pixel Addict, flickr.com, CC]*

Figure 3.1. *A naked man jumping on the bed on a chilly morning [Credit: Pixel Addict, flickr.com, CC]*

> **A naked man jumping on the bed in front of the single-pane window is giving off not only more views than he's getting back but also more heat.**

Later, after you've cooled down from your exercise on this cold January day, you start feeling the chill. Hmmmmm. The thermostat says it's 70 °F in the house. So why are you cold?

Building science has the answer to your discomfort. Comfort depends, of course, on internal factors—metabolism, activity, the hot flashes of menopause—but four primary factors from outside your body affect your comfort as well.

The one that gets all the attention is air temperature (technically, dry bulb temperature),

Every object radiates heat. The amount of radiant heat it gives off depends on its temperature (to the 4th power), surface area, and emissivity. (That last item is the property of a material that determines how much radiant heat it will emit. See Chapter 10.) So, a naked man jumping on the bed in front of the single-pane window is giving off not only more views than he's getting back but also more heat. The surface of the window is much colder and gives off far less heat, so the net flow of radiant heat is away from the man in his birthday suit. He's cold!

In your home, the surfaces all around you have a big effect on your comfort, whether you're in the raw or not. You're giving off heat, and so are they. If they're cooler than you, you lose heat to them. If they're warmer (think bonus room in summer), you gain heat from them. If you keep the air temperature at 70 °F in winter, the closer your walls and windows are to that temperature, the more comfortable you'll be.

Obviously, a home with single-pane windows and uninsulated walls will have colder surfaces in winter. On cold days, you feel the chill almost as soon as the heat goes off because those surfaces quickly suck the heat right out of your body. That's why insulation and air sealing are so important. A good building enclosure is critical to comfort, especially for the threadbare. But even when you're dressed, you don't want to lose excess heat to a bad building enclosure.

The takeaway is that you can enjoy comfort in your home without cranking up the heat to 90 °F. You just need to make sure the inner surfaces of your building enclosure have a high enough radiant temperature. You achieve that by having good insulation, reduced thermal bridging (described later in this chapter), and a robust air barrier.

Do Women Like to Be Warmer Than Men?

The battle of the thermostat is a continuing source of news stories, but how real is it? Do women in general prefer warmer temperatures than men do? The short answer to this perennial question is: It's complicated. A lot of research has shown that men and women generally prefer similar thermal conditions, but of course that can't be the end of the story. The endless stream of news stories, cartoons, and even television commercials is testament to the different experiences of men and women.

Research has shown that women lose less heat than men, but they also generate less heat. That mostly evens things out between men's and women's preferences, but there's more to the story. A lot of the research on thermal comfort was done in carefully controlled environments with subjects who are young college students. Things get messier when we try to understand what happens in real buildings with people of all ages.

We know from this chapter that six main factors affect a person's comfort. As you already know from your experience with real buildings, those conditions aren't uniform throughout a building. Some areas are warmer or cooler because of windows, heating and cooling systems, or other factors. A person in one chair might be perfectly comfortable, while another person sitting nearby feels an uncomfortable draft. Or an older person might be bundled up and still cold at a temperature that has others in the room shedding layers and fanning themselves. Age, weight, activity level, and genetics all can play a role in metabolism's effect on comfort.

Clothing is another important differentiator between men and women. Take a look at news programs where a man and a woman are in front of the camera. The man usually wears a button-down shirt, tie, and coat (and probably an undershirt as well), while the woman may be wearing a sleeveless dress. Immediately, we see an imbalance in how men and women address one of the six factors of comfort.

We're adding to the research database on this topic all the time. For now, we can say that the issue is a bit more complicated than the research shows. Buildings aren't as controlled in the real world, and people aren't as uniform.

Figure 3.3. *Yes, women can experience the same temperature differently from men.* [Credit: Jerzy Kociatkiewicz, CC 2.0, flickr.com]

You Need Cooling

When I was a runner, I had direct experience with temperature regulation in the human body. In winter, I was always faced with the choice of how to dress for the conditions I'd encounter during a run. It usually came down to whether I wanted to be uncomfortable at the beginning or at the end of the run. If I put on enough clothing to be okay at the start, I'd be stripping down and figuring out how best to carry the extra layers once I got warmed up. On the other hand, if I wore just enough to be comfortable later in the run, I'd suffer being too cold at first.

As you know from the Robert Bean quote at the beginning of this chapter, building science is really more about people than about buildings. If you don't understand how the human body responds to its environment, you can't understand what we need buildings to do. And that brings us back to my running in the cold experience and this thing called thermoregulation, the process that keeps your core internal temperature stable.

Misconception #1: Winter Cooling

The first misconception about human thermoregulation is that we need to cool off in summer and warm up in winter. The language we use to describe keeping our bodies comfortable in winter isn't accurate. We don't need to warm up. Well, most times we don't anyway. If you fall through the ice and are stuck in a freezing cold pond for a few minutes, your body cools too much, and you really do need to warm up. It's called hypothermia, and it can kill you.

Under normal circumstances, however, our bodies need constant cooling, even in winter. That's because the human body is a lot like an internal combustion engine. It takes in fuel, puts it through chemical transformations, and generates waste heat. It's easy to understand our need for cooling in summer. In winter, though, our bodies still need to cool. It's just that we need to shed less heat than in summer because the environment around us is cooler, providing a kind of hidden cooling.

We regulate the amount of cooling our bodies do in a number of ways. As I mentioned at the

Myth: A Good Heating and Cooling System Is All You Need for a Comfortable House

I recently received an email with the subject line "Discover how air becomes comfort." When I clicked the link, the page I landed on said, "Find the air conditioner that makes your indoor space comfortable." Consider the names of some companies in the heating and air conditioning business: Absolute Comfort, Assured Comfort, ComfortMaker . . . . The problem with that line of thinking is that it's just not true.

As you see in this chapter, comfort isn't just about the air temperature. It's also a result of the radiant temperature, air speed, and humidity in the room. Further, the actual people in the room have varying comfort levels based on their clothing and metabolic rate.

If the statements and company names I led with were more accurate, they'd be something like:
- *Discover how air aids comfort.*
- *Find the air conditioner that makes your indoor space less uncomfortable.*
- *Assisted Comfort*
- *ComfortHelper*

beginning of this section, one method is with clothing (insulation). We add or remove layers to adjust the rate of cooling. Another part of my running example is important, too. The amount of cooling we need changes with activity level. If you're sitting on a chair in a cool room reading a book, you might need a couple of layers plus a sweater. Go out for a run on a chilly day, and you may be OK with shorts, a long-sleeve shirt, and no gloves. Or go jump on the bed for a while, and you'll be stripping down to your socks.

The human body cools primarily through the skin, and scientists have found that a person reading in a chair generates about 350 British Thermal Units (BTU) per hour of heat. Scaling that for the average adult, it's about 18.4 BTU per hour per square foot of skin area. If you've ever used the cardio machines at the gym, you may have noticed that they show your output in calories, watts, and mets. Well, now you know what a met is: It's 18.4 BTU/hr/sf.

Misconception #2: Psychology

The other misconception about human thermoregulation and comfort is that it's an objective factor that can be calculated. Certainly, we can quantify heat loss from the human body. Just take a look at Chapter 9 in the ASHRAE *Handbook of Fundamentals*. You'll see equations for the energy balance between the body and its environment, heat storage, sensible heat loss from the skin, evaporative heat loss from the skin, respiratory losses, and more. Oh, we know how to quantify this stuff!

But don't forget ASHRAE's definition of thermal comfort: "that condition of mind that expresses satisfaction with the thermal environment and is assessed by subjective evaluation." As I've already pointed out, thermal comfort depends on each person's own judgment, based on sensory data from all over the body and interpretation by the brain.

Comfort is about more than the type of insulation in your walls and the type of heating and air-conditioning system you have. It's about the human body and the mind. A good building enclosure and a well-designed mechanical system can go a long way to helping you be comfortable, but in the end, comfort happens within a range of conditions.

The Factors Affecting Comfort

ASHRAE's thermal comfort standard lists six factors that affect our comfort. They are:

1. Metabolic rate
2. Clothing insulation
3. Air temperature
4. Radiant temperature
5. Air speed
6. Humidity

The first two are personal factors. Metabolic rate is a measure of your energy use. Recall that your body is a heat engine, turning fuel into mechanical energy and heat. It's similar to a power plant turning fuel (e.g., coal or gas) into heat that spins a turbine that generates electricity. Not all the heat can turn into usable energy, however, so

a human body and a power plant both must deal with that excess heat somehow. Remember, you need cooling! And the higher your metabolic rate, the more cooling you need. Your metabolic rate depends on the nature of your particular body—everyone is different—and on your activity level.

Clothing, of course, insulates the body from its surroundings. In winter, that's a good thing. In summer, it can slow down the body's cooling process. We all know that when you're too warm, you can take off excess clothing to cool off. No mystery here.

The last four are environmental factors. Air temperature gets all the attention, but as we know from the naked man jumping on the bed, radiant temperature can be just as important. The radiant temperature comes from the temperature of all the objects surrounding you in a room. A high radiant temperature on a summer day can negate a nice, cool air temperature, making you uncomfortable even though the thermostat says you should feel good.

Moving air can be good or bad. When you come into a house after playing basketball on a warm day, standing in front of a fan or air conditioner vent feels great. Once you've cooled off, though, moving air may feel uncomfortable, even on a summer day. And in winter, air moving across your skin is almost never a good thing.

Humidity primarily affects comfort when air and radiant temperatures are higher. One of the ways the human body gets rid of excess heat is through evaporative cooling. You know: Sweating. Perspiring. Glistening. Because evaporation can remove a lot of heat, sweating is an excellent cooling mechanism. But if the humidity in the room is too high, sweat doesn't evaporate completely. Thus, your body doesn't cool as well in warm, humid conditions.

Looking at Figure 3.4, you can see how complex the study of comfort is. The body has 166,000 sensors spread across the skin area. A group of people in a room might have different metabolism, activity levels, and insulation values in their clothing. Then there are all the different thermal impacts coming at them from the environment. They feel the temperature, movement, and humidity of the air. They feel the radiant heat exchange with all the objects within sight of their body. And because each person occupies a different part of the room, they each feel the thermal impacts differently. One might feel more draft. Another is standing closer to a cold, single-pane window. It seems like a crap shoot, right?

There's good news here, though. Yes, the variations can be enormous, but we have a good idea of how to minimize discomfort from all the research that's been done. The first thing to understand is that for each person, comfort occurs in a range of conditions based on those six factors. We also know that most of what we do to make homes more energy efficient also makes them more comfortable. But you do have to pay attention to some comfort-specific details that go beyond energy efficiency.

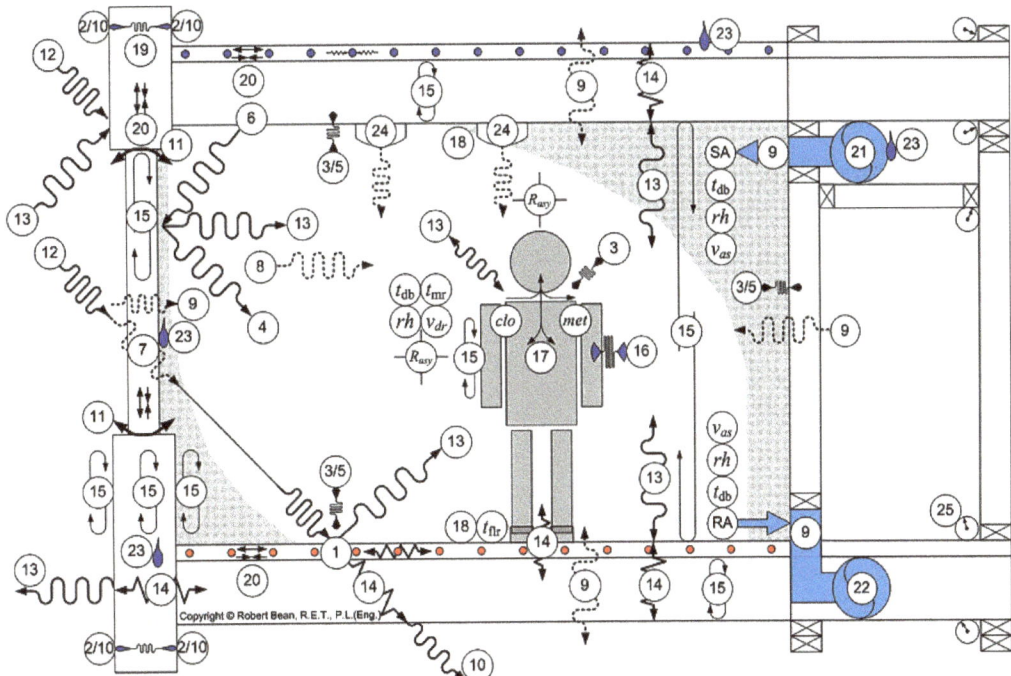

Figure 3.4. *Thermal interactions between a person and their environment [Courtesy of Robert Bean]*

10 Ways to Make Your Home Comfortable

Now that we understand that comfort is more than just the air temperature, we can lay out some prescriptions for achieving thermal comfort in homes. In designing, building, operating, or improving a home, we have the power to change the four general factors (air temperature, radiant temperature, air speed, and humidity). The two personal factors (metabolic rate and clothing) are mostly outside the purview of building professionals. I say mostly because we do take them into account sometimes. For example, we know people who are exercising will have a higher metabolic rate and need more cooling and add more humidity to the air, so it's good to account for that in home exercise rooms.

Now, let's look at some ways we can enhance thermal comfort by considering the four general factors. Since we're early in the book, you may need to come back to this section after learning the building science behind some of the issues presented here.

1. Comfort Begins with the Building Enclosure

When designing a new home, you have complete control over size, shape, orientation, and other factors relevant to comfort. Many people think comfort is solely the product of the heating and cooling system, but the architect actually has a huge influence on comfort. A complex design with a lot of corners, chopped-up attics, and large west-facing windows may be so difficult to heat and cool that some rooms are unusable a good part of the time. Yes, you can put in a mechanical system that will put the air temperature in the sweet spot for comfort. But if the radiant temperature is off, the humidity too high, or drafts are blowing at your neck, you're not going to be comfortable. So, start with the building enclosure to achieve true thermal comfort.

2. Use Passive Strategies First

Using passive strategies first is almost another way of saying the same thing as starting with the enclosure. The comfort that comes from a properly insulated, airtight enclosure with well-thought-out windows has no operational costs associated with it. You pay for the comfort provided by mechanical systems (heating, cooling, dehumidification, humidification, fans) on your energy bills. Also, as mentioned already, mechanical systems can't always overcome problems baked into your building enclosure.

3. Make It Airtight

A house does not need to breathe! Air that leaks in from outside can make it harder to have a comfortable air temperature. It can get into your floors, walls, and ceilings, taking the radiant temperature out of the comfort zone. It can create drafts. And it can raise the indoor humidity to uncomfortable levels. Airtightness solves a lot of problems, as you'll see throughout this book.

4. Insulate Fully

Radiant temperature doesn't get nearly as much attention as it deserves, but it has a huge effect on comfort. It's not solely an insulation problem—airtightness and windows also affect it—but insulation is usually the biggest factor in floors, walls, and ceilings being too cold or too hot. The more thermal resistance you put in the insulated parts of the building—including windows—the more likely it is that the radiant temperature will be in the thermal comfort range.

5. Reduce Thermal Bridging

Insulation is great, and the more, the better. Houses, though, usually have insulation that's interrupted by wood. Those pieces of wood have much lower thermal resistance than insulation does. Thus, they act as thermal bridges, places in the building enclosure that transfer heat more easily between inside and outside. One way to reduce the effect of these thermal bridges is to reduce the amount of wood. Yes, you can do that. The first way to reduce the amount of wood in a new home is to design a simpler house. The more complex the house, the more wood it will use in corners, window and door openings, and transitions, such as where a roof meets a wall. Designing a simpler house with fewer of those tricky areas will reduce thermal bridging. Even simpler houses use more wood than they really need. You can tackle that by using advanced framing—methods that allow you to reduce the amount of wood and increase the amount of insulation—or by covering the outside of the house with continuous insulation. (See Chapters 10 and 11.) Whatever way you do it, less thermal bridging means better radiant temperatures indoors.

6. Put the Right Amount of Window Area in the Right Places

When I was a window cleaner in Seattle—a place not known for houses that need air conditioning—I went into some homes facing west to enjoy the beautiful views of Puget Sound. Guess what? They can get too hot on sunny afternoons. I'm not saying houses shouldn't take advantage of the views. But you've got to think carefully about how much window area you really need to do that. Floor-to-ceiling windows bring in or lose a lot of heat, and no one is going to lie on the floor admiring the view. And how high do those windows need to go? A lot of houses with big windows would have the same beautiful views with significantly less window area. Those rooms will be more comfortable, too.

You can characterize the amount of window area in a house by looking at the ratio of the window area to the exterior wall area. An important factor in determining what your window-to-wall ratio should be is the orientation. Ideally, windows that face west should have the lowest ratios, especially in climates that require cooling. West-facing windows add to an already high afternoon cooling load. East-facing windows are almost as bad, but they have the advantage of bringing in extra solar gain in the morning when the outdoor temperatures are lower. South-facing windows are easily shaded with overhangs, so they don't have to add as much to the cooling load. North-facing windows are great for bringing in daylight without adding solar gain. Energy modeling can help you make decisions about window area, but it's best to keep the east and west window-to-wall ratios at about 10 percent or less. You can go up to about 20 percent with south windows and up to about 40 percent on the north side.

Keep in mind the overall effect of the windows, too. Windows have lower R-values than walls, so the more window area you have, the more heat you lose in winter and gain in summer. A higher window-to-wall ratio makes it harder to maintain a good radiant temperature inside the house.

7. Use Exterior Window Shading

In addition to paying attention to house orientation and the window area, be sure to take advantage of shading. And here's a little secret: Exterior shading is always better than interior shading because it keeps the heat out of the house. Once the heat comes through the glass, it's inside the house. Interior shading can reflect some heat back outside or keep it between the shades and the window, but it can't keep it outside of the house.

Especially on south-facing windows, overhangs are a great way to provide exterior shading. They don't need to extend out very far to keep the heat out in summer. Sunny days in spring or fall can be more difficult, but they're not as bad as afternoon sun hitting west-facing windows. To shade the windows on the east or west sides, you need a large overhang, perhaps 10 or 20 feet deep, or a nice shade tree. If you're designing a porch or carport for the house, consider putting it on the east or west sides where it can provide that shading. An inexpensive option for exterior shading is to use solar screens. They're like insect screens but are designed to reduce the amount of sunlight that gets to the window. Unfortunately, they cut down on visible light and views as well. Permanently mounted exterior structures can do the job, too.

8. Don't Blow Air on People

Only after dealing with the building enclosure and the related passive comfort strategies is it time to consider the mechanical systems. One of the first comfort strategies to use in that realm is not to blow conditioned air directly on people. To achieve that, you have to design the supply vents properly. The first step is locating them where they won't blow air on people. Then choose the right type of supply vent. In a bedroom, for example, find out where the bed is (or will be) and then put in the right type of supply vent to ensure that the conditioned air blows away from the bed.

One reason not to blow air on people is that the air they feel probably won't be at room temperature. It will have mixed with some air by the time it reaches them, so it won't be as warm or cool as the air coming out right at the vent. That air may still be warmer or cooler than is comfortable, though. And if the heat comes from a heat pump, it may occasionally blow cool air during the defrost cycle, when it goes into air-conditioning mode to melt frost accumulating on the outdoor unit. The other reason is that moving air isn't comfortable in the cooler parts of the year. No one likes a draft when they're trying to keep warm.

9. Use Smaller Equipment Blowing Less Air

A high percentage of heating and cooling systems are oversized. (See Chapter 12 for a full discussion of heating and cooling loads.) It's good to have some excess capacity for those times when the weather is really hot or really cold. The problem is that most systems are grossly oversized for the design load. To make it even worse, the actual heating or cooling load on a house at any given time is almost always below the design load. The result is heating systems and air conditioners that come on for a short time and then go off. (I'm assuming fixed capacity equipment, which is what's in most houses.) That short cycling will blast the house with conditioned air and then go off, causing more noticeable changes in the indoor temperature.

The solution is to install smaller equipment, which will stay on longer and blow air into the house at a lower rate. That in turn creates more uniform indoor conditions, with better mixing of the air and also dilution of pollutants. The lower air flow rate also makes it less likely that you'll feel uncomfortable drafts. Another way to achieve the same goal is to use variable capacity heating and cooling equipment. When the load is smaller, the equipment runs at a lower rate, again providing more uniform conditions and better comfort.

10. Heat with Lower-Temperature Air

Another way to even out indoor temperature swings in winter is to use air that's heated to a more moderate temperature. The air temperature in most homes in winter is somewhere around 70 °F. On the one hand, when that air goes through a furnace, its temperature usually rises 40 °F to 70 °F. That would put 110 °F to 140 °F air coming out of the vents. It's usually closer to the middle of that range, though; say 125 °F. On the other hand, a heat pump heats the air to about 95 °F, about 30 °F lower than furnace air. Lower temperature air means more air flow to deliver the same amount of heat, and that helps even out the temperatures in a room, much like the lower air flow rates of right-sized equipment.

Chapter Takeaways

- Comfort results from the thermal signals received by the 166,000 sensors in our skin and then sent to the brain.
- ASHRAE has identified six factors that determine thermal comfort. Two of them are personal, and four are environmental.
- This chapter lists 10 ways to make a home more comfortable.

CHAPTER 4

Energy Use in the Home

What got me started down the path I'm on is energy conservation. I was in sixth grade during the oil embargo in 1973 and a senior in high school during the Iranian revolution in 1979. Those global events resulted in energy prices skyrocketing and gas stations running out of fuel. Now that we're facing the huge challenge of an overheating global climate because of our centuries-long history of burning fossil fuels, we have another reason to save energy.

In 2020, residential buildings accounted for 12 percent of all the energy consumed in the United States and 32 percent of the electricity generated based on the energy consumption chart from Lawrence Livermore National Laboratory (Figure 4.1). The sum of residential and commercial building energy use was 22 percent of our total energy use and 57 percent of our electricity use.

The good news is that the shocks we received from the 1973 and 1979 energy crises changed our energy trajectory. The total amount of energy used in all US residential and commercial buildings hasn't changed much in 40 years. In 1978, this sector consumed 18.6 quadrillion BTUs, and in 2020 the number was 20.2 quads. (A quad equals a quadrillion BTUs.) Because the number of buildings is much greater now, that represents a significant improvement in energy efficiency.

> **"Energy consumption is the most tangible way to understand the importance of efficiency."**
> —Dejah Leger

The US Census shows an increase of about 52 million housing units from 1980 to 2018, a 60 percent jump. The average energy use per housing unit went from 114 million BTU in 1980 to 77 million BTU in 2015. That's a 32 percent drop in energy use per household. And it didn't happen because people changed the thermostat and lived with less comfort. It happened because we made our homes much more efficient.

Another interesting statistic in the 1978 to 2020 comparison is the percentage of residential and commercial building energy provided by electricity. It was only 20 percent in 1978 and grew to 46 percent by 2020. There's a lot of talk now about going all-electric with buildings in an effort to decarbonize our energy use, and we'll get into that later in this chapter.

How much better can we do? Does fuel type matter? Should you install photovoltaic modules to generate your own electricity? Let's take a look.

What Is Energy?

"All truths are easy to understand once they are discovered," Galileo is reported to have said. This thing called energy may seem easy to grasp now, but it took centuries for physicists to wrap their minds around such an abstract concept. The malleability of energy made it especially difficult because energy can show itself as motion (kinetic energy) or in stillness (potential energy). Through continual probing, scientists discovered that motion, position, light, electricity, magnetism,

The equivalence of the different forms of energy and the knowledge of how to convert among them is one of the most important scientific and technological discoveries in history.

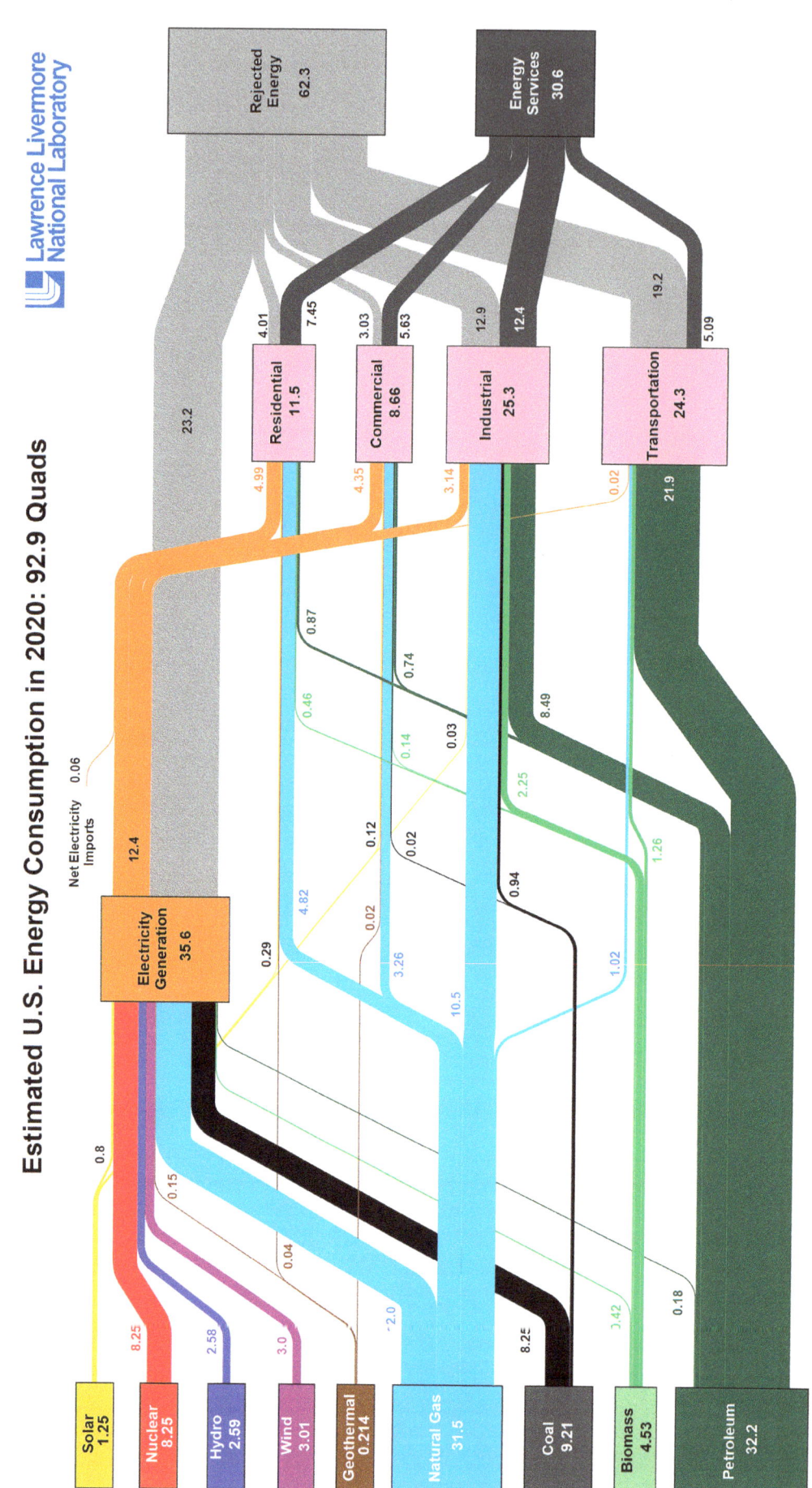

Estimated U.S. Energy Consumption in 2020: 92.9 Quads

Lawrence Livermore National Laboratory

Figure 4.1. *US energy consumption by source and end use for the year 2020 [Chart from Lawrence Livermore National Laboratory]*

heat, and more were all tied together by the same thing: energy. The equivalence of the different forms of energy and the knowledge of how to convert among them is one of the most important scientific and technological discoveries in history.

In this book, we'll limit our discussion to a narrow subset of the whole field of energy. We'll cover electricity, of course, because it constitutes a great portion of the energy delivered to—and now, produced at—our homes. The chemical energy stored in natural gas, propane, fuel oil, and wood is also an important form of energy for houses. But the form of energy we'll spend the most time on in this book is heat. As Henry Gifford, the author of *Buildings Don't Lie*, wrote, "Heat is the ultimate form of energy because all energy is either heat now or on its way to being transformed into heat."

So, what exactly is energy? Most physics books define it simply as the ability to do work or make a physical change in something. For example, electrical energy comes into your home and runs through the high-resistance filaments in your toaster, drying out your bread and turning it a nice golden brown. Another example is a water heater in which natural gas combines with oxygen in the combustion process, resulting in heat that changes the temperature of the water. You get the idea.

All these different forms of energy exist, and they can change from one to another. Heat is often involved in the conversion because we either start with it or are looking to make it. Even if we're trying to convert the mechanical energy of the wind to electrical energy, some of the mechanical energy becomes heat. One hundred percent efficiency is difficult to achieve. What we do know is that whatever amount of energy we start with is exactly equal to the amount of energy we get after the conversion.

Indeed, that's such a fundamental concept that it's one of the most important laws of nature: the **law of conservation of energy**. It's so important, in fact, that physicists explained an apparent violation of this law by postulating the existence of dark energy, which comes into play at the largest scales of the universe. Dark energy, supernovae, and the Big

Bang theory (the scientific theory, not the show!) are fascinating topics, but let me point out that on the smaller scale of what happens here on Earth, the law of conservation of energy has never been disproven through countless experiments. That law applied to energy conversion processes involving heat is called the **first law of thermodynamics**.

Energy is essential to the way we live in the modern world. We use far more energy in our daily lives than our ancestors did because we have far more energy available. Because of the abundance of energy, our homes have central heating and air conditioning, hot water, refrigeration for our food, and outlets in every room so we can plug in the myriad devices we use every day.

The history of how we got here is fascinating. In 1890, the typical house didn't have indoor plumbing, electricity, or natural gas. Nor did it have the kind of comfort we enjoy today. Along with mechanical heating in the early 20th century, homes started getting insulation. It had been used on a small scale before but came onto the scene in a bigger way in the 1920s. That change led to moisture problems that fueled the development of building science in North America. (See the story of peeling paint in Chapter 6.) As it turns out, the heat we wasted through uninsulated walls helped keep things dry, so saving energy required us to get smarter about building enclosures.

And then came the two big shocks to the global oil market in the 1970s, which forced us to get serious about insulation, airtightness, and the other aspects of high-performance homes. Since the 1970s, we've made great progress in our understanding and application of building science and energy conservation. Because of the tremendous amount of relatively cheap energy we have access to in the modern era, we've enjoyed much easier and more comfortable lives than our ancestors experienced. But the energy field is changing rapidly, as are the global economy and the environment. Today, the average house uses far more energy than it needs to and is less comfortable and healthy than it can be. We've got work to do. But first, we need to understand energy use in houses.

Energy Use in the Home **47**

How Is Energy Measured?

The first thing to understand is that energy is energy is energy. We can state the amount of energy in the same unit, no matter what type of energy we're talking about, such as electricity, propane, or an anvil falling from the sky. If we want to compare the electrical energy used by a heat pump to the chemical energy used by a gas furnace, we can find the appropriate conversion factor to convert them. Yes, you can talk about therms of electricity or kilowatt-hours of natural gas. When you want to do an accurate comparison—and we'll do some in this chapter—you *must* have the same units for all energy sources.

Unfortunately, the way we measure energy is a mess. Homes use different types of energy, each with their own set of units (e.g., kilowatt-hours for electricity and therms for natural gas). Sometimes, different utility companies use different units for the same type of energy (e.g., therms or million British Thermal Units, MMBTU, for natural gas). Then we have cases where the unit used is not even a unit of energy (e.g., hundred cubic feet for natural gas, which is a volume). And don't get me started on the mix of both Greek and Roman prefixes (e.g., CCF for hundred cubic feet, MJ for megajoule). Also, most of the world uses the metric system, officially known as the International System (abbreviated S.I. for the French version, *Système International*). Finally, we have to distinguish between a quantity of energy and the rate at which it's used, which is made even more confusing by one particular unit: the watt. So yeah, it's a mess, but let's make some sense of it here.

Energy

Energy is what you get charged for by the utility. It's the amount of heat you lose through the enclosure and that needs to be replaced by your heating system. It's the calories in the oatmeal you had for breakfast. It's a quantity measured over some defined period of time.

Here's a quick rundown on energy units and their abbreviations for the two most common types of energy used in houses:

Electricity	kilowatt-hour (kWh)
	joule (MJ)
Natural gas	therm
	hundred cubic feet (CCF)
	million British Thermal Units (MMBTU)
	cubic meters (m^3)

Propane, fuel oil, and kerosene are liquid fuels measured by volume (gallons in the United States, liters in metric countries). And that might help you understand why some types of energy are measured in volume units. Raw fuels, like those three and natural gas, are measured at the meter by the volume of the fuel. Then the utility company applies the energy factor for the type of fuel to convert to energy.

Another way we talk about energy in the world of building science is in terms of the heat that's lost from the house in winter or gained in summer. We use heating systems to replace the heat lost and cooling systems to remove the heat gained. In the United States, we use the British Thermal Unit (BTU) as the standard unit for heat. In metric countries, it's typically the watt-hour (Wh), kilowatt-hour (kWh), or megajoule (MJ).

Power

Power is the rate at which energy is transferred. It's the energy per unit time.

$$Power = \frac{Energy}{time}$$

When you say, "That furnace has a heating capacity of 15,000 BTU per hour," you're describing the heating power of the furnace. Another example is a 14-watt light bulb, which uses 14 watts of power when it's turned on.

Did you notice there was no "per second" or "per hour" with the watt? There it is, the unit that gives so much trouble. Power is energy per unit time, but there seems to be no per hour or per second or any other kind of time unit in a watt. The problem is that the time unit is hidden. Here's how a watt is defined:

1 watt (W) = 1 joule per second (J/s)

Watts and kilowatts are units of power, which is energy per unit time. The kilowatt-hour, on the other hand, is a unit of energy, even though, yes, it does seem to have time in the unit. The equation for power can be solved for energy to yield:

$$\textbf{\textit{Energy = Power x time}}$$

So, a kilowatt-hour is indeed a unit of energy because it's a unit of power multiplied by a unit of time. It's the same type of calculation as multiplying your speed (miles or kilometers per hour) by the time (hours) to find the distance traveled (miles or kilometers).

We'll be dealing with power and energy and their respective units frequently in this book, so if this is unfamiliar to you, you can come back to this section. There is also an appendix on units and conversion factors at the end of the book.

How Do Homes Use Energy?

Each home is different, but we can look at data collected by the US Energy Information Administration (EIA) to see what's happening with homes in the United States. The pie chart in Figure 4.2 is from the 2015 Residential Energy Consumption Survey done by the EIA and shows the percent of energy used for the major end uses in an average American household. Heating the conditioned space is the largest chunk of the pie at 43 percent, with "other" coming in second at 26 percent. Water heating is third at 19 percent. Air conditioning comes in at a paltry 8 percent, followed by refrigerators at 3 percent.

Air conditioning takes a lot of abuse as climate-killing wasted energy, but space heating, as you can see in the chart, uses much more energy than air conditioning. Two other factors, however, make air conditioning worse than it appears here. One is that the energy used by air conditioners mostly comes from electric power plants, whereas the energy for a lot of space heating comes from combustion on site. We'll discuss the significance of site and source energy later in this chapter. The other way air conditioners can make climate change worse is that their refrigerants sometimes leak into the atmosphere. Refrigerants are the special substances that make air conditioners work, and each refrigerant molecule can be as bad as 1,000 or so carbon dioxide molecules.

Of course, a pie chart for energy use averaged over all the homes in the whole United States doesn't give you the kind of narrow guidance you need for what you should do with your particular house. One way to get a little closer is to use the EIA data for your region. The EIA separates the data into four major regions, nine sub-regions, and even a couple of sub-sub-regions. Figure 4.3 shows the 2015 energy use data for homes in the South.

As you'd expect, homes in warmer climates do less space heating and more air conditioning. What you may not have expected, however, is that the South still uses more energy for space heating than for cooling. Obviously, you need to drill

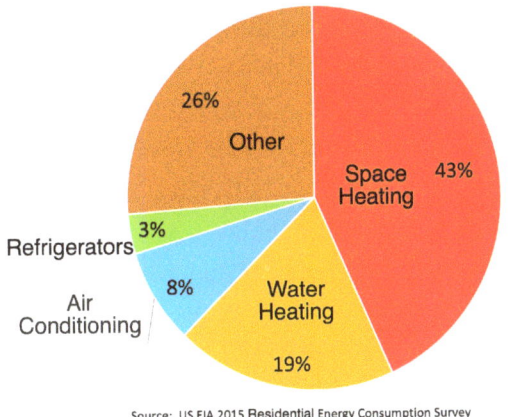

Average US Household Energy Use
Whole Country

Source: US EIA 2015 Residential Energy Consumption Survey

Figure 4.2. *Average household energy consumption by end use for the entire United States [Data from US Energy Information Administration]*

down a bit further because a home in a place like Weeki Wachee, Florida, will almost certainly use more energy for air conditioning than for heating. Averages for a country, region, state, or province are helpful in seeing the big picture, but you need more specific information for your home.

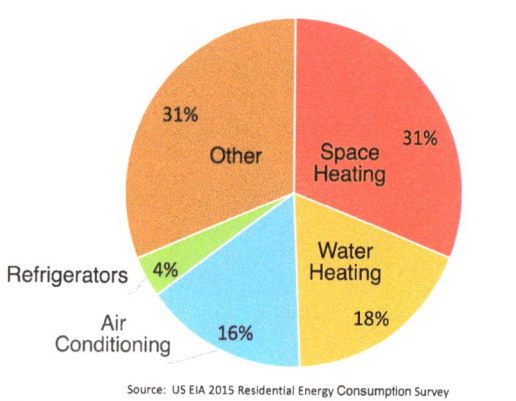

Figure 4.3. *Average energy consumption by end use for homes in the South region*

Figure 4.4 is the same kind of pie chart, but this time it's for a particular house, a 1940s bungalow in Atlanta, Georgia. You can see that space heating is the dominant user of energy in this home. That's because Atlanta does have some cold weather in the winter, this house was mostly uninsulated, and the furnace was old and inefficient. If you're trying to fix an existing home, this is the information you need. It's obvious that addressing space heating should be the first priority for this homeowner.

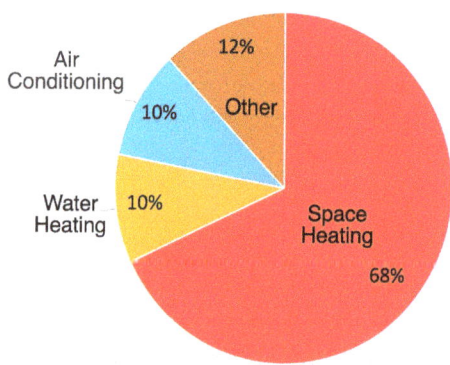

Figure 4.4. *Energy consumption by end use for a 1940s bungalow in Atlanta, Georgia (Data shown are from energy modeling software, not actual use.)*

Let's take a look at one more pie chart. Figure 4.5 is from the house I built in 2001 in Georgia, and it shows what happens to the proportions when you have a really efficient house. In the two average homes and the one particular home above, heating and cooling account for about half or more of the total energy consumption. In an energy-efficient home, heating and cooling can be a third or less of the energy consumption.

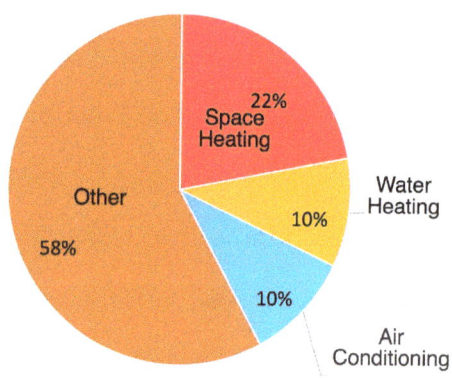

Figure 4.5. *Energy use for a super-efficient house in Georgia (Data shown are from energy modeling software, not actual use.)*

Some of the takeaways from these charts are that for the typical home, heating and cooling are what you should focus on first. Reduce those loads as much as you can, first by improving the airtightness, insulation, and windows, and then by using more efficient heating and cooling equipment, including the distribution system. Once you do as much as makes sense for you with those pieces of the pie, then you go after the water heating, refrigerator, lights, and appliances to see how much you can reduce those.

One thing to know about these pie charts is that they don't tell the whole story when you look at them separately. What percentage of energy goes to the various end uses is good to know, but so is the size of the pie. Once you've reduced the heating and cooling consumption, you're dealing with a smaller pie. The three pie charts in Figure 4.6 show this effect.

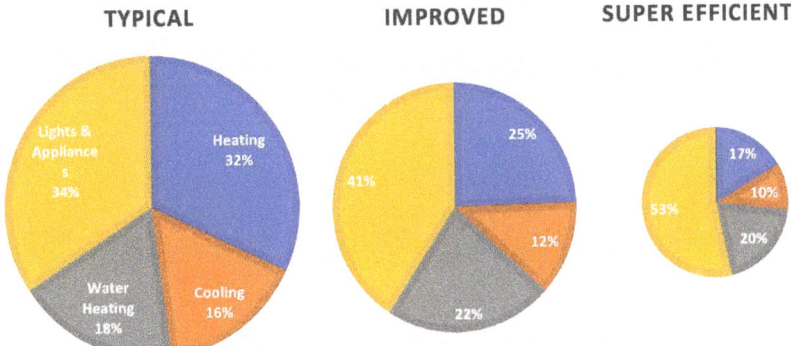

TYPICAL

Lights & Appliances 34%
Heating 32%
Water Heating 18%
Cooling 16%

IMPROVED

25%
41%
12%
22%

SUPER EFFICIENT

17%
10%
53%
20%

It's easy to get hung up on whatever part of the pie looks the biggest, but remember that the whole pie shrinks as you make a house more energy efficient. Sixty percent of 100 is a lot less than 30 percent of 1,000.

Figure 4.6. *As a house gets more energy efficient, the percentages in the pie chart of consumption change. Heating and cooling decrease the most, while the lights and appliances slice often increases as a portion of the total consumption. A key point to keep in mind is that the size of the pie is shrinking.*

Finding How Energy Is Used in a Home

If you want a pie chart showing the proportions of various energy end uses for the house you're working on, you have two options. You can use an energy modeling tool to calculate how much each of the end uses should use or you can measure actual energy consumption. Let's look at these two ways of understanding how energy is used in a house.

When designing a new home, there's nothing to measure yet, so you have to do energy modeling. Some architects use software that can do the necessary calculations, but there are other ways to do it, too. If you're getting the house certified in a program like ENERGY STAR® or Passive House, the certifier will have access to software like Ekotrope, REM/Rate™, or WUFI Passive® that does the calculations. The certifier will do the analysis and include the results in the reports they provide you. To do it yourself, you can pay for the license for energy modeling software like REM/Design™ or WUFI Passive, or you can try a free one like BEopt from the US Department of Energy or HOT2000 from Natural Resources Canada.

Energy modeling won't be as accurate as measuring the actual energy use, and the output depends strongly on the accuracy of the inputs. There's an old computer programming acronym for this: GIGO, which stands for "Garbage in; garbage

out." Some inputs have more effect on the results than others, and it takes experience and patience to understand how to do energy modeling well.

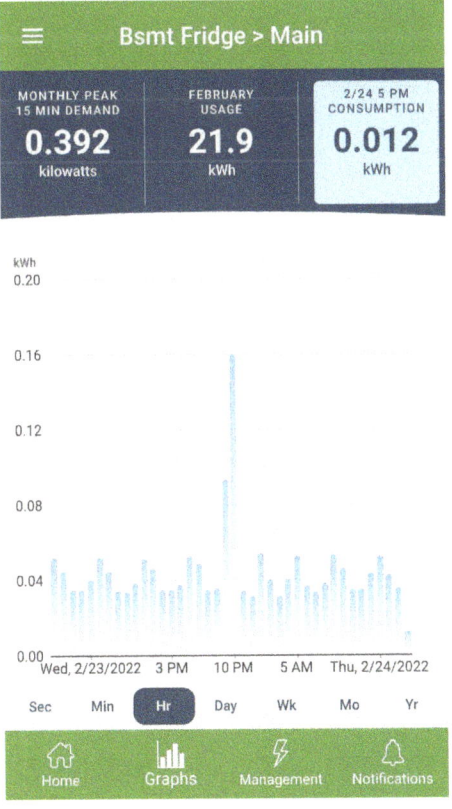

Figure 4.7. *An electricity monitoring system can show you how much electricity you use for individual circuits in your home or for plug-in devices, like a refrigerator.*

The other option to create your pie chart is to monitor the end uses. Of course, you have to have an occupied house to do this. A lot of devices on the market can monitor your electricity use. Plug-in energy monitors directly give you the energy used by plug-in electrical loads, like a refrigerator, lamp, or dehumidifier. Some devices monitor individual circuits in the house through sensors installed at the electrical panel. Another class of these devices clamps onto the main wires bringing electricity into your home and then disaggregates the total signal based on knowledge of the electrical signatures of individual devices. If you're lucky, your electric utility company is already doing that for you through the smart meter on your home and providing you with the data.

Natural gas consumption is a bit more difficult unless you have only one gas appliance. Smart meter disaggregation may be coming for this fuel, too, but individual metering of gas appliances is probably your best option if you really want the separate data. Since you probably have only a few gas appliances in the home, the cost of installing meters on each of them may be affordable enough for you. (Or you could do like I did and replace your gas appliances with electric appliances, and this problem goes away.)

Energy Use Intensity

Another way you can get a handle on your home energy use in an existing home is to calculate the energy use intensity (EUI). To do so, you simply divide the total energy used in a year for all fuels by the conditioned floor area of the house. All you need is 12 months of energy bills and the size of the house.

The electricity consumption is usually given in units of kilowatt-hours (kWh). Natural gas could be in therms, hundred cubic feet (CCF), cubic meters, or something else. Fuel oil and propane are sold by the gallon. The first step is to take those 12 months of bills and convert all of the fuels you used to the same unit. I prefer kilowatt-hours, but you could also do British Thermal Units (BTU), megajoules (MJ), or any other unit of energy. If you choose something other than kilowatt-hours, you'll need to adjust the numbers on the scale to find where your house falls in the range from super-efficient to energy hog.

kWh/ft^2	kWh/m^2	Description
<5	<54	Super efficient
5 to 10	54 to 108	Efficient
10 to 15	108 to 161	Moderately efficient
15 to 20	161 to 215	Inefficient
>20	>215	Energy hog

Table 4.1. *Energy use intensity (EUI) is a measure of how energy efficient a house is.*

Table 4.1 shows a scale of energy use intensity in kWh per square foot and kWh per square meter. Once you calculate the EUI for your home, you can see where it falls on the scale, and that will give you a good idea of how much savings are available to you. If your house is in one of the top two categories, you still can find some savings, but it's going to be a lot harder than if your house is inefficient or worse, an energy hog. Note that the ranges in Table 4.1 apply to typical homes that don't have features that use huge amounts of energy, like a heated swimming pool, hot tub, or greenhouse. Also note that the ranges in the table depend on the climate where a house is located. It's not easy to get to the super-efficient range in Anchorage, Alaska, whereas a home in Santa Monica, California, might qualify as efficient without doing much of anything special.

One thing missing from that calculation, however, is the impact of weather. If the 12 months of energy bills you chose included an extremely cold winter, for example, your EUI will come out higher than if you had looked at energy bills from an average year. You can account for the weather by dividing your EUI by the total number of degree days (see Chapter 5) for the 12 months you're using. That calculation yields a weather-normalized energy use intensity.

Site Energy versus Source Energy

Up to this point in our discussion of energy, we've mostly ignored an important distinction. Every mention of home energy use up to now has referred to site energy. As its name implies, that's the energy the house uses onsite. When you burn natural gas in a furnace, the site energy is the entire energy content in the gas you burn, which is the number of therms, hundred cubic feet, or cubic meters the gas utility charges you for. When you use electricity, the site energy is the number of kilowatt-hours you get charged for. Pretty simple, right?

Source energy is where things get more complex. To get at it properly, we need to define another two types of energy:

- **Primary energy:** A raw fuel that is used in the home, like natural gas or firewood.
- **Secondary energy:** A form of energy that was first generated by another type of energy with the conversion happening offsite. For example, electricity generated by the burning of coal at a power plant is secondary energy.

Now we can define site energy and source energy.

Site energy: This is the energy used within the boundary of the site. For electricity, it's the kilowatt-hours you get billed for. For gas, it's the amount that flows through your gas meter. For propane, it's the amount used from your tank. Each fuel delivered and used at the site counts toward the total site energy, whether it's a primary or secondary energy.

Source energy: This is the energy used onsite plus the energy that went into getting that energy onto the site. For electricity, it's the kilowatt-hours you get billed for plus the kilowatt-hours of energy that are "consumed in the extraction, processing, and transport of primary fuels such as coal, oil, and natural gas; energy losses in thermal combustion in power generation plants; and energy losses in transmission and distribution to the building site."[6]

Source energy accounts for losses in both primary and secondary energy. The source energy for a primary energy, like natural gas, factors in the energy losses that occurred during storage, transport, and delivery of the gas to the house. The source energy for a secondary energy, like electricity, factors in the losses that occurred when the original source (coal, gas, wind . . .) was converted to the secondary energy (electricity) as well as the losses when the electricity is transmitted and distributed to the site.

If all you care about is how efficient your house is, the site versus source distinction doesn't really matter. Site energy is what you focus on. Source energy comes into play when you're looking at the environmental impact of the energy your house uses.

Here's an example. When an electric power plant burns coal, it takes about 100 kWh of coal energy to generate 35 kWh of electricity for the grid. To get those 35 kWh from the plant to the house results in another 5 kWh of losses, so the net electrical energy delivered to the house is 30 kWh. The ratio of source to site energy in this case is 100/30, which equals 3.33. That number is called the source energy factor.

Source energy comes into play when you're looking at the environmental impact of the energy your house uses.

6. A Common Definition for Zero Energy Buildings, US Department of Energy, 2015

If an all-electric house gets all of its electricity from a power plant that uses only coal, the source energy factor for their energy would be 3.33. Let's extend this example and say the house uses 10,000 kWh per year, which is about average for all households in the United States. The two metrics for this house would be:

Site energy   10,000 kWh
Source energy 10,000 x 3.33 = 33,333 kWh

The homeowners of this house used and paid their electric utility for 10,000 kWh of electricity, but behind the scenes, it took about 33,000 kWh of energy for them to get those 10,000 kWh. Let that sink in for a minute. The 10,000 kWh of energy used was only a third of the energy in the fuel that made the electricity. The other two-thirds was considered waste heat and most likely dumped into a nearby body of water.

Most electricity delivered to homes, however, is generated by a mix of fuels. Electricity generated by natural gas, for example, has a lower source energy factor. The resultant source energy factor of electricity depends on the entire mix of fuels. For the United States, the source energy factor for electricity was 2.8 in 2020. For Canada, the number is 1.96, which indicates a more efficient mix of fuels and a lot of hydroelectric power. Also, the source energy factor for electricity changes with time. (See the next section for more on this.)

For primary fuels used in the home, the source energy factor is close to 1. For example, natural gas in the United States has a source energy factor of 1.05. Table 4.2 below lists source energy factors for both primary and secondary energy types for the United States and Canada.

Some energy-efficiency and green building programs, like the Phius Passive House program, have requirements based on source rather than site energy. To meet the requirements, you have to calculate the total source energy using source energy factors specified by the program.

The preceding discussion provides a basic overview of source energy, but we need to emphasize two important points:

• National source energy factors may be different from local source energy factors and don't give you the true picture of a building's impact on the environment.
• Source energy factors change with time. (See "Reasons to Go All-Electric" later in this chapter.)

This is about as deep as we're going with this discussion. It's an interesting topic, and I encourage you to look at some of the resources at the end of this book if you'd like to learn more.

Energy Type	U.S. Ratio	Canadian Ratio
Electricity (Grid Purchase)	2.80	1.96
Electricity (Onsite Solar or Wind - regardless of REC ownership)	1.00	1.00
Natural Gas	1.05	1.01
Fuel Oil (No. 1,2,4,5,6, Diesel, Kerosene)	1.01	1.01
Propane & Liquid Propane	1.01	1.04
Steam	1.20	1.33
Hot Water	1.20	1.33
Chilled Water	0.91	0.57
Wood	1.00	1.00
Coal/Coke	1.00	1.00
Other	1.00	1.00

Table 4.2. *Source energy factors from the ENERGY STAR Portfolio Manager Technical Document, August 2019*

Comparing a Gas Furnace to a Heat Pump

The discussion of energy use intensity and source energy factors is still a bit abstract. Let's make it more real by doing a little comparison. If you have a gas furnace, you heat your house with a primary energy, but what if you replaced your gas furnace with a heat pump? Before we look at the numbers, note that since gas and electricity are sold in different units, you have to convert one of them so you can compare apples to apples, or in this case, kilowatt-hours to kilowatt-hours.

	Site energy	Source energy
Gas furnace (therms)	285 therms	299 therms
Gas furnace (kWh)	8,350 kWh	8,768 kWh
Heat Pump	2,700 kWh	7,560 kWh

Table 4.3. *Comparison source energy for a gas furnace and a heat pump.*

The assumptions built into this comparison are that the gas furnace has an efficiency rating of 95 AFUE and the heat pump has an efficiency rating of 10 HSPF. Both are high-efficiency heating systems. The annual heating load for the house is 7,933 kWh, or ~27 million BTU. (See the appendices or Chapter 13 for explanations of AFUE and HSPF. Also note that this calculation is a bit squirrely because AFUE and HSPF aren't really meant for this, but it's good enough to illustrate our point here.)

When you look at the site energy column, it's obvious we can't do an accurate comparison of energy use with that quantity. If that's all there were to it, the heat pump would win every time since it uses a third the amount of site energy as the gas furnace. And that's where source energy comes in. The source energy column shows how much energy was in the fuel that was burned at the plant or lost in delivering that heating energy to the house.

If all you're interested in is the effect of the furnace or the heat pump on your utility bills, comparing the energy used by the gas furnace or the heat pump energy doesn't help you. In this case, you need to compare the cost of running each piece of equipment. Table 4 shows that comparison using the heating energy from above for typical gas and electric rates offered in Georgia. (Electricity rates in the United States range from about $0.10 to $0.23 per kWh, with Hawaii at $0.34. Natural gas rates range from about $1 to $2 per therm. These rates include taxes and fees.)

	Energy Used	Rate	Annual Cost
Gas furnace	285 therms	$1.20/therm	$342
Heat pump	2,700 kWh	$0.12/kWh	$324

Table 4.4. *The cost of heating with a gas furnace versus a heat pump.*

You have to be careful with this calculation, too, because each utility charges a rate for the energy they sell but also has taxes and fees piled on top. Try to account for the full cost in doing an actual comparison like this.

For the example shown here, it's a wash between an electric heat pump and a gas furnace based on source energy or costs. That conclusion could change, though, for an area with different gas and electricity rates. But how do they compare on the basis of carbon emissions? In 2020, the Rocky Mountain Institute (RMI) did an analysis showing that a heat pump beats a gas furnace using that metric in 46 out of the 48 contiguous states in the United States. (Wyoming and Utah were the outliers.) Even in Georgia, a heat pump beats a gas furnace—by a lot! According to the RMI analysis, a gas furnace in Georgia will emit 130 pounds per million BTU of CO_2 over its lifetime versus 52 pounds per million BTU of CO_2 for a heat pump. Another study in the scientific journal *Nature* showed similar results, with heat pumps emitting less carbon in 53 of 59 world regions.

Reasons to Go All-Electric

When you start looking at source energy in terms of impact on the environment, it can guide you to decisions about which types of energy to use in a house and which to avoid. One factor that can inform your decision is which way source energy factors are trending. In this section, we'll look at what's been happening with the source energy that goes into generating electricity.

Figure 4.8. Less and less electricity is generated by burning coal each year [Credit: stanze, flickr.com]

The burning of fossil fuels has put a lot of carbon dioxide into the atmosphere, leading to a sharp rise in global temperatures since the Industrial Revolution began. As a result, there's a move to decrease the use of burning fossil fuels. Natural gas has been touted as a "clean" fossil fuel that puts less carbon dioxide into the air than coal and so might help with the transition to a clean energy economy, but cities in California, Massachusetts, and in other states are banning or looking to ban natural gas in new buildings.

Why are they abandoning natural gas? Even though gas puts less carbon dioxide into the air than coal does, its carbon emissions are still appreciable. Replacing gas appliances in your home with their electric counterparts, however, doesn't eliminate gas altogether. Gas is still used to generate electricity in North America, as are coal, nuclear, hydropower, wind, and solar.

To understand the move away from natural gas, we need to see the big picture. Let's take a look

at electricity production over the past few decades. The most recent energy flows diagram from the Lawrence Livermore National Lab (LLNL) is shown in Figure 4.1 earlier in this chapter. It's a complex diagram showing the inputs on the left, with the size of the line proportional to the amount of energy. (This particular type of data representation is called a Sankey diagram, the most famous of which shows the attrition in Napoleon's army as they invaded Russia in 1812.) The charts below show some of the illuminating trends in source energy used to generate electricity.

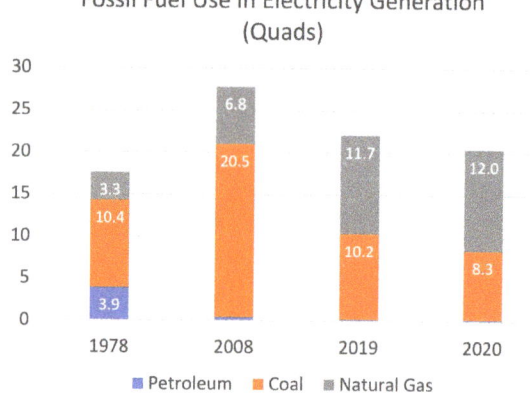

Figure 4.9. *The amount of source energy from fossil fuels used to generate electricity. [Data from Lawrence Livermore National Laboratory.]*

The first chart (Figure 4.9) shows the amount of energy used to generate electricity from three different fossil fuels in 1978, 2008, 2019, and 2020. The unit here is the quad, short for a quadrillion BTU. The amount of natural gas in the mix increased over that time, but coal and petroleum both dropped significantly. Petroleum's big drop occurred right after the two oil shocks of the 1970s, and coal's decline came after 2008.

The second chart (Figure 4.10, opposite) presents the same data for all the fossil fuels (petroleum, coal, and natural gas) but as a percentage of all the source energy used to generate electricity. These charts make it clear that fossil fuels used to generate electricity are losing ground to cleaner energy sources, both as a percentage and on an absolute energy use scale.

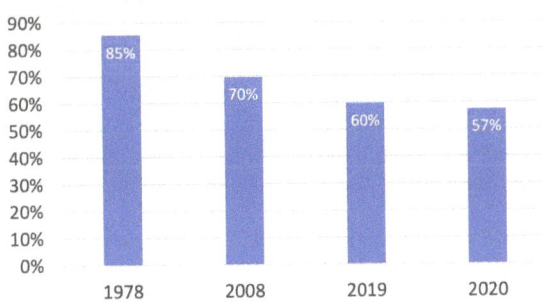

Fossil Fuel Use in Electricity Generation (Percent)

Figure 4.10. *Fossil fuels as a percentage of the total source energy used for electricity generation. [Data from Lawrence Livermore National Laboratory.]*

The third chart (Figure 4.11) illustrates where some of coal's lost market share is going: wind and solar. The cost of wind and solar is finally dropping—and fast! In the 11 years from 2008 to 2019, the source energy contribution of solar and wind to US electricity generation increased by a factor of 10. And it's still rising quickly.

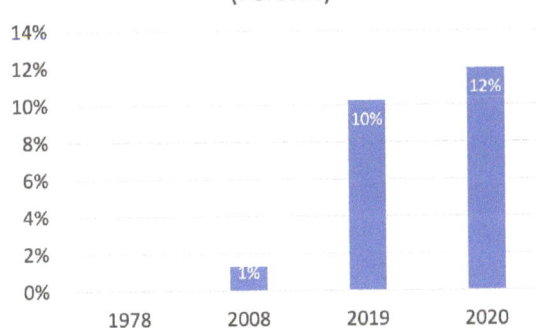

Solar & Wind in Electricity Generation (Percent)

Figure 4.11. *The percentage of solar and wind used for electricity generation in the United States. [Data from Lawrence Livermore National Laboratory.]*

The big takeaway from these data is clear: Electricity keeps getting cleaner. Petroleum is out almost completely. Coal is disappearing rapidly. And solar and wind are taking off. Even with the natural gas portion increasing, the electricity mix in the United States is decarbonizing, as we've gone from having 85 percent fossil fuels in the electricity fuel mix in 1978 to 57 percent in 2020. The source energy factor for electricity reflects

this trend, as it has gone from 3.37 in 2006[7] to 2.80 in 2019 in the United States (Table 4.2).

When you have to make a choice between electricity and natural gas, it's clear that electricity is the better choice for the environment. Natural gas is not getting cleaner. And there are indications that natural gas may start going the way of coal as we get further into the 2020s. (See Jeremy Rifkin's book *The Green New Deal* for more on that topic.)

In addition to being better for the environment, electricity may well be better for your pocketbook. A 2019 whitepaper from Pecan Street, a research and policy organization, found that converting from natural gas space heating to a heat pump could save Texas homeowners from $57 to $452 per year.

Finally, of course, having an all-electric home makes it easier to offset your energy use with site-generated solar power if you install photovoltaic modules. My house is on the path to net zero energy use. I changed out the old gas water heater with a new heat pump water heater and replaced the gas furnace with ducted mini-split heat pumps. Then I had the gas meter removed.

The next time someone tells you that electric cars, heat pumps, or electric water heaters don't help the environment because they use dirty coal, you can respond by saying, yes, coal still may be part of the mix, but it's decreasing rapidly. Electricity is getting cleaner all the time.

Figure 4.12. *The gas meter at my house (left) and the gas line after I had the meter removed in 2019 (right)*

7. Source: Energy and Emission Factors for Energy Use in Buildings (Deru and Torcellini 2006)

Net Zero Homes

Net zero anything means you have a quantity that flows in two directions. Some flows in; some flows out. The net result of the two flows is zero. Net zero energy is just what it sounds like. All homes use energy, and most are net negative. The energy flows only one way. But if a home also produces energy onsite, it will offset some of the energy used. If the onsite production equals the amount of energy used, that makes it a net zero energy home.

It matters, though, how that onsite energy is produced. In programs and laws that require or incentivize net zero energy buildings, the onsite energy must be produced by renewable means. If you want to do that with a house, that generally means photovoltaic (PV) modules onsite, usually on the roof. Wind energy is possible, but it's often not appropriate at the scale of a single home.

Another important factor is timing. Intrepid early adopters have been producing solar electricity for decades in their off-grid homes with batteries for storage. If they had enough battery storage and used only solar electricity, they could achieve net zero electricity. If they brought in no other fuel—propane for heating, for example—they got all the way to net zero energy.

The concept of net zero energy didn't really get going, however, until grid-tied photovoltaic systems became feasible in the mid-1990s. With that development, a homeowner could produce their own solar electricity without having to invest in an expensive, maintenance-requiring battery storage system. The electricity grid became their storage system. During the daytime when the sun is shining, the PV system produces more electricity than the home is using, and the excess electrical power goes into the grid. At night, the flow goes the other way.

The electric utility tracks the flows in both directions and provides the homeowner a credit on their electricity bill if they send more electricity into the grid than they withdraw. That's more likely to happen when solar energy is plentiful during summer and less likely during the dark days of winter. If, over the course of a year, the PV system sends the same amount of energy into the grid as the house pulls from the grid, that's a net zero energy house.

Sounds simple, right? Well, it turns out to be a bit more complex because there are several ways to define what net zero means. Here are six of them.

1. Net Zero Site Energy

This is the standard way of talking about a net zero energy house. Based on site energy, a net zero house produces as much energy onsite as it uses onsite over the course of a year. If the house uses 10,000 kWh, it's got to produce 10,000 kWh or more. It's all about what happens onsite, as described in our definition of site energy earlier in this chapter.

This description of net zero site energy doesn't account for the type of energy used, though. Electricity is simple. Where this becomes important is if the building uses natural gas, propane, or some other type of primary energy instead of only electricity.

Let's say your home has a natural gas furnace, and it's 95 percent efficient. For every 95 kWh of heat that your home needs, your furnace must burn 100 kWh of natural gas. Net zero site energy, then, means you've got to provide 100 kWh of site-generated electricity to balance out the energy used by the gas furnace.

If, on the other hand, you had a heat pump, it might need 40 kWh of electricity to pump the same 95 kWh of heat into your home. Rather than having to produce 100 kWh of electricity, then, you'd need to produce only 40 kWh to balance consumption and production.

As you can see from this example, this definition

of net zero neglects the energy used in the production of electricity powering the heat pump (the source energy). Needing to provide only 40 kWh of onsite production for the heat pump versus 100 kWh for the furnace means this definition favors electricity over gas or other primary fuels.

2. Net Zero Source Energy

A net zero source energy house produces as much energy as it uses, but you have to account for all the energy used from fuel extraction to delivery. The way you do that is simple: You multiply the energy flowing in both directions by their respective source energy factors.

For an all-electric house, the site and source definitions of net zero energy are equivalent. Using the source energy factor discussed earlier in this chapter, each kWh of electricity used in the house comes at the cost of 2.80 kWh of source energy. And for each 2.80 kWh of electrical source energy used, you need to export 2.80 kWh of electrical source energy. That's a 1:1 ratio, so for each kilowatt-hour of electricity delivered to the house, you need to export 1 kilowatt-hour of electricity. This table lays out the calculation.

	Site energy	Source energy factor	Source energy
Delivered electricity	10,000 kWh	2.80	28,000 kWh
Exported electricity	10,000 kWh	2.80	28,000 kWh

A good way to visualize the calculations, if it helps, is to go left-to-right in the row showing delivered energy (10,000 x 2.80 = 28,000) and then right-to-left in the exported energy row (28,000 ÷ 2.80 = 10,000). The reason is that you know how much site energy was used (delivered), and you're looking for how much site energy you need to produce.

Now let's look at some numbers for natural gas. Here's a similar table to the one above, except this time we're looking at the delivered energy being natural gas, whereas the exported energy stays the same (electricity).

	Site energy	Source energy factor	Source energy
Delivered gas	2,000 kWh	1.05	2,100 kWh
Exported electricity	750 kWh	2.80	2,100 kWh

This time we need only 750 kWh of renewable electricity produced on site and exported to the grid to cover 2,000 kWh of natural gas energy used onsite. So, instead of having to produce 1 kWh of electricity for each 1 kWh of natural gas consumption, you need to export only 0.38 kWh for each kilowatt-hour of natural gas used. In the section on site and source energy, I gave the US national average for electricity of 2.80, which means that for each 2.80 kWh of natural gas burned, you'd have to produce 1 kWh of electricity. This definition favors natural gas.

3. Net Zero Energy Costs

A net zero energy house based on energy costs is one in which the house earns as much money from selling renewable electricity produced onsite as it pays for energy delivered to the house. It's an appealing definition to accountants, I suppose, and of course everyone would like to be net zero or better in energy costs. Wouldn't you rather get money from your electric utility instead of having to send money to them?

The problem is that even with the same energy balance, a house may be net zero one year and not the next simply because of changes in the price of energy. In addition, utility companies often pay you their avoided cost rather than the same amount you pay them for the kilowatt-hours you buy. That means you'll need more onsite production than you would by using the definitions based on site or source energy.

4. Net Zero Total Emissions

A house that achieves net zero based on total emissions produces enough emissions-free renewable energy to offset the emissions from the electricity they buy from their utility. How easy this is to do depends greatly on the type of energy used and the location. For example, a house in the Pacific Northwest, which has a high percentage of electricity generated by emissions-free hydroelectric plants, can achieve net-zero energy emissions without much difficulty because there aren't a lot of emissions associated with the electricity they buy.

5. Net Zero Carbon Emissions

Because climate change is the biggest of our environmental problems, many have narrowed the focus to carbon and carbon-equivalent emissions. Another name for offsetting carbon emissions is carbon neutrality. When zero-carbon renewable energy produced onsite balances out the carbon dioxide emissions of the grid electricity, the house achieves net zero carbon emissions.

6. Net Zero Renewable Energy Certificates

The sixth type of net zero energy home is not like the others. The previous definitions all require onsite production of renewable energy. This net zero definition instead uses renewable energy generated offsite through the purchase of what's called renewable energy certificates (REC). This may be the only path available for your home if your house and lot are shaded or if you live in a condo or apartment.

RECs are basically a tool for markets to track the amount of renewable energy delivered. For example, when the power lines connected to your house send electricity in for you to use in your water heater, it's just electricity. The electrons in the wires jiggle back and forth and transmit energy into your home. If you get that electricity from your utility, you get whatever they're sending, which could be electricity from the power plant nearest your home, a mix of power generated by different plants owned by your utility, or even power imported from other utilities 1,000 miles away. When you purchase RECs, you're paying for renewably generated electricity being added to the grid, possibly by your neighbor with a sunny, south-facing roof covered with photovoltaic modules or a wind farm in another state or province.

Net Zero Energy Priorities

It's easy to get lost in the details of the different definitions, but some important points jump out when you step back and look at the bigger picture. Here are a few.

Conservation first. You can achieve net zero energy with an energy hog of a house, but it'll cost extra, and you may not have enough space on your roof for all the photovoltaic modules you'll need. If you reduce your energy use first, achieving net zero becomes a lot easier.

Measured, not just designed. True net zero energy status should depend on actual performance as measured by the amounts of delivered and exported energy. Modeling the energy use and production during design is helpful and even necessary for program certification, but you don't get to claim net zero energy just because of those calculations. Few houses perform as modeled.

Adding renewable to the energy grid is good. Even if you don't hit net zero, you're still helping chart the course for a clean energy future.

About the Name

I've used the term "net zero energy" in this book. Sometimes you'll see the words transposed and the same concept called "zero net energy." Either is fine. In 2015, though, the US Department of Energy adopted "zero energy" as the proper name to describe these buildings. I'd like to support the DOE here, but I just can't. To me, "zero energy" implies zeroes all around: zero consumption, zero production. I like the qualifier "net" because it makes it clear that we're interested in an energy balance.

Existing Home Improvement Case Study

Danny Orlando, a retired EPA employee, steadily worked to make his Atlanta, Georgia, home more energy efficient. The graph in Figure 4.13 shows the reduction, month by month, starting in 1994. The callouts show the work he did along the way.

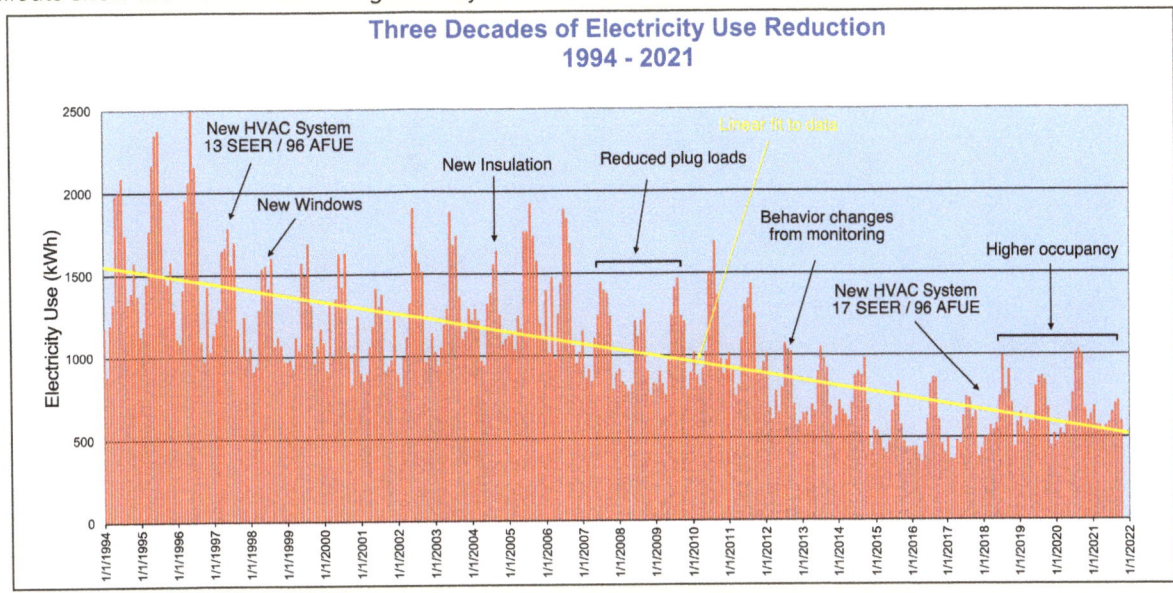

Figure 4.13. *Danny Orlando's electricity use over 28 years steadily decreased because of the improvements he made.*

- He reduced the electricity consumption of his plug loads (the things you plug into an outlet) between 2007 and 2009 by getting rid of a stereo system and waterbed and switching to smart power strips, which can turn off devices to prevent them from drawing power when they're not in use.
- The behavior changes in 2012 stemmed from installing a whole-house electricity monitor. By watching the total power being used, he and his family were able to shave off some unnecessary electricity consumption.
- In 2017, Orlando's household grew in number and in hours occupied. He retired from the EPA that year and was home more often. He also had a stepson and his mother move into the house. They installed a new range and ate at home more. And then the COVID lockdown of 2020 hit.

The changes Orlando made to the building enclosure and heating and cooling equipment helped significantly, too. New windows and more insulation are indicated on the graph, but the insulation also came with another important step. Orlando did air sealing in the attic before the new insulation went in. (See Figure 11.23.)

All this shows that by making improvements over time, you can reduce your energy use significantly while also improving your indoor environmental quality.

Chapter Takeaways

- Energy is an abstract concept that took scientists a long time to understand.
- We now can quantify with great accuracy the energy we use in our homes. We can calculate how much goes to different end uses (e.g., heating, cooling, lights . . .).
- Energy use intensity (EUI) is a good metric for finding out just how energy efficient a house is.

- The energy we use in homes is not simply the amount we pay for on our utility bills. That is the site energy. The source energy can be much higher, especially for electricity.
- Going all-electric can be better for indoor air quality, comfort, and the environment. Electricity does not have combustion safety problems, can result in better sizing for heating systems, and keeps getting cleaner.

Part 2
The Building Enclosure

CHAPTER 5

Building Science 101

If you're trying to run a bath but the tub leaks almost as quickly as you fill it, do you need to get more water flowing through the faucet or fix the leak? The answer is obvious. You fix the leak. When the bathtub is our house, however, and the stuff that's leaking is energy, a lot of people jump to the wrong answer. The house is just the house, they think, and if there's a problem heating or cooling it, the fault must lie with the heating and cooling system.

Unfortunately, most homes leak a lot of energy, and many people think there's just not much they can do about that. Maybe they add some insulation to the attic, attach a little bit of weatherstripping to the front door, and caulk around the windows. The truth, however, is that the energy leaking through the floors, walls, and ceilings can be reduced greatly, making the house more comfortable, healthier, durable, and quieter—and less expensive to operate.

Before you focus on the heating and cooling system as the source of problems, you need to consider the building enclosure. If it leaks heat, you might have cold surfaces in winter or warm surfaces in summer that lead to comfort

> *"We live in a society exquisitely dependent on science and technology, in which hardly anyone knows anything about science and technology."*
> —Carl Sagan

problems. Cold surfaces can collect water, leading to mold growth and health problems. Excess heat flow through the building enclosure leads to high energy bills. Excess air flow through the enclosure can lead to poor indoor air quality, noise, drafts, and high energy bills. A lot can—and does—go wrong with the building enclosure. That's where it all begins.

We're going to cover a lot of ground in this chapter, but we can organize it all around three fundamental principles:

1. A house is a system.
2. A house should control the flows of heat, air, and moisture.
3. A house should be tailored to its climate.

Understand and apply those principles, and your house will treat you well.

A House Is a System

Just as the human body has many cells, tissues, and organs that handle innumerable tasks and must work in harmony, a house likewise has many subsystems that must work in harmony. Stewart Brand's shearing layers (Chapter 1)—site, structure, skin, services, space plan, and stuff—all play a role. They're also all interconnected. A failure in the site can cause the structure and skin to fail. For example, a water drainage problem that keeps the foundation wet can cause water

to wick up into the wood framing, rotting it, damaging the drywall, and growing mold.

As we'll see in this chapter, the building enclosure (structure and skin in Brand's layers) is one of the most important parts of a house, and it's responsible for a lot. It's got to keep the wind and rain out, of course, but our demands have gone way beyond that. We want the house to stay warm in winter, cool in summer, and dry year-round. It shouldn't let water in to grow mold, rot the structure, or invite moisture-seeking pests into the house. We'd like it to stop outdoor noise from coming in. And we want it to play its part in keeping us healthy. The building enclosure does those things by controlling the flows of heat, air, and moisture.

But the building enclosure can't do all those things alone. The mechanical systems also play important roles. We need heating and cooling systems to help with comfort, and we also need ventilation systems to remove indoor air pollutants and moisture. A poor choice in design can lead to serious problems years later, as can replacing an original piece of equipment with one inappropriate for the house.

Figure 5.1. *Insulation and air barrier compromised by the "cable guy"*

The building enclosure and mechanical systems interact with other parts of the house, too. For example, if a cable guy removes insulation to run a new line and doesn't put it back or air-seal the hole he drilled, the home's performance will suffer. Everything is interconnected. The hip bone's connected to the back bone, you know. One of the big problems with houses is that on many new construction and home improvement projects, there's no one trained to see the house as a system. They're all wearing their blinders, doing their own thing. That's why the cable guy removes the insulation and drills a hole without fixing the damage to the building enclosure (Figure 5.1). Even most building or remodeling contractors don't see a house as a system. Their primary job is to manage the flows of money, materials, and labor.

> *Taking the blinders off lets you see the world of possibilities that's always been there, just waiting for you to look.*

As we go through the rest of this book, my goal is to give you a good feel for the interconnection of the various components of a house. When you get it, you'll be able to perform a simple act like turning on an exhaust fan and you will immediately think about the air leaking in from the garage. Or when you consider putting up vinyl wallpaper, you will wonder what that might do to the flow of moisture through that wall and if it could result in mold. Taking the blinders off lets you see the world of possibilities that's always been there, just waiting for you to look.

The Building Enclosure

Let's begin with a definition: The building enclosure is the boundary between conditioned space and the various types of unconditioned spaces surrounding the house. Some of those unconditioned spaces are:

- Attic
- Garage
- Crawl space
- Basement
- Outdoor air
- Ground

Figure 5.2 on page 65 shows the conditioned space in blue with the dark blue line representing the building enclosure. The orange parts at the top are unconditioned attic spaces. The orange at the bottom is an unconditioned crawl space. The brown area is the ground. The outdoor air around the house is the color of the page.

Defining the building enclosure is critical. Whether you're designing a new house or fixing an old one, you've got to know where to put the air barrier and the insulation and where you need to control liquid water and water vapor. Get those details wrong, and the home's performance will suffer.

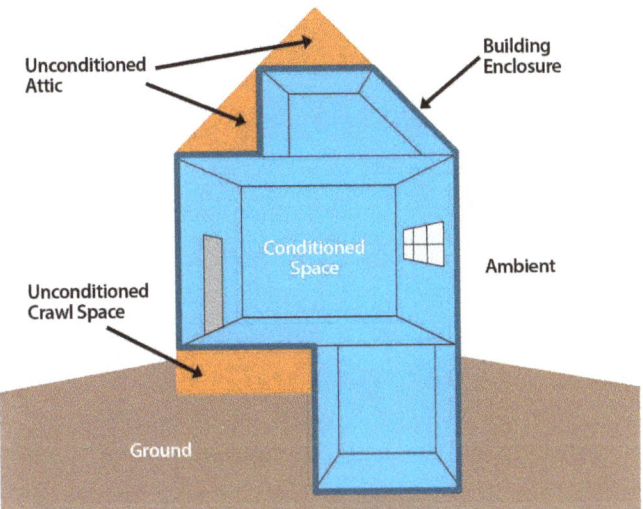

Figure 5.2. *The building enclosure of a house with unconditioned attic, crawl space, ground, and outdoor air surrounding the conditioned space inside.*

The building enclosure is one of the most important topics to understand in all of building science. It can affect all of the indoor environmental quality factors we discussed in Chapter 1, as well as the operation of the mechanical systems in the house, the durability of the house, and even the value of the house. The definition in here is pretty simple. We need to add more complexity, though, and that starts

with looking at the building enclosure itself as a bunch of subsystems that also are made up of subsystems.

Materials, Assemblies, and Enclosures

One of the most important lessons I learned about buildings is always to be aware of what level of the building is under consideration. In addition to Brand's shearing layers, another kind of classification is helpful. Whether we're talking about the building enclosure, the structure, or the exterior and interior finishes, we need to know whether the object of our attention is a material, a building assembly, or a building enclosure.

A building enclosure is composed of building assemblies (floors, walls, windows, ceilings, etc.). A building assembly is composed of materials (wood, drywall, insulation, etc.). Keeping that in mind can help you sort through misleading information. For example, if a company claims their product, a material, has a certain R-value, but that product reaches that R-value only in a properly detailed assembly, then their claim is misleading. Foil-faced bubble wrap is a good example here. The material itself has an R-value of about 1, but manufacturers sometimes claim R-values as high as 15. In those cases, they're giving credit to the material for the performance of the whole assembly. I'm not saying radiant insulation is a bad thing, but it's important to understand what is being contributed by a single material and how much of the performance relies on the entire assembly.

Controlling the Flows of Heat, Air, and Moisture

Moisture, air, and heat are forms of matter and energy. Heat, as we saw in the past chapter, is a form of energy. Air is the stuff we breathe, a form of matter that's a mixture of different gases and vapors, primarily nitrogen and oxygen. Moisture

is a form of matter that might interact with a house–or with you–in any of its three states, solid, liquid, and vapor. Because of the variety of forms moisture takes, it is described by a variety of terms: water, H_2O, ice, steam, water vapor, and humidity.

These three forms of matter and energy—moisture, air, and heat—are connected in many ways. Here are just three.

- Air can leak through a building enclosure, carrying heat and moisture with it.
- Heat can leave a material, cooling it off enough that it collects moisture from the air.
- Moisture can evaporate, lowering the temperature of the air as the water absorbs heat in the phase change from liquid to vapor.

Is there a ranking of importance of these flows of moisture, air, and heat? Why, yes. But before we rank them, let's split moisture into two forms. The interactions of moisture with a house occur mainly in its liquid and vapor states,[8] and liquid water and water vapor behave differently. So, the flows of moisture, air, and heat are actually the flows of liquid water, water vapor, air, and heat. As for the relative importance of the four, Joseph Lstiburek, PhD, PE, puts them in the following order:

- Liquid water
- Air
- Water vapor
- Heat

From a design and construction perspective, liquid water is the most important because the majority of building damage related to the four flows is caused by liquid water. Floods that bring water up into a house, plumbing leaks that go unnoticed, or rain getting into parts of a house where you don't want it can cause major damage or even completely destroy a house. Moisture accumulating in porous materials also can create indoor air quality problems because the moisture encourages the growth of mold and the invasion of pests. Controlling liquid water is the first priority.

The reason air flow outranks water vapor is that uncontrolled flows of air across the building enclosure can carry heat and water vapor. As we'll see in Chapter 9, a lot more water vapor can move with air flows than by the slow spreading out of vapor due to its random molecular motion in the

air. In a way then, water vapor is kind of in both second and third places in this ranking. But air flow is still more important because it also moves heat. Further, air moving across the building enclosure can carry pollutants such as carbon monoxide from the garage into the living space. Let's say it again: A house does *not* need to breathe!

> *Air moving across the building enclosure can carry pollutants such as carbon monoxide from the garage into the living space.*

Although heat is in last place in the priority list above, it is the one that often gets most of the attention. That's because heat is the only one with an associated operational cost. When the architect, builder, and trade contractors do their jobs well, you shouldn't have to think about controlling liquid water, air, or water vapor, except during the occasional maintenance or remodeling. You don't get a monthly bill for the amount of rainwater kept out of the house or the amount of air that didn't leak in from the garage, attic, or outdoors. But you do get monthly bills for the amount of energy you use because of heat that leaks out of the house in winter or into the house in summer. That energy has implications for your finances and also for clean air, global warming, and environmental justice.

The laws of thermodynamics are the science behind the flow of heat. We'll discuss all four of them in Chapter 10, but the two most important takeaways for building science are:

1. Heat flows when there's a temperature difference.
2. Heat flows from warmer to cooler objects.

Those two principles hold no matter the mechanism by which heat flows. Conduction, convection, and radiation all depend on temperature differences. The rate at which heat

---

8. Yes, snow sits on the roof and piles up around the base of a house in colder climates, but it usually doesn't create a problem until it melts and becomes liquid water.

flows depends on how it's flowing and on things like surface area and the nature of the materials.

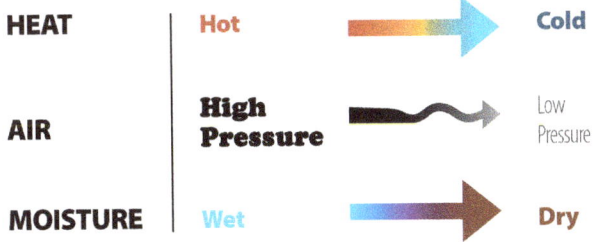

Figure 5.3. *The flows of heat, air, and moisture*

Now that we've mentioned the direction of heat flow, we should list the directions of all of the flows in one place.

- Liquid water flows from higher elevation to lower elevation by gravity.
- Liquid water flows from higher concentration to lower concentration by capillary action or diffusion.
- Air flows from higher pressure to lower pressure.
- Water vapor flows from warmer to cooler (most of the time).
- Water vapor flows from higher concentration to lower concentration.
- Heat flows from warmer to cooler.

Air and heat are the simpler ones because they each follow a simple rule of flowing from higher to lower pressure or temperature. The four rules above for water in the liquid and vapor states seem more complex. The one thing that binds them all, though, is that they all flow from higher to lower.

The key to a good building enclosure is controlling all four of these flows. Failure to do so can result in all kinds of problems, from comfort to indoor air quality to high energy bills to complete house failure. This is serious business.

Control Layers

Now that we've seen the need to control the flows of heat, air, and moisture, how do we do that? With control layers, of course. We have four things

to control (liquid water, air, water vapor, and heat), so there are four control layers. Here are the control layers matched with what they're controlling:

- Liquid water: water-resistive barrier (WRB), flashing
- Air: air barrier
- Water vapor: vapor retarder
- Heat: insulation

One of those four, however, is not like the others. Building codes require building enclosure control layers for liquid water, air, and heat in every climate. Using vapor retarders to control water vapor moving through the building enclosure, though, isn't generally required in warmer climates. We'll cover this in Chapter 9. They are only required on air conditioning ducts in humid climates.

In Chapters 7 through 10, we'll cover the details on the various types of control layers. For now, though, keep in mind that you don't always need separate products or materials for the different control layers. Sometimes one product can be the control layer for more than one of the four flows. For example, a water resistive barrier's main function is to be the control layer for liquid water, but it could also control air and water vapor. Along the same lines, closed-cell spray polyurethane foam can be the control layer for all four.

Alignment of the Control Layers

To properly control the flows of moisture, air, and heat, control layers need to be in the right places. The key is knowing your climate and your building assemblies. What good would it do to put the liquid water control layer beneath the drywall on the inside of a wall? If you did that, you'd be giving wind-driven rain free access to all the materials outside that location. Wood, concrete, and other porous materials in the structure would suck up as much water as they could. Some insulation materials (e.g., fiberglass, cellulose, open-cell spray foam) would get soggy and lose their effectiveness. Stuff would rot, grow mold, and invite termites. You've got to put things in the right places.

The liquid water control layer usually goes as far outside as you can get it. That means just under the cladding in most cases, but it also could be between the exterior insulation and sheathing. The air barrier works well on the outside, as does the insulation. If a vapor retarder is needed, it may go on the interior (cold climate), the exterior (hot or cold climate), or in the middle of the building enclosure (double-stud wall).

Figure 5.4. *Air-permeable insulation like fiberglass must be aligned with an air barrier. In this house, it wasn't.*

One part of aligning the control layers that's frequently messed up is getting the insulation and air barrier right. Some insulation types allow air to move through them. Fibrous materials like mineral wool, cellulose, or fiberglass are mostly air, with pathways that connect all that air. There's nothing wrong with that. The key is making sure that air doesn't move through it. You do that by putting air-permeable insulation in contact with the air barrier. In walls, it needs to be encapsulated on six sides. In Figure 5.4, you can see fiberglass insulation with a paper facing. There's no air barrier on either side of that wall, though, as you can tell because you can see right through to the other side with one piece of fiberglass pulled aside. The other way to ensure alignment of the control layers for heat and air flow is to use an insulation material that controls both, such as rigid foam board and spray foam insulation.

The Pen Test

A few years ago, the US Environmental Protection Agency published a document titled *Moisture Control Guidance for Building Design, Construction, and Maintenance*. It's an excellent resource full of useful information about indoor air quality, fundamental building science principles, and controlling moisture. One of the most important tools in it is the pen test described in Appendix A of that document. During the design phase, the architect can do the pen test to ensure the continuity of the control layers—and mark the control layers on the plans. Then during construction, the contractor should review the pen test and pay special attention to any tricky areas. This test is both simple and powerful, and it can prevent a lot of pain down the road.

To do the pen test, you simply pick a spot on a section in the plans and then trace the control layers for heat, and air, and liquid water (rain). If you have to pick up your pen at any point, you've discovered a flaw in that particular control layer.

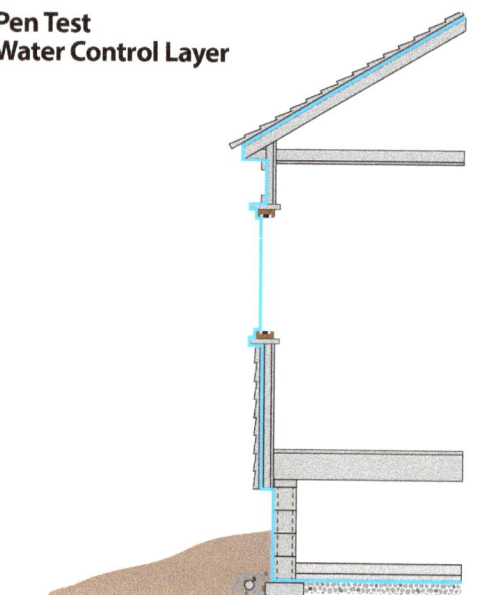

Figure 5.5. *In this pen test diagram, the blue line shows where the liquid water control layer should be.*

Figure 5.5 shows a sample liquid water control layer pen test diagram. You can follow this control layer (the blue line) from the roof membrane all the way down to the polyethylene sheet under

Learning to look at the building with "pen test eyes" can go a long way toward making buildings that work properly.

the slab in this section. You need to pay special attention at every transition from one material or assembly to another and where the openings for windows, doors, and penetrations are.

The same principle applies to the heat and air control layers, and you can see the examples in the EPA's moisture control guide. (See resources.) These three control layers don't always follow the same path. For example, the water control layer will always be along the roofline, but the air and heat control layers are often at the ceiling below the roof.

One final note about the pen test: It starts with design. The builder then goes over the plans and makes sure they understand how to do it right. But then comes the most important part: execution! Once construction begins, all kinds of unanticipated obstacles pop up. Changes get made on the fly, and what was a continuous line on paper now gets chopped up. And that's where the pen test shows its real value—as long as someone is in charge of control layer continuity on the job site. Even if the plans don't show a critical flashing detail or an electrician cuts a penetration that wasn't on the plans, the control layer enforcer can catch and fix those problems. Learning to look at the building with "pen test eyes" can go a long way toward making buildings that work properly.

A House Should Be Tailored to Its Climate

One of the fundamental principles of building science is that a building must be suited to its climate. When it's not, problems can ensue. Maybe the house is not as efficient as it should be. Maybe it's worse. Put plastic between the drywall and framing of your exterior walls in Ottawa, and it can help control vapor drive from the interior air and its associated moisture problems. Put that plastic in the same place in Georgia, and you may rot the walls.

The first thing to know about climate zones is that we divide them up based on two parameters: temperature and moisture. The fancy word for this type of division is hygrothermal. Building Science Corporation has a nice map of the hygrothermal regions of North America (Figure 5.6).

The International Code Council has a more fine-grained and quantitative approach to climate zones in the United States, as shown in Figure 5.7 from the 2021 version of the International Energy Conservation Code (IECC). Each zone has a number, starting with 0 for the hottest areas (none in the United States) and going up to 8 (the coldest parts in Alaska).

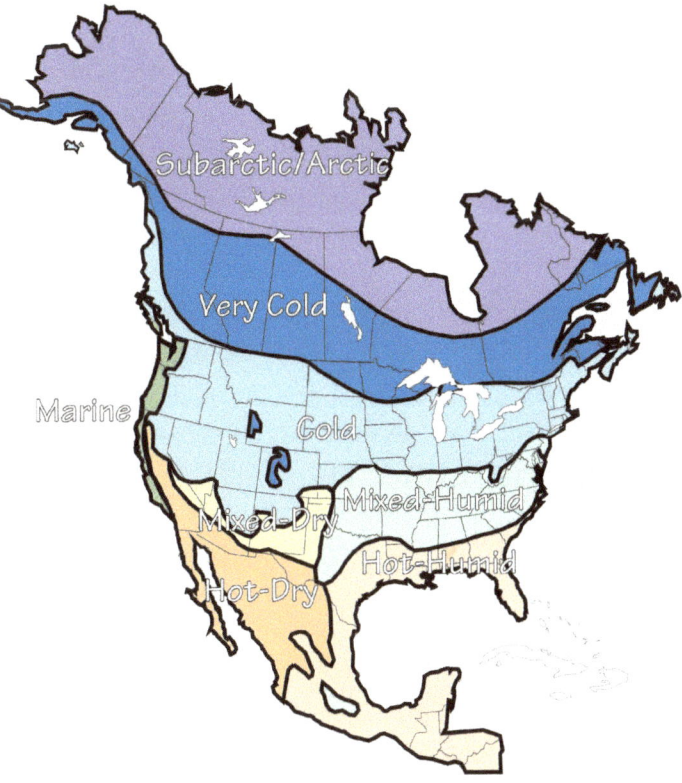

Figure 5.6. *The major hygrothermal regions of North America [Courtesy of Joseph Lstiburek]*

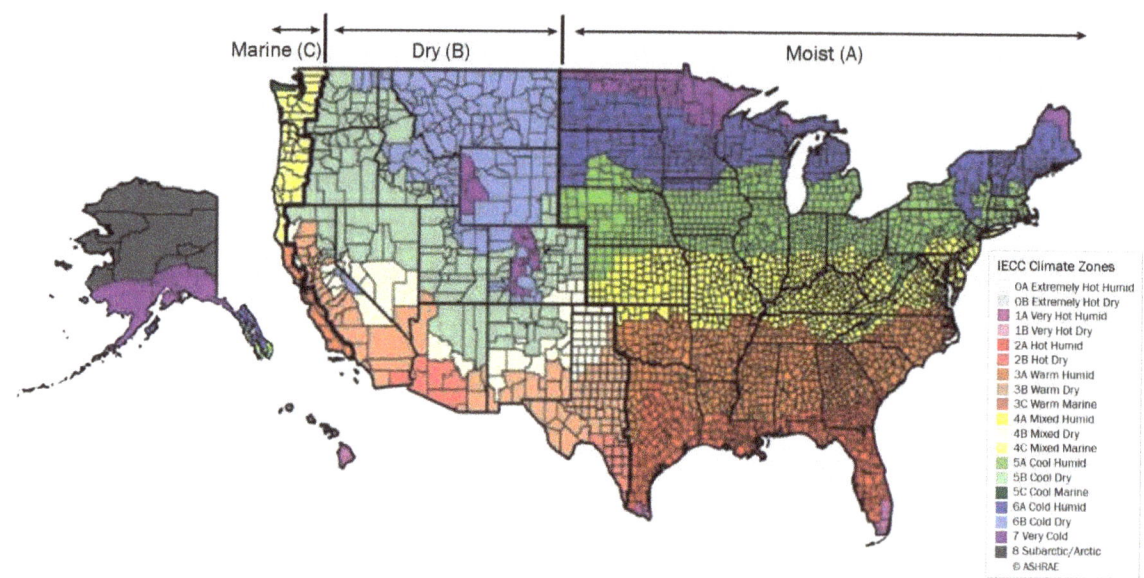

Figure 5.7. *The US climate zones used in the 2021 International Energy Conservation Code [Source: US Department of Energy, Building America Solution Center]*

Temperature Divisions

The number of each zone tells you how warm or cold it is. Although temperature is the primary way we talk about how hot or cold a place is, that's not a full description of what separates these climate zones. It's not just how cold or how hot the place gets. It's based on accumulated temperature calculations called degree days. Basically, heating degree days combine the amount of time and the temperature difference below some base temperature, and cooling degree days do likewise for temperatures above a base temperature.

For example, let's use the most common base temperature for heating, 65 °F. If the temperature stays at 55 °F for 24 hours, you've accumulated 10 heating degree days (HDD). It's the same for cooling degree days (CDD). The IECC uses 50 °F for the cooling base temperature, so if the temperature is 90 °F for 24 hours, you've got 40 CDD. For heating and cooling, you add up the total number of HDD or CDD for the whole year, and that tells you how hot, cold, or mild the climate is. (See the resources for more degree days information.)

Table 5.1 shows how the IECC uses the number of cooling degree days for climate zones 0 through 5 and the number of heating degree days for climate zones 3 through 8. In zones 0 through 2, cooling dominates. In zones 3 through 5, heating and cooling both matter. In zones 6 and higher, it's mostly about heating.

Zone Number	Thermal Criteria	
	IP units	SI units
0	CDD50 °F: > 10,800	CDD10 °C: > 6,000
1	CDD50 °F: 9,000 to 10,800	CDD10 °C: 5,000 to 6,000
2	CDD50 °F: 6,300 to 9,000	CDD10 °: 3,500 to 5,000
3	CDD50 °F: ≤ 6,300 *AND* HDD65 °F: ≤ 3,600	CDD10 °C: < 3,500 AND HDD18 °C: ≤ 2,000
4	CDD50 °F: ≤ 6,300 *AND* HDD65 °F: 3,600 to 5,400	CDD10 °C: < 3,500 AND HDD18 °C: 2,000 to 3,000
5	CDD50 °F: ≤ 6,300 *AND* HDD65 °F: 5,400 to 7,200	CDD10 °C: < 3,500 AND HDD18 °C: 3,000 to 4,000
6	HDD65 °F: 7,200 to 9,000	HDD18 °C: 4,000 to 5,000
7	HDD65 °F: 9,000 to 12,600	HDD18 °C: 5,000 to 7,000
8	HDD65 °F: > 12,600	HDD18 °C: > 7,000

Table 5.1. *The IECC climate zones are defined in terms of cooling degree days (CDD) and heating degree days (HDD) at the base temperatures indicated. [Adapted from the IECC]*

Note that the climate zone map for your local code may be different. With the 2021 IECC, the map changed. About 10 percent of the counties in

Myth: A House Needs to Breathe

I've heard this statement from a lot of people over the years, many of them home builders. The idea is that when you make a house airtight, you trap the air inside and the level of indoor air pollution just keeps rising. Materials can outgas nasty chemicals. Cooking dumps particles into the air. The dog keeps doing its thing. So, you need to make sure the house has enough random holes in the building enclosure to keep the air fresh, right?

Wrong! A house cannot be too tight. Yes, an airtight house can have problems, but it's not because of the air sealing. Leaky houses often have the same problems or worse. The problem here is the lack of systems thinking.

Here are three problems that the proponents of "breathing houses" think they're able to solve with random leaks:

1. Poor indoor air quality (IAQ)
2. Backdrafting of combustion appliances
3. High humidity leading to mold growth

If a leaky house is the solution to the first of these problems, how exactly does that work? Those random holes are going to bring air into the house from places like the smelly garage, the moldy crawl space, and the dirty attic. "Ah, yes. This house needs to suck in some air through that dead squirrel in the attic."

No! The solution is laid out in Chapter 2. It's a combination of airtightness, source control, filtration, ventilation, and other measures. We understand this now. Random leaks don't bring in fresh air, so we seal up the house and make it as airtight as possible and then intentionally bring in air from a location where we know it will be as fresh as possible.

Problem number 2 above, backdrafting combustion appliances, can be dangerous. When air is coming down the exhaust flue and into the house, the exhaust gases aren't going up the flue pipe. That changes the combustion process, making it more likely to generate carbon monoxide and then dump it into the house. Not good.

My first suggestion for avoiding backdrafting is to avoid combustion appliances. Go all electric, and your water heater will never poison your family with carbon monoxide. If that's not something you want to do, at least get sealed combustion appliances.

The third problem, high humidity, is actually helped by airtightness. In a humid climate, most of the water vapor is outdoors. If your house is too humid, where do you think that moisture is coming from? Seal up the house, and then look for other ways to control humidity like a properly designed, installed, and maintained air-conditioning system, bathroom exhaust fans, and a kitchen range hood. Because of enhanced building codes and the way air conditioners work (Chapters 12 and 13), many homes now also need supplemental dehumidification.

The need for materials that don't trap moisture is true for many houses. Unless you're in a heating-only or cooling-only climate, like Minneapolis or Miami, putting plastic in your walls can trap moisture and grow things. Houses don't need to breathe, but they do need to be able to dry out when they get wet.

Here, then, are three rules that we could substitute for this myth about houses needing to breathe:

• People need to breathe.
• Don't mix combustion air and people air.
• Houses need to be able to dry.

the United States changed to a different climate zone, with most of them going to warmer zones (lower numbers). If you're in one of those swing counties and your state currently uses an earlier version of the code, you'll need to use the earlier climate zone map. One of the states that changed the most is Wisconsin, with 45 of 72 counties (63 percent) moving to warmer climate zones.

Moisture Divisions

Notice that the IECC map also shows how moisture impacts the climate zones. Generally, it's moist to the east, dry to the west, and marine along the West Coast. I remember driving across Texas from west to east in the summer of '88 and feeling the humidity hit us when we crossed that black line west of Dallas. It's real!

As a matter of fact, people have known about that line since the 19th century. It lies pretty close to the 100th meridian of longitude and divides the part of the United States that gets enough rain to farm without irrigation from the dry side that requires irrigation.

The IECC has three main moisture divisions. How they determine which one you're in is based mainly on annual average temperature and precipitation, and it gets a bit complex. The way you determine which climate zone you're in is much easier. You just look it up. Not many people even have to think about it much because most of us don't live near a black line separating moist from dry climates. And if you're in a marine climate, you live on the West Coast. Here are brief descriptions of the three moisture divisions.

Moist (A): This is designated by the letter A after the climate zone number. Most of the United States is designated as moist, as you can see on the map in Figure 5.7.

Dry (B): This is the western part of the country except for most of the coast.

Marine (C): This is nearly the entire West Coast. Only the southern California coastline is excluded.

It's All in the IECC

Wherever you read building science, you're likely to run into someone talking about climate zones, and if you don't know the exact definitions, it can be a bit confusing. Now you've got my little summary here, but you can always get a copy of the IECC as well. It's updated every three years, and your state may be one or more cycles behind. In addition to the basic definitions above, the IECC also tells you county by county what the local climate zone is.

For those of you outside the United States, your building codes (and energy code, if you have one) may define climate zones differently, so be sure to check them first. If for some reason you wanted to compare to the United States and see where the IECC definitions would put your location, you'll need to get a copy of the code and dig in. They do give SI units, though, as you can see in Table 5.1, so you don't have to worry about conversions.

Chapter Takeaways

- A house is a system.
- The building enclosure separates conditioned space from various types of unconditioned space.
- Controlling the flows of heat, air, and moisture is critical. This is done by control layers in the building enclosure.
- A house needs to work in the climate where it's located.
- Climate zones are based on the amount of heating and cooling needed as well as the amount of rainfall and humidity.

CHAPTER 6

Understanding Moisture

Water is responsible for most building failures. Whether it's rotten walls, roof leaks, or wet basements, water has a way of causing problems that are a bane to homeowners and can be expensive, too. What makes them worse is that they often don't show themselves until serious damage is done. The good news—unless you've already got moisture damage—is that they're largely preventable. The first step is understanding where moisture comes from, how it moves, and when it's okay to let it keep flowing.

Sources of Moisture

The first step in solving water problems when you have them or figuring out how to prevent them is to understand the source of the moisture. Where is it coming from? If you don't know that, you have little hope of solving the problem. Water can come from outside the house or inside. It can come from the sky, the ground, or the air. Its source can be natural or artificial. Here are the most common moisture sources that damage homes.

Groundwater: A house might sit in a naturally wet area, perhaps even right on top of a spring. Sometimes water coming up from the ground is an infrequent occurrence related to extreme weather, such as if your house is in a 100-year flood plain and you get that flood. Other times the ground wets the bottom of the house every spring, every time it rains, or every time you're out of money. The keys to solving groundwater problems are having a foundation appropriate for the site, making sure the ground around the house is sloped away from the foundation, and using the right waterproofing techniques on the foundation.

> *"The three biggest problems in buildings are water, water, and water."*
> —*Gus Handegord*

Figure 6.1. *Bulk water in a crawl space: The source was a backyard that sloped toward the unprotected crawl space wall.*

Rainwater: Precipitation, whether rain or snow, will put a house's moisture defenses to the test. When water hits a house from above, the roof is the first place it may gain entrance. Just getting the water off the roof, however, doesn't mean the house is safe. The gutters may direct all that rainwater or melting snow right into the foundation. Rain that hits the walls will test the moisture management details around all the windows, doors, and transitions.

Figure 6.2. *Heavy mold growing on floor joists: The water heater had a leak and sprayed water all over the crawl space for a long time before it was discovered. [Courtesy of David Goulding]*

Plumbing: One of the worst plumbing leaks I've heard about was a water heater in a crawl space. It had a leak that sprayed a fine mist of water into the crawl space over an extended period of time. The result, as you can guess, was catastrophic. That crawl space became one of the worst mold farms in the history of houses. In general, plumbing leaks are bad news, but the kind that aren't discovered for a long time tend to do the most damage.

Construction moisture: Lumber brought to a construction site often still has a lot of moisture in it. Even if it didn't come laden with moisture, it may get wet sitting out in the weather before it's used or when the house gets rained on before it's dried in. Some construction materials—concrete, drywall, and cellulose insulation—contain a lot of water that evaporates over time. If those wet materials are not allowed to dry, they can cause problems.

Outdoor air: In humid climates, the outdoor air carries a lot of water vapor. When that humid air gets into a house through infiltration or ventilation, comfort and indoor air quality may suffer, and condensation may occur on cooler surfaces.

Occupants: The people who live in the house also add moisture, mostly in the form of water vapor. Cooking, cleaning, showering, and breathing all add to the indoor humidity (Figure 6.3). Having a lot of indoor plants, pets, or aquariums adds even more moisture that must be dealt with.

HVAC systems: Air conditioners reduce indoor humidity when they run by condensing water vapor on the cold coil and sending the liquid water to the outdoors or to a plumbing drain. Condensate leaks, however, are common. Heating systems also can add to the moisture load in a house. High-efficiency furnaces produce liquid water by condensing the water vapor in the exhaust gases from the combustion process. If the condensate from an air conditioner or condensing furnace leaks—and it does sometimes—it can create problems. Another type of HVAC moisture, however, is more than just a plumbing leak. Unvented gas, kerosene, or propane space heaters produce a lot of water vapor. In homes with poor building enclosures, this can result in wet surfaces from condensation and mold as moisture gets into porous materials.

When you discover a moisture-related problem, the source of the water isn't always obvious. A bit of building science history illustrates that point beautifully.

Figure 6.3. *Occupants generate a lot of moisture indoors from breathing, showering, cooking, and cleaning. [Credit: Rochelle Hartman, flickr, CC2.0]*

The Story of Peeling Paint

Back in the 1920s and 1930s, homebuilders began adding insulation to the walls of the houses they built. Then something strange started happening. Painters began refusing to paint new homes that had insulation in the walls. Why? Because they'd often be called back to repaint those houses when the paint began peeling after a short time. This problem led to some interesting early research in building science—and a decades-long recommendation that still leads to problems.

Insulation and the Early Building Science Researchers

In his excellent book, *Water in Buildings,* Bill Rose lays out the US history of building science research spurred by the paint-peeling episode of those early adopters of insulation. On the first page of that chapter, Rose outlines a set of moisture management practices that developed in the period from 1937 to 1942. I'll abbreviate his six bullet points to three:

- Insulated buildings can have moisture problems because the exterior cladding and sheathing stay colder.
- Water vapor from the indoor air diffuses through the wall and settles in the cold cladding and sheathing.
- Vapor barriers are the solution to the problem.

It's a fascinating history, and Rose goes into the details of the people who advanced the theory of vapor diffusion and vapor barriers, the papers they wrote, and nearly two full pages on the 1952 condensation conference.

One of the most amusing parts is how the National Paint and Varnish Association got involved and declared war against water. Figure 6.4 is a cover of one of the booklets they published in the early 1950s. Written near

Figure 6.4. *Cover of a booklet promoting misguided advice about vapor barriers in walls*

the beginning of the Cold War, they villainize moisture much the same as McCarthy maligned communists. For example:

They seem innocent enough, these three pools of moisture: the milk from the bottle, the steam from the shower, the vapor rising from the whistling tea kettle. But are they? Oh, no, they're up to no good. Where do they go from here? Believe it or not, they have an engagement. At the "dewpoint"—if you please.

Yeah, we can laugh now, but back then building professionals and homeowners alike were practicing their duck-and-cover drills at the slightest hint of water vapor!

Will the Real Culprit Please Stand Up?

Those early building scientists did some good research and advanced our knowledge of buildings considerably. One researcher found that a material's wetness is related to its temperature in what Rose calls the **Fundamental Rule of Material Wetness**: Cold materials tend to be wet, and warm materials tend to be dry.

The problem, though, was that the industry focused almost entirely on moisture diffusion and the need for vapor barriers. (These are also the guys who gave us vented crawl spaces, which we'll get to in Chapter 11.) A chemist named F.L. Browne got it right way back in 1933. Yes, he mentioned diffusion as one mechanism for the wetting of walls and peeling of paint, but he also called out "poor carpenter work or faulty design," as quoted by Rose.

That is, the bigger problem was bad flashing details, which allowed rainwater to get into the building assemblies—and then stay there. Before insulation, it didn't matter as much because of the Fundamental Rule of Material Wetness. Uninsulated walls stayed warmer and thus drier. With insulation in the walls, the cladding was colder, which meant it had less tolerance for bad flashing.

So, the moral of the story is not to jump to conclusions. We learned a lot about vapor diffusion, but our decades-long obsession with vapor barriers was counterproductive and hindered us from learning the more important lesson: It's generally more important for building assemblies to be able to dry than it is to prevent wetting by vapor diffusion.

> *It's generally more important for building assemblies to be able to dry than it is to prevent wetting by vapor diffusion.*

I'll give the last word to Bill Rose on this topic: "Given the fact that a very small percentage of building problems (1 to 5 percent at most in the author's experience) are associated with wetting by water vapor diffusion, the argument for enhanced drying potential becomes much stronger."

When Is the Humidity Low Enough to Open the Windows?

One way the dew point can be helpful is in deciding when it's okay to open the windows. Relative humidity is a terrible gauge for that. Let's say the outdoor relative humidity is 50 percent while your indoor air is also at 50 percent. If the outdoor temperature is 90 °F when you open the windows, your indoor humidity will rise. At 75 °F and 50 percent relative humidity, your indoor air will have a 55 °F dew point. The outdoor air, at 90 °F and 50 percent, has a dew point of 69 °F. Open the windows to that, and you're bringing in more humid air!

A good humidity threshold for deciding when to open the windows is a dew point of 60 °F or below. You can check the dew point on your weather app. Before you open the windows, be sure to check the outdoor air quality, too, though. You can find apps for that as well.

Figure 6.12. *Dew point is a great way to decide if it's too humid outdoors to open the windows. If the dew point is above about 60 °F, keep the windows closed.*

The Properties of Water

Water is one of the most interesting substances in the universe. We live most of our lives between the temperatures of 0 °F and 100 °F, and in that range, water can be solid, liquid, or vapor. (This also assumes normal atmospheric pressures.) The only reason this seems normal is because we're used to it. How many other substances can exist in even two states at normal temperatures and pressures? All the other gases in the air remain in the gaseous state under normal conditions. Yes, we can solidify carbon dioxide, and we can liquify oxygen and nitrogen, but those require refrigeration technology because the phase changes require temperatures of -109 °F, -130 °F, and -320 °F.

Water's ability to exist in three states at normal conditions impacts atmospheric science, the human body, and buildings. For example, snow can damage a house by melting on the roof because too much heat from the home leaks into the attic (ice dams). Heavy rains and high temperatures in summer can increase the humidity, interfering with your body's ability to use evaporation to cool itself. Water vapor in your home's indoor air can accumulate in porous materials, causing mold growth and attracting termites and carpenter ants.

The Direction of Moisture Flow

In the previous chapter, we found out that the second law of thermodynamics governs the direction of flow for moisture, air, and heat. The general rule is that these three flows go in the direction of more to less, whether it be air pressure, concentration, or temperature. Some people say the rule for moisture is that it always flows from wetter areas to drier areas. But what about water falling off the roof into a big puddle? That's wet to wet. What about lots of spread-out, individual water vapor molecules in the air coming together to form a drop of liquid water? That's drier to wetter, so that general rule about wet to dry can't be true.

Water is a complex substance with many unusual habits. The second law of thermodynamics is likewise complex and unusual. The key is to understand the second law in its broader context. The two forces responsible for moisture flow are gravity and the electrostatic force.[9] What the second law actually says for moisture flow is that, without the input of additional energy, those forces will move water to lower energy states. When liquid water drips off the roof, it loses gravitational potential energy. The kinetic energy it gained on the way down becomes heat when it hits the puddle. So, in the case of liquid water, the flow is from high elevation to low elevation.

When water vapor condenses into a drop of liquid water, the kinetic energy of the vapor molecule becomes heat, and the resulting drop of liquid water is in a lower energy state. But why does it condense? We'll get into this in more detail later, but generally water vapor condenses into the liquid state when it finds a cool surface. You've probably never seen condensation appear on the outside of a hot frying pan. (I say "probably" here because it all depends on the dew point of the water vapor near the pan relative to the temperature of the pan. We'll discuss dew point in a bit.) So, in the case of water vapor condensing, the flow is from warm to cool.

The last example here is water vapor that doesn't change phase. If you boil water on the stove, steam comes up off the surface of the water. Then what? It doesn't hover right there over the pot, getting more and more concentrated until

---

9. By the way, there are three fundamental forces in the universe. Any force you can think of can be shown to be either gravitational, electro-weak, or the strong nuclear force. You know about gravity already. The electro-weak force is electromagnetism combined with one type of force seen in atomic nuclei. The strong force is what holds protons and neutrons together in a nucleus.

it forms a little cloud that starts raining in your kitchen. No, it spreads out. The stuff you see, by the way, isn't water vapor. Individual water molecules are far too small for the human eye to see. What you see are clusters of water molecules, and they quickly break up until you have individual water molecules floating around. Then their kinetic energy keeps them moving and spreading out. This water vapor flow is driven by vapor pressure, but you can think of it as being driven by the difference in concentration. So, in the case of water vapor in a space, the flow is from higher vapor pressure (or concentration) to lower vapor pressure (or concentration). That's essentially a wet-to-dry flow.

We can summarize the second law of thermodynamics for moisture flow as:

- Moisture flows from higher elevation to lower elevation.
- Moisture flows from warmer to cooler.
- Moisture flows from higher vapor pressure to lower vapor pressure (or concentration).

As with heat flow and air flow, moisture flows from a place where some physical quantity (elevation, temperature, or vapor pressure) is higher to where it's lower. But the flows of heat, air, and moisture have something more in common. All three flows are driven by the move to lower energy states when they're available.

The Electrical Nature of Water

Now, let's discuss the electrostatic forces that drive some of the moisture flow. Each water molecule, H_2O, contains two hydrogen atoms and one oxygen atom. The water molecule also happens to be bent (Figure 6.5). Because of how the three atoms share electrons, the side of the molecule with the hydrogen ends up with a slight positive charge, and the oxygen side gets a small negative charge. It is electrically polar.

Figure 6.6, each water molecule can form weak bonds, called hydrogen bonds, with four other water molecules.

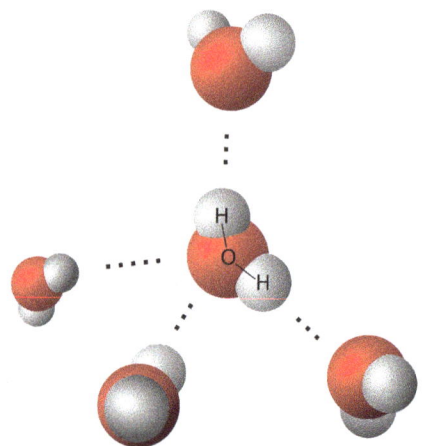

Figure 6.6. *The polarity of water molecules attracts other water molecules.*

One consequence of water's polarity is that it's a liquid at higher temperatures than similar molecules. Carbon dioxide, for example, is a linear, nonpolar molecule and cannot exist in the liquid state unless the pressure is five times normal atmospheric pressure. If water were like carbon dioxide, the low parts of the Earth's crust wouldn't be filled with water. Mountains would have no snow. And I wouldn't be writing this

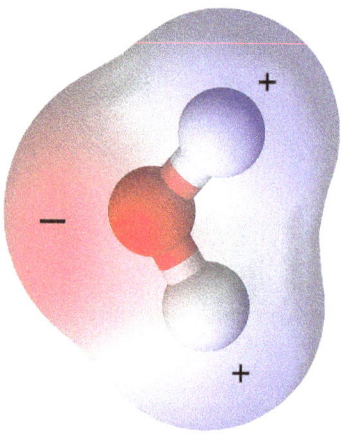

Figure 6.5. *A water molecule*

When you put a bunch of water molecules together, the polarity of the individual molecules causes them to attract each other. Like charges repel, and unlike charges attract. As you see in

because we humans would not exist, at least not in the form we do now.

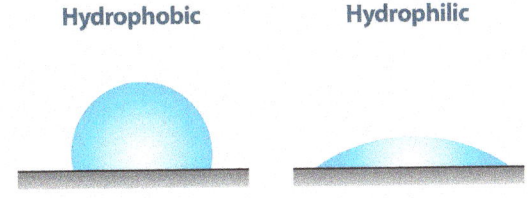

Hydrophobic   **Hydrophilic**

Figure 6.7. *How water interacts with different materials depends on which attraction is stronger—water for itself (hydrophobic) or water for the other material (hydrophilic).*

Here's another interesting fact about the polarity of water molecules. When you put water in contact with another material, what happens depends on which attraction is stronger: water for itself or water for the other material. When the water is more strongly attracted to itself, as you see on the left side of Figure 6.7, we call the other material hydrophobic, or water fearing. When the water is more strongly attracted to the other material than to itself, we say that material is hydrophilic, or water loving.

Water Vapor and Porous Materials

Things start getting fun when we take a look at what happens when water vapor interacts with porous materials. If you have such a material (drywall, wood, concrete, cellulose, etc.) with humid air around it, water vapor will find its way into the pores. If the material is hydrophilic, water vapor will start sticking to the walls of those pores. When a surface pulls water out of the air like this, we call the material hygroscopic. We also say that it has hygroscopic water on the surfaces.

Another word you need to know here is "adsorbed." Something that's *adsorbed* sticks to the surface. Something *absorbed*, on the other hand, is pulled into the volume. A pie thrown in your face is adsorbtion. A pie you eat is absorption. Water molecules adsorb because they stick to the walls of the pores rather than getting pulled into the bulk of the material. As they do, the molecules build up in layers.

The water that adsorbs to the pore walls of hygroscopic materials is not really liquid, solid, or vapor. Why? Because the energy changes that occur when it sticks or unsticks (adsorbs or desorbs) don't match the energy changes that happen during freezing, melting, evaporation, or condensation. So, when wood and drywall are in a humid environment and pull in a lot of water vapor because they're hygroscopic materials, the process isn't strictly condensation, which forms droplets of liquid water. It's adsorption, which forms layers of water.

The amount of water vapor adsorbed in the pores of hygroscopic materials depends on the type of material, the temperature, and the relative humidity. The moisture content of a material varies with relative humidity, and each type of material has its own characteristic relationship of how the moisture content varies with humidity (Figure 6.8).

At very low humidity, the moisture content of the material is low. As the humidity increases, the moisture content increases. For each unit of humidity rise in the middle range of relative humidity, the moisture content increases at a steady pace. But at a certain point, the moisture content begins to spike upward at a much greater rate. At that point, the pores are beginning to fill up with

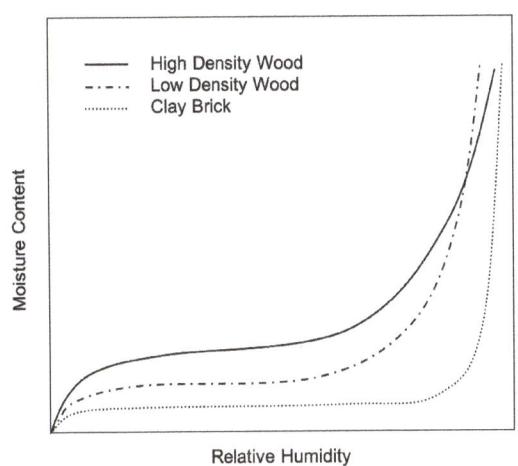

Figure 6.8. *Sorption isotherm curves for several porous building materials [Courtesy of Chris Timusk, PhD]*

water molecules, and the water starts acting more like a liquid. (Graphs of moisture content versus relative humidity are called sorption isotherms, and they are a great help to building scientists.)

Capillary Action of Liquid Water

Recall that the two forces that move water are gravity and the electrostatic force. Water in the liquid state will flow from one place to another by gravity as it seeks a lower level (e.g., that low spot in the basement). Water also flows by its electrostatic attraction to other materials. This can be in the opposite direction that gravity wants the water to go because the electrostatic force is a much stronger force than the gravitational force. Gravity is easy to understand, and we'll discuss how to prevent and solve moisture problems driven by gravitational flows in Chapter 7. Let's turn our attention now to the more interesting flows driven by electrostatic attraction.

Houses are built from and filled with myriad porous materials, and the pores usually have an affinity for water. If a porous material has one end sitting in water, for example, the pores, or capillaries, will begin filling with water. The movement of water

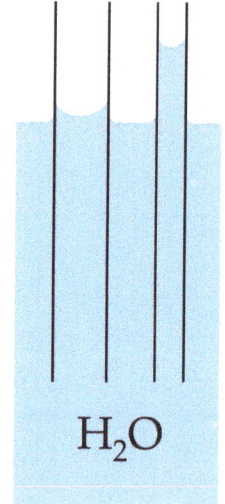

Figure 6.9. *Water rises in tubes by capillary action, and it rises higher in smaller tubes. [Credit: MesserWoland Wikimedia Commons, CC 3.0]*

through capillaries depends on how hydrophilic, or wettable, a surface is and on how small the capillary is. The smaller the capillary, the higher the water can rise in it, as shown in Figure 6.9. This type of moisture flow is called capillary action.

The photo in Figure 6.10 shows the capillary rise of water in a brick. After 64 minutes, the water has climbed three-quarters of the way up the brick.

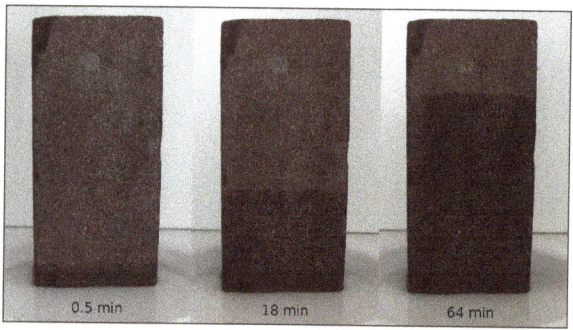

Figure 6.10. *Water rises in these porous bricks through capillary action.*

Think of a foundation with no waterproofing sitting in saturated soil. Concrete has many pores that can wick water up above the level of the soil. The same is true of wood. When water wicks up from the foundation, it can find other porous materials that allow it to move even farther. Bad window flashing, with gravity pulling the water down, is one way to rot a band joist. A wet foundation, with capillary action pulling water up, is another.

Water Vapor and Moist Air

The study of water vapor is endlessly fascinating. Water in the vapor state usually doesn't exist by itself, as a pure substance. It mixes with the air in greater or lesser amounts, and it's that mixture of dry air and water vapor that's so interesting. In fact, the study of moist air is a branch of science with its own name: psychrometrics. In a hot desert, the percent of the air that's made up of water vapor may be only a few tenths of a percent by mass. The most humid air that occurs naturally here on Earth contains about 3 percent water vapor by mass. Water vapor concentration can vary so widely because of water's unusual ability to exist as a liquid, solid, or vapor at normal atmospheric temperatures and pressures.

Moist air is a mixture, not a pure substance. All that means is we can separate the components by physical processes like condensation or freezing. The two major components are dry air and water vapor, and dry air itself is also a mixture. Table 6.1 shows the major components. In addition to those shown, dry air has small amounts of neon, helium, krypton, and other gases.

Component	Content by Volume
Nitrogen (N_2)	78.08 percent
Oxygen (O_2)	20.95 percent
Argon (Ar)	0.93 percent
Carbon dioxide (CO_2)	0.04 percent

Table 6.1. *The top four components of dry air, by volume*

Dew Point Temperature

The first thing to understand is that water vapor floating around in the air interacts with the materials in contact with the air. As in the example of morning dew on the grass, water vapor can condense on materials if their temperature is low enough. The dividing line between condensing and not condensing is the dew point temperature. When the temperature of a material is above the dew point, we don't get condensation. When it's below the dew point, condensation occurs. And the lower the temperature of a material, the more water vapor will condense out of the air.

Figure 6.11. *Condensation on a single-pane window*

Each of those elements and compounds has its own set of properties, but there's one important thing they have in common. It's also the thing that distinguishes dry air from water vapor. The dry air components don't change phase at the normal temperature and pressure ranges we deal with. Unless the temperature drops below -148 °F (-100 °C)—and no place on Earth gets that cold—all of the dry air components exist in the gas phase only. They don't condense out of the air.

But water vapor regularly condenses out of and evaporates back into the air. When the temperature drops at night, we sometimes wake up in the morning to find dew on the grass and on our cars. When the sun hits the grass later in the morning, the dew starts evaporating and will return to the air as the temperature rises.

But what exactly is the dew point temperature? You can think of it as just another way of talking about the concentration of water vapor. The more water vapor is in the air, the more humid it is and the higher the dew point temperature. A high dew point means condensation is more likely. On a hot, humid day in 2016, I visited Daniel Boone's house in Missouri. Figure 6.11 shows one of the windows of the house. The condensation is on the outside of the glass. The room on the other side of the single-pane window was air conditioned. The dew point temperature outdoors was 75 °F, so the outer surface of that glass had to be below 75 °F to create that much condensation. When you run the air conditioner on high outdoor dew point days in a house with single-pane windows, this is what can happen.

We use dew point to our benefit with dehumidifiers. Air passes over a cold coil whose temperature is below the dew point. Water vapor condenses, and the air gets drier. When we're talking about parts of a building, though, we'd rather not have water vapor condensing on materials, whether that's bathroom windows, crawl space band joists, or vinyl-covered walls. Accidental dehumidification is generally not a good thing.

The more water vapor is in the air, the more humid it is and the higher the dew point temperature.

Three Important Points about Dew Point Temperature

1. The dew point is a temperature.

I've certainly been guilty of using the shorthand term "dew point" and will continue to do so. It's important to remember, though, that whenever we talk about dew point, we're talking about a temperature. It's not a place or time or event. It's a temperature. And the dew point temperature tells us when condensation like you see in Figure 6.11 will happen. It tells us about the potential for condensation but not the actual occurrence.

2. The dew point temperature is a property of the air.

More correctly, the dew point temperature is a property only of the water vapor in the air. But we're here on Earth. Our atmosphere and buildings are filled with both the dry air components (nitrogen, oxygen, etc.) and water vapor, so it's okay to say the dew point temperature is a property of the air. And that property is related to the concentration of water vapor in the air. The more water vapor per volume of air, the higher the dew point temperature will be. (The dew point temperature is also related to pressure.)

3. Materials have a temperature, but not a dew point.

Dew point temperature is a property of a material in the vapor phase. That glass in the window in Figure 6.11 is definitely not a vapor. It's a solid material. It has a temperature. But it doesn't have a dew point temperature unless you vaporize it.

Avoiding dew point confusion.

The point I'm trying to make here is that condensation is the result of two separate properties coming into alignment: the dew point temperature of the air and the surface temperature of a material in contact with the air. The air has its dew point temperature. When a nearby surface has a temperature at or below the dew point temperature, condensation occurs. Dew point temperature and material temperature are two separate things.

There are other important facts about dew point temperature, too. In this section, my focus is on condensation only. That's what you see in Figure 6.11, or on the bathroom mirror after your shower. Water vapor interacts differently with porous materials like drywall and wood, though. See "Water Vapor and Porous Materials" on page 79 for more on that topic.

Dew Point Temperature versus Relative Humidity

Most people are used to thinking about humidity in terms of relative humidity, a 0 to 100 percent scale. My goal is to get you to think about humidity in terms of dew point temperature rather than relative humidity. Why? Because relative humidity is misleading. That whole "relative" thing is slippery.

For example, building industry professionals who deal with moisture problems tell me they regularly see both temperature and relative humidity in the 90s (Fahrenheit and percent, respectively). It's a common misconception. One builder said, "Where I live, it gets up to 98 °F and 95 percent relative humidity."

I don't doubt those people. It's just that their timing is off. Yes, hitting temperatures in the 90s, even up to 98, is certainly possible in the majority of the United States. And having relative humidity at 90 percent or higher is also possible, especially in the Eastern states. They just don't happen at the same time. When they do, new records may be set.

Yes, meteorologists and climatologists keep records of such things as highest dew point. Dew point is the quantity you have to look at for humidity records because it actually tells you something about how much water vapor is in the air. Relative humidity tells you how close you are to saturation (100 percent), which happens when the water vapor starts condensing out as you try to add more.

Let's look at some dew point records. Table 6.2. shows the three highest dew points recorded in the United States.

You're probably wondering now about the rest of the world. The highest dew point temperature ever recorded was 95 °F on July 8, 2003, at Dhahran, Saudi Arabia. The air temperature at the time was 108 °F, making the relative humidity a relatively dry-sounding 68 percent.

Yes, a 90/90 day for air temperature and relative humidity is possible. It happened at least once, and it set a record. But those are far from normal conditions. An 80/80 day, however, is quite likely on the humid side of North America. The dew point in those conditions is 73 °F. If you live in Houston, Mobile, or Tampa, that's about the low end of dew point for you in summer. In Atlanta, that's about where we top out.

Here's one more perspective on dew point: When you keep your house at recommended design conditions of 75 °F and 50 percent relative humidity, the dew point is 55 °F. That's comfortable. Even an indoor dew point of 58 °F in summer is still comfortable to most people.

The weather app on your phone probably shows the dew point for your location, so if you get in the habit of looking at it, you'll have a better idea of the humidity than if you go by relative humidity. Here in Atlanta, our normal summer range is from the mid 60s to the low 70s. On the coast of the Gulf of Mexico, it's usually in the mid to upper 70s and even into the 80s. In Nevada, the average dew point in summer is less than 50 °F, and minimum dew points can be below 0 °F!

Location	When	Dew Point	Air Temperature	Relative Humidity
Appleton, Wisconsin	7/13/95	90 °F	101 °F	71%
Melbourne, Florida	7/12/87	91 °F	95 °F	88%
New Orleans, Louisiana	7/30/87	90 °F	91 °F	97%

Table 6.2. *Dew point temperature records in the United States*

Chapter Takeaways

- Water in homes can come from several sources.
- Controlling liquid water (rain, plumbing leaks, etc.) is more important than controlling water vapor because in most cases, liquid water can result in more wetting.
- Water flows from high to low. That could be from high to low elevation, high to low concentration, or high to low temperature. These aren't absolute directions of flow in every case because water can flow from high to low concentration while flowing from low to high elevation (capillary action).
- The water molecule is electrically polar, which governs much of its behavior.
- The study of the mixture of dry air and water vapor is called psychrometrics.
- For many purposes, the dew point temperature is a better gauge of humidity than is relative humidity.
- Porous materials interact with water vapor in the air, accumulating and releasing water vapor based on the relative humidity.
- Sorption isotherms show the relationship between the moisture content of porous materials and the relative humidity. Each material has characteristic curves that depend on the nature of the materials.

CHAPTER 7
Controlling Liquid Water

Now that we understand the properties of water, we can discuss controlling it. Because liquid water is the most important one to control, we'll begin there. The exterior of a house is covered with some kind of cladding, like brick, siding, or stucco on the walls and shingles, metal, or tile on the roof. Although the cladding stops a lot of the rain from getting through to the materials behind, it doesn't stop all of it. Wind, for example, can drive rain through gaps and into the space behind the cladding. That's why we need a liquid water control layer back there.

Before we get into the details, though, let's discuss vocabulary. Here are some important terms used for this part of the building enclosure:

Water control layer: Combination of the drainage plane, flashing, and other liquid water management details on the outside of a house. Sometimes it's called the liquid water control layer or the rain control layer.

Drainage plane: Water-repellent materials used in the field of roofs or walls to drain the

> **"You can't trust water: Even a straight stick turns crooked in it."**
> –W.C. Fields

liquid water, integrated with flashing and other liquid water management details to form the continuous water control layer. They may also act as the water vapor control layer, or they may allow water vapor to pass through. Common types include house wrap, building paper, and peel-and-stick membranes. (More on this below.)

Water-resistive barrier (WRB): Another term for the material used as a drainage plane; it's also called water-resistant barrier, weather-resistant barrier, or weather resistive barrier.

Flashing: Components that divert water away from parts of the building. It must be integrated with the drainage plane and is used around windows, doors, and transitions, such as where a roof meets a wall.

Drain the Rain

Draining a house properly is the aikido of building science. Just as an aikido master uses an opponent's momentum against him, an effective liquid water control layer incorporates slopes and diverters to keep water moving down and out from a house. Here's Joseph Lstiburek, PhD, PE, explaining the objective:

"The fundamental principle of water management is to shed water by layering materials in such a way that water is directed downwards and outwards out of the building or away from the building." [10]

The water wants to go down, and you design and install a series of layers that will ensure it also goes out. Down and out is the rule for draining the rain (Figure 7.1).

Think of it in personal terms. When you wear rubber boots, rain pants, and a raincoat, you have to put them on correctly to stay dry in the rain. You don't tuck the rain pants into your boots or your raincoat into your pants. You layer them the other way to keep the rain moving down and out.

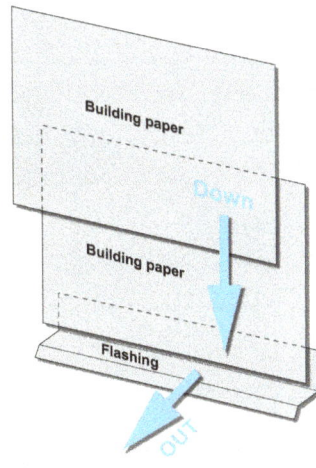

Figure 7.1. *Layer your liquid water control materials to keep the water moving down and out from the house. [Courtesy of Joseph Lstiburek]*

10. RR-0103: Water Management, https://www.buildingscience.com/documents/reports/rr-0103-water-management/view, (9/15/01)

Roofs and Overhangs

Roofs will be exposed to more water than any other part of the house. It's essential that they're designed well and detailed properly. The surface of the roof will be covered with asphalt shingles, metal roofing, clay tiles, or some other material that will repel water and keep it moving down and out from the house. Most houses have sloped roofs, which aids greatly in draining the rain. Intersecting roof sections create valleys that concentrate water, and they require special attention. Penetrations, chimneys, dormers, and other features that interrupt the flow of liquid water also require special attention—or elimination from the design altogether.

Speaking of design, the two main roof problems that lead to water damage are lack of maintenance and poor design. Maintaining the roof is one of the most important responsibilities of homeowners. Delaying inspections, repairs, or replacement only leads to trouble. Roof maintenance on existing homes with poor design is even more critical. Homes still in the design process can be spared future problems by avoiding trouble spots. Here are a few.

Figure 7.2. *The poor design of this roof-wall intersection causes debris to collect and may result in water damage.*

Roofs that slope downward into a wall: Figure 7.2 shows a roof with a wall intersecting on the downward slope. The area between wall and roof section has a cricket, a built-up section to provide more slope to divert the water from the wall. That narrowing passageway for water is a great trap for debris. The house was brand-new when I took the photo and already had a nice collection of pine straw and sticks. This part of the house should have been designed differently.

Figure 7.3. *A dormer and a chimney intersect on a roof, creating obstacles to the downward flow of water.*

Dormers and chimneys: Figure 7.3 shows a roof with two obstacles to the downward flow of water: a chimney and a dormer. By itself, the chimney wouldn't cause much of a problem. It's not at the eave, so there's not so much water hitting the upper side of it. But then they put a dormer right there to slow down the water. Maybe a well-designed cricket will keep this house dry. Maybe it won't. They didn't have to rely on the cricket, though. They could have eliminated the problem with good design. They could have eliminated the chimney, eliminated the dormer, made the dormer smaller, moved the dormer a bit to the right (although then that valley below the dormer becomes a problem), or even just added a proper second floor and moved the roof higher.

Dead valleys: Figure 7.4 shows a mid-century modern house with a dead valley, a horizontal valley created by the intersection of two roof sections. The butterfly roof certainly looks interesting, but think of what happens when it rains. I'm sure they built up a little bit of slope in that dead valley, but still, there's not a lot of room for error here. Delay just a bit on maintaining that roof, and you've got a living room full of water.

Figure 7.4. *A butterfly roof creates a dead valley. Note the white primer near the gutter, indicating recent repair work.*

Height of chimneys and penetrations: The greatest amount of water will be at the bottom edge of a roof. The ridge will have only the water that falls on the ridge, but every step down the roof carries the water that falls on that part plus all the water that drained to that part from farther up. It makes sense, then, to put chimneys and penetrations through the roof as high up as possible, so less water impinges on them. Figure 7.5 shows a house where the builders compounded their errors by putting a chimney at the bottom edge of the roof and also by putting it right at the bottom of a valley.

Roof funnels: The house in Figure 7.6 funnels most of the water from the front of the house to two small areas, indicated by red circles in the photo. The small gutter to the right of the front door is unlikely to be able to handle anything more than a light rain. Anyone coming to the front door when it's raining better have a big umbrella and a rain suit!

Figure 7.5. *The chimney for this house in a cold climate sits right at the bottom of a valley.*

Overhangs: The last topic to discuss here before moving on to walls is something that is a tremendous aid in keeping walls dry. When a roof has overhangs that extend out beyond the wall, less rain hits the cladding. Less rain on the cladding means less water behind the cladding, and less water behind the cladding means less water that can find weak spots in the water control layer and get into places where we don't want it. Less water behind the cladding also means less likelihood of damage if wood does get wet. A study from British Columbia[11] found a correlation between the depth of an overhang with the likelihood of water damage.

Figure 7.6. *This roof funnels water to two points, indicated by circles in the photo.*

11. Survey of Building Envelope Failures in the Coastal Climate of British Columbia by Morrison Hershfield Limited (1996)

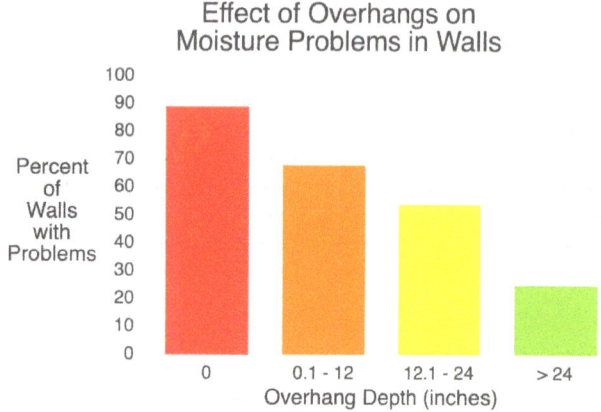

Effect of Overhangs on Moisture Problems in Walls

Percent of Walls with Problems

100
90
80
70
60
50
40
30
20
10
0

Overhang Depth (inches)

0   0.1 - 12   12.1 - 24   > 24

Figure 7.7. *Overhangs reduce the likelihood of moisture problems occurring. [Adapted from Morrison Hershfield paper]*

(Figure 7.7). With no overhang, there's a 90 percent chance of problems. With a 2-foot overhang, that number drops to less than 30 percent.

The big lesson here is that the design of a roof is critical. Once you know what to look for, you can look at a set of plans or a house and see if there are any trouble spots. Yes, some of these problems can be fixed with really good water management techniques and materials, but others will resist any kind of mitigation short of redesigning and rebuilding the roof. Of course, it's best to catch these problems in the design phase, long before the house is ever built.

Drainage Planes for Walls

The easiest place to drain liquid water from a wall is across the field of a wall. The drainage plane, one component of the water control layer, does that job. Here we'll look at six of the most common types of drainage plane materials used on walls.

Before jumping in, let me point out that these six drainage plane materials can be put into three groups. First, there are the products that come on rolls: felt, house wrap, and peel-and-stick membranes. For these, proper layering is essential. Start at the bottom with the first run. The second pass should overlap with the first by at least 6 inches. Where the installation results in vertical seams between pieces of the drainage plane material, the overlap should be 6 to 12 inches, and the seam must be taped. If the drainage plane also acts as the air barrier, you need to tape all the seams and seal any penetrations or tears. This last part applies mainly to house wrap because felt doesn't get taped, and peel-and-stick membranes should already be sealed by the adhesive on the backside.

The second type of drainage plane is the board type. If ZIP System® sheathing or foam board act as your drainage plane, they need to be sealed at all the seams and transitions. Foam board manufacturers have special tapes for their foam

board, and you're likely to risk moisture damage if you use anything else. ZIP sheathing also has its special tape, but some people prefer to use a liquid-applied sealant instead of tape. Make sure to press the tape firmly, usually with a special roller. That's how you get good adhesion, eliminate pockets that might allow water behind the tape, and qualify the installation for the warranty.

The final type of drainage plane material is the liquid-applied membrane. You apply this material with a brush, roller, or sprayer. Integrating with openings, penetrations, and transitions, when done properly, results in a watertight drainage plane.

Figure 7.8. *Felt paper worked well on the house I built.*

Felt paper: There's nothing wrong with going old-school and using asphalt-saturated felt or

Grade D building paper. It can work well to control liquid water. I used it on the house I built back in 2001 (Figure 7.8).

If you start digging into the differences between felt and building paper, you'll find that felt is the term used for roofing materials and building paper is what's recommended for walls. Building paper, also called asphalt-saturated kraft building paper (ASK), has to meet the ASTM D-779 test criteria, and when it does, it's called Grade D building paper.

Another interesting tidbit is the naming of felt. You'll hear people refer to 15-pound felt or 30-pound felt. That terminology is obsolete. Now we have number 15 (#15) and number 30 (#30) felt. It used to be that 15-pound felt weighed 15 pounds per square (100 square feet). Number 15 felt, however, might weigh only half of that, depending on the manufacturer. In the end, either felt or building paper can work as your water control layer.

With felt, building paper, or other drainage planes that come on rolls, you start at the bottom of the wall and work your way up. That gives you the proper layering you need to keep water moving down and out.

House wrap: This water-repellent material comes on rolls much wider than building paper, which results in less lapping to worry about. To install it, you wrap the house as if it were a giant gift, beginning at the bottom and working your way up to keep water moving down and out. House wrap can do a great job of controlling liquid water that gets behind the cladding, if it's detailed properly and you choose the right material.

Figure 7.9. *House wrap on the exterior walls of a house acts primarily as the liquid water control layer.*

There are two main types of materials used in house wraps: woven and nonwoven. Both types are meant to allow water vapor to pass through while draining the liquid water, but the important difference between them is how they achieve that vapor permeability. The woven types, which are often sold with a store's or builder's name emblazoned across the material, are perforated with lots of tiny holes to allow vapor to pass through. The nonwoven types, with brands such as Tyvek®, Typar®, and Weathermate™, are made of synthetic fibers that have pores that allow water vapor to diffuse through. That may sound like the same thing, but it's not. The perforated holes in the woven types allow water vapor to move through, but they also allow liquid water through. The pores in the nonwoven types allow only vapor through. If you want the best house wrap, choose a nonwoven type. Nonwoven house wrap costs more than the woven types, but the water control layer will be worth the investment.

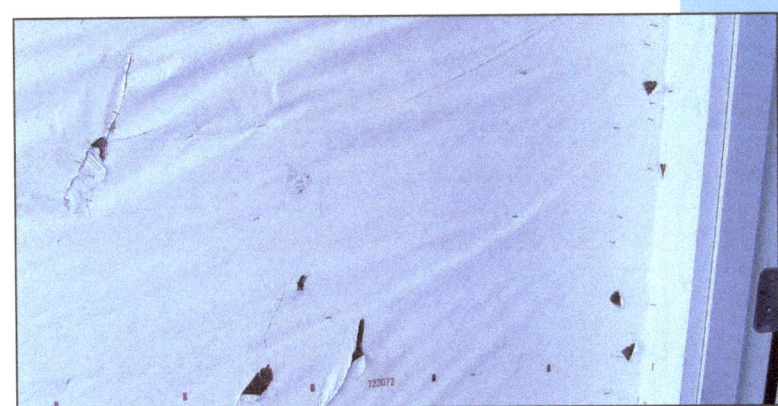

Figure 7.10. *Tears in house wrap are common during and after installation. This section is particularly bad and may even have trouble controlling liquid water as well as air.*

House wrap, more than the other drainage plane materials, seems to have people confused. Ask 100 building professionals what it's for, and more than half of them are likely to tell you it's a vapor barrier or an air barrier. Most house wraps are not vapor barriers. In fact, they're made to be vapor permeable so building assemblies can dry out. And although a lot of house wraps can act as the air barrier, they often do a poor job at stopping air leakage because of untaped seams, unsealed penetrations, and holes (Figure 7.10). Always remember that house wrap's first job is to protect the sheathing from liquid water.

Structural sheathing with integrated drainage plane: This drainage plane has become popular over the past decade, but you've most likely heard it called something else. The most common brand is ZIP System® sheathing from Huber Engineered Woods. It's an oriented strand board (OSB) with a special membrane adhered to the wood at the factory. The membrane resists liquid water so it can be a great liquid water control layer.

Figure 7.11. *ZIP sheathing with taped seams*

The seams have to be sealed to complete the water control layer, and that's what the black stripes are in Figure 7.11. In fact, the product is actually called ZIP System because it's a system, not a single product. The sheathing must be installed with either the specially made tape or a liquid-applied sealant. The tape works well—when installed properly. It needs to be rolled for good adhesion, and, like most tapes, it doesn't stick well to dirt. If you don't like tape, you can use a liquid-applied sealant at the seams. This product also works well on sloped surfaces.

Huber also sells a version of ZIP sheathing bonded to polyisocyanurate foam insulation. It's called ZIP Insulated R-Sheathing, and you can get it with enough insulation to give you R-3, R-6, R-9, or R-12. The insulation is continuous,

but there's one difference from most exterior continuous insulation: The insulation is between the sheathing and the framing instead of outside the sheathing. The OSB sheathing will get cold in winter, and you may not be able to use this product in areas needing more structural support from the sheathing. But it does work well and save labor, and it has become very popular.

This type of sheathing has another advantage, too: Taped sheathing with a membrane is an excellent air control layer.

Rigid foam sheathing: Although it's best to have a drainage plane behind it, foam board can be used as both sheathing and drainage plane if you tape the seams. The photo in Figure 7.12 shows foam board installed over OSB sheathing. The foam board seams are partly taped in the photo. As the workers continue installation, they'll finish taping the rest of the seams.

Figure 7.12. *Rigid foam sheathing can be used as a drainage plane behind the siding.*

Because of greater interest in high-performance homes and also because energy codes are starting to require it, more new homes are getting exterior insulation. So, if you're already using foam board on the outside, it's possible to use it as your only drainage plane. Tape the seams, flash the openings, and your rain will drain down the plane. To minimize the chances of water getting through the horizontal seams, which are the most at risk, use Z-flashing (Figure 7.13). Attach it to the back side of the upper piece, send it through the horizontal seam, and then fasten it to the top of the bottom piece of foam board, as shown.

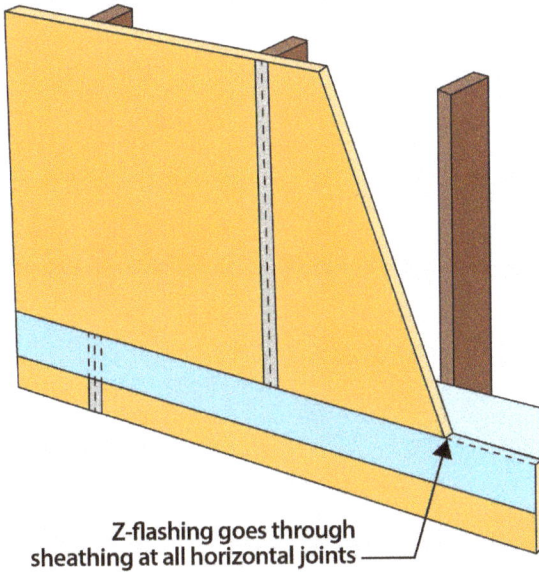

Z-flashing goes through sheathing at all horizontal joints —

Figure 7.13. *Z-flashing goes through the horizontal joints to keep water moving down and out. [Adapted from Building Science Corporation diagram]*

Not all foam sheathing, however, has the code approval to act as the drainage plane. Sometimes foam shrinks, or the tape gets damaged. If that happens, there goes your defense against water. If you tape the foam board and put another drainage plane behind it, then you've got a belt-and-suspenders drainage plane, which should be an iron-clad defense against water. The best practice is to put the primary water control layer behind exterior foam insulation whenever possible.

Liquid-applied membrane: This type of drainage plane is still rare for most above-grade walls, but it is used a lot on below-grade foundation walls. The black color you see on the house in Figure 7.14 isn't the cladding. It's a liquid-applied membrane that will serve as both the water and air control layers. The final result is similar to the ZIP System, but it's applied in the field rather than the factory.

Figure 7.14. *Liquid-applied drainage plane (the black stuff)*

One really nice property of liquid-applied membranes is the ease of integrating them with flashing around openings and at transitions. Just spray, brush, or trowel it on, and you get a good seal. And again, proper installation is critical.

Peel-and-stick membranes: Another way to get your drainage plane without having to nail or staple it to the sheathing is with water-repellent materials you stick to the sheathing. Also called fully adhered sheet membranes, they're similar to other sheet membranes like felt or house wrap. Detailing around the openings and transitions can be tricky. Peel-and-stick membranes have been used mostly on roofs in cold climates, but new products that allow some water vapor to pass through are being used more in mild and even hot climates now.

Figure 7.15. *Peel-and-stick membrane acts as the drainage plane on this house under construction in Austin, Texas.*

Flashing

The drainage plane is a critical part of the liquid water control layer, but even the best product installed perfectly isn't good enough. You can have the best rain jacket in the world, but you'll still get wet if you tuck it into your rain pants. Remember, the rule for controlling liquid water is to have it move down and out, getting it away from the house. That's why it's important to pay close attention to the flashing, the parts of the water control layer that keep water out of joints, seams, and interfaces.

I can't cover all the types of flashing details you might need, so let's illustrate the principles of flashing with two of the places where it's needed most: around windows and doors and where a sloped roof intersects a wall.

The diagram in Figure 7.16 is the 12th step in the flashing recommendations from Pacific Northwest builder Hammer & Hand. The flashing details began with liquid-applied flashing (red) around the window opening, followed by a transition strip at the bottom (blue), and then the first two courses of the drainage plane (grey). The drainage plane here could be felt, house wrap, or peel-and-stick membrane. Note that in getting the rain to drain down and out, we have to start at the bottom and work our way up with the various materials.

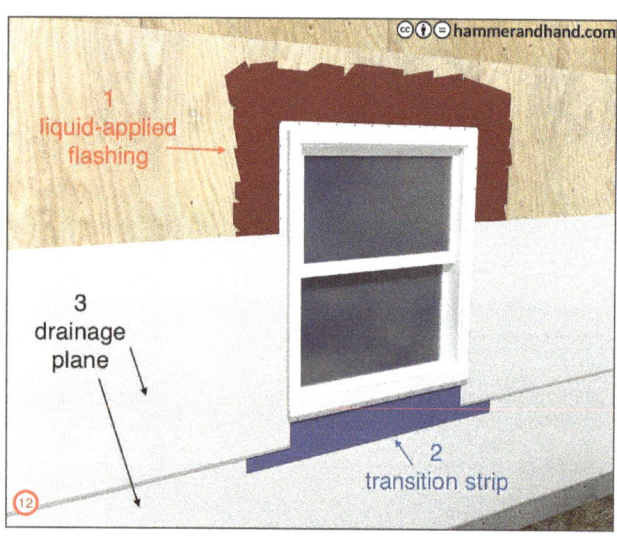

Figure 7.16. *A new window is being installed with the first few steps in the flashing completed. [Credit: Hammer & Hand]*

Figure 7.17. *Head flashing goes over a window, door, or in this case, a ledger board for a deck.*

Flashing around Windows and Doors

Windows and doors interrupt the continuity of the drainage plane and must be integrated with the drainage plane to keep water from finding a way into those sensitive areas.

As water drains down a wall, either outside or behind the cladding, it encounters the top of the window. To keep the water moving down and out at the top of a window, you can use a special piece of flashing called a head flashing (Figure 7.17).

Figure 7.18 shows Hammer & Hand's diagram (number 16 in the series) of the head flashing installed above the window. The vertical blue strips are pieces of tape temporarily holding the drainage plane up. They used liquid-applied flashing material (pink) at the top edge of the head flashing and then pulled the drainage plane material down over the top. The only thing left to do after that is install the cladding.

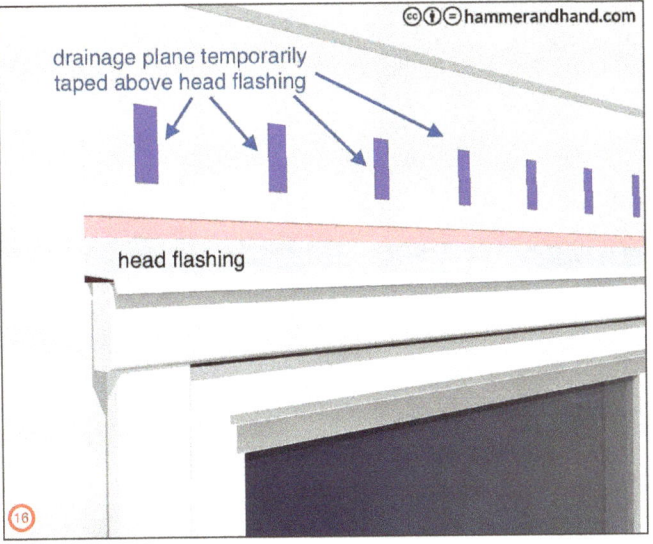

Figure 7.18. *Head flashing goes over the top of the exterior window trim. [Credit: Hammer & Hand]*

Figure 7.19. *Improper flashing at roof-wall intersections can lead to significant water damage. In this case, having a window in the line of fire made things worse.*

Flashing When a Roof Intersects a Wall

The second example when flashing is really needed is one that can cost homeowners a lot of money and goes wrong way more often than it should. When a roof intersects a wall, the damage usually occurs to the wall at the bottom edge of the roof. Figure 7.19 is a perfect example of how badly this can go. That roof had step flashing at the roof-wall intersection, but the lack of proper integration—and possibly the absence of a drainage plane— led to the wall rotting out and needing expensive repairs.

You can find many different methods and materials prescribed for this application, and most of them incorporate similar techniques. Here's an abbreviated look at the method described in Hammer & Hand's *Best Practices Manual*. Their method has a lot of redundancy, but with the amount of water that washes over roofs, this is not a place to skimp on materials or labor. Spend the time and money needed to get it right.

Figure 7.20 shows the bottom of the roof-wall intersection after the first several steps. (Note this is diagram 11 in this series. See the Hammer and Hand manual for full details.) At this point, they've installed liquid-applied flashing (red), a piece of transition membrane (blue below red), drip edge, peel-and-stick, roofing felt, kickout flashing, the first course of roofing shingles, and step flashing. All are layered appropriately to keep the water moving down and out.

After continuing up the roof with the step flashing and shingles, another piece of peel-and-stick membrane is applied over the step flashing (Figure 7.21). The drainage plane on the wall has been installed up to the point where the other flashing details begin, with the transition membrane (blue) pulled over the top of the drainage plane.

In Figure 7.22, the drainage plane membrane is installed around the transition, lapping over the peel-and-stick membrane that's installed over the step flashing. The wall is now ready for siding.

Figure 7.20. *Flashing details at the intersection of a roof and a wall are critical. [Credit: Hammer & Hand]*

Figure 7.21. *Step flashing and roofing are complete. Peel-and-stick has been installed over step flashing. Wall drainage plane is being installed. [Credit: Hammer & Hand]*

Figure 7.22. *The drainage plane is complete, and the wall is now ready for siding. [Credit: Hammer & Hand]*

At this point, you may be wondering how this works with brick veneer or exterior insulation or a flat roof. Yes, you'll run into many variations in materials and assemblies that require different flashing techniques. The basic principles, however, are the same. Keep the water moving down and out. Build in redundancy. Use good materials appropriate for the application.

Sealing Penetrations

In addition to flashing at openings for windows and doors and at roof-wall intersections, you need to pay close attention to any place where pipes, wires, or other services cross the control layers. Without a clear plan in place before making any penetrations, these holes often go unsealed (Figure 7.23). When they do get sealed, it's usually done poorly. Caulk and tape are not enough here.

If you want control layer holes that don't leak, you need to plan ahead for every hole and use a multi-step approach to making sure it's sealed well. (If you want control layer holes that do leak, you're reading the wrong book.) The *Best Practices Manual* from Hammer & Hand also has great details for flashing penetrations.

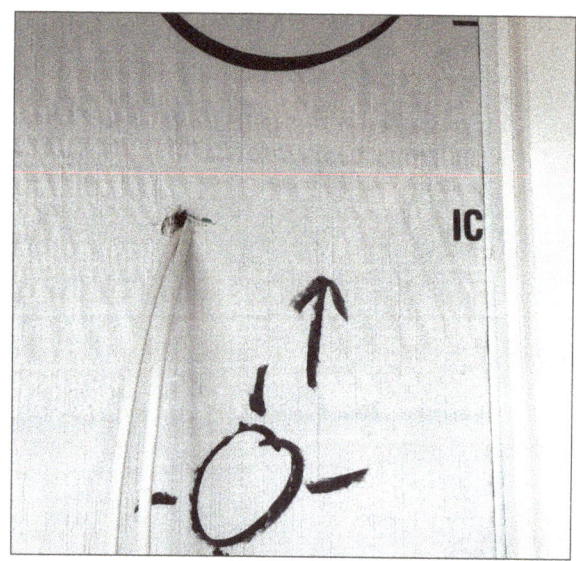

Figure 7.23. *An electrical wire pushed through a hole in the drainage plane: Without a clear plan in place before such penetrations occur, they often end up as sources of water and air leakage.*

Figure 7.24 shows several of the flashing components for a clothes dryer vent from the Hammer & Hand manual. Here are the steps to take to ensure your control layer penetrations don't leak.

1. You can't see the first component in Figure 7.24, which is the sealant applied to the gap between the sheathing and the duct.
2. Apply a liquid flashing (red) around the hole.
3. Attach a transition strip (dark blue) below the hole.
4. Install the drainage plane (white). Do the lower course first, putting it beneath the transition strip at the bottom.
5. The next course goes over the transition strip, with a strip cut above the hole and taped back temporarily.
6. After installing the wall cap, attach a rigid head flashing (grey).
7. Cover the top edge of the head flashing with sealant (pink).
8. Bring the drainage plane down over the top part of the head flashing.

9. The wall is now ready for siding.

The same technique works for other types of penetrations. If you're installing a ventilated rain screen (next section), you'll need to adjust for that. See the Hammer & Hand manual for full details.

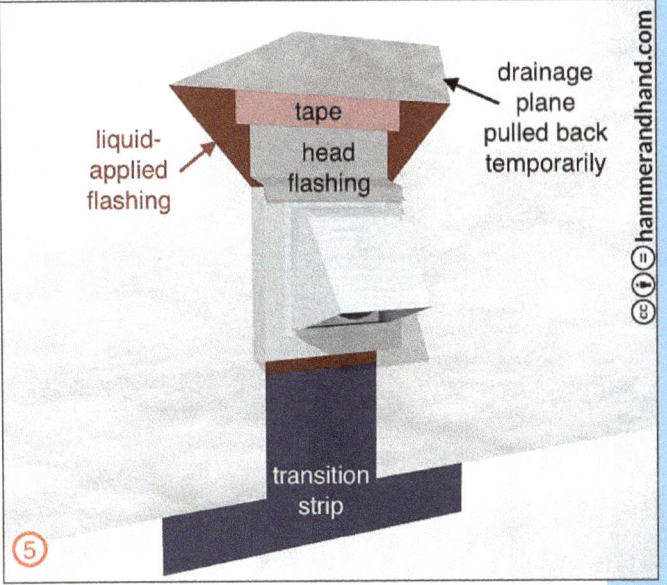

Figure 7.24. *Flashing a penetration through the drainage plane is a multi-step process. [Credit: Hammer & Hand]*

Ventilated Rain Screens

Having a good drainage plane and flashing details is essential to controlling liquid water. There's one more thing you can do to make your walls even better able to control water, and that's to add a gap between the cladding and the drainage plane. Without a gap, water that gets behind the cladding may run into roadblocks on its way down. If siding is nailed directly to the wall, it will delay water's trip to the ground. If water sits trapped against the drainage plane, it may find a weak spot and get behind the membrane. It may also get into the cladding, causing the paint to fail sooner than it should.

Putting a gap there does a few things to help. First, having that gap means less water makes it all the way to the drainage plane. Second, the water that does reach the drainage plane is able to move downward unimpeded. Third, if the gap is connected to the outdoor air at the bottom and top of the wall, excess water vapor is vented out with the air movement.

The details of a rain screen are important. To ventilate the rain screen cavity, the wall must have openings at the top and the bottom. But allowing air behind the cladding also could let bugs into the gap, and we don't want wasps or other bugs building their nests there. In Figure

7.25, you can see an insect screen at the bottom of the rain screen cavity. The top of the wall also needs to have a screen.

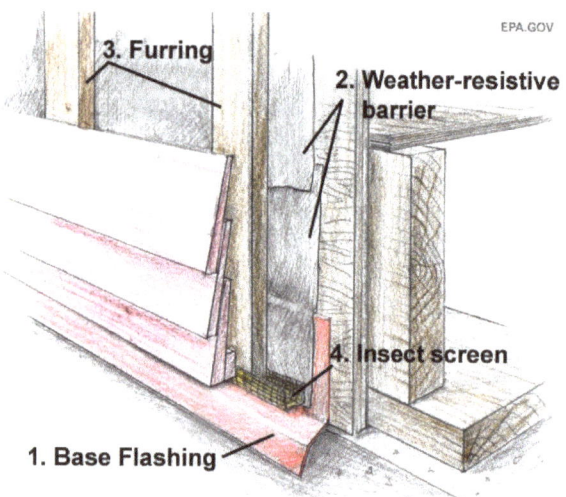

Figure 7.25. *Ventilated rain screen details for fiber cement siding on furring strips showing the insect screen at the bottom [Credit: US EPA]*

How does one get a gap behind the cladding? Brick veneer, if done correctly, has a built-in gap. With siding, stucco, or another kind of cladding, one way to get that gap is with furring strips (Figure 7.26), which are pieces of wood typically ¾ inch thick nailed or screwed to the wall. The cladding is then attached to the furring strips. Openings at the bottom and top of the wall allow air to move through the cavity, helping to keep things dry.

Another common method to create a rain screen is to install a plastic mesh over the drainage plane. Some of these materials come with house wrap on one side, thus saving a step in the installation process.

Figure 7.26. *A vented rain screen created by attaching furring strips to the exterior of the foam board*

Chapter Takeaways

- The primary objective is to keep liquid water moving down and out.
- The water control layer includes a drainage plane and flashing.
- Roofs and overhangs that are designed to shed water easily result in fewer problems.
- Many different products and materials can perform well as the water control layer, but proper installation is critical.
- Use a multi-layered flashing approach to keep water out of weak areas, like windows, roof-wall intersections, and penetrations for wiring and other services.
- Ventilated rain screens aid the drying of water that gets behind cladding on walls.

CHAPTER 8
Controlling Air

Air may come in second to rain in our hierarchy of the four substances we need to control (rain, air, water vapor, and heat), but it's more important in at least one respect. The rain that lands on our house is not something we intentionally take into our bodies. The air, however, goes into our lungs about 20,000 times per day. We breathe about 200 gallons of air each day. As we saw in Chapter 2, that air can be laden with all manner of bad stuff: particulate matter, volatile organic compounds, carbon monoxide, and on and on.

Air can hurt you. The pollutants it carries can make you sick. The moisture it carries can damage building materials and help to grow mold, which makes some people ill. That same moisture can rot structural materials and make buildings fall down. The heat that air carries results in comfort problems and excess energy use. The sound waves it carries can diminish indoor environmental quality.

> *"Buildings are complex three-dimensional air flow networks driven by complex air pressure relationships."*
> —Joseph Lstiburek, PhD, PE

This chapter doesn't explain how to solve all those problems. We've already stated that source control, filtration, and ventilation are important factors in indoor air quality, and those topics are covered elsewhere in this book. The purpose of this chapter is to understand the properties of air and how to control it. We know a house doesn't need to breathe. The goal is for it to be as airtight as possible and still have good indoor air quality. The first step is installing a good air control layer, which is usually called the air barrier. It's one of the most important parts of a house—and one that gives you a lot of bang for your buck.

Understanding Pressure

Before we look at the dynamics of air flow in a house, let's understand what air pressure is. Put your hand out, palm up. Believe it or not, you're holding about 200 pounds of air in your hand. You may have heard that standard atmospheric pressure is 14.7 pounds per square inch. Your hand is probably in the range of 15 square inches. Thus, the amount of pressure pushing down on your hand is about 200 pounds.

Well, then, you may wonder, "Why doesn't it feel like I'm holding 200 pounds?" The secret is that air—a fluid[12]—is a sneaky substance. In this case, it sneaks around to the other side of your hand and pushes up with that same force of about 200 pounds. Two hundred pounds pushing down. Two hundred pounds pushing up. It feels like nothing because that's the net result of those two forces pushing in opposite directions.

In this example, gravity is the source of the pressure, but we can also get pressure in fluids from fans or pumps. Pressure is defined as the amount of force per unit area (think pounds per square inch). In the example of your hand, it's the weight of all the air above your hand. Even though the pressure is due to gravity, the air presses in all directions, not just downward. That's why the air also pushes up on the back side of your hand.

An empty beer can provides another good

12. A fluid is a gas or liquid. The word comes from the Latin "fluere," which means "to flow."

example of air pressure. When it's sitting on a counter, it has air inside and air outside. The pressure against the walls of the can comes from both directions equally, so nothing changes. But if you put a little water in the can and boil it, the can fills with water vapor. That forces some of the air out of the can. By removing the can from the heat, screwing the top on the can, and then letting it cool, the water vapor condenses inside the can. Now the air inside the can is less dense than the air outside, and thus pressure is lower inside than outside. As you watch the can from outside, it gets crushed because of the difference in pressure.

Now let's apply this to buildings. The beer can is now the wall of a house. The air inside the house pushes outward on the wall, while the air outside pushes inward. If the air inside is connected directly to the air outside—through an open door or window, say—the pressure should be the same in each direction and nothing happens, as with 200 pounds of air on each side

Figure 8.1. *Air pressure crushed this aluminum beer can. It can crush a 55-gallon drum the same way.*

of your hand. If, however, the house is closed up, we may have a pressure difference between inside and outside. Unlike the beer can, though, the walls are usually strong enough to handle the pressure difference. But there are other consequences.

Positive and Negative Pressure

In building science, we use the terms *positive pressure* and *negative pressure* a lot. Both terms express the pressure relationship between two different locations. Both positive and negative pressure refer to a differential pressure, the pressure in one place with reference to the pressure in another place. When you measure the air pressure in your tire, you're measuring the difference in pressure between the inside of the tire and the outside of the tire.

So, both positive pressure and negative pressure are differential pressures. The additional descriptors—positive or negative—tell you the direction air will flow if there's a pathway. The pressure inside your tire, when inflated, is

positive pressure. Poke a hole in the tire, and the air flows out. If a house is described as having positive pressure, that means the pressure inside the house is higher than outside. Open a window, and air flows out of the house. We normally do blower door tests at negative pressure by setting up a fan and sucking air out of the house. Some ventilation systems put positive pressure inside the house (Chapter 17). Dryers, range hoods, and bathroom exhaust fans can induce negative pressure in the rooms where they're located. Air ducts operate at positive pressure on the supply side and negative pressure on the return side. Combustion appliance exhaust flues operate at positive or negative pressure, depending on the type of venting.

Figure 8.2. *Analog pressure gauge with two hoses attached to the pressure taps*

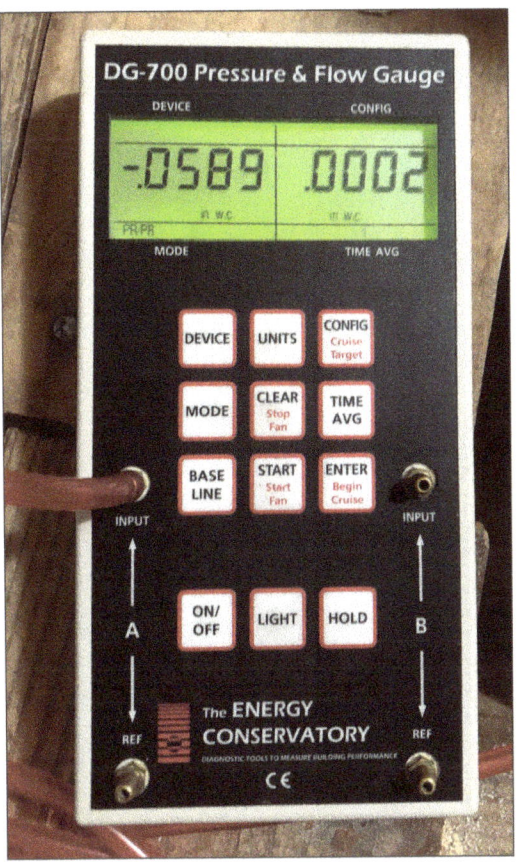

Figure 8.3. *Differential pressure is what digital manometers, analog gauges, and tire gauges measure. The model above has two channels (A and B), each with two pressure taps (input and reference).*

We measure differential pressures in houses most often with analog pressure gauges and digital manometers. Every measurement comes from the difference in pressures felt by a sensor that's exposed to air coming in through two pressure taps. Figure 8.2 shows an analog gauge with two tubes connected to the pressure taps on the left side. The scale is calibrated in a unit called inches of water column (iwc), named for the height a column of water rises when subjected to a pressure difference. This unit is a small unit of pressure that's useful for measuring the pressures we deal with in houses. The Pascal is the metric unit for pressure and is used in airtightness testing.

Figure 8.3 shows a digital manometer that has two sets of pressure taps and can make two separate measurements of differential pressure. Each channel (A and B) has two taps (labeled INPUT and REF in the photo). One of the two taps (input) on the left side (channel A) is connected to a red tube. You can't see it in the photo, but the other end of that tube is inside

a duct. The pressure in the tube is the same from the end of the tube in the duct all the way to the manometer. The other tap (reference) on channel A is not connected to a hose and thus measures the pressure in the space around the manometer. The number displayed (-0.0589 iwc) is the difference in pressure between the duct where the red tube is connected and the air around the manometer.

If a gauge has no hoses connected to it, the pressure difference should be zero. The right side of the manometer in Figure 8.3 has no tubes connected to the taps. There should be no difference in pressure for the air near the two taps, and indeed that's what the manometer shows. It's reading 0.0002 iwc, which is essentially zero.

How to Determine If a House or Room Is Under Positive or Negative Pressure

When I was a graduate student, the University of Florida's basketball arena had a fabric roof held up by air pressure. They replaced it with a hard roof before I left, but it was always fun going to watch a game, and not just for the game. As I entered, I'd get hit with a strong wind because of the massive positive pressure they kept the place under.

In a case like that, it's easy to know whether the building was under positive or negative pressure, but with homes, you're dealing with smaller pressure differences. Since we know that air moves from higher to lower pressure areas, the direction of air movement tells us which side is positive. Here are five ways to use that directional flow to find out whether a house or room is positively or negatively pressurized.

1. **Feel for the air flow.** Use your hand or your face.

2. **Feel for the air flow with a wet hand.** Wetting your hand makes it more sensitive to air flow because water evaporating from your skin makes it cooler.

3. **Hold a piece of tissue in the opening.** Using a piece of tissue makes it easier to show the direction of air flow to others.

Figure 8.4. *With the house depressurized during a blower door test, you can feel for air leakage from rooms by closing the door to a small crack.*

4. **Use a smoke device.** Figure 8.15. shows a smoke stick being used to show air movement.

5. **Measure the pressure difference with a manometer.** By putting a tube into one of the spaces and standing with the manometer in the other, you can see which has the higher pressure.

For the first four of these methods, you're looking for a qualitative result: positive, negative, or neutral. To aid your measurement, you can make the hole as small as possible to increase the velocity of air flow. With interior rooms, you can do that by closing the door until there's just a small slit allowing air to move through. This technique is especially helpful when doing a blower door test to find which rooms might be the leakiest. If you want to get semi-quantitative, you could use an anemometer to get a rough idea of the air flow rate coming through the crack.

The Two Requirements for Air to Move

Will a pressure difference result in air leakage? Only if another requirement is also met: A pathway exists between the positive and negative pressure areas. For air to move, both of them must be present:

- Pressure difference
- Pathway

The air pressure inside a balloon, for example, is higher than the pressure outside. The air stays in the balloon, though, as long as there's no hole. A house can act similarly. When a house is closed up and there's a pressure difference between inside and out, the surfaces of the building enclosure have air pressing harder from one direction than the other. If, going back to our earlier example, the air below your hand suddenly disappeared, leaving a vacuum in its wake, you'd feel those 200 pounds of air pressing down on your hand.

> *When a pressure difference and a pathway exist, air will move from higher pressure to lower pressure.*

Likewise, a pressure difference across a house forces air to move through the holes in the building enclosure, from the side with higher air pressure to the side with lower pressure. The bigger that pressure difference, the more air that will move through the holes. The bigger the area of the holes, the more air will move across the building enclosure.

There's a really important point here that needs to be emphasized. When a pressure difference and a pathway exist, air will move from higher pressure to lower pressure. As with heat flowing from hot to cold and moisture moving from wet to dry, this is a consequence of the second law of thermodynamics.

One case when we create a pressure difference intentionally is during a blower door test. The airtightness professional turns up the blower door fan to create a given pressure difference (often negative 50 Pascals) and then measures the amount of air moving through the fan. More air flowing through the fan means more air leaking in the enclosure. Understand this simple principle of physics, and you've unlocked one of the most important principles of building science.

Three More Principles of Air Movement

Now we know that to get air moving from one place to another, there must be a pressure difference and a pathway, and the air will move from higher pressure to lower pressure. When air is flowing, it follows the laws of physics, so we can extrapolate a few other principles that help us understand what's happening.

Larger pressure differences result in more air flow. The caveat here is that we're talking about a house (or room or duct system) where the pathways don't change. When all we do is increase the pressure difference, the amount of air flow will increase. Likewise, when we decrease the pressure difference, the air flow decreases. The mathematics of this relationship is well known and used extensively in testing houses for airtightness. It's not a linear relationship, which would cause the air flow to double when the pressure difference doubles. Pressure difference and air flow rate, nonetheless, do go up together and down together. Also, air flow rate changes less than the pressure difference. If the pressure difference doubles, for example, the air flow rate will go up but won't double.

Figure 8.5 shows the relationship between pressure and air flow for three identical houses. As you can see, the increase in the air leakage rate starts flattening out with increasing pressure. Although it's beyond the scope of this book, this kind of pressure and air flow relationship also can provide information about the types of pathways through which the air is moving. When the air flow pathways are narrow slits, the air flow rate changes with pressure in one way. When the pathways are round holes, the air flow rate changes with pressure in a different way. Those differences show up in the shape of the data plotted in graphs like Figure 8.5.

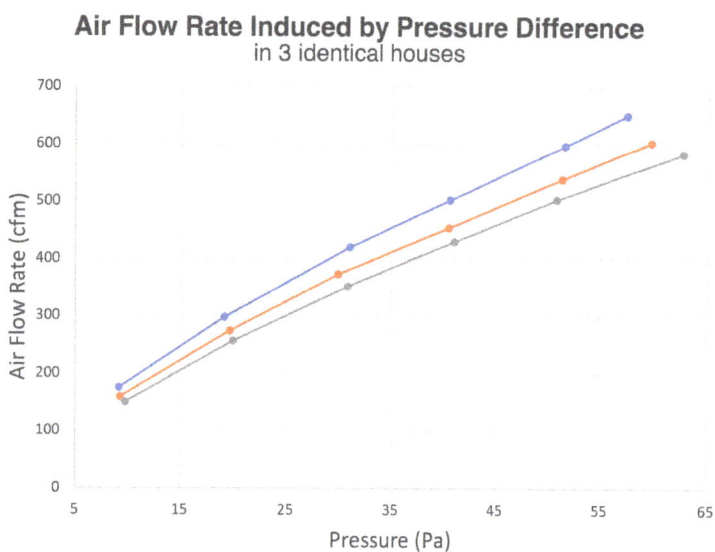

Air Flow Rate Induced by Pressure Difference
in 3 identical houses

Figure 8.5. *As the pressure difference across the building enclosure increases, so does the air leakage. The data here are from tests done on three identical new homes.*

Air flowing in equals air flowing out. When an exhaust fan is running, the air that moves out of the house will be replaced by an equal amount of air coming into the house. Seems obvious, right? Well, it's not strictly true. If you think through the whole operation of the fan, you'll understand why.

For a brief time when the fan first starts up, it changes the pressure difference across the

building enclosure. That happens by removing more air from the house than is replaced by outside air coming in. During the time the pressure is changing, the amount of air leaving the house is greater than the amount of air entering. That's the only way to get a pressure difference. The time it takes to reach equilibrium is relatively short, but it depends on how tight the house is. Greater airtightness means a longer time to reach equilibrium, but we're talking seconds, not minutes. At equilibrium, the amount of air flowing into the house equals the amount of air flowing out of the house.

In all discussions of air moving across the building enclosure throughout the remainder of this book, we'll assume the system has come to equilibrium and the rate of air leaving the house is exactly equal to the rate of air entering the house. One more possibly useful bit of information for you: You'll often see the term "infiltration" used to describe how leaky a house is, but infiltration is only one side of the equation. Infiltration is the air leaking into the house. Since it's matched by an equal amount of air leaking out of the house, we can just as accurately use the term "exfiltration." Or we can be air flow direction neutral and just call it air leakage.

Air takes the pathways of least resistance. When you put a pressure difference across the building enclosure, it has multiple pathways to move through. The number and size of those pathways determine how airtight the house is. An exhaust fan near a large, round hole connected to the vented attic will have an easy time pulling in air from outside. An airtight house with only a few small holes and narrow slits will make it harder for air to come in when an exhaust fan is turned on.

When there's a pressure difference between the house and outside, air may flow through all of the pathways. The amount of air flowing through each hole will depend on the resistance to air flow and the actual pressure difference at that hole. Even holes of the same total area and with the same pressure difference across them can have different amounts of air flow. A narrow crack under the baseboard, for example, has more resistance to air flow than an equal-sized round hole in the floor and will move less air.

> **The amount of air flowing through each hole will depend on the resistance to air flow and the actual pressure difference at that hole.**

Also, we normally speak of these pathways as holes in the building enclosure, but as the quote from Joseph Lstiburek, PhD, PE, at the beginning of this chapter states, the air leakage sites are actually three-dimensional pathways that connect the indoor air with interstitial air and with outdoor air. Indoor air might go into a light switch on a first-floor interior wall, travel up through the wall cavity, find a joist bay between the first and second floors, and exit through a gap around exhaust fan termination. Those wall and floor cavities are called interstitial spaces, and they can connect the indoor air with the outdoor air when not properly sealed.

Likewise, the pressures aren't so simple. The pressure inside a house can vary from place to place depending on the proximity of central air-conditioning return or supply vents, exhaust fans, combustion appliances that use indoor air, openings to the outside, or wind. Closed doors also can create pressure differences inside a house. The pressures inside interstitial spaces can vary as well. The result of all this is that a house is exactly as Dr. Lstiburek described it: a "complex three-dimensional air flow network" with the flows "driven by complex air pressure relationships."

We don't need to be intimidated by that fact, though. When we understand those air flow networks and pressure relationships, reducing the effect of uncontrolled air flow is much easier.

Three Sources of Pressure Difference

Pressure differences and pathways are both necessary, so let's examine them in more detail, beginning with pressure differences. Where do they come from? There are three important sources in buildings: the stack effect, wind, and mechanical systems. Let's look at each individually.

Stack Effect

The stack effect is usually explained as warm air rising. It's related to the large-scale pressure differences in the atmosphere and to smaller-scale pressure differences that happen between the inside and outside of buildings. Those building pressures result from temperature differences and building height. Remember that air pressure in the atmosphere varies with height, so the pressure on the outside of a building is higher at the bottom and lower at the top, just as the air pressure at Galveston Beach is higher than that on top of Whistler Mountain. The pressure inside the building depends on the density of air, which depends on temperature.

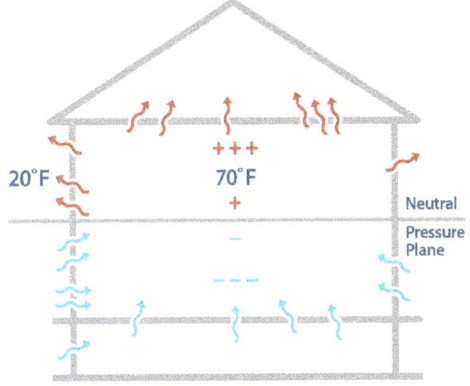

Figure 8.6. *The pressure changes with height inside the house, with the most negative pressure at the bottom and the most positive pressure at the top.*

Warmer air is less dense and rises inside a house. That creates a positive pressure (relative to outdoors) at the top of the building and a negative pressure at the bottom, as shown in Figure 8.6. If the house has pathways for air leakage, air will leak out where the inside pressure is positive relative to outside pressure, and it will leak in where the pressure is negative. That is, air leaks out at the top and in at the bottom. Figure 8.7 shows the stack effect in a different way.

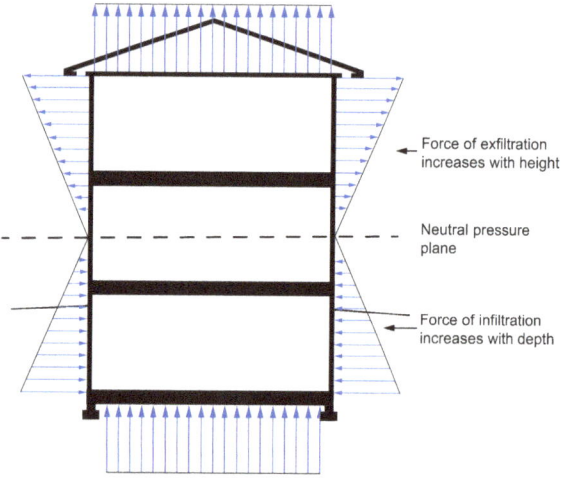

Figure 8.7. *Stack effect pressures on a building [Courtesy of Joseph Lstiburek]*

The illustration in Figure 8.6 shows the pressure differences from the bottom to the top of this house. At the bottom, the pressure is most negative. At the top, the pressure is most positive. Going from the bottom to the top, the pressure gets more positive with each increase in height. At some point, the pressure difference between inside and outside the house is zero. We call that neutral pressure, and the plane that slices through the house where the pressure is neutral is called the neutral pressure plane. That plane isn't necessarily halfway up from the ground because the configuration of air leakage pathways and sources of pressure difference may move it closer to the ground or to the ceiling.

Figure 8.8. *On a cold day in Boston, the tarps at the top of this building are being pushed outward, and the tarps at the bottom of the building are being pulled inward. That's a visual example of the stack effect in action.*

The stack effect creates pressure differences across the building enclosure that change with height. We know that if a pathway connects two areas with different pressures, air will move. So, at the bottom of a house where there's negative pressure, air moves from outdoors to indoors. At the top where the positive pressure is, air leaks out of the house. At the neutral pressure plane, no pressure difference means there's nothing to move the air one way or another, so you could open a window there and not have air leakage (assuming neither of the other drivers, wind or mechanical systems, is creating a pressure difference).

As mentioned above, the stack effect varies with the temperature difference between inside and outside the building. For most places, that means it's going to be strongest in winter. Take Gainesville, Florida, for example. In summer, the design temperatures are 75 °F indoors and 92 °F outdoors. That's a temperature difference of 17 °F. In winter, the design temperatures are 70 °F indoors and 33 °F outdoors, for a difference of 37 °F. In Atlanta, our winter and summer temperature differences are 47 °F and 17 °F. For Minneapolis, they're 76 °F and 13 °F. You have to go to a place like Phoenix to find a higher temperature difference in summer (38 °F) than in winter (28 °F).

Figure 8.9. *Revolving doors were invented to combat the stack effect. [Credit: Hernán Piñera, CC 2.0]*

The other factor that influences the strength of the stack effect is building height. The taller the building, the larger the pressure differences can be. Have you ever opened the door in the lobby of a tall building in winter and been hit with a strong, cold breeze from outside? That's the stack effect. Here's a bit of trivia for you. Because the stack effect can steal a lot of heat from a tall building when the ground floor doors open, a clever person in Germany invented the revolving door. The original German name, *tür ohne Luftzug*, translates to "door without draft of air."

One final note about the stack effect is that the direction of air flow changes from winter to summer. In winter, warm air rises, like a bubble in water. In summer, the warmer, less dense air is outdoors. The indoor air is cooler and more dense. The result is that holes high and low in a house will allow cool, dense air to fall out of the lower holes, drawing warm, less dense air in through the upper holes (Figure 8.10). This is sometimes called the reverse stack effect.

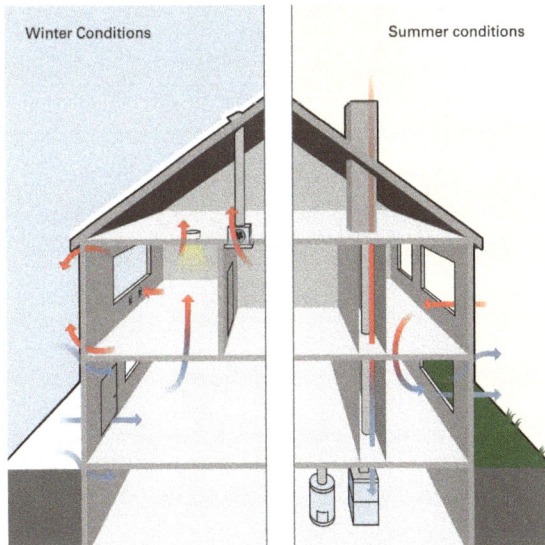

Figure 8.10. *The stack effect is the term for air moving through a building due to density and pressure. In winter, warm air rises through a house, but it changes direction in summer as cool air falls. [Courtesy of The Energy Conservatory]*

Wind

When the outdoor air moves, we call it wind. As the wind blows from one side of a house to the other, it creates pressure differences. Remember that air has mass, and moving air has energy and exerts pressure. On the side of the house getting hit directly by the wind, there's a negative pressure inside the house. If a window is open, the wind will blow right into it. On the other side of the house, there's a positive pressure inside the house, so if a window is open over there, air will move from the house to the outdoors. Moving air creates pressure differences.

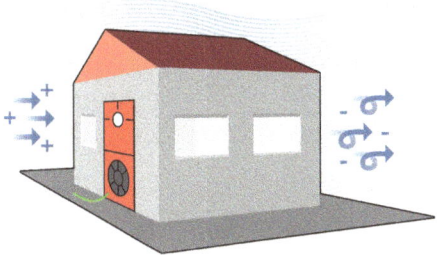

Figure 8.11. *Wind blowing on a house creates a positive pressure on one side and a negative pressure on the other side. [Courtesy of The Energy Conservatory]*

Mechanical Systems

The last driver of pressure differences is mechanical systems. When you turn on the range hood, clothes dryer, or bath fan, air is exhausted from the house. Sending air out through a fan creates a negative pressure in the house. That means air must come in through pathways in the building enclosure.

Exhaust fans aren't the only mechanical systems that create pressure differences, though. One that can drive a significant amount of air leakage is your central forced-air heating and air-conditioning system. Imagine, for example, that a supply duct in the unconditioned attic has completely fallen off its connection. Instead of sending conditioned air to the house,

it's now dumping it into the attic. The return duct is still pulling just as much air as it's supposed to, though, so the house develops a negative pressure whenever the heating and cooling system runs with that supply duct disconnected in the attic. Even closing bedroom doors can create pressure differences in the house. (See Chapter 14.)

Let's put the scale of the various drivers of pressure difference in context now. Wind and stack effect in low-rise residential buildings are usually in single digits when measured in Pascals. On a really windy or cold day or in a taller home, it might get up to 20 Pascals. Mechanical systems can put a house under a pressure difference of tens of Pascals. In airtight homes, they can drive the pressure to more than 100 Pascals.

The Air Barrier Is a System

Now that you know air leakage happens only when there's both a pathway and a pressure difference, you know how to reduce it. Seal the pathways and reduce the pressure differences. To minimize stack effect pressures, you can build a shorter house, set the thermostat back, or choose a milder climate. Wind pressures are governed mainly by where you build, although wind breaks can help. Mechanical systems are the wild card for pressure differences, and I'll cover that in later chapters. We want to minimize pressure differences, but the primary way to reduce air leakage in houses is to get rid of the pathways as much as possible.

The air control layer, also called the air barrier, is the pressure boundary for the house. That's where the air leakage occurs. It is not, however, a single product or something that appears magically once a house is complete. In new construction, it's a system that must be designed and installed with great care. As with

the water control layer, the critical parts are the interfaces between different sections of the air barrier. Some of those critical parts are where a wall meets a roof or foundation, at the junction between a window and a wall, and wherever penetrations occur in the building enclosure. The pen test (Chapter 5) is a great way to get those details right.

Figure 8.12. *New home jobsite sign stressing the importance of the air barrier [Courtesy of 475.supply/ProClima]*

The above-grade walls and the roof will have a liquid water control layer that also can serve as the air barrier. Some water control layers are easier to use as an air barrier than others, but all should be detailed carefully to ensure airtightness. Every interface, junction, and penetration must be planned, not dealt with as the need arises during installation. And the air barrier must be maintained during the entire construction process because it will be under constant assault. Figure 8.12 shows a sign used on jobsites where the builder cares about airtightness and wants to ensure everyone working on the house will think twice before adding any potential air leakage pathways to the enclosure. It's also a good idea to think like this even when doing things like punching through a wall to add a new faucet on an existing home.

The good news is that when you pay attention, it's not hard to achieve good airtightness when building a new home. We've built houses for so long with the false idea that they need to breathe that we're still just scratching the surface after a decade of improved building codes. When Georgia started requiring mandatory air leakage testing of all new homes in 2011, many home builders suddenly had to reduce the air leakage of their homes by 50 to 100 percent. In shooting for the state-mandated threshold, some builders overshot the mark and built homes that were nearly twice as airtight as the code required. What was the difference? They paid attention to the details!

Measuring Air Leakage

Now that we've covered the principles of air flow, we're ready to apply them to the job of measuring the air leakage of a house. The basic idea of testing for air leakage is that we use a fan to apply a pressure difference across the building enclosure of the house. Then we measure the rate of air flow that results from that pressure difference. This works because we know a pressure difference will cause air to move through any pathways in the building enclosure.

The question is, how do we measure the amount of air flowing as a result of the pressure difference? We can't go around the house and measure how much air flows through each of the leaks. But we can use a fan calibrated for a specific relationship between pressure and air flow rate. When the air moves through the fan at a specific pressure, the calibrated pressure-flow relationship tells us how much air is flowing through the fan. Once the house comes to equilibrium at a stable pressure, the air flowing out of the house equals the air flowing into the house. Boom! Now we know how leaky the house is.

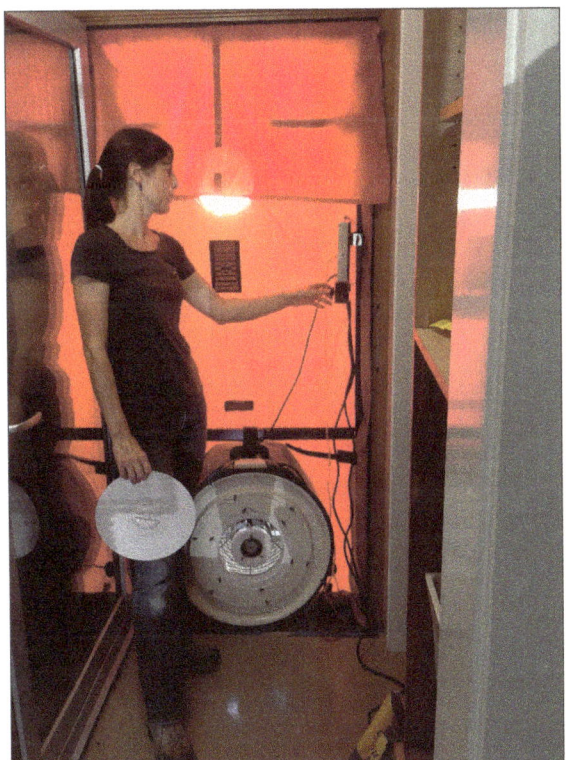

Figure 8.13. *A blower door test measures the infiltration rate of a house by using a fan to create a pressure difference and then measuring the rate of air flow through the fan.*

We can do this test at either a positive pressure or a negative pressure. Normally it's done at a negative pressure because the leakage measured will be a little bit higher at a positive pressure. Why? It's because of intentional air leakage pathways used to exhaust air from bathroom fans, range hoods, and clothes dryers. Those ducts have dampers that allow the air to move out of the house but are supposed to stop the air coming in. Negative pressure, thus, results in a lower air leakage rate. From here on, I'll assume negative pressure when talking about these airtightness tests, but it could be either. In some cases (e.g., vermiculite insulation in the attic), you want to do a positive pressure blower door test to prevent pollutants from being pulled indoors from attics, crawl spaces, and garages.

Let's back up a little bit and describe the test. We use a fan installed in a special frame that goes into a door or window to create a pressure difference between the inside and outside of the house (Figure 8.14). It's usually installed in a door, so we call it a blower door. To put the house under negative pressure, the fan blows air from the house to the outdoors. The negative pressure allows air to come into the house through all the leaks.

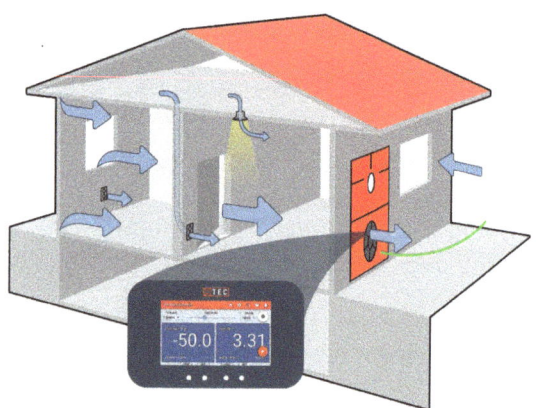

Figure 8.14. *Setup for a blower door test with the house under negative pressure [Courtesy of The Energy Conservatory]*

We know from the past section, though, that pressure differences can arise from other sources,

too. There could be stack effect, wind, and mechanical systems other than the blower door. What do we do about that? The easy one is mechanical systems. We simply turn off anything that moves air between inside and outside or that could create a pressure difference, including exhaust fans, dryers, ducted heating and air-conditioning systems, and atmospheric combustion appliances.

The pressure difference created by wind and stack effect is usually small. The way we handle it is to do the blower door test with much higher pressure differences. We also measure the baseline pressure difference, which is the pressure difference between the house and outdoors with the house set up for the blower door test and the fan turned off. Let's say the baseline pressure difference is positive 2 Pascals, and we want to do the blower door test at negative 50 Pascals. Since we want the pressure difference to be 50 Pascals lower than our starting pressure, we adjust the speed of the blower door fan until the house is at negative 48 Pascals. On windy days, the pressure can fluctuate a lot, so you either can wait and do the test when it's less windy, you can do several tests and average the results, or you can do the blower door test at a range of pressures, usually between 15 and 60 Pascals.

Speaking of blower door test pressure, 50 Pascals has come to be the standard test pressure for houses. Even when the test is run at a range of pressures, as mentioned above, the resulting air flow rate is often stated for the pressure of 50 Pascals. As we'll see in the next section, the pressure for any air leakage result is usually given as a subscript on the result.

In addition to making sure the blower door is the main driver of the test pressure difference, we need to get an accurate reading from the air leakage pathways. A closed bedroom door, for example, could reduce the amount of air leakage coming from that room during the test. Likewise, having an exterior window open would inflate the air leakage. To get the best result, we open all interior doors and close all exterior doors and windows.

A blower door test is simply a way of using the principles of air flow to find out how leaky a house is.

When a house has a basement, you have to decide whether the door to the basement should be open or closed for the test. Most of the time it's going to be open, but in some older houses the basement may be outside the building enclosure, and the door would be closed for the test. To make that determination, look for the location of insulation and the presence of heating and cooling in the basement. If the insulation is on the basement ceiling and it's not conditioned, exclude the basement from the test. If the basement is conditioned or the insulation is on the foundation walls, include the basement. You can also run the blower door test both ways and see which part of the enclosure is the better air barrier. With attics that have insulation on the roof deck instead of the attic floor, the attic hatch or pulldown stairs should be open for the test.

That's it. A blower door test is simply a way of using the principles of air flow to find out how leaky a house is. We create a specific pressure difference with a calibrated fan. We set up the house to account for other sources of pressure difference and make sure we're accurately measuring air moving across the building enclosure. Then the amount of air moving through the fan at a specific pressure tells us how leaky the house is at that pressure.

Specifying Air Leakage Rates

The initial result from a blower door test is the **air flow rate** at the specified pressure difference. In the United States, we use cubic feet per minute (cfm) for air flow rate, so a typical blower door result might be given as 550 cfm_{50}. The subscript indicates the pressure difference across the building enclosure that yields a leakage rate of 550 cfm, in this case 50 Pascals. (Other parts of the world use liters per second or cubic meters per hour for flow rates and Pascals or centimeters of water column for pressure.)

The only problem with using the air flow rate at 50 Pascals is that it doesn't factor in the size of the house. If I told you, for example, that I have a friend who weighs 150 pounds (68 kg), you don't know anything about whether he's morbidly obese, anorexically skinny, or somewhere in between. If I tell you he's 7 feet tall (2.1 m), you know he's skinny. The body mass index is a single number that accounts for both weight and height, and we need something similar for air leakage.

The most common way of accounting for the size of the house is to use the volume. The air leakage rate divided by the volume gives us the air change rate. What's an air change? When a volume of air equal to the volume of the house changes with outdoor air, there's been one air change. With the blower door running to maintain a pressure difference of 50 Pascals, we can express the result in air changes per hour at 50 Pa, or ACH_{50}. (Going from cfm_{50} to ACH_{50} also includes converting minutes to hours.) The nice thing about air changes per hour (at any pressure) is that it doesn't matter which set of units you use for the air flow rate. Whether you start with cubic feet per minute or cubic meters per hour, all units lead you to the same result when you get to air changes per hour.

The nice thing about air changes per hour is that it doesn't matter which set of units you use for the air flow rate.

The only problem with measuring air leakage rates in air changes per hour, however, is that it's not a good way to compare the air leakage of different houses. Yes, it's the unit used almost universally (including in building codes), but volume would be the proper way to account for house size only if air leakage happened throughout the volume of the house. It doesn't. Air leakage occurs at the surface of the building enclosure. A better way to bring in the house size is to use the surface area. Dividing the air leakage rate by the surface area of the building enclosure yields a result sometimes called the enclosure leakage ratio, or ELR.

To grasp the real meaning of the various metrics, remember that the first result of an air leakage measurement is the air flow rate at the pressure difference of the test (cfm_{50}). It's the volume of air per unit time. Because that tells you nothing about how much leakage you might expect based on the size of the house, we take the air flow rate and divide by a number representing the size of the house. Table 8.1. shows the three most used metrics.

Metric	Abbr.	Comment
Air flow rate	cfm	Doesn't account for house size
Air changes per hour	ACH	Divides by volume of house
Enclosure leakage ratio	ELR	Divides by building enclosure surface area

Table 8.1. *Three metrics for airtightness test results*

The next step is talking about the effect of pressure difference on air leakage rates. Blower door test results for homes are usually presented as the air leakage rate, air changes per hour, or enclosure leakage ratio at a pressure difference of 50 Pascals. Homes don't always have a pressure difference of 50 Pascals across the building enclosure, though, so the next step is to convert the air leakage rates during the blower door test to so-called "natural" air leakage rates. We need to know the "natural" air leakage mainly for calculating the amount of energy lost to infiltration as well as calculating the contribution of infiltration to the heating and cooling loads.

Extrapolating down from the test pressure to "natural" pressure is where using volume, not surface area, makes more sense. Whether it's the air flow rate in cubic feet per minute or the air change rate in air changes per hour, the heat and energy scale with the volume of air moving across the building enclosure at "natural" pressures. (The models for this extrapolation are complex and left out of this book.) These calculations allow us to go from cfm_{50} or ACH_{50} with the blower door running to cfm_{nat} or ACH_{nat}, which are estimates of the amount of air leakage when the house is operating under "natural" conditions.

It's important to understand that the extrapolation from blower door test pressures to "natural" pressures introduces a lot of uncertainty into the air leakage rate. For example, duct leakage, range hoods, or powered attic ventilators can create large pressure differences across the building enclosure. Those pressures can swamp the estimates of the natural air leakage, which model stack effect and wind but not mechanical systems.

Putting the various metrics in context, we can say that you want the lowest air flow rate (cfm_{50}) you can get when you do a blower door test. When judging the airtightness of a house (e.g., for building codes or program certification), the air flow rate per unit of building enclosure surface area is the best metric. When modeling energy consumption or heating and cooling loads, you need an estimate of the "natural?" air leakage rate (cfm_{nat} or ACH_{nat}).

The natural air changes per hour is good for one other thing, too. A blower door test calculated as ACH_{nat} is a great way to get across the idea of air leakage. The leakiest house I've measured came in at 13,000 cfm_{50}, which extrapolates to 1.0 ACH_{nat} for that particular house. A homeowner is likely to understand the impact better if you tell them that, on average, they lose all the conditioned air in their house every hour. That amount of loss means having to heat or cool all new air every hour.

Airtightness Goals

If you have an existing home and want to make it airtight, what's a good number to shoot for? Likewise, if you're building a new home, what should be your goal for airtightness? Of course, you should make it as airtight as possible, but let's put some numbers on these metrics to put them in context. Here are the ranges for the four main air leakage metrics when testing houses for air leakage. The low-end numbers represent high levels of airtightness. The high-end numbers represent extremely leaky houses.

Metric	Low end	High end
cfm_{50}	<100	>10,000
ACH_{50}	<1	>20
ELR	<0.1	>2
ACH_{nat}	<0.1	>2

Table 8.2. *Range of values for super tight and super leaky houses under the four main airtightness metrics*

One threshold is to compare a house to what the code requires. For much of the United States, the state and local codes are based on the model codes created by the International Code Council (sometimes called the I-codes). The International Energy Conservation Code contains the airtightness requirements. For mixed and cold climate zones, the threshold is 3 ACH_{50}. In the warm climate zones (0-2), the threshold is 5 ACH_{50}. When building a new home, 3 ACH_{50} is pretty airtight, but you can do better. Passive House certification requires 0.6 ACH_{50} or 0.06 cfm_{50} per square foot of enclosure area. If you're improving an existing home, 5 ACH_{50} is a good number to shoot for. Depending on the house and your budget, you may not be able to reach it, but it's still a good target. My 1961 ranch house is at 8.8 ACH_{50} now (late 2021), and my goal is to get it below 5 ACH_{50}.

Using a Blower Door to Find Leaks

Blower doors are useful for more than providing an estimate of the airtightness of a house. They're also great at helping to find leaks that need to be sealed. One way to do this is by walking around the house with the blower door running and feeling for air movement. With the interior doors open, air from each room has a large path to the blower door. By closing a bedroom or basement door until there's just a narrow slit of opening left, you can get an idea of the amount of the leakage from that room by putting your face or hand near the opening to feel for air flow. The worst rooms are usually the ones that have plumbing (bathrooms, kitchens) or those with connections to attics, crawl spaces, and garages.

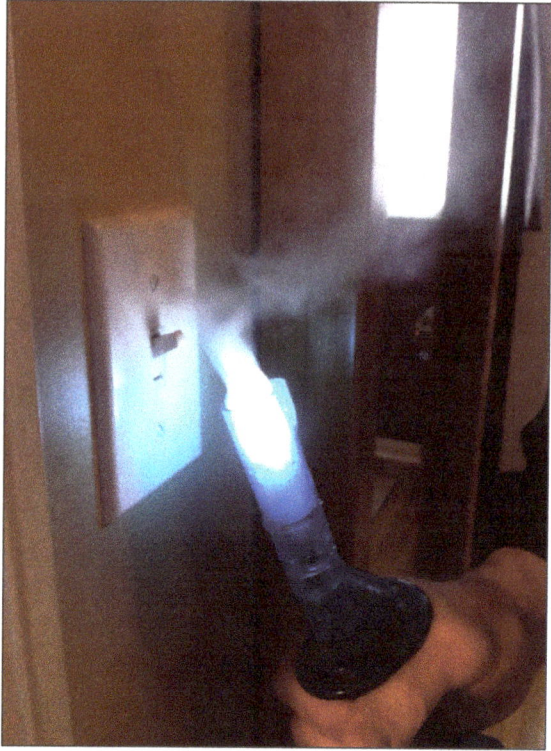

Figure 8.15. *Looking for air leakage during a blower door test: Notice the smoke blowing away from the switch as air leaks into the house.*

If feeling with your hand or face doesn't tell you anything, you can lick your fingers to detect smaller air flows. Another way to look for leaks is to use visual cues. A piece of tissue or a smoke pencil are the standard ways to do that. Figure 8.15 shows air leaking into a house through an electrical switch during a blower door test. Notice that the smoke is blowing up and to the right. (Of interest here is that this switch had recently been air-sealed with a foam gasket behind the switch plate. Those gaskets may work to stop air from leaking out around the perimeter of a switch or outlet, but they do little to stop air leaking through the switch or outlet.)

On a larger scale, you can use a theatrical fog machine to find air leaks in the whole house. Close up the house and pressurize it with a fan. Then blow theatrical fog into the house through the fan. When you go outdoors or into the attic, crawl space, or garage, you should see where the "smoke" is coming out. A word of warning, though: Before doing this, be sure to let the neighbors know your plan. Otherwise, you may get a visit from the fire department with sirens blaring.

Where Should the Air Barrier Be Located?

Where to put the air barrier may seem obvious, but this question has many dimensions—literally. Let's look at the question of air barrier location from three perspectives.

First, most houses in North America are built with framing lumber that creates frames for the floors, walls, and ceilings. The building assemblies aren't solid pieces of a single material, as a concrete wall is, but the assemblies have an outside, an inside, and interstitial[13] spaces in between. The outer surface has sheathing, control layers, and cladding. The inside has the inner surface, with drywall and perhaps a vapor retarder. The in-between part

has wood framing and cavities that may be filled with insulation. This kind of structure creates interstitial spaces. Much of the air leaking through the enclosure passes through these spaces to enter or leave the house.

These three-dimensional building assemblies mean that air can leak in at one location, travel through the interstitial spaces, and come out somewhere entirely different. During a blower door test, for example, you can feel air coming in through switches and outlets even when they're on interior walls that aren't part of the building enclosure. (See Figure 8.15.) The air traveled through the interstitial space (the empty wall

13. The word *interstitial*, although uncommon, is the perfect word for this part of a building enclosure. It refers to the spaces between, as the openings between the string and knots in a net. The noun is *interstices*.

cavity) to get to the switch or outlet. The place where the air came in might have been the wiring penetration at the top of the wall, allowing unconditioned attic air to travel several feet before entering the living space.

Think about the complexity of the structure of a framed house. A hole in one part allows air to get in. That air can move through a floor, wall, or ceiling, looking for a hole or crack that lets it get into the house. The distance could be a few inches, or it could be 30 feet. The air keeps going, though, pushed by a pressure difference. It's like ants getting into a house through the basement, traveling through interstitial spaces, and coming out in the kitchen, drawn by the crumbs they find there.

Now that you understand this kind of air leakage, you probably can guess the best place to put the air barrier. It's on the outside of the structure. Keep all unconditioned air out of the interstitial spaces. That solves most problems associated with air leakage. (The one that it doesn't solve is moist, indoor air getting into wall cavities and condensing on the back side of cold, exterior sheathing. For that, the best solution is exterior insulation, which we'll cover in Chapter 11.)

Interior air barriers used to be a thing. Building scientist Joe Lstiburek even wrote a book on the airtight drywall approach in the mid-1980s. Air barriers on the interior side of the structure certainly can keep unconditioned air out of the house, but they're not ideal. One big drawback with interior air barriers is the potential for moisture and mold on the backside of drywall in humid climates. In an air-conditioned house, the drywall will be cool in summer. Without an exterior air barrier, humid, outdoor air can get into a wall cavity, find that cool drywall, and get the drywall wet enough to damage it or grow mold.

Another problem with interior air barriers is that they're not tamper-proof. When someone makes extra holes trying to hang a picture or doesn't seal a gap around a new thermostat, they've compromised the air barrier.

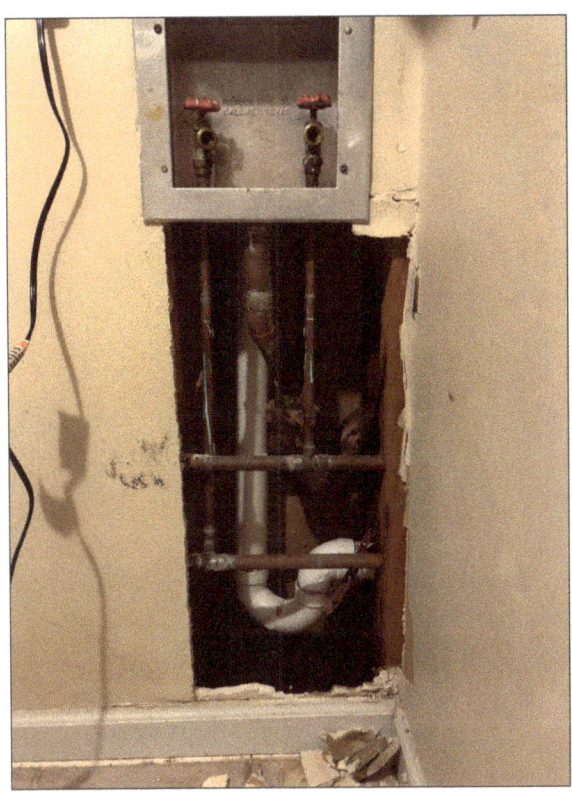

Figure 8.16. *If the drywall serves as the air barrier and then the plumbing is repaired but they don't seal the hole, a lot of air can leak.*

When it's a choice between the inside and outside of the structure for the location of the air barrier, the outside is the better choice. But there's another option. Some super-insulated walls are really thick, and often the air barrier goes somewhere in the middle. That's a really good place to put the air barrier because it's protected from damage from both sides.

The second perspective of air barrier location has to do with its relation to the thermal control layer (i.e., insulation). For insulation to do its job of limiting the flow of heat, it needs to be free of air flow. The most commonly used insulation in homes is fiberglass, which is air permeable. When air flows through fiberglass or any other air-permeable insulation, it loses some of its ability to resist heat flow. The implication here is that the air barrier needs to be right next to the insulation. For example, you can't have an effective building enclosure if you put your air barrier at the subfloor over a vented crawl space and the insulation on the foundation walls. The air barrier needs to be aligned with the insulation. Air-impermeable insulation materials (e.g., spray foam) have this alignment built in because the insulation is also the air barrier.

> **The air barrier needs to be aligned with the insulation.**

The third perspective of this question is the decision about whether buffer spaces should be included or excluded. The air barrier is at the boundary between conditioned and unconditioned spaces. In complex buildings, it's sometimes difficult to see exactly where that boundary is—or should be. For indoor air quality reasons, we know a house needs a robust air barrier separating a garage from the living space. Basements, however, are often included, and that's generally the best choice because of how difficult it is to isolate the basement from the living space above it.

To find the best place to put the air barrier with buffer spaces, you need to evaluate the pros and cons of each choice. How will including or excluding the buffer space affect indoor air quality? How easy will it be to do the air sealing? Which will be easier to insulate? Crawl spaces and basements are usually better kept inside the building enclosure. Attics can go either way, although it's easier and less expensive to put the air barrier at the attic floor. We'll explore the pros and cons of some of these choices in Chapter 11.

Types of Air Sealing Materials

An air barrier is a system composed of different materials. Some of those materials might also act as control layers for liquid water, water vapor, and heat. Some of those materials are part of the structure. Others are part of the finish.

One thing common to all materials used as part of an air barrier is that they should meet the requirements of an air barrier material. Just as we can test the air leakage of a whole house (i.e., building enclosure), we can test how much air leakage occurs through any material when we put a pressure difference across it. For materials, the threshold used in some building codes and standards is 0.0039 cubic feet per minute per square foot (0.02 liters per second per square meter) at a pressure difference of 75 Pascals. Dr. Lstiburek was involved with settling on that number, and he came to it by using drywall as the standard. As a result, any material classified as an air barrier must be at least as good as drywall at resisting air flow.

Let's look at the types of air barrier materials you may use.

Materials for Large Areas

Many people think of air sealing as what happens at those places where you apply caulk or tape. But the vast majority of air is kept out of a house by the large expanses of the building enclosure covered by sheet or roll goods. The exterior wall sheathing may be the primary air barrier, or maybe the sheathing is covered with house wrap or a peel-and-stick membrane. The following are some of the most common large area air barrier materials.

Drywall, plywood, oriented strand board (OSB), concrete, house wrap, liquid-applied membrane, aluminum foil, glass, sheet metal, and rigid foam

(Note that OSB by itself may not qualify as an air barrier material. In practice, this weakness usually matters only when you get below about 1.5 ACH$_{50}$.)

Materials for Gaps and Holes

To create a continuous air barrier around the entire enclosure, the large area materials must be sealed with other materials where they connect to each other and to other materials. For this we use a variety of materials, most of which can stick to the large area air barrier materials:

Caulk, tape, liquid flashing, gaskets, backer rod, and spray foam

The key with air barrier materials is to choose the best one for the job. Some need to cover large expanses and act as the liquid water control layer (plywood, house wrap, peel-and-stick membrane). Others should be able to seal the seams between adjacent pieces of those large air barrier materials (tape, liquid-applied flashing). Still others are for sealing gaps and cracks (caulk, spray foam). Some need to be vapor permeable. Each also has its own installation procedures that need to be followed and its own properties related to adhesion, durability, vapor permeability, and other characteristics that matter.

Critical Locations for Air Sealing

I've spent many hours inspecting, testing, and air sealing homes, and I still haven't seen all the ways air barriers get compromised. Here's my (admittedly incomplete) list of places to focus your attention to get a more airtight house. I'll start at the bottom of the house and work my way up.

Slabs and Foundation Walls

Concrete slab: Whether it's in a basement, crawl space, or slab-on-grade construction, concrete slabs can be a source of air leaks. It's not the concrete itself that leaks, though. It's the places where different pieces of concrete come together or where there are holes in the concrete. And regular air isn't always the biggest problem. The air that leaks from the ground includes soil gases like water vapor, methane, and radon.

To make your house more airtight, seal the joints at the perimeter where the slab meets the foundation walls. Seal around any plumbing or other penetrations. Seal any cracks that open up. (Sealing a slab doesn't solve all radon problems, so have your house tested or buy a radon monitor.)

Foundation walls: Treat foundation walls like vertical slabs. Seal the joints, penetrations, and cracks. Walls made of concrete masonry units (CMU) are leakier than poured concrete walls because the blocks themselves aren't airtight and neither is the mortar holding them together. If you want to get your air leakage as low as possible, you need to cover CMU walls with a material that can act as a real air barrier. In an encapsulated crawl space, for example, the foundation walls get covered with sealed plastic sheeting or closed-cell spray foam. Also, these walls sometimes have blocks with open cells (Figure 8.17), which provide another air leakage pathway, so seal any open blocks, too.

Figure 8.17. A concrete block wall with cells open to the basement

Framed Floor over Unconditioned Space

Bathtub drain hole: This part of a house has myriad air leakage pathways. One of the biggest is the hole for the bathtub drain. Rigid foam and spray foam work well to seal it (Figure 8.18).

Figure 8.18. *A bathtub drain hole sealed with rigid foam and spray foam.*

Open chase: Chases are hidden cavities in a house to provide space for air ducts, exhaust vents, or plumbing pipes. Often, they start in a basement or crawl space and go up into the attic. An open chase can be a source of a lot of air flowing through interstitial spaces. They need to be sealed with a material for large openings, as with the bathtub hole.

Wiring penetrations: If an electrician has drilled a hole through the air barrier, it needs to be sealed. These holes are usually sealed in newer homes because fire codes require it.

Sill plate: This is the board that lies flat on top of a foundation wall. The foam gasket that goes under the sill plate helps close larger gaps but by itself does not provide a sufficient air seal. You still need to use caulk or spray foam to finish the job.

Rim and band joists: At the perimeter of a framed floor is either a rim joist or a band joist. Sometimes they sit on top of a sill plate on a foundation wall, sometimes on a top plate of another framed wall. The leakage pathways here occur where the joist sits on the plate and at any penetrations through the band joist.

Cantilevers: Where a framed floor extends out past a foundation or framed wall, you need to make sure the cavities are sealed at all edges and penetrations. In addition, the joists should be blocked and sealed at the point where the cantilever meets the wall it rests upon. Figure 8.19 shows this done for a wall separating the garage from the house, but it's the same process for a cantilever.

Garage joists: Similar to cantilevers, joists over a garage must be blocked and sealed to seal off this interstitial pathway. (See Figure 8.19.)

Figure 8.19. *Blocking between joists over a garage as they cross the wall separating the garage from the house [Source: US Department of Energy Building America Solution Center]*

Above-Grade Walls

Fenestration: Window and door openings should be sealed with real air barrier materials. Stuffing fiberglass into the gap is fine as a backing material for caulk or spray foam but is not an air barrier itself.

Penetrations: As with all other parts of the building enclosure, penetrations need to be air sealed (in addition to being properly integrated into the water control layer).

Sheathing seams: The seams between adjacent pieces of wall sheathing should be sealed, either by being covered with a properly detailed house wrap or sealed with an appropriate tape or flashing material. This applies to where the sheathing meets the rim and band joists, too.

Dropped soffits above cabinets: When cabinets don't go all the way to the ceiling, often the builder will build a soffit to go over the top of the cabinets. Many such soffits have no air barrier to keep air from moving from an unconditioned area through the interstitial spaces, down into the soffit and from there into the walls. You can tell if that's the case with a blower door test or an attic inspection.

Attic Floor

Open chases: This is the top end of a hidden building cavity used for ducts, pipes, and vents. Cover the opening with sheet metal, rigid foam, or another large area air barrier, and then seal all the edges and penetrations. If a metal flue pipe from a combustion appliance comes up through the chase, you'll need to use sheet metal to seal around the flue and be sure to keep all flammable materials away from the flue.

Figure 8.20. *An open chase in an unconditioned attic can be the source of a lot of air leakage.*

Top plates: The board across the top of framed walls is called the top plate. In most site-built houses, you can see the top plates from the attic. The ceiling drywall is butted up to the top plates, but there's usually a small gap between the drywall and the top plate. That gap can be hundreds of feet long, though, and it can contribute considerable air leakage. Seal it with caulk, spray foam, or gaskets.

Penetrations: A lot of a home's electrical wiring goes through the attic, and electricians drill holes in the top plate to get the wires down to switches and receptacles in walls. Seal those holes with caulk or spray foam.

Electrical junction boxes: Lights, ceiling fans, and other electrical devices mounted in the ceiling allow air to leak around the edge of the junction box as well as through it. Seal it with materials approved for contact with wiring.

Exhaust fans: Where exhaust fans are in the ceiling, there's often a gap around the edge that needs to be sealed.

Recessed can lights: Older can lights have very leaky cans. One way to seal them is to use foil-faced rigid fiberglass to build a box over the whole fixture and seal the edges with spray foam. Prefabricated can light covers also are available. A better solution is to replace those lights with new fixtures rated as insulation contact, airtight (ICAT). Because of how much lighting has improved in recent years, this will reduce lighting energy, too.

Whole-house fan: Older homes that still have a whole-house fan in a hallway have a huge air leak (and uninsulated area). The best bet is to remove the fan altogether and patch the hole with drywall. If you live in a place where a whole-house fan makes sense, you can replace the old one with a more efficient model that also closes tightly when not in use. Tamarack Technologies makes nice ones.

Roof Deck

The alternative to putting the air barrier at the attic floor is to insulate and air seal the roof deck. In some ways, the roof deck is easier to seal than the attic floor, but it does make for a more expensive lid on the building enclosure.

Eaves: The place in the roof deck that causes the most air-sealing problems is where the roof meets the top of the above-grade walls. It's easier to get right in new construction because the prep crew can get to the eaves easily before the ceiling drywall is installed. To prep that area, install baffles or blocking to stop the foam from shooting out into the soffit.

Roof penetrations: Plumbing stacks, exhaust fan vents, and other penetrations all need to be sealed.

Combustion flues: Flues from fireplaces, furnaces, boilers, and water heaters need special attention because foam insulation that's not fire-rated should not be put in contact with a flue that can get hot. Sealed combustion appliance flues are generally cool enough to have insulation in direct contact with the flue, but it's important to check with the manufacturer's required clearances.

Attic ventilation: If the building enclosure is at the roofline, the attic does not get vented. All ridge vents, gable vents, soffit vents, roof vents, and powered ventilators should be removed or sealed.

(Using an exhaust fan to control humidity in the attic is different because it pulls conditioned air up from the living space below and operates at much lower air flow. See Chapter 11.)

Attic Kneewalls

Attic-side sheathing: An attic kneewall separates conditioned space from an unconditioned attic. It should have a sealed air barrier material applied to the attic side of the wall and sealed completely.

Top plates: Some kneewalls are built without top plates. When air sealing an existing kneewall that does not have a top plate, install blocking and air sealing so the kneewall cavities are enclosed on all six sides.

Floor joists: The floor joists going from the unconditioned attic to beneath the adjacent conditioned space should be blocked and sealed. Otherwise, you have a huge interstitial air leakage problem.

Vaulted ceilings: Rafters for a vaulted ceiling typically rest on top of the kneewall. If you see fiberglass batt insulation at the end of the vaulted ceiling rafter bays, install and seal blocking to prevent air from going through or beneath the insulation.

Don't Caulk the Windows of Your Existing Home!

The section heading here is an exaggeration. It grew out of my frustration with the annual parade of autumnal advice for homeowners to weatherstrip doors and caulk windows to prepare for winter. Why would I say not to caulk the windows in an existing home? Because doing this will reduce your total air leakage by only a small amount. The bigger leaks are in your crawl space, basement, and attic. That's not to say that air leaks around windows and doors aren't important. They can cause uncomfortable drafts, and they can bring in unfiltered air. It's just that they're usually a small amount of the total air leakage.

Figure 8.21. *The large hole for the bathtub drain lets a lot of air leak into the interstitial spaces of a house.*

That's reason number one that caulking and weatherstripping aren't going to help a whole lot. When you've got big holes in the ceiling or floor, the gaps around the windows and doors pale in comparison. For example, there's the bathtub hole in the floor (Figure 8.21). The open chase to the attic is another biggie. In Figure 8.22, the mechanical closet had no ceiling.

Figure 8.22. *This mechanical closet in a condo had no ceiling to separate it from the attic. The louvered doors on the closet were air leakage superhighways.*

Occasionally contractors or homeowners put really crazy holes in the ceiling. For example, my in-laws had a hole cut in their kitchen ceiling (Figure 8.23). The best I could figure was that the contractor who remodeled their kitchen a few years before thought their refrigerator needed to be vented to the attic.

Before I reveal the other problem with caulking and weatherstripping, let's review two of the fundamental principles of air leakage covered earlier in this chapter.

- For air to leak across the building enclosure, you need two things: a pressure difference and a pathway.
- Pressure differences are created by wind, stack effect, and mechanical systems.

To address the problem of air leakage, we should minimize pressure differences and seal up pathways wherever possible. Let's begin with pressure differences. You can't do a whole lot to reduce pressure differences created by wind on

an existing home without making some radical changes outdoors. The best way to prevent it from stealing conditioned air from your home is to reduce the pathways.

Figure 8.23. *This large hole in the ceiling seems to have been intended to vent heat from the refrigerator into the attic.*

Mechanical systems can create pressure differences, too. One of the hidden sources of this type of pressure difference is unbalanced duct leakage, and sealing the ducts is the answer. Another hidden source related to ducts is not giving supply air a pathway back to the return vent. (Both of these are covered in Chapter 14.) Exhaust fans, including the clothes dryer, are another. You have some control here, but you shouldn't compromise indoor air quality or moisture control by running fans less than necessary.

That leaves the stack effect. Warm air rises inside the home because it's less dense than cold air. You end up with positive pressure at the top of the house and negative pressure at the bottom. (See Figure 8.6.) Because more air flows through a leakage pathway when there's a bigger pressure difference, you'll get more air leaking at the bottom and the top of the house than you do in the middle. In fact, you could open a window in the middle and get very little air leakage if you're at what's called the neutral pressure plane, where the pressure inside equals the pressure outside.

One of the hidden sources of pressure difference is unbalanced duct leakage, and sealing the ducts is the answer.

The common advice for winterizing your home is likely to be ineffective because of the two reasons I described here:

• The big holes are in the floor and ceiling.
• The big pressure differences are at the top and bottom of the house.

Air leakage is one of the biggest problems with homes, so it's worth going after it. Just be smart about it and go for the biggest leaks first. Those standard tips for winterizing a home may give you a warm and fuzzy feeling, but they won't give you a warm and cozy house.

Chapter Takeaways

• Air is a fluid that has weight. Air pressure at the Earth's surface is due to the weight of all the air above.
• Relative pressures between two places can be expressed as positive or negative, depending on which of the two places has the higher pressure.
• Air flow requires a pressure difference and a pathway.
• Larger pressure differences result in more air flow through the same pathway.
• The air flowing into a house equals the air flowing out.
• Air takes the pathways of least resistance.
• Pressure differences in houses arise from the stack effect, wind, and mechanical systems that move air.
• The air barrier—the control layer for air—is a system, not a single product or component.
• A blower door is the tool used to measure the air leakage of a house.
• Air leakage rates can be specified in many ways. We discussed three: air flow rate (cfm), air changes per hour (ACH), and enclosure leakage ratio (cfm per square foot of enclosure area).
• Because of the way houses are built, many places must be air sealed because they are susceptible to air leakage.

CHAPTER 9
Controlling Water Vapor

A homeowner in Atlanta was having health problems after moving into a new house. He complained of a musty smell in the house. He had already had some work done on the house a few months before he called me, but his symptoms hadn't gone away. In addition, the house developed a new symptom: water spots on the basement ceiling from a sweating duct above the drywall.

When I looked at the house, he had the drywall removed from beneath the sweating ducts, and a contractor had insulated them. Also, he showed me some discolored areas on the exterior siding (Figure 9.1) that lined up perfectly with the air conditioner vents on the other side of those exterior walls. He had humidity problems.

> **"The air was already drunk with humidity when I stepped outside on that first morning."**
> —Alexandra Horowitz

humidity problem that's really an air leakage problem. And then there are the times when high humidity is the result of mechanical system failure. The key to solving humidity problems—or moisture problems in general—is to figure out where the moisture is coming from or why it's not being removed. Only then will you know the proper way to tackle it.

When you identify an air leakage problem, the solution is always the same: Improve the air barrier system. Liquid water is similar. Some people think the solution for most water vapor problems is to use a vapor barrier. Not true. We have multiple ways to control water vapor, including:

- Air sealing
- Insulation
- Vapor retarders
- Air conditioners
- Ventilation systems
- Dehumidifiers

Figure 9.1. *Condensation on uninsulated ducts in exterior walls was the cause of humidity damage on the siding of a house in Atlanta.*

Water vapor confuses people in many ways, and not just because of the relative humidity issue I discussed in Chapter 6. Sometimes we see a liquid water problem that really began as a humidity problem. Other times we have a

The homeowner with the sweating ducts in Atlanta has a water vapor problem that's both an air leakage and an insulation problem. If humid outdoor air weren't in contact with those ducts, he wouldn't have that problem. And if those ducts were insulated properly, humid air wouldn't condense on them.

Let's see if we can make some sense of this sticky topic.

Two Important Moisture Principles

Cold Air Is Dry Air

It's easy to be fooled about moisture when you use relative humidity as your measure of it. Here's an example. It's a cold, nasty day outdoors with freezing rain coming down. Let's say the temperature is at the freezing point of water (32 °F), and the outdoor relative humidity is 100 percent. Sounds humid, right? Well, it's humid for that temperature. Relative humidity is the humidity relative to a particular temperature. But what happens if, through ventilation or infiltration, some of that outdoor air comes into your house. When that air warms up to 70 °F, the new relative humidity will be an arid 20 percent.

This principle comes into play in a number of ways. It explains why a leaky house can be too dry in winter. It also gives us a way to reduce indoor relative humidity in winter, if that's ever necessary.

The Fundamental Rule of Material Wetness

As stated by Bill Rose in his book *Water in Buildings*, temperature and moisture are connected.

"Cold materials tend to be wet, and warm materials tend to be dry."

The story of peeling paint discussed in Chapter 6 illustrates this important rule. Home builders started insulating the exterior walls of houses, and some of them had trouble with moisture causing the paint to peel. Moisture can get to the wall sheathing and siding in a number of ways, but the one that can put the most water there is poor control of the rainwater hitting the house.

Controlling the liquid water using the principles from the past chapter isn't the end of the story, though. Insulated walls still have cold sheathing and, as stated above, cold materials tend to be wet. The key is keeping all moisture sources away from cold sheathing. Drainage planes and flashing remove most of the potential for water. The next largest source of water is the indoor air, and that water vapor can reach the cold sheathing in two ways: air leakage and diffusion.

The Primary Rule for Preventing Accidental Dehumidification

Several years ago, I read a building science paper where the authors used the term "accidental dehumidification." They were describing cases where you take water vapor out of the air and put it in places where it can cause problems, for example condensation that drips down a window and rots the sill or a humid crawl space that causes floor joists to grow mold and ducts to sweat. Accidental dehumidification is a great term. Having a lot of water vapor in the air doesn't by itself cause problems—aside from the comfort issue associated with the human body's

> *Having a lot of water vapor in the air doesn't by itself cause problems. It's the accidental dehumidification that causes problems.*

reduced evaporative cooling. It's the interaction of that water vapor with surrounding materials that gets a house into trouble. It's the accidental dehumidification that causes problems.

The good news is that we can prevent accidental dehumidification and humidity damage with one simple rule:

Keep humid air away from cool materials.

This rule, of course, immediately raises two questions: How humid is humid? How cool is cool?

The best way to answer both questions is with dew point. The amount of water vapor in the air determines the dew point temperature. We can say the air is humid if there's any chance it could come into contact with materials that have temperatures near or below the dew point. A material is cool if its temperature is below the dew point of any nearby air.

With porous materials—like wood, drywall, and concrete—focusing on the dew point is a simplification because they accumulate water as a function of relative humidity. (See sidebar in Chapter 6, page 79.) It's not a simple on-off switch that happens at the dew point. Still, though, the dew point is a good metric. The fundamental rule of material wetness says cool materials are usually wetter than warmer materials. If a material happens to be at or below the dew point of the surrounding air, it's going to be wetter than we want it to be.

Figure 9.2 shows what can happen when humid air meets cold surfaces. The band joist, floor trusses, and subfloor in this crawl space are saturated on a cold day. The house was still being framed, and it got so wet that water was even dripping from the plastic pipe. In this case, the problem resulted from a wet crawl space under an unheated house on a cold day during construction. Although this condition was temporary, it's best to think through what might happen even when a house is being built because wood this wet can grow mold. If you look closely

Figure 9.2. *Saturated wood in a crawl space on a cold winter day*

at the photo, you can see evidence that it's already happening.

Now, back to the rule and what it tells us to do. We have two ways to keep humid air away from cool materials. We can reduce the humidity of air near cool surfaces. Or we can raise the temperature of the materials.

Method 1: Reduce the Humidity

If the humidity is too high, you have a few options. You can cut off the source of water vapor, dehumidify the air with mechanical systems, or ventilate with drier outdoor air. Obviously, cutting off the source should come first because running mechanical equipment takes energy, which isn't free, and buying the equipment takes money. You bring in the mechanical solution when you've gone as far as you can with passive methods.

Reducing indoor humidity. Potential sources of indoor humidity include activities like cooking, showering, and breathing any time of year. Cooking and showering should be done with exhaust fans running to remove the moisture (and pollutants). Other sources of indoor humidity include people, pets, plants, humidifiers, clothes drying racks, and indoor water features. If you're using any of these to keep the relative humidity up in winter, make sure to change your behavior with the seasons. In humid summer weather, turn off the humidifier, put plants outdoors, dry your clothes outdoors or in a dryer, and perhaps limit the use of that fountain in your foyer.

Some special cases bear mentioning here, too. Aquarium aficionados with several tanks often find they need a dehumidifier to keep the humidity under control. A house with an indoor pool, hot tub, steam shower, or connected greenhouse, naturally, needs careful engineering to ensure it doesn't add excessive humidity to the indoor air. That usually means separation, ventilation, and dehumidification.

With crawl spaces, you can reduce the humidity a number of ways. You can encapsulate the crawl space and dry out the humid air. Or you could make sure the humid crawl space air doesn't come anywhere near surfaces that might be below the dew point. Fiberglass batts in the floor probably won't get you there because air can move through them. You'll need to use spray foam or put an air barrier (usually rigid foam board) over the bottom of the floor joists.

Keeping humid air out of interstitial spaces. A cold climate wall with no exterior insulation may have wet, moldy sheathing if indoor air gets into the wall cavities. A typical indoor temperature is 70 °F in winter. With 50 percent relative humidity, the dew point of indoor air will be 50 °F. If you keep the indoor relative humidity at 40 percent in winter, that drops the dew point to a safer 45 °F. Outdoor temperatures in winter can be much lower than that in cold climates, though, so you need to keep the water vapor in the indoor air from making its way through the wall and finding the sheathing. That essentially reduces the humidity in the wall cavities, thus reducing the chance of serious moisture problems.

The main way to keep water vapor out of building cavities is with air sealing. (See the section on air sealing solving most humidity problems later in this chapter.) In some cases, though, you may need a vapor retarder because

diffusion can bring enough water vapor to the cold sheathing to create a wet mess. This is a cold climate problem, and it happens mainly in highly insulated assemblies. With a lot of insulation in the wall, less heat flows through to the exterior sheathing, so the sheathing stays colder. Colder materials can accumulate more water. Even though diffusion is a slow process, a significant amount of water vapor can move through the wall over the course of a winter.

That's when you need a vapor retarder to keep the indoor water vapor away from the cold exterior sheathing. It might be vapor retarder paint on the drywall. It could be vapor retarder sheeting, like polyethylene, between the drywall and the framing. (Don't run out to buy a roll of poly just yet, though. I'll have more to say about that later in this chapter.) Or you could use a special membrane called a smart vapor retarder. Vapor retarders come in different strengths, which I'll describe later in this chapter.

In addition to keeping humid, indoor air away from cold, exterior sheathing, we also want to separate humid, outdoor air from cool, indoor drywall. This is a hot or mixed humid climate problem. A continuous air barrier is the best way to achieve this, but in some cases, you might want to consider an exterior vapor retarder to reduce vapor diffusion. Figure 9.3 shows what can happen to the back side of drywall in a warm,

Figure 9.3. *Mold is growing on the backside of interior drywall because humid air found a cool surface. [Courtesy of Chris White]*

humid climate. The black areas are mold growing on the paper backing on the drywall because humid outdoor air infiltrated through the wall and found the cool drywall. That moisture kept the drywall wet enough to make the mold happy. A good exterior air barrier would have gone a long way to preventing this problem, but vapor diffusion through a perfect air barrier could also allow enough moisture in to cause problems.

Reducing humidity with mechanical systems. Dehumidifiers are the answer in some cases, but they aren't the only type of mechanical system that can be used to reduce humidity. Air conditioners do this while cooling the air. Exhaust fans remove humidity at the source (bathrooms and kitchens). Exhaust fans also reduce the humidity in winter by bringing in outdoor air. (Cold air is dry air!) They also work to reduce indoor humidity year-round in a dry climate because they pull in dry outdoor air. Sometimes, though, air conditioners and exhaust fans aren't able to handle the humidity load, and that's when you need a dehumidifier.

Method 2: Raise the Temperature of the Materials

Now that you've got your humidity under control, let's talk about the temperature of the materials. We need to figure out where our humid air might come into contact with materials below the dew point temperature. Let's begin with walls.

Think of a wood-framed wall. Moving from inside the house to outside, the basic assembly consists of drywall, framing or cavity insulation, sheathing, and cladding. Where's the humid air? In summer, it's outside if you live in a humid climate. The exterior of an insulated wall won't go below the dew point in summer because your air conditioner can't make it so cold indoors that the siding or sheathing drops below the dew point (unless you have some bad thermal bridging or an uninsulated duct in the wall). The back side

of the drywall on the inside of the wall, however, can drop below the dew point. A good exterior air barrier keeps the humid air away, but in a really humid climate, you still may need an exterior vapor retarder to limit water vapor getting through by diffusion.

Looking now at a cold weather issue, a place where raising the temperature can help is at that cold sheathing we discussed in method 1. There I recommended using interior air sealing or vapor retarders to keep water vapor away from the cold surface. Method 2 is to keep materials warm if they might see humid air, and we can do that here by putting insulation outside of the sheathing. That insulates the sheathing from the cold, outdoor air, keeping it above the dew point temperature of any indoor air that might find its way to the sheathing.

> *Bulk water from bad flashing, stupid roof design, and failing gutters causes a lot more problems than water vapor.*

Keeping Things Dry

Water vapor probably gets more attention than it deserves in our discussions of moisture problems in buildings. Bulk water from bad flashing, stupid roof design, and failing gutters causes a lot more problems than water vapor. Still, water vapor does matter. If you're reading this on a cold winter day, you can rest assured that in a house with poorly insulated walls and unvented space heaters, condensation is dripping down a bathroom window somewhere and mold is growing. Maybe it's even happening in your house.

If you can identify a problem resulting from humid air, you have two ways to deal with it: reduce the humidity or keep materials warmer. Otherwise, you could end up with accidental dehumidification, and that's usually not a good thing.

Air Sealing Solves Most Water Vapor Problems

Water vapor can move in two ways. It can jiggle its way with the air or through porous materials (diffusion), and it can be carried along with air as pressure differences cause the air to move from one place to another. Which do you think moves more water vapor? As with most building science questions, the correct answer is: It depends.

You know from the past chapter that the amount of air leakage depends on the pressure difference and the size and shape of the pathway. Diffusion depends on the concentration of water vapor, the temperature, and the vapor permeability of the material it's diffusing through. It's certainly possible to have a wall assembly through which vapor diffusion is a bigger factor than vapor transport with air leakage. In fact, some high-performance wall assemblies do just that. But many houses have high air leakage rates and can easily move a lot of water vapor into a wall assembly.

Figure 9.4 shows what can happen in extremely cold weather. At the top, water vapor is shown diffusing through a 4-foot-by-8-foot section of drywall. Over the entire heating season, the amount of water vapor that got through that drywall was ⅓ quart. At the bottom is another sheet of drywall, this time with a small hole (one square inch). The pressure differences over that heating season resulted in 30 quarts of water getting through the hole.

Compared to air leakage, even porous materials like drywall act as vapor retarders because they slow down the flow so much. And it doesn't take long for some houses to have five coats of paint on the drywall, which slows down diffusion even more. The problem with most houses with accidental dehumidification is air leakage. By making the house as airtight as possible, you also greatly reduce the likelihood of moisture problems caused by water vapor. Air sealing is the first step in controlling water vapor.

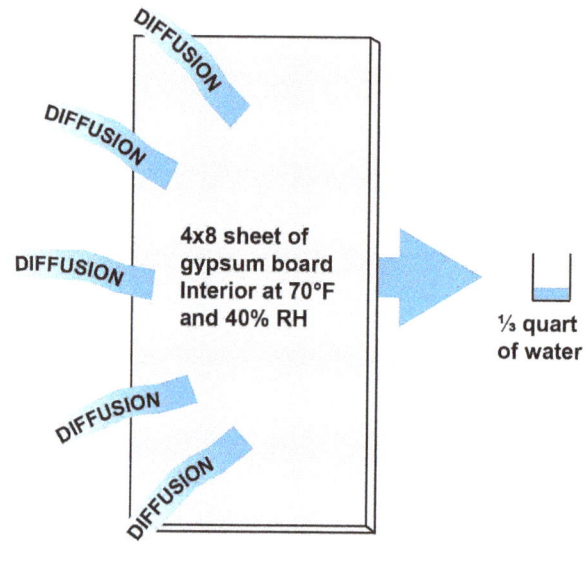

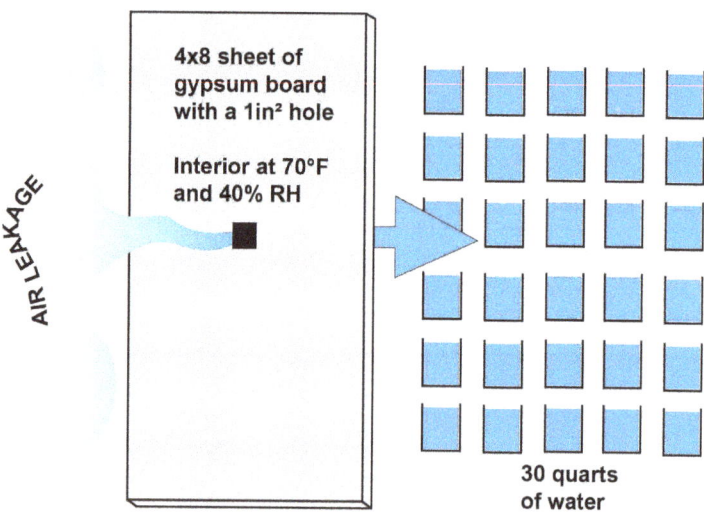

Figure 9.4. *Air leakage can move much more water vapor through a wall than diffusion can. The example here is for extremely cold outdoor conditions. [Courtesy of Joseph Lstiburek]*

What Happens When You Put a Plastic Vapor Barrier in Your Wall?

Before we get into vapor barriers and vapor retarders, let's take a look at what happens inside walls that have a sheet of plastic (typically polyethylene) intended to stop the diffusion of water vapor. We'll look at four possible scenarios of walls with a vapor barrier either inside or outside and in either hot, humid, or cold weather. Let's see which scenarios are most likely to result in accidental dehumidification by letting humid air be close to cool surfaces.

Scenario 1: Plastic Inside; Hot, Humid Weather

One sunny summer day, I was in Charleston and saw condensation on the outside of a window at 1 o'clock in the afternoon. The dew point of the outdoor air was 78 °F. The window had a single pane of glass. The air conditioner was running in the house, so the indoor temperature was probably 75 °F or below. When the humid outdoor air hit the cool window, condensation resulted.

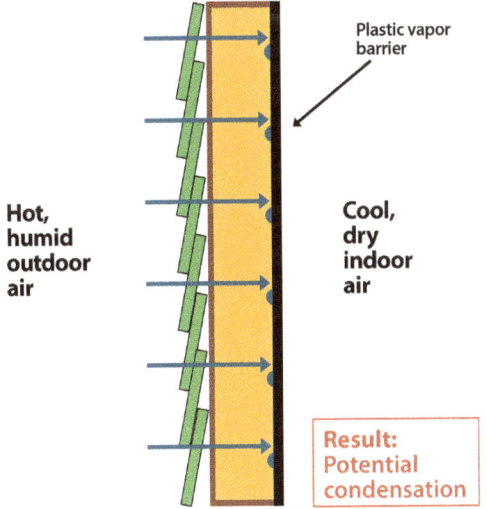

Plastic vapor barrier

Hot, humid outdoor air

Cool, dry indoor air

Result: Potential condensation

Figure 9.5. *Plastic on the inside of a wall in hot, humid weather. The arrows show the movement of water vapor. The wall has insulation in the cavities.*

Now, imagine that pane of glass is actually a sheet of polyethylene (vapor impermeable plastic sheeting). Next, imagine that a layer of drywall separates the poly from the indoor air. Then build a wood-frame wall outside the poly, complete with cladding and air-permeable insulation in the cavities. Will that poly be protected from the outdoor humidity? Or might it, like the window I saw, be dripping with condensation?

If it's a typical wall, chances are good that water vapor in the outdoor air will get into the wall cavity through air leakage, eventually finding the sheet of poly, pressed up against the drywall. If that wall allows outdoor air to infiltrate and the poly is below the dew point, condensation is the likely result. If those conditions last long enough, the condensed water will run down the poly, get the wood framing wet, and begin to grow mold and rot out the wall.

Without poly beneath the drywall, water vapor hits the drywall and some diffuses through to the drier (in summer) indoor air. Enough water may accumulate in the drywall to cause problems, but by installing a sheet of poly there, you cut off that drying mechanism. Water that finds its way into walls can stay there longer and do more damage.

Scenario 2: Plastic Inside; Cold Weather

In cold weather, a sheet of poly on the interior side of a wall probably won't cause problems (Fig. 9.6). The humid air is indoors, and the dry air is outdoors. The sheet of poly still cuts off drying to the indoors, but it keeps the water vapor in the humid indoor air away from the cold surfaces inside the wall.

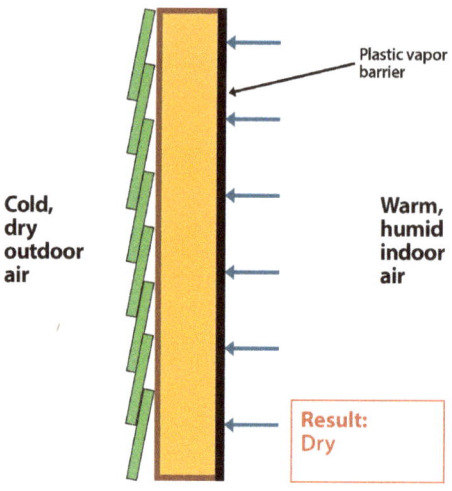

Figure 9.6. *Plastic on the inside in cold weather*

Back in the early days of insulation, this is what building scientists proposed as the solution for walls that wouldn't hold paint. It didn't solve the paint problem, though, because water vapor from the indoor air wasn't the main source of moisture. Plus, as you know now, vapor retarders slow diffusion, but most water vapor moves with air leakage.

Scenario 3: Plastic Outside; Cold Weather

Plastic on the outer surface of a wall in cold weather could cause problems (Fig. 9.7). The humid air is indoors. The cool surface is the sheathing, assuming no exterior insulation. If water vapor diffuses or infiltrates into the wall cavity and finds the cool surface, moisture problems can occur.

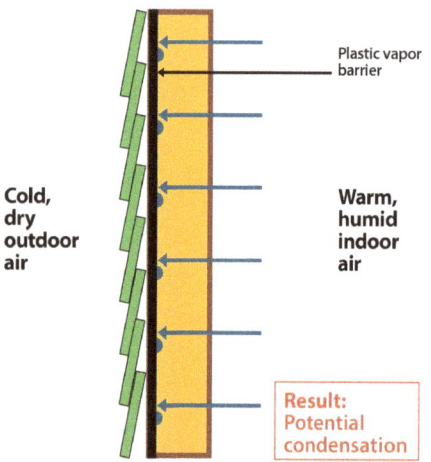

Figure 9.7. *Plastic on the outside in cold weather*

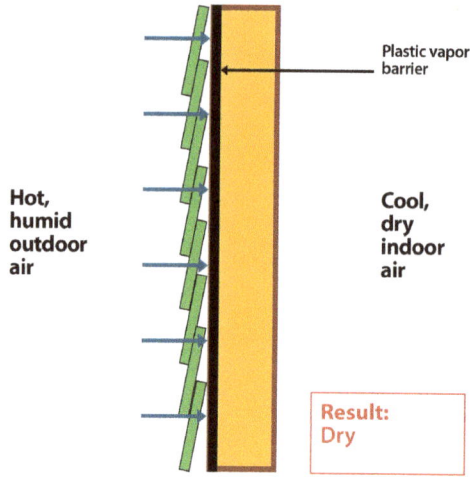

Figure 9.8. *Plastic on the outside in hot, humid weather*

Of course, you can have moisture problems here even without the exterior vapor barrier. Recall: The fundamental rule of material wetness is that cold materials tend to be wet.

Scenario 4: Plastic Outside; Hot, Humid Weather

Problems occur with a vapor barrier when it prevents drying to the drier space. In a building with air conditioning during hot, humid weather, the drier space is indoors. The humid air is outdoors. The wrong place to put a vapor barrier is on the inside because any humid air that gets into the wall cavity is blocked from drying to the inside.

If the vapor barrier is on the outside, as in Figure 9.8, it prevents the humid air from diffusing into the wall cavity and finding the cold surface on the other side of the cavity, the back side of the drywall. So, like a vapor barrier on the inner surface in cold weather, putting one on the outer surface in hot weather isn't likely to cause a moisture problem due to vapor diffusion.

In all four of these scenarios, we need to keep in mind our earlier lessons on controlling water vapor as well as some broader issues. First, reducing air leakage is the most important way to control the movement of water vapor. Plastic sheeting can act as an air barrier as well as vapor barrier, but it's easily damaged during construction. Second, remember the rule for controlling humidity: Keep humid air away from cool materials. Third, putting plastic in the walls of a house isn't a good idea if the house has both heating and air conditioning. It can work in Maine, where air conditioning is rare, and it can work in Miami, where heating is rare. Don't do it in Maryland, though, because if you choose the location for the vapor barrier based on heating, you'll be wrong in cooling season and vice versa.

What's the Best Indoor Relative Humidity?

The relative humidity of indoor air affects health, comfort, durability, and energy consumption. The main factors that determine the indoor relative humidity are climate, season, infiltration, ventilation, heating, air conditioning, dehumidification, humidification, activities, materials, and numbers of people, plants, and pets. Because water vapor can move so easily from one place to another and from one state to another (vapor-liquid-solid), you may see large swings in indoor relative humidity, especially in localized parts of a house. For example, when you take a shower, the relative humidity in the bathroom spikes to nearly 100 percent. Or stand at the front door with the door open on a cold day, and the relative humidity drops 15 percent in the living room.

So, relative humidity impacts several of the end results we want from our homes. It's affected by many factors. And it can have large swings in short times. Low relative humidity happens more often in wintertime—cold air is dry air—and in dry climates. High relative humidity in indoor air is generally a summertime phenomenon because higher temperatures evaporate more water into the air. High relative humidity also occurs in home with greater airtightness and higher occupancy. Fortunately, it's pretty easy to figure out how low or high to keep relative humidity. Let's start with the most important factor: health.

Health and Relative Humidity

The Sterling chart, shown in Chapter 2 (Figure 2.2 on page 24), illustrates the health impacts of humidity. It shows the relative strengths of biological and chemical factors as they change with relative humidity. Some problems (respiratory infections and ozone production) get worse as the humidity decreases. Other issues (fungi, mites, and chemical interactions) get worse as the humidity increases. And still other problems (bacteria, viruses, allergic rhinitis, and asthma) both get worse as the relative humidity decreases and as it increases. The best place to be for health reasons is in the middle of the 0 to 100 percent range, with 40 to 60 percent relative humidity being the ideal range.

This chart has been used in countless classes, articles, and presentations since it was introduced in 1986, but there's an important nuance that some people miss. The height of those bars—which go up uniformly and at the same slope for each factor as the relative humidity either decreases or increases—is not based on quantitative data. The authors of the original paper themselves say, "The shape and height of the bars in the figure are only suggestive." So, yes, 40 to 60 percent relative humidity is ideal for health reasons, but it's not a hard-and-fast rule. You're not necessarily going to get a respiratory infection as soon as your house drops below 40 percent nor have an infestation of dust mites when the relative humidity goes to 61 percent.

But don't crank up that humidifier just yet. Forty percent may be a good minimum relative humidity for health reasons in the abstract, but your house may not be able to handle that much humidity.

Wintertime Indoor Relative Humidity

Beyond health reasons, low relative humidity causes static electricity to build up and become annoying. No one likes to be shocked when they reach for a doorknob. Low relative humidity also can dry out wood and other building materials, creating gaps that increase infiltration or diminish the strength of the bonds. Because low relative humidity is typically a wintertime problem, more infiltration leads to more cold, dry air entering the home, making the situation even worse.

The Sterling chart recommends 30 to 60 percent relative humidity as ideal for health reasons. Keeping a house at 60 percent in wintertime, however, can lead to trouble in a cold climate where cold weather persists for many months. At 60 percent and 70 °F, the dew point is 56 °F. In a cold climate, keeping the indoor air at such a high dew point temperature is asking for trouble. You can do it, but you've got to have a really good building enclosure that ensures none of the humid air will find materials with temperatures below 56 °F. When the outdoor temperature is 10 °F, do you have confidence in your home?

> **Keeping a house at 60 percent relative humidity in wintertime can lead to trouble in a cold climate where cold weather persists for many months.**

What about 40 percent relative humidity and 70 °F? The dew point for that condition is 45 °F. Can the air in your house find any materials at that temperature? If your average January temperature is 20 °F and you live in a house built in 1950, the answer is probably yes. That's

why it's safer to settle for 30 percent and 70 °F, which corresponds to a dew point temperature of 37 °F. A lower dew point means less likelihood of materials getting wet, staying wet, growing mold, and rotting.

Figure 9.9 shows a house in Kansas where the building enclosure didn't stop the cold from getting to the interior drywall. Yes, that's frost in the corner. At the time the photo was taken, the outdoor temperature was -5 °F, and the indoors was 66 °F and 49 percent relative humidity. Now, 49 percent relative humidity isn't horrible—unless it's really cold outside and your insulation doesn't work. The reason their humidity was so high was that they have eight kids and kept the humidifier going 24/7. The dew point indoors was 46 °F, and the below-zero-windy weather outdoors found a weak spot in this home's building enclosure. The attic ventilation made things worse by channeling frigid air directly beneath the insulation, cooling that frozen corner you see in the photo.

Figure 9.9. *Frost formed on the ceiling and walls inside a house because of poor insulation. [Courtesy of Erik Henson]*

The colder the climate, the lower you want to keep the indoor relative humidity in winter if you don't have a really good building enclosure. In Atlanta, we occasionally see temperatures below 10 °F, but that's rare. Our typical winter has temperatures mostly in the 30s to 50s Fahrenheit, with an occasional dip into the 20s. At those temperatures, the materials usually won't stay cold for long enough to get wet and stay wet. In Minneapolis, however, temperatures can stay below 0 °F for weeks at a time. That can cause a lot of wetting—even with 40 percent relative humidity—so separating the humid air and keeping materials warm is critical.

The good news with indoor humidity in winter is that it's self-regulating, in a way. Cold air is dry air, so infiltration keeps the indoor air from getting too humid. If you've got an airtight house, all you need to do is ventilate more if the humidity starts getting too high. So, airtightness helps to keep the indoor air from getting too dry, and ventilation is the solution to air that's too humid when it's cold outside. Those are your two primary ways to control the indoor humidity in winter.

In really cold climates, you probably want to limit the humidity to about 30 percent in winter. If the house isn't airtight, though, don't run for that humidifier just yet. Air sealing is a more sustainable solution when air leakage is responsible for dry indoor air.

Houses in hot-humid and mixed-humid climates often have the opposite problem. When cold weather occurs in short bursts between longer periods of warmer weather, keeping the indoor relative humidity below 60 percent can be a challenge. On days when the outdoor temperature is mild and the humidity high, the air conditioner won't help much because it makes the house too cold. That's when you either resign yourself to living with the higher humidity until the next cold front comes through, or you close up the house and use a dehumidifier.

Air sealing is a more sustainable solution than running a humidifier when air leakage is responsible for dry indoor air.

Summertime Indoor Relative Humidity

High dew points in warm weather can lead to comfort problems. Our bodies need more cooling in warm weather, but high humidity makes it harder. We have more trouble cooling by evaporating water from the skin (i.e., sweating) because there's already so much water vapor in the air. In an air-conditioned house, the standard design conditions call for a temperature of 75 °F at 50 percent relative humidity. That's smack-dab in the middle of the total relative humidity range (0-100 percent) and also in the middle of the Sterling chart recommended range (30-60 percent).

In a humid climate, 50 to 60 percent relative humidity can be plenty comfortable. Yes, with air conditioning and maybe a dehumidifier, you can get down to 40 or 45 percent, but do you need to? Health and building durability don't require that. One area that does suffer if you try to dehumidify to 40 or 45 percent is energy consumption. It takes more energy to run your air conditioner or dehumidifier to achieve 40 to 45 percent humidity than it does to keep in the 50 to 60 percent range. If you can be comfortable and healthy with the relative humidity below 60 percent, and your house shouldn't grow mold or start rotting in those conditions, why use the extra energy to dehumidify further?

The Confusing World of Vapor Barriers and Vapor Retarders

Before we get into the details of those things meant to reduce the diffusion of water vapor, let's talk about words. When you talk to building professionals, you may hear a lot of references to "vapor barriers." Sometimes they refer to house wrap as a vapor barrier. In most cases, though, house wrap doesn't stop water vapor. House wrap's main purpose is to control the liquid water that gets behind the cladding. Sometimes the kraft paper facing on insulation is called a vapor barrier. Is it? Maybe, but that depends on your definition of vapor barrier. And then there's the term "vapor retarder." Is that the same as a vapor barrier?

Water vapor can move in two ways: swept along with a volume of air (moving because of a pressure difference and a pathway) or by the random motion of molecules (diffusion from wet to dry). Air barriers control the first kind of movement. Both vapor barriers and vapor retarders control the second. Air barriers are defined by how much air moves through a material, assembly, or enclosure at a certain pressure difference. The vapor resistance of a material is defined similarly by the rate at which water vapor moves through a material. Called vapor permeance, this rate tells you how much water vapor moves across a certain amount of area of a given thickness at a given vapor pressure difference. The US unit for this is the perm, and lower numbers mean less vapor flow.

Every material has a greater or lesser ability to allow water vapor to diffuse through to the drier side. A bit of confusion creeps in here because we can specify that ability as either the material's permeability or its permeance. Both tell how easily water vapor moves through a material, with higher numbers indicating more movement. The difference is that permeability doesn't depend on thickness, but permeance does. It's like the difference between density and weight. Permeability is like density. Permeance is like weight. A ⅜-inch sheet of plywood may have the same density as a ¾-inch sheet of the same type of plywood, but it has half the weight. Similarly, both sheets of plywood have the same permeability, being made of the same material. But the thicker sheet has roughly half the permeance. Permeance, unlike weight, decreases with thickness because there's more material for water vapor to get through.

When you're studying the properties of materials to use in construction, you'll often see a perm rating. That's short for permeance, which means that it already factors in the thickness. For example, if you're thinking of using extruded polystyrene (XPS) foam board insulation in your walls, you'll find in your research that one particular brand says the perm rating drops from 1.1 to 0.7 to 0.6 as the thickness goes from 1 inch to 2 inches to 3 inches.

In other words, as the thickness increases, water vapor has a harder time making it through, and the perm rating drops. So, materials with lower perm ratings are better at slowing the movement of water vapor. If the perm rating is low enough, we call the material a vapor retarder. If it's really low, we call it a vapor barrier.

The International Residential Code (IRC) updated its definition of vapor retarders in 2007 to include three classes of vapor retarders:

Class 1: ≤ 0.1 perm (vapor impermeable)
Class 2: 0.1 to 1.0 perm (vapor semi-impermeable)
Class 3: 1.0 perm to 10 perms (vapor semi-permeable)

People who understand this issue reserve the name "vapor barrier" for class 1 vapor retarders because they pretty much stop all movement of

Vapor Properties of Materials

Type	Material	Permeance (perms)
Permeable	Tyvek Home Wrap	54
	Drywall	56
	Plaster on wood lath	11
	Building paper/felt	30
	Open-cell spray polyurethane foam insulation	10 (5")
Semi-permeable	Oriented strand board (OSB)	2-3
	Plywood	0.3-9.4
	Expanded polystyrene (EPS)	>1 (3")
	Extruded polystyrene (XPS)	1.5 (0.5") 1.1 (1")
Semi-impermeable	Extruded polystyrene (XPS)	0.7 (2")
	Closed-cell spray polyurethane foam insulation	0.9 (2")
	Vapor retarder latex paint	0.8-0.45
Impermeable	Polyethylene film	0.06
	Aluminum foil	0.01

Table 9.1. *Vapor properties of some common building materials. Note that the permeance values are approximate. They vary from one manufacturer to another, from one product line to another, and even in the same product when the composition changes. To do calculations involving permeance, be sure to get actual data from the manufacturer.*

water vapor. When you call oriented strand board (OSB), asphalt-coated kraft paper, or closed-cell spray foam a vapor barrier, you're missing that vapor permeance isn't a black-and-white issue. That's why we have three classes of vapor retarders in the United States.

Another way this issue is framed is to refer to materials as vapor-open or vapor-closed. Again, though, that's putting it in black-and-white terms. Perhaps the best way to discuss the vapor properties of materials is by using the descriptive terms shown with their definitions above.[14]

Do You Need a Vapor Retarder?

The question of whether or not to use a vapor retarder is commonly misunderstood as a yes-or-no, black-and-white issue. In 2001, when I embarked on my homebuilding experience, I was at the front end of my building science education. I had read about vapor barriers, but a lot of what's written on this topic is a confusing mess.

If you've read Chapter 6 and this chapter, you already have a much better understanding of this issue than I had in 2001. Here's a quick summary of what I've written about water vapor so far in this book:

- Water is often the biggest problem with houses, and liquid water is a much bigger problem than water vapor.

14. If you go looking for more information on permeance, you'll find a distinction between wet cup and dry cup measurements. The descriptive terms apply to the dry cup values.

- The primary rule for preventing water vapor damage is to keep humid air away from cool materials, either by reducing the humidity, raising the temperature of materials, or by separating humid air and cool materials.
- Ventilation in colder weather or dehumidification in warmer weather can reduce the humidity.
- Exterior insulation can keep the temperature of materials above the dew point.
- Air leakage can move a lot more water vapor than diffusion does, so an air barrier does most of the vapor control you need.
- A building assembly's ability to dry out is generally more important than stopping the diffusion of water vapor.
- When you do use assemblies that need to slow down vapor diffusion, you need to know how well all the materials in that assembly transport water vapor by diffusion. The materials specified may already have a low-enough permeance for the whole assembly, making an additional vapor retarder unnecessary.

In short, most vapor control is done with methods other than vapor retarders. Sometimes, though, you do need to limit the amount of vapor diffusion through an assembly. One case where you need a vapor retarder is when you have an unvented attic with open-cell spray foam insulation against the roof deck in a cold climate (IECC climate zones 5 and higher). In fact, this is required by the International Residential Code.

Open-cell spray foam insulation is vapor permeable or semi-permeable, depending on the thickness. Because humid air and cold materials do what they do, water vapor in the humid attic air can diffuse through the open-cell spray foam and accumulate in the cold roof deck. To prevent the roof deck from getting wet and staying wet over the course of a winter, you can install a class 2 vapor retarder. An alternative would be to keep the roof deck warmer by also installing insulation on top.

Another case where a vapor retarder is required is when you have thick walls with a lot of insulation on the conditioned space side of the sheathing and none outside. The more insulation in the wall, the colder the sheathing will be in winter. And we know about humid air (inside the conditioned space in winter) and cold materials (the wall sheathing). Even the most airtight walls may not be able to keep the sheathing dry. A class 2 vapor retarder—which could be a vapor retarder paint—can prevent the sheathing from getting wet.

A few other situations that require a vapor retarder are beneath a concrete slab, on foundation walls, and on the ground in a crawl space. In Chapter 11, we'll go deeper into some specific examples of assemblies and spaces where vapor control is needed.

Chapter Takeaways

- Controlling water vapor is not simply a matter of installing a vapor control layer.
- Cold air is dry air. When you heat it up, the relative humidity is very low.
- Cold materials are generally wetter than warm materials.
- To prevent humidity from causing problems, keep humid air away from cool materials.
- Because more water vapor moves with air flow than by diffusing through materials, air sealing is one of the best ways to control humidity.
- Indoor relative humidity should be between 30 and 60 percent. Homes with weak building enclosures need to stay near the bottom end of that range in winter.
- The higher the water vapor permeance of a material or assembly, the more easily water vapor can pass through a material.

CHAPTER 10
Controlling Heat

The control layer for heat is insulation. Insulation helps to keep heat out of the house in summer and in the house in winter. When it's hot outdoors, you rely on more than just air conditioning to keep cool inside your home. It's not the only factor—airtightness and windows play significant roles as well—but it's a crucial one. Recall from Chapter 5 that heat flow depends on the temperature difference, the area, and how resistive the assembly is. The wood, drywall, and other materials also resist heat flow—and we're happy to count their contributions—but we mainly rely on insulation to slow down the flow of heat.

We can rank all materials by how well they slow down the flow of heat. This is called their thermal resistance, or R-value. Special testing labs use expensive devices to measure the thermal resistance of materials and assign a number to them. We call that number the R-value and discuss it more in the next section. Also,

> *"All heat is of the same kind."*
> —*James Clerk Maxwell*

in this chapter, we'll look at how the R-value of the material isn't the same as the R-value of the assembly and how thermal bridging can make you uncomfortable, cause moisture problems, and lead to high energy bills.

As mentioned above, the R-value depends on the material, so we'll look at several different kinds of insulation and their properties. You want to make sure you choose one that's right for your application. And then you want to install it properly as well. Poor installation reduces the effectiveness of insulation. Finally, we'll look at the question of how much insulation you should install. (As usual, the answer is, "It depends.")

Heat Flow

Heat is energy on the move. That's why you almost always see the word "heat" connected with another word, like "flow" or "transfer." What causes that flow of energy is a temperature difference because heat flows from something at a higher temperature to something at a lower temperature. For example, heat can flow from hot outdoor air through a wall assembly and into the cooler indoor air. It can flow from the hot exhaust gases of a natural gas furnace into the cooler heat exchanger. It can even flow from cold outdoor air into the even colder refrigerant flowing through the outdoor coil of a heat pump.

The biggest takeaway here is that heat flows from a warmer material to a cooler one. That behavior is part of the **second law of thermodynamics**.

Temperature

To measure heat flow, we need to know temperature. We have many ways to do that now. Because so many materials have properties that change with temperature, it's easy to calibrate and use them to measure temperature. It could be the volume of mercury in a glass tube (mercury thermometer), the voltage developed by two dissimilar metals (thermocouple), the thermal radiation emitted by an object (infrared thermometer), or others.

Then we need a scale for our temperature readings. The fellow who invented the mercury thermometer, Daniel Fahrenheit, also came up with a scale so he could relate the change in volume of the mercury in the tube to the temperature change.

The freezing and boiling points of water are easy reference points that can be used to calibrate a thermometer. For the Fahrenheit scale, those points are at 32 °F and 212 °F.

Then there's the scale used by 95 percent of the world: Celsius, named for the 18th-century Swedish astronomer Anders Celsius. The freezing and boiling points of water on that scale are at 0 °C and 100 °C. Because the Celsius degree is 1.8 times larger than the Fahrenheit degree, converting between the scales is a chore. But here's one reference point for you that you probably won't forget (and maybe you won't have to experience it either): The two scales cross at -40 degrees, which means -40 °F = -40 °C. Because they're the same, we can call that -40 °FC, which also could stand for -40 °Freaking Cold!

What exactly is temperature, though? It's familiar to all of us since childhood, but let's explore the concept behind the idea that's ingrained in our minds from decades of experience. We know that solids, liquids, and gases are composed of small particles called molecules and atoms. When we measure the temperature of a substance, we're getting a sense of how energetic those small particles are. Higher temperatures mean more kinetic energy of the molecules; lower temperatures mean less kinetic energy.

Think of a mercury thermometer. If we move a thermometer from, say, an air-conditioned living room to the hot backyard, the mercury will expand and rise in the glass tube. Eventually it stops. Why? A physicist would say the thermometer has come to equilibrium with its surroundings. In everyday language, that just means they're at the same temperature. And because this object happens to be a calibrated thermometer, that's how we know what the temperature is in the backyard.

Let's take it a step further. We know the thermometer is in thermal equilibrium with the air surrounding it because the two have been

in contact long enough that the mercury isn't rising anymore. The air, likewise, is in thermal equilibrium with a rocking chair on the porch. Can we then say the rocking chair is in thermal equilibrium with the thermometer, and thus at the same temperature, even though they're not in contact with each other?

> *Higher temperatures mean more kinetic energy of the molecules; lower temperatures mean less kinetic energy.*

Yes, we can. The thermometer and the rocking chair don't exchange heat directly to come to equilibrium with each other. (Assume the thermometer and chair don't exchange radiant heat with each other and do have equal radiant heat transfer with their environment.) They do both exchange heat with the air, though, so if the thermometer is in equilibrium with the air and the same air is in equilibrium with the rocking chair, then the thermometer is in equilibrium with the rocking chair, too.

The exercise may seem obvious, but it's significant. In fact, it's so obvious (in hindsight) and significant that it's the zeroth law of thermodynamics. Because heat flows due to temperature differences, we have to know those temperatures to calculate the amount of heat flow. Being able to design a thermometer that tells us the temperature of the thermometer and also the stuff around it makes that possible.

Heat Flow by Conduction

When we put cold next to warm, the kinetic energy in the warm thing's molecules gets transferred to the cold thing's molecules. Heat moves from higher temperatures to lower temperatures. Let's say the cold thing is a steel pole and the warm thing is your tongue. When you put your warm, wet tongue on that cold, steel pole outdoors, thermodynamics rules the day. Heat moves from your tongue into the cold steel. That causes your body to send more heat to your tongue as it cools, but if the temperature is below freezing, it may not be enough.

Steel is a good conductor of heat, so the pole whisks heat away from your tongue faster than your body can replenish it. Once the temperature of the tip of your tongue gets to the freezing point of water, the liquid moisture on your tongue starts turning to ice. It fills the crevices and pores in both your tongue and the steel pole, forming a strong bond between the two. Try pulling away too quickly, and you'll leave part of your tongue on the pole. (Or so I've been told. We didn't have freezing steel poles on the Gulf Coast of Texas and Louisiana when I was growing up.) The way to break the bond is to bring the heat. Pouring warm water over the tongue-pole connection will work, as heat conducts energy from the water to the tongue and pole.

It's the same with buildings. Warmer materials conduct heat into adjacent cooler materials, whether that's the outdoor air and a house's siding, indoor air moving over the cold air-conditioner coil, or the water in your electric water heater in contact with the heating element. We use this fact to do all kinds of calculations for a building, such as a heating and cooling load calculation, which determines how much heating and cooling capacity a house needs (Chapter 12).

Note that heat flow by conduction can occur in solids, liquids, and gases. It's not something that happens only in solids.

Heat Flow by Convection

When solids transfer heat by conduction, they do so particle by particle, as the intense jiggling of one particle imparts some of that kinetic energy to its neighbors, which then send the energy to their neighbors. Unlike solids, with their atoms and molecules locked into relatively fixed positions, fluids are materials that flow. We're talking liquids and gases here. Heat transfer from jiggling neighbor to jiggling neighbor can happen in liquids and gases, too, but fluids have another way to transfer heat: Because the particles are energetic and can move, they can take their energy with them.

Consider a day at the beach. You know those nice breezes that come off the water toward the beach? That's heat transfer by convection. This may seem a bit confusing because the sea breeze is moving horizontally, but the driving force of natural convection is gravity.

The air right over the ocean has a tall column of more air sitting on top of it, as does the air sitting on top of the land. If either were just a single column of air with nothing surrounding it, the air at the bottom would be sent moving in all sideways directions. Imagine holding an open tube of toothpaste just above the countertop and squeezing the tube. That's what would happen. But that column isn't alone, and the surrounding columns of air also want to move sideways if they can.

Figure 10.1. *A sea breeze is a great example of a convective loop that arises from warming and cooling air.*

In the morning when there's no breeze, the air at the bottom isn't moving. The air over the land and the air over the water are pushing equally hard against each other. Stalemate. But as the sun gets higher in the sky and heats everything up, the land gets hotter than the ocean. As the land gets hotter, the air above it gets hotter. As the air gets hotter, its molecules zip around faster, spreading out as they do. The density of the air over the land decreases. The density of the air over the water doesn't decrease as much.

Now the battle over spreading out changes, and the air over the water wins. It moves toward the low-density air over the land, pushing it up. The warmer, less dense air rises and eventually cools, replacing the air over the ocean that dropped down as it squished the lower ocean air onto the land. Now, we've got a cycle happening, and it's called a convective loop.

This kind of heat transfer is called natural convection. It happens with sea breezes and also in many other circumstances, such as water in a pot being heated on the stove, warm air rising up to the second floor in your house in winter, and the air inside uninsulated walls.

Let's take a look at the example of an uninsulated wood-framed wall (Figure 10.2). A volume of air inside a cavity is bounded by wood framing members on left, right, bottom, and top, wood sheathing on the outside, and drywall on the inside. It's a cold winter night, and the higher temperature is inside the house. The drywall is warm, and the sheathing is cold. The enclosed air in contact with the cold sheathing loses heat to the sheathing. That air gets cold and dense, causing it to fall toward the bottom of the cavity. At the bottom, it pushes up the lighter, warmer air heated by its contact with the warm drywall. As the warm air crowds the top of the cavity, some of it comes into contact with the cold sheathing, thus cooling, getting denser, and then falling again. And now we have heat transfer by a convective loop inside the wall cavity.

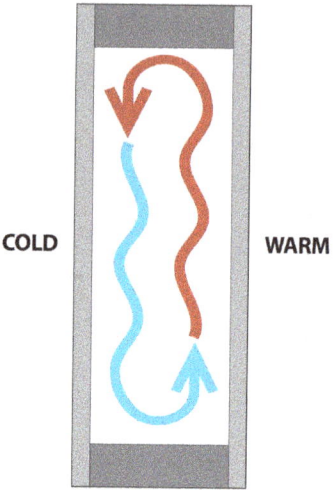

Figure 10.2. *Convective loop in an uninsulated wall*

In this example, we've seen two ways of transferring heat from the warm side to the cold side. The air in contact with the cold sheathing transfers heat through conduction, as does the air in contact with the warm drywall. The movement of air inside the cavity, going through its cycle of cooling and falling followed by warming and rising, is heat transfer by convection.

But that's far from the end of the story for this uninsulated wall. A significant portion of the heat transfer within the wall occurs via a third mechanism, and that's next.

Heat Flow by Radiation

Conduction and convection both require matter to move heat from warmer to cooler places. Radiation is different. When radiant heat moves from one place to another, it doesn't need any matter in between. Think of the sun, 93 million miles away, sending abundant radiant energy through empty space to Earth.

In conduction, jiggling molecules bump into their neighbors, spreading their energy in the process. In convection, jiggling molecules move from one place to another, carrying their jiggling energy with them and (perhaps) depositing it somewhere else. In radiation, jiggling molecules emit electromagnetic radiation, which then travels until it is absorbed by matter somewhere else.

Jiggling molecules emit electromagnetic radiation, which then travels until it is absorbed by matter somewhere else.

Where does that electromagnetic radiation come from? Molecules are made of atoms, and atoms are made of electrically charged particles (protons and electrons). The energy of jiggling atoms and molecules can accelerate the electrically charged particles within, and that acceleration results in electromagnetic radiation. Any object with a temperature above absolute zero will emit such radiation. This is every object in the universe because the **third law of thermodynamics** says that no object can ever get all the way down to absolute zero. When this radiation is in the infrared part of the spectrum (plus visible and some ultraviolet), it's often called thermal radiation.

This whole thing is fascinating on many levels. First, thermal radiation isn't just a uniform quantity that's always the same. No, thermal radiation is composed of electromagnetic waves with varying wavelength. Figure 10.3 shows the intensity of radiation for a range of wavelengths. Each curve represents the thermal radiation from an object with a specific temperature, shown at the peak of the curve. Note that as the object gets hotter, the peak wavelength is shorter and the intensity is higher.

Everything with a temperature radiates heat, even if you can't see it. You're radiating infrared heat right now as your body seeks to rid itself of the heat given off by your metabolism. When you put a piece of bread in the toaster, the filament gets red hot and radiates in the infrared part of the spectrum and also in the visible as well. And yes, the radiators in a hydronic heating system give off infrared radiation, too (although they deliver most of their heat via convection).

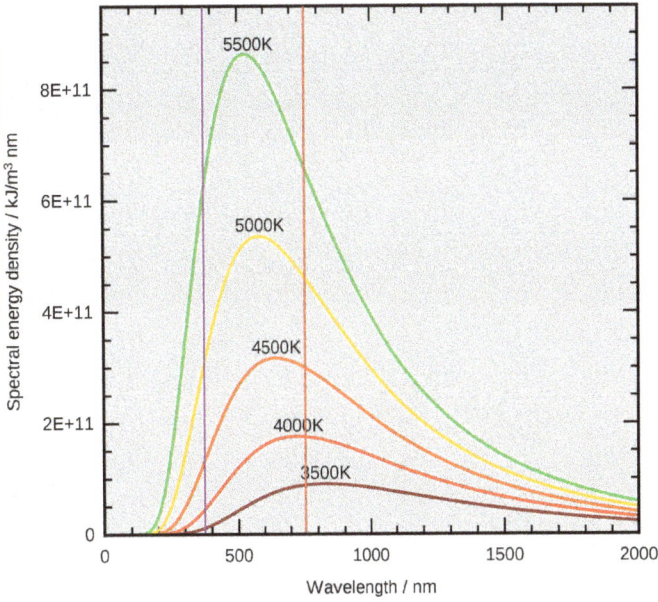

Figure 10.3. *Intensity of thermal radiation as a function of wavelength for objects at various temperatures. Visible light has wavelengths of about 380 to 750 nm, between the violet and red vertical lines shown on the graph.* [Credit: 4C, Wikimedia Commons, CC 3.0]

How does this apply to buildings? When you put a temperature difference across a building assembly, it's likely that all three modes of heat transfer will occur—conduction, convection, and radiation. In the empty wall cavity we discussed in the previous section, conduction and convection both move energy from the warm side to the cool side. But so does radiation. Here's how it works.

As noted above, every object will send out thermal radiation with wavelengths and intensities based on the temperature of the object. Obviously, the warm drywall will radiate heat into the uninsulated cavity. Much of that heat will be absorbed by the cold sheathing. But the cold sheathing also radiates heat back toward the warm drywall. Because it's at a lower temperature, however, the amount of thermal radiation it sends to the drywall will be less than it absorbs from the drywall. So, the net flow of thermal radiation is what matters, and in this case that's from the warm drywall to the cold sheathing.

Another example of radiant heat transfer is a big single-pane picture window in an older house. It's a cold night and you're sitting near the window with the heat cranked up. The air in the room is toasty, yet you feel uncomfortably cold. Why? A big part of it is radiant heat transfer. That single-pane window is cold. Your body is warm. You're radiating a lot more heat to the window than it's radiating back to you, so your body cools faster than you'd like. In addition, that cold surface can get a convective loop going in the room, just as the uninsulated cavity did, so you may feel a draft as the cooled air drops down to the floor near the window and then rises as it warms again.

We'll get into some applications of radiant heat transfer related to attics, bonus rooms, and more in the next chapter.

Calculating Heat Flow

When heat flows across parts of the building enclosure, all three mechanisms—conduction, convection, and radiation—are in play, often at the same time. Also, building assemblies are not uniform. They vary in type of material, density, resistance to heat flow, and other ways. That complexity leads to a complex, three-dimensional pattern of heat flow, too. And that leads to the need for complex equations to describe that flow. Fortunately, for most practical purposes, calculating heat flow through building assemblies can be done with a simple equation.

$$Q = U \times A \times \Delta T$$

Q is the rate of heat flow, measured in BTU per hour in the United States.

U is the conductance of the material through which the heat is flowing.

A is the area of the assembly.

And ΔT is the temperature difference.

Even if you're not familiar with conductance, you probably have heard of R-value, which is the resistance to heat flow. Those two quantities are reciprocals of each other.

$$R = \frac{1}{U} \quad \text{and} \quad U = \frac{1}{R}$$

The heat flow equation is usually stated in terms of the conductance, U, but you can use the relationship between U and R to show it in terms of the R-value.

$$Q = \frac{1}{R} \times A \times \Delta T$$

This equation is for heat flowing through materials and accounts for much of the heat flow through a building enclosure, the walls of a duct, or any place where matter lies between two areas of different temperature. We use it for floors, walls, ceilings, doors, windows, and ducts. When you have an assembly, like a wall, this equation actually accounts for the radiation and convection within the wall as well as the conduction.

This is not the only equation needed for calculating heat flow in buildings, however. If you sit in front of a west-facing window on a sunny summer afternoon, you'll feel the radiant heat flowing through the window. Heat moves through the glazing (the transparent part of a window or door) in windows all three ways—conduction, convection, and radiation—and each has its own equation. The radiant transfer can be significant, so we need to include it in calculations for annual energy use and heating and cooling load calculations.

Another way that heat moves into or out of a house is with air. In fact, the heat in air also moves into or out of the house in two forms. When cold air leaks into a house in winter or hot air leaks into a house in summer, it must be heated or cooled to the indoor temperature. The heat associated with temperature changes is called sensible heat. The other kind of heat is called latent heat, and it is associated with the water vapor mixed in with the air. That form of heat affects cooling only because it can reduce our bodies' ability to use evaporative cooling. We'll have more to say about sensible and latent heat in Chapter 12.

Heat transfer is a quantitative relationship between matter and energy. Because this book focuses more on concepts than calculations, however, I'll omit the other heat transfer equations here. If you'd like to go deeper into the mathematics, see the resources and appendices at the end of the book.

Temperature and Phase Changes

Most of the time, when you put two objects next to each other and heat flows from the warmer to the cooler, the temperature of the cooler object rises, and the temperature of the warmer object falls. If left together long enough, they come to equilibrium and have equal temperatures. Heat flow and temperature changes go together, at least sometimes.

In other cases, though, heat flows from one object to another with no temperature change. Consider a pot of water on the stove. With the burner on, heat flows into the bottom of the pot and then into the water. Initially, the temperature of the water rises. Once the temperature reaches the boiling point, however, the water temperature stays the same. Heat is still flowing into the water, but now we have a different phenomenon taking over: a phase change. The energy from the burner now goes into transforming the water from the liquid state to the vapor state.

Refrigerators, air conditioners, heat pumps, and dehumidifiers all rely on phase changes.

Phase changes are important in houses, and not just when you boil water. Refrigerators, air conditioners, heat pumps, and dehumidifiers all rely on phase changes. These devices can transfer a lot more heat from one place to another when the heat turns a liquid into a vapor than

when it simply increases the temperature of that same liquid. (See Chapter 12.) Phase changes are also important in the operation of air conditioners and dehumidifiers because they condense water vapor from the air to reduce the humidity.

Phase changes can be put to use within a building enclosure, too. Phase change materials built into walls or other assemblies can intercept a lot of heat as it tries to invade or escape from a house. Then there are all the other ways that water changing phase can affect a house and the people within, such as ice dams, frost heaving, condensation inside building assemblies, and evaporation from your skin.

The point to remember here is that heat transfer doesn't always result in a temperature change. Whatever happens, though, the first law of thermodynamics will hold, and the total amount of energy will be conserved.

Thermal Expansion and Contraction

Another interesting thing that happens when heat flows into or out of something is that the material can expand or contract. Heat is energy, which causes atoms and molecules to move more. As molecules vibrate faster, they take up more space. On a larger scale, the material expands. This is called thermal expansion. When heat flows out of a material, the reverse happens: Molecules vibrate slower, they take up less space, and the material contracts, which is called thermal contraction.

This property isn't as important for the amount of heat flow involved as it is for what it can do to buildings. One consequence of thermal expansion and contraction is that the places where materials meet—joints and seams—are subject to stresses over time. Years of expanding and contracting can tear a building apart. For example, sealants and adhesives can be pulled away from the materials they were bonded to, leaving gaps for air and moisture to move through. A house that was airtight at first can become leakier as it ages. Using sealants and adhesives that are elastic enough to move with thermal changes can keep those gaps sealed and those materials held together for a longer time.

Another way that thermal expansion is planned for in a building is in the use of expansion joints. Look at a driveway or sidewalk. At regular intervals, you'll see a gap that allows the concrete to expand without buckling or shrink without tearing itself apart.

Thermal expansion occurs in materials like concrete, masonry, steel, various types of plastic, and other building materials. Wood also expands and contracts, but moisture is the main cause there, not heat. Whether the cause is heat or moisture, what usually causes problems is the difference in the amount of expansion or contraction. One way to minimize those changes in size is to minimize temperature and moisture changes. We'll look at that in the next chapter.

The Laws of Thermodynamics

Entire books have been written about the laws of thermodynamics. I'll cover them here in one short section. To understand how houses work, you don't need to know Clausius's interpretation of the second law of thermodynamics or what happens at absolute zero. We can condense this immense body of knowledge into just a few sentences.

Zeroth Law of Thermodynamics

Heat won't flow from one object to another unless there's a temperature difference. This is the concept of thermal equilibrium I discussed early in this chapter when defining temperature. If a rocking chair is in thermal equilibrium with the air, and the air is in thermal equilibrium with a thermometer, then the rocking chair is also in thermal equilibrium with the thermometer.

First Law of Thermodynamics

Work can be converted to heat, heat can be converted to work, and heat can move from one object to another, but no energy is ever lost or created in those changes. This is a form of the law of conservation of energy. This and the second law are the basic principles that make heating and cooling systems work. It says we can make a warm place warmer or a cool place cooler by doing some work to move heat. The first law also explains why we have to pay to keep our homes warm in winter and cool in summer. In winter, for example, heat escapes from the house. Because we cannot create energy, we have to pay to replace the heat lost from the house if we want to stay warm.

Second Law of Thermodynamics

The most likely way you've heard of this law is in the statement that heat flows from warmer to cooler objects. It's a bit broader than just giving the direction of heat flow. It also gives a direction for the flows of moisture—wet to dry—and air—high pressure to low pressure (See Fig. 5.3). It's an important law with many implications. It introduces the concept of entropy, a measure of disorder in a system, and explores the reversibility and irreversibility of processes as well as indicating the direction of time. As you might suspect just from this brief explanation, entire books, careers, and even lives have been devoted to this law alone.

The second law's impact on building science is enormous. It tells us that heat is going to flow into the house on a hot summer day. Even though it wouldn't violate the first law just for heat to flow unassisted from a cooler place to a warmer place, we know that doesn't happen. If that could happen, it would be possible for the same thing to happen inside the house. One side of a room, for example, could get hot enough to fry a person while the other side became cold enough to turn their housemate into a popsicle.

The second law's impact on building science is enormous.

Air source heat pumps are a perfect example of the first and second laws. With them, we can move heat from a cold place to a hot place or vice versa, but only by doing work. The work in a vapor-compression driven heat pump (Chapter 13) is the key to getting heat to flow backward, from cold to hot. That work done by a heat pump creates a temperature in the outdoor unit that's lower than the outdoor air, resulting in heat flowing from cold outdoor air into an even colder heat pump coil. The indoor part of the heat pump gets hotter than the indoor air, so again, heat flows from hot to cold.

Third Law of Thermodynamics

It's impossible to reach a temperature of absolute zero. That's really all I need to say about that one. The only way to get close enough to absolute zero for this law to matter is in a low-temperature research lab. If you live in a low-temperature lab, you need a different book . . . and maybe a different life.

The Relevance for Building Science

The big takeaway is that two of the laws of thermodynamics do the heavy lifting in building science. The first law tells us that all of the energy transformations that happen in homes must obey the law of conservation of energy. The second law tells us that not every process that conserves energy is going to happen. Even though heat could naturally flow from cold to hot and not violate the first law, the second law tells us that never happens. Those two laws together underlie a lot of the processes that happen in buildings.

The Laws of Thermodynamics Summarized

Here's a quick summary of the four laws to help you remember them:

Zeroth Law: Thermal equilibrium
First Law: Conservation of energy
Second Law: Heat flows from hot to cold
Third Law: Absolute zero is impossible

Other summaries of the laws of thermodynamics explain them differently. Here's one tongue-in-cheek version of the first, second, and third laws:

- You can't win; you can only break even.
- You can only break even at absolute zero.
- You can't reach absolute zero.

Taking it a step further, Ginsberg's Theorem, named for the poet Allen Ginsberg, gives another version of the first, second, and third laws:

- You can't win.
- You can't break even.
- You can't get out of the game.

Insulation Is the Primary Control Layer for Heat

Control layers are the parts of a building enclosure that control the flows of liquid water, air, water vapor, and heat. In the broadest sense, the entire building enclosure controls heat flow because all the materials in it add some resistance. The air barrier, of course, controls a whole lot of heat flow, as we discussed in Chapter 8. The majority of homes, though, allow more heat to cross the building enclosure by conduction through the floors, walls, ceilings, windows, and doors. Except for windows, the primary heat control layer is insulation. For windows, it's also insulation, in a sense, but it comes in the form of confined gas between multiple panes of glass and microscopic coatings on the glass.

> **When heat flows through a building assembly, it uses all three modes of heat transfer: conduction, convection, and radiation.**

The amount of heat that flows through a building assembly (a wall, for example) depends on three factors: the temperature difference, the area (length times width), and how resistive the assembly is. Changing any of those factors is a way to control heat flow, of course. You can reduce the temperature difference by adjusting the thermostat. You can reduce the area by building a smaller house. You can make the building enclosure more resistive to heat flow by insulating and air sealing.

The resistance to heat flow comes primarily from the material we call insulation, although most of the materials in our home's building enclosure also resist heat flow. When heat flows through a building assembly, it uses all three modes of heat transfer: conduction,

convection, and radiation. Materials that are good insulators reduce the effect of each mode.

But where do we put insulation? In North America, we mostly build houses framed with wood. That frame has cavities between the wood framing members, and that's where we stick the insulation. The result is a partially insulated building because wood isn't nearly as good at controlling heat flow as insulation. (More on that in the upcoming section on thermal bridging.)

It helps to think of the building enclosure as a whole to see where you should focus your efforts on reducing heat flow. For example, if you're building a new house, it's easy to add lots of insulation to the ceiling, but at a certain point you'll get more bang for your buck by improving the walls.

Likewise, a typical window these days has an R-value of about 3.5. Putting in better windows or reducing window area may do more to reduce your heat flow than going from R-20 to R-30 walls.

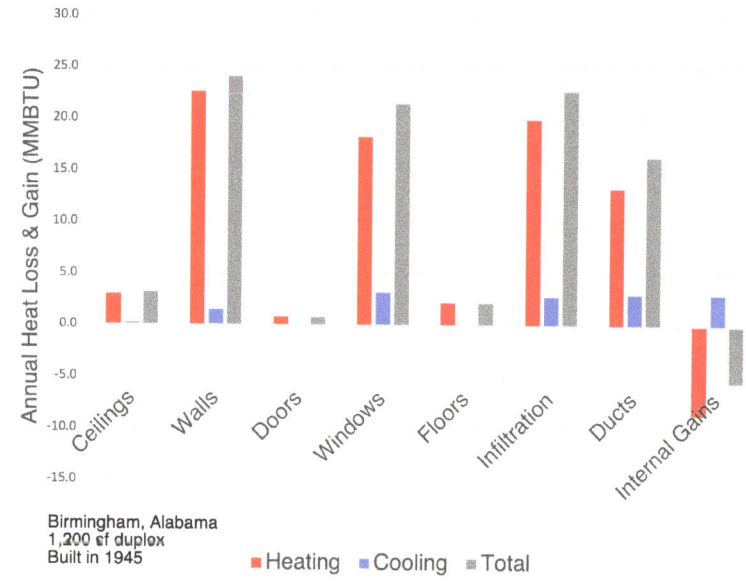

Figure 10.4. *Finding the amount of heating or cooling load associated with each component can tell you where to focus your efforts on improving a house or design.*

Figure 10.4 shows the results of modeling the annual energy consumption of a 1,200-square-foot duplex in Birmingham, Alabama. The red columns show the contributions to the heating consumption, the blue columns show where the cooling consumption comes from, and the grey columns show the sum of heating and cooling use. The first thing to notice is that this house uses much more energy for heating than for cooling. (And yes, it really is in Alabama.) You can see that there's not a lot of difference between the heating and total consumption for every component. The four largest contributors to the annual heating and cooling use are the walls (uninsulated), infiltration, windows, and ducts. Those are the areas where you should focus your improvement efforts for this house. Adding more insulation to the attic or installing a storm door will do little to lower energy bills.

Another point of interest here is the internal gains. They're the second-largest source of cooling energy consumption, so using more efficient lights and appliances would be the way to reduce that part of the load. But internal gains are a small part of the total consumption and actually help more with winter heating than they hurt with summer cooling. Internal gains are relatively small for the Birmingham duplex because it's an older, inefficient home.

In efficient new homes, internal gains can dominate consumption for both heating and cooling. The graph in Figure 10.5 shows this effect in a 1,300-square-foot house in Nashville, Tennessee. This is related to the changing proportions of contributors to energy consumption we saw in Chapter 4. When a house gets more energy efficient, the heating and cooling parts of the total consumption pie shrink and the consumption due to lights and appliances grows. See the shrinking pie charts of Figure 4.6 on page 51.

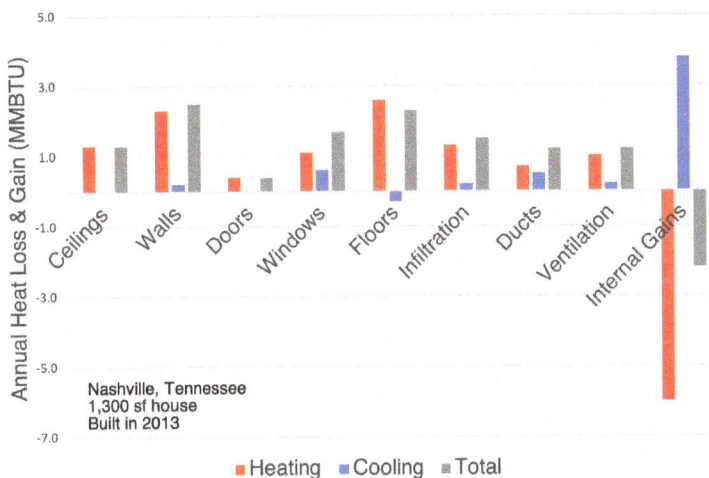

Figure 10.5. *Annual energy consumption for heating and cooling in this energy-efficient house in Nashville, Tennessee. Internal gains contribute more than any other component.*

What Is R-Value?

We talk about R-value all the time. "I've got an R-19 wall," or "Code requires R-38 in my ceiling." But what do those numbers mean? What is this thing called R-value? As is the case with so many topics in building science, the first answer to these questions is, "It depends."

We can divide the meanings of R-value into two groups. The first group we can call a rated R-value, and the second group we can name a real-world R-value. (In fact, we can divide the properties of many materials and products into these two groups.) Both groups measure essentially the same property: a material's resistance to heat flow. However, there is an important difference between the two that's worth understanding.

Rated R-Value

Rated R-value is a regulated number. When the United States saw energy prices soar after the 1973 Arab oil embargo, a lot of scammers sold insulation products with unbelievably high R-values. Even some people who weren't scammers claimed R-values that were too high because of the way they tested their products. The US Federal Trade Commission (FTC) stepped in and instituted what's now called the FTC R-value Rule.

This regulation requires any company selling insulation to label it with an R-value that comes from one of four approved test methods. As it turns out, this regulation is still needed and enforced. In 2013, a company selling "insulating" paint claimed an R-value of 100. The FTC hit them with the largest fine they had ever issued: $350,000.

The first thing to know about rated R-valued is that it's a static number. It's the result of a test done at specific conditions. Because R-value is a measure of heat flow, those conditions are basically the temperature difference across the tested material, with requirements for controlling other factors (air flow, moisture, etc.). The test for insulation R-value is usually done with a temperature of 50 °F on one side and 100 °F on the other, and with the material placed horizontally. See the problems? First, nobody keeps their house at 50 °F when it's 100 °F outdoors, or vice versa. Second, walls are not horizontal; they're vertical. Yet the amount of resistance measured in that test is the number that gets stamped on the material. As with the efficiency rating of a car, "Your mileage may vary." Still the rated R-value is a helpful number because you can use it to compare one insulation material to another.

> **In wall cavities, air-permeable insulation needs to be completely encapsulated on all sides.**

Real-World R-Value

Unlike the rated R-value, the real-world R-value[15] is a dynamic number. In other words,

the actual R-value of an insulation material that's installed by real people in a real building assembly changes. Here are some factors that affect it:

- Temperature difference
- Air flow
- Moisture
- Compression, missing insulation, and other installation problems

Temperature is the only factor you don't have much control over. For a specific house in a specific location, the temperature difference across the insulation changes with the weather, the time of day, and the season. As a result, the resistance of the insulation changes. For example, an R-13 fiberglass batt may range from R-12 at 110 °F to R-14 at 10 °F. (Yes, most insulation gets better in cold weather and worse in hot weather.)

The other factors on the list are mainly related to installation and building failures. Some insulation materials, like fiberglass and cellulose, allow air to move in and out. (They are air permeable.) They're meant to be installed with a certain amount of air between the fibers, but they often are compressed. Compression itself isn't a problem, but it does lower the R-value. For example, an R-19 fiberglass batt installed in a 2x6 cavity will be compressed about ¾ of an inch. The result is that it performs as an R-18 batt.

Compression can create a problem, however, when it results in a wall cavity not being filled with insulation. The open spaces (voids) allow convective loops to move heat more rapidly. Also, air flowing through an insulation material because of air leakage can degrade its R-value. Water getting into the insulation can also lower its R-value. It's best to avoid these problems by making sure the air and water control layers do their jobs. In wall cavities, air-permeable insulation needs to be completely encapsulated on all sides. It also must completely fill the cavity.

Another way that R-value varies is when you

---

15. Strictly speaking, we should use the term *thermal resistance* for real-world values. As mentioned earlier, *R-value* is a regulated term, and it applies only to insulation materials that have been tested according to the FTC rules.

change from looking at the R-value of a material, to that of an assembly, to that of an entire enclosure. The real-world R-value of a material should be close to the rated R-value, if it was installed properly. The R-value of an assembly averages all of the layers and pathways for heat flow in the assembly, which we'll look at in more detail in the next section. The R-value of an enclosure averages the R-values of the assemblies in the whole building enclosure.

The point is not to get too hung up on stated R-values. Next time you see R-30 on an insulation sheet or read people arguing on the Internet about the R-value of a double-stud wall, remember that R-value isn't a fixed number. That's not to say we should be sloppy about load calculations, energy modeling, or code compliance, though. R-value is still an important number.

Five Types of R-Values

When you hear someone talk of R-value, they usually mean the rated R-value of just the insulation. But what's the real-world R-value of a wall or ceiling? Insulation makes up only a part of each. There's also wood, drywall, sheathing, cladding, and anything else that might be in the assembly.

If we use R-value to describe only the insulating properties of the insulation installed, we neglect the insulation value of the other layers in a building assembly. When heat moves through a framed wall, it can go through the part of the wall where the insulation is (the cavity) or the part of the wall where the framing is. Those are two different pathways.

Within each pathway, heat flows through a series of layers. For heat going through the cavity, where the insulation is, those layers can include drywall, insulation, sheathing, cladding, air films, and other materials. Adding up their individual R-values gives the total R-value.

Similarly, when heat goes through the pathway where the wood framing is, it travels through all the layers that go all the way across the wall (air films, drywall, sheathing, and cladding). The only difference is that the heat goes through wood instead of insulation in the middle of the wall. Because wood has about one quarter the R-value of insulation, that pathway is considered a thermal bridge.

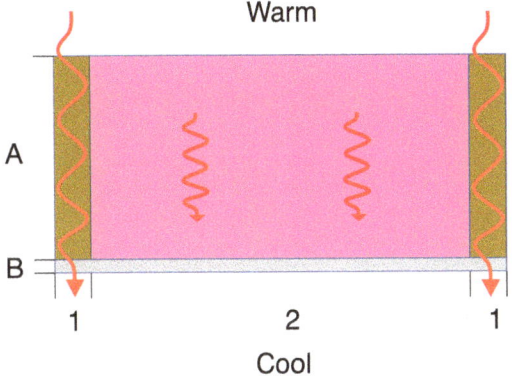

Figure 10.6. *Heat can flow through two types of pathways in this wood-framed ceiling assembly: wood (1) or cavity (2). The cavity should have insulation. This diagram also shows two layers: wood or cavity (A) and drywall (B).*

When you factor in the different layers and pathways for heat flow, the overall R-value of an assembly is different from that of the material (insulation) only. But how do you factor in the other materials? You know the answer: It depends. Here are five ways you can talk about R-value, beginning with the one we covered in the past section. For purposes of calculating the other four ways, we usually use the rated R-values. In other words, we don't usually adjust for temperature, air flow, or moisture, although we do sometimes adjust for the quality of installation.

Material R-Value

This is the R-value as discussed in the past section. This is the type of R-value referred to by building codes.

Figure 10.7. *The center-of-cavity R-value includes only the layers through the cavity, where the insulation is.*

Figure 10.8. *Clear-wall R-value includes only studs, plates, and cavity insulation.*

Figure 10.9. *Whole-wall R-value includes all the framing and insulation but not windows and doors.*

Figure 10.10. *Overall R-value includes everything.*

Center-of-Cavity R-Value

This is the R-value taken through a point in the wall containing the most insulation. This R-value would include all the layers: interior air film, drywall, insulation in the center of the cavity, sheathing, cladding, and exterior air film. The result would be the sum of the individual R-values but would neglect the thermal bridging effects of the framing.

Clear-Wall R-Value

This is the R-value for the exterior wall area containing only insulation and framing materials necessary for a clear section with no windows, doors, corners, or connections between other enclosure elements such as roofs, foundations, and other walls. To get this R-value, you have to average the two pathways for heat flow: through the cavities and through the framing. (Note: You can't just average the R-values, though. You have to average the U-values and then convert to R-value in the end. See Appendix F for details.)

Whole-Wall R-Value

This is the R-value for the whole opaque wall, including the thermal performance of the clear wall area, with insulation and structural elements, and also typical enclosure interface details, including wall-to-wall (corners), wall-to-roof, wall-to-floor, wall-to-door, and wall-to-window connections. This R-value includes everything but the heat flow through fenestration (windows and doors). Like clear-wall R-value, it also is an average of resistance to heat flowing through the cavity and framing pathways.

Overall R-Value

This is the R-value of the whole wall, including fenestration. Because windows and doors have significantly lower R-values than opaque walls, the overall R-value will be the lowest of these five types of R-value. To calculate the overall R-value, you do an average similar to that for whole-wall R-value, but it will include the pathways for windows and doors.

We already know the limitations of material R-value. Center-of-cavity R-value will be higher than material R-value because it includes other layers in the assembly, but it doesn't include any thermal bridging effects. That makes it a poor choice for comparing one wall to another. Clear-wall R-value is better, but it doesn't include enough of the thermal bridging because it ignores corners, intersecting walls (T-walls), and other important thermal bridges.

Whole-wall R-value is really what you want to know when comparing one wall assembly to another for a particular house. In new home construction, complex building enclosures rule the market. Look at all the corners, roof-wall intersections, and other complexities in Figure 10.11. At least on the front of this house, there's not a whole lot of clear-wall area.

Figure 10.11. *Many new homes have complex building enclosures. Corners, windows, and roof-wall intersections add framing and reduce the whole-wall R-value.*

This is a house being built to the minimum levels required by code in Atlanta, so they used R-13 insulation in the walls. They're putting half-inch drywall on the interior and half-inch oriented strand board (OSB) on the exterior with brick and stone cladding. The windows have an R-value of about 3.5. My estimates of the five types of R-value for this house are:

- Insulation   R-13
- Center-of-cavity   R-15
- Clear-wall   R-14
- Whole-wall   R-10.5
- Overall   R-8.7

Here's my explanation of the calculation behind these numbers.

Center-of-cavity R-value. This is simply the result of adding the R-values of the layers, which includes the indoor air film, drywall, insulation, sheathing, cladding, and outdoor air film.

Clear-wall R-value. I calculated a clear-wall framing factor (ratio of framing to insulated cavity area) of about 13 percent using 9-foot-high ceilings to find the clear-wall R-value. Because we have two pathways for heat flow, we have to do an area-weighted average, and the framing factor gives us the weights: The cavities compose 87 percent of the area, and the framing is 13 percent.

Whole-wall R-value. I estimated a framing factor of about 30 percent to find the whole-wall R-value. The difference between those two framing factors is that the clear-wall framing factor includes only main studs and plates whereas the whole-wall framing factor includes all studs (main, kings, jacks, etc.), plates, corners, T-walls, and headers.

Overall R-value. Now we have three pathways to factor into the calculation: cavities, framing, and windows. (There are no doors in the part of the house shown in this photo.) I estimated 60 percent wall cavities, 20 percent framing, and 20 percent windows.

Of the five types of R-value explained here, the most useful are the whole-wall and overall R-values. Whole-wall is the one you want when comparing different wall assemblies, say a double-stud wall versus a standard wall with continuous exterior insulation. Overall R-value is the number to look at when you're trying to minimize heat flow through the wall and fenestration. It can be helpful when looking at changes in window area or type compared to improvements in whole-wall R-value.

The thing to remember here is that the R-value in your walls, floors, and ceilings isn't the same as the R-value of the insulation you put in them. Oh, and one more thing: The R-value you calculate according to the definitions above isn't a static number. It changes with temperature and other factors.

Thermal Bridging

A thermal bridge is part of a building assembly with a lower R-value than what surrounds it. Wood framing has a lower R-value than a cavity filled with insulation, so it's a thermal bridge. The wall in a standard wood-frame home has a framing factor of about 23 percent. That means nearly one quarter of the wall is wood, and only 77 percent of the wall is really insulated. The walls on the front of the house in Figure 10.11 have a higher framing factor because there's more wood in and around corners, intersections, and openings for windows and doors. You can see the effect of that in the whole-wall R-value. The wall has R-13 insulation in it, but all that thermal bridging from the wood brings the whole-wall R-value down to R-10.5, a 19 percent reduction. Compared to the center-of-cavity R-value, the framing reduces the R-value by 30 percent.

Let's look at a more extreme example that may be costing you more than you realize. Attic pull-down stairs or hatches often are uninsulated. You may have had your attic insulated to R-38, but an uninsulated attic access is a severe thermal bridge. Let's be generous and give it an R-value of 1. Let's also ignore the details of framing in the insulated part of the ceiling and say that your whole-ceiling R-value is 38.

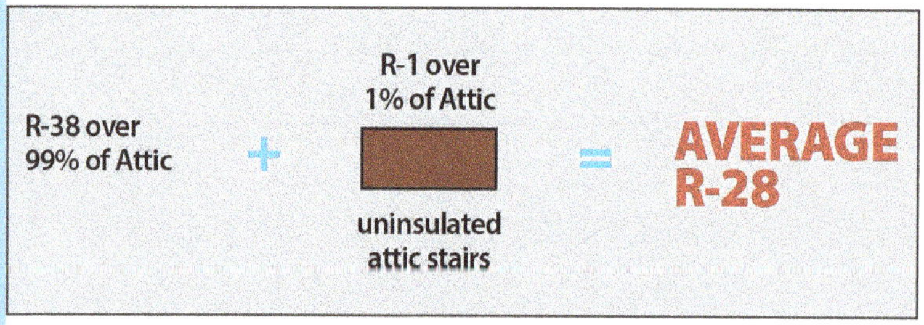

If your attic is 1,000 square feet in area and the attic access is 10 square feet, you might think that only 1 percent of the area being uninsulated would have minimal effect on the heat flow and R-value. And you'd be wrong. When you calculate the average R-value, it's not R-38 or R-37 or even R-35. It's a mere R-28. That's a 27 percent loss of R-value because of a thermal bridge that takes up only 1 percent of the ceiling area. Is your mind blown? (There are insulated covers you can buy to address this problem. Some builders make their own.)

Clearly, thermal bridges matter. The good news is that it's relatively easy to make big improvements in a home's overall R-value by reducing thermal bridges. The big secret is continuous insulation. The not-quite-so-big secret is advanced framing or other types of structures, like structural insulated panels or insulated concrete forms.

Attics: When you insulate the floor of an attic, getting a layer of continuous insulation is easy. You simply blow enough insulation to go above the ceiling joists. If a ceiling is framed with 2x8 lumber, for example, the first 7.25" of insulation won't be continuous because it will only fill the cavities between the joists. But every inch of insulation beyond that is a continuous layer of insulation. That dampens the thermal bridging of the framing. Roof trusses are made with a 2x4 board (3.5 inches high) along the bottom, which results in more continuous insulation. Then you have to find any places that don't get covered with the blown insulation (e.g., your attic access) and get them insulated, too. Easy peasy.

Insulated rooflines: Rather than insulating the floor of the attic, you can put the insulation on the roof. It can go either beneath the roof deck, above the roof deck,

R-38 over 99% of Attic + R-1 over 1% of Attic (uninsulated attic stairs) = **AVERAGE R-28**

Figure 10.12. Attic with 99 percent of the area insulated to R-38 while 1 percent, the uninsulated pulldown stairs, has only R-1

or a combination of both. To do this with spray foam insulation from the attic, make sure to spray foam over the rafters, not just between them. To do continuous insulation on cathedral ceilings, you can put rigid insulation on top of the roof deck. Rigid insulation on top of the roof works for attics, too. (See Chapter 11.)

Walls: So many ways of building and insulating walls have been developed that I can't cover them all here. We'll look at some in Chapter 11. Advanced framing techniques reduce the amount of framing in a wall but don't eliminate it. The two main methods of getting insulation in walls are continuous insulation on the exterior and double-stud walls.

Foundations: Insulating foundation walls and slabs with spray foam, rigid foam, or mineral wool are common ways to reduce or eliminate thermal bridging in a foundation.

The Passive House movement is focused first and foremost on building robust building enclosures. Reducing thermal bridging is one of the key tenets of their protocols. Whether you go as far as Passive House or not, you really should take thermal bridging seriously.

Types of Insulation

When it comes to insulation, you have a lot of choices. You can go rigid or fluffy. You can get insulation that stops air flow or lets air pass through. Some insulation materials let water vapor move through them, and others don't. Some insulation is brightly colored, and others are dull. (This is a mostly irrelevant factor.) Some insulation fills cavities easily, and others require more care to install properly. Some are natural materials, and others release volatile organic compounds. Let's look at the properties, forms, and types of the main insulation materials used in North America.

Insulation Properties

R-value: The primary property of insulation is its ability to resist heat flow, as measured by its R-value. This property varies with temperature, density, moisture content, and air flow. Moisture and air flow should be handled by the other control layers for materials that are susceptible to thermal degradation. In most cases, R-value fluctuations due to changing temperature are irrelevant when choosing or installing insulation. (Some polyisocyanurate products are the exception.) Insulation density is important when designing a building enclosure or installing insulation.

Air permeable: The most common insulation materials used in houses don't stop air movement. Some may slow it more than others but not enough to qualify as an air barrier. Air-permeable insulation needs to be protected from air flowing through it by being adjacent to the air barrier. These insulation materials include fiberglass, cellulose, mineral wool, cotton, and sheep's wool. You may hear low-density air-permeable insulation referred to as "fluffy stuff" sometimes.

Air impermeable: In some cases, the thermal control layer itself reduces air flow enough to qualify as an air barrier, too. Spray foam and foam board are in this category.

Vapor permeable: All air-permeable insulation is also vapor permeable. Open-cell spray foam is the only foam—spray or rigid—that is vapor permeable, although expanded polystyrene (EPS) is semi-permeable as long as it's not too thick.

Vapor impermeable: Recall from Chapter 9 that we classify vapor retarders as class 1, 2, or 3, with lower numbers meaning less likely to allow water vapor to move through. Closed-cell spray foam and the three types of rigid foam are either class 2 or class 3 vapor retarders when looking only at the foam. But foam board comes with facings and films that may knock them down to class 1. Check the specifications.

Insulation Forms

Batts: Also in the form of blankets or rolls, batts are made of an insulation material held together with adhesive binders. They're made to the thickness and dimensions of common framing cavities. For example, a standard R-13 fiberglass batt is 3.5 inches thick and 15 inches wide to fit in a 2"x4" cavity framed at 16" on center. Batts work best when the cavities they're used in are free of obstructions like pipes, wiring, and miscellaneous framing. If the batts don't fill the entire cavity—including those little spaces behind electrical junction boxes, pipes, and other obstructions—they don't work as well as they should. Materials used in batts include fiberglass, mineral wool, cotton, and wool.

Figure 10.13. *Unfaced fiberglass batt insulation in a wall*

Blown: Fibrous insulation materials that come in smaller pieces are good fodder for machines that fill cavities by blowing the insulation out of a hose. This form is most often used in attics, but it can be used in walls and even ceilings insulated from below. When used in walls that are open at the time of application, blown insulation will be either held in place by a thin mesh fabric stapled to the wall or with adhesive binders or water mixed in with the insulation before it's blown. In existing homes, it can be installed using the drill-and-fill method, which is exactly what it sounds like. (Drill holes either in the siding or drywall, insert hose, and fill cavities.) When insulating ceilings from below, the insulation can be held in place with fabric first, but then ideally it will be supported by a rigid material to prevent sagging. Blown insulation is better than batts at filling small, nonuniform spaces created by wires, pipes, and other obstructions. One thing you have to watch out for with blown insulation is that it doesn't get installed at a low density that causes it to settle. Check the specifications for the correct density. Some materials used in blown form are fiberglass, cellulose, mineral wool, cotton, and sheep's wool.

Sprayed: Foam insulation expands upon release when sprayed from a gun with a small nozzle. When this spraying happens in the building, it's called spray foam. It requires precise equipment and skilled operators to install spray foam correctly. When it's done right, it's a great insulation material that can fill cavities, act as the air barrier, and, in the case of closed-cell spray foam, manage moisture. Because of its adhesive properties, it sticks to the materials it's sprayed onto, so there's no need for netting to hold it in place. It also expands to fill spaces well.

Rigid: When foam insulation is created in a factory and cut into boards, the result is foam board. There are three major types of this kind of insulation (covered below). But foam board is not the only kind of rigid insulation. Mineral wool and fiberglass also come in rigid form, but they are used differently. Rigid foam and mineral wool insulation can be used as exterior continuous insulation, beneath slabs, and on attic kneewalls. Rigid fiberglass is sometimes used for ducts and is called ductboard for that reason. Another type of rigid insulation that's not common in North America is Foamglas®, which starts off like the making of fiberglass but then is turned into a foam instead of fibers.

Insulation Materials

Fiberglass: As its name says, this material is made of glass fibers. Fiberglass is made from new or recycled glass that's melted and spun into long fibers. They're held together with binders. Batts can have a kraft paper facing on one side or be unfaced, as in Figure 10.13. This is the most common insulation material for new homes in the United States, accounting for about 70 percent of the market. Most of the fiberglass installed is in batt form, with loose fill fiberglass used mainly in attics. Rigid fiberglass is used mainly for duct systems. The R-value depends on the density, and it varies from 3.5 to 4.4 per inch of thickness.

Mineral wool: This material is similar to fiberglass except it's made by melting rocks instead of glass. Mineral wool is more rigid than fiberglass, which makes it easier to install properly. It also comes in batt, loose-fill, and rigid forms with R-value ranging from 3.5 to 4.4 per inch.

Cellulose: Made from recycled paper with fire retardants, cellulose comes in loose-fill form. Because much of it comes from recycled newspaper and manufacturing, it doesn't require high temperatures like fiberglass and mineral wool, and so cellulose has a low embodied energy.[16] It has a higher density than fiberglass, and it also can help to reduce infiltration. Their R-value ranges from 3.6 to 3.9 per inch.

Cotton or sheep's wool: These materials can be good environmental choices because they're natural and have low embodied energy. Unfortunately, their performance as a building material hasn't been a great success. In batt form, they're at least as difficult to install as fiberglass. They're difficult to cut, and fitting them to the cavity can be a problem. Blowing loose-fill cotton or wool is a better bet than using batts.

Spray foam: Spray polyurethane foam (SPF) insulation comes in two types. Open-cell SPF, also called low-density or half-pound foam (because its density is 0.5 lb/ft^3), has an R-value of about 3.8 per inch. Closed-cell SPF, also called medium-density or 2-pound SPF, has an R-value of about 6.5 per inch. Open-cell is generally less expensive than closed-cell, but both are more expensive than fiberglass, mineral wool, and cellulose. Open-cell is vapor permeable, and closed-cell is vapor semi-impermeable (class

2), depending on thickness. In cold climates, you need to put a vapor retarder on the interior side of open-cell spray foam. In warm, humid climates, you need to condition the air in attics encapsulated with open-cell SPF.

Foam board: Rigid foam products come in three types.

Expanded polystyrene (EPS) is the white foam used in beer coolers and disposable coffee cups. If you look closely, you'll see that it's made of many small beads of foam. Some EPS has graphite added to it, which changes its color to a dark grey and gives it a higher R-value. Structural insulated panels (SIPs) and insulated concrete forms (ICFs) are typically made with EPS. It comes in different densities for different applications, but the standard EPS is about R-4 per inch. With graphite, it's about R-5 per inch.

Extruded polystyrene (XPS) is denser than EPS and comes in colors that help you identify the manufacturer (pink for Owens Corning, blue for Dow, green for Kingspan). XPS is about R-5 per inch. With graphite, XPS can get up to about R-6 per inch.

Polyisocyanurate, often called polyiso, is a yellowish foam board with the highest rated R-value of the three types. Some brands of polyiso have the problem of gases condensing inside the foam cells in cold weather, which reduces the R-value. (Recall from earlier in this chapter that the R-value of most insulation materials gets higher in cold weather.) If you use polyiso in a cold climate, you may not get the full R-value when you need it most. Keep in mind, though, that if you put more than a couple of inches of it on the exterior, only the outer part will be subject to the reduced R-value. The inner parts of the polyiso foam board will stay warm enough to avoid the condensation problem. Polyiso is about R-5.5 per inch.

Reflective: One way to control the radiant part of heat flow is with a material that reflects the heat instead of just slowing it down. The way to do this is with reflective foils. Reflective metal roofs are a great way to keep radiant heat out of the attic.

16. Most of the energy discussion in this book is focused on operational energy (e.g., the energy used by a lightbulb or air conditioner). But the energy that went into making something (e.g., insulation or a whole house) is important, too, and that's what embodied energy is.

Foil-faced insulation, roof decking, and bubble wrap also reduce radiant heat flow, but their effectiveness depends on several factors. Depending on how they're used, materials that reduce radiant heat flow may be called reflective insulation, radiant barriers, or low-emissivity (low-e) coatings.

It's not just by reflection that these materials work, though. Emissivity is a complementary property that tells you how easily a material radiates heat away. A material that gets hot and radiates heat easily has a high emissivity. Think asphalt pavement on a hot summer day. A material that doesn't radiate much heat when it gets hot has a low emissivity. This would be like a stainless steel slide on the playground on a hot summer day. You can put your hand right above it and not be able to tell that it's hot. But jump on the slide while wearing shorts, and your bare legs will feel the heat by conduction.

Emissivity and reflectivity are two sides of the same coin. When one is high, the other is low, so a highly reflective material has a low emissivity. Sometimes low emissivity is the property you need to reduce radiant heat transfer. For example, if a roof absorbs a lot of solar heat, that heat conducts down through the roofing materials. The underside of the roof decking gets very hot, and it radiates heat down into the attic. Putting a radiant barrier beneath the roof deck cuts the amount of radiant heat flow significantly and can help reduce cooling bills in hot climates. (If you do a really good job air sealing and insulating the attic floor, though, radiant barriers may not be cost effective.) Similarly, a low-e coating in a window keeps heat inside the house in winter by getting warm and then not radiating much of that heat to the outdoors.

Insulation Wrap-Up

Insulation comes in many forms and materials. Each has its benefits and drawbacks. Some work better than others for a specific application, so learning their properties is important. Understanding your priorities and goals allows you to make the right choice.

Installation of Insulation Matters

As important as understanding the different types of insulation is, getting it installed well makes the difference between a high-performance building enclosure and an average one. It's not enough to get insulation in wall cavities or sprayed to the underside of a roof deck. Look at the following three installation issues to make sure you get the most bang for your insulation buck:

1. There's enough insulation.
2. It fills the space properly.
3. The other control layers do their jobs.

Issue #1: Enough Insulation

After you decide what R-value you're going for, whether you have enough insulation depends on two factors: thickness and density. For example, let's say you're aiming for R-19. An insulation that's rated at R-3.5 per inch has to be 5.5 inches thick to achieve an R-19 total, which is standard for a 2"x6" wall cavity. Fiberglass and mineral wool batts aren't usually a problem here because they're manufactured to ensure proper R-value for enclosed cavities. But when the insulation is installed in cavities that don't get covered or aren't completely filled, knowing the thickness, density, and R-value per inch is critical.

Here's an example that ties back to the section on thermal bridging. Recall that an uninsulated attic access (R-1) that makes up only 1 percent of an attic that's otherwise insulated to R-38 reduces the average R-value of the entire attic to R-28. A similar reduction in R-value happens when you have the right average thickness of insulation, but it varies in thickness. Let's say you have an R-38 attic that requires 12 inches of depth. (That's R-3.2 per inch.) If half of the insulation is only 8 inches deep and the other half is 16 inches deep, you have an average of 12 inches of insulation, but it doesn't average to R-38. The actual R-value would be less than R-34. The half that's not deep enough is a thermal bridge, allowing significantly more heat to flow than is saved by the deeper half. Figure 10.14 shows how the average R-value changes as the insulation depth gets less uniform.

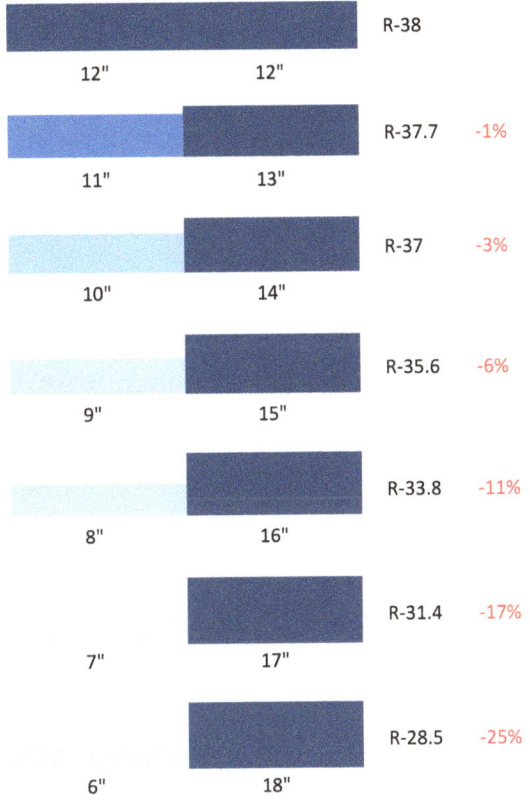

Figure 10.14. *Reduction in R-value for the right amount of insulation installed unevenly. Instead of 12" depth everywhere, this attic has 50 percent of its area with less insulation (left) and 50 percent with more insulation (right).*

As you can see, when the insulation is shorted only an inch or two over half the attic and increased by that amount on the other side, the hit to R-value isn't too bad (-1 percent and -3 percent). A 3-inch short on the left side, though, knocks 6 percent off the R-value, and beyond that you're in double digits, which is unacceptable.

Another way poor installation of insulation can reduce R-value is by getting the correct amount over part of the attic and shorting the other part. Figure 10.15 shows this scenario. The top line shows perfect installation of a uniform 12" depth of insulation. The next five lines show the R-value and percent reduction in R-value when various portions of the attic are shorted by 4".

As you would suspect, the 4-inch short becomes painful quickly. Even 10 percent of the attic shorted 4 inches knocks your R-value down by 5 percent. With 50 percent of the attic insulation reduced by 4 inches, the average R-value is down by a whopping 20 percent.

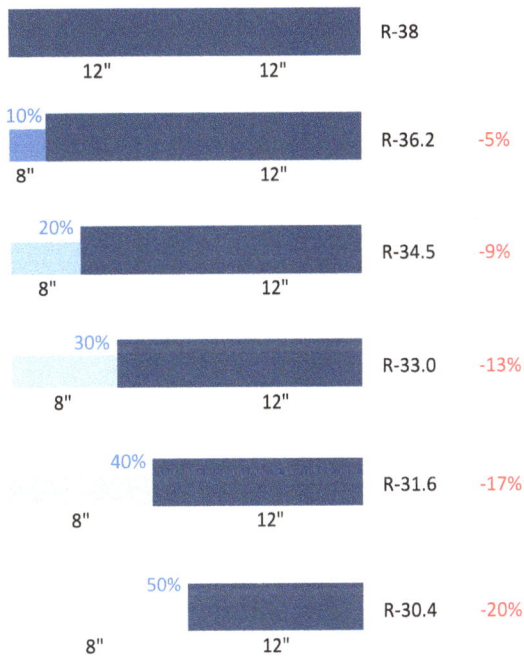

Figure 10.15. *Reduction in R-value for the wrong amount of insulation, poorly distributed. This attic has the specified 12" of insulation in some areas (right) and 4" less insulation (left) in the percent of area indicated.*

The big takeaway here is that installing the right amount of insulation should be based on a minimum depth, not on an average depth. If the R-38 attic had the same amount of insulation but instead of varying from 8 to 16 inches, it varied only from 11 to 13 inches, the average R-value would be 37.8. If it varied from 10 to 14 inches, the average R-value would be 37.0. In the second scenario, likewise, a 4-inch reduction in thickness over part of the attic drops the R-value more than I would want.

Installing the right amount of insulation should be based on a minimum depth, not on average depth.

Be careful, though. The amount of R-value you lose for each inch of depth depends on the R-value per inch of the insulation. If you use insulation that comes in at R-6.4 per inch (e.g., closed-cell spray foam) rather than R-3.2 per inch, you can't afford to lose as much depth. With the lower value, a 2-inch deficit knocks R-6.4 off your total. With the higher value, a 2-inch deficit knocks you down by nearly R-13.

Issue #2: Filling the Space

The installation issue of filling the space may seem to be the same as getting enough insulation, but the two are different. Here's an analogy: When you see a bedspread pulled up and a lump beneath it, you may think there's a person in the bed. But sometimes you pull the bedspread back and find that it's actually a bunch of dirty clothes, carefully placed into a human-shaped lump. The same is true with insulation. Sometimes installers do a job that looks good on the surface, but underneath lies a lump of problems.

This is where you have to do some detective work. The insulation needs to fill the cavities completely, and some of the places that are hard to fill aren't visible without digging in there. Filling the space is most difficult with batt insulation, so you have to pull it out and check. Here are the tricky places to look:

- Around and behind electrical junction boxes
- Around electrical wires
- At the perimeter of cavities
- Around pipes
- Around extra framing
- In non-standard width cavities

The easiest cavity to insulate is one with no obstructions. You cut the batt to the right length and width and expand it to fill the whole cavity. With obstructions in the cavity, you have to cut notches for junction boxes and extra framing members. For wires, you can cut a slice in the insulation or pull the fibers apart and slide them over to embed the wire in the insulation rather than pressing it against the wire and creating an empty pocket. When pipes are in the cavity, you cut and shape the batt to completely fill the space around it. The best way to handle the perimeter is to make sure the batt is cut to the right dimensions. It should be just slightly larger than the cavity so that it fills the space completely without much compression.

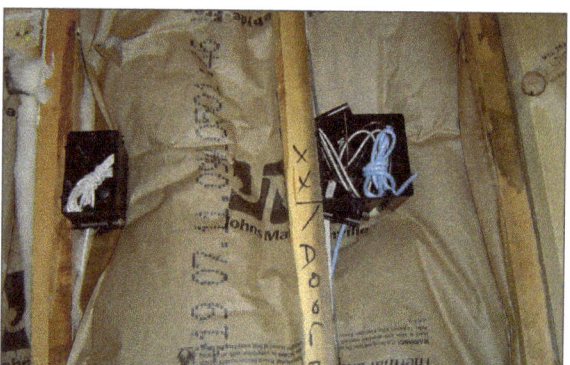

Figure 10.16. *Fiberglass batts installed improperly by not cutting to fit around and behind the electrical junction boxes*

Blown or sprayed insulation generally fills the spaces, so there's not much to check in that regard. The main checks for these types are in issues number 1 and number 3.

Issue #3: Control Layers

Some insulation is a control layer for heat only. Other insulation is a control layer for both heat and air. Still other insulation is a control layer for heat, air, and water vapor. When you check the installation quality of insulation, you need to understand the properties of the insulation itself. For example, open-cell spray foam is vapor permeable. When it's installed in a cold climate, it needs to have a vapor retarder.

The air barrier is one of the biggest issues with installation quality. When air-permeable insulation goes into a building assembly, it must be adjacent to a good air barrier because air moving through the insulation reduces its R-value. Insulation in vertical wall cavities needs to be enclosed completely to prevent convection from decreasing the effectiveness of the insulation. Insulation in horizontal cavities (floors and ceilings) is not required to be completely enclosed, but it will be better protected from damage and gravity if it is enclosed. Even when it's not enclosed, though, insulation installed horizontally must be next to the air barrier. (See Chapter 8 for air barrier information and Chapter 9 for the water vapor control layer.)

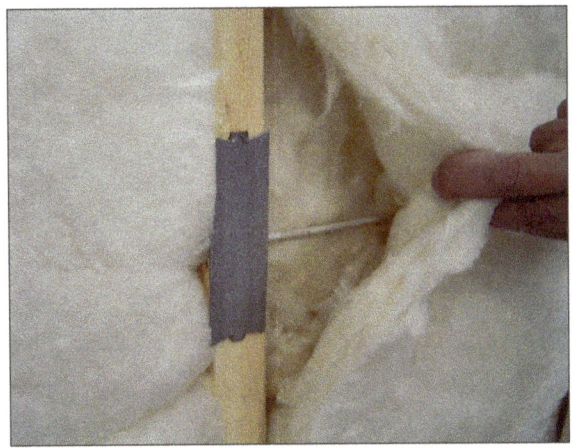

Figure 10.17. *Properly installed fiberglass batts have insulation on both sides of wires.*

How Much Insulation Do You Need?

The amount of insulation you put into a house depends on several factors:

- Your priorities
- Your budget
- The type and location of the building assembly

If your goal is to build a resilient house, one that can keep you warm for days or weeks if the power goes out in a winter storm, you'll want a lot of insulation. If instead you prioritize cost-effectiveness above resilience, you'll put in less insulation. You may even decide that the minimum required by code is enough. Different people have different priorities.

Different people have different budgets, too. The most common insulation types are one of the least expensive materials you can put in a house, and adding more doesn't add much to the insulation cost. It can add significantly to the total cost, however, because more insulation can mean thicker walls, and building thicker walls means more lumber and more expensive windows and doors. On the other hand, adding more insulation to an attic usually adds minimal additional cost because it often doesn't change the structure.

Rather than continuing to add more insulation to the already insulated parts of a house, at some point you do more to control heat flow by looking to reduce the thermal bridges. In the attic, that would be the attic access, above the exterior walls, and any place where the framing isn't covered (or isn't covered deeply enough). In walls, it's the framing and windows.

But there's another issue lurking in the shadows of this discussion. Not every inch of insulation you add gives you the same amount of reduction in heat flow. If you start from zero, the first inch of insulation gives you the most reduction. Each successive inch reduces the heat flow less than the previous inch. The term for this effect is *diminishing returns*.

Sometimes people selling more expensive insulation try to talk their customers into going with less insulation than they should have. Their reasoning is that the diminishing returns of additional insulation make it unnecessary. Diminishing returns is a real phenomenon, but it's easy to abuse. For example, take the chart in Figure 10.18. If you start with an uninsulated wall cavity and look at the reduction in heat flow for each R-2 of insulation added to the wall, you might think it would be silly to go beyond about R-10. But you'd be wrong.

The Diminishing Returns of More Insulation
4400 HDD, 1000 sf wall area

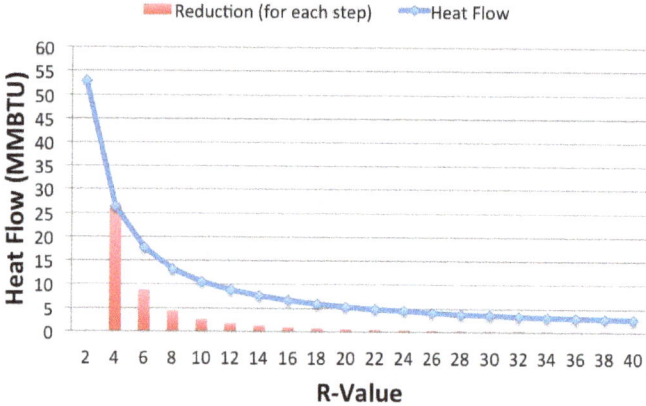

Figure 10.18. *The first few inches of insulation provide the greatest benefit. Beyond that, the diminishing returns add more cost with less benefit. But you have to be aware of the baseline for comparison. In this case, the starting point is an uninsulated wall.*

The first thing wrong with that argument is that the calculation should not start with an uninsulated wall. That's not allowed by code, so why even look at it? We need to start with something realistic. In much of North America, 2x6 walls are the standard, and Figure 10.19 shows how much the heat flow diminishes with R-20 as the baseline. As you can see, it's not nearly so dramatic a drop-off as when you start from zero.

Going Beyond R-20 in Climate Zone 4
4400 HDD, 1000 sf wall area

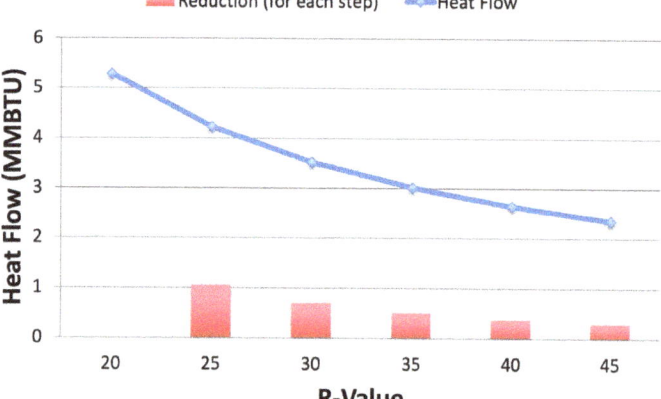

Figure 10.19. *When R-20 is used as the baseline, the diminishing returns of additional insulation don't look as bad.*

A better way to show the benefit of adding more insulation is to show the percent reduction in heat flow as you increase the R-value from 20 to 45 in increments of R-5. Figure 10.20 shows the same heat flow curve as the previous graph. But instead of showing the amount magnitude of the reduction (in millions of BTU in this case), now the red columns represent the cumulative percent reduction in heat flow for each step. Going from R-20 to R-25 reduces the total heat flow by 20 percent. The reduction as we go from R-20 to R-30 is 33 percent. And going from R-20 to R-40, the total heat flow drops by 50 percent. One easy generalization pops out of that last step: Doubling the R-value cuts the heat flow in half, no matter what the starting point is.

Going Beyond R-20 in Climate Zone 4
4400 HDD, 1000 sf wall area

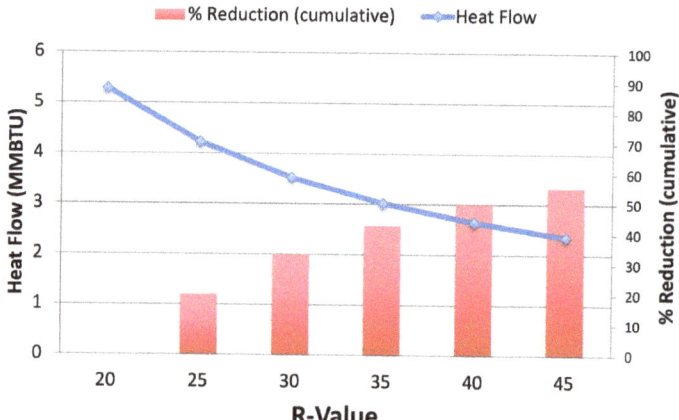

Figure 10.20. *Showing the reduction in heat flow as a cumulative percent reduction is a better way to see the benefit of adding insulation. (Note that the percent reduction is plotted on the righthand vertical axis.)*

The key point is that you shouldn't base your decision on a salesperson's claims about diminishing returns. Decide on your priorities, your budget, and what's possible with the type of structure in your house. Modeling tools can help you decide how far is reasonable to go with the insulation and other measures to control heat flow.

Doubling the R-value cuts the heat flow in half, no matter what the starting point is.

Windows: Thermal Bridges with Benefits

Insulation is for the opaque parts of a building enclosure. The weakest part of most thermal control layers, though, is the windows. Currently, windows cannot match the thermal performance of walls, but that doesn't mean we should get rid of them. They provide important benefits: escape routes (for emergencies and teenagers), daylight, views, and natural ventilation. Also, even though windows can lose a lot of heat in cold climates, they also may add more heat to a house through solar gain than they lose if designed properly. We can certainly minimize the heat transfer through them, however, so let's start by understanding heat flow through windows and the types of windows.

Recall that heat moves through windows by conduction, convection, and radiation. (I'm assuming reasonably airtight windows.) Conduction is the flow of heat by the jiggling of atoms and molecules in a material caused by a higher temperature on one side than the other. Different materials and configurations of materials can slow that jiggling. Both the window frame and the glazing can conduct heat, so we have to look at both. Convective loops within the gas-filled window also can result in heat transfer. Radiation transfers heat through a window mainly through the glass, but window frames can radiate heat, too.

The Two Most Important Window Specifications

When doing energy modeling or load calculations for homes or deciding which windows to buy, you don't need to know the details about the number of panes of glass, frame material, or the presence of low-emissivity coatings. Two numbers tell you what you need to know about how well the window will control heat flow: U-factor and Solar Heat Gain Coefficient.

U-factor: Officially, this property is called heat flow conductance, but most people call it U-factor or U-value. It's the reciprocal of the R-value, or heat flow resistance, and it's used in the equation to determine the rate of heat flow (covered earlier in this chapter). The U-factor is the number you have to include when you want to find the average R-value for an assembly, which is simply a collection of heat flow layers and pathways. The U-factor for a window may include the frame and the glazing, or it may be the center-of-glass value. Make sure you know which one you have.

The lower a window's U-factor is, the better the window is. This follows from the fact that higher R-values are better, and U-factor is the reciprocal of R-value. A typical U-value for a double-pane window with a low-e coating is about 0.3. That would give it an R-value of about 1 ÷ 0.3, which is 3.3. When putting new windows into a house, you should look at 0.3 as the upper limit for the U-factor. Your building code may require a lower U-factor. A nice high-performance window will have a U-factor of about 0.15 (R = 6.7). Table 10.1 shows approximate U-factors, R-values, and solar heat gain coefficients for different window types. The actual values will vary with frame type (metal, wood, etc.), spacing between panes of glass, type of gas used between panes of glass, and location of low-e coatings.

Window Type	U-factor	R-value	SHGC
Single pane	1	1	0.9
Double pane	0.5	2	0.75
Double pane, low-e coating	0.3	3	0.2-0.7
Triple pane, low-e coating	0.1	10	0.15-0.6

Table 10.1. *Approximate specifications for different window types.*

Solar Heat Gain Coefficient (SHGC): This window property tells you how much of the solar radiation hitting a window gets transmitted all the way through to heat up the conditioned space inside. As with window U-factors, this number derives from the proportion of heat transmitted through the entire window assembly, including the frame. Thus, a window with a larger frame will have a lower SHGC compared to the same size window with the same kind of glass but a thinner frame. That's why a wood-frame single pane window has a lower SHGC than a metal-frame single pane window.

The SHGC ranges from a low of 0 to a high of 1. The upper limit of SHGC that you'd want to use varies by climate zone, orientation of the house, and shading. For warm climates where houses need more cooling, 0.3 is a good upper limit. For homes with less cooling and more heating, going with a higher SHGC can help a bit with heating in winter, at least on sunny days. In moderately cold climates, consider going up to 0.4. In really cold climates, 0.5 will help capture more free solar heating on sunny days.

But there's a caveat to going with a higher SHGC: The only windows where this would help are the ones facing south. Those facing southeast and southwest might be okay, too, but they're harder to shade in summer. (See the sidebar on passive solar houses on page 161 for a caution about using different SHGC windows on different sides of the house.) Also, lower SHGC values aren't just for keeping heat out of the house in summer. They help keep the heat in the house in winter, which is why you still want low SHGC on non-south-facing windows in cold climates. And lower SHGC values also bring the U-factor down.

NFRC Label

Most windows in the United States now have a label with the relevant specifications. The National Fenestration Ratings Council (NFRC) has standards for testing windows, and NFRC labels show the U-factor, SHGC, and other information. Three other window specifications are showing up on these labels more frequently: visible transmittance, air leakage, and condensation resistance. All three are important to consider in addition to U factor and SHGC.

Visible transmittance is just what it says: the proportion of visible light that gets all the way through the window. A good lower limit there would be 0.4. Below that, the house will feel darker, and the view from indoors may be a bit grey.

Air leakage is a relative newcomer to window labels. It's not on all windows. If your window has that number, look for 0.3 or less.

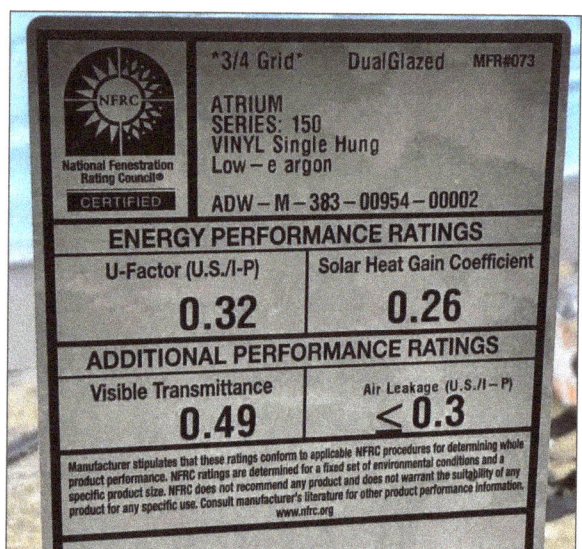

Figure 10.21. *An NFRC window label showing the U-factor, SHGC, visible transmittance, and air leakage*

Condensation resistance is a number between 0 and 100, with higher numbers for windows that are better at resisting condensation.

Frames, Panes, and Coatings

The frame material and construction details play a large role in conduction. Metal, of course, is a good conductor of heat, so it's best to avoid metal-framed windows. Yes, you can get metal-frame windows that have a thermal break to interrupt the path for heat conduction, but other materials generally make better frames. Wood, vinyl, and fiberglass are all better at resisting heat flow than metal, and they don't need to rely on a thermal break. Frames made of vinyl or fiberglass aren't solid material, so some manufacturers improve their U-factors by filling the open cavities with foam insulation.

Glass itself is a conductor of heat. A window with a single pane of glass, therefore, will allow a lot of heat to leave the house in winter and enter in summer. The first big advance in improving window performance was using multiple panes of glass. When you add a second pane of glass and separate the two by an air space, conduction slows significantly. The U-factor for a single-pane window is about 1, whereas a double-pane window is about 0.5. (Lower is better.) The conductance is affected by the depth of the air gap and what kind of gas is in that space. Plain air is good, but gases like argon and krypton are better because

Should You Use High-SHGC Windows in a Passive Solar House?

In 2001, I embarked on a huge project. I was going to build a passive solar house in Georgia. This type of house is designed to capture heat from the sun to reduce your need for other heat sources. In the Northern Hemisphere, that means having a lot of window area facing south. I had read about such houses in the 1970s and 1980s. My thesis advisor in graduate school built one in Florida in the 1990s. Now it was my turn.

It didn't take long, though, before I ran into the question about what kind of windows to put in. Trying to capture solar heat means you want a high solar heat gain coefficient, right? But high SHGC also means higher U-factor, so you lose more heat when it's not sunny. I called the Southface Energy Institute in Atlanta for guidance, and they told me to go with low-SHGC windows. That's what I did, and it worked out just fine (Figure 10.22).

Designers and energy modelers in the Passive House community understand this issue better than most. They've told me that trying to "tune" the heat loss and heat gain by using windows with different SHGCs on different sides of the house is not a good strategy. First, windows in a Passive House often gain more heat than they lose, but it's mainly because they lose so little. Second, when you choose windows with different SHGCs, they often have different tints because of the different coatings. When you can see both types of windows from the same place, the difference in how the windows look can be distracting.

Figure 10.22. *House designed to have south-facing windows fully shaded at the summer solstice (above) and fully exposed to the sun at the winter solstice (below)*

In a cold climate, it's fine to use windows with a slightly higher SHGC. In a mixed or hot climate, go with the lowest-SHGC windows you can afford. In both cases, use the same windows all the way around. In the house I built, most of our windows had a U-factor of 0.35 and SHGC of 0.31. Because of the amount of south-facing window area on the house, we got lots of light and also good passive solar heating on sunny winter days.

they're less thermally conductive. Check the manufacturer's specifications or NFRC label to see how these things affect the numbers.

The second big advance in window technology in the past 50 years has been the addition of low-emissivity, or low-e, coatings. Combined with multiple panes of glass, these coatings have improved window performance dramatically. U-factors and solar heat gain coefficients have gone from about 1 all the way down to 0.2 and

below. Low-e coatings work by absorbing heat from the warm side. Then the coating holds onto the heat or conducts it into the glass while preventing that heat from radiating to the other side the way uncoated glass would. This process slows the transfer of heat a lot, allowing a home to retain more of its heat in winter and keep more heat out in summer. It's the same principle behind reflective insulation we discussed earlier in this chapter.

Window Orientation, Area, and Shading

Controlling heat that moves through windows isn't a job that should be left to the windows alone. Yes, you can go with lower solar heat gain coefficients, but that's not always enough. Here are some other ways to reduce heat flow through windows.

First, of course, the designer of a new home may be able to minimize the amount of east- and west-facing windows. Windows facing those directions are hard to shade from morning and afternoon sun, and they will increase the cooling load on the house more than north- and south-facing windows. Of the two directions, east-facing is preferable to west-facing. Solar gain in the afternoon from the west is worse than solar gain in the morning from the east because the outdoor temperatures are higher in the afternoon. On the other hand, windows facing south can help bring heat into the house on sunny winter days when the sun is lower in the sky. When the sun is higher in the sky in summer, it doesn't penetrate the house much and thus doesn't add as much heat through south-facing windows. North-facing[17] windows are great for bringing in natural light because direct sunlight rarely comes in these windows except early in the morning or late in the evening in the summer.

Second, overhangs and other external shading devices on windows help keep the heat out and the cooling loads lower. South-facing windows are relatively easy to shade with overhangs because the sun is higher in the sky when direct solar heat gain is a problem. East- and west-facing windows will need porches, carports, or trees to keep unwanted heat out of the house. And as mentioned, north-facing windows will get little solar gain and don't need to be shaded.

Third, minimizing window area reduces heat gain. One easy place to do that is at floor level. Instead of having floor-to-ceiling windows, have the bottom of the window a couple of feet or so off the floor. This will rarely affect the view or the amount of daylight coming in through the windows, but it will improve the building enclosure's ability to limit heat flow. Also, overhangs and shading devices don't have to be as large for smaller windows. The best time to reduce window area is when the house is still in the design phase. Consider the location and sizes of windows as well as the window-to-floor area and window-to-wall area ratios. Every square foot of R-4 window you can replace with R 13 or R 19 wall leads to a better and less expensive building enclosure.

17. Those of you in the Southern Hemisphere should transpose north and south in this discussion. But you know that.

Use a Laser Pointer to Find Low-E Coatings

If you have an existing house and want to know if the double-pane windows have low-e coatings, there's an easy way to do it. Actually, there are two easy ways to do it: one expensive and one cheap. You could spend $200 or so on a low-e coating detector that you hold up to the window. Or you could use light.

When I first learned of this technique, the recommendation was to light a match in front of a window and count how many reflections you see. Henry Gifford describes a better way to do it in his excellent book *Buildings Don't Lie*. Use a laser pointer instead of a match and put a piece of paper near the window to catch the reflections. Then you examine the spots to tell what kind of window you have.

Each surface of the window will create one reflection. A single-pane window will create two reflected spots, one for each surface of the glass. A double-pane window will show four spots because the glass has four surfaces. If any of the four surfaces of a double-pane window have low-e coatings, the spot for that surface will appear brighter. With triple-pane windows, you'll see an additional two spots. (Single-pane windows may have tints or films applied to them, but low-e coatings are mostly applied to the inner surfaces of multi-pane windows because the coatings are easily damaged.)

One thing to watch out for here is aiming the laser at too great an angle. The closer the beam is to being parallel to the plane of the glass, the more reflected spots you'll see. The reason is the light will create multiple reflections from each surface as the light bounces around inside the glass. Keep the laser as close to perpendicular to the window as you can. Another thing to watch out for is a laser that doesn't make a round spot. Try rotating the laser pointer if you have trouble.

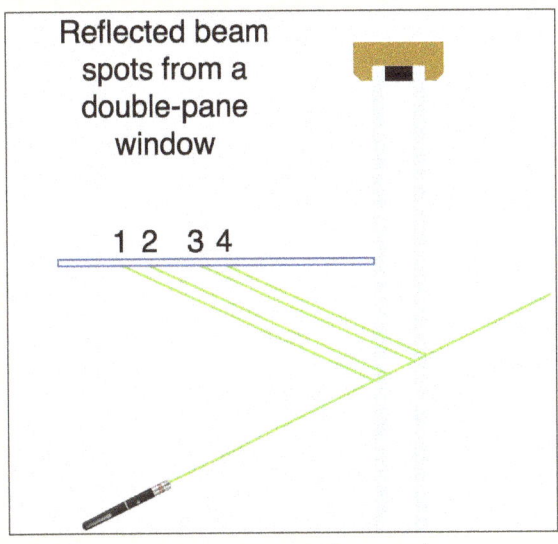

Figure 10.23. *A laser pointer aimed at a window creates a reflected spot for each surface it hits.*

Figure 10.24. *The four numbered spots are the reflections from the four surfaces of the two panes of glass. Spot number 2 is brighter, indicating the presence of a low-e coating.*

How Much Do Windows Affect a Home?

Windows are thermal bridges. The best windows available have an R-value of only about 12. More affordable windows are in the R-3 to R-6 range. Wall R-values are in the 13 to 15 range on the low end, and some cold-climate homes have R-40 walls or even higher. Whether you put an R-4 window in an R-13 wall or an R-12 window in an R-40 wall, windows are the weakest link (like the uninsulated attic hatch in a well-insulated attic).

Conduction and radiation through windows suck heat out of the house in winter and give heat easy entry in summer. Cooling loads can increase dramatically when windows take a direct hit from the sun's rays. Windows typically add more to the cooling loads than to heating loads because of direct solar gain on sunny days. But how much? Figure 10.25 shows that the windows contribute 19 percent to the heating load in a 4,000-square-foot house in Virginia. That's not too bad.

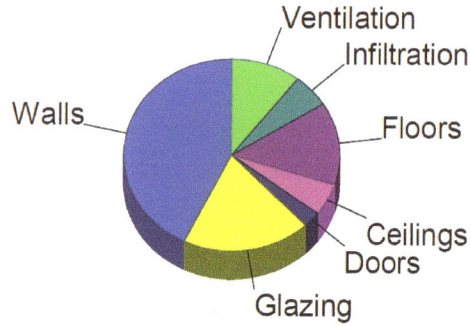

Figure 10.25. *The windows (glazing) make up 19 percent of the design heating load for a 4,000-square-foot house in Virginia.*

The cooling load in this house, however, is dominated by heat gain through the windows (Figure 10.26). Nearly half of the total peak cooling load comes from the windows for this particular house.

Those two pie charts come from a heating and cooling load calculation. They're used for sizing heating and cooling equipment, so it's a peak load. Another way to look at the effect of windows is to look at the annual heating and cooling loads. I don't have that kind of energy model for this house, but the relationship is similar to the peak loads. Most of the time, windows cost more for cooling than they do for heating. The percentages and actual loads vary for different houses because of the type of windows, window-to-wall area ratios, and shading, but they're always the weak link in the building enclosure.

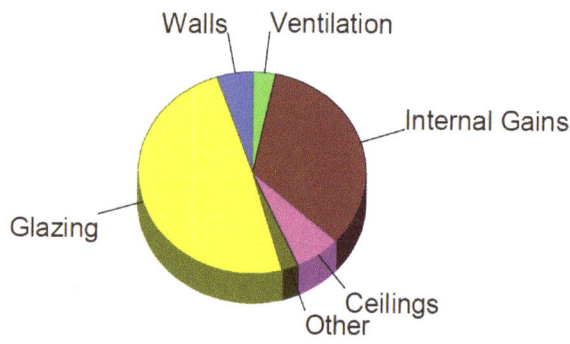

Figure 10.26. *The windows (glazing) make up 49 percent of the design cooling load for the same 4,000-square-foot house in Virginia.*

Plotting Your Window Strategy

Windows are the Achilles' heel of the thermal control layer. Getting the best window you can afford is one way to limit the amount of heat that flows through them, but I've mentioned several other ways, too. Here's a quick summary:

1. Put majority of windows on north and south sides of house.
2. Reduce window area.
3. Use overhangs or shading devices on east, south, and west sides.
4. Choose windows with a U-factor less than 0.3.
5. Choose windows with an SHGC appropriate to the climate:
   a. < 0.3 for cooling climates
   b. 0.4 to 0.5 for heating climates

You can't eliminate the thermal penalty of windows, but you can reduce it greatly by following this guidance.

Other Measures for Controlling Heat

In addition to the heat that flows through the floors, walls, ceilings, and windows, a few other sources result in heat gain or heat loss. Air leakage, of course, is an important one, and we covered that in Chapter 8. Other ways that heat enters or leaves a house are through whole-house ventilation (Chapter 17), duct systems in unconditioned spaces (Chapter 14), lights, and appliances. The only ones not covered elsewhere in this book are lights and appliances, so let's look briefly at how they affect heating and cooling.

The first thing to know about lights and appliances—or anything that uses electricity inside the house, really—is that pretty much all the electricity they use gets turned into heat inside the house. The only exception would be any light that escapes through the windows, but that would be a small fraction of the energy converted from electricity into light, motion, sound, or other forms. In winter, that heat reduces the need for heat from the heating system, so it's a benefit. It's generally less efficient, however, than just using the heating system. In summer, the heat from electricity use adds to the cooling load and will need to be removed. Using more efficient lights and appliances helps in both winter and summer.

> *Pretty much all the electricity used by lights and appliances gets turned into heat inside the house.*

Chapter Takeaways

- The key to measuring heat flow is being able to measure temperature. The Zeroth Law of Thermodynamics gives us a way to do that.
- Heat flows by conduction, convection, and radiation.
- We can calculate the amount of heat flowing across a building assembly if we know the area, thermal resistance (or conductance), and temperature difference.
- Phase changes and thermal expansion and contraction also play important roles in how buildings perform.
- The four laws of thermodynamics underlie all aspects of heat. The first and second laws have the most bearing on building science.
- The R-value of materials and assemblies is of great importance.
- Insulation materials have several properties that affect the performance of a building enclosure.
- The installation quality of insulation is critical to reducing heat flow.
- Thermal bridges are places in the building enclosure with lower resistance to heat flow.
- The reduction in heat flow of each additional inch of insulation is less than the inch before it. This is known as *diminishing returns*, but be aware of what the reference for comparison is when making judgments.
- Windows are often the weakest link for heat flow in a building enclosure. Follow the best practices in this chapter to get the most out of your windows.

CHAPTER 11

Integrating Control Layers with Shearing Layers

That house in Atlanta with damaged siding because of uninsulated ducts in the exterior wall (Figure 9.1 on page 121) had the intermingling problem. The house with the wire poked through the drainage plane (Figure 7.23 on page 94) had the intermingling problem. And just about every insulated house in the United States has the intermingling problem. You'll see plenty of examples of the problem in this chapter. The problem, of course, is the one alluded to in the chapter title. The control layers for water, air, vapor, and heat can and do intermingle with three of the Stewart Brand's shearing layers: structure, skin, and services (Figure 1.3 on page 15). The more they intermingle, the harder it is for the control layers to control water, air, vapor, and heat.

Think of the thermal control layer. When you put insulation between studs in a traditionally framed wall, it doesn't insulate the house completely because the insulation is interrupted by studs, headers, plates, and other framing members. To make it worse, the insulation shares space in those same cavities with some of the services—electrical wires, plumbing pipes, and sometimes even heating and air conditioning ducts. Then

> *"Poor building envelope design, especially fenestration, requires more robust HVAC systems to compensate. Get the envelope right, then start worrying about the HVAC system."*
>
> –Sonia Barrantes, PE

those wires, pipes, and ducts poke through the skin, rupturing the water and air control layers. It's actually quite messy and inefficient.

Let's take a look at some of the types of structures used in houses. If you're building new, you get to choose which one to use. If you have an existing home, you're stuck with what you have (unless you have a really big budget). In either case, understanding the structure is important if you want to get the most out of the house. In this chapter, we'll look at some of the most common structures used in houses, with a quick overview of how to control the heat, air, and moisture flows through them. The succeeding chapters will go into greater detail about controlling those flows.

The Perfect Enclosure

Before we get into foundations, wall systems, and other structural issues, let's look at an ideal case. When Brand's shearing layers of structure, skin, and services intermingle, problems arise. Insulation installed in the cavities created by a traditional wood structure subjects the wood framing to the vagaries of the outdoor environment. The resulting thermal and moisture changes cause the structure to swell and shrink

with the seasons. That's not good for the control layers. It's not good for the structure either.

Imagine, though, that the structure is completely protected by the control layers. For that to happen, all of the control layers would have to be outside of the structure. With insulation outside of the structure, thermal expansion and contraction are greatly minimized. With the air barrier outside the structure, humid,

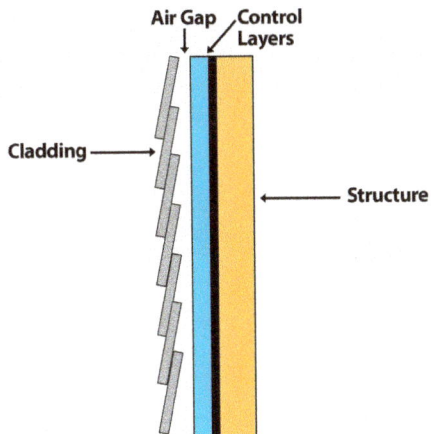

Figure 11.1. *The Perfect Wall has all control layers outside of the structure.*

hot, cold, or polluted air has no access to the structure or the indoors. With the liquid control layer outside the structure, the porous materials stay dry and intact and are less attractive to pests like termites and carpenter ants.

Such a system is not only possible but also a reality in many homes built over the past few decades. Joseph Lstiburek, PhD, PE, a former Canadian who's a smart guy with a PhD in engineering (and a lot of attitude), has been promoting the "Perfect Wall"[18] for a long time. And it works . . . if you do it right. The key is connecting all the control layers as you go from the top of the wall to the bottom of the wall, across windows, doors, and penetrations. When you apply the same idea to the floors and ceilings of a house, you get the Perfect Enclosure. Again, the key is connecting the control layers to keep them continuous, and the pen test (Chapter 5) is the tool to help you do that.

The Perfect Enclosure, unfortunately, is not a slam dunk. To do it on existing homes, you usually rip off the outer layers of the house. Even on new homes, it's difficult because it's not what construction workers are used to doing. When you do something different, you either have to do it yourself, spend a whole lot of time supervising, or—if you're really lucky—have a trained crew that knows what they're doing. And it's more expensive, mainly because of the difficulty issue but also because you're going above and beyond the code-minimum house.

In reality, you can get many of the advantages of the Perfect Enclosure with a few key changes. With crawl spaces and basements, for example, it's often best to put the insulation on the inside of the foundation walls, not the outside. With walls, you can split the insulation. Put enough of it outside the structure to limit the thermal expansion and contraction and moisture cycling. Then put the rest of it in the cavities (if you choose a structure that has cavities).

What we need here is an addition to the six shearing layers. The control layers for water, air, and heat should be a seventh shearing layer. Put them between the skin and the structure and make them continuous. That would represent a paradigm shift in the traditional way of building, and we've already made some progress toward it.

Construction crews already know about the water control layer. We just need to expand that awareness to the air and thermal control layers.

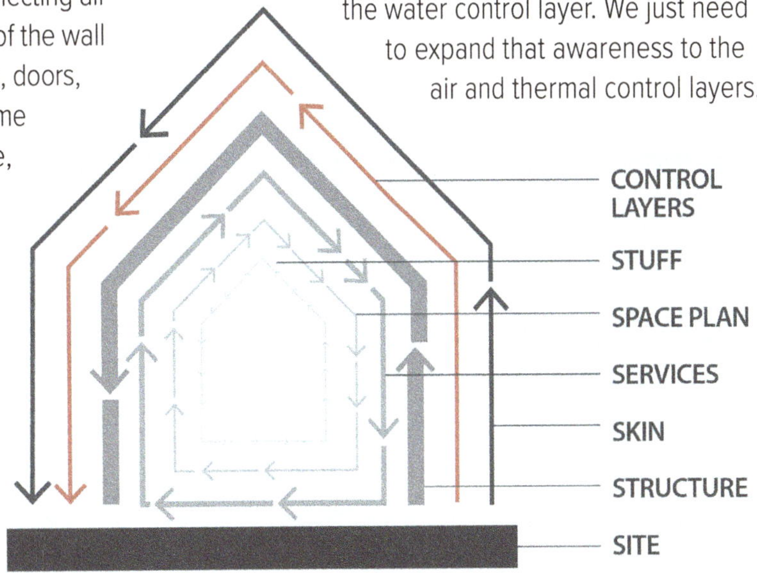

CONTROL LAYERS

STUFF

SPACE PLAN

SERVICES

SKIN

STRUCTURE

SITE

Figure 11.2. *Stewart Brand's shearing layers of change with a seventh layer added for the control layers [Adapted from How Buildings Learn, by Stewart Brand]*

18. Dr. Joe, as he is known, has been at the forefront of building science since the 1980s and is quick to say that Neil Hutcheon should get the credit for the Perfect Wall. He does claim credit for "The house is a system," but he'll probably be remembered more for his colorful presentations and for hosting the annual Building Science Summer Camp.

Foundations and Floors

The three main types of foundations are the concrete slab on grade, crawl space, and basement. Each has its advantages and disadvantages in terms of how easy it is to control the heat, air, and moisture flows through them and their effect on indoor environmental quality. You'll need to make the choice about foundation type based on your site characteristics, budget, and preferences. A basement costs more than a crawl space, which costs more than a slab, but you get more space with each step up the cost ladder. A crawl space will never be finished space, but some are useful for storage. A basement can be left unfinished or become part of the living space.

Concrete Slab on Grade

The least expensive foundation is a slab on grade. It's also usually the easiest to incorporate into the building enclosure. When the bottom of the building enclosure is a concrete slab, there's no buffer space to worry about. The house stops at the slab.

Controlling heat flow: Insulating a slab can be straightforward. Heat flows from the house through a concrete slab and into the ground at a lower rate than it flows through the slab and into the air. That makes the perimeter of the slab, some of which is probably above grade, the most important place to insulate. In milder climates (IECC climate zones 1-4), that's probably the only part of the slab that's cost-effective to insulate in many cases. An exception would be a slab with a radiant heating system embedded within the concrete or applied to the surface. The main obstacle to insulating a slab in warmer climates is termites. If they're in your area, you'll need to be extra careful to block any pathway termites may have to tunnel through the insulation and find the wood they're looking for. But the good news is that an uninsulated slab can provide free cooling, so don't automatically think you have to insulate it.

> *You know there are two kinds of concrete, right? Cracked and not yet cracked.*

Controlling air flow: Concrete is a good air barrier material. That doesn't mean you can't get air leakage at the slab, though. You know there are two kinds of concrete, right? Cracked and not yet cracked. As concrete cures, it shrinks a little bit. Then cracks open up as it tears itself apart (just as Stewart Brand said). Gaps appear around the plumbing pipes that come up through the slab. Those cracks and gaps can connect the indoor air with the gravel, soil, or sand beneath the slab. But gravel, soil, and sand aren't solids. They're mixtures. Between the individual solid parts, there's space that's filled with soil gas, which is similar to air. It's not exactly air, though, because it contains methane, radon, water vapor, odors, and other gases at higher concentrations than you find them in air. You don't want those things coming into your house. So, those gaps around plumbing fixtures and any other penetrations through the slab need to be air-sealed. The other area that needs to be air-sealed is the transition from slab to exterior walls.

Controlling moisture flow: Because concrete is a porous material, pouring a slab right on top of the ground with no moisture barrier is a good way to pull water out of the ground and keep the slab wet. You don't want that. The standard way of separating the concrete from the potentially wet ground beneath is to:

1. Put down a layer of gravel on top of the cleared site.
2. Then put a layer of plastic sheeting material on top of the gravel.

The standard plastic sheeting used in the United States is polyethylene that's 6 mils thick (called "6 mil poly"). While 6 mil poly may meet the requirements of your building code, it's not likely to pass the test of time. Because one mil equals one thousandth of an inch, a layer of 6 mil poly isn't very thick. With workers walking across it to lay the rebar and work the concrete, it's likely to get torn in many places. (Remember that it's sitting on top of gravel.)

Better moisture barriers are available. They're thicker (10 to 15 mils), and some are reinforced, making them less likely to be punctured before or during the concrete pour.

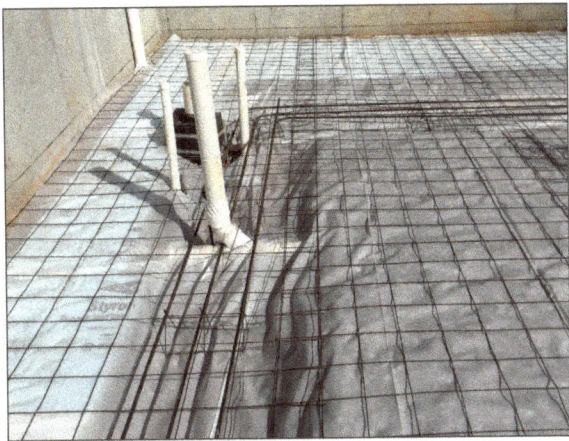

Figure 11.3. *The prep for a concrete slab includes a plastic moisture barrier. This one is 10 mils (0.010 inch) thick, which provides better resistance to damage than the standard 6 mil barrier. [Courtesy of Luis Imery]*

But there's more to it than just putting a layer of plastic on top of the gravel. As usual, the devil's in the details. Ideally, every penetration through that plastic needs to be sealed with the appropriate tape or sealants to keep moisture and soil gases from squeezing through those weak points. Manufacturers of the higher-quality materials also have sealants and techniques for this purpose. In reality, perfect sealing isn't required, so do the best you can. Remember: You get only one chance to do this right. You sometimes get chances to upgrade the control layers in the above-grade walls when you remodel, but what you put beneath a slab is there—or not there—for the life of the building.

The concrete sits on a layer of plastic, which stops liquid water and water vapor from getting into the slab. The plastic sits on top of gravel. Sand or another fine aggregate is never appropriate beneath the plastic. The spaces between grains of sand are small. If there's water in the ground below the sand, capillary action can bring it up. Even though you've got that plastic there to stop water from moving into the concrete, you don't want to put it to the test unnecessarily. For the same reason, the ground around the slab (and the other two foundation types as well) should slope down as it moves away from the house.

To keep water in the slab from moving into the wood framing, you can put a material that's impermeable to moisture between the framing and the slab, such as foam gaskets. They may help to control the air flow, too, but they usually need some caulk to complete the air barrier there.

Crawl Space

There are two types of crawl spaces: open and enclosed. An open crawl space is one in which the house sits on piers or stilts, with no foundation walls around the perimeter. An enclosed crawl space has foundation walls around the entire perimeter. With open crawl spaces, you have one option for the location of the heat, air, and moisture control layers: the floor over the crawl space. With enclosed crawl spaces, the control layers can be at the floor above the crawl space or at the foundation walls and ground.

An enclosed crawl space costs more because you've got to build foundation walls around the perimeter and then build a floor that sits atop those walls. With both open and enclosed crawl spaces, you get space below the floor for plumbing, electrical, and HVAC as well as storage in some cases.

Controlling heat flow: You have two options here. You can insulate the framed floor above the crawl space (both open and enclosed), or you can insulate the foundation walls (enclosed). The majority of homes with crawl spaces put the insulation in the floor above and leave the crawl space unconditioned. It's possible to make that work, but you're fighting an uphill battle. Well, actually it's a downhill battle because those fiberglass batts so often used to insulate the floor will fall down over time (Figure 11.4). Even when the batts are still in place, they don't insulate as well as they could because of the many obstacles in the joist bays: wiring, plumbing, ducts, framing. The best way to insulate the cavities in a floor above a crawl space is with spray foam insulation. A foam-free alternative would be to fill the cavities with blown or batt insulation and then put a sealed air barrier below the floor joists.

Figure 11.4. *Crawl space floor insulation that has fallen down*

Insulating the foundation walls of a crawl space is the other way to control heat flow with an enclosed crawl space. It can be done on the inside or outside of the foundation walls. Inside is easier to do, though, and won't be subject to damage from lawn equipment, kids, and other outdoor hazards. The insulation materials used must not absorb water. The most common insulation types used here are rigid foam board or closed-cell spray foam insulation. Mineral wool would be the best foam-free choice.

In some cases, a house with insulation on the crawl space walls also has insulation on the ground. It's easiest to do this when the house is being built because the ground in a crawl space is almost always uneven and occasionally a topographic nightmare. I've been in crawl spaces with huge tree stumps. Ground insulation throughout a crawl space is best when you have some protection for it, and a thin slab does the job well. (This kind of slab is often called a "rat slab," which is typically 2 inches thick instead of the standard 4 inches.) An alternative to insulating the entire crawl space floor is to extend the foundation wall insulation into the ground another 2 to 4 feet, with the deeper insulation needed in colder climates.

Controlling air flow: If the insulation is in the floor above the crawl space, that floor needs to be airtight. With an open crawl space, a lack of air sealing means outdoor air gets into the house. That doesn't sound so bad. But some open crawl spaces also serve as carports and storage for lawn equipment, pesticides, and other sources of air pollutants. If that contaminated air comes in, your indoor air won't be healthy. And if the crawl space is enclosed, it may have high humidity, mold, and other air pollutants that you don't want in the house either. Air sealing a floor over a crawl space is a difficult job but a necessary one in these cases.

By putting insulation on the foundation walls of an enclosed crawl space, you're making a different choice about the location of the building enclosure. That means the air barrier needs to be on the foundation walls, too. One of the biggest pathways for air movement between an enclosed crawl space and outdoors is the foundation vents. They must be sealed up. The other places to focus your air-sealing attention in this case are the band joist above the foundation walls and the crawl space access door. All penetrations must be sealed, and the crawl space access door, if it goes anywhere but the living space, must be made airtight.

Controlling moisture flow: Controlling liquid

water on the roof and exterior walls will keep rainwater from getting in through the floor over the crawl space. Sloping the ground away from the foundation keeps the rainwater from getting into the crawl space. If the ground in the crawl space does get wet, however, groundwater may get into the house through capillary action. Liquid water will move up through the foundation walls and piers and into the wood framing.

The solution is to put a piece of water-impermeable material at the top of the foundation walls and piers (Figure 11.5). The material will act as a capillary break to prevent the moisture from rising farther and wetting the wood framing. This applies regardless of whether the crawl space is insulated at the floor above or the foundation walls.

Figure 11.5. *A capillary break separates the concrete foundation from the wood framing.*

To control water vapor, we first need to recall that far more water vapor moves by being swept along with the air than by diffusion. Thus, air sealing the floor over the crawl space or the foundation walls handles most of the water vapor control needed for crawl spaces. That stops water vapor in the outdoor air from being brought into a crawl space. It also stops humid air in the crawl space from being brought into the living space above. (See "Why a Vented Crawl Space Doesn't Work in a Humid Climate" on page 172.)

Air sealing, however, doesn't solve all

problems. High humidity in the crawl space can cause hardwood floors to buckle, rot the floor joists and subfloor decking, and create a hospitable environment for mold and pests. If the control layers are at the subfloor on top of the joists and the humidity below is high, those joists will adsorb moisture from the humid air. To prevent the joists from getting too wet, the air barrier needs to be at the bottom of the floor joists.

Another way to control water vapor moving into the floor joists is to control the humidity below the floor. You can't do that with an open crawl space nor with an enclosed crawl space that's connected to the outdoors with foundation vents. But if you have an enclosed crawl space and seal it up to the outside, then you can control the humidity in that space. You can put the insulation either at the floor above or on the walls. But you must isolate the crawl space from the outdoors.

Figure 11.6. *An encapsulated crawl space is a much less scary place to visit when you have to. And it keeps the humidity under control. [Source: US Department of Energy, Building America Solution Center]*

In addition to sealing the foundation walls, you need to put a vapor barrier on the ground to prevent water from evaporating into the crawl space. When you isolate an enclosed crawl space from the outdoor air and cover the ground with plastic, you're creating what's called an encapsulated, conditioned, sealed, or closed crawl space. I generally call them either conditioned or encapsulated crawl spaces. Encapsulating a crawl space is a big job, and handling all the details necessary is beyond the scope of this book. The general principle, though, is to seal it up completely at the foundation walls and insulate, ideally also at the foundation walls.

Basement

A basement is really just a tall crawl space. They're more expensive than slabs or crawl spaces, especially if they include finished space. The control layers here should follow the recommendations for conditioned crawl spaces above. As with crawl spaces, basements sometimes are outside the building enclosure and sometimes inside. It's generally best to put them inside the building enclosure, with control layers around the perimeter of the foundation walls and beneath the basement slab. However, if the basement has exposed dirt walls and floor and is vented to the outdoors, treat it like a conditioned crawl space and seal it up with a good vapor barrier. The details for including the basement inside the building enclosure are the same as for slabs and crawl spaces above.

Why a Vented Crawl Space Doesn't Work in a Humid Climate

I once went into a vented crawl space in Atlanta and measured a temperature of 70 °F and 92 percent relative humidity (Figure 11.7). That translates to a dew point of about 68 °F. It was a sunny August day, and the outdoor conditions were 90 °F and 52 percent relative humidity. Which air was more humid?

If you want to say it's the crawl space air but think this might be a trick question, your intuition is good. The outdoor air, even though it's 40 points lower on the relative humidity scale, is more humid. The dew point of that air was 70 °F.

Dew point, as discussed in Chapter 6, tells you how much actual water vapor is in the air. And the outdoor air on that August afternoon had more water vapor in it than the crawl space air. Astonishing!

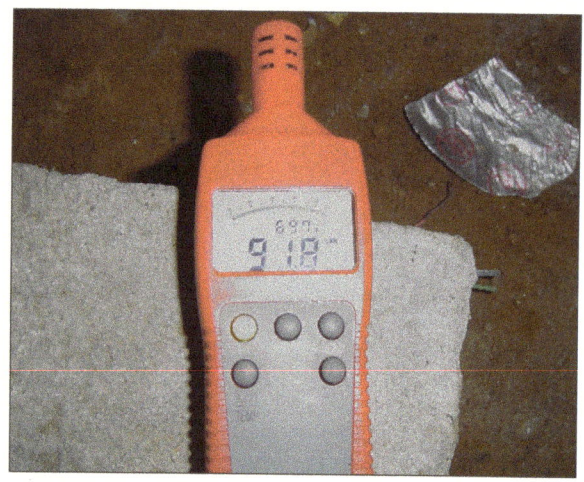

Figure 11.7. *The humidity looks really high in this vented crawl space. Is it possible the outdoor humidity was even higher?*

Until you get used to dew point temperature, that is. So, when outdoor air entered the crawl space, it actually made the crawl space more humid. That's the exact opposite of the intended result for venting a crawl space.

We can also look at it from a relative humidity angle. If some of that outdoor air enters the crawl space and cools to 70 °F, its relative humidity goes to 100 percent. One reason the crawl space had lower humidity than the outdoor air was probably leakage of dry air from the duct system.

Above-Grade Walls

Ah, above-grade walls—the movie stars of the building enclosure. They get far more attention than ceilings and floors. They have more style and adornments than ceilings and floors, too. Let us enter this subject not as adoring fan or exploitative paparazzo, but as practical homeowner, shrewd builder, or sensible designer. We're looking for a wall design that's an excellent vehicle for robust control layers, that's easy to build, and that will continue to do its job for decades with minimal maintenance. The options are plentiful, so let's focus here on the most often used wall types. (See Appendix E for definitions and images of wood frame construction terms.)

Traditional Wood Framing

Most houses in the United States are built with dimensional lumber (2x4s, 2x6s, etc.). This method is often called stick building because dimensional lumber looked so puny to the old-school timber frame builders. Older stick-built houses used balloon framing, but that method has been abandoned for platform framing because of fire codes, the reduced availability of long timber, and the difficulty of working up high on the studs before the second floor was built. In a two-story balloon-framed house, you built the foundation and floors and then built the walls from the first floor all the way up to where the roof started. Then you hung the second floor inside the walls. This type of framing tended to result in houses that burned to the ground quickly because the walls acted like chimneys, allowing air and fire to move quickly through the structure.

On the other hand, to build a two-story platform-framed house, you build, in order, the foundation and floor, first-story walls, second floor, second-story walls, second-story ceiling, and roof. The floors (except for a slab) and ceilings are framed with dimensional lumber

(2"x6" to 2"x12"), I-joists (10" to 16" high), or open-web trusses (18" to 24" high). The walls are usually framed with 2"x4" or 2"x6" dimensional lumber. And the roof is framed with dimensional lumber (2"x6" to 2"x12" rafters) or with engineered trusses (2"x4" framing members held together with gusset plates).

All of these structures get covered with sheathing (also called decking on the roof), which is mostly oriented strand board (OSB) in new homes these days, although some new homes are still sheathed with plywood. In older homes, the wall sheathing, as well as the floor and roof decking, may be 1"x6" boards nailed across the studs, joists, or rafters. That structure is what holds everything together and keeps the house from falling down.

The advantage of traditional wood framing for a house is that you won't have trouble finding workers who have experience with this method. It's also relatively inexpensive, and the materials are easy to find. In addition, no building official will ever question your sanity when you submit plans for a traditionally wood-framed house, as they might if you want to build out of something less common like straw bales.

What we care about here, though, is how the structure helps or hinders the building enclosure and its control layers. In that regard, traditional wood framing has some shortcomings. Traditional framing doesn't inherently present trouble for the liquid water, air, and water vapor control layers. Liquid water must be controlled at the skin of the building, at and behind the cladding. Air flow can be controlled at the outside or inside, although many new homes have the air barrier at the outer wall sheathing.

Water vapor control isn't like air and water control. In most parts of the enclosure, it's more important for a house to be able to dry than it is to stop the diffusion of water vapor. In a hot, humid climate (zones 1A and 2A), you may need a vapor retarder on the outside of the wall. In a cold climate (zones 5 and higher), you may need a vapor retarder on the inside. Yes, the control layers get messed up all the time, but that's because builders haven't had to pay much attention to the control layers until recently when building codes have ramped up their requirements. It's certainly possible to build a traditionally framed house and have good, continuous control layers for liquid water, air, and water vapor.

The control layer most affected by traditional wood-framed structures is insulation. It requires more depth than the other control layers, which can be thin sheets of material. Because insulation takes more space and this type of structure has cavities between the studs, that seemed like the natural place to put the insulation.

> *Cavities make up about 75 percent of the surface area of walls in a traditionally framed house, which means the wood framing is about 25 percent.*

The only problem is that we don't have continuity of the thermal control layer when the only place we put it is in the cavities. Cavities make up about 75 percent of the surface area of walls in a traditionally framed house, which means the wood framing is about 25 percent. And that means 25 percent of the walls are insulated with wood, which has a quarter of the R-value of most insulation types. Heat flowing between inside and outside can flow through the cavity where the insulation is, or it can flow through the wood framing. Because wood is about three times more conductive to heat flow than is insulation, a considerable amount of

the heat loss in winter or heat gain in summer will happen through the wood framing. When insulation is interrupted and extra heat flows through the interruptions, we call those more thermally conductive parts thermal bridges. (See Chapter 10.)

If you want to stick with this type of structure, you have a few options for making the insulation more effective.

Option 1: Make the walls thicker. Instead of 2x4 walls, build with 2x6 or 2x8 studs. You get more insulation in the cavities, and you also get more insulation from the wood framing because it's thicker, too. A 2x4 gives you about R-4, and a 2x6 gives you R-6.

Option 2: Use advanced framing techniques. Corners, T-walls, and headers are easy places to change the framing without diminishing the structural strength at all. Instead of 25 percent wood, you can reduce the amount of wood to less than 20 percent of the surface area.

Option 3: Install continuous insulation over the exterior sheathing. You could put all your insulation on the outside, leaving the cavities empty, or you could put just enough to make the thermal bridging insignificant.

Most traditionally framed houses are a mess when it comes to insulation because of thermal bridging (and poor installation, but that's a separate issue). Using one or more of the options above can bring a standard wood-framed wall into the high-performance world while still retaining the advantages of stick building. To go even further, it's usually best to choose a different type of structure.

Staggered-Stud Walls

A baby-step away from the standard wall is the staggered-stud wall. This type of wall uses two sets of wall studs nailed to bottom and top plates that are wider than the studs. For example, the studs are usually 2x4s and the plates 2x6s or 2x8s. One set of studs lines up with the inner side of the wall while the other set of studs is flush with the outer side. The studs are staggered because the plate isn't wide enough to align the inner and outer studs. Because none of the studs go all the way through from the inside to the outside, thermal bridging from the studs is greatly reduced. The plates and framing around windows and doors still go all the way through and act as thermal bridges. (See Figure 11.8.)

Figure 11.8. *A staggered-stud wall, like the double-stud wall, eliminates the thermal bridging from wall studs.*

Staggered-stud walls have more insulation and reduced thermal bridging. Staggered-stud walls are also more difficult to frame than standard walls. Also, framing around doors and windows gets complicated because of the staggering. Getting the rain, air, and vapor control detailed properly is no more difficult in the staggered-stud wall than the standard wall because they all should be at the exterior sheathing.

Traditional Wood Framing Plus Exterior Continuous Insulation

A 2x4 wall with exterior continuous insulation would be better than a staggered-stud wall because it can have as much or more insulation with all thermal bridging eliminated from the wall. Exterior continuous insulation, sometimes call "outsulation," eliminates all thermal bridging because it can cover not only

the studs but also the bottom and top plates, extra framing around windows and doors, and even the band joists.

In addition to helping with thermal bridging, continuous insulation keeps the sheathing warmer when the insulation is outboard of the sheathing. In cold climates, humid air from inside the house sometimes gets into wall cavities. If the exterior sheathing isn't covered by exterior insulation, the sheathing will be cold. And cold materials can suck up water vapor. If the sheathing stays wet long enough, it can grow mold. It can rot. The siding falls off. Your friends stop visiting. It's a problem! Putting enough insulation on the exterior side of the sheathing keeps it warm enough to prevent this problem.

Figure 11.9. *This Habitat for Humanity home under construction in Maine is getting 2-inch foam board installed over the exterior sheathing.*

Foam board is the most common insulation type used in this application, but mineral wool also works (Figure 11.10). Foam board can be used as the air and water control layers, but it's better to have another set of air and water control layers behind the foam board. It's less subject to damage during construction or degradation due to the cycling of temperature and moisture. For mineral wool, the air and water control layers will be on the back side of the exterior insulation.

Figure 11.10. *Mineral wool insulation is an alternative to foam board for exterior continuous insulation. [Courtesy of ROCKWOOL]*

Continuous insulation on the exterior presents an attachment challenge. Attaching the insulation is easy because it's lightweight, but the cladding has to go on over the insulation. Fiber cement siding, stucco, or stone veneer, however, has some heft and needs good support. The good news is that plenty of work has been done on attaching cladding over thick exterior insulation, and long screws are the answer. Figure 11.11 shows a building science experiment with weights hanging from various types of foam board installed as it would be on the exterior of a wall, and Figure 11.12 shows the weight suspended from the insulation with a gauge measuring any movement. After many months in place with more weight than would normally be supported, the deflection was negligible.

Figure 11.11. *Strength testing of several kinds of foam board insulation installed on the exterior of a wall*

Figure 11.12. *Thick foam board insulation undergoing a strength test*

Another way to use foam board to get continuous insulation is with a product that integrates the insulation with the sheathing. Huber's ZIP System® R-sheathing is the dominant product in this category. But there's a difference from installing foam board to the outside of the sheathing. The foam board on ZIP R-sheathing goes between the sheathing and the framing. As with foam board installed all the way to the outside, ZIP R-sheathing eliminates thermal bridging. The difference is that the sheathing is not protected by the insulation with this product. The sheathing can get cold in winter. Does it matter? Probably not much. Yes, the sheathing stays cold, but the foam board isolates it from the water vapor inside the house. The bottom line here is that ZIP R-sheathing works, but it would be better to have the exterior insulation to the outside of the sheathing.

Traditional framing with exterior continuous insulation, on either side of the sheathing, solves the problem of thermal bridging. Builders have been using this technique successfully for decades. The model building code in the United

States now requires continuous insulation in climate zones 4 and colder, and this is the most common way to meet the requirement.

Double-Stud Walls

Another way to solve the thermal bridging problem is with two sets of framed walls with a gap between for more insulation. The double-stud wall is like the staggered-stud wall, except you put enough space between the inner and outer studs that you can line them up across from each other. The insulation you use could be cellulose, fiberglass, open-cell spray foam, closed-cell spray foam, or some combination. You can make the wall thicker or thinner to adjust the amount of insulation in the wall. Thermal bridging through both the studs and the plates is eliminated. This is what staggered-stud walls really want to be.

Figure 11.13. *A double-stud wall has two sets of studs aligned with each other with a spacious gap in between. This wall allows for a lot of insulation and eliminates thermal bridging through the studs. [Source: US Department of Energy, Building America Solution Center]*

Figure 11.13 shows a double-stud wall. It has two sets of studs and about a foot of depth for a wall that will come in at R-30 or higher. The two sets of walls here were framed separately and sit on separate bottom plates. Some double-stud walls are connected with plywood or oriented

strand board (OSB) at the top and bottom plates (Figure 11.14).

The liquid water control layer goes behind the cladding and outside of the sheathing. The air barrier can go in the same place, or you could put it between the two sets of studs. Figure 11.14 shows a double-stud wall with the air barrier made of sealed OSB or plywood nailed to the inner set of studs. The advantages of this method are that the air barrier is better protected in the middle of the wall than it is on the outside or the inside of the whole assembly, and rigid materials hold up better than membranes and tape. A disadvantage is that you have to insulate twice, once from the inside and again from the outside.

Double-stud walls are like ZIP R-sheathing in that they also let the sheathing get cold. A lot of people fret over cold sheathing getting soggy in super-insulated walls, but Maine home builder Dan Kolbert calls this the Yeti of building science: often discussed but rarely seen. Again, just because the sheathing stays cold in winter doesn't mean it gets wet. With liquid water control protecting the wall from exterior moisture and insulation and air sealing protecting the sheathing from interior moisture, it can stay cold and dry through the winter. Still, as with ZIP R-sheathing, exterior insulation is the less risky way to go.

Structural Insulated Panels

Another way to construct a house is with a sandwich of sheathing (the bread) and rigid foam (the peanut butter). Keeping to the PB&J metaphor, the spray foam at all the connections is the jelly. The most common type of structural insulated panel (SIP) uses oriented strand board (OSB) for the sheathing and expanded polystyrene (EPS) for the foam insulation. Other types are also available.

Building a house with structural insulated panels (SIPs) is easier than some of the previous structures I discussed. In fact, I built a house with structural insulated panels in 2001, and I had never built anything bigger than a bookcase before undertaking the project. I did get a good set of panel plans and hired a consultant for the first couple of days on the project. I also had an experienced builder to help me take the house from basement to dried-in structure.

Different companies have different methods for connecting the panels. Some eliminate all thermal bridging where the panels join by using connecting pieces (called splines) with foam in the middle. The house I built used wood splines between each two panels. The standard width for the panels is 4 feet, though, so there's a lot less thermal bridging with "studs" 4 feet apart rather than 16 inches apart. Using structural insulated panels for the roof requires wood splines for structural support, but again, they're 4 feet apart. You could always put exterior continuous insulation on the outside of the walls or roof to reduce the thermal bridging from the wood splines.

The advantages of SIPs are reduced thermal bridging and easier control of heat, air, and moisture. Solid insulation embedded in panels means that sealing the joints and penetrations is straightforward. I had never seen or done a blower door test before building with SIPs, and I measured an air leakage rate of 1.7 air changes per hour at 50 Pascals (ACH_{50}) when I tested the house upon completion. Controlling liquid water is no different than doing so for the other types of structures mentioned above. You can use house wrap, fluid-applied membranes, felt, or another type of liquid water control layer.

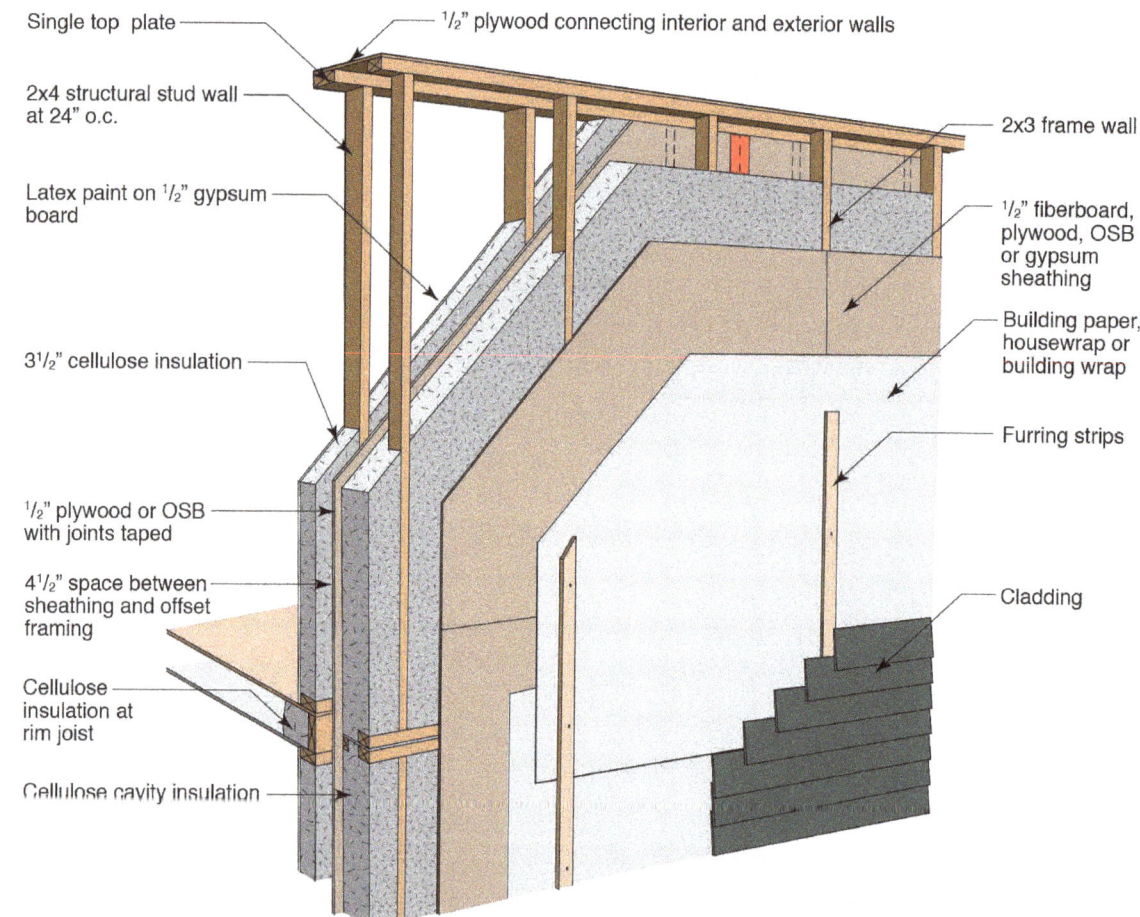

Figure 11.14. *Double-stud wall construction, as recommended by Building Science Corporation [Courtesy of Joseph Lstiburek]*

Figure 11.15. *Structural insulated panel construction: Wall panels get stood up and attached to the already nailed-down bottom plates.*

Figure 11.16. *The first wall section we installed in the house I built*

The panels themselves have a low vapor permeability, so you must make sure that the walls can dry. The interior OSB can dry only to the inside of the house, so don't put plastic under the drywall. The exterior OSB can dry only to the outside, so it needs a gap. See the section on rain screens in Chapter 7.

SIP homes are stronger than many stick-built homes. They have survived hurricanes in neighborhoods where all the other houses were destroyed.

The big caution for building with SIPs is that you must make sure all the seams, joints, and penetrations are air-sealed to the hilt. This is especially true at the top of the house because the stack effect will put pressure on any weakness in the air barrier. Some SIP houses have required extensive repairs to the sheathing after only a few years because of air leaking through.

John Semmelhack in Charlottesville, Virginia, built a SIP house in 2008. As his family grew, he added onto the house in 2015 and discovered that some of the OSB on the roof and the upper part of the wall was damaged. The problem was not the overall airtightness of the whole building enclosure. He was almost Passive House tight at a little over 0.6 ACH_{50}. The problem was the concentrated leakage through seams at the top of the house because of the stack effect. That put humid air from inside the house in contact with cold surfaces, and you know what happens then.

Figure 11.17. *Moisture damage to the upper part of the wall of John Semmelhack's house [Courtesy of John Semmelhack]*

Semmelhack repaired his roof, but what could you do differently to avoid this problem? One simple change would make the difference between needing repairs in less than 10 years and a SIP house that lasts for decades. When

John and I built our SIP houses, the air barrier was the whole panel. The weak part was at the connections between panels. Before we connected two panels, we sprayed can foam on both sides to stop air leakage. As Semmelhack found out, though, even a few small areas of air leakage can damage your enclosure.

One step in solving the problem is to put a continuous air barrier on the outside of the panels. Peel-and-stick or fluid-applied membranes would work well. But that's not going to be enough. Warm, humid air inside the house can cause problems through convective looping in the seams between panels (Figure 11.18). Thus, the other important step in ensuring your SIP house won't rot is to seal the inside.

Figure 11.19. *Insulated concrete forms connected and reinforced [Source: US Department of Energy Building America Solution Center]*

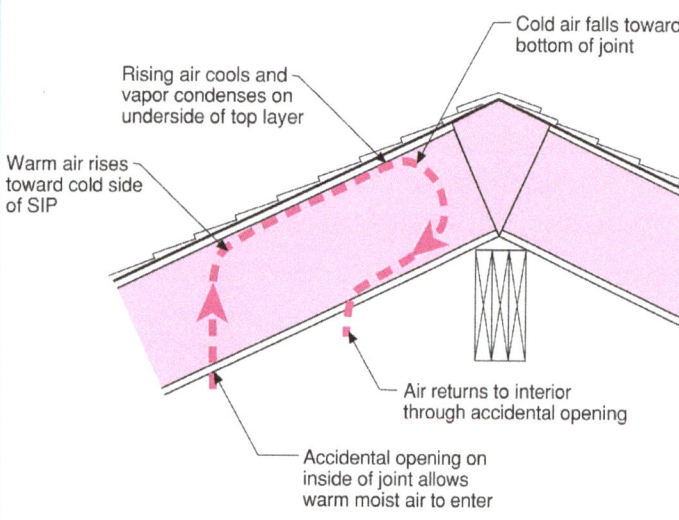

Rising air cools and vapor condenses on underside of top layer

Cold air falls toward bottom of joint

Warm air rises toward cold side of SIP

Air returns to interior through accidental opening

Accidental opening on inside of joint allows warm moist air to enter

Figure 11.18. *Convective looping within the seam of a structural insulated panel roof [Courtesy of Joseph Lstiburek]*

Insulated Concrete Forms

Like structural insulated panels, insulated concrete forms (ICFs) are a way to sandwich structure and insulation materials together. In this case, insulation (usually expanded polystyrene) is the bread of the sandwich, and concrete is the peanut butter and jelly. Plastic or metal ties hold the inner and outer foam layers of the form together.

The forms stack together with tongue-and-groove connections. As you assemble the forms, you put rebar in the gap where the concrete goes to improve the structural strength of the walls. Then you pour the concrete between the two foam layers of the forms. Unlike with regular poured concrete walls, though, you leave the forms in place because they provide the thermal control layer. Then you attach drywall on the interior and a water control layer (if necessary) and cladding on the exterior. Some manufacturers say you don't need to add a water control layer because the foam itself will keep things dry.

Figure 11.20. *Insulated concrete form construction [Source: US Department of Energy Building America Solution Center]*

A bunch of different companies make insulated concrete forms in several different styles. Flat panel, waffle, and post-and-beam are the most common, but they all do essentially the same thing. If you're interested in going this route, explore your options before settling on one type.

Insulated concrete forms have several advantages. The foam on both sides gives you a lot of wall insulation. Many ICFs have a continuous R-22, but you can get forms with higher R-values. Because the walls are solid concrete with foam on both sides, it's easy to make them airtight. They're also quieter, more fire resistant, and more critter-proof than wood-frame homes.

And because they're concrete, the walls are strong. The owners of an ICF home in Cape Coral, Florida, heard a noise in the living room after going to bed one night. When they got up to investigate, they saw a pair of headlights shining through the living room window. A car traveling at 90 miles per hour had crashed into the house. The only damage to their house was a small section of the exterior finish and the foam on that part of the wall. The car, however, was totaled.

Kohta Ueno's Top Three Lids

How you design the building enclosure at the top of the house—the lid—is critical. When you look at the building science literature and at what people are actually doing, you'll see a lot of different designs for the lid. You can make most of them work, but some are easier to do and more forgiving than others. Kohta Ueno is an engineer with Building Science Corporation who has helped with a lot of lids that work and studied a lot that have failed. Here are his top three designs for this part of a house.

1. **Vented attic:** This is the most prevalent and the least expensive option. It's been around a long time, and we know how to make it work. The keys are aggressive air sealing of the attic floor, well-installed insulation (including over the exterior walls), and keeping mechanical equipment and ducts out of the attic.

2. **Insulation on top of the roof deck:** If you really want a conditioned attic, the best way to do it is to put the insulation and the air barrier above the roof sheathing. This method works either with all insulation on top of the deck or a hybrid of some above and some below. If you go with the hybrid method, you need to follow the ratio rule (discussed later in this chapter) to keep the roof sheathing temperature above 45 °F. Ueno recommends using fibrous insulation on the underside because it's less expensive and makes it easy to find roof leaks. Putting insulation on top works in every climate. It protects the structure from variations in temperature and moisture. It's recommended to provide some conditioning in the attic to control humidity in humid climates.

3. **Closed-cell spray foam insulation on the underside of the roof deck:** If you're going to condition the attic by putting all the insulation on the underside of the roof deck, closed-cell spray foam is your best bet. As with Ueno's first and second choices, it works in every climate. You can save some money by installing a layer of closed-cell spray foam under the roof deck first and then getting the rest of your R-value with open-cell spray foam or fibrous insulation. If you go this route, you'll need to follow the same ratio rule as with the hybrid method in Ueno's second choice. (See the section on conditioned attics later in this chapter.)

Ceilings and Attics

Every part of a house faces its own stresses. Foundations have to fend off water, radon, and critters. Walls hold up the roof, let light and people in, and hide the electrical wiring. The top of the house has its challenges, too. Warm, sometimes humid, air rises in the house, courtesy of the stack effect. Roofs soak up great quantities of solar energy during the day, mainly because of dark asphalt shingles, especially at times of the year when you'd rather they didn't. That absorbed heat then can conduct downward through the layers of roofing. And of course, rain falls on the roof, and snow collects and melts there. All this means that the air, heat, and water control layers at the top of the house are critical.

> *Roofs soak up great quantities of solar energy during the day, mainly because of dark asphalt shingles, especially at times of the year when you'd rather they didn't.*

Roof leaks are a common failure of the water control layer, of course. Ice dams in cold climates, sweating ducts in humid climates, and excessive heat flow through the ceiling in all climates are failures of thermal and air control layers.

With the top of the house, you have choices about where to put the control layers. The liquid water control layer always goes on top of the roof. The thermal and air control layers can be configured in one of three ways. They can go at the ceiling plane with an unconditioned attic above. They can be at the roofline with a conditioned attic below. Or they can be at the roofline (sloped or flat) with no attic.

Ceiling Under Unconditioned Attic

Most single-family homes as well as the top-floor units in some multifamily buildings have an unconditioned attic at the top of the house. It's a buffer space that's neither indoors nor outdoors. It usually has insulation on the floor and, ideally, an air barrier beneath the insulation. The unconditioned attic in such a house can be nearly as cold as outdoors in winter and much hotter than outdoors in summer. If the house is more than a few decades old, the attic is probably one of the nastiest parts of the house, a place that causes comfort, indoor air quality, durability, and energy use problems for the owners (Figure 11.21).

Figure 11.21. *Nasty attic in an old house: The insulation is filthy and has lost much of its R-value through losing its loft over time. The opening around the chimney is a huge thermal bypass.*

In newer homes, attics are nice and clean at first. The insulation is installed evenly, and the ceiling is airtight (Figure 11.22). Or at least that should be the case. Lack of building codes, lack of enforcement, or complex designs can lead to attics that have problems from the get-go. Sometimes an attic is fine at inspection time, and then the cable guy or another trade comes in, moving and compressing insulation and occasionally not sealing holes or putting the insulation back when they're done. Other times, a homeowner goes into the attic and messes up the insulation and air barrier. Then there's the issue of critters. Roaches, wasps, mice, rats, squirrels, raccoons, bats, birds, and more will take up residence in your attic if they have an opportunity. Over time, the state of an unconditioned attic will decay, so plan for inspections, maintenance, and renovations of the control layers as your house ages.

Figure 11.22. *The attic in a new home is nice and clean with a good air barrier and evenly installed insulation.*

An unconditioned attic is usually the most cost-effective way to design the top of the house. The materials and labor for the control layers are relatively inexpensive. The key is to make sure the attic floor is airtight. Then cover it with a generous amount of insulation and make sure it is evenly distributed. Ventilating an attic with outdoor air can keep it cooler in summer and drier in winter, but it may not provide much real benefit to the house.

Controlling air: When air sealing the floor of an unconditioned attic, follow the guidance in Chapter 8. It's critical to get all the air sealing done before insulating because once you put the insulation in place, you don't want to disturb it to fix air leaks. Also, make sure that any trades-people who could penetrate the air barrier do so

before air sealing or that they understand their responsibility for getting their holes air sealed if they do it afterward. In new construction, getting all the trades scheduled in the right order can be a challenge.

> *It's critical to get all the air sealing done before insulating because once you put the insulation in place, you don't want to disturb it to fix air leaks.*

I like to tell people who are considering home performance improvements not to insulate the attic. Then I pause before telling them they need to deal with the air barrier first. Older homes often had little to no thought given to an air barrier at the ceiling plane, and consequently they are quite leaky. Air leaks through the obvious places like recessed can lights and attic hatches. The hidden air leaks, though, often steal a lot more conditioned air than the obvious ones. (Some of the main ones are open chases, unsealed top plates, and recessed can lights. See Chapter 8.) Make the attic floor as airtight as possible before even thinking about putting in more insulation.

Newer homes, especially those that get blower door tested, have better air barriers. Depending on how the home was built, though, you may still have room for improvement. If the attic insulation is in good shape, a blower door test can guide you to how much air sealing may be warranted. But if the insulation is in good shape, it's going to be hard to get into the attic and really seal things up. If the insulation is old and nasty, have it removed, do your air sealing (Figure 11.23), and then reinsulate. An excellent resource for air sealing an attic is the Attic Air Sealing Guide and Details, a free download from Building Science Corporation.[19]

---

19. https://www.buildingscience.com/documents/guides-and-manuals/gm-attic-air-sealing-guide/view

Figure 11.23. *The attic floor should be thoroughly air sealed before installing insulation. [Courtesy of Danny Orlando]*

Controlling heat: Fiberglass is the insulation used on the floor in most attics, and cellulose also works well here. Usually it's loose-fill insulation blown in with a machine. One of the keys to success is to achieve the correct density. Insulation blown in with too much air will have depth but not density. Another key is uniformity of depth, as explained in Chapter 10.

Figure 11.24. *Blown fiberglass insulation in an attic: Make sure the installers use plenty of depth markers.*

Fiberglass batt insulation on the attic floor isn't as common as it once was, but some builders still insulate this way. It's more difficult to fill the space completely because of obstructions like wiring, framing, ductwork, and plumbing. If you go with this method, the best way to do it is to use two layers of fiberglass batts. Place one between the joists, cutting and notching where necessary. Then run

another set of batts across the top, perpendicular to the direction of the joists (Figure 11.25). This method prevents heat from moving through gaps between insulation and joists. It also puts a nice, thick layer of continuous insulation across the joists.

Occasionally you'll find mineral wool insulating attics. Some older houses have other materials, like vermiculite, which may contain asbestos (Chapter 12). Whatever kind of insulation you use, it needs to fill the space completely. I like blown insulation for attics because it's easier to get insulation around the many obstructions and blow it over the top of the joists to cover the thermal bridges.

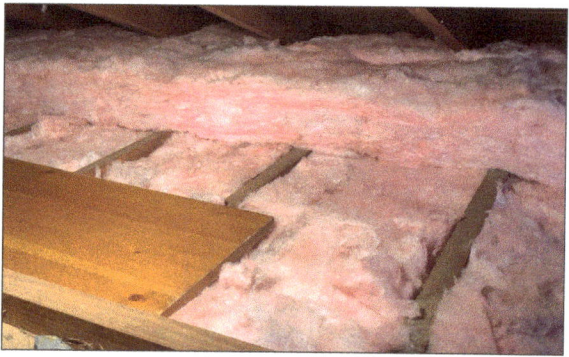

Figure 11.25. *Fiberglass batt insulation installed properly in an attic: The first layer of batts goes between the ceiling joists, filling the bays completely. The second layer goes across the top of the joists, perpendicular to the first layer.*

Using spray foam insulation on the attic floor is another option, but it's rarely done, for several reasons. First, you don't need the adhesive properties of spray foam to keep insulation on that surface because gravity does it for you. Second, for most attics, the surface you're covering is drywall, which is an air barrier material by itself. Sealing the leakage sites with spray foam (Figure 11.23) and then covering the attic floor with blown insulation is much more cost effective. Third, spraying foam on the attic floor encapsulates wiring and other services, making it more difficult to change them later. Open-cell foam tears away easily, but you can forget about easy electrical repairs if you have closed-cell spray foam on the attic floor.

Controlling moisture: The good news here is that sunshine helps keep attics dry. Bill Rose, in his wonderful book, *Water in Buildings,* wrote, "If there are moisture problems in attics, we may consider that they are due to a strong excess moisture load, a lack of sunlight, or both. Of all the parts of a building, the easiest to keep dry is the attic."

With an unconditioned attic, controlling the flow of heat and air does most of the work in preventing a "strong excess moisture load" in the attic (barring roof and plumbing leaks). Most of the moisture that gets into an attic comes with air entering the attic. In winter, the humid air is inside the house. A good air barrier keeps that moisture out of the attic. In cold climate homes lacking a good air barrier between the attic and the living space, condensation and frost can form on roofing nails, decking, framing, and any other surface below the dew or frost point. Sometimes the moisture accumulation in an attic can be so bad that mold grows and the roof rots.

Figure 11.26. *Frost on roof deck and nails in unconditioned attic. Air leakage from living space below is the source of the moisture. [Courtesy of Todd Abercrombie]*

In hot or mixed humid climates, winters don't stay cold long enough to cause serious condensation problems from interior moisture getting into the attic. In summer, however, the moisture is outdoors. When humid outdoor air enters an attic, it can cause a different set of problems. A poor air barrier can let humid attic air into the house, raising interior humidity and making the air harder to condition properly. With an airtight attic floor, that humid air won't get into the house through air leaks, so that avoids one potential problem.

Figure 11.27. *Condensation beneath plastic on top of attic floor insulation. [Courtesy of Todd Abercrombie]*

The other potential problem with warm, humid air in the attic is condensation on anything that might be below the dew point. Mostly that problem occurs with air handlers and ducts carrying cold air on humid days as well as the condensate line from the air conditioner. Burying ducts, partially or completely, in the attic insulation can make condensation worse because the outer jacket will be cooler. And the humid attic air isn't stopped by fluffy insulation. It's possible to bury ducts in attic insulation in a humid climate, but you need to have more insulation on the ducts themselves (i.e., between the duct and the vapor barrier jacket on the duct insulation). The model code currently says you need to use R-13 on buried ducts in climate zones 1A, 2A, and 3A.

Another place where condensation occurs is where two ducts are touching or very close to each other. Again, the outer jacket is cold and can be below the dew point. The more humid your climate, the more condensation on ducts is an issue. (I'm looking at you, Gulf coast and Atlantic seaboard.)

Attic ventilation: Now let's talk about the controversial issue of ventilating unconditioned attics with outdoor air. First, powered attic ventilators are almost never a good idea. Yes, they can keep the attic cooler in summer than a passively vented or unvented attic. One problem, though, is they sometimes do that by stealing conditioned air from the living space. These fans, mounted in the roof deck or a gable end, typically move 1,000 to 2,000 cubic feet of air per minute, which can easily pull air from the living space through an unsealed attic floor. In some cases, they can present a safety hazard by backdrafting a natural draft gas water heater and putting carbon monoxide into the home's air.

Powered attic ventilators are almost never a good idea.

I looked at a house once that had mold growing near a bathroom exhaust fan because the powered attic ventilators were sucking humid outdoor air through the bath fan duct. Even in the best-case scenario, the energy used to run the fans often ends up being higher than any savings on cooling the living space. If you really want to keep your attic cooler, invest in a reflective or light-colored roof. Or let the attic get hot and keep the heat out of the house with good insulation and air sealing.

Even passive ventilation, although required by building codes, doesn't always do what its proponents claim: prevent condensation in the attic, minimize the chances of getting ice dams, extend shingle life, and reduce cooling costs. The issue that led to ventilation requirements in building codes is preventing condensation. But does it work? Building science researchers at the University of Illinois believe there's little data to support the idea that ventilated attics don't have moisture problems. Bill Rose, one of those researchers, wrote in *Water in Buildings*, "It is always preferable to reduce an excess moisture source than to presume its existence and hope to dilute it with outdoor air."

One reason attic ventilation doesn't always help with condensation is that wind is the main driver for passive ventilation. Attics usually don't have enough height to generate much stack effect. The main reason attic ventilation doesn't always work, though, is that the moisture that causes problems in attics comes from the living space below. That occurs either because the house has excessive humidity in the winter, the ceiling isn't air sealed properly, or both. Thus, air sealing is the best way to prevent attic condensation in winter.

Similarly, excessive heat entering the attic is what causes ice dams. Air sealing and insulation are much more effective at preventing ice dams than attic ventilation is. And they're definitely better than the quick-fix solution of putting electric resistance heat on the roof.

Having said that, sometimes attic ventilation does help with moisture problems. Remember, cold air is dry air, so diluting the attic with outdoor air can dry it out. Engineer Kohta Ueno says enough marginal cases are helped by venting that he wouldn't recommend not doing it.

The warm climate, summer problems of shingle life and cooling costs also show little improvement from attic ventilation. Shingle life can be shortened by higher temperatures, and asphalt shingles do stay cooler in a ventilated attic. But the effect is small, with only about 6 percent reduction in temperature. Changing the color of the shingles from black to white drops the shingle temperature by 25 percent, on the other hand. As Bill Rose wrote, "Attic ventilation does not deserve the attention it has received in relation to shingle durability."[20]

For the second problem, cooling costs, attic ventilation supposedly reduces cooling costs in the house. Yes, ventilation can keep the attic cooler, but that doesn't translate to lower air-conditioning costs. In days of yore, when insulation wasn't required and no one had ever heard of thermal bypasses, keeping the attic cooler certainly could keep the house cooler. With modern building codes requiring R-38 or higher for nearly the entire United States in addition to verified airtightness, there's little heat flowing into the house even from the hottest attics.

20. From *Water in Buildings*, by William Rose (p. 203)

Yes, ventilation can keep the attic cooler, but that doesn't translate to lower air-conditioning costs.

The bottom line is that attic ventilation may or may not help cooling costs. It could make things worse if it makes the attic colder without removing much of the moisture. Your first lines of attack should be air sealing and insulation. But if you're going to have an unconditioned attic in a cold climate, it's safest to include venting. Why? Because it's often the difference between success and failure when an attic is on the edge. Yeah, you may not extend your shingle life or save much on your cooling costs. But allowing outdoor air to move through the attic in winter may just be the difference between a dry attic and condensation on the roof deck.

Tricky parts: The best-case scenario for an unconditioned attic is that the house has a simple roof design and an attic floor at the same level throughout. That makes air-sealing and insulating relatively easy. Homes with changes in ceiling height, tray ceilings, vertical walls separating unconditioned attic from conditioned space, lots of recessed can lights, distinct attics separated by cathedral ceilings, and other complexities can be a nightmare to air seal and insulate.

Changes in ceiling height are easy to air seal and insulate. Unfortunately, in many homes these areas don't get air sealed and insulated properly, as you can see in the photo of a home I worked on (Figure 11.28). The uninsulated wall area is even greater than you can see in that photo, too, because the stud bays are open all the way down, as shown in Figure 11.29.

To make changes in ceiling height work properly, the stud bays need to be blocked and sealed to keep hot or cold attic air away from the uninsulated drywall. That turns the bottom parts of those walls into regular partition walls (i.e., conditioned space on both sides). If they're

not connected to unconditioned spaces, they don't need insulation in the cavities. Then the top part of the wall, the attic kneewall separating conditioned space from unconditioned attic, must be air sealed and insulated. If the kneewall is less than about a foot in height, mounding up a lot of blown insulation against it may be all you need. Otherwise, the kneewall should be insulated and then have air-sealed sheathing on the attic side of the wall. Another way to handle it is with spray foam insulation, which is what I did in this house. It both air seals and insulates the kneewall, and it also blocks attic air from getting down into the partition wall. Figure 11.30 shows the change-of-ceiling height kneewalls of Figure 11.28 after filling the bays with fiberglass batt insulation and then spraying closed-cell spray foam over it.

Figure 11.28. *A change in ceiling height results in attic kneewalls that need to be air sealed and insulated but sometimes aren't.*

Figure 11.29. *The uninsulated attic kneewall area extends to the full height of the kneewall in this house.*

Figure 11.30. *The kneewall of Figure 11.28 has been sealed and insulated with closed-cell spray foam over fiberglass batts.*

A tray ceiling is another way a ceiling height changes, and the solution is the same. If the vertical part is short, blown insulation may be all you need after air sealing everything. Otherwise, treat the kneewalls as described above.

And speaking of kneewalls, some homes have a lot of them, sometimes at full height. The way they've been handled in the past (and even today, depending on where you live) is just to put fiberglass batts in the open cavities on the attic side of the kneewall. As you can see in Figure 11.31, that method doesn't work well. Figure 11.32 shows one of the effects of not air sealing kneewalls. The dark areas are dirt that got trapped in the fiberglass when air leaked through the kneewall at unsealed penetrations and joints.

Figure 11.31 *Typical attic kneewall insulated with fiberglass batts and no attic-side sheathing*

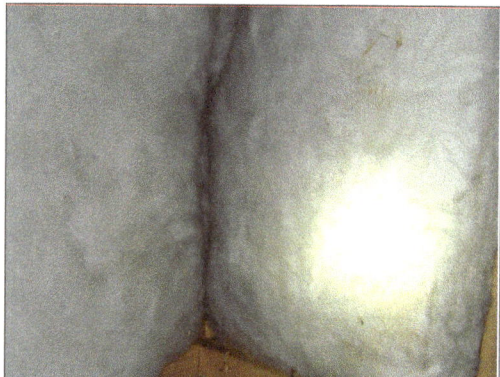

Figure 11.32. *The dark areas in the insulation of this kneewall are dirt captured in the fiberglass when air moves through unsealed leakage sites.*

It's fine to insulate kneewall cavities with air-permeable insulation. You just need to sheathe the attic side of the kneewall with an air barrier material

Figure 11.33. *An attic kneewall sheathed with extruded polystyrene foam board and sealed with spray foam*

afterward and then air seal it. The kneewall in Figure 11.33 is sheathed with extruded polystyrene (XPS) and sealed at all the seams and penetrations.

A common problem with ceilings is recessed can lights, which are a common source of air leakage. The good news is that lighting has improved tremendously. The old-style can light that protrudes above the ceiling in a leaky, difficult to insulate mess is becoming obsolete as smaller, sealed LED fixtures take their place. Sometimes, though, a homeowner doesn't want to change the fixtures (yet), so you have to find a way to air seal and insulate them. In the case of old can lights that are neither airtight nor rated for insulation contact (IC-AT), you can make a box out of fiberglass ductboard to cover them (Figure 11.34). Tape the seams, use caulk or spray foam to seal the edges, and you've got a sealed can light that's ready to be buried in blown insulation. You also could use prefabricated can light covers and save yourself a bit of work.

Figure 11.34. *This fiberglass ductboard box covers a leaky recessed can light in the ceiling.*

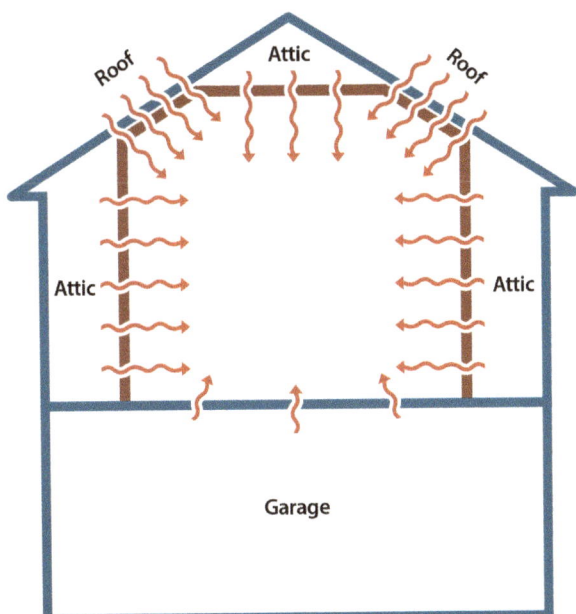

Figure 11.35. *A bonus room can have a lot of exposed surface area, much of it to attic spaces. As a result, these rooms can be very difficult to cool in summer.*

A bonus room, which is a finished room over the garage (thus called a FROG in some regions), often has floors exposed to attic air because of poor understanding of the building enclosure. The bottom center area of Figure 11.36 shows floor joists that extend from an unconditioned attic to the floor of the bonus room. Because the space above the bonus room floor is conditioned, allowing attic air to get into those joist bays accelerates the heat flow between the bonus room and the attic. It also allows attic air to find its way into the living space, potentially creating an indoor air quality problem. This was my sister's house in Florida, and they had to abandon that room most of the year. The solution, of course, is to block and seal those joist bays and fix the knee walls.

Figure 11.37 shows the missing part of the building enclosure beneath the attic kneewalls. The pen test (Chapter 5) would have revealed this problem quickly.

The final tricky part I'll discuss is identifying or finding the parts of the attic that need to be insulated and air sealed. Houses often get chopped up into a complex network of building assemblies and buffer spaces surrounding the conditioned space, and it's not always easy to see where the building enclosure is. Occasionally, for example,

a house design creates two separate main attics separated by a cathedral ceiling in the center of a house. Bonus rooms often have small attic spaces on each side, sometimes with no access after the drywall is installed. Bump-outs with attic above are easily overlooked, especially if they also have a different ceiling height. For new construction, doing a pen test (Chapter 5) on the plans is the best way to identify any tricky areas. In existing homes, you have to explore the attic and the house thoroughly, looking for every surface that separates conditioned space from unconditioned space.

Conditioned Attic

Unconditioned attics are generally the most cost-effective way to insulate and air seal the top of the house, but they have their weaknesses. An alternative is to put the insulation and air barrier at the roofline and create a conditioned attic. This method requires at least as much attention to detail as putting the control layers at the attic floor. It's also more expensive in most cases and comes with its own set of potential problems.

Figure 11.36. *Bonus room floor joists going from unconditioned attic space to beneath conditioned space before (top) and after (bottom) blocking and sealing the joist bays. [Courtesy by Jim Breitenbach]*

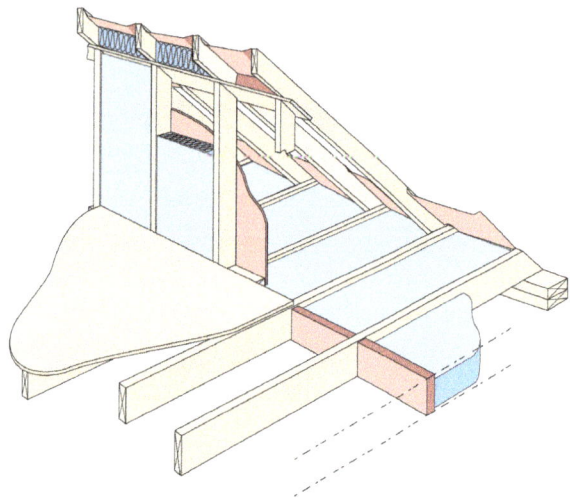

Figure 11.37. *When floor joists beneath an attic kneewall have no blocking or air sealing, air from the attic can flow into those joist bays, stealing heat from the room in winter, making it warmer in summer, and potentially making indoor air quality worse. [Courtesy of Southface]*

Creating a conditioned attic, though, also comes with some significant benefits, most of which stem from the attic staying closer to interior conditions.

- Any HVAC components in the attic—air handler, ducts, ventilation system—will have less heat loss in winter and less heat gain in summer.
- Anyone who has to be in the attic— electricians, HVAC technicians, homeowners' children—will find the conditions much more tolerable.
- Mechanical equipment, ducts, and other parts of the home's services should last longer.
- The attic becomes a better place to store stuff.

So how do you make a conditioned attic? I've already given you the simple answer: You move the insulation and air barrier to the roofline. The reality is more complex, of course. You can make a conditioned attic in a number of ways. The insulation and air barrier can be on top of the roof deck. The insulation and air barrier can be beneath the roof deck. Or the insulation and air barrier can be incorporated into the roof deck.

All insulation on top of roof deck: Putting

all of the insulation on top of the roof deck is the ideal way to go. As I discussed in the section on the Perfect Enclosure, controlling heat and air on the exterior of the structure helps protect the structure, provides easier access to services (wiring, etc.), and usually results in less thermal bridging and better insulation performance.

Figure 11.38. *Installing rigid foam insulation on top of roof deck. [Courtesy of Dan Kolbert]*

What type of insulation works for this purpose? Most sloped roofs insulated above the roof deck use rigid foam. Expanded polystyrene, extruded polystyrene, and polyisocyanurate all work. Closed-cell spray foam is an option for flat roofs. Another option is semi-rigid mineral wool. Whereas rigid foam can give you additional levels of airtightness, especially if you use two or more layers with the seams staggered and taped, mineral wool is air permeable. If you choose any type of air-permeable insulation for the exterior (roof or walls), all of your airtightness will have to come by sealing the roof deck itself.

In putting insulation on top of the roof deck, you don't want to put an air gap or ventilation channels between the insulation and the roof deck. That will reduce the effectiveness of the insulation by separating it from the assembly you're trying to insulate. Likewise, if you're using rigid foam, you don't need to worry about installing a vapor retarder. The foam itself will have low vapor permeance. You do, however, need a good air barrier. Because more water vapor moves with air flow than through diffusion, any air leakage at the roof deck can cause moisture to accumulate, and you don't want air leaking into the insulation sandwich on top of your roof.

Climate Zone	Ceiling R-value
0-1	30
2-3	49
4-8	60

Table 11.1. Minimum R-values required for ceilings by the 2021 International Energy Conservation Code

Putting all your roof insulation above the roof deck makes things simple. As long as you use enough insulation, the roof deck stays warm enough in winter to avoid the risk of accumulating moisture from the humid air in a conditioned attic. If you go by current building code requirements, you'll have enough. Table 11.1 shows the minimum insulation required by the residential building code (2021 IRC and IECC) for each climate zone. (Tradeoffs with other building enclosure components may allow you to use less insulation. Check your local building code.)

All insulation below roof deck: This method is the most common way to create a conditioned attic because it's easily done with spray foam insulation. With good oversight, it can be done correctly.

Spray foam isn't the only way to encapsulate an attic with insulation beneath the roof deck, however. In the past few years, building codes have begun to accept air-permeable insulation against the bottom side of the roof sheathing with the addition of something called a vapor diffusion port. Let's talk about control layers before we dive into those details, though.

As usual, every building assembly needs to have an air barrier and insulation. If you use spray foam insulation, both control layers are incorporated into the same material. If you use the fluffy stuff (i.e., air-permeable insulation), it's got to be installed adjacent to a good, continuous air barrier. You've also got to have enough insulation, installed uniformly, and filling all the space it's supposed to fill. (See Chapter 10.)

Vapor control is critical in attics insulated from beneath. In cold climates, your best bet is to use closed-cell spray foam. If you really want to use open-cell spray foam, building codes require you to install a vapor retarder with it in climate zones 5 and colder. The reason is the same one we've been discussing: moisture accumulation in the roof sheathing from humid indoor (attic) air.

In warm climates, moisture accumulation in the sheathing also can be a problem, but it's mainly a summertime problem. The problem arises when an attic is encapsulated but not directly conditioned. The humidity can reach high levels during the daytime, especially when the sun is shining. At night, the humidity drops as the water vapor diffuses through the spray foam and finds the cooler roof sheathing. It hangs out there until the next day, when the sun comes up and drives the water back down into the attic air. This ping-pong effect repeats daily and intensifies, as more and more water vapor finds its way into the attic. The warmer and more humid the climate, the more the roof sheathing is at risk of rotting.

Whether you encapsulate an attic with spray foam or air-permeable insulation, you need to consider the attic as conditioned space. That means conditioning the air, which you can do in one of three ways:

1. Supply conditioned air from the heating and cooling system.
2. Exhaust attic air with a small exhaust fan.
3. Dehumidify the air.

In a dry climate, use one of the first two methods. In a humid climate, use any of the three or some combination. I like the exhaust method because it can keep attic air out of the living space, which also solves the problem of odors from the attic getting into the house. By exhausting air, you put the attic under a slight negative pressure. As long as the attic is properly sealed, the air removed from the attic is replaced with conditioned air from the living space.

For the exhaust method to work well, you've got to get the details right.

- The attic must be sealed airtight to the outdoors.
- Ensure the exhaust fan pulls air from high in the attic.
- Use one or more high-efficiency exhaust fans to provide 50 cfm per 1,000 square feet of attic floor area.

One way to tell if the attic is airtight to the outdoors is to do the feel test while the blower door is running, as described in Chapter 8. To do that here, you stand near the attic access and close it most of the way. If the attic is airtight, you should feel little air coming through the gap. Another way is to do zonal pressure diagnostics during a blower door test. If that test indicates that the attic is much more connected to the living space than to the outdoors, the attic is sealed well. Yet another method for this is to fill the house with theatrical fog while putting the house under positive pressure. From outdoors, you should be able to see if the fog is coming out from the attic. (Caution: Alert the neighbors before doing this test so they don't call the fire department.)

The first two methods are affected by intentional openings you may have put in the ceiling, however. To use the exhaust method in the attic, you need those openings to allow conditioned air to be pulled into the attic. They interfere when trying to determine the airtightness of the attic because they allow air to move freely, thus changing how much air you'll feel at the attic access and the zonal pressure difference. You can cover them temporarily for the test.

Regarding those intentional openings, you can add transfer grilles in the ceiling if there's not enough open area to allow enough replacement air to get into the attic. Closets can be a good place for these grilles because the grilles are hidden and the air flow helps keep the closet from smelling stale.

Some insulation on top of roof deck, some beneath (hybrid assembly): Rigid foam is more expensive in labor and materials than many of the insulation types that go into building cavities. Putting lots of it on top of the roof thus makes it a more expensive roof. You can reduce costs, though, by splitting up the insulation. Put some above and some below the roof deck. But splitting the insulation across the roof deck isn't as simple as if you put it all on top because of the potential for moisture accumulation. This is mainly a cold climate issue, where the roof can stay cold and wet for long periods if you get it wrong. In warmer climates, the roof deck may absorb moisture in cold weather but then dry out between cold fronts. If you're in a climate zone with moisture risk, you've got to have the right balance of above-deck and below-deck insulation. What some call the "ratio rule" helps you know what that balance is. Let's look at the science behind the ratio rule and then discuss the rule itself.

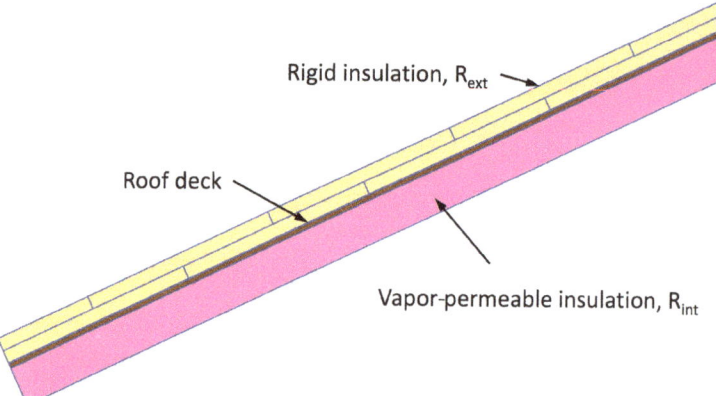

Figure 11.39. *Hybrid roof assembly with some insulation above the roof deck and some below*

When you put insulation on the exterior of a roof (and it's the same for a wall), it keeps the sheathing warmer. That's a good thing. Recall from Chapter 6 that warmer materials are generally drier than cooler materials (Bill Rose's fundamental rule of material wetness). You need a minimum thickness of exterior insulation, though, to keep the average wintertime temperature of the sheathing above the dew point of the air in the attic, about 45 °F. But when you also put insulation beneath the roof deck, it slows the flow of heat from the space below and makes the roof deck cooler. Put enough insulation below the roof deck without increasing the R-value above the deck and you start running into the risk of moisture accumulation in the roof deck again. The answer is to put more insulation on top of the roof deck.

> *You need a minimum thickness of exterior insulation to keep the average wintertime temperature of the sheathing above the dew point of the air in the attic, about 45 °F.*

I know what you're thinking. "If the moisture is coming from inside, can't we use a vapor retarder in the attic to keep moisture from reaching the roof deck?" That's a good thought, but we already have a low vapor permeance above the deck, especially with rigid foam. Think polyisocyanurate with foil facing, extruded polystyrene, or expanded polystyrene on top of oriented strand board or plywood. Consequently, there won't be much drying to the outside. If we limit drying to the inside as well, we could create problems. If the roof deck gets wet and can't dry in either direction, it will stay wet. When it stays wet long enough, it rots.

This also means you have to be careful about what type of insulation you install beneath the sheathing. Fiberglass, cellulose, mineral wool, and others in the "fluffy stuff" category would be fine because they're vapor permeable. Open-cell spray foam also works because it's vapor permeable. Using closed-cell spray foam, rigid foam, or any other insulation that acts as

a vapor retarder is a bad idea. Likewise, putting polyethylene or any type of vapor retarder on the rafters could cause problems.

As with putting all of the insulation on top of the roof deck, you don't want an air gap or ventilation between the insulation and the roof deck, and you don't need a vapor retarder on top of the roof deck. You do need the roof deck to be airtight, though.

The model code (2021 IRC) makes it easy if you want to go with the code-minimum R-value using the prescriptive compliance path. There's a table showing the minimum R-value for the insulation on top of the roof deck for each climate zone. In the warm climates (zones 1 through 3), the minimum is R-5. The minimum is R-35 in climate zone 8. See Table 11.2 for all the numbers.

That minimum R-value on top of the roof deck, though, assumes you're not going above the minimum required total insulation. For example, in climate zone 5, the total ceiling insulation required by the 2018 code is R-49. The minimum on top is R-20. That means you'd have to put R-29 below the roof deck. If you decide to go above code and put R-38 on the underside, now you'll have to add more to the top side, too. But how much? The code tells you only how much you need to put on top when you're doing the required total R-value.

Never fear! This is where the "ratio rule" comes into play, and Table 11.2 has the answer. It shows, by climate zone, the minimum you need on the exterior to prevent moisture accumulation in the sheathing, the total R-value you need to meet the prescriptive insulation requirement, the amount you need to put below the sheathing if you do the minimum on top, and the minimum percentage of the R-value you need on top if you go with higher total R-values.

Here's an example. Say you're building a house in climate zone 5 and want to do a hybrid insulated roof assembly with R-60 total. From the table, you can see you'd need 41 percent of the insulation to be on top of the roof deck. R-60 times 0.41 is 24.6, so that's the R-value you'd

Climate Zone	R_{ext}	R_{total}	R_{int}	Ratio
1	5	30	25	17%
2-3	5	38	33	13%
4C	10	49	39	20%
4A & 4B	15	49	34	31%
5	20	49	29	41%
6	25	49	24	51%
7	30	49	19	61%
8	35	49	14	71%

Table 11.2. *Requirements for minimum exterior R-value (R_{ext}), total R-value (R_{total}), the amount of interior insulation (R_{int}) and percentage of R-value needed on top of the roof deck (Ratio) [adapted from 2021 International Residential Code, Table N1102.1.2 and Table R806.5]*

need on top of the roof deck. With R-25 on top, you'd then install R-35 beneath the roof deck. Those amounts of insulation on either side should keep the roof deck warm enough to stay dry.

The actual numbers in the table, specifically the minimum R-values needed on top of the roof deck, come partly from science and partly from politics. All of the minimums there are probably higher than you need for the science, so if code's not an issue, you can go a bit lower. In the warm climate zones (1-3), you can put whatever minimum R-value you want on top. The colder your climate, though, the closer you'll want to stay to those ratios.

The science behind this is based on keeping the moisture content of the roof deck below 20 percent through the winter. One way to get there is by keeping the roof deck above 45 °F. There are tools available that let you calculate the sheathing temperature with various levels of insulation. For outdoor temperature, use the average temperature for the coldest three months in your location. The indoor temperature is 68 or 70 °F.

Cathedral Ceilings

If you think houses with attics can be tricky, cathedral ceilings can be trickier. These are sloped ceilings with insulation above or below the roof deck and a finished ceiling beneath the rafters. Many of these ceilings have problems with moisture, air, and heat flow, costing the people who live beneath them money, comfort, and repairs. The principles for detailing them correctly are much the same as for the other insulated rooflines discussed in this chapter, but there are some important differences.

The insulation at the roofline can be above the roof deck, beneath the roof deck, or both above and beneath. You can insulate cathedral ceilings with either type of spray foam (closed-cell or open-cell), fluffy stuff, rigid foam, or rigid mineral wool. And cathedral ceilings can work either with or without venting, but the venting decision must be based on the particular details of the cathedral ceiling you're building and the type of roof framing.

The first thing to do is find out what your building code requires for minimum R-value. Next, decide where the insulation will go (above, below, or both) and what type you're going to use. Then, determine whether you're going to vent the ceiling or not. Those decisions all play into the details of the cathedral ceiling type that will work for you.

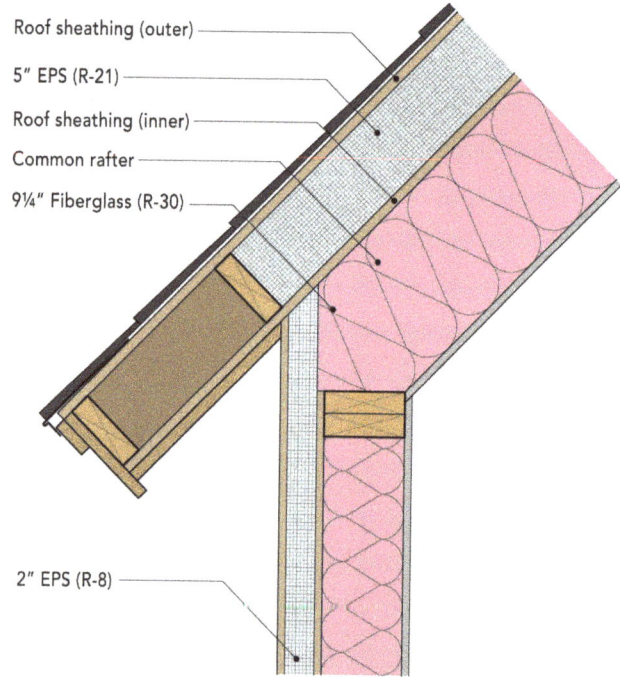

Roof sheathing (outer)
5" EPS (R-21)
Roof sheathing (inner)
Common rafter
9¼" Fiberglass (R-30)
2" EPS (R-8)

Figure 11.40. *Detail for an unvented cathedral ceiling [Credit: Alexandra Baczek, copyright The Taunton Press, Inc.]*

Whether you vent a cathedral ceiling or not depends on the type and location of the insulation. If you put any insulation on top of the roof deck, you don't want to vent the assembly, except maybe above the exterior insulation. If you're using air-impermeable insulation below the roof deck, don't vent the assembly.

If you're insulating with air-permeable insulation only and putting it all below the roof deck, venting between the insulation and the roof deck is both recommended and stupid. It's recommended because indoor air in winter is humid, and indoor air has a nasty habit of finding its way through air-permeable insulation to reach the cold roof sheathing. It's stupid because you have to detail the venting in a way that you probably won't get it built properly. And to make it worse, the details are nigh impossible to do correctly on anything but the simplest roof: a single gable. Even if you don't rot your roof, the energy and comfort penalty of using fluffy stuff in cathedral ceilings can be significant. The takeaway here is that you should forget about

using fluffy stuff against a cold roof deck. Just put air-impermeable insulation against the roof deck, either above or below, and save yourself a lot of grief. (And definitely don't put can lights in there!)

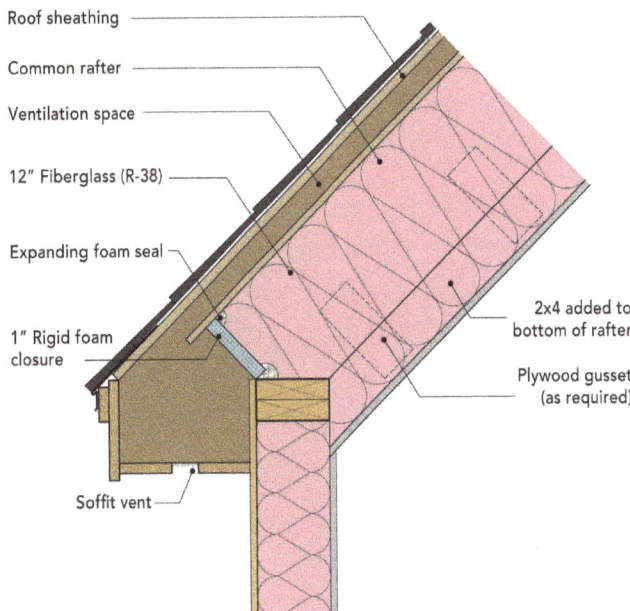

Figure 11.41. *Detail for a vented cathedral ceiling [Credit: Alexandra Baczek, copyright The Taunton Press, Inc.]*

Labels in figure:
Roof sheathing
Common rafter
Ventilation space
12" Fiberglass (R-38)
Expanding foam seal
1" Rigid foam closure
Soffit vent
2x4 added to bottom of rafter
Plywood gusset (as required)

Other Types of Structures

This chapter is not an exhaustive list of all the types of building enclosures, assemblies, or details you can choose when renovating or building a home. Some other options include log cabins, adobe, straw bale houses, tiny houses, aerated autoclaved concrete block, rammed earth, EarthShips, and more. If you're building with some of these other material, assembly, or enclosure options,

apply the basic principles of moisture, air, and heat flow. Insulation and air barriers are generally easy to figure out because you can't reduce heat and air flow too much. Moisture is where things get tricky, but going with common enclosure details can make things easier. The more uncommon the enclosure details you choose, the harder it may be to get everything right and prevent moisture problems.

Chapter Takeaways

- The perfect enclosure would have all control layers outside of the structure.
- Controlling the flow of heat, air, and moisture through foundations, walls, and ceilings can be done in many ways.
- When building a house, you can choose from many different types of structures, each with its advantages and drawbacks.

Part 3
The Mechanical Systems

CHAPTER 12

The Fundamentals of Heating and Air Conditioning

The outdoor air gets cold in winter (although the "cold" in Miami is different from the cold in Calgary). It gets hot and, in some places, humid in summer. A good building enclosure separates us from harsh outdoor conditions, but by itself it's almost never enough to provide the kind of comfort most people want inside their homes. In winter, heat flows from indoors to outdoors. A mechanical heating system adds heat to the indoors to make up for the heat lost. In summer, heat flows from outdoors to indoors, and air conditioners capture that heat and move it back outdoors.

Back in the 1970s when the superinsulation movement got going in Canada and the United States, some of the early pioneers in that field thought that with enough airtightness and insulation, a house could get by without any additional heating or cooling. A lot of this work was done in cold climates, and the idea was that the body heat of the people inside and the heat given off by lights and appliances along with a bit of solar heat collected during the daytime would keep the house warm enough without a heating system. The only mechanical system needed, they thought, would be a ventilation system with heat recovery. Because they were pursuing houses without active heating or cooling, some of these pioneers[21] decided in the early 1980s that a good name for such a house would be "passive house."

A few decades later, we know that, although

> *"What she loved most about America, Eilis thought on these mornings, was how the heating was kept on all night."*
>
> —Colm Toibin

it's possible to build a house without active heating and cooling, it's generally not practical. Even houses certified by Passive House programs have heating and cooling systems. The best way to build or improve a house is to start with the enclosure to minimize the heating and cooling loads and then put in a really good heating and cooling system. But a high-performance heating and cooling system is more than a piece of equipment with a high efficiency rating. It's one that keeps the people warm in winter and cool in summer without them even noticing it. That means they don't hear it. They don't feel air blowing on them from the vents. And no matter where they are in the house, they're comfortable.

Achieving those objectives takes forethought. It takes designers who understand the principles of physics that lead to heat loss and heat gain across the building enclosure, as well as the different forms of heat, and the effects of windows, internal heat sources, and more. In short, it takes design. Let's start there.

---

21. William Shurcliff, PhD, a Harvard physicist and tireless advocate for super-insulated houses, seems to have been the first person to use the term "passive house" in relation to this kind of house.

Designing Good Heating and Air-Conditioning Systems

The only way to get a high-performance heating and air-conditioning system is to design it using proven design methods based on the laws of physics. Unfortunately, far too many homes are saddled with poorly performing systems for which the design decisions were based on rules of thumb. Folklore. Urban legends. Fortune cookie lottery numbers. No, you can't determine how much heating and cooling a house needs from the floor area alone. Nobody can select the right heating and cooling equipment without a proper load calculation. And a 6-inch duct shouldn't be moving 200 cubic feet per minute of air.

> *Far too many homes are saddled with poorly performing systems for which the design decisions were based on rules of thumb.*

It takes time to become proficient at designing heating and air-conditioning systems. The best designers are those who have done enough designs to understand the nuances of the various steps involved and who also get feedback from the performance of their designs. In this chapter, I'll cover the four basic steps of HVAC design, first in overview and then in more detail. I'll wrap up with a discussion of the benefits of using a third-party HVAC designer.

Because so many houses have air conditioning now, I'm going to limit the discussion of heating and cooling systems in this book to those that use air to distribute the heating and cooling throughout the house. Such forced-air systems can be ductless, like wall-mounted mini-split heat pumps, or ducted, like a central heating and air-conditioning system.

The main alternative to forced air is hydronic distribution, where the heating and cooling is distributed via water. Also, I'm going to use the initials "HVAC" (heating, ventilating, and air conditioning) in addition to "heating and cooling" or "heating and air conditioning" even though we won't get to ventilation until Chapter 17.

99 Percent, 1 Percent, Winter, and Summer

The winter and summer design temperatures are also called the 99 percent and 1 percent design temperatures, as explained in this chapter. A quick way to figure out whether the 99 percent design temperature is the winter or summer design temperature is to remember a single word. The same word works for the 1 percent design temperature, too. And the word is: above.

The 99 percent design temperature must be for winter because it's the temperature that a location stays above 99 percent of the time (on average). For example, if the 99 percent design temperature is 17 °F, the actual temperature will be above 17 °F 99 percent of the time. Likewise, the 1 percent design temperature is the temperature a location goes above only 1 percent of the hours in a year.

Easy peasy, right? If you're above a design temperature 99 percent of the time, that must be a low number, so it's for winter. If you go above a design temperature only 1 percent of the time, it's a high number, so it's for summer.

The Four Steps of HVAC Design

The steps described in this section generally apply to both forced-air and hydronic systems, but I'm going to flesh out the details in this chapter with forced-air distribution in mind.

Step 1 – The load calculation: The proper way to design a heating and air-conditioning system is to begin with a room-by-room load calculation. This step determines how much heating and cooling each room in the house needs. It also provides the total heating and cooling loads, which you need to know for step 2. In terms of heat transfer, the load calculation tells you how much heat the house loses in winter and gains in summer. To keep the house comfortable, you need a heating system that can provide as much heat to the house as the house loses when it's cold outdoors, and you need a cooling system that can remove as much heat from the house as the house gains when it's hot outdoors.

The heating load is related only to maintaining the temperature in the house. The cooling load, however, has two components. The larger part of the cooling load is maintaining temperature, as with heating, but in a humid climate an air conditioner must dehumidify, too. The temperature part of the cooling load is called the sensible load, and the humidity part is called the latent load.

Step 2 – Equipment selection: With the heating and cooling loads in hand, the designer reviews and selects the equipment that can provide both the right amount of heating in winter and cooling in summer. Which air conditioner, heat pump, furnace, or boiler is a good fit for the calculated loads and homeowner preferences? With forced-air cooling systems, this selection is critical because every piece of equipment has different characteristics: Sensible and latent capacities, the amount of air moved, and the static pressure in ducts are key attributes applied to the design in the next stages.

Step 3 – Duct design: Once the heating and cooling load calculations and equipment selection are done, the designer tackles the distribution system. The equipment selection determines the total amount of air flow as well as the air flow needed for each room. Now it's just a matter of deciding where the air handler will be located and then delivering the heated or cooled air from there to the individual rooms. The underlying principle of duct design is to use the pressure created by the blower to deliver the correct conditioned air to each room by pushing it against the resistance created by the ducts and fittings.

Step 4 – Duct terminations: The duct design gets the required heating and cooling to a room. The other important part of designing the distribution system is figuring out how best to put that heated or cooled air into the room. The questions answered here are: Where will the supply vents be located? Where will the return grilles be located? What type of register, diffuser, or grille (collectively called vents) will be used? How big does each vent need to be? Good choices at this step eliminate drafts or inadequate mixing.

It's possible to provide enough conditioned air to a room but still have comfort problems because the conditioned air doesn't spread out in the room. Or you might feel uncomfortable drafts from poor supply vent placement. The good news is that a house with a good building enclosure isn't as sensitive to the supply duct terminations.

Figure 12.1. *The HVAC design protocols from the Air Conditioning Contractors of America (ACCA): Manuals J, S, D, and T*

These four steps are covered by four official protocols published by the Air Conditioning Contractors of America (ACCA). They are:

- Manual J: Heating and cooling load calculations
- Manual S: Equipment selection
- Manual D: Duct design
- Manual T: Duct terminations (registers, diffusers, and grilles)

From here on, I'll use the names of these protocols (e.g., Manual J) interchangeably with their descriptions.

Calculating Heating and Cooling Loads

Every house loses heat in winter and gains heat in summer. The laws of thermodynamics tell us that when there's a temperature difference, heat flows from the warmer area to the cooler area. In winter, that heat flow is from indoors to outdoors (heat loss). In summer, the flow is from outdoors to indoors (heat gain). We slow down the rate of heat transfer with air sealing, insulation, and good windows, but unless you're determined to go the super-insulated, passive solar route, you'll still need a mechanical heating system to make up for the heat loss in winter. And unless you live in a place with mild summers, you'll probably want some cooling to get rid of the heat gained on hot days. In a humid climate, you'll also want a way to reduce the indoor humidity in summer.

Before you choose your heating and cooling equipment, you have to know how much heating you need in winter and how much cooling in summer. That's where the Manual J load calculation comes in. But load calculations require time and attention to detail, so many HVAC contractors instead rely on rules of thumb to determine the sizes of the cooling systems they install. Usually, their rule of thumb is based on the amount of conditioned floor area, and contractors in many areas of the United States use 400 to 600 square feet per ton as their rule. Using that rule, a contractor might put a 4-ton air conditioner in a 2,000-square-foot house (500 square feet per ton).

The correct way to size an air-conditioning system is to begin with a heating and cooling load calculation.

The correct way to size an air-conditioning system is to begin with a heating and cooling load calculation. Manual J is the standard way to do this for homes, and it is mandated by most building codes in the United States. It's usually done with computers these days. You enter all the relevant data into the Manual J software, the computer does the calculations, and then you get the results for how much heating and cooling the house needs overall as well as how much it needs for each room in the house.

How Much Heating Do You Need?

The Manual J protocol lays out all the details for calculating winter heat loss and summer heat gain. Heating and cooling loads share a lot of the same types of calculations, but there are some significant differences. I'll cover heating first because it's simpler.

Figure 12.2 shows the major contributions to the heating load. The majority is the heat loss through the building enclosure, including the conductive losses through the floors, walls, and ceilings and the heat lost by air leakage. Another contribution is the heat lost when the heating system or its distribution system (air ducts or hydronic pipes) is in unconditioned space. Heat from the warm air inside a duct or pipe conducts through the duct or pipe and its insulation. Worse, warm air inside ducts can leak out from a poorly sealed duct system. The other contribution to the heating load is intentional air exchange between indoors and outdoors for ventilation or combustion air for heating or water heating equipment.

Heating

Heat loss through:
• floors
• walls
• ceilings
• windows
• doors
• ducts
• air leakage
• duct leakage

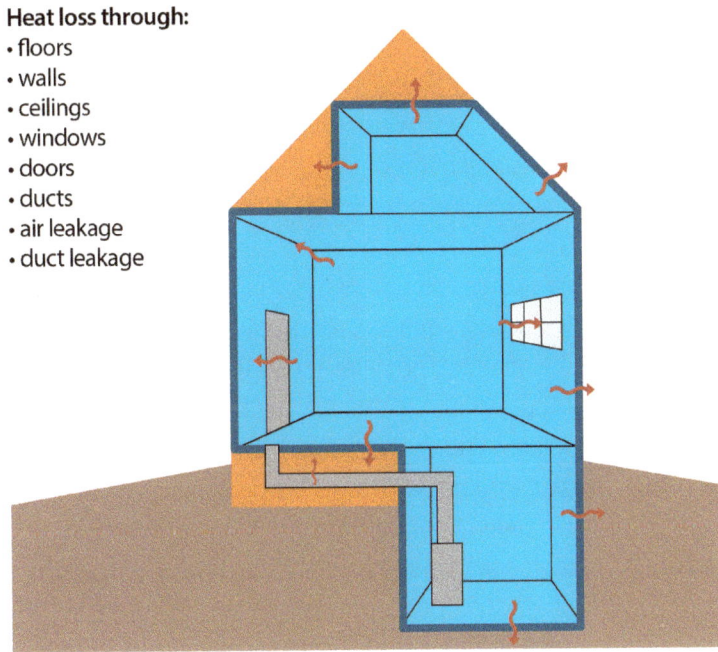

Figure 12.2. *Factors that contribute to the heating load on a house*

Of course, the amount of heat needed also depends on the outdoor and indoor temperatures because the rate of heat flow through the building enclosure depends on the temperature difference. Choosing the right design temperatures is a critical part of the HVAC design process. Let's look first at the outdoor winter design temperature.

Each hour of the year has an average outdoor temperature. By analyzing all those average temperatures, we can find the dividing line between the coldest hours of the year and all the rest of the hours. A year has 8,760 hours total. So, we can find the 87.6 hours, or 1 percent of the total, with the coldest temperatures for a given location. The temperature that separates

those 87.6 hours from the remaining 99 percent of the hours in a year is called the 99 percent design temperature. That's the winter design temperature we use for heating load calculations. (Some designers use the 99.6 percent design temperature, which covers all but 35 hours per year on average.) Because weather varies from year to year, the outdoor winter design temperature is based on temperature data averaged over a 20- to 30-year period.

The standard indoor design temperature for winter is 70 °F. The designer can override both of those design temperatures, but it's usually best not to go too far away from the recommended design temperatures unless you have good reason to change (e.g., a tricky microclimate that differs significantly from the local design temperature, as can happen in mountainous areas).

Now, you may be wondering if something is missing. I've mentioned the ways a house can lose heat in winter, and that determines the size of the heating system. But what about the heat given off by people, pets, lights, and appliances? And what about the heat that comes in through the windows? Don't you get to count that heat so you can put in a smaller heating system? I'm glad you asked.

Let's talk about how a load calculation is done. By choosing the 99 percent design temperature as the outdoor temperature we use in the load calculations, we've made a choice to look at how much heating a house needs for only a few hours a year. The outdoor air is above that temperature 99 percent of the time. The other 87.6 hours per year, the outdoor air will be at or below that temperature. In other words, the heating load we calculate is larger than the actual load the great majority of the time. Occasionally the outdoor temperature will be right on our 99 percent design temperature. For about 87.6 hours per year, the outdoors will be colder than our design temperature (on average).

The reason that's important is that the outdoor temperature is most likely to drop to the 99 percent design temperature at night, and that's when the peak heating load occurs. In most places, the sun won't be shining in the windows at night, so it won't help out with the heating. (In those places where the sun does shine at night, it's summertime so it still may not help.) Also, because the coldest temperatures happen in the wee hours, people are usually in bed, not baking a turkey or playing video games.

So, the answer to those questions is that you don't count the heat added by people, pets, lights, appliances, or sunshine in the load calculation. If your area hits the winter design temperature during the daytime or when the teenagers are playing video games, leaving lights on, and making popcorn, your heating system is called on to do a little less of the heating. But on those cold nights when the teenagers are away, your heating system is able to keep the house warm.

How Much Cooling Do You Need?

Cooling a house is similar to heating in many ways but with some significant differences. As with heating, the biggest part of the cooling load is usually the heat flow through the floors, walls, and ceilings (including windows, doors, and skylights). Much of that heat flow is due to the temperature difference across each part of the building enclosure, but the cooling load includes a form of enclosure heat flow not included in the heating load. In addition, the heat gains from air leakage, cooling equipment and ducts in unconditioned spaces, and ventilation all add to the cooling load.

The drawing in Figure 12.3 shows the major factors that contribute to the cooling load on a house. These include:
- Orientation of the house (because of solar gain through windows)
- Insulation levels of the floors, walls, and ceilings
- Framing details: spacing, depth, and other factors that influence the overall R-value of the building enclosure
- Window types: single, double, or triple pane; low-e coatings; U-factor and solar heat gain coefficient (SHGC)
- Window shading
- Amount of heat and moisture given off by people, pets, lights, and appliances
- Indoor and outdoor design temperatures and humidity

One of the big differences between heating and cooling loads is that the sources of heat we excluded from the heating load do count toward the cooling load. People, pets, lights, and appliances all give off heat, and sunshine coming in through windows and skylights adds heat to the interior. The peak cooling load, therefore, occurs during the daytime, when the sun is shining and the people are active. The solar gain through windows and skylights is a form of radiant heat transfer, and it can overwhelm the cooling load in parts of the house with a lot of glazing. It also can change the timing of the cooling loads. One room may have its peak load in the morning and another in the late afternoon, and that timing can lead to imbalances in indoor temperature if both rooms are controlled by the same thermostat.

The indoor and outdoor design temperatures for cooling work the same way as for heating. The indoor design temperature specified in Manual J is 75 °F. The outdoor design temperature is the temperature that a location exceeds only 1 percent of the time over the course of a year (87.6 hours). It's not the record high temperature for a location or the average high temperature in summer. It's a specific temperature obtained by looking at decades of data. Only 1 percent of the time, on average, will the outdoor temperature be above the 1 percent design temperature.

Cooling

Heat gain through:
- floors
- walls
- ceilings
- window conduction
- doors
- ducts
- air leakage
- duct leakage
- window solar gain
- internal loads

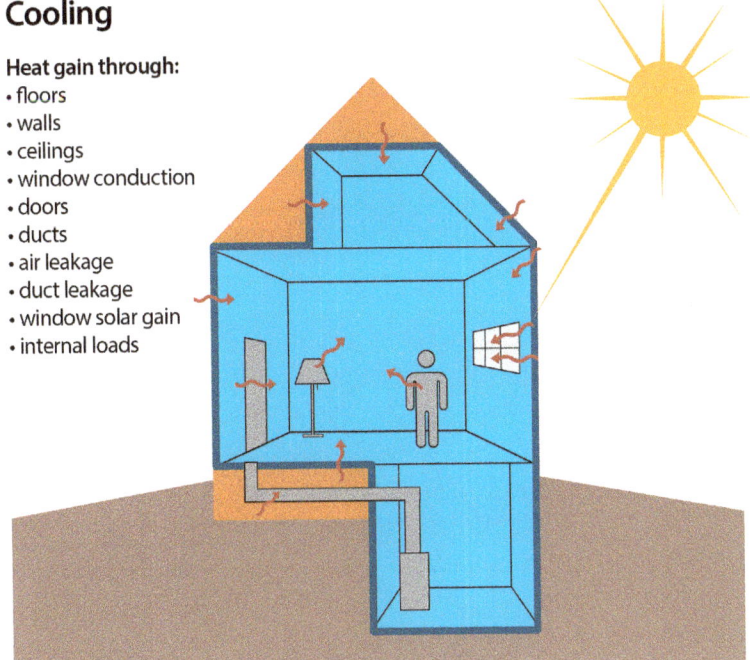

Figure 12.3. *Factors that contribute to the cooling load on a house*

Sensible and Latent Heat

Another big difference between heating and cooling loads is that heating loads deal with only one kind of heat, and cooling loads have two: sensible heat and latent heat. Sensible heat is the kind of heat related to the temperature. When a house gains heat in the summer and the air conditioner is turned off, the indoor temperature will rise. Turning the air conditioner on removes heat and lowers the temperature. The same kind of thing happens in winter with heat loss from the house. In both cases, we're talking about sensible heat, which is all about temperature. To maintain a comfortable indoor temperature in winter, we need to add sensible heat to the house to make up for the heat lost by the house. To maintain a comfortable temperature in summer, we need to remove the sensible heat gained by the house.

> **Latent heat is the heat associated with humidity.**

Latent heat is the heat associated with humidity. Yes, it's a form of heat because it takes energy to remove it, just as it takes energy to remove sensible heat. Water vapor in the air has a lot more kinetic energy than liquid water, so to get that water vapor into the liquid state requires removing the excess kinetic energy. When water vapor condenses on the cold coil of an air conditioner (or dehumidifier), that excess energy is transferred in the form of heat to the cold coil and then the refrigerant making the coil cold. (More on how all that works is coming in the next chapter.) The latent heat in a house comes from two places: humidity entering the house from outside (infiltration or ventilation) or humidity generated inside the house (breathing, cooking, showering, etc.).

The best way to understand the meaning of sensible and latent heat is to think of heating water through a temperature change and a phase change. Let's say you have 1 pound of liquid water that's right at the freezing point, 32 °F. Because a British Thermal Unit is defined as the amount of heat it takes to raise the temperature of 1 pound of water 1 degree Fahrenheit, we can use that relationship (1 BTU per degree) to figure out how much heat it takes to raise the temperature of our pound of cold water all the way to the boiling point. From 32 °F to 212 °F is 180 °F, so it takes 180 BTUs to heat 1 pound of water from freezing to boiling.

Once we get it to the boiling point, however, the relationship changes. As we continue adding heat, the temperature stops rising, and the water begins to boil. The definition of the BTU doesn't help us now because we're dealing with a phase change, not a temperature change. What we need to know is the latent heat of vaporization for water, which is the amount of heat needed to vaporize 1 pound of water. That number is 970 BTUs per pound for water at the boiling point. Figure 12.4 shows the difference between heating 1 pound of water to the boiling point and then boiling that water. A phase change for a given material can involve a lot more heat transfer than a temperature change. (Note that, as with the boiling point temperature, the latent heat of vaporization depends on temperature and pressure. The value of 970 BTU per pound applies to water at its boiling point and vapor pressure at standard atmospheric pressure and temperature.)

Sensible & Latent Heat for Water

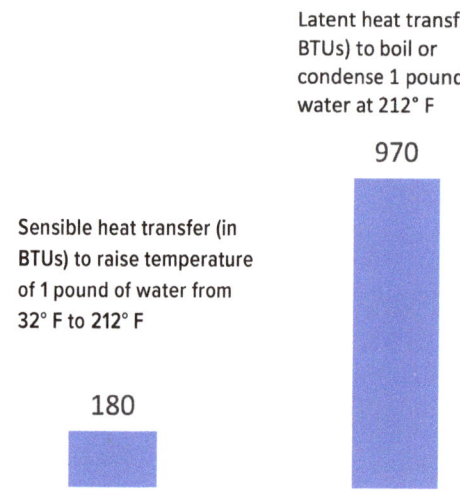

Latent heat transfer (in BTUs) to boil or condense 1 pound of water at 212° F

970

Sensible heat transfer (in BTUs) to raise temperature of 1 pound of water from 32° F to 212° F

180

Figure 12.4. *Starting with 1 pound of liquid water at the freezing point, it takes 180 BTUs of sensible heat to raise the temperature of the water to the boiling point and then 970 BTUs of latent heat to boil that same pound of water.*

If you're wondering what heating and boiling a pound of water has to do with air conditioning, let me connect the dots here. When you turn the processes around, the numbers are the same. Let's say we start with a pound of water vapor at the boiling point, condense it all, and then lower the temperature to the freezing point. To condense the pound of water requires the removal of 970 BTUs of heat. To lower the temperature of that water from the boiling point to the freezing point requires 180 BTUs. It's a reversible process.

When humid air goes through an air conditioner, two things happen. One, the temperature of the mixture of dry air and water vapor decreases. That's sensible cooling. Two, in addition to the temperature dropping, some of the water vapor condenses. That's latent cooling. The actual amount of heat lost from the water vapor will be more than 970 BTUs per pound, though, because it occurs at a lower temperature. Let's make things easy here and just round to a nice even 1,000 BTUs per pound. (It's actually more like 1,060, but we're close enough here.)

The above example of the pound of water is a good illustration of the difference between sensible and latent cooling, but it's not an exact analog for air conditioning. The reason for this came up in the last paragraph. With the pound of water, both the sensible and latent heat transferred only into or out of the water. In air conditioning, the sensible heat transfers from the mixture of dry air and water vapor, whereas the latent heat transfers from the water vapor only. So, the 1,000 BTUs per pound of latent heat transfer still applies, but the 1 BTU per pound per degree does not because that relationship applies only to liquid water, not to a mixture of dry air and water vapor. For air, the relationship is different, but we know how to calculate the amount of both sensible and latent heat removed from air as it goes through an air conditioner. (See "Sensible and Latent Heat Calculations" on page 206.)

Thinking of it in terms of comfort may make more sense, so to speak. In winter, our thermal comfort depends primarily on temperature, with humidity having no great significance. Yes, low humidity does affect our skin and mucous membranes, but winter humidity is more of a health concern than a thermal comfort one. On the other hand, in summer, our thermal comfort can be affected greatly by humidity. I know. I was born in Houston, Texas, and I've lived most of my life in the southeastern United States.

Sensible, Latent, and Total Cooling Loads

Because there are two kinds of heat to remove, cooling loads are presented as two numbers: the sensible cooling load and the latent cooling load. The sensible cooling load is the larger of the two numbers. The total cooling load is the sum of the sensible and latent loads.

In a dry climate like Albuquerque, New Mexico, the latent load can be negative. In terms of its effect on the cooling needed in a house, a negative latent load counts as zero because the cooling system won't need to remove water vapor.

At the other end of the humidity spectrum, a house in a place like Houston can have a high latent load. In a leaky, older house in a humid climate, the latent load might be 30 percent of the total cooling load. Much of the indoor humidity in such a house comes from outdoors. An airtight house in a humid climate can have a latent load less than 10 percent of the total cooling load.

Sensible and Latent Heat

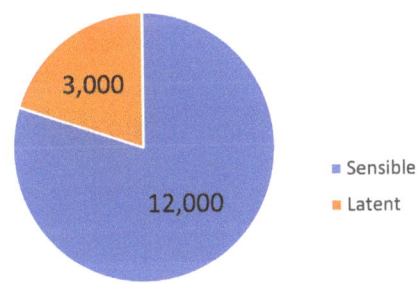

Sensible Heat Ratio (SHR) = 0.8

Figure 12.5. *An example of sensible and latent cooling loads, in BTU per hour: The sensible heat ratio is the sensible cooling load (12,000 BTU/hr) divided by the total cooling load (15,000 BTU/hr).*

Describing the balance of sensible and latent loads with percentages is common in the air conditioning industry. I've been talking about latent load as a percentage of the total cooling load, but that's not the way it's normally given. Instead, manufacturers of air conditioning equipment specify a sensible heat ratio (sometimes called sensible heat fraction), which is the ratio of the sensible load to the total cooling load. A house in Albuquerque with 0 percent

In most cases, the Manual J calculation gives you a cooling load that will be 10 to 20 percent higher than the actual cooling load at design conditions.

latent load would have a sensible heat ratio of 1.0, or 100 percent. That leaky house in Houston with a 30 percent latent load would have a sensible heat ratio of 0.7, or 70 percent.

In dry climates, the latent load isn't an important factor in cooling a house. In humid climates, it's critical. You should never choose an air conditioner for a humid climate home based on the total load alone. To provide enough of both kinds of cooling, an air conditioner has to be able to satisfy both the sensible load and the latent load.

Putting Cooling Loads in Context

Once you have the cooling load calculation results, you have a lot of information to make informed choices on cooling equipment. You know the total cooling load, of course, but you also know how much sensible and latent cooling capacity you need. Also you should know how much heating and how much cooling each room in the house needs if you're planning to design the duct system.

Here's another little nugget for you. If you do a load calculation correctly, without inflating any numbers to add more load, you still end up with a number that's bigger than the amount of cooling the house actually needs. In most cases, the Manual J calculation gives you a cooling load that will be 10 to 20 percent higher than the actual cooling load at design conditions. So, you already have a built-in buffer. There's no need to add extra people to the house or make the window specifications worse than they really are.

Sensible and Latent Heat Calculations

To find the amount of sensible heat energy removed from air passing over a cold air-conditioning coil, we need to know three parameters: the temperature of the air before it's cooled, the temperature of the air after it's cooled, and the air flow rate. The difference in those two temperatures, called ΔT, and the air flow rate, q, combine in the following equations to find the amount of heat removed from the air passing over the coil.

Sensible heat: $h_s = 1.08 \times q \times \Delta T$

To find the amount of latent heat energy removed from air passing over a cold air-conditioning coil, we again need to know three parameters: the humidity of the air before it's cooled, the humidity of the air after it's cooled, and the air flow rate. The two humidities are actually a different measure of humidity than the standard relative humidity we're used to. It's a kind of absolute humidity called the humidity ratio and written w_{gr}, and you can find it by measuring the temperature and relative humidity of the air entering and leaving the coil. The equation for latent heat removal looks similar to the one for sensible heat except for the number out front and the difference in humidity ratio, Δw_{gr}, rather than temperature.

Latent heat: $h_L = 0.68 \times q \times \Delta w_{gr}$

The numbers that appear in the two equations, 1.08 and 0.68, look like constants, but they're not. They depend on the density of air and on the heat capacity. For air-conditioning purposes, the heat capacity can be considered constant. The density of air, however, changes with elevation, so when you do this calculation for a place like Salt Lake City, with an elevation of about 4,200 feet above sea level, you need to make a slight adjustment.

Example: A home is at the standard indoor design conditions of 75 °F and 50 percent relative humidity. Those are the values of temperature and relative humidity entering the air conditioner. The final condition of the air is 55 °F and 90 percent relative humidity. (Even though the air conditioner removes water vapor from the air passing over the coil, the relative humidity ends up higher for the air leaving the air conditioner because the temperature is lower.) Those conditions of entering and leaving air correspond to a ΔT of 20 °F and humidity ratios of 64.92 and 58.09 grains per pound, resulting in a Δwgr of 6.83. The house is at sea level and has a 2.5 ton air conditioner that moves 1,000 cfm of air. Here's how the calculations work out:

$$h_s = 1.08 \times q \times \Delta T = 1.08 \times 1{,}000 \; cfm \times 18°F = 19{,}440 \; \tfrac{BTU}{hr}$$

and

$$h_L = 0.68 \times q \times \Delta w_{gr} = 0.68 \times 1{,}000 \; cfm \times 6.83\tfrac{gr}{lb} = 4{,}644 \; \tfrac{BTU}{hr}$$

These numbers are the rates of sensible and latent heat removal by the air conditioner. The total rate of heat removal is the sum, or 24,084 BTU/hr. The sensible heat ratio (SHR) would be 19,440 ÷ 24,084 = 0.81.

Choosing the Right Cooling Equipment

Selecting heating and cooling equipment is commonly based on guesswork. Of course, when you don't have an actual load calculation for a house, guesswork is really the only way you can select equipment. The next thing to understand about this step is that the load calculation does not tell you what size piece of equipment you need, as you'll see shortly.

For residential HVAC design, the way to choose the right heating and cooling equipment is to use the Manual S protocol from the Air Conditioning Contractors of America. This method describes how to look at the equipment performance data and match it up to the heating and cooling loads for the house. Selecting heating equipment is different from selecting cooling equipment, so let's look at them separately, beginning with cooling.

One of the first things to know about air conditioners is what the heck a ton is. Both heating and air conditioning loads and capacity are measured (using the old-fashioned units used in the US) in BTU per hour. Because of the history of cooling, though, we often use the ton as a unit of cooling capacity. Before Willis Carrier patented the modern air conditioner, melting ice was the cooling method of choice. Naturally, engineers like to quantify things, and they found that the ice would absorb 12,000 BTUs of heat per hour to melt 1 ton (2,000 pounds) of ice in 24 hours. Thus, a ton of cooling capacity equals 12,000 BTU per hour.

With air conditioners and heat pumps in cooling mode, matching equipment to the cooling load is tricky because the cooling capacity of the equipment changes with outdoor temperature. For example, a 3-ton air conditioner probably won't give you 3 tons of cooling at your design conditions. Also, the total capacity of an air conditioner isn't the right number to focus on. You need an air conditioner that will meet both the sensible and latent loads. You might have a house that needs a total of 2 tons of total cooling and 1.8 tons of sensible cooling (SHR – 0.9). A typical 2-ton air conditioner might provide only 1.5 tons of sensible cooling, so you have to go to a 2.5-ton air conditioner to ensure you can meet both the sensible and latent loads.

> *A 3-ton air conditioner probably won't give you 3 tons of cooling at your design conditions.*

In addition to an air conditioner's capacity depending on the outdoor conditions, it also depends on the indoor conditions and other factors like the rate of air flow through the system. The air flow, in turn, depends on which speed the blower is set to run at as well as the amount of resistance in the duct system. These factors all send a good designer to the manufacturer's expanded performance data, which shows the cooling capacity for a piece of equipment at different indoor and outdoor temperatures, different indoor relative humidities, and different air flow rates.

Another aspect of choosing an air conditioner is keeping the total, sensible, and latent cooling capacities all within acceptable limits, as specified by Manual S. For total cooling capacity, the limit varies from 15 to 35 percent higher than the total cooling load, depending on the type of system (single speed, two speed, or variable speed). The sensible capacity needs to meet at least 90 percent of the sensible load. The latent capacity needs to meet 100 percent of the latent load but not more than 150 percent. It's a balancing act, but good HVAC designers understand the importance of these selection criteria.

Choosing the Right Heating Equipment

Heating is different. With some kinds of heating systems (furnaces, boilers, and electric resistance), equipment selection is straightforward. The capacity of this type of heating equipment is constant—no matter how warm or cold it is outdoors. All you need to do is find a piece of equipment that's rated to provide at least as much heating as the load calculation shows the house needs.

With heat pumps, however, the selection process is trickier because the heating capacity changes with outdoor temperature. The colder it is outdoors, the less heat the heat pump can send into the house, as discussed in Appendix G. That means you need to use the manufacturer's data to find the heating capacity at the design temperature for the house. However, even that makes the process sound simpler than it is because many times you end up choosing a heat pump that doesn't have enough heating capacity to meet the heating load at the design conditions. Why? Because you need to select a heat pump based on cooling capacity. Then, if that results in a heat pump that can't meet the heating load, you need an auxiliary heating system.

As with cooling equipment, Manual S specifies limits for the size of heating systems that depend on the type of system. Electric resistance heating systems generally need to be sized between 95 percent and 175 percent of the heating load. Furnaces can be oversized by 40 percent in some cases and by as much as 200 percent in others. Boilers can be oversized by 25 percent to 50 percent. Heat pumps don't have sizing limits for heating because you base the size on the cooling requirements, and then you get what you get for heating. If it's not enough, you add auxiliary heat, as mentioned previously.

Oversized Air Conditioners and Rules of Thumb

Would you buy a pair of pants twice your size so you have that extra capacity just in case you might need it? Sadly, that's how many contractors look upon heating and cooling equipment capacity. Those Manual S sizing limits I discussed don't get used for a great number of the systems installed in homes because many contractors use rules of thumb to decide what size equipment to install. Usually, the rule is based on square footage of conditioned floor area, and contractors in many areas generally use the rule of 1 ton of air conditioning capacity for each 400 to 600 square feet of floor area.

In the HVAC world, people usually talk about load and capacity in terms of square feet per ton instead of tons per square feet. That means that higher square feet per ton numbers mean lower cooling loads and smaller air conditioning systems. It can be a bit confusing, but you'll get used to it quickly. Think of higher square feet per ton numbers as better because they mean you have a more efficient house that doesn't need as much cooling.

Every house is unique. Rules of thumb almost never provide an accurate estimate of the heating and cooling loads.

Anyone who sizes a heating or air conditioning system using a rule of thumb is making two mistakes. First, every house is unique. Rules of thumb almost never provide an accurate estimate of the heating and cooling loads. For example, rotating a house by 90 degrees could change the cooling load by 25 percent or more. (A wall full of windows on one side of the house could do that.)

Second, using a rule of thumb based on floor area conflates the first two steps of the design process: the load calculation and the equipment selection. The reason this rule of thumb method sort-of works is that it's a worst-case procedure. For new, poorly built homes or older, unimproved houses, a heating and cooling system sized this way may have about the right capacity. For most others, they'll be oversized.

Now, you may think having a bigger system is better, but the Texan way doesn't always prevail in HVAC. In the case of air conditioning, oversized cooling systems can result in higher cost. That extra capacity isn't free, you know. It also can reduce comfort. An oversized system blasts the house with cold air for a few minutes and then shuts off. A smaller system blowing air into the living space at a lower rate provides more uniform temperatures and, depending on the details, better air mixing. (These reasons not to oversize also apply to heating.)

What we find is that most newer homes—even in hot climates—have square feet per ton numbers significantly higher than 400 to 600. Even 1,500 square feet per ton or higher isn't unusual. That means a contractor using 500 square feet per ton is installing an air conditioner that's three times larger than it should be. In a 3,000-square-foot house, for example, the rule-of-thumb installer might put in 6 tons of capacity, whereas they probably should be installing only 2 to 3 tons of air conditioning capacity.

My rule of thumb is 1,000 square feet per ton for newer houses. I don't mean that's how I do sizing. That's just my quick check to see if a system might be oversized. If that calculation comes out close to 500 square feet per ton, I assume the installer didn't do a load calculation, or if they did, they fudged the numbers. If it's 1,000 square feet per ton or more, it may be okay. But that applies to the above-grade parts of a house. Basements are often closer to 2,000 square feet per ton for newer houses.

Figure 12.6 shows the breakdown for some of the load calculations we've done at Energy Vanguard recently. The data come from 75 homes, and the numbers plotted here are for the 167 individual zones in the houses. All the homes included here are in hot climates with an outdoor cooling design temperature greater than 90 °F. Only 53 of the 167 zones came in lower than 1,000 square feet per ton. A mere 20 zones were below 700 square feet per ton. That means only 12 percent of the zones in this group might have been okay having equipment sized at 400 to 600 square feet per ton. The average load for these 75 homes, as you can see on the chart, was about 1,200 square feet per ton.

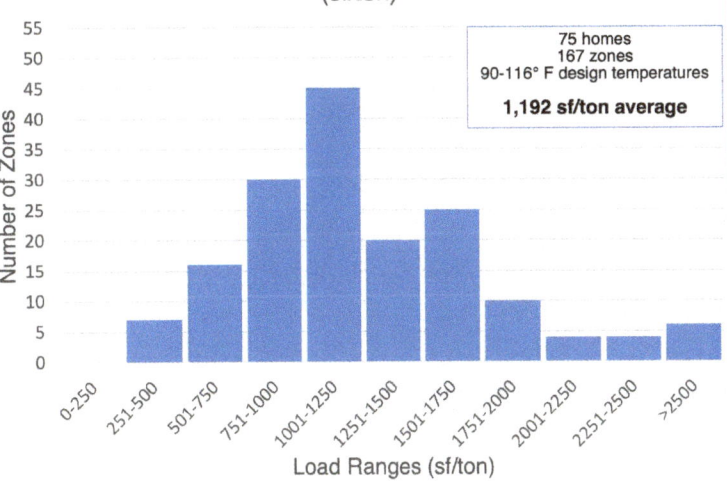

Figure 12.6. *Cooling loads expressed as square feet per ton for houses in hot climates*

"But wait," you say, "cooling load isn't the same as air-conditioner size. Didn't you tell me that you have to adjust the air-conditioner size when you do Manual S?" Why, yes. I did. Most of the time, the air-conditioner capacity will be larger than the cooling load. And I've looked at the same group of homes to see how that comes out. Figure 12.7 shows the results of that analysis. This time there are 63 homes included in the data. (It's not 75 because some of those in the previous chart were jobs where we did only the load calculation and did not select equipment.)

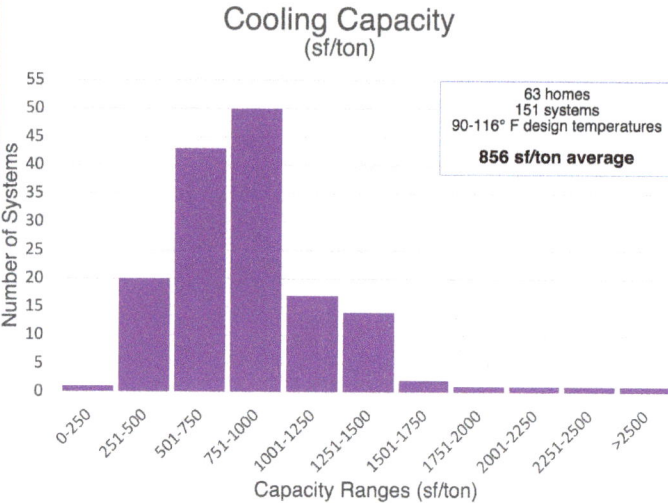

Figure 12.7. *The designed cooling system capacity usually comes out higher than the cooling load.*

In those 63 homes, we selected 151 individual heating and cooling systems. As you can see, the columns have shifted to the left here, indicating that the air conditioning equipment we chose was larger than the loads. That's why the average capacity of the systems we selected was 856 square feet per ton, making our average capacity 28 percent higher than the average cooling load (1,192 square feet per ton). But there's a catch. I used the nominal capacity for the systems we selected. The actual capacity from the manufacturers' expanded performance data would show less capacity. The real square feet per ton number here would probably be about 1,000. And remember, even right-sized systems still will be oversized because Manual J loads are 10 to 20 percent higher than the actual cooling loads.

Here are a few more important points on sizing air conditioners:

1. No matter the number, you shouldn't use square feet per ton to size air conditioners. The average of the data in the load graph is 1,192 square feet per ton, but you can't use that to size air conditioners. You have to do an actual load calculation because it's not just the total cooling load that matters. You need to know how much of it is sensible and how much is latent.

2. If you tell me your load calculations average 400 to 600 square feet per ton for new homes, I assume you're not doing them correctly. Is it possible that homes meeting current building and energy codes need that much air conditioning? Yes. They do if they have a lot of window area, they face west, and/or are in states with weak codes. When Mike MacFarland was a home performance contractor in California, he got 1,500 square feet per ton for retrofits. He built a new net zero energy home and achieved 3,350 square feet per ton. And their design temperature is 102 °F, so don't tell me this doesn't apply in Florida or Arizona.

3. You need room-by-room load calculations to get the air flow right. Contractors who use whole-house rules of thumb rarely get the right amount of conditioned air for individual rooms.

4. The square feet per ton you get from Manual J is a bit inflated, even when you do it correctly. Experienced HVAC designers find that when you follow the Manual J and S procedures religiously, you still end up with 15 to 40 percent excess cooling capacity.

5. It's easy to get whatever load you want when you do a Manual J load calculation. Easy ways to add load include putting in the wrong values for windows, factoring in too many people, using exaggerated design temperatures, and applying the wrong orientation. If you want 500 square feet per ton, it's not hard to produce a Manual J load calculation that gives you that number. But don't do that!

Designing an HVAC system starts with proper sizing. Look at the square feet per ton number you get to see if you're in the ballpark. If the number is less than 1,000 square feet per ton for newer homes, either the number is wrong or the house isn't as efficient as it should be.

Look at the square feet per ton from a load calculation to see if it's in the ballpark. If the number is less than 1,000 square feet per ton for newer homes, either the number is wrong or the house isn't as efficient as it should be.

Designing the Distribution System

Once you've found the heating and cooling loads for the house and have selected the proper equipment to meet those loads, you're ready to think about distributing that heating and cooling throughout the house. The load calculation tells you how much heating and cooling each room in the house needs. The equipment you choose determines how much air will be delivered to each room for heating and cooling. Now it's just a matter of connecting the rooms to the equipment with ducts and then getting the air adequately mixed in each room. That's the purview of Manual D.

Although the concept sounds simple, the reality can sometimes be an exasperating endeavor for both the designer and the installer. Getting a duct from the equipment to a room often means figuring out how to get it past a bevy of obstacles—beams, plumbing pipes, concrete walls—without adding too much resistance. Occasionally, the designer has a slam-dunk, easy-peasy house to run ducts in . . . and then the owner decides to turn part of that attic into another room. Then there's the mechanical room. It seems few architects understand how much space is really needed to set up an air handler and the ductwork around it.

Figure 12.8. *An air handler stuffed into a small closet makes the designer's and installer's jobs much harder. It also makes it likely the system will not perform optimally.*

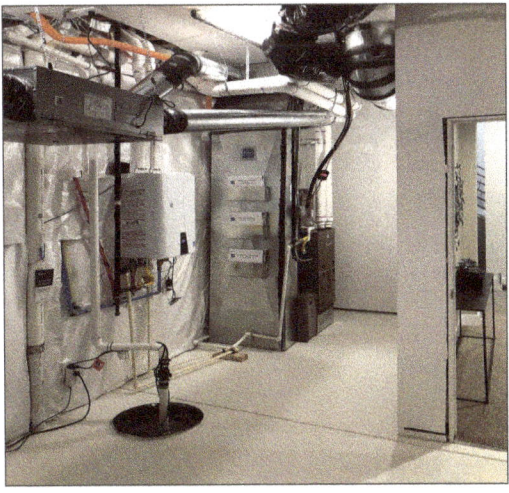

Figure 12.9. *A spacious mechanical room makes good design possible. [Source: US Department of Energy, Building America Solution Center]*

But HVAC designers find a way to make it happen. We rarely get the ideal design, but even in the most difficult houses, we do our best to come up with a design that delivers the conditioned air to where it needs to go—without wasting a lot of energy on excessive resistance in the ducts. And if we can't, we can always hope the client will go for ductless systems.

We'll get into some of the nitty-gritty of duct systems in Chapter 14, but here are a few parameters you need to work with. Of course, we've got to deliver the right amount of air to each room. For that air to deliver the required heating or cooling, it has to be at the right temperature. That's partly a function of the equipment and partly a function of the ducts. We don't want our 55 °F air from the air conditioner to enter the room at 65 °F. Having the ducts properly sealed and insulated helps tremendously, but it's not enough. The velocity of air moving through the ducts must be appropriate for the space those ducts are located in. The air can move relatively slowly when the ducts are in conditioned space, but the air must move faster when the ducts are in an unconditioned space, such as a hot, unconditioned attic in Florida.

Designers and installers also need to understand the properties of different types of ducts and the fittings that connect them. When it's all done well, the air flow, temperature, and pressures in the ducts are where they need to be. And where they need to be is what we'll discuss in Chapter 14.

Consider Third-Party HVAC Design

Getting the heating and air-conditioning systems in a house right isn't easy. In many cases, the HVAC contractor is in charge of the whole process, making all the decisions about the type, size, and location of the equipment and the ductwork. And many houses have HVAC systems that severely underperform. Because there's little thought put into good design, the duct system often has far too much resistance to move the air efficiently. That in turn feeds into the rule-of-thumb equipment sizing method that leads to equipment that's two or three times larger than it needs to be. This slapdash approach is almost guaranteed to result in problems with comfort, humidity, efficiency, and noise.

The resulting indoor environmental quality of such houses is far below what should be acceptable. The only reason it's accepted at all is that contractors who do this kind of work have a lot of company. That makes it easier for them to get away with telling unhappy homeowners that what they're experiencing is "normal."

Some HVAC contractors understand the importance of the design principles described in this book. And they know how to apply them. They start with an assessment of the building enclosure to make their load calculations as accurate as they can. They also probably charge more than rule-of-thumb contractors. Builders or homeowners who find these contractors should use them.

But be wary. Sometimes contractors who promise to do load calculations and have the software to do it can't stop themselves from adding extra load. They do so by increasing the number of occupants; changing floor, wall, or ceiling areas; or using the worst-case orientation for the house. If you apply the 1,000 square feet per ton metric I described earlier, you may be able to tell if they've fudged the numbers for a new home.

If your contractor won't do proper design, your best bet is to hire a third-party designer and then find another contractor willing to implement it. A knowledgeable third-party designer probably won't have a financial interest in selling you bigger equipment or unnecessary add-ons. They also are likely to spend more time on your design than a contractor would. Contractors make money by doing jobs as quickly as possible, and design is often given short shrift in their business model. Third-party designers help you get that step right.

Chapter Takeaways

- HVAC design includes the heating and cooling load calculation, equipment selection, duct design, and grille and register selection.
- Air conditioning requires careful attention to both sensible and latent cooling loads and equipment capacity.
- In most cases, properly using Manual J, the main load calculation protocol in North America, results in loads that are 10 to 20 percent higher than the actual loads.
- Using a third-party HVAC designer may get you a better design for your heating and air-conditioning systems.

CHAPTER 13

Heating and Air-Conditioning Equipment

Heating and cooling a house can be done with different types of equipment. Some equipment only does heating, other equipment only does cooling, and still others do both heating and cooling. You can go all-electric with your choice of equipment, or you can cool with electricity and heat with the combustion of fossil fuels or wood. You also have the option of providing some of your heat with solar energy. I've already stated my preference for all-electric homes back in Chapter 4, but I'll lay out the types of combustion equipment for people who get their heat that way. Also, you can heat and even cool your house using

> *"America is a great country. I've been in the south, in the center and in the north. I like it. Americans are very good people. There's just too much air-conditioning."*
> —Mario Balotelli

water as the fluid that distributes the heating or cooling, but my focus here is on systems that use air distribution, blowing it throughout the house using ducts or directly into rooms using ductless heating or cooling equipment.

Cooling with Air Conditioners and Heat Pumps

An air conditioner is really a heat pump. (So are refrigerators and dehumidifiers.) They all do the same thing: pump heat from a cooler place to a warmer place. They do so with a special substance called a refrigerant (often called Freon because that was the brand of early refrigerants) and mechanical equipment that causes the refrigerant to change its temperature, pressure, and phase. In doing so, it picks up heat in one location and delivers it to another location.

The term "heat pump," however, is used in a more specific way. It's an air conditioner that can cool by running the refrigerant through the system in one direction, and it can heat by running the refrigerant the other way. We'll talk about the heating side of heat pumps later in this chapter, but for the remainder of this section, I'll use the term "air conditioner" to refer to both air conditioners and heat pumps in the cooling mode. Now, let's get back to what these things do.

In summer, a house gains heat from the outdoors, which is hotter, and from indoors, where people, pets, lights, and appliances give off heat. The way to cool a house is to remove the excess heat gained from those various sources. It's like bailing out a boat.

Does this direction of heat flow created by an air conditioner—from indoors to outdoors—jibe with your personal experience? Actually, you may think the opposite. After all, the most obvious effect of an air conditioner is that it blows cold air out of the vents. An air conditioner seems to be adding "coolth" the way a heating system adds warmth. The explanation for that seeming paradox is coming up.

The reality, however, is different. Although a heating system does add warmth, an air conditioner does not add coolth; the net result is that it subtracts warmth. It does so by exploiting the Second Law of Thermodynamics: Heat flows from hot to cold. When room temperature air flows over a cold air conditioner coil, heat flows from the warmer air into the cold coil. Then the refrigerant flowing through the coil carries that heat outside the house and dumps it outdoors. And again, heat flows from hot to cold, so the part of the air conditioner dumping the heat has to be hotter than whatever part of the outdoors is receiving that heat.

How an Air Conditioner Works

Let's dive just a bit deeper into this process. An air conditioner coil gets cold because cold liquid refrigerant flows through it. As heat flows from the air into the coil, the refrigerant picks up enough heat to boil. That's why the cold coil of an air conditioner is called an evaporator coil. We know from our study of latent heat in the last chapter that phase changes like this can transfer a lot more heat than simple temperature changes. That's why we use refrigerants with special properties. They're tuned to boil at just the right temperature and pressure to allow an air conditioner to pick up a lot of heat relative to the amount of refrigerant flowing through the coil.

> **Phase changes can transfer a lot more heat than simple temperature changes.**

But they also need to be able to dump that heat efficiently to the outdoors. Most air conditioners give that heat up to the outdoor air. And they even work in a place like Phoenix, Arizona, when the outdoor temperature is 115 °F. The Second Law of Thermodynamics doesn't care what the temperature is. Heat will still flow from hot to cold   or in this case, from hotter to hot even when the cooler side (the outdoor air in this case) seems really hot to us. To get heat to flow from the outdoor part of an air conditioner into

hot air, the air conditioner has to be hotter. In our example, if it's 115 °F outdoors, the outdoor air conditioner coil dumping heat needs to be hotter than 115 °F.

When heat flows out of the refrigerant in the outdoor coil, the refrigerant changes phase again. It condenses, going from vapor to liquid. The outdoor coil is thus called the condensing coil.

The two parts of the air conditioner we've discussed already are the indoor (evaporator) coil, which picks up heat from inside the house, and the outdoor (condensing) coil, which dumps that heat to the outdoors. But two other parts make the whole thing work. The part that makes the refrigerant cold is the expansion valve. Several different kinds exist, but the basic principle behind all of them is that when a fluid moves from a higher-pressure region to a lower-pressure region, the temperature drops. It's not a perfect analogy, but it's similar to what happens when you use a can of compressed air to clean off your computer keyboard or a cartridge to fill a bicycle tire. As the compressed gas is released from the can or cartridge, it expands and gets cold.

The other essential part of an air conditioner is the compressor. This component does two jobs. It's the pump that pushes the refrigerant through the line, and it's also the temperature elevator. Just as dropping the pressure of the refrigerant lowers the temperature, adding energy to increase the pressure also raises the temperature.

In both cases—temperature drop at the expansion valve and temperature rise at the compressor—the temperature changes are mainly a function of pressure changes, not heat loss or heat gain. That's important because we don't want to lose or gain heat anywhere except at the two coils.

Putting all four parts together, we have the evaporator coil, the compressor, the condensing coil, and the expansion valve. Figure 13.1 shows these four components, along with the state of the refrigerant at different parts of the cycle. There are also fans blowing air over the two coils to aid the heat exchange process and distribute the conditioned air inside the house.

COOLING

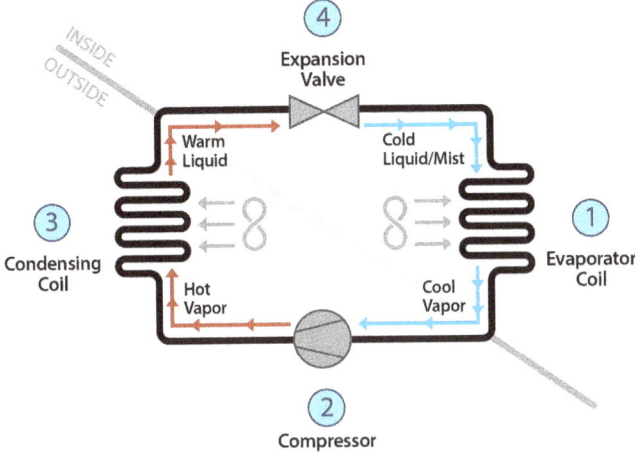

Figure 13.1. *The refrigeration cycle of a typical air conditioner involves four main components: the evaporator coil, the compressor, the condensing coil, and expansion valve. The inside/outside line shows which components are indoors and which are outdoors.*

Heating with Heat Pumps

As mentioned earlier, a heat pump is simply an air conditioner that can run in reverse. An air conditioner uses boiling refrigerant to pick up heat from indoors and then deposit that heat outdoors by condensing the refrigerant. A heat pump does the same thing in cooling mode, but it also can move heat in the other direction when in heating mode.

A lot of people have difficulty grasping the idea that cold outdoor air can heat a house. Really, though, it's no different than what air conditioners and refrigerators do. In all three cases, the cooler space has heat pumped out of it, and that heat is moved to the warmer space. It's easy to understand that an air-conditioned house still has a lot of thermal energy, but how about a

Before we leave this section, let's talk about the thing that makes all this possible: the refrigerant. It goes through a cycle that has it evaporating, being compressed, condensing, and then being decompressed. The pressure, temperature, and phase of the refrigerant all change in the different parts of the cycle, but it always stays fairly close to the saturation point. That is, it's never too far from changing between the liquid and vapor phases.

Changing refrigerants, as we've had to do to reduce damage to the ozone layer and to reduce their global warming potential, isn't an easy thing to do. Each refrigerant has its own operating characteristics. A new one may absorb more heat or operate at higher pressures, for example. Changing refrigerants means using different components (evaporating and condensing coils, compressor, expansion valves) that are suitable for the different properties. It's rare that a heat pump can work well with different refrigerants.

> **A heat pump is simply an air conditioner that can run in reverse.**

refrigerator? To keep the freezer compartment at 0 °F, the system has to keep pumping heat out of there. That's the same thing a heat pump does.

Now, how does extracting heat from cold outdoor air actually work? Well, as with a heat pump in cooling mode, the refrigerant picks up heat by evaporating in the evaporator coil (Figure 13.2). It dumps heat by condensing in the condensing coil. In cooling mode, the evaporator coil is indoors, whereas in heating mode it's outdoors. Again, the Second Law of

Thermodynamics rules the day, so getting heat out of air that's 30 °F means the evaporator coil must be at a temperature below 30 °F.

HEATING

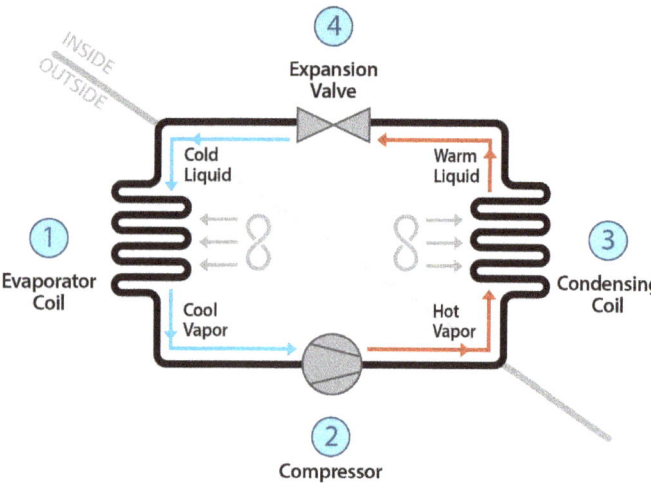

Figure 13.2. *The refrigeration cycle for a heat pump in heating mode: Note the condensing and evaporator coils have switched places, and the refrigerant flows in the opposite direction from an air conditioner. The inside/outside line shows which components are in which box for a split system.*

Generally, the evaporator coil will be about 20 °F below the outdoor temperature in heating mode, so if it's 30 °F outdoors, the outdoor coil will be about 10 °F.

Once heat starts flowing from the cold outdoor air into the colder outdoor coil, the refrigerant warms up and eventually evaporates. As we know, that phase change can absorb a lot of heat, which then travels through the system to the other coil. When refrigerant carrying that extra heat flows to the indoor coil, it first passes through the compressor. That jacks up the temperature so that it's higher than the indoor air temperature. Then the refrigerant passes through the (indoor) condensing coil, where it gives up that heat to the indoor air blowing over the coil. That causes the refrigerant to condense back to a liquid. The next step is the expansion valve, which lowers the refrigerant to a temperature below that of outdoor air, and we start the cycle again.

And that's how you can heat your home using cold outdoor air!

Two Ways of Packaging Air Conditioners and Heat Pumps

We can classify air conditioners and heat pumps in a number of ways. One way to classify them is by the location of the four parts in an air conditioner: evaporator coil, compressor, condensing coil, and expansion valve. If those four parts are all in the same place, it's a package system. If the four components are separated into two boxes, it's a split system.

Package Systems

In "package" systems, all four components are in the same box. The three main types of package systems are window units, package terminal units, and ducted package units. (A package terminal unit is often called a PTAC, short for

package terminal air conditioner. It could just as well be a heat pump, but PTHP is too hard to pronounce.)

The main differences between the three main types of package systems are their size, shape, and use.

- Window units are usually for smaller spaces (although I've lived in houses cooled with a single window unit).
- Package terminal units are the kind of system you often see in hotel rooms. They go through the wall and blow air directly into the room, like a window unit.
- Ducted package units are larger systems that sit completely outdoors and have two large ducts for return and supply air.

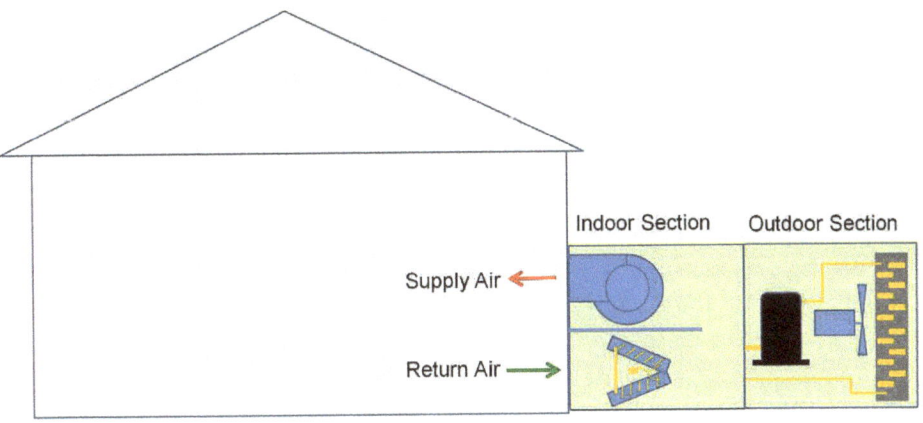

Indoor Section   Outdoor Section

Supply Air

Return Air

Figure 13.3. *A package unit air conditioner or heat pump has all mechanical components and refrigerant in one box that sits outdoors. The ducts go into the house behind the sheet metal in this photo. [Source: US Department of Energy, Building America Solution Center]*

Package systems have some advantages. Because everything is in one box that sits outdoors, they take up less space indoors. They also don't need to have the refrigerant level adjusted when installed because everything is connected and self-contained from the factory, like a refrigerator.

Also, package systems have disadvantages. For window units and package terminal units, the big drawback is noise because the compressor, the biggest noisemaker in air conditioners, sits right there in the window or wall. One drawback for ducted package units is that at least a little bit of the conditioned air side of the system is outside the building enclosure, so it needs to be well insulated. Another negative is that either there's a pretty big hole in the building enclosure for those ducts, or the ducts stay outside the building enclosure.

Figure 13.4. *The supply and return ducts for a package unit go through the wall and attach directly to the outdoor unit.*

Split Systems

The other type of air conditioner is a split system. As its name makes obvious, the four components aren't all in the same place. Rather than having everything all in one box like a package unit, a split system has two boxes: one indoors and the other outdoors. The best names for these two pieces are—wait for it—the indoor unit and the outdoor unit. They have other names, too. The indoor unit (or parts of it) is called the air handler, fan coil, or evaporator coil. The outdoor unit (or parts of it) is called the condenser, condensing unit, and compressor. Location-based names generally work best, though, because in a heat pump, the locations of the evaporator and condensing coils switch when you go from cooling to heating. (See previous section.) Let's look at these two boxes now.

Figure 13.5. *The supply and return ducts for a package unit go through the wall and attach directly to the outdoor unit.*

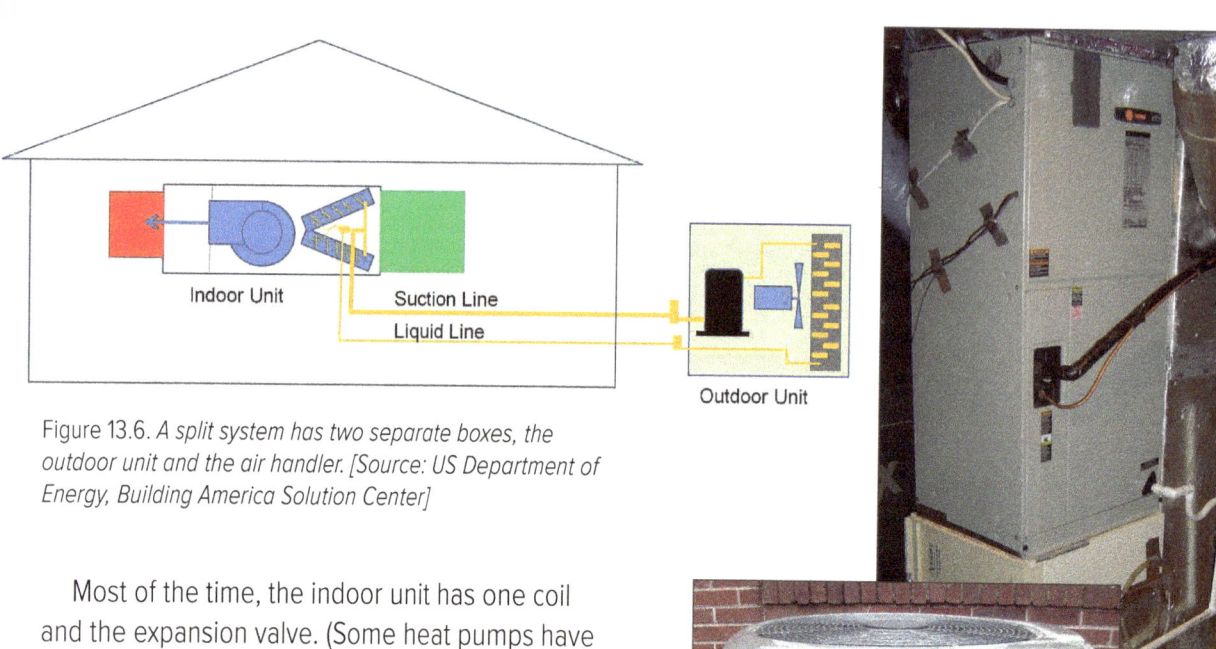

Figure 13.6. *A split system has two separate boxes, the outdoor unit and the air handler. [Source: US Department of Energy, Building America Solution Center]*

Most of the time, the indoor unit has one coil and the expansion valve. (Some heat pumps have the expansion valve in the outdoor unit.) Some indoor units also include the fan that blows air across the coil, pulling the air first through the return ducts and then sending it to the house through the supply ducts after cooling or heating the air as it moves across the coil. Other times, the indoor part of the air conditioner is a smaller box with the coil and the expansion valve, and it's coupled to another box that contains the blower. That second indoor box with the blower is usually a furnace.

The outdoor unit contains the compressor and the other coil (and in some cases, the expansion valve). It usually sits in the backyard or on the side. It's a metal box that makes noise and blows hot air out through a grille on hot summer days. It's connected to the indoor unit with electricity and two copper refrigerant lines.

One big advantage of a split system is that you can put the noisiest part of the system, the compressor, in an isolated part of the yard where you won't hear it much (but your neighbors may if it's on the side of the house). The indoor unit is relatively quiet, and, with good design, it should be practically unnoticeable.

Figure 13.7. *The air handler (top) is connected to the outdoor unit (bottom) with refrigerant lines and electrical connections.*

Separating the components in a split system can be more efficient, too, because the heating and cooling parts of the equipment can be closer to where the heating and cooling are needed. A drawback is that the amount of refrigerant needed will vary from system to system because the length of the refrigerant lines varies from system to system. Having site-modified refrigerant lines also increases the likelihood of refrigerant leaks.

Three Types of Air-Conditioner or Heat-Pump Capacity

A second way of categorizing air conditioners and heat pumps is by how much heating and cooling they can provide. By how much, I'm not referring to, say, a 2-ton versus a 3-ton air conditioner. What I'm talking about is whether it provides a fixed capacity when it's running (single-stage) or has the ability to change the amount of heating or cooling it puts out (multi-stage or variable capacity). Most homes have fixed capacity systems, but mini-split heat pumps are starting to gain traction here in the United States, as are multi-stage systems. What does all this mean? Let's find out.

Fixed-Capacity Heat Pumps

A fixed-capacity (single-stage) heat pump has only two modes: on or off. When the thermostat in a house says it's time for more heating or cooling, it kicks on and ramps up to its full speed almost instantly. When the thermostat is satisfied, the power shuts off, and the system sits idly, waiting to roar up to full capacity again upon the next signal from the thermostat. You can think of a single-stage heat pump as a car without gears or accelerator. When you turn it on, you're going full speed. The only way to stop is to turn off the engine. That would be a terrible way to design a car, but it's sort of okay for heating and cooling equipment.

The advantage of fixed-capacity (single-stage) equipment is simplicity. It's either on or off, so the controls needed are straightforward. Because this type of system is so common in homes, finding people to work on it and getting parts for it are relatively easy, too. It's also usually the least expensive of the three types we're discussing here.

The biggest disadvantage of a fixed-capacity (single-stage) heat pump is that it's terrible at matching the actual load on the house. Remember the three types of heating and cooling loads discussed in Chapter 12. A single-stage system is oversized for most of the year, sometimes by a huge amount.

That oversizing is the source of another downside of fixed-capacity systems. When the system is putting out a lot more heating or cooling than a house needs, people inside the home get blasted every time the system comes on. That's not a recipe for thermal comfort.

And that's where the other two types come in.

Multi-Stage Heat Pump

Because the heating and cooling loads on a house go up and down throughout the course of a day as well as through the seasons, it makes sense to have heating and cooling equipment that can change their capacity. The simplest way to do that is with a two-stage system. Such a piece of equipment has two modes of operation: a low capacity (or speed) and a high capacity. Imagine the car from our previous example that has no gears or accelerator. The engine is either on or off, and when it's on, it's going full speed. A two-stage heating or cooling system is like that except it now has two engines. You can turn one engine on to go one speed, or you can turn them both on when you need to go faster.

Because the preponderance of heating hours and cooling hours occurs with a house under part-load conditions, a properly sized two-stage system will operate at its lowest capacity most of the time. On the really cold or hot days, the system will shift to the high-capacity mode because the demand is higher.

A two-stage system, therefore, offers a huge improvement in efficiency and comfort over a

Mini-Split Heat Pumps

Ah, mini-splits. They're all the rage in the world of high-performance homes. But what exactly are they? Unfortunately, the terminology around this technology is confusing because it's used inconsistently by different people. Let's start at the beginning.

The term "mini-split" itself refers to a split-system air conditioner or heat pump with a smaller capacity than conventional systems. In that sense, a mini-split is just what its name says it is.

Where it gets confusing is in the different ways manufacturers make these lower-capacity, split-system heat pumps. For example, a mini-split can have a conventional fixed-capacity compressor or an inverter-driven variable capacity compressor. So, a mini-split could be a conventional heat pump that's just smaller. Or, it could be a smaller heat pump with variable capacity. No one talks about the former type, though, so when you hear the term "mini-split," you should think of the inverter-driven compressor with variable capacity.

Another confusing area is that with this type of heat pump, the outdoor unit can be connected to one indoor unit (referred to as one-to-one), or it could be connected to multiple indoor units. Some people distinguish these two types by using the term "mini-split" only for the one-to-one configuration and "multi-split" whenever you have more than one indoor unit on a single outdoor unit.

And then there's the issue of the type of indoor unit. Some are ductless, and they come in different flavors: wall-mounted, ceiling cassettes, and floor-mounted. Others are ducted, and they come in horizontal ducted or multi-position types. Some people use the term "mini-split" only for ductless indoor units. Others refer to any type of split system with smaller capacity as a mini-split, no matter whether the indoor unit is ducted or ductless.

I use the term "mini-split" for all of the above. Since mini-splits with fixed-capacity compressors are rare, you don't really need to worry about confusion there. If you're talking to someone about mini-splits, you should be able to tell from the context how they use the term. If not, ask them to clarify.

Inverter-driven mini-split heat pumps are the future for high-performance homes. I've got them in my home, and it's what we specify in a majority of our HVAC design jobs at Energy Vanguard. Their high efficiency and variable capacity that can ramp down to very low values are perfect for super-insulated, airtight homes, and they work well in less efficient homes, too. They give you a couple of other benefits, too. Their lower capacity means you can zone your heating and cooling with separate pieces of equipment. And using separate pieces of equipment provides resilience. If one heat pump stops working, you can still heat or cool the parts of the house that have operable equipment.

One final point here concerns the one-to-one configuration. If you want the highest efficiency, the best zone-to-zone control, and the most resilience, use only one indoor unit on each outdoor unit. Multi-split systems can work fine, but they're not as good as one-to-one setups.

fixed-capacity system, but it doesn't end there. Multi-stage equipment also comes with three, four, or even five stages. Manufacturers do this by using clever compressor tricks. Because heat is moved by the refrigerant, multi-stage equipment simply needs the ability to run the refrigerant through the system at different rates.

When you start looking at multi-stage equipment, an important concept to understand is turndown ratio. It's the ratio of the highest to the lowest capacity, and it's a good number to know when picking equipment. For example, one 4-ton, 5-stage air conditioner runs at 1 ton of capacity on its lowest stage. The turndown ratio is 4 ÷ 1, or 4-to-1. That's a good turndown ratio. The same manufacturer also offers a 2-stage system with a low end that's 83 percent of maximum. With such a small difference between low and high stages, that 2-stage system doesn't provide much of an advantage over a single-stage system and may not be worth the extra cost.

Variable Capacity Heat Pumps

As you go from two stages to several stages, the capacity difference between any two stages gets smaller and smaller. If your mind goes to calculus when you hear about gaps getting smaller, you may be thinking about that gap becoming infinitesimally small. And yes, it's been done. That's the variable capacity system we discuss now.

In a variable capacity system, instead of having a discrete set of stages, this type of system can vary its capacity continuously between its low end and its high end. They usually modulate with special electronic controls on the compressor, and the term "inverter-driven compressor" applies to most variable capacity systems. Theoretically, these systems can have turndown ratios as low as 10-to-1. In the real world, getting down to 4-to-1 is good.

Perhaps the most common type of variable capacity heat pumps is mini-split heat pumps. In addition to being able to vary the capacity continuously, mini-splits also come in smaller total capacity than do conventional systems. Conventional systems generally don't come in sizes smaller than 1.5 tons (18,000 BTU/hr), but you can get a mini-split as small as 0.5 ton (6,000 BTU/hr), and smaller ones are coming soon. And that's good because it allows for better zoning in a house. You can use one

system to heat and cool the bedrooms, one to do the common areas, and a third for a sunroom with lots of windows—and thus lots of cooling load.

Aside from the advantage of smaller capacities, mini-splits have surprisingly quiet outdoor units. You have to get right next to them to hear anything, and even then it's barely audible. Another advantage is efficiency. The ductless units have SEER ratings and HSPF that beat any conventional fixed-capacity or multi-stage system.

> *Mini-splits have surprisingly quiet outdoor units. You have to get right next to them to hear anything, and even then it's barely audible.*

The biggest disadvantage of variable capacity heat pumps is cost because these systems can be significantly more expensive than fixed-capacity systems. Also, even with the low-capacity units available, ductless mini-splits are often still too large to put one in every room because they'll be running at the bottom end of their capacity range. One final potential drawback is that some of the ducted mini-split air handlers have blowers that can't produce much pressure. They can work fine, though, with proper duct design and installation.

One other issue to mention regarding both multi-stage and variable capacity systems is air flow. When the compressor modulates the refrigerant flow, both the indoor and outdoor blowers need to be able to modulate as well. Ideally, when the system is operating at 50 percent of its full capacity, the blower also would be at 50 percent. That doesn't always happen, though. (Related: See "Speed versus Capacity" on page 222.)

Speed versus Capacity

The world of buildings and mechanical systems is full of confusing terminology. When we talk about single-stage, multi-stage, or variable capacity, it's clear—or it should be—that we're referring to how much heating or cooling the system can produce. Many people in the industry, however, use the terms single-speed, multi-speed, and variable speed to describe these systems. Before I knew better, I thought those terms referred to the fan speed. That's why I prefer to use the words "stage" and "capacity" in these descriptors.

Here's another confusing aspect of using the word "speed." A single-stage air conditioner has a fan that operates on a single-speed. But that fan has wiring that allows it to be set at different levels (e.g., low, medium, and high). Yes, once you know the lingo, it's clear, but why not use language that's less confusing to people who are never going to be experts? I'll stick with stage and capacity when talking about rates of heating and cooling, and I'll reserve the term "speed" for fans and air flow.

Heat Sources and Sinks for Air Conditioners and Heat Pumps

Air conditioners and heat pumps move heat from one place (the source) to another place (the sink). In cooling mode, they move heat from indoors (the source) to outdoors (the sink). In heating mode, they move heat from outdoors (the source) to indoors (the sink). But outdoors is a big place, and we have options for where to dump that heat in summer when it's the sink or where to pull it from in winter when it's the source. Two forms of heat pump technology have arisen, based on what acts as the sink or source: the outdoor air or the ground or water.

Outdoor Air as Source or Sink

The lion's share of air conditioners and heat pumps use the outdoor air as the heat sink or source. That metal noisemaker out in the yard in summer is dumping heat from indoors into the outdoor air, as discussed earlier in this chapter. The trick is to make the outdoor coil hotter than the outdoor air, which is the job of the compressor. In winter, the outdoor unit extracts heat from cold air by making the outdoor coil colder than the outdoor air. This type of system is called an air-source air conditioner or heat pump. (The word "source" here refers to the outdoor air being either a heat source or a heat sink.)

The big advantage of using outdoor air as the sink or source is cost. Compared to systems that use the ground or water as the sink or source, air-source heat pumps are far less expensive. It's not so much the equipment itself, but the connection to the sink or source that makes these systems expensive or not. One disadvantage is that air has less heat capacity than the ground or water, so it's harder to dump or draw heat there. Related, air temperature can change significantly, and that affects the capacity and efficiency of air-source equipment. The hotter it is on a summer afternoon, the more energy an air conditioner will use to dump heat into that hot air. The same applies to drawing heat from outdoor air on those really cold nights. And of course, the disadvantage known to everyone who has been around them is noise. Conventional air conditioners and heat pumps can be annoying, especially when they come on with a bang. Mini-splits, however, are nearly inaudible.

Ground or Water as Source or Sink

Because of air's relatively low heat capacity, a clever person some time ago got the idea to use the ground or water as the outdoor heat sink and source for heat pumps. Soil, rock, or water has a much higher capacity for storing thermal energy than air, so both the efficiency and capacity of a ground- or water-coupled heat pump can be higher than they are for an equivalent air-source heat pump.

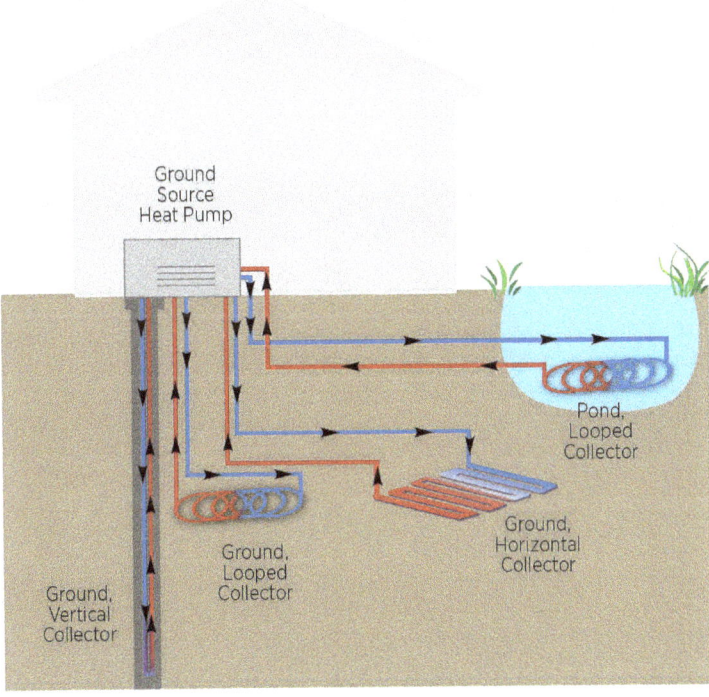

Figure 13.8. *A ground-source heat pump, showing different types of collectors that exchange heat with the ground or water [Source: US Department of Energy, Building America Solution Center]*

Also, as we know from the past section, the efficiency and capacity of an air-source heat pump can vary greatly as the weather changes. The ground temperature, however, is fairly constant year-round once you get about 20 feet below the surface, and it's roughly equal to the average air temperature of the location.

Those cooler-than-summer-air temperatures and warmer-than-winter-air temperatures make ground- or water-coupled heat pumps more efficient than equivalent air-source heat pumps. They also can keep the capacity much more constant over a heating or cooling season.

Most of these systems use the soil or rock in the ground as the source or sink, but some use groundwater or surface water. Engineers have different names for them based on the way they exchange heat, but the two names you're most likely to hear are geothermal heat pump and ground-source heat pump. They're most often called geothermal heat pumps, but that name is inaccurate since they're not tapping into the heat generated by Earth's inner layers. There's no steam, no geysers, no magma. Let's dispense with that marketing name and use a more accurate term: ground-source heat pump. Even that isn't the best name, though, because sometimes the ground acts as a heat sink, not a heat source. The best name would be ground-coupled heat pump.

The basic idea for the outdoor heat exchange in most systems is to circulate a fluid through a closed loop of pipes that are in contact with the ground. Those pipes can be in the form of slinky loops buried horizontally in trenches or vertical pipes in bore holes that can be hundreds of feet deep (Figure 13.9). The fluid in the pipe is a mix of water and antifreeze that's moved by a circulator connected to the indoor unit. The pipes are in contact with soil, water, or a special grout to aid heat transfer. When the heat pump runs, the water-antifreeze mixture moves through the pipes, transferring heat from the fluid to the ground in summer and from the ground to the fluid in winter. The cooled or heated fluid then goes back to the indoor unit to participate in the indoor heat exchange, which works the same way as in an air-source heat pump.

Moving that water-antifreeze mixture through the pipes is also the hidden weakness in this type of heat pump. With air-source heat pumps, the fan blowing air over the coil doesn't have to do a lot of work. Air is light. Water is heavy. Ground-source heat pumps exchange heat more efficiently, but they use more energy moving the working fluid than air-source heat pumps. That extra energy use reduces the efficiency of the whole system.

Figure 13.9. *A bore hole for a ground-source heat pump: A pipe carries a working fluid down and back up, exchanging heat with the ground along the way.*

There are many ways to design ground- or water-coupled heat pumps. Some have one loop for both the indoor and outdoor heat exchange, and it contains refrigerant. Others have two separate loops: the outdoor loop with a water-antifreeze mixture and the indoor loop with refrigerant. Still others have a closed loop for the outdoor part. Some have open loops, which are more efficient but also banned in some places because they can deplete aquifers or contaminate wells.

The advantages of ground-source heat pumps come with a hefty price tag. The indoor components are mostly the same as air-source units, but the outdoor heat exchanger can be pricey. Drilling a lot of vertical bore holes can double the cost compared to air-source heat pumps . . . and that's if you're lucky. It could cost four or five times as much, depending on how many bore holes you need and whether or not they hit rock when they're drilling. Tax credits can lower the cost significantly, though, so find out what's available if you're considering this technology.

In short, ground-source heat pumps can make sense in some cases, but inverter-driven air-source heat pumps are often the better way to go.

Air-Conditioner and Heat-Pump Efficiency

Efficiency is something we can quantify with simple arithmetic. If we know what it is that a device is producing (the output) and what it takes to make it work (the input), we can calculate the efficiency. Really, it's just a measure of how much bang you get for your buck. Here's the equation:

$$Efficiency = \frac{Output}{Input} = \frac{Bang}{Buck}$$

In the world of air conditioners, heat pumps, and furnaces, a bewildering array of efficiency terms exists. But they all share in common that they're a measure of how much bang you get for your buck: the output energy (heating or cooling provided) divided by the input energy (electrical or combustion energy).

The various definitions differ in a number of ways because the devil's always in the details. The output and input values used in the equation above depend on the operating conditions. For example, with the thermostat set to cool a space to 72 °F, the output cooling and input electricity will both be different than if the thermostat is set to 75 °F. That's why the different efficiency terms below are defined precisely in standards.

Without getting into all those details, we can look at some of the ways the efficiency definitions differ. For example, some definitions apply to the instantaneous, steady-state ratio of output to input while a system is operating and don't account for on-off cycles or changes in efficiency over the course of a season or a year. Others do factor in those annual or seasonal changes, and the name of the rating indicates that with the words "annual" or "seasonal." And then there's the real-world versus rated efficiency, which is similar to real-world versus rated R-value we talked about in Chapter 10. Here are the main efficiency ratings you might run across when it comes to most heating and air conditioning equipment.

Seasonal Energy Efficiency Ratio (SEER)

This rating is a measure of the cooling efficiency of air conditioners and heat pumps. It averages the output and input over a typical cooling season. In the United States, the calculation is cooling output in BTUs divided by electrical input in watt-hours. Even though we're dividing energy by energy, we don't end up with a unitless quantity because the two types of energy are measured in different units. You may never see the units stated, but when you see an air conditioner listed as 13 SEER, you now know that means the efficiency is 13 BTU per watt-hour. The higher the number, the more efficient the cooling system. The minimum SEER required in the United States is 13 or 14, depending on whether you're in a colder or warmer part of the country and on what type of cooling system you have. (See Table 13.1)

Heating Season Performance Factor (HSPF)

When an air-source heat pump runs in heating mode, the same calculation as above results in the Heating Season Performance Factor. You could think of HSPF as a wintertime SEER, and SEER as a summertime HSPF. As with SEER, higher HSPF means greater efficiency. It's the heating output in BTUs divided by the electrical

input in watt-hours. Because it takes more energy for heat pumps to heat in winter than it does for them to cool in summer, the HSPFs are lower than the SEERs. The other difference is that HSPF is harder to pronounce than SEER.

Annual Fuel Utilization Efficiency (AFUE)

Furnaces and boilers have a different efficiency rating because the output results from burning a fossil fuel (natural gas, propane, or heating oil) rather than using electricity to move heat around. And because the output and input are both measured in the same units, we end up with a percent efficiency. For example, a 95 AFUE furnace will deliver 95 BTUs of heat for each 100 BTUs of fossil fuel energy that go into the furnace. Keep in mind that this isn't the instantaneous, steady-state thermal efficiency of the furnace because the word "annual" indicates that the output and input are averaged over a typical heating season.

Furnaces and boilers come in two types, as we'll discuss in the next section. The standard type operates at an efficiency of about 80 AFUE, and the high-efficiency condensing units are in the 90 to 98 AFUE range. An AFUE of 100 is the unattainable theoretical maximum.

Also, I've indicated that this rating applies to heating equipment that burns fossil fuel, but it's also used in a couple of other places. Wood-burning heating systems can be rated in AFUE, as can the so-called electric furnace, which uses electric resistance heat. Because electricity can be converted to heat with an efficiency of 100 percent, if you see 100 AFUE on the yellow Energy Guide label on a piece of equipment, that means you're looking at an electric furnace.

Coefficient of Performance (COP)

The coefficient of performance is different from the three previous efficiency ratings in that it's not averaged over a whole heating or cooling season. It can be used for heat pumps, air conditioners, and refrigerators (different kinds of heat pumps, really), but unlike SEER and HSPF, the calculation uses the same units for the input and output. And unlike AFUE, it's not capped at 100 percent. That's because heat pumps aren't turning a fuel into heat; they're using electricity to move heat from one place to another.

In fact, a COP of 1, which is like 100 percent efficiency, would not be good because most heat pumps have COPs that range from 2 to 6. An electric furnace has a COP of 1 because it turns one unit of electricity into one unit of heat. A typical heat pump in heating mode might have a COP of 3 at design conditions, meaning it moves 3 units of heat into the house for each unit of electricity consumed to do the work. On a really cold night, however, the COP might drop to less than 2. Even in the coldest weather, heat pumps in heating mode have a COP that's almost always above 1. If you don't see the implication of that on the use of the emergency heat in your heat pump, hang on and we'll come back to it in the section on electric resistance heat later in this chapter.

Energy Efficiency Ratio (EER)

The energy efficiency ratio is for cooling efficiency and is defined almost the same way as SEER. The difference is that EER is calculated for specific operating conditions of indoor and outdoor temperature and relative humidity, whereas SEER is calculated over a typical cooling season, averaging in the temperature changes and cycling losses. Ground-source heat pumps have their cooling efficiency rated in EER and their heating efficiency measured in COP. They're both really the same calculation. It's simply a matter of whether you express the output and input in the same units (COP) or different units (EER). EER values are lower than SEER, with a 13 SEER air conditioner having an EER of about 11.

System Type	Efficiency
Split-system air conditioner	14 SEER northern states 15 SEER southern states
Package air conditioner	14 SEER
Split-system heat pump	15 SEER/8.8 HSPF
Package heat pump	14 SEER/8.0 HSPF
Furnace	80 AFUE
Ground-source heat pump, closed loop	17.1 EER/3.6 COP

Table 13.1. *Minimum efficiency requirements for heating and cooling equipment in the United States*

Understanding HVAC Efficiency Ratings

Let's make some sense of all this now. The first thing to know is that when you see a piece of heating or cooling equipment labeled with a particular number in one of those efficiency ratings, that's a fixed value based on operating conditions defined in a standard. For example, SEER is calculated using set indoor conditions (80 °F and 50 percent relative humidity) and a range of outdoor temperatures with an amount of air-conditioner runtime specified for each temperature range. It doesn't factor in actual climate data for different locations. So, if you have a 13 SEER air conditioner, you're unlikely to get 13 BTU/hr of cooling for each watt-hour of electricity you use because the conditions at your house are different than the test conditions for the rating. The same is true for HSPF, AFUE, COP, and EER values given in product specifications. When you see those ratings on product labels, they're not going to help you to figure out exactly how much energy you'll use. What they are good for is helping you compare the efficiency of one piece of equipment to another of the same type.

And speaking of types of heating and cooling equipment, these different efficiency ratings are used for different kinds of equipment. SEER and EER are for cooling systems, HSPF and AFUE are for heating systems, and COP could be used for heating and cooling systems—although it's usually applied to heating. Larger air-source cooling equipment is covered by SEER. Smaller air conditioners (window units) and ground-source heat pumps use EER for cooling. HSPF is for heat pumps in heating mode, and AFUE is mostly for fuel-burning equipment like furnaces and boilers (with the electric furnace exception mentioned earlier).

But if you're savvy, you can find the actual efficiency of heating or cooling systems. You just need to measure the output energy for heating or cooling and divide by the input energy. The calculation for heating is straightforward because you can find the heating output of a furnace or heat pump by measuring the air flow rate and the temperature rise as the air goes through the heating equipment.

Finding the efficiency of air conditioning systems is more complex because the cooling output includes both sensible and latent components. You'd need to find how both the dry bulb temperature and humidity change as the air goes through the system in addition to the air flow rate.

For both heating and cooling, the input energy is straightforward, but you have to get the right equipment to measure it. To find the electrical energy input, you need monitors that measure and record the voltage and current (Figure 13.10). For split-system air conditioners, you need to measure both the outdoor and indoor components. With furnaces, you have to measure the gas, propane, or heating oil input and also the electrical input because these types of equipment use both a fossil fuel to burn for heat and electricity in the blower to move the heat around the house.

Another important point about efficiency metrics is that they don't provide an easy way to make a direct comparison of the efficiency of two types of equipment that use different fuels. For example, consider a natural gas furnace and an electric furnace (strip heat). Even though they're both labeled with an AFUE, a direct comparison would lead to an inaccurate conclusion. A condensing gas furnace may have an AFUE of 95, whereas an electric furnace is 100 AFUE. Does that make the electric furnace more efficient? No. The fuel for the gas furnace was delivered right to the house, but the electricity used

in the electric furnace was generated at a power plant by using a mix of fuels—coal, gas, nuclear power, wind, or others. You have to factor in how that electricity was generated to truly compare gas versus electricity. (See the discussion of site versus source energy in Chapter 4.)

Figure 13.10. *You can see four circuit sensors, two main sensors, and the communications box for the monitoring system in this electrical panel. (Not all circuits have monitors, and the whole panel isn't shown.) [Courtesy of John Semmelhack]*

Here are the key points to remember about the energy efficiency of HVAC equipment:

- They're all based on the same definition of output heating or cooling energy divided by the input energy.
- Some are averaged over a whole heating or cooling season (SEER, HSPF, AFUE).
- Some are based on the output and input energy at specific conditions (COP, EER).
- Some have mixed units for the output and input energy (SEER, HSPF, EER).
- Some use the same units for output and input energy (AFUE, COP).
- You can measure the efficiency of heating and

cooling systems if you have the right equipment.

- There's not an easy way to compare different types of equipment or different types of fuel.

Of course, other efficiency ratings exist, and other types of equipment use some of the ratings mentioned here. If you understand these ratings, you'll have a good handle on the energy efficiency of systems that deliver their heating and cooling through the air.

Fuel-Fired Combustion Equipment

Although I'm partial to heat pumps, heating equipment that gets its heat from the combustion of a fuel isn't going away anytime soon. Many existing homes already are set up for combustion equipment, including the meters, pipes, tanks, or racks. Converting these houses to electric heat may be too expensive, especially if it means upgrading the electrical service. So, let's look at the options for combustion equipment that uses forced-air distribution: furnaces, combi systems, and woodstoves.

Furnaces and Boilers

This is the type of heating system used in many homes. Most furnaces run on natural gas, but some furnaces burn propane or heating oil. The concept of heating with a furnace is simple. The combustion of a fuel releases heat. Much of the heat is in products of combustion. Those exhaust gases get sent to the outdoors through a flue, the furnace's exhaust pipe. On their way out of the house, the exhaust gases travel through a heat exchanger. As they move through, the exhaust gases cool down by transferring heat to the metal heat exchanger. On the other side of the heat exchanger—and sealed from the exhaust gases—air or water from the house moves across the heat exchanger, picking up the heat from the hot exhaust gases and distributing it to the house.

Boilers do the same thing furnaces do: burn a fuel to create heat. The difference is in where they put that heat. A furnace puts the heat into air to be sent throughout the house. A boiler puts the heat in water. And here's a little secret for you:

Most boilers don't actually boil water. They just make hot water. Steam systems do still exist, but they're rare in most places. That's about all I'm going to say about boilers here as I'm going to focus on air distribution systems.

An important thing to note about heat exchangers is that they're designed for a relatively tight tolerance of temperatures. If heat exchangers run too hot, the metal can crack, leaking exhaust gases into the air being sent to the living space. If heat exchangers run too cool, they could be below the dew point temperature of the water vapor in the exhaust gases. (The combustion of methane produces a lot of water vapor!) If the inside of the heat exchanger gets wet and stays wet long enough, it can corrode. A leaky heat exchanger can put exhaust gases into the indoor air. One of those exhaust gases is carbon monoxide, so be sure to have a low-level carbon monoxide monitor if you have any combustion appliances.

Furnaces have changed a lot over the years, and you can find old, inefficient, and potentially unsafe models still in use. You can also find modern, super-efficient furnaces with variable capacity. As mentioned in the section on annual fuel utilization efficiency (AFUE), furnaces come in two basic flavors: standard and condensing.

Standard furnaces: Many furnaces have an efficiency of about 80 AFUE. They turn 80 percent of the energy in the fuel into heat that can be delivered[22] to the house. Where does the other 20 percent go? Mostly up the flue with the exhaust gases. With that much heat in the exhaust gases, the flue can get quite hot, so this

---

22. I say "can be delivered" because if ducts run through an unconditioned space like a vented attic, duct leakage and conductive loss through the ducts aren't counted in the AFUE rating. Also, the 80 AFUE is based on standard conditions, not the conditions at your house.

type of furnace will have a metal flue. That's your first clue as to whether it's a standard furnace or not. Another characteristic of the standard furnace is that it draws air from the space around the furnace to use in the combustion process. To get that air to the burner, the furnace cabinet usually has louvers on the front panel.

Figure 13.11. *Standard efficiency furnace. The metal flue and louvered cabinet indicate the type of furnace.*

Whenever you have combustion appliances in a house, it's important to make sure they're safe. Any furnace you buy now is relatively safe from backdrafting, one of the main hazards of combustion equipment. (See Chapter 2.) Older furnaces, however, used what's called natural draft to vent the exhaust gases up the flue and out of the house, and those furnaces can be backdrafted relatively easily. A combustion appliance can put carbon monoxide into a home's air if the exhaust gases don't go up the flue, so if a house has a natural draft furnace, it should be replaced as soon as possible. Upgrading to a condensing furnace

will be more expensive than a standard furnace, but the savings will be significant, and the new furnace will pay for itself quickly.

Condensing furnace: The second type of furnace harvests a lot of the waste heat that goes up the flue in a standard furnace. They're able to do so because much of that waste heat is in the form of latent heat in water vapor, which is one of the primary combustion products of hydrocarbons like natural gas, propane, and heating oil. In a condensing furnace—and the name gives away its energy-saving trick—the exhaust gases pass through a secondary heat exchanger that cools down the exhaust below the dew point of the water vapor. The water vapor then condenses in that heat exchanger and is drained out of the furnace. The net result is that a condensing furnace can produce 90 to 98 units of heat for each 100 units of energy in the fuel, with an AFUE ranging from 90 to 98.

Figure 13.12. *High-efficiency furnace. Note the two plastic pipes, one that brings in combustion air and the other to send out the exhaust gases.*

Identifying a condensing furnace is easy. Look for a plastic flue instead of a metal one. In addition, there's likely to be a second plastic pipe that brings in combustion air rather than drawing it from the surrounding space. The second pipe is there because condensing furnaces have sealed combustion chambers, and the pipe brings in outdoor air to prevent creating negative pressure in the house. The intake pipe is sometimes omitted on furnaces installed outside conditioned space. The other clue to identifying condensing furnaces is the pipe coming out of the furnace to drain the condensed water vapor.

As with air conditioners and heat pumps, condensing furnaces come with different ways of managing capacity. They can have fixed capacity, two or more stages, or variable capacity. By ramping down to lower capacity, multi-stage or variable capacity furnaces can improve comfort on part-load days. And most days are part-load days.

Hydronic Air Handler/Combi System

A hydronic air handler has two heat exchangers to heat the living space in a house. First, a fuel is burned to heat water. Then the water circulates through a heat exchanger in an air handler that sends the heated air through ducts to heat the space. This type of system is also called a combi system because the whole system provides both space heat and hot water to the house. Another name for it is hydro-air system.

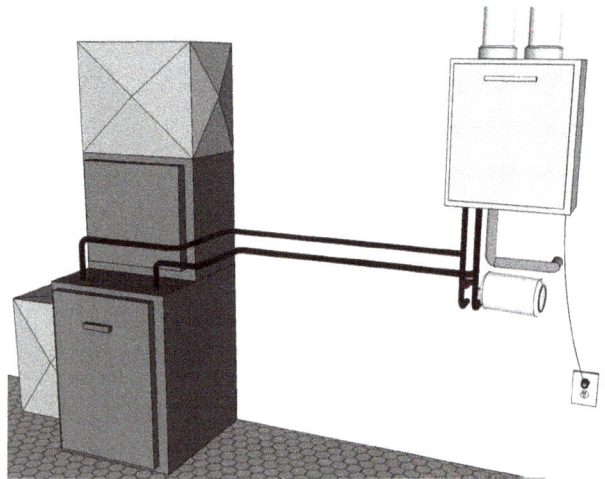

Figure 13.13. *Combined hot water and space heating system, called a combi system. The two components are connected by two pipes that send hot water from the tankless water heater (right) to the air handler (left) and back. [Source: US Department of Energy, Building America Solution Center]*

Combining a water heater (tankless or storage) with a space heater is a clever way to have only one combustion device serve two needs. The hydronic air handler has two other advantages. Many furnaces come with their smallest heating capacity in the 40,000 BTU/hr range, but some hydronic air handlers have heating capacities less than 20,000 BTU/hr. Even better, the controls on modulating equipment can ramp the capacity down further. Smaller units are better suited to smaller loads, providing more comfort and less noise. Another advantage of the combi system is that a hydronic coil can be paired with a heat pump to serve as the auxiliary heat for those cold spells when an air-source heat pump can't provide enough heat.

Woodstove

Burning wood for heat harkens back to our early human ancestors' discovery of fire. Open wood-burning fireplaces are a bad idea for indoor living space because they suck a lot of heat out of the house when they're in use. The main heating benefit they provide is the radiant heat felt by anyone near the fire. While they're burning, however, they pull in a lot of air from the home and send it up the chimney. Thus, the net effect of this way of burning wood is heat loss.

A woodstove solves that problem by keeping the fire contained in a metal box that draws much less air than an open wood-burning fireplace. They generally use only about 15 cubic feet per minute of air from the house once the fire is established, or about a third of what a properly installed bathroom fan exhausts from the house when it runs.

Woodstoves can be a good source of supplemental heat for homes with heat pumps. Even a gas furnace won't run without electricity, so woodstoves can also serve as backup heat when the power goes out. If you live in an area with plentiful sources of firewood and are willing to do the work, a woodstove can be a good source of heat. Some areas don't allow them, however, because of the smoke they put in the air, so check the laws where you live before you decide to install a woodstove.

Electric Resistance Heat

One hundred percent efficient! That sounds great, doesn't it? That's what you get with electric resistance heat, but, sadly, it's not as good as it sounds. Electricity is a fantastic way to move energy and then convert it to other forms, such as motion (think fans and blenders) or heat. When electricity runs through a material with high-electrical resistance, like the filaments in your toaster or blow dryer, it becomes heat. And every kilowatt-hour of electricity used becomes one kilowatt-hour of heat. That's 100 percent efficient. In the technical terms we've covered in this chapter, the coefficient of performance for electric resistance heat is 1. But that's a poor use of electricity because heat pumps have COPs that range from 2 to about 6. Why would you want to get one unit of heat for each unit of electricity when you can get 4?

Figure 13.14. *Electric resistance installed in the air handler for a heat pump*

Electric resistance heat, also called strip heat, is used to toast bread, dry hair, and heat houses. Two of those are appropriate uses. (No one would pay $500 for a heat pump toaster.) Using electric resistance for space heating can make sense in some cases, but it's best to avoid it in most cases. Plug-in portable space heaters use electric resistance and can make sense sometimes. However, supplying all the heat for a house with electric resistance rarely makes sense. If the total heating load is really low, it might make sense. For example, one of the first Passive Houses in North America had a heating load so small it could be heated with a blow dryer.[23] But specifying an electric furnace for a full-size house with a significant heating load is insane and will cost the homeowners a lot, especially in areas with high electricity rates. In some areas—like my home state of Georgia—electric resistance is not allowed for primary space heating.

The strip heat used for auxiliary heat in heat pumps can be okay if it's controlled properly and is used for a relatively small amount of the total heat supplied to the house. One problem with electric resistance heat in heat pumps is that sometimes homeowners are told—even by HVAC technicians—to set their thermostats for emergency heat on cold days. That immediately increases their electricity bill because now they've gone from using a heat pump with a COP of 2 or more most of the time to using all strip heat with its COP of 1. The heat pump, with proper controls, is designed to add in enough strip heat to meet the space heating needs while still using the heat pump compressor for as much as it can do. There's no need to override that functionality.

Other Ways of Heating and Cooling

As I mentioned, my bias is toward heat pumps. And I like forced-air distribution for heating and cooling houses. Those are not the only ways to deliver comfortable indoor conditions, though.

Let's look at some of them here: radiant heating and cooling, hydronic heating and cooling, and evaporative cooling.

23. A 1,500-watt blow dryer supplies heat at the rate of about 5,000 BTU/hr.

Radiant and Hydronic Heating and Cooling

The first thing to know here is that both radiant and hydronic refer to the distribution of the heating and cooling. You can do either radiant or hydronic heating and cooling with equipment we've already described: heat pumps, fuel-fired combustion, or electric resistance.

A lot of people lump these two types of systems together, but radiant heating and cooling does differ from hydronic heating and cooling. Radiant systems, as the name implies, deliver heating or cooling to a room via the process of radiation. Recall that any object that has a temperature will radiate heat away and that all the other objects in its view are doing the same. The net flow into or out of any object depends on its temperature relative to the temperature of its surroundings and also on how well it emits and absorbs heat (its emissivity). A floor, wall, or ceiling panel that's significantly cooler than other parts of a room will absorb heat. A panel that's warmer will radiate heat away.

One really nice thing about radiant heating and cooling is that a lot of how we experience comfort comes from the radiant temperatures of our surroundings. (See Chapter 3.) By using radiant panels to keep cooler in summer and warmer in winter, you'll probably find that you're more comfortable with the indoor air temperature higher in summer and lower in winter.

Hydronic systems use heated or chilled water to deliver the heating or cooling. The "hydro" part of hydronic should tip you off that water is involved. The "onic" part is because the early 20th-century steam and hot water advocates wanted their heating systems to sound as cool as electronics.

The difference between radiant and hydronic is simply the stage of delivering heating and cooling. Hydronic refers to the connection between the equipment and the space being heated or cooled. Radiant tells you how the heating or cooling is delivered to the space once it gets there. A system could be both hydronic and radiant, it could be radiant but not hydronic, or it could be hydronic but not radiant.

Hydronic and radiant: Radiant floor heating systems often get their heat from hot water running through pipes embedded in a concrete slab or attached beneath flooring materials. The hot water usually comes from a boiler in another part of the house.

Radiant but not hydronic: Some radiant panels get their heat from electric resistance tapes in the floor. Portable radiant heaters often rely on strip heat. If you've ever sat on the patio at a restaurant on a chilly evening, you've probably been warmed by a gas-burning radiant heater. No water is involved in any of those because the equipment generating the heat isn't separated from the space that needs the heat.

Hydronic but not radiant: Old-style radiators are heated by hot water running through them. Even though they're called radiators, most of their heat transfer into the room is by convection, not radiation. Sitting on the floor, they're surrounded by the coolest air in the room. As the air around them heats up, it rises, creating convective loops and spreading the heat throughout the room. The same is true of hydronic baseboard heaters.

Using radiant systems for your primary heating and cooling requires floors, walls, or ceilings that get heated or cooled. Those panels then heat or cool the people in the space. When using hydronic radiant panels, most systems use a boiler to heat water and do heating only. If you want to do radiant cooling, you'll need a system that's essentially an air conditioner or heat pump except that the indoor fluid that distributes the cooling is water rather than air. (This would be an air-to-water cooling system, with outdoor air being the heat sink and water in the hydronic system being the heat source.) Also, with radiant cooling in a humid climate, you need to maintain good control of the indoor humidity to prevent moisture problems. Radiant panels can be cooled to 70 °F or below, and outdoor dew points can be 75 °F or higher in some places. Without an airtight enclosure and good dehumidification of the indoor air, this system can lead to moisture and mold problems.

Advocates of radiant heating and cooling often claim that it beats forced-air heating and cooling systems in comfort. Yes, it's absolutely true that by keeping a house's mean radiant temperature lower in summer and higher in winter, radiant systems help with thermal comfort. But a good building enclosure is the starting point for controlling mean radiant temperature. And putting radiant heating or cooling panels on a bad building enclosure is as bad as increasing the size of the heat pump because someone believed that a house needs to breathe. (Aaarrgh!)

If we start with a well-insulated, airtight building enclosure, both forced-air and radiant systems can work well. In fact, a 2017 study found that "radiant and all-air spaces have equal indoor environmental quality, including acoustic satisfaction, with a tendency towards improved temperature satisfaction in radiant buildings."[24] If you live in a place where you can find skilled, knowledgeable radiant contractors and that's what you want, go for it. Just don't let anyone convince you that a good building enclosure with forced-air heat pumps can't be just as good.

Evaporative Cooling

The final type of system I'll mention here is the evaporative cooling system, or swamp cooler. The way the most common types work is by using a fan to blow air over a wet material, evaporating water into the air stream. To get liquid water into the vapor phase requires heat, and that heat comes from the air. So, the air temperature drops as sensible heat converts to latent heat. The cooler, more humid air is blown into the house, making it more comfortable as long as the humidity is kept low enough.

Swamp coolers used to be popular in hot, dry climates, but they have fallen out of favor in recent years. Why? They cost less to install than air conditioners, use less energy, are easier to fix, and provide lots of ventilation air. On the downside, they can't cool a house as much as an air conditioner, use a lot of water, and require frequent maintenance. Because of the high humidity of the air exiting the cooler, ducts and other metal components rust out and need to be cleaned or replaced frequently. There are some health hazards as well. Mosquitoes sometimes breed in them. Bringing in a lot of outdoor air in an area with wildfires raging is a problem, as is turning them off to keep the smoke out when it's hot outdoors. And of course, all that water can put mold, bacteria, and other bad stuff in the indoor air.

Chapter Takeaways

- Air conditioners and heat pumps move heat from a cool place to a warmer place.
- The refrigerants in air conditioners and heat pumps go through changes in pressure, temperature, and phase to transfer heat from a cooler to a warmer place.
- Heating and cooling systems come all in one box (package unit) or in two boxes (split system).
- Heating and cooling equipment comes with one of three types of capacity: fixed capacity (single-stage), multi-stage, or variable capacity.
- Air conditioners and heat pumps can use the outdoor air, the ground, or a body of water as the heat source and sink.
- We have many ways of measuring the efficiency of heating and cooling systems, but they all result from a calculation of the output divided by the input.
- Furnaces and boilers come in standard and condensing models. Condensing models are more efficient and safer.

24. Compairing temperature and acoustic satisfaction in 60 radiant and all-air buildings, Karmann et al., Building and Environment, Vol. 126, Dec. 2017

CHAPTER 14

Moving Conditioned Air around the House

In 2004, I got called to look at someone's home. It was a hot summer, and the owner told me she couldn't get the second floor of her home to cool below 85 °F. I packed up my blower door, duct tester, and other equipment and went to have a look. The house had two air conditioning systems, and the second-floor system was in the unconditioned attic. I questioned her for a bit and then went up into the attic. The problem was immediately obvious. A large piece of return ductwork (the vertical return plenum) had fallen away from the air handler. The result was that most of the air pulled into the system was hot attic air. There's no way to cool 110 °F air adequately. Her house was uncomfortable not because her air conditioner failed, but because her duct system failed.

Figure 14.1. *This disconnected return duct in an unconditioned crawl space sucked up all kinds of nasty air, including the emissions from a decaying possum. [Courtesy of E3 Innovate]*

> **"If ducting looks a mess, it probably is."**
> —Charles H. Beach, PE

This case is one of a gazillion where homeowners have trouble with heating, cooling, humidity, noise, or indoor air quality because of a failure of the duct system. Take the room that couldn't get cool because the supply duct for that room fell off in the crawl space. Or the condo I used to live in, where we'd have to turn the television volume up whenever the system came on. Or the house in Tennessee that had a disconnected return duct sucking up nasty, humid air from the crawl space . . . and then a possum died right next to that open duct (Figure 14.1)!

The conditioned air generated by your heat pump, furnace, or other equipment must be delivered properly. When it's done right, distributing heating and cooling throughout a home leads to a comfortable, healthy, durable, and efficient home. Oh . . . and a silent one, too. Sadly, however, many homes miss the mark on many or all of those goals. In this chapter, I'll cover some of the most important factors in distributing heating and cooling. The focus here will be on forced-air distribution.

The Fundamentals of Using Air to Move Heat

A forced-air heating or cooling system is just a big air recirculating machine. It pulls in room-temperature air from the living space, changes the temperature (heating and cooling) and water vapor content (cooling) of the air, and then sends that air back into the living space. It sounds so simple. What could possibly go wrong? Well, let me list some of the requirements to make such a system perform optimally.

- Ducts need to be sized properly to move the

right amount of air efficiently and quietly.

- Ducts need to be insulated to prevent condensation in humid climates and to deliver air at the correct temperature in all climates.
- Air going into the equipment needs to be filtered to keep the internal components clean.
- High-efficiency filtration requires additional care with filter selection and sizing.
- Vents for supply air need to be sized and located to allow for proper mixing of conditioned air with room air.
- Supply vents need to be located properly to avoid blowing air directly on occupants to prevent comfort problems.
- Return air pathways must be present for every room with a supply vent.
- Intakes for return air need to be designed carefully to keep resistance low.
- Duct fittings, which turn or split the air flow, must be chosen carefully to limit the overall resistance to air flow in the duct system.
- Ducts need to be installed properly.
- Ducts need to be made as airtight as possible, especially if they are in an unconditioned attic or otherwise outside of the conditioned space.

Before we get into the details of those requirements, let's start with the fundamentals. Forced-air heating and cooling equipment is a box with a fan (in addition to the coils, heat exchangers, and the other components needed

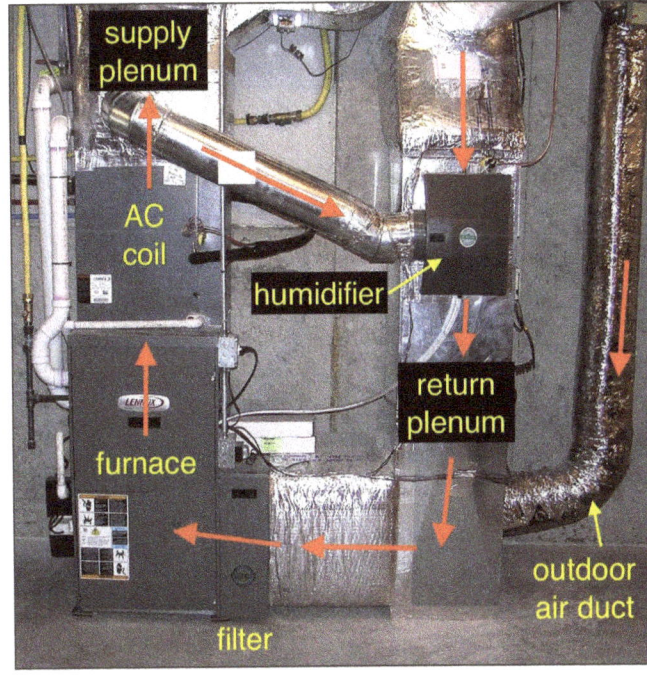

Figure 14.2. *A typical forced-air heating and cooling system. This one also has a humidifier and a duct bringing in outdoor air for ventilation. Red arrows show the direction of air flow through the system. [Source: US Department of Energy, Building America Solution Center]*

for the heating and cooling). Air gets pulled into one side of the box and pushed out the other. The box is called an air handler.[25] The intake side is called the return side because air from the living space is returning to the unit for more heating or cooling. The output side is called the supply side because it supplies conditioned air to the living space. The return and supply duct sides usually have large boxes called plenums attached to the air handler.

Going Ductless

One way to distribute heating and cooling throughout a house is to do it with refrigerant rather than air. That's what ductless heat pumps and air conditioners do. Instead of ducts that send air to a bunch of rooms, you have a small system that generates heating and cooling and blows that air directly into the room where it's

needed. Ductless systems are almost always high-efficiency inverter-driven mini-splits that do either heating and cooling (heat pumps) or cooling only (air conditioners).

The keys to using ductless units effectively are:
- *Size them properly.* Putting a ductless unit in every room in the house adds unnecessary

25. HVAC pros usually distinguish between air handlers and furnaces, but for our purposes, I'll use the term "air handler" for any forced-air heating or cooling system cabinet with a blower and ducts.

expense, and it also results in far more capacity than most houses need. A 6,000 BTU/hr ductless unit, the smallest size many manufacturers make, in a bedroom with a load of 1,500 BTU/hr will run at the bottom of its capacity range most of the time. In a case like this, the variable capacity of the system provides little to no benefit. It also costs more to install extra equipment.

- *Match the system type to the needs of the homeowner.* Ductless units come in various types: wall-mounted (the most common), ceiling cassettes, and floor-mounted. Some can be disguised by incorporating them into cabinetry or other features.
- *Choose a unit with the proper air flow characteristics.* The air flow patterns from each type of unit differ, so look at the specifications and find one that accommodates the needs of the room.

I prefer to use ductless units in places where they work well. That includes common areas with enough heating and cooling load to be able to use the full capacity of the system. Another good place for ductless units is any room that needs to be zoned separately from other parts of the house. The sunroom shown in Figure 14.3 is a good example. The large amount of window area makes it difficult to heat and cool this room with the same system that serves the adjacent rooms. On the other hand, bedrooms rarely justify their own ductless units because the loads are too small.

Figure 14.3. *A ductless mini-split heat pump serving a single room*

Two Types of Duct Systems

In designing a duct system, you have options. First, you need to choose whether to go with a trunk-and-branch layout or a radial duct system. In the former, a large supply duct—the trunk— runs throughout the house or zone, with smaller branch ducts coming off of the trunk to deliver air to the various supply vents. In the latter, the ducts "radiate" off of the supply plenum. Sometimes the duct runs in a radial system branch on their way to the supply vents.

Both trunk-and-branch and radial duct systems can perform well when designed properly. However, radial systems have gotten a bad reputation because so many duct systems that weren't properly designed use this strategy (Figure 14.6). A

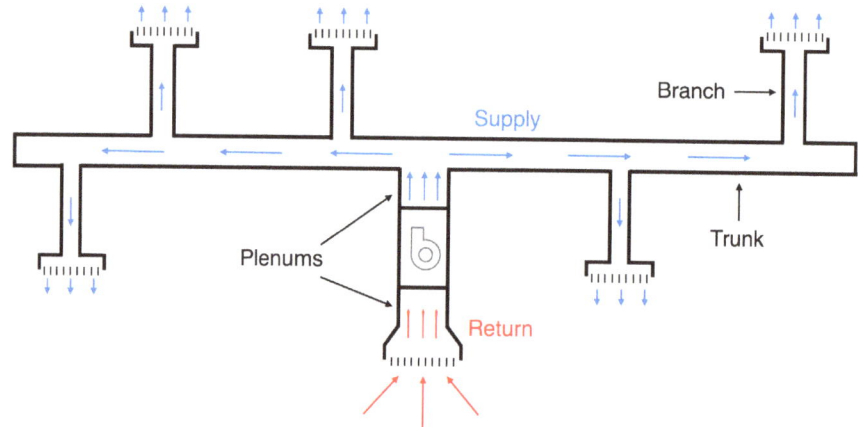

Figure 14.4. *Trunk-and-branch duct system*

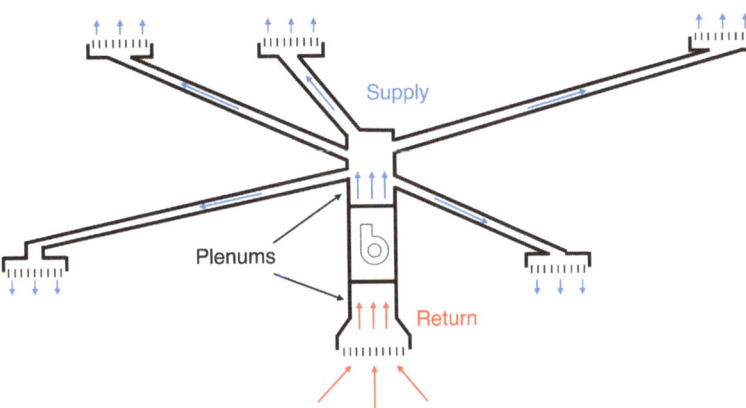

Figure 14.5. *Radial duct system*

Figure 14.6. *An example of a poorly designed radial duct system, sometimes referred to as a ductopus. My friend John Poole in Connecticut saw this photo and exclaimed, "Release the Kraken!"*

poorly designed radial duct system is sometimes referred to as a "ductopus." It has almost no chance of delivering the right amount of conditioned air to each room. But a properly designed duct system of either type is possible, and it's a beautiful sight to behold—and not because it's shiny!

Types of Ducts

In addition to the two types of duct systems, the ducts themselves come in a few different varieties. The most common types you'll see are flexible, sheet metal, and rigid fiberglass. Another type that is unfortunately all too common in homes is the site-built duct, which uses a building cavity to move air. Let's take a closer look.

Flexible Ducts

Usually called flex duct or just flex, this type of duct has three parts: the inner liner, the insulation, and the outer jacket (Figure 14.7). Each part is critical and serves a different purpose.

- The inner liner is the pressure boundary for the air flow. It's made of plastic with a helical coil of wire to keep it from collapsing.
- The insulation is to reduce the amount of heat gain or heat loss that happens to the air traveling through the duct, of course.
- The outer jacket keeps the insulation from being damaged and, in humid climates, prevents condensation on the inner liner.

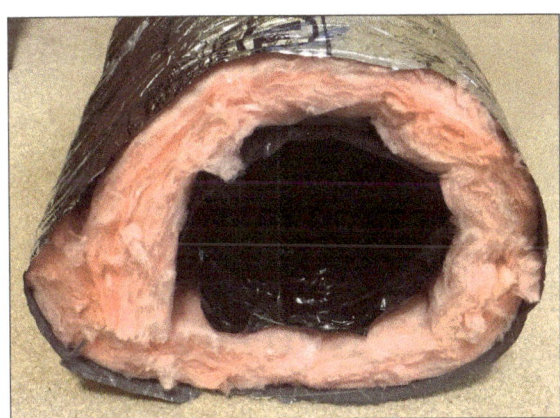

Figure 14.7. *Flex duct has three parts: the inner plastic liner, the insulation, and the outer jacket.*

Flex duct is relatively inexpensive and easy to install. Unfortunately, those characteristics lead to many problems. Installers often use too much flex because it's cheap, and they contort it in ways that add a lot of extra resistance to the air flow. I could fill a book with photos of very bad duct systems (like the ductopus of Figure 14.6), but instead I'll focus on how to do flex duct properly in the next section.

Sheet Metal Ducts

Also called rigid duct or hardpipe, this type of duct requires a higher level of design behind it than does flex duct. Installers don't just show up at a house with a bunch of sheet metal in the back of their truck and then figure out how they're going to make it work. Ducts in older houses were usually made of sheet metal, but the low cost and ease of installation of flex are making hardpipe more of a specialty product today.

Advantages of hardpipe include lower resistance to air flow, less susceptibility to damage, and a longer lifespan. Most of the time, it looks better than flex duct, too. But sheet metal ducts do have their drawbacks. Straight duct sections come in flat panels that have to be snapped together. Then you have to seal and insulate the ducts after assembling.

The leakage issue is significant because hardpipe can be leakier than flex. It has a lot more places for air to leak through. Every section of straight duct has a seam running along the whole length. Then you've got the joint where two pieces are connected, and that happens every 3 to 5 feet for hardpipe, whereas flex duct can go 25 feet with no longitudinal seam and only two joints where hardpipe would have about six joints. All those joints and seams leak if they're not sealed. Then there are the sheet metal fittings (elbows, takeoffs, etc.), which have even more places to leak.

Figure 14.8. *Sheet metal duct has many places that can leak. In this photo, all seams, joints, and holes are sealed with mastic.*

In short, sheet metal is a good duct material, but even poorly designed and installed hardpipe costs more and requires more work than flex duct. Design and install it well, as you should with any duct, and it will serve you well.

Rigid Fiberglass Ductboard

In some places, ductboard is used for nearly the entire duct system. It comes in big sheets and is cut to size onsite. As with flex duct, it comes pre-insulated, in this case, because it's made of insulation. It has a foil facing on one side and exposed fiberglass on the other side. Because the foil goes on the outside, the inner surface is rougher than sheet metal or flex duct pulled tight. It's got more potential leakage sites than flex duct but less than hardpipe. Ductboard is easy to fabricate onsite and reduces noise transmission more than flex or hardpipe.

Figure 14.9. *This ductboard supply trunk line in an unconditioned attic has split open, dumping a tremendous amount of conditioned air into the attic.*

In my opinion, the biggest disadvantage of ductboard is its structural weakness. I've seen all kinds of duct systems fall apart, but ductboard seems to fall apart more spectacularly, as it did in the story I opened this chapter with as well as the one shown in Figure 14.9. Ductboard is held together primarily with tape and staples and has some heft. If it's not supported properly, it falls apart at the joints. When it falls apart, large amounts of unconditioned air leak out of or into the duct system. With a lot of leakage, the system loses heating or cooling capacity and causes comfort, indoor air quality, and efficiency problems.

Site-Built Ducts

The previous three duct types have their problems, but none is banned from homes. Site-built ducts aren't banned completely (yet), but they are banned for use as supply ducts in most building codes and as return ducts in some local and state codes.

As you might suspect from the name, site-built ducts are places where the building itself is used as part of the pathway for the air moving through the system. The most notorious of these is the panned joist return. This is where a piece of sheet metal (usually, although I've seen cardboard used, too) encloses a section of a floor joist cavity, and the return duct is connected to a hole in the sheet metal (Figure 14.10). That depressurizes the enclosed joist cavity, which is then connected to a grille in the floor or to a duct that goes to a grille in the wall. You'll usually see panned joists in a basement or crawl space. Duct systems that use panned joist returns are extremely leaky.

Two other parts of the house are sometimes used as ducts also: wall cavities and the space between a base cabinet bottom shelf and the floor beneath. The only reason it's done is to make installation easier. However, the potential problems of using building cavities for ducts should outweigh the convenience factor. Every part of the duct system that moves air between supply or return vents and the air handler should be made of approved duct materials only.

One of the reasons for this is that when wood or drywall are used as part of the duct system, they are hard to seal properly, so the duct leakage will be higher. Another is that people don't respect building cavities used as ducts. Most people wouldn't think of drilling through an actual duct to run a pipe or wire, but they do cut and drill through panned joist returns, wall cavity ducts, and cabinets. Still another reason is that when you pressurize or depressurize a floor, wall, or cabinet cavity, you may be sending or pulling air to or from other places, like a damp, smelly crawl space.

Using building cavities as supply ducts is banned by the model code because of the temperature extremes. Wood and drywall expand and contract at different rates than duct materials, and that can cause gaps to open up and excess leakage to occur. Worse, when air conditioning in humid climates, cold air in poorly sealed building cavities can lead to mold growth. This is especially true with toe kick grilles in kitchen or bathroom cabinets, where water leaks can make things bad in a hurry.

Figure 14.10. *Panned joist return in a vented crawl space. Also be careful with white tape on ducts in old houses because it may contain asbestos.*

Figure 14.11. *Sheet metal duct (near hand) for toekick grille protected from construction damage before cabinet installation*

The best practice here is to avoid unlined building cavities for moving air and instead use only approved duct materials. The toekick duct awaiting cabinet installation (Figure 14.11) is a good example. A sheet metal duct will connect the supply duct in the crawl space to the toekick grille. The wood around it protects the duct from damage during construction.

Two Causes of Resistance to Air Flow in Ducts

Air moving through a duct is hampered primarily by two factors: friction and turbulence.

Friction

The first factor hampering air moving through a duct is friction, or air resistance. The roughness of the surfaces either helps or hinders the air flow. The smoother the surface, the more easily the air moves. The rougher the surface, the more resistance there is to the flow.

The smoothness or roughness of the duct surface depends on a few factors. The duct material is one of those factors. For example, sheet metal is smoother than fiberglass ductboard. Another factor is how well the duct is installed, particularly with flex duct. If you pull flex tight, it's not much different than sheet metal. However, if you leave it slack, the friction goes up quickly with the undulations in the surface as the sections of helical wire get closer together and the plastic gets wrinkled. A third factor is cleanliness. The more dirt accumulates in ducts, the greater the friction.

Air Turbulence

The second cause of reduced air flow is turbulence. When air flowing through a duct comes to a turn, a place where the air flow splits, or an obstruction in the airstream, the nice flow lines of smooth air flow turn into a sloppy mess, resulting in a duct system that's more resistant to air flow. The key here is to pay close attention to any place in the duct system where you turn the air, split the air, or put obstacles in its path (e.g., dampers).

The net effect of friction and turbulence is the overall resistance of the duct system. In a properly installed system, can you guess which one of those factors is bigger than the other? Hint: It's turbulence. From a practical standpoint, the implication is that you need to pick fittings—those duct components that turn, split, or in some way interrupt the air flow—that result in less turbulence whenever possible.

Figure 14.12. *Flex duct that's not pulled tight adds a lot of resistance to the air flow.*

Measuring the Resistance

We discussed measuring pressure differences in Chapter 8. To get a handle on the resistance to air flow in a duct system (or across a filter, as we'll see in Chapter 15), that's the physical quantity that matters. As air moves through a duct, the static pressure decreases. The amount of reduction is a measure of the resistance. When air moves through a nice straight section of smooth sheet metal duct, the pressure drops slowly. When the air moves through a bad-fitting or a restrictive filter, the pressure drops quickly.

We can measure the pressure change between any two parts of a duct system to find the resistance in that section. That section could be a straight section of duct. It could be a fitting. Or it could be across the cabinet that contains the blower, which is an air handler or furnace. Measuring the pressure drop across the air handler gives you the total external static pressure (TESP). That number gives you a measure of the resistance of the entire duct system, including the filter, grilles, registers, dampers, fittings, and duct sections. A typical air handler runs best with a TESP of 0.5 inch of water column (iwc) or lower.

In a duct system that uses sheet metal, the resistance due to the fittings will dominate. The same is true for a duct system with straight sections of flex duct with the inner liner pulled tight. In many houses, though, the majority of the duct system is made of flex, and it's installed poorly (Figure 14.12). In cases like that, improving the straight sections can have a huge impact on the air flow. Sometimes it helps a lot to add or change fittings, too. And that takes us into the next topic . . .

Choosing the Right Duct Fittings

A duct system is made up of two types of components: fittings and the sections of duct between fittings. Flex duct systems eliminate many of the fittings because the installer often turns the air with the duct itself rather than installing fittings to do that. Similarly, with ductboard systems, some of the fittings are made of ductboard rather than specially manufactured from sheet metal. Does it matter?

Sheet metal fittings have a leg up on using flex or ductboard without fittings. The reason is that it's a lot easier to predict how they'll behave in a duct system. That's because fittings are made in standard forms, and the amount of resistance they add has been measured.

The way resistance to air flow is measured in a duct system is by measuring how much the pressure decreases from one point to another. Straight, clean sheet metal ducts have a certain amount of pressure drop per unit length. Although ducts in homes are rarely 100 feet long, the resistance is stated as the pressure drop per 100 feet because the pressure drop for just 1 foot is an annoyingly small number. Stating the resistance per 100 feet changes, for example, a friction loss of 0.0008 to 0.08. The former number would be in units of iwc per foot and the latter in iwc per 100 feet.

Fittings can have a larger effect on the air flow than straight ducts, and the way we describe that is by measuring the pressure drop as air moves through the fitting and then comparing it to the pressure drop in a piece of straight duct. For example, we can say that the pressure drop in a particular fitting is equal to the pressure drop in 50 feet of straight duct. And that number even has a special name: equivalent length.

Figure 14.13 shows two fittings that both do the same thing. Each is a transition from a round duct to a rectangular opening meant to hold a supply vent, which then sends the conditioned air into a room. But these two fittings have very different effects on the air flow. The upper fitting has an equivalent length of 20 feet, while the fitting below is equivalent to 50 feet. These numbers tell you that you should avoid that fitting with the higher equivalent length if you can. It's always best to keep the resistance as low as possible.

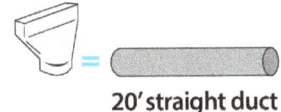

20′ straight duct

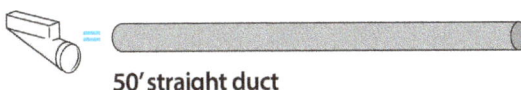

50′ straight duct

Figure 14.13. *The equivalent length of two types of fittings compared to the length of straight duct with the same resistance*

With sheet metal fittings, you can look up the equivalent lengths and use them in designing, installing, or retrofitting a duct system for better air flow. With flex duct, ductboard, or site-built ducts, it's hard to know what the effect on the overall resistance might be because every occurrence is different. Even if you incorporate flex or ductboard into your duct system, it's best to use sheet metal fittings to turn or split the air.

Before we go on, let me leave you with a general rule for fittings. The way to achieve low

The way to achieve low resistance in ducts is to make all transitions as gradual and smooth as possible.

resistance is to make all transitions as gradual and smooth as possible. This applies to turning the air in a single duct, splitting the air flow, or changing the size of a duct. Gradual and smooth are good; abrupt and sharp are bad.

Turning the Air

Let's look at one of the most common sources of resistance in ducts: turning the air. This is something that we can accomplish in different ways. First, let's give up on the common method of just bending a run of flex duct to turn the air. Figure 14.14 shows how that's often done, and it's immediately obvious that this turn violates the gradual-and-smooth rule. In addition to the turn here being too sharp, it's difficult to pull the inner liner tight when the duct is also turning the air. Even when the duct is turned more gently, the liner can't be pulled as tight as it can in a straight piece of flex duct (Figure 14.12), and it will be more resistive to air flow.

What are your options if you're not going to turn the air with flex duct? Fittings, of course, and the ones used for turning air are called elbows. Let's do a little terminology first. An elbow has two sections. The outside of the turn is called the heel. The inside of the turn is called the throat.

Now, take a look at that elbow in Figure 14.15 on page 243. What jumps out at you is that nice round turn, right? Well, that's only part of the story, and in fact, it's not the most important part. That rounded curve on the heel of the elbow does help, but the sharp 90-degree corner on the throat of the turn hurts the air flow far more than the round heel. Think of cars going around a racetrack. If the racetrack's turns were like this

duct fitting's, the cars on the inside would either have to slow down to a crawl to make the turn or their inertia would carry them across the track, probably causing multiple crashes. The same thing happens in a duct, and the crashes are called turbulence.

Figure 14.14. *It's easy to turn the air with flex duct, but turns like this will add a lot of resistance to air flow. [Photo by Energy Vanguard]*

No, the way to cut resistance in an elbow is to make it as gradual and smooth as possible.

The elbow in Figure 14.16 is about the same size as the one in Figure 14.15, but it has a rounded throat rather than the sharp 90-degree turn. The equivalent lengths tell the story. The equivalent length for the elbow with the sharp throat is 75 feet for a square rectangular duct, whereas the one with the round throat is only 30 feet.

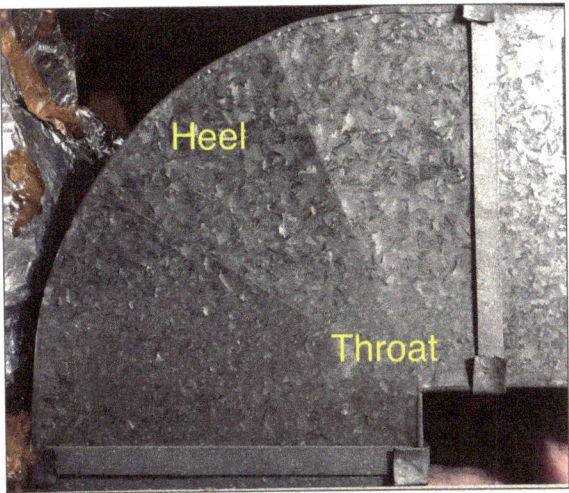

Figure 14.15. *A sheet metal elbow with a radius heel and a sharp throat*

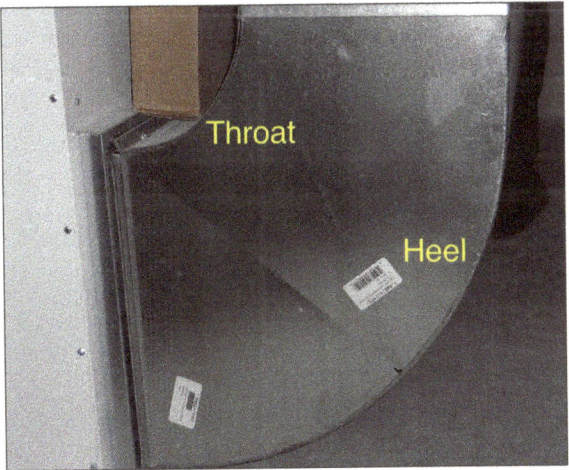

Figure 14.16. *A sheet metal elbow with a radius heel and, more importantly, a radius throat.*

But what do you do if you've got an ugly square elbow that you can't change because there's not enough room for one with a nice gradual turn? If you can't make it gradual and smooth on the outside, then do it on the inside, in the air stream itself. The way to do that is with turning vanes. These are little curved air foils

mounted several to a rack and installed inside the elbow. The rack extends from the throat to the heel and gently turns the air, preventing it from slamming into the opposite side of the duct. These devices greatly reduce turbulence.

The previous elbow photos show turns in rectangular sections of duct. Round duct needs turns, too, and Figure 14.17 shows a nice one. It's made of one piece of sheet metal, has a nice gradual turn, and is about the best you can do with turns in round duct.

The one-piece round elbow, although great for air flow, isn't as common as the type made of three, four, or five pieces. Figure 14.18 shows a four-piece elbow, which has an equivalent length about a third to a half larger than the one-piece elbow (20 feet vs. 15 feet, or 30 feet vs. 20 feet). The multi-piece elbows have the advantage of being more than just a 90-degree turn. Those pieces that make up the elbow rotate to any angle to connect two pieces of ductwork.

Figure 14.17. *A smooth, one-piece elbow is best for air flow.*

One place where flex duct is often used to turn the air—and shouldn't be—is at the boot, the metal box on the back side of a ceiling, wall, or floor to which the register or grille connects from the finished space side. A few problems can result from this practice. First, not getting a gradual enough turn increases turbulence. Second, it's hard to pull the inner liner tight enough to reduce resistance. Third, trying to pull the inner liner tight can result in excess tension that causes the duct to fail. So not only is this practice bad for air flow when all the air stays in the duct, but losing conditioned air when it fails makes it even worse.

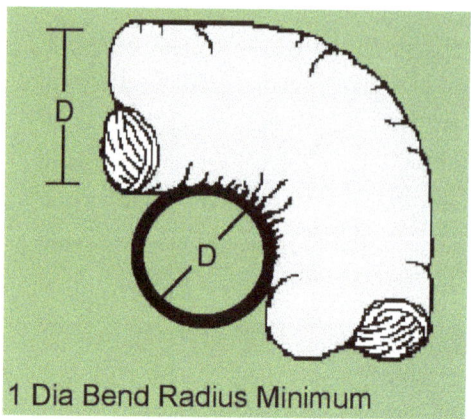

Figure 14.19. *The Air Duct Council recommends a bend radius of one duct diameter when turning flex duct. [Courtesy of Air Duct Council]*

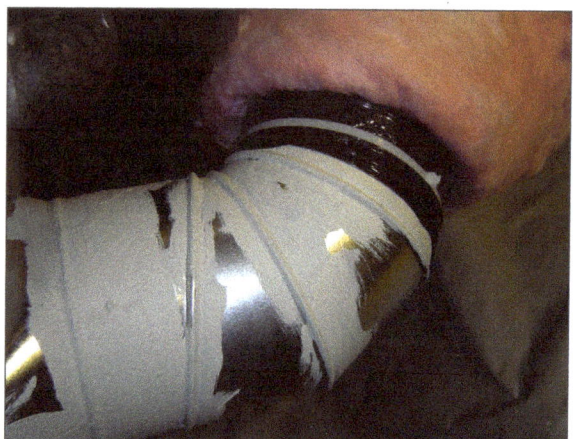

Figure 14.18. *Elbows with three, four, or five sections are more common than one-piece elbows.*

Let me backtrack a bit now and say that it is possible to use flex duct to turn the air and still get good air flow. The Air Duct Council is the trade association for the flex duct industry, and they've published a guide on how to install flex duct properly. If you follow their advice, you should be able to get good air flow. The guide says, "Keep bends greater than or equal to one (1) duct diameter bend radius." Figure 14.19 shows what they mean by a bend radius. There's even a nice product (the Malco FDS1) that will provide support for turning the air with flex duct (Figure 14.20).

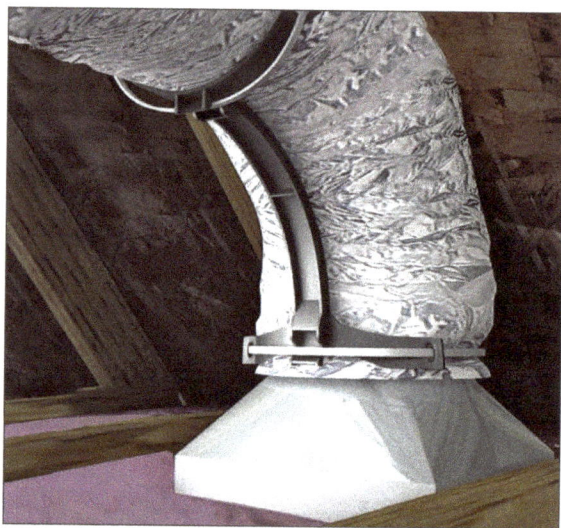

Figure 14.20. *Using a support for turning flex duct can help make the turn gradual enough to keep resistance low. [Courtesy of Build Right/Malco]*

To close here, let me repeat the general rule for fittings: Gradual and smooth are good; abrupt and sharp are bad. And if you can't make it gradual and smooth on the outside, do it on the inside with turning vanes.

Duct Size, Velocity, Resistance, and Air Flow

The relationships among duct size, velocity, and resistance are important factors in getting good air flow in ducts. Here's what it boils down to:

- Bigger ducts mean lower velocity.
- Lower velocity means lower resistance.
- Lower resistance means better air flow.

The first thing to understand here is that bigger ducts mean lower velocity, and smaller ducts mean higher velocity. That's important because the resistance to air flow changes with

Two Rules for Flex Duct

Flex duct can work well in duct systems when it's done properly. One way to ensure a good installation is to follow these two rules:

1. Use flex duct only for straight runs. If you need to turn the air, use a fitting.
2. Pull the inner liner tight. Leaving slack in the inner liner increases resistance to air flow.

It's possible to get good air flow from flex duct even if you use it to turn the air, but you'll have to do it gradually while still keeping the inner liner tight. If you're doing it yourself or have an installer you trust, go for it. If not, put these two rules into your contract.

velocity. The faster the air is moving, the higher the resistance will be. The implication here is that if you want low resistance to air flow in your duct system, make the ducts really big. That, of course, makes the need for compromise obvious because the bigger we make the ducts, the more space they take up.

Figure 14.21. *The air velocity changes when the duct size changes. The larger the duct, the lower the velocity and vice versa.*

It's not just about space, however. Any ducts in unconditioned space will lose more heat in winter and gain more heat in summer if we make them bigger because they'll have more surface area, which is where heat transfer happens. Worse, slower moving air in bigger ducts will experience larger changes in the temperature of the conditioned air when those ducts are in unconditioned space. For example, if you keep 58 °F air moving slowly through a 120 °F attic, it may gain enough heat to rise several degrees by the time it gets thrown into the conditioned space.

In short, the duct design compromise boils down to these variables:

- Duct size
- Blower power
- Location of ducts

Let's start with the first two. Ideally, you want large ducts with low velocity and low resistance. You can't always do that, though, so sometimes you have to work with smaller ducts that have more resistance. One way to overcome that resistance is to design a duct system with less total resistance (i.e., better fittings) so the blower in the air handler still can move a sufficient amount of air. If you must have smaller ducts and have done the best you can with the total resistance but still can't move enough air, you need to use a higher speed on the blower or install a more powerful blower.

The location of the ducts affects the design because you don't want too much heat transfer between the air in the ducts and their surroundings. We want that 58 °F air traveling through the hot attic to be delivered to its destination at a temperature as close to 58 °F air as possible. Thus, you want smaller ducts and higher velocity. That means more resistance and more blower power.

Residential duct systems are designed for supply air to move at maximum velocity of 900 feet per minute. If the ducts are running through conditioned space, the velocity can be significantly lower to reduce resistance, which reduces the energy needed to move the air. At Energy Vanguard, we typically shoot for about 400 feet per minute for supply ducts in conditioned space. If the ducts are running through an unconditioned crawl space, we might run the velocity a bit higher, in the 500 to 600 feet per minute range. When the ducts are in an unconditioned attic and not buried in insulation, we use 600 to 800 feet per minute in our designs.

To summarize, you should use large ducts with low velocity in conditioned space whenever you can. In unconditioned attics, go with smaller ducts and higher velocity. No, don't do that. Just get those ducts out of the unconditioned attic!

Putting Conditioned Air into the Room

One question comes up frequently when discussing low air velocity in ducts. As we'll see in this section, we want the supply air to come out of the vents with enough velocity to shoot into the room and mix well with the air that's already there. But if we use big ducts with low velocity, will we be able to do that? Or will the conditioned air from large ducts just dribble out of the vent and sit there without mixing throughout the room?

The answer is found in something you've probably done before. If you have a garden hose and no nozzle, how do you shoot the water across the yard? You put your thumb over the end to reduce the size of the hole at the end of the hose. This does the same thing we discussed above with the air in a duct getting faster when you reduce the size of the duct. And that's how we can get low velocity air from the duct to shoot out into the room at a higher velocity.

The magic is in the engineering data provided by the manufacturers of grilles and registers. To get supply air to mix well in a room, you want it to come out of the vent at about 600 to 700 feet per minute. Then, you have to choose a type of grille or register that matches the needs of the room. If the air needs to get across a 20-foot-long room, you need a grille or register that has a throw of 20 feet. Throw is the distance the air travels from the vent to a point where its velocity has dropped to some lower value. A common ending velocity to use is 50 feet per minute, but manufacturers sometimes use other numbers.

Figure 14.22. *The distance air moves into a room after leaving the supply register—the throw—works the same way as water leaving a garden hose. Larger area means lower velocity and shorter throw. Smaller area means higher velocity and longer throw.*

Another important characteristic of grilles and registers is the spread of the air flow. If you're putting air into a wide room, you probably want to use a grille or register that will spread the air out across the width of the room. The type of grille or register you choose will determine whether you get more throw, more spread, or a good balance (Figure 14.23). Some vents come with fixed vanes, and you get what you get for the air flow rate arriving at the vent. Other vents have adjustable vanes that allow you to change how much throw and spread you get.

Finally, the amount of throw and spread you

get from a vent is more important with houses that have poor building enclosures. When you have a lot of heat gain, heat loss, or infiltration happening in a room, getting the conditioned air to mix quickly in the room can overcome the enclosure deficiencies and make the room more comfortable. However, the better the building enclosure, the less important is the mixing from the vent. That's not to say that it's not important. Cold air puddling on the floor or warm air hovering at the ceiling might still lead to comfort problems. You need to shoot that air out of the vents with enough velocity to do some mixing. You don't have to be as quick with the mixing in an airtight, well-insulated house that has good windows.

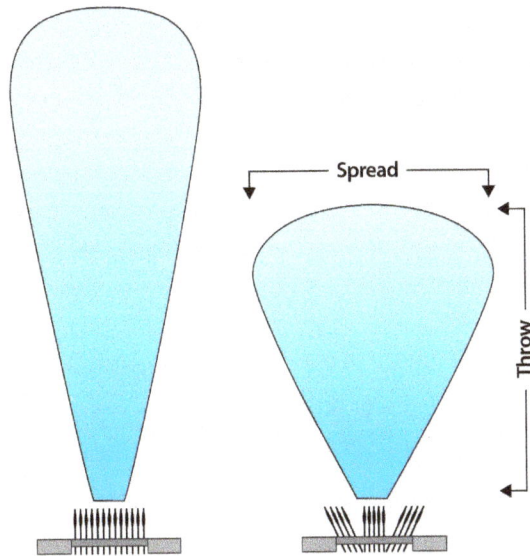

Figure 14.23. *The throw and spread are determined by the velocity of the air and the angle of the vanes on a grille or register.*

Options for Return Air

One of the problems with many duct systems is getting the air back to the air handler or furnace to be heated or cooled again. The supply vents push the conditioned air into the rooms, and the return vents pull it back for more conditioning. In many duct systems, a lot of the resistance is on the return side. Grilles that are too small, duct fittings with too much resistance, and high-resistance filters can kill the air flow.

But think about the return side of the duct system and how it compares to the supply ducts. When conditioned air leaves the air handler, it goes through the supply plenum. Whether it then enters a trunk line or a set of radial ducts, the air splits multiple times because most rooms in a house have at least one supply vent. Even in a house with dedicated return vents for the bedrooms, an air handler is pulling air from far fewer vents than it's supplying air to. Fewer pathways often mean less area and greater resistance. So, the first thing to know about return air is that you need to think big.

The first thing to know about return air is that you need to think big.

The second thing to know is that you must have return air pathways for every room that has a supply vent. Common areas in a house that are all open to each other aren't a problem. As long as there's a properly sized return vent in that area, the air delivered to those rooms can make its way to that return. Think about air supplied to the kitchen with a return vent in the living room. With no closed doors between those rooms, the air can move easily from the kitchen to the return vent in the living room.

The lack of return air pathways is mainly a problem with bedrooms. Their doors can be closed, and without adequate return pathways, the supply air is trapped in them. The two main ways to provide such pathways are (1) with dedicated return vents connected to the return ducts that send the air directly to the air handler or (2) with passive pathways through jumper ducts, transfer grilles, door undercuts, or some combination of those. Either method can work well.

A common way to determine how well a bedroom's return air pathway works is to measure the pressure difference between the bedroom and the hall while the air handler is running. A difference of 3 Pascals or less is generally thought to be okay and is the threshold for homes certified in the ENERGY STAR new homes program. With a manometer, you find out how good your bedrooms are at getting the return air back to the air handler.

In the condo I used to live in, one bedroom had a pressure difference of nearly 7 Pascals before I lowered it to 1.7 Pascals by installing a return air pathway in the bottom of the door (Figure 14.24). Some bedrooms can have much worse pressure differences than that. I've heard of one that was as high as 40 Pascals.

The other rooms in the house that get closed off are bathrooms and laundry rooms. Because they usually have exhaust fans or clothes dryers that exhaust air from the room, they usually don't get return vents. Other rooms that may be closed sometimes, like pantries or walk-in closets, might need some kind of return air pathway.

Figure 14.24. A Perfect Balance® return air pathway from Tamarack Technologies installed in the bottom of a bedroom door in my condo dropped the pressure difference from 6.7 to 1.7 Pascals.

Figure 14.25. The jumper duct shown here is a duct connected to vents in two rooms and acts as a return air pathway. [Courtesy of Mike MacFarland]

Getting a Handle on Duct Leakage

Duct leakage is a big deal. It's one of the top energy wasters in homes. Researchers at Lawrence Berkeley National Lab found that duct systems leak about 10 percent of the supply air they move and 12 percent of the return air, on average. In far more homes than you might suspect, the main culprit is a disconnected duct (Figure 14.26), but a typical duct system has a lot of other leaks, too.

Here are the main places where duct leakage occurs:

- Connection between a duct and a fitting
- Seams in rigid duct and plenums
- Seams and joints in fittings
- Air handler cabinet
- Punctures and penetrations

Many homes have ducts in unconditioned spaces, and that's where duct leakage hurts the most. Leaky supply ducts lose air that was heated or cooled but then never made it into the house to benefit the people. Leakage on the return side makes the system do extra work because it pulls in air from a crawl space or attic that needs a lot more conditioning than return air from the conditioned space.

Figure 14.26. *This disconnected duct was blowing a lot of conditioned air into an unconditioned crawl space.*

Worse, air that leaks into the return ducts may be really unhealthy, too. Nobody goes into a crawl space, attic, or garage to get fresh air. Many HVAC systems don't have good filtration, so a lot of the polluted air will make it into the living space. Even if your system has really good filtration, return duct leakage will result in filters that get dirty far more quickly than they should.

What about ducts that are completely inside conditioned space? You won't have the problems mentioned above, but you still could have comfort and indoor air quality problems. If a properly designed system is supposed to deliver 100 cubic feet per minute of air to a room but half of it leaks out before it gets there, that room won't be comfortable. It may even result in more energy use if the people adjust the thermostat to make the room comfortable.

In addition, return ducts with filter grilles (which is where I like the filters to be) should definitely be sealed because duct leakage there will come in after the filter and bring its load of dust, particulates, and spiders all the way to the heating and cooling equipment. This return duct leakage can hurt the performance of the equipment, and it can also create indoor air quality problems by feeding mold and algae on the air-conditioning coil as well as sending nasty stuff back into the living space.

The Sucking and the Blowing: A Lesson in Duct Leakage

The energy costs and comfort problems described above are a direct consequence of duct leakage. But duct leakage has a sneaky way of wasting even more energy, creating more comfort problems, and making the indoor air quality worse. These secondary effects of duct leakage stem from the location of the leaks and the balance of leakage between the supply and return ducts.

Duct leakage inside a building enclosure isn't terrible because the air is still in the conditioned space. Leakage outside—in an unconditioned attic, crawl space, basement, or garage—is what you really pay for. And if that duct leakage is different for the return ducts than it is for the supply ducts, you pay twice. Take a look at Figure 14.27.

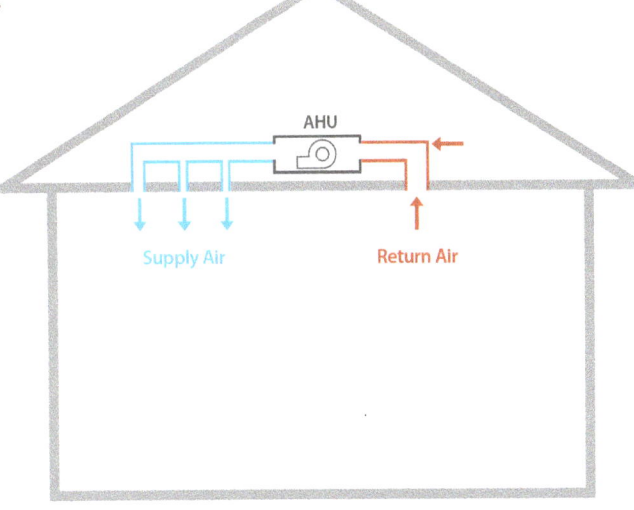

Return Duct Leakage

Figure 14.27. *A house with duct leakage only on the return side*

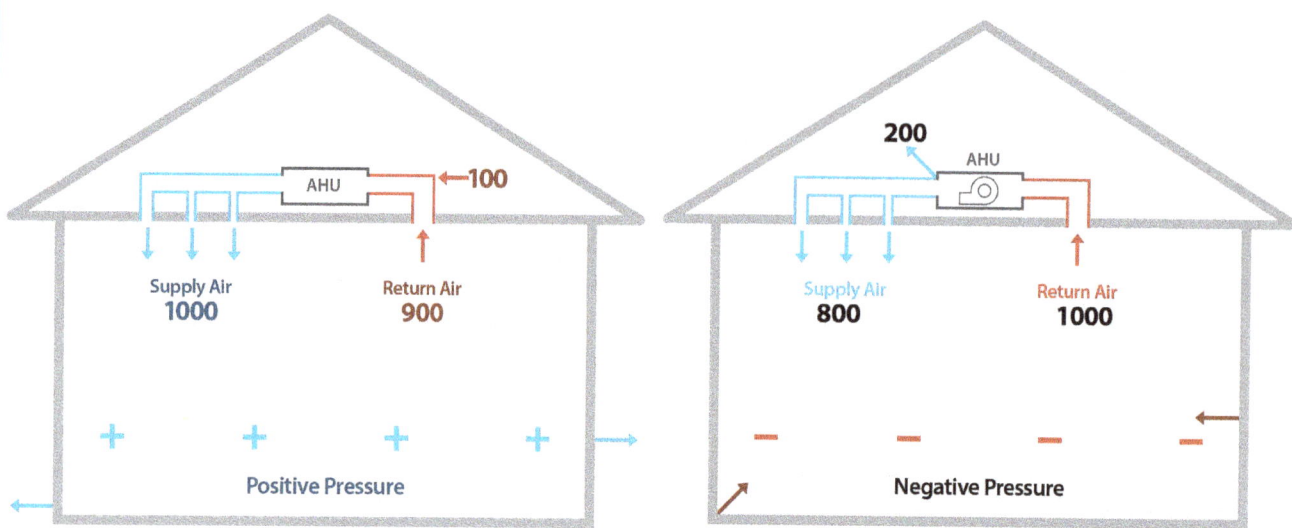

Figure 14.28. *Return duct leakage leads to positive pressure in the house, which leads to exfiltration.*

Figure 14.29. *Supply duct leakage leads to negative pressure in the house, which leads to infiltration.*

In this case, all of the leakage is on the return side of the duct system, the side that pulls air back to the air handler. If 1,000 units of air move through the air handler, 1,000 units are being supplied to the house because there's no supply duct leakage. But less than 1,000 units of air are being pulled from the house because some of the return side air comes from the attic.

The numbers don't really matter here, though. The real takeaway is what happens to the pressure in the house because of this imbalance in air flow. We're pulling less air out of the house than we're putting into it. The result of that imbalance is that the house develops a positive pressure relative to the outside when the air handler is running. That means air in the house will find places to leak to the outside, wasting some of the energy just put into that air. We can summarize it thus:

Return duct leakage ⇨ *positive pressure* ⇨ *exfiltration*

Likewise, the duct leakage could be all on the supply side, the ducts that send conditioned air back into the house. Figure 14.29 shows that scenario.

We can summarize the effect of supply duct leakage thus:

Supply duct leakage ⇨ *negative pressure* ⇨ *infiltration*

The two scenarios described above have either all return duct leakage or all supply duct leakage, but all that really matters is that the duct leakage is unbalanced. You'll probably have leakage on each side. If return leakage dominates, the house pressure goes positive. If supply leakage dominates, the house pressure goes negative. Here's an easy way to remember what happens:

Return leaks blow.
Supply leaks suck.

To find out if you have unbalanced duct leakage, use the method in the sidebar "How to Determine If a House or Room Is Under Positive or Negative Pressure" on page 100 to determine if your house has positive or negative pressure.

So, what do you do if you have unbalanced duct leakage? Seal the duct leaks, perhaps paying more attention to the leakier side. The lower you get the total duct leakage, the less imbalance you're likely to have. For example, if a duct system has a total leakage of 500 cfm, an imbalance of 100 cfm is certainly possible. But if the total leakage is only 25 cfm, which is where you might start calling a duct system airtight, the imbalance cannot be any higher than 25 cfm.

Sealing Ducts

Although I still run across people who think "a house needs to breathe," I've never met anyone in the world of home building, remodeling, or improvement who says "a duct system needs to breathe," at least not with the same meaning. Most professionals recognize the need for airtight ducts, especially when those ducts are outside the building enclosure.

You have several options for sealing ducts, but the three best are mastic, mastic tape, and Aeroseal.®

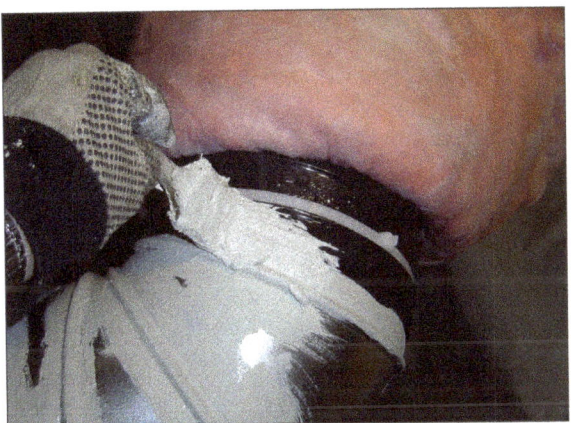

Figure 14.30. *Putting mastic on the connection between a piece of flex duct and a metal elbow.*

Mastic

This material is a thick paste you spread onto any parts of the duct system that can leak. It's great for sealing leaks in irregular shapes, like the multi-part rigid elbow shown in Figure 14.30. Make sure to coat the surfaces completely and don't be afraid to use a lot of mastic. One saying popular among duct sealers is to put it on "thick as a nickel." You want the mastic to be thick enough even after it dries and shrinks, so lay it on thickly.

Mastic Tape

This sealant is a foil-backed tape with a thick layer of adhesive, typically butyl. It has performed well in tests done by Lawrence Berkeley National Lab, and it can stand the test of time. It works best where you don't have to do tape origami because of an irregular shape. As with any tape, proper installation is the key. The surface needs to be clean and dry, and you need to press the tape firmly onto the surface with a roller or squeegee.

Duct sealing always should be done in conjunction with air flow measurements and a duct system retrofit or replacement if necessary.

Aeroseal

Aeroseal is great for existing homes with inaccessible ducts. This is a brand name, and you have to hire an Aeroseal contractor to install it for you. The material itself is a water-based polymer that is suspended in air during installation. The installer closes up the duct system, attaches a blower, and pressurizes the ducts with the polymer-filled air. As the air escapes through leaks in the duct system, the material collects at those openings and gradually seals them. The installer monitors the pressure in the duct system to determine when the ducts are sealed adequately.

All three of the above methods work well. Deciding which to use is a matter of personal preference, budget, and time constraints. Some contractors use Aeroseal because their duct installers are more valuable when they're actually installing ducts rather than sealing them. Another benefit of Aeroseal is that it can ensure the ducts will pass code-required duct leakage tests, which can save on having to go back and do more sealing. If you have more time than money, mastic or mastic tape works great.

Before we leave the topic of duct sealing, I need to issue a caution and a warning. First, the caution: Avoid the ubiquitous cloth-backed "duct tape." It dries out, shrinks, and degrades quickly. As it loses its adhesive properties, it also loses its sealing ability. Another kind of tape to avoid for duct sealing is the thin foil-backed tape. It may have the UL-181 label indicating that it's rated for ducts, but in testing done by Lawrence Berkeley National Lab, it didn't perform any better than tapes without the UL-181 label.

Next, the warning, which is more serious. Sealing a duct system may result in some unintended consequences that could be worse than the problem you're fixing. And that topic deserves its own heading.

CAUTION: Sealing Leaky Ducts Can Cause Problems

If you have a restrictive duct system, sealing the ducts may reduce the air flow enough to freeze the evaporator coil, burn out the compressor, or crack the furnace heat exchanger. A cracked heat exchanger can put carbon monoxide into the home's air. Duct sealing always should be done in conjunction with air flow measurements and a duct system retrofit or replacement if necessary.

The test to determine your system's tolerance for duct sealing is a relatively simple test of the total external static pressure (TESP), often just called a static pressure test. It's a measure of the pressure difference across the air handler or furnace and provides a result you can compare with the manufacturer's recommended static pressure.

The first step is to find out what type of motor your blower has. (See "Two Types of Blower Motors" below.) If it has a constant air flow motor, sealing the ducts is less a safety issue and more a problem with operating cost. The system will use more energy with a more restrictive, higher static pressure duct system, but it will do its best to maintain proper air flow.

For example, let's say you have a system rated for a static pressure of 0.5 inches of water column (iwc) at the design air flow. If you measure a static pressure of 0.8 iwc, that means the air flowing through the system is likely to be significantly lower than the system was designed for. If your system has a blower powered by a constant speed motor, higher static pressure will mean lower air flow. If it has a constant air flow motor, the system will do its best to maintain proper air flow, but it will do so at the cost of more energy use.

Two Types of Blower Motors

Blower motors come in two types: permanent split capacitor motors and electronically commutated motor. What's the difference?

A permanent split capacitor (PSC) motor operates at one speed when it's running. (There is some dependence on the load, so calling it a fixed-speed motor is an approximation.) The wiring is usually set up so that it has different speeds available (e.g., low, medium, and high), but that's generally a permanent setting once the system is commissioned. PSC motors come on at full speed and stop abruptly, which can be hard on the system.

An electronically commutated motor (ECM) is a direct current motor that can be controlled to run at constant speed, constant torque, or constant air flow. Constant speed ECMs are used in the outdoor unit of some air conditioners and heat pumps. An air handler with an ECM will usually be set for constant torque or constant air flow. A constant air flow ECM is the type that can increase the operating cost on a bad duct system as they try to overcome the extra resistance. A constant torque ECM will behave similarly to a PSC motor as the resistance goes up.

Can You Save Money by Closing the Vents in Unused Rooms?

The answer, like most things in building science, is "It depends." Closing supply vents inside a house is like sealing ducts. It can increase resistance to air flow and have unintended consequences. When you close one supply vent, the system will probably still work just fine. However, closing off a significant amount of the total air flow can lower the air flow enough to freeze the evaporator coil or crack the furnace heat exchanger. Manufacturers don't like paying out on warranties, so it's unlikely that low air flow will damage a compressor, but it can cause the compressor to shut down. When that happens, you lose all heating or cooling until you get it running again.

Why? When you close vents, the pressure inside the duct system increases. That increases the resistance to air flow. Depending upon the type of equipment you have, you might end up with higher energy bills, damaged heating and cooling equipment, or a trip to the hospital.

Another problem that could result from closing vents is mold growth. Keeping one room cooler than the rest of the house in winter means the walls, windows, and other surfaces will be cooler. But the room is still connected to the air in the rest of the house, and indoor air in winter has enough humidity

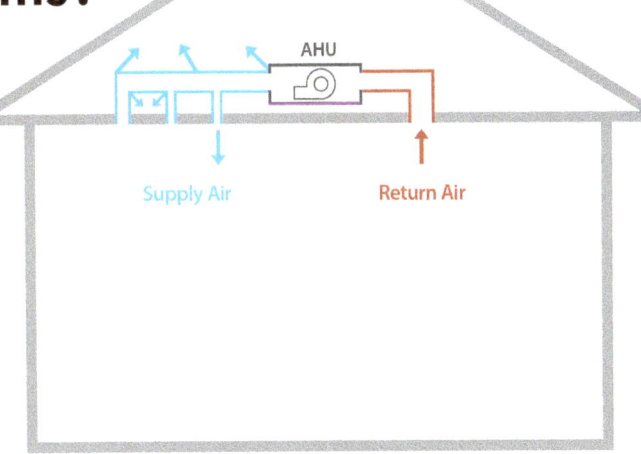

Closed Supply Vents

Figure 14.31. *One thing that can happen when you close supply vents is increased duct leakage because of the higher pressure in the duct system.*

to cause problems when it finds cool surfaces. When porous walls accumulate water vapor from the air in that cool room, mold can grow.

So yes, you can adjust supply vents to change the air flow patterns in rooms to improve comfort, but you have better options to save money on heating and cooling bills. Make the house more efficient with air sealing, duct sealing (keeping in mind the caution above), adding insulation, and possibly replacing windows.

Chapter Takeaways

- When ducts are designed and installed poorly, air distribution of heating, cooling, and ventilation through air is subject to problems of efficiency, comfort, noise, and indoor air quality.
- Duct systems can be in either trunk-and-branch or radial design.
- Some types of ducts and duct components are better than others.
- The two primary causes of reduced air flow are friction and turbulence.
- Fittings, which turn or split the air, add more resistance to air flow than straight sections of duct.
- Flex duct can work well if you follow good design and installation protocols.
- Duct leakage can be a huge problem in itself, and it can also lead to other problems: increased air leakage through the enclosure, combustion safety problems, and poor indoor air quality.

CHAPTER 15
Filtration of Indoor Air

As a kid, I was fascinated when sunlight would stream through my bedroom window and illuminate all the tiny particles floating in the air. As an adult who understands building science, I now know that those particles are usually the least of our worries from a health perspective. Yes, the mix of skin flakes, dust mite carcasses, and other miniscule detritus that's light enough to float may end up on your air conditioner coil. Once there, it can create biofilms, which can put more bacteria, fungi, and odors into your indoor air.

The good thing about the stuff that's big enough to see in a ray of sunlight is that it's easy to filter with both an HVAC system and your upper respiratory system. Keeping it off your air conditioner coil prevents biofilms from building up. And because it's too big to penetrate deep into your lungs, it may be an allergen, but it's unlikely to get into your bloodstream and cause more serious problems. Of course, it depends on what exactly is in that stuff. If those particles include substances known to be health hazards—virus-laden droplets, for example—all bets are off.

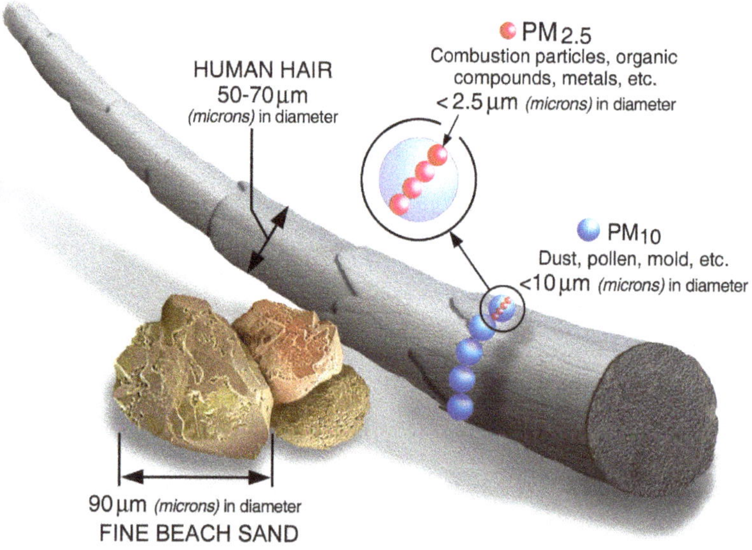

> **"Good filtration is like a breath of fresh air."**
> —Mike Steffes

Now let's focus on the stuff you can't see. Indoor air quality (IAQ) researchers have established that little bitty invisible pieces of stuff that float around in the air are bad for human health. Of course, being scientists, they don't call it little bitty invisible pieces of stuff. They call it particulate matter (PM) or particulates. And it turns out that the really small pieces—the stuff that's 2.5 microns (0.0000025 m, or 2.5 μm) or smaller, abbreviated $PM_{2.5}$—is worse than the bigger stuff because it can penetrate deeper into the lungs and find its way into your bloodstream. (See Chapter 2 for more information on healthy homes.)

The particles floating around in your home's air, especially $PM_{2.5}$, are bad for indoor air quality and thus can be a health hazard. That's not the only kind of indoor air pollutant, however.

Gases like ozone, radon, and carbon monoxide also worsen indoor air quality. The standard type of filter in your central HVAC system is actually a particulate filter because it captures only the particles, like dust, smoke, mold spores, and virus-laden aerosols. That's the focus of this chapter. In the section on filter types, I'll describe the main types of particulate filters and then mention some of the others that are available. If you want to remove gases like ozone from your home, the best method is source control first and then ventilation.

The good news is that particles are easy to remove from the air. We know

HUMAN HAIR
50-70 μm
(microns) in diameter

● PM 2.5
Combustion particles, organic compounds, metals, etc.
< 2.5 μm *(microns)* in diameter

● PM 10
Dust, pollen, mold, etc.
<10 μm *(microns)* in diameter

90 μm *(microns)* in diameter
FINE BEACH SAND

Figure 15.1. *The scale of the particles floating around in your air [Source: EPA]*

how to filter out both the larger particles you can see and the small ones that are such a serious health risk. First, I should point out that the majority of the $PM_{2.5}$ found in homes comes from outdoors (unless you smoke or burn a lot of candles or incense), so your first line of defense is airtightness. (A house doesn't need to . . . oh, you know this by now.) That won't handle all of the particles, though, because your indoor activities generate more. And that's when you need filtration.

One more thing before we dive in: I apologize in advance for all the initials and acronyms in this chapter. I've mostly written everything out in this book, but I just can't bear to write out things like Minimum Efficiency Reporting Value every time it comes up.

The Basics of Filtering a Home's Air

If you've got a forced-air heating and cooling system, it recirculates and filters the air in your home every time it runs. The effectiveness of your system's ability to filter the indoor air depends on several factors, including:

- Filter efficiency
- Air velocity
- Runtime
- Amount of particulate matter on the filter
- Electrostatic charge
- Filter thickness
- Filter porosity
- Size of fibers
- Size of particles

Most of the items on the list affect the filter effectiveness in one direction. By definition, more efficient filters capture more particles. Lower velocity of air generally results in more particles captured. The dirtier a filter gets, the more particles it captures unless it started with an electrostatic charge (electret filter). As electret filters load, their ability to capture particles decreases at first, but if they get dirty enough, they'll capture more particles again. Although loading a filter with dirt may help it stop more particles, the added resistance to the air flow may result in less filtered air as less air is able to go through the dirty filter. It may also result in problems with heating and cooling, and it could even damage the equipment.

Benefits of Filtration

A good particulate filtration system can:
- Keep the HVAC equipment clean
- Keep the ducts clean
- Improve functioning and efficiency of heating and air-conditioning systems
- Reduce the amount of dust in the house
- Remove allergens and other health-impairing particles from the air

Filtering dust and other particles keeps them from collecting on the air conditioner coil, which gets wet. Wet dirt is good for gardening. It's not good to have a garden in your air conditioner. The name for that farm on your coil is biofilm, which is just a fancy name for a slimy layer of algae, mold, and bacteria. When biofilm collects on your AC coil, the resistance to air flow increases, affecting the functioning of both your air conditioner and heating system. It can also blow the waste products of biofilm metabolism into the air, which may cause allergic reactions or illness.

However, many heating and AC systems don't provide all those benefits because they don't do a good job filtering. In fact, some are downright terrible at removing dust, particulates, bacteria, viruses, and mold spores. So, before we go on to the basics of good filtration, we need to look at why so many filters are so bad at doing this simple job.

Six Reasons Your Filter Isn't Improving Your Indoor Air Quality

One of the primary methods to deal with these visible and invisible particles is to filter them out of the indoor air. In most homes, the only filtering of the air that happens is in the heating and air-conditioning system. But if you think you're covered because you have a forced-air system with a filter, let me give you a few reasons why that filter that you so dutifully change may not be helping your indoor air quality (IAQ). (You do change your filter, don't you?)

1. No Filter

It's true. If there's no filter in the filter slot, you're not going to get any filtration. And yeah, it really happens. Sometimes someone removes a filter because it's in a difficult spot to reach, like a crawl space. Other times they take it out and forget to put it back in. Still other times...well, who knows! All kinds of things happen. If you do not have a filter, you are not improving your indoor air quality, and you're also getting dirt in your duct work, blower, air-conditioner coil, furnace heat exchanger, and everything else in there.

Figure 15.2. *This HVAC system has a filter slot with no filter, and, to make it even worse, no cover over the filter slot.*

I took the photo in Figure 15.2 in a nasty, damp crawl space in Atlanta. Notice the filter slot near the middle of the photo? Not only is the cover missing, but so was the filter. I took the picture on a hot, muggy day in August. Imagine all the nasty stuff getting sucked in there and sent through the system and into the house.

2. Filter Bypass

How about the filter in Figure 15.3? That's some serious bypass. They put a nice, deep media filter in that's capable of filtering out a lot of nasty stuff in the air. But they installed it incorrectly, so quite a bit of air going through the system was passing right by the filter—instead of through it. Bypass means you're not cleaning all of the air.

It doesn't take a fancy filter to get bypass, though. Plenty of standard 1-inch fiberglass filters don't fit well, are the wrong size, or get jammed into the slot incorrectly. When that happens, filter bypass reduces your filtration efficiency.

Figure 15.3. *A fancy filter incorrectly installed, resulting in a lot of bypass*

3. Not Enough Runtime

Filters can clean the air only when air is going through them. When the system is off, no filtering happens. You may be thinking, "Aha! Yet another reason not to install an oversized heating and air-conditioning system." Hang on there. The problem with that thinking is that when you put in a smaller HVAC system, you also have less air flow. The filtration volume is the product of those two quantities:

Filtration volume = Air flow x runtime

You can double the runtime by cutting the system size in half, but at the same time you're also cutting the air flow in half. That means the filtration volume stays the same.

One way some IAQ advocates tell people to get more runtime is to put the fan on the "On" position instead of on "Auto." That's a nice idea, and it does work. But it also may increase your energy bills if you have an inefficient blower and duct system. Worse, it may create new indoor air quality problems in a humid climate during cooling season. When the air-conditioner compressor cycles off, the coil warms up and evaporates the condensed water and puts it back into your air. Thus, you could be making your IAQ worse by raising the humidity. I did an experiment with this in my home a few years ago, and the relative humidity quickly rose to 70 percent.

The best thing to do here is size your system properly, keep the fan on the "Auto" position, and get as much filtering as you can with your system. If you have an efficient blower motor and are in a dry climate or running your system with a dry coil (e.g., in wintertime), using the fan on the "On" setting can help. Of course, the best thing to do is focus on minimizing the stuff in your indoor air by doing source control, air sealing, and mechanical ventilation—both local (bathrooms and kitchen) and whole house. If that still doesn't do it for you, it may be time to add a standalone fan with a filter that will run more and get you a higher filtration volume.

4. Not Enough Flow

Now you know that flow and runtime go together. So, it follows that not enough flow also impacts your filter's ability to help IAQ. This is a common problem for a couple of reasons. First, many return ducts and filters are sized too small. That increases the resistance in the system, which reduces air flow. Second, some people don't change their filters often enough. (I know this doesn't apply to you, right?) Again, the result is high resistance and low air flow.

Figure 15.4. *The pressure drop across this filter (a measure of resistance to air flow) is nearly 9 times higher than is recommended. Some of that resistance is due to the dirt on the filter, but much of it is because the filter area is too small.*

The system in Figure 15.4 had both problems. The pressure drop across the dirty filter and coil in this system was a super high 0.9 inches of water column (iwc). That pressure drop is nine times higher than recommended by the Air Conditioning Contractors of America. With a clean filter, it was still six times too high, at 0.6 iwc.

5. Low-Efficiency Filter

You can install a standard 1-inch fiberglass filter. It's not going to do much for your IAQ because it's basically designed to keep dog hair,

Two Reasons to Avoid Most Electronic Air Cleaners

A slew of electronic air cleaners have gained a foothold in the home indoor air quality market. They include photocatalytic oxidation (PCO), ionizers, ozone generators, electrostatic precipitators, and germicidal ultraviolet lamps. These devices have gotten a lot of attention as the companies making them have ramped up their marketing to capitalize on the COVID-19 pandemic.

One of these, ultraviolet lamps, is a proven technology used in hospitals and other places that need really clean air. However, they're often not appropriate for homes because of the level of engineering required to design them properly. Another, the electrostatic precipitator, uses electric fields in place of (or in addition to) standard filters. It can be a good way to reduce waste sent to the landfill.

The air cleaners to watch out for are the additive types. They add something to the air in an attempt to remove the bad stuff, but those additives often do more than just remove the bad stuff.

Marwa Zaatari, PhD, a mechanical engineer and IAQ consultant, examined three claims made by additive electronic air cleaner companies: reduced particle counts, deactivation of the SARS-COV-2 virus, and the removal of formaldehyde and volatile organic compounds. She found that manufacturers' claims are either false or can't be verified by independent researchers.

Reason number one to avoid additive air cleaners: As Dr. Zaatari found, a lot of electronic air cleaners don't do what they say they do. There are no standards or regulations they have to follow. They can devise their own tests of effectiveness, keep the test methods to themselves, and claim almost whatever they want.

Reason number two to avoid additive air cleaners: They may actually be bad for indoor air quality. They may produce ozone, which is protective in the Earth's stratosphere, but harmful here at the surface. Here's what the US Environmental Protection Agency says about ozone:

When inhaled, ozone can damage the lungs. Relatively low amounts can cause chest pain, coughing, shortness of breath, and throat irritation. Ozone may also worsen chronic respiratory diseases, such as asthma, and compromise the ability of the body to fight respiratory infections.

Some release formaldehyde. Some may even put carbon monoxide into the indoor air. It's the byproducts of these systems that can cause problems.

In short, it's best to stick with non-additive technology when possible. If you need a stand-alone air cleaner in your house, buy one that's a HEPA filter with a high clean air delivery rate (CADR). (The CADR is the air flow rate multiplied by the efficiency of the filter. For example, an air cleaner that moves 300 cubic feet per minute through a filter that has an efficiency of 85 percent for the $PM_{2.5}$ range would have a CADR of 300 x 0.85 = 255 cfm.)

dead spiders, and lost socks from getting into the air handler. Yes, and dust, too. But it won't filter out the small particles that present more of an IAQ problem.

The standard rating system for filters is minimum efficiency reporting value (MERV). (See later in this chapter for more on MERV ratings.) The higher the MERV number, the more stuff you filter out. For example, a 1-inch fiberglass filter is about a MERV-2. MERV-10 removes half of the $PM_{2.5}$, but IAQ experts recommend MERV-13 or higher because it removes more than 85 percent of little, bitty, invisible lung penetrators. A MERV-13 filter also removes 50 percent of the even smaller particles, $PM_{1.0}$ and smaller. On the other hand, MERV-10 filters don't have to remove any particles that small.

But there's a caveat here: High-MERV filters can decrease the air flow if your system isn't designed to handle them. The next two sections will explore this issue in depth and show you how to do it right.

6. Not Filtering Outdoor Air

Some whole-house mechanical ventilation systems are designed to use the heating and cooling ducts to distribute outdoor air. With the central-fan-integrated-supply type of mechanical ventilation (see Chapter 17), a duct from the outdoors is connected to the return side of the duct system. Occasionally, a designer or installer doesn't pay attention and connects that outdoor air duct to the return side downstream of the filter.

Oops! When that happens, you're putting unfiltered outdoor air straight into your ducts, where it can make the ducts, blower, and heating and AC components dirty as well as send more particulate matter and other outdoor air pollutants into your indoor air. Because the biggest source of $PM_{2.5}$ in many homes is outdoor air, make sure you filter outdoor air before introducing it into your home.

Filtration can be an important part of good IAQ. Unfortunately, you need to overcome some significant obstacles if you want to clean up your air. Jeffrey Siegel, PhD, of the University of Toronto, has been studying the effectiveness of filtration in real homes. He found that the filtration effectiveness in those homes ranged from 15 to 45 percent.[26] No one who understands this issue and has seen the filtration in homes would be surprised by this poor performance.

Types of Filters

Before we dive into the details of filter types, let's first divide the world of filtration into two groups: central HVAC system filters and stand-alone filters. The latter has its place and garnered a lot of attention during the COVID-19 pandemic. We'll focus mainly on central HVAC system filters here, but see the sidebar "The Corsi-Rosenthal Box and Other DIY Box Fan Filters" on page 261 for a high-MERV standalone filter you can make yourself—for less than it would cost you to get a small tattoo of a MERV-2 filter (i.e., less than $100 US).

The standard filters used in central HVAC systems are made with a matte of fibers from fiberglass, polyester, polypropylene, cotton, or other materials. Here are the three basic options for fibrous media filters:

- Fiberglass filters
- Washable filters
- High-efficiency fabric filters

Fiberglass filters: The fiberglass filter is the inexpensive, standard, disposable filter. They're almost always only 1 inch thick. You can find thicker versions, and the extra thickness improves the filter efficiency a bit. But these filters still won't capture many of the small particles. This type of filter is intended mainly to protect the equipment by keeping the larger particles from accumulating in the ducts, blower, and heating and cooling components. It will do little for your indoor air quality.

Washable filters: Reusable or washable filters are often promoted as a way to save money by never having to buy filters again. You have to clean them regularly, and they're supposed to last a long time. Most washable filters are less efficient at capturing particles from the air than are fabric filters. They generally remove only the larger particles.

26. "Residential Filtration" by Jeffrey Siegel, PhD, *ASHRAE Journal,* Nov. 2019

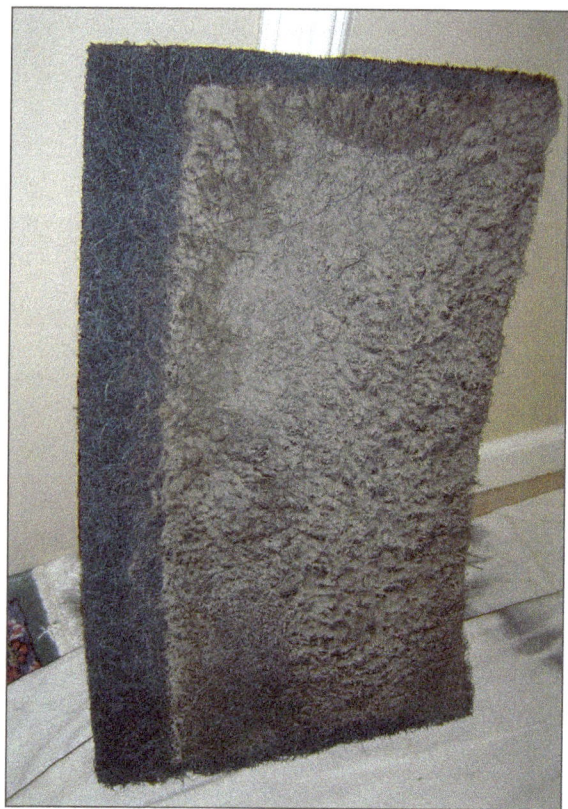

Figure 15.5. *Do you really want to expose yourself to the pollutants on a dirty filter by having to clean it?*

Then there's the washing. Your filter collects gunk you don't want to breathe. Some indoor air quality researchers actually study that stuff, and they've found it to have a wide range of pollutants that are best not disturbed: lead, cadmium, semi-volatile organic compounds, flame retardants, microbes, and skin flakes. And because of the

microbes, sometimes that dirty filter turns into its own little ecosystem. Keeping in mind an image of those nasties on the filter, imagine taking your washable filter and cleaning it out. In your kitchen sink. You've done a good job collecting that stuff, and now you're going to expose yourself to it—unless you're wearing full personal protective equipment and washing it outdoors.

High-efficiency fabric filters: The best of the three options is the high-efficiency fabric filter. These most often come with pleats in the fabric, which add more surface area, and the most common thicknesses are 1 inch to 4 inches. Like the fiberglass and washable filters, high-efficiency fabric filters work by collecting particles the way pulling a net through water can catch algae, fish, and whatever else is too big to go through the holes in the net. It's a sieving process. But that's not all. Even particles that are smaller than the holes sometimes get captured because of sticking after a direct impact or getting pulled in by electrostatic attraction.

In general, the more efficient filters are the ones that give the passing particles more opportunities to get caught. Smaller pores, thicker media, and more surface area all help. In the next section, we'll look at the three main ratings systems for filter efficiency. The good news is that even though the numbers are different, higher is better on all three scales.

Filter Ratings: MERV, FPR, and MPR

When you go shopping for filters, you may be confronted with different ratings for filter efficiency. The three main ratings you're likely to see are MERV, FPR, and MPR.

Minimum Efficiency Reporting Value (MERV)

The standard rating system for filters is called minimum efficiency reporting value (MERV). When

I say it's the "standard" rating system, I mean it. It's defined in an ASHRAE standard (52.2), which specifies the conditions under which the testing must be done and the performance required to meet each MERV level. Higher-MERV filters remove more particles from your air. They also remove smaller particles. A typical 1-inch fiberglass filter is MERV-2. The top end of the scale is MERV-16.

Before we go further, we need to define

The Corsi-Rosenthal Box and Other DIY Box Fan Filters

If your central HVAC system doesn't do a good job with filtration, you can always add a standalone air cleaner. A portable HEPA air cleaner is proven technology, but they can by pricy. For about $100 or less, you can build your own standalone air cleaner with a very high clean air delivery rate (CADR). All you need is a box fan and one, two, four, or five high-efficiency filters. MERV-13 is the minimum filter rating you should look for.

Figure 15.6. *A portable DIY high-efficiency air cleaner, made with a box fan and four MERV-13 filters*

The simplest way to make such an air cleaner is to tape a MERV-13 filter to a box fan. The problem with a single filter, though, is that there will be more resistance to air flow (pressure drop) and thus lower air flow. You can tape two filters together, doubling the filter area and improving the air flow. Or you could turn your DIY air cleaner into a cube by using four or five filters, as shown in Figure 15.6. That's the Corsi-Rosenthal version, named for Richard Corsi, PhD, PE, an IAQ researcher, and Jim Rosenthal, who owns a filter company.

With all the concern over airborne transmission of COVID-19, these devices have really taken off. Schools, community groups, and families have gotten in on the action, and you can find a lot of information about them online.

the three general size ranges of particulate matter (PM).

- PM_{10} – 3.0 to 10.0 microns
- $PM_{2.5}$ – 1.0 to 3.0 microns
- $PM_{1.0}$ – 0.3 to 1.0 micron

The words making up the MERV acronym are a bit unwieldy, but the "minimum efficiency" part is the most important. For example, for a filter to get a MERV-13 rating, it must filter out a minimum of 90 percent of the PM_{10}, a minimum of 85 percent of the $PM_{2.5}$, and a minimum of 50 percent of the $PM_{1.0}$. Table 15.1 shows the percentage of particles removed by size range of particle and the MERV rating of the filter.

As you can see, you've got to go to at least MERV-10 to remove half of the $PM_{2.5}$. But you really should think of MERV-13 as the minimum because it removes more than 85 percent of little, bitty, invisible pieces of stuff. With the COVID-19 pandemic, ASHRAE recommended at least MERV-14.

MERV	0.3-1.0 μm	1.0-3.0 μm	3.0-10.0 μm
16	≥ 95%	≥ 95%	≥ 95%
15	≥ 85%	≥ 90%	≥ 95%
14	≥ 75%	≥ 90%	≥ 95%
13	≥ 50%	≥ 85%	≥ 90%
12	≥ 35%	≥ 80%	≥ 90%
11	≥ 20%	≥ 65%	≥ 85%
10		≥ 50%	≥ 80%
9		≥ 35%	≥ 75%
8		≥ 20%	≥ 70%
7			≥ 50%
6			≥ 35%
5			≥ 20%
4			< 20%
3			< 20%
2			< 20%
1			< 20%

Table 15.1. *The percentage of small particles filtered out for MERV 1 through 16*

Filter Performance Rating (FPR)

The Home Depot sells a lot of filters. Rather than use MERV ratings, they decided to create their own rating system, which they call filter performance rating (FPR). The details of their testing are a bit murky, but their website explains some of what goes into it. They look at how well a filter catches both large and small particles and rank the filters on a scale of 1 to 10. From that, they do a weighted average using those percentiles:

> *Sixty percent of the rating is determined by the filter's ability to capture large particles, 30 percent is determined by its ability to capture small particles, and weight gain over the filter's lifetime determines the final 10 percent.*[27]

Here are the four FPR categories of ratings you'll find on filters:

- 1-4: Good
- 5-7: Better
- 8-9: Best
- 10: Premium

Home Depot must be using a different definition for the word "best" than the one I'm familiar with because their premium is better than best. If you're wondering how FPR compares to MERV, the Home Depot website has a section on that. They start by saying, "FPR-10 is similar in strength to MERV-20, since they are both the highest rating value."[28] They're not in tune with the MERV scale, however, because it goes only to 16. Some filters on their website have both an FPR and a MERV rating, and at least one with an FPR of 10 is shown as equivalent to either MERV-8 or MERV-13.[29] Clearly, this isn't clear. Is an FPR-10 the same as MERV-16 or MERV-13 or MERV-8? Who knows!

Home Depot also doesn't provide easily available information on the sizes of what they call large and small particles, so it's hard to know what you're getting with a particular FPR rating. When you combine that with the difficulty of comparing FPR to MERV, it seems the best you can do with this scale is to use it as a rough guide. If you want to filter out as much of the $PM_{2.5}$ as you can, stick with the FPR-10. Better, find one that also has a MERV rating and go with MERV-13 or higher.

> **Buy filters with a MERV rating whenever possible.**

Microparticle Performance Rating (MPR)

As with Home Depot's filter performance rating, the microparticle performance rating (MPR) was developed by a company with a financial interest in the sale of filters. In this case, it was 3M, the maker of the Filtrete™ line of filters. Unlike MERV and FPR, the MPR measures the effectiveness of a filter's capturing only the smallest particles on the MERV scale: 0.3 to 1.0 micron. Their website says, "Your filter's MPR (Microparticle Performance Rating) indicates its ability to capture tiny particles between 0.3 and 1 micron in size."

Chances are good that if a filter captures a lot of the small particles, it will capture even more of the larger particles. The scale just won't tell you anything about how well it does with particles larger than 1.0 micron. And we should note that 2.5 microns, near the upper limit of $PM_{2.5}$, is in the group of larger particles not covered by MPR. However, apparently they do measure the larger particles because they provide information comparing MPR to MERV, including a table of capture efficiency data showing the three ranges of particle sizes used in the MERV scale.

Like MERV and FPR, the MPR system uses

27. From https://www.homedepot.com/c/ab/best-air-filters-for-your-home/9ba683603be9fa5395fab90e10394fb, accessed on 5/18/2020.

28. From https://www.homedepot.com/c/ab/best-air-filters-for-your-home/9ba683603be9fa5395fab90e10394fb, accessed on 5/18/2020.

29. From https://www.homedepot.com/p/Honeywell-16-in-x-20-in-x-1-in-Elite-Allergen-Pleated-Air-Filter-Case-of-12-91001-011620/203225883, accessed on 5/18/2020.

a numerical scale on which higher numbers indicate better filtration. The MPR scale, however, uses much larger numbers. Their basic filter is rated at 100, and their most efficient filter is rated at 2800. The MPR-2800 would qualify as a MERV-14. So, even though 3M emphasizes the smallest size range of particles, their best filter does not qualify for the highest MERV rating.

My recommendation is to buy filters with a MERV rating whenever possible. All three ratings have their problems, but even Home Depot and 3M state on their websites that MERV is the industry standard for rating filters. If you want a filter to improve your indoor air quality and not just protect the heating and air-conditioning system, go with MERV 13, FPR-10, MPR-1900, or higher. But make sure you can do that without reducing air flow and possibly damaging your system. (The next section covers that aspect of filtration.)

The Path to Low Pressure Drop across a High-Efficiency Filter

How can we get a high-MERV filter and have it filter well without causing problems with the air flow in the heating and cooling system? The answer is simple: Make the filter big enough. In our Energy Vanguard office, we have a Mitsubishi ducted mini-split heat pump, and I have two in my home. All three air handlers have MERV-13 filters, and none has a problem with resistance to air flow through the filter. Let me show you what's possible.

High-MERV Filters with Low Pressure Drop

In our office, we have a filter that's 20"x20" and 4" deep in a cabinet near the ducted mini-split air handler. Our pressure drop is 0.06 iwc (Figure 15.7). In my home, I have three 16"x25"x2" MERV-13 filters on two ducted mini-split air handlers. All three also come in at around 0.06 iwc pressure drop. That's low compared to what you might expect for a MERV-13 filter.

The Manual D duct design protocol (Chapter 14) says to allow 0.10 iwc for a filter, and that's for a standard 1-inch deep MERV-2 filter, not a 2-inch or 4-inch MERV-13. Ask contractors what the pressure drop across a high-MERV filter is, and they'll probably tell you something like 0.25 iwc because that's where a lot of them come in.

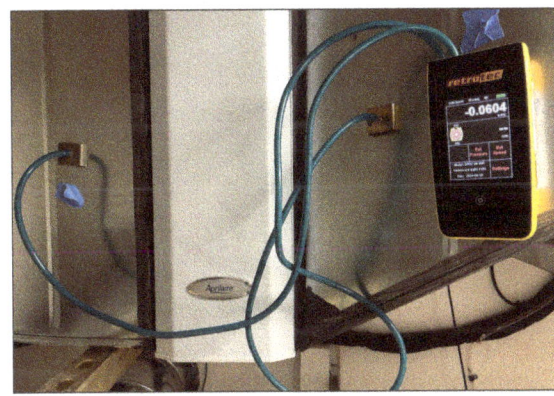

Figure 15.7. *The pressure drop across our MERV-13 filter is a very low 0.06 inch of water column (iwc.).*

When we measured the air flow in our office system, we got 363 cfm. The ratio of filter area to air flow is 0.008 sf/cfm, or 3.1 square feet per ton when converted using 400 cfm/ton of capacity. Getting a 0.06 iwc pressure drop across a MERV-13 filter is great. The key to whether it's a good number or not is how well it fits in with the total pressure drop in the system compared to what's allowed (the total external static pressure, or TESP). In our case, it's fine. We've got 0.2 iwc total external static pressure to work with, and our measured result was 0.1 iwc.

A Simple Rule of Thumb for Low Pressure Drop across a High-MERV Filter

I've discussed data from four MERV-13 filters now. All are lower than you'd measure across many of the MERV-13 filters installed in the wild, and I've given you the key to achieving similarly low pressure drops. It's simply to increase the filter area relative to the air flow rate.

The systems in our office and my house above have ratios of filter area to air flow between 3.1 and 4.4 square feet per ton. You don't have to go that high, though; 2 square feet per ton works fine. With smaller-capacity mini-split heat pumps, getting filter sizes to 2.5 or 3.0 square feet per ton isn't that hard. With conventional systems, it's not so easy. For example, with a 2.5-ton system at 3.0 square feet per ton, you'd need 7.5 square feet of filter area, or a 30"x36" filter, but you'd have a hard time finding one that size. You could instead install two 18"x30" filters. But if you use 2.0 square feet per ton, the resulting 24"x30" filter (or equivalent) is much easier to find space for, and you can still get a low pressure drop.

So, here's your rule of thumb for filter sizing:

Filter area = 2.0 square feet (or more) for each 400 cfm of air flow

One other feature to pay attention to is the back side of the filter. To reduce turbulence, you want a good 6 inches of space behind the filter before the air enters a smaller duct. Figure 15.8 shows one of the sheet metal boxes above a filter grille in my home. Originally, I had little space between the filter and the sheet metal backing, and this retrofit decreased my filter pressure drop about 30 percent.

Do these things (and size your ducts properly), and you won't have to worry about high pressure drops across your filters.

Figure 15.8. *The back side of one of the filter grilles in my home: There's a lot of space to calm the air down before it enters the duct.*

How Often Should You Change the Filter?

Rules of thumb for sizing air conditioners are dumb. We've already discussed how they don't work when determining what size heating and air-conditioning system you need. Another area where a rule of thumb dominates is in replacing the filter in your air conditioner (or heat pump or furnace). Change it every 30 days, right?

Is 30 Days the Answer?

When you buy standard 1-inch fiberglass filters for your HVAC system, the instructions on the package usually say to change it every 30 days. This advice gets repeated dutifully by a lot of people and organizations trying to help. And the truth is, you won't cause any problems by changing your filter every 30 days (unless it needs changing sooner).

Changing the filter every 30 days is a hassle, though. In spring and fall, the filter generally won't get as dirty as summer and winter because you're not running the heating and cooling as much, so you can get by with changing it less frequently. And in a house that doesn't have much infiltration or duct leakage and that has a low level of dust overall, the filter can stay clean longer even when being used a lot. If you have pets that shed a lot, return vents in the floor, or some other reason that you get a lot of stuff in your indoor air, you need to replace the filter more frequently.

Figure 15.9. *Don't let your filter get this dirty!*

And then there's the issue of the type of filter. Standard 1-inch fiberglass filters are cheap, so changing them every 30 days won't cost you much. But I've already told you that you should be using high-MERV filters. Changing them every 30 days is not so easy for the pocketbook because they're more expensive.

How About Replacing Filters When They Look Dirty?

The easiest way to approach filter replacements is to go by a visual inspection. Rather than replace the filter every 30 days, that rule of thumb should be changed to inspect the filter every 30 days. When it's as dirty as the filter in Figure 15.9, it's probably past time to replace it. If you look at the filter after a month of use, and it still looks relatively clean, it should be fine to leave it in.

With high-efficiency filters in properly

designed systems, just looking at the filter may not be enough. It's possible for them to keep performing well with only a small impact on resistance to air flow if you do the things recommended in the past section (i.e., keep the ratio of filter area to air flow at 2 square feet per ton or more). For that situation, we need a better metric than visual inspection.

Measure the Pressure Drop Across the Filter

High-efficiency filters can hold more dust. There's more surface area in thicker, pleated filters, so when they capture the same amount of dirt as a standard 1-inch filter, the increase in resistance isn't as much. John Semmelhack, a Virginia consultant and contractor, said this about measuring the drop to determine when it's time to replace a filter:

Our general rule is that when the pressure drop across the filter doubles from the initial, clean pressure drop, it's probably time for a change. With big, deep filters this can take a loooooooooong time, and the filters will look absolutely disgusting well before the pressure drop would indicate that it's time for a change.

Figure 15.7 in the previous section shows the setup for measuring pressure. To do this, you need a device that measures small pressure changes (a digital manometer or an analog pressure gauge), one or two static pressure probes, and some vinyl hose to connect the probes to the gauge (Figure 15.10).

Once you have the items needed to measure the pressure drop, you'll have to drill a hole in the return ductwork on each side of the filter. If you're measuring the pressure drop across a filter grille, you just need one hole because one side of the filter is open to the room where the filter grille is installed. In Figure 15.7, I used two static pressure probes, one inserted in each hole, because the filter is in a cabinet embedded in the return duct. Each probe has a piece of hose connecting the probes to the input and reference pressure taps on the gauge.

Figure 15.10. These are the things you need to set up a gauge to monitor the pressure drop.

A digital manometer isn't the least expensive way to do this, though. You can get a decent analog pressure gauge for about the cost of this book. Make sure to get one with a range of 0 to 0.5 iwc. If you ever have a filter with a pressure drop approaching the upper limit of that gauge, you have a problem.

What About the Total System Pressure?

I need to point out one more thing here: Waiting for your pressure drop across the filter to double will work only for a filter and duct system that are designed properly. If you put in a MERV-13 filter and the pressure drop across a brand-new, clean filter is 0.15 iwc, which would not be uncommon in poorly designed systems, you shouldn't let that filter load to the point where the pressure drop is 0.3 iwc. The pressure drop across the dirty filter may push over what's allowed for the total external static pressure.

If you want a performance-based method for deciding when to change a filter, you've got to make sure your duct system and filter design are appropriate. If they're not, you should fix those problems so you can get it to the point where a doubling of the filter pressure drop is your signal to change the filter.

Chapter Takeaways

- Fibrous media filters can remove harmful particles from the indoor air.
- The effectiveness of a filtration system depends on many factors.
- Many filters don't do a good job of filtering the air.
- Additive air cleaners, which add chemically active particles to the indoor air, may not clean the air as well as the manufacturers claim and may create harmful pollutants through chemical reactions.
- Filter ratings can be confusing. The MERV rating scale provides the best guidance on the level of filtration you can expect.
- You can get high-efficiency filtration with low resistance by sizing the filter appropriately.

CHAPTER 16

Dehumidification

You know those days in spring and fall when the temperature is about 70 °F and it's cloudy and humid outdoors? Maybe it's raining. It's too cool for the air conditioner to run and too warm for the heat. Whether you open the windows or not, it's going to be humid indoors. You can either wait out the muggy weather and let the indoor relative humidity float above 70 percent, or you can use a dehumidifier. That's not the only case where a dehumidifier can help, but it's an important one.

> *"The absence of suffocating humidity and carnivorous plants was appreciated."*
> —Brandon Mull

Excess humidity can have a negative impact on indoor air quality, thermal comfort, and durability. Moisture floating around in the house can collect on cool parts of the building enclosure. It can aid mold growth. It can keep viruses active and bacteria alive. It makes it harder for our bodies to use evaporative cooling to rid ourselves of metabolic waste heat. Oh, and it can rot your house, too.

In some situations, the air and thermal control layers help by keeping the temperature of any materials above the dew point. In cold weather, ventilating more can reduce the indoor humidity. Still, 21st-century homes in humid climates occasionally need additional help reducing indoor humidity. And for high-performance homes with low cooling loads in humid climates, supplemental dehumidification has become essential.

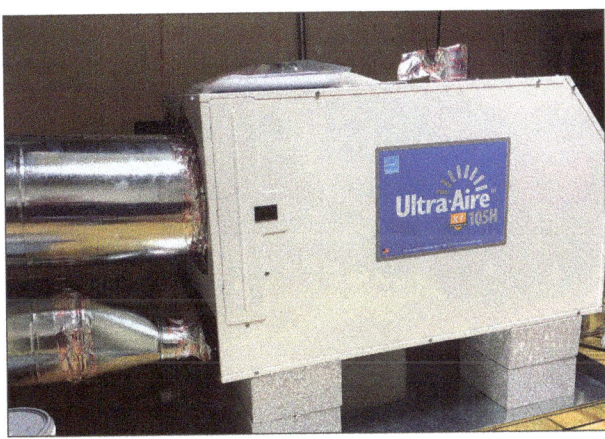

Figure 16.1. *A ducted whole-house dehumidifier*

How Dehumidifiers Work

A dehumidifier works the same way a refrigerator, air conditioner, or heat pump works. A refrigerant pumped through the system goes through phase changes that absorb and release heat. The absorber of heat is the evaporator coil, which gets cold enough to cool air and condense water vapor. (See Chapter 13.) Refrigerators, air conditioners, and dehumidifiers have different purposes, so the design changes depending on whether the primary need is getting low temperatures (refrigerators), cooling and dehumidifying indoor air (air conditioners), or condensing water vapor. However, the basic principles are the same.

Because an air conditioner's primary purpose is cooling the air, it has to send the heat it collects from the indoors to the outdoors. That's why air conditioners are always connected to the outdoors, either by having the components split into two separate boxes (a split system), by having a unit that is half inside and half outside (a window unit or package terminal air conditioner), or by having a unit that's all outdoors with ducts connecting it to indoors (a package unit).

A dehumidifier differs from an air conditioner in that the focus is solely on removing water vapor from the air. Most dehumidifiers are package units, with a single cabinet containing all the components. Unlike an air conditioner, a dehumidifier is not connected to the outdoors, so all the heat stays inside the space it's dehumidifying. Recall from Chapter 12 that air conditioners remove both sensible heat (temperature) and latent heat (humidity) from the house.

A dehumidifier, in contrast, simply converts latent heat to sensible heat. All of that newly converted sensible heat—plus the heat from running the dehumidifier—stays in the house. An air conditioner dries and cools the air. A dehumidifier dries and warms the air. That's an important consideration when deciding how to set up and use a dehumidifier.

Do You Need a Dehumidifier?

Let's look at some scenarios to see what conditions might indicate the need for a dehumidifier.

Cold outdoors: When it's cold outdoors, you shouldn't need a dehumidifier. Cold air is dry air, so ventilating the house with outdoor air will provide the drying you need. Yes, this works for basements, too, but people often use dehumidifiers there because basements are usually cooler than the rest of the house.

Indoor relative humidity less than 60 percent: When the relative humidity stays below 60 percent without a dehumidifier, you don't need one. If it's that high in winter, you may need more ventilation if you have weak areas in the building enclosure. Single-pane windows will become an accidental dehumidifier, for example, if you keep the relative humidity in the 50+ percent range while outdoor temperatures are in the 40s Fahrenheit. In summer, humidity between 50 and 60 percent is still in the range of thermal comfort and shouldn't cause indoor air quality or durability problems.

Mild and dry outdoors: You know the days. It's beautiful and sunny outdoors on a perfect spring or fall day. As with cold weather, you may be able to do all the drying you need to do by ventilating with outdoor air.

Mild and humid outdoors: These are some of the worst times for humidity. It's 70 °F and raining (or about to rain or recently finished raining). The outdoor relative humidity is 90 to 100 percent. On the Gulf Coast, this can happen from October through April. The farther north you go, the more it's just a spring and fall phenomenon. It's the kind of weather that forces you to let the muggy air invade your house if you don't have supplemental dehumidification because the air conditioner won't dehumidify, at least not without making the house uncomfortably cold. This is the perfect weather for a dehumidifier, but do you have enough of those days for it to matter?

Hot and humid outdoors: Ah, summer! It's warm and muggy in the morning and hot and muggy in the afternoon. The air conditioner runs to keep you cool, but does it keep the indoor air dry? Maybe. Most air-conditioned homes don't have a problem with high humidity in summer. The air conditioner runs long enough, even if it's oversized, that it does a good job removing moisture.

Some homes, however, do have a problem keeping the humidity low on hot summer days. One reason is that the air conditioner is grossly oversized out of negligence. Another is that the air conditioner is grossly oversized because the cooling load on the house is much lower than the smallest air conditioner available, which happens with super airtight, highly insulated homes. The smaller the home, the worse this problem becomes, and it can be extreme in apartments and condos. Yet another reason is that the house has too much infiltration and duct leakage.

High-performance house: A robust building enclosure with a lot of insulation and a well-sealed air barrier reduces the cooling load so much that it can be difficult to find an air conditioner small enough for the house. Even with right-sized air conditioning, the sensible load is often so low that the air conditioner won't run enough hours per day to dehumidify well. Then you have the issue of more efficient air conditioners having less capacity to remove moisture. The result of all this is that the more insulated and airtight a house is, the more likely it will be to need supplemental dehumidification in a humid climate.

Other factors: In addition to the scenarios above, the need for a dehumidifier is affected by moisture from inside the house. For example, a damp crawl space or basement can raise the humidity in the whole house. The number of people in the home is also a factor because each person generates moisture by breathing, bathing, and cooking. Indoor activities matter, too. A family with several aquariums is going to have higher relative humidity. Indoor pools, hot tubs,

and water features, of course, deserve special attention regarding humidity control. Finally, the type of air conditioner you use may affect your need for a dehumidifier. For example, mini-split heat pumps don't have as much moisture removal capacity as standard air conditioners.

In the end, adding supplemental dehumidification is often necessary for apartments, condos, and low-load houses in humid climates. Likewise, it's getting to be necessary for code-built homes in hot, humid climates because the energy code has improved so much. For everyone else, it's probably a subjective call. How many of those moderate but muggy days are you willing to let the indoor relative humidity float up above 70 percent? If you're looking for tight control of the indoor conditions, you'll want a dehumidifier.

> *The more insulated and airtight a house is, the more likely it will be to need supplemental dehumidification in a humid climate.*

Dehumidifier Types

You can dehumidify in several ways. As mentioned above, ventilating with dry outdoor air dehumidifies the indoor air through dilution. Running an air conditioner on warm days dehumidifies as it cools the indoor air. Sometimes you need a dehumidifier because the outdoor air isn't dry enough, and the air conditioner doesn't run enough. In this book, that means a mechanical dehumidifier (as opposed to a desiccant or other type of dehumidifier).

A mechanical dehumidifier is what most people simply call a dehumidifier. It is a heat

pump, though, just as an air conditioner or a refrigerator is a heat pump. (See Chapter 13.) They all use a compressor, coils, and refrigerant to move heat from one place to another. The dehumidifier, though, is designed to maximize the condensation of water vapor rather than the sensible cooling of the air. In fact, most dehumidifiers don't do any sensible cooling because the whole process happens in a self-contained unit. They just convert latent heat to sensible heat. Let's talk about the two types of dehumidifiers: room dehumidifiers and whole-house dehumidifiers.

Room Dehumidifiers

When the average person thinks of a dehumidifier, they picture a small standalone unit. A room dehumidifier is a self-contained unit that sits in the space you want to dehumidify. The liquid water that results from the dehumidification usually goes into a tank built into the unit, and it has to be emptied manually when it fills up. Some dehumidifiers let you drain the water through a tube to avoid having to empty the tank. The most commonly available models remove about 20 to 30 pints of water per day (Figure 16.2).

Figure 16.2. *A standalone dehumidifier*

The advantages of this type of dehumidifier are that they are relatively inexpensive and easy to use. You just set it where you want it, plug it in, and let it do its thing. The downsides are that they are noisy, are not particularly energy efficient, provide relatively little dehumidification, and can't be used remotely. Some units also have had safety problems in recent years, leading to massive recalls. The low capacity of room dehumidifiers means that you may need to buy more than one to do the amount of dehumidification you need. Also, if you don't have a way to drain it with a tube, you have to keep emptying the tank whenever it fills up. The dehumidifier in Figure 16.2 is draining through a hose into a basement sink.

Whole-House Dehumidifiers

The more sophisticated way to control the humidity in a home is to use a whole-house dehumidifier (also called a ducted dehumidifier). These dehumidifiers generally have higher capacity, better energy efficiency, the capability for ducting, and higher cost. The ability to move the air through ducts means that you can install the unit remotely, which helps keep noise out of the space you're dehumidifying. Ducting also lets you pull air from multiple places and distribute the dehumidified air around the house. Even better, you can run a duct from the outdoors to the intake side and use your dehumidifier to ventilate the home as well. In hot, humid climates, this is a good strategy. (See Chapter 17 for more on ventilating dehumidifiers.)

Yes, ducted dehumidifiers are more expensive. But they have higher capacity, too, so one ducted dehumidifier can do the job of two or more standalone dehumidifiers. When comparing the cost of standalone to ducted units, be sure to account for the cost of additional standalone units. Ducted dehumidifiers are also more energy efficient, which means that the higher upfront cost will come back to you in lower operating cost.

Dehumidifier Capacity and Energy Use

Dehumidifiers are characterized mainly by their moisture removal capacity, which is measured in volume of liquid water produced per unit time for a given temperature and relative humidity. The other specification you should check when buying a dehumidifier is its energy consumption.

The US Department of Energy (DOE) has standards for testing and rating both of those quantities, and there's something a bit odd about them. For some reason, they decided to rate capacity in pints per day, whereas energy efficiency is rated in liters per kilowatt-hour.

Noise is another important factor to consider when buying a dehumidifier. And air flow rate is important when deciding on how to duct a whole-house dehumidifier.

Capacity: Dehumidifier capacity, of course, depends on the conditions of the air entering the unit. The warmer and more humid the entering air, the greater the capacity will be. The standard used for testing and rating dehumidifier capacity changed in 2020, so when shopping for a new one, you may notice that they don't seem to have as much capacity as they used to have. Before 2020, dehumidifier capacity was based on air entering at 80 °F and 60 percent relative humidity. The 2020 change dropped that to 65 °F and 60 percent relative humidity for standalone dehumidifiers and 72 °F and 60 percent relative humidity for whole-house dehumidifiers. The change means that what used to be a 30 pint per day standalone dehumidifier now is rated at about 20 pints per day using the new test conditions, and a 70 pint per day model is now rated at about 50 pints per day.

The good news is that the new standards are closer to the actual operating conditions of many dehumidifiers. The other good news is that despite the revised capacity ratings, that 30 pint per day dehumidifier still does exactly the same amount of dehumidification it used to do.

Energy efficiency: On the energy efficiency side, the official ratings give you a way to compare one dehumidifier to another. The old energy efficiency rating for a dehumidifier was called the energy factor. The new one is called the integrated energy factor (IEF), and it now includes standby losses. Both are given as the volume of water produced per unit of electricity used: liters per kilowatt-hour (L/kWh). A low-efficiency unit might have an energy factor as low as 1 L/kWh, whereas the most efficient models can have efficiencies of 3 L/kWh or more.

The efficiency requirement for a dehumidifier to get the ENERGY STAR label is a bit confusing. The threshold needed for standalone dehumidifiers depends on the capacity of the dehumidifier, and there are three ranges. The threshold for whole-house dehumidifiers depends on the size of the dehumidifier case. Table 15 shows how all this shakes out.

Standalone

Capacity (Pts/day)	IEF (L/kWh)
≤ 25.00	≥1.57
25.01 to 50.00	≥ 1.80
≥ 50.01	≥ 3.30

Whole-House

Case Volume (ft³)	IEF (L/kWH
≤ 8.0	≥ 2.09
> 8.0	≥ 3.30

Table 16.1. *Criteria for standalone and whole-house dehumidifiers to get the ENERGY STAR label*

Keep in mind that the term "energy factor" is like seasonal energy efficiency ratio (SEER) for air conditioners. It's the efficiency when tested using the DOE standard. However, as with the miles per gallon efficiency ratings for cars, your efficiency may vary. You already know that the capacity of a dehumidifier changes with the temperature and relative humidity of the air entering the unit, and those variables affect the energy efficiency as well.

For room dehumidifiers, the entering air conditions are the only variables that affect the efficiency. (That assumes the dehumidifier is operating properly with a clean filter and the correct air flow.)

For whole-house dehumidifiers, the fan energy use can change, too. A restrictive duct system has a different effect on the fan energy than a low-resistance duct system. The direction of the effect—more energy use or less energy use—depends on the type of fan motor. Just be aware that ducts add another variable. Then there's the issue of how the dehumidifier fan is controlled. Some fans run only when the unit is dehumidifying. Others can

How to Measure the Energy Efficiency of a Dehumidifier

The energy efficiency of a dehumidifier is the result of a simple calculation:

$$\text{Energy efficiency} = \frac{\textit{volume of water produced}}{\textit{energy used}}$$

Measuring the water produced is easy. Dehumidifiers don't produce it at a great rate, so you can simply capture it in a bucket over a 24-hour period and measure how many pints or liters of water the dehumidifier condensed from the air. For example, if you have a 50 pint per day dehumidifier, you'll catch about 50 pints if the air being dehumidified is at the rated conditions (65 °F and 60 percent relative humidity). Because 50 pints equals 6.25 gallons, you'll need to measure and empty the bucket once before the 24-hour period is over if you're using a 5-gallon bucket. At the end of the 24 hours, your total volume of water collected goes into the numerator in the equation above.

The other part of the equation is the energy used. Nearly all dehumidifiers made for home use plug into standard electrical outlets, and that makes measuring the energy use simple. You can find a gazillion brands of electricity monitors for plugin devices, many with Wi-Fi built in so you can see the energy use on your smartphone. Now you just need to get that number for the same 24-hour period that you're measuring the water, do the little arithmetic above, and voilà! You have the actual energy efficiency of your dehumidifier. Even better, you could do it for a longer period and get a better idea of the long-term average efficiency.

Measured Energy Factor (L/kWh)

Mode	Avg	Low	High
Continuous	**1.55**	1.29	1.90
Intermittent	**1.30**	1.08	1.52

Table 16.2. *The results of measuring the energy factor for a standalone dehumidifier: The official rated efficiency for this model was 1.85 L/kWh.*

I did that little experiment with a standalone dehumidifier in my home and got the results in Table 16.2. The two rows in the table show the difference in efficiency when the dehumidifier ran continuously versus the days when it went on and off many times throughout the day. The takeaway here is that you'll save money by putting the humidifier on a timer so it can run continuously.

move air even when the compressor isn't running, usually when the dehumidifier also is being used as a ventilator. To measure the actual energy use of your dehumidifier, see the sidebar "How to Measure the Energy Efficiency of a Dehumidifier" above.

Humidity Sources in Homes

The dehumidification load in a house can come from several potential sources of moisture: infiltration, ventilation, foundation, internally generated moisture, materials that get wet because of poor water control details, and even from water vapor diffusing through the building enclosure. Infiltration brings humidity with it, so the higher the outdoor humidity and the leakier the house, the more this source contributes.

Ventilation is like controlled infiltration. Spot

ventilation—bath fans and range hoods—exhausts air from the house, resulting in outdoor air leaking in and bringing all its humidity along for the ride. That moisture gets dealt with only when it makes its way to an air conditioner or dehumidifier.

Whole-house ventilation brings moisture in, too, but the amount and method of dealing with it depends on the type of ventilation system. (See Chapter 17.) Exhaust-only whole-house ventilation brings in outdoor humidity through leaks in the building enclosure. That moisture gets removed when it finds an air conditioner or dehumidifier. Supply-only ventilation may do the same as exhaust-only, or it may send the ventilation air directly into the air conditioner or a dehumidifier.

> **The people themselves in a house are a source of moisture, in more than one way.**

An energy recovery ventilator (ERV) sends moisture in the outdoor air right back outdoors—but not all of it. Most ERVs still allow 35 to 55 percent of the humidity in the outdoor air to enter the house.

Foundations are in contact with the ground. If there's not a good liquid water control layer on the foundation, it gets wet. When the foundation gets wet, it can evaporate moisture into the crawl space, basement, or living space. If there's no capillary break, water may also wick up into the main part of the house.

Finally, the people themselves in a house are a source of moisture, in more than one way. Every exhaled breath puts water vapor into the indoor air. So do cooking, washing dishes, bathing, and exercising. The more people and the more activity they do, the more humidity there will be. And if they have moisture-generating hobbies, like aquariums, the dehumidification load can shoot up even more. Houseplants and pets also add to the humidity. Every drop of water you give to the plants, for example, ends up in your indoor air.

Sizing Dehumidifiers

Getting the right size air conditioner is important if you live in a humid climate because you want it to be able to dehumidify as much as it can. That means sizing the air conditioner as close to the cooling load as possible, and not grossly oversizing it. Bigger is not better for air conditioners.

Dehumidifiers aren't as sensitive to proper sizing because they do only one job: remove moisture from the air. The concern here is getting one that's up to the task. Buy one too small, and the space won't dry out as much as you'd like. Buy one too big, though, and it just doesn't run as often. It does the job you want it to do, but it may be noisier and will probably cost you more upfront.

Take a look at dehumidifier marketing information, and you'll see that the most recommended method for selecting one with the proper capacity for your needs is to use a rule

of thumb. As with the main air conditioner rule of thumb, this rule is based on floor area. More sophisticated recommendations might also factor in the application and the level of humidity. For damp basements or crawl spaces, you'll need more capacity. For drier spaces, less capacity may be okay.

Here's what you can do to come up with a size for your application. Check out different manufacturers' recommendations, and then do a little calculation. For example, Santa Fe recommends that their 70 pint per day dehumidifier is appropriate for 1,800, 2,200, or 2,600 square feet of floor area. The difference among the recommendations is whether the dehumidifier is for a basement/crawl space or for supplemental dehumidification for the living space. Now here's the calculation. Divide the capacity (pints per day) by the floor area (square feet). Here's what the numbers come out to for those three scenarios above.

Floor Area (sf)	Capacity/Floor Area (pts/day/sf)
1,800	0.039
2,200	0.032
2,600	0.027

Table 16.3. *Ratio of capacity to floor area for a 70 pint per day dehumidifier, as recommended by Santa Fe Dehumidifiers*

The ratios are in about the same range for the other dehumidifiers that Santa Fe sells, too. It's generally in the 0.03 to 0.04 pints per day per square foot range. Other companies may recommend higher ratios. I've seen some as high as 0.1 pints per day per square foot. In our HVAC design business at Energy Vanguard, we generally size dehumidifiers using the Santa Fe ratios, and it works out fine.

Options for Dehumidifier Ducting

You can duct a dehumidifier in several different ways.

- It can have its own duct system, independent of any other ducts.
- It can have its own intake and send dehumidified air into the heating and cooling system ducts.
- It can have the intake on the return side of the air handler and send dry air into the supply duct in what's called the bypass method.
- It can have both ducts attached to one side of the heating and cooling ducts in what's called the injection method.
- It can draw in outdoor air to dehumidify and send into the house for ventilation.

Let's look at each of these options, but first, let's clear up the language issue so you know which ducts and which air I'm talking about.

Dehumidifier air: the air of primary interest here

Intake air: the air going into the dehumidifier, which could be indoor air or a mix of indoor and outdoor air

Dry air: the air coming out of the dehumidifier

Main air: the heating and cooling air

Main ducts: the heating and cooling system ducts

Return ducts: intake ducts of the heating and cooling system

Supply ducts: the ducts sending heated or cooled air to the house

Independent Ducts

Keeping the intake and dry air ducts independent of any air flows powered by other fans is the best way to go. The ducts can be sized appropriately for the air flow in each section, and you don't have to worry about fighting the pressure created by other fans. At its simplest, this setup would have a single intake vent and a single supply vent with the dehumidifier between the two. It could also have multiple intake or supply vents.

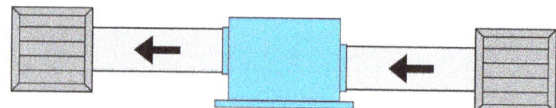

Figure 16.3. *The ideal way to duct a dehumidifier is to have completely independent ducts.*

Dry Air Sent into Air-Conditioning Ducts

This method adds complexity. Now you've got two air streams powered by two different fans. You've also got dry air being combined with main air. In addition, both of those systems usually operate intermittently. Sometimes the dehumidifier will send air into the main ducts without the air handler moving air. Other times the air handler will be running when the dehumidifier isn't. And still other times both systems will run at the same time.

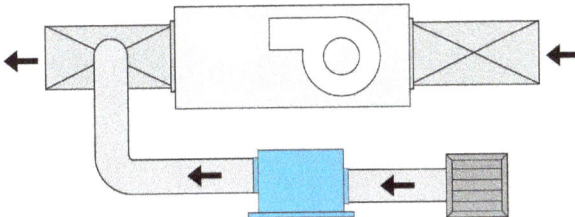

Figure 16.4. *If you have an independent intake vent for the dehumidifier and want to use the air conditioning ducts to distribute the dry air, duct the dry air into the supply side of the air conditioner.*

The big issue you may not be aware of is to which side of the air handler you should send the dry air. Many people naturally want to put it into the return side because that's where air goes into the air handler. Also, because the dry air is warmer than the rest of the air, it seems like it should go through the air conditioner to get cooled. There's just one little problem with that. In summer, the air conditioner's job is to cool and dehumidify the air from the house. If you mix dry air in with the return air, the air conditioner won't dehumidify as well. Consequently, the dehumidifier runs more, the air conditioner still runs about the same amount of time, and you use more energy.

A better method is to put the dry air into the supply duct. If you do it this way, you need to pay attention to two things. First, the temperature of the supply air will increase when the dehumidifier is running because the dry air is warm. Second, you probably need to increase the size of your supply ducts to handle the additional air flow. Both of those effects tell us that the dry air should be a

relatively small amount of the total air flowing in the supply duct.

Bypass Method

In this setup, the dehumidifier intake is connected to the main return duct, and the dry air is sent into the main supply duct. The dehumidifier acts as a bypass. Most of the air goes through the air handler to be heated or cooled. A smaller portion goes through the dehumidifier, and the two air streams mix again on the downstream side. This method minimizes ductwork, distributes the dry air throughout the house or zone, and doesn't reduce the moisture removal capacity of the air conditioner.

Because you've got two fans pulling air from the house, you'll need to increase the size of the main ducts to accommodate the extra air flow of the dehumidifier. You also need to do two other things for this method to work properly.

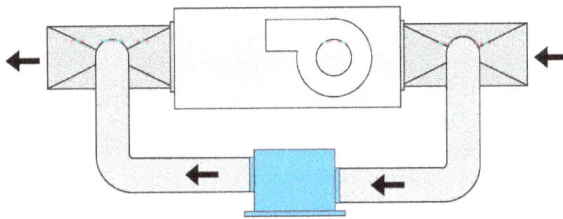

Figure 16.5. *If you don't have space for any extra ductwork, the bypass method is an acceptable substitute.*

First, the dry air side of the dehumidifier needs to have a backdraft damper installed that prevents supply air from flowing backward through the dehumidifier. Remember, we have two fans trying to have their way with the air, and some configurations could result in air moving the wrong way. Also, when the dehumidifier isn't running, the backdraft damper prevents the main air from going through the dehumidifier back to the return duct, creating a short circuit.

Second, you need to prevent the other kind of short circuit. When the air handler isn't running and the dehumidifier is, the dry air could get pulled back through the air handler to the intake side of the dehumidifier. One solution is to put a damper in the return side that prevents backflow. The other solution is to wire the dehumidifier to the air handler to ensure the air handler always runs whenever the dehumidifier is running. More air handler runtime means more energy use but also better distribution of the dry air.

Injection Method

Here the intake and dry air sides of the dehumidifier are both connected to the same side of the air handler. As with putting only the dry air into the main ducts, the best place to put a dehumidifier using this method is on the supply duct side. With cooler air coming into the dehumidifier, the capacity of the dehumidifier will be lower. The efficiency, however, will be higher because the intake air will be close to the dew point already.

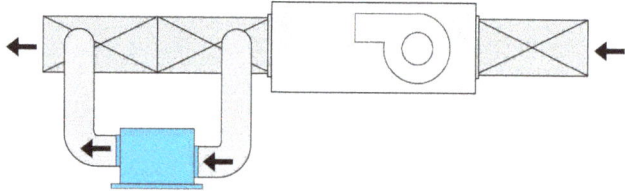

Figure 16.6. *In the injection method, both the intake and dry air ducts are attached to the same side of the air conditioner. Here they're shown on the supply side.*

The problem here is that when the weather is hot, the air conditioner often can do the necessary dehumidification by itself (when sized properly). The dehumidifier isn't needed in that case until the air conditioner runtime is low. To use this method, you need to wire the two appliances together, so the air handler runs whenever the dehumidifier runs. For a house in a hot, humid climate like Florida, though, the dehumidifier and air conditioner may run simultaneously for many hours a year, and this method can spend more of its runtime operating at higher efficiency. Not every dehumidifier is capable of being ducted this way because the colder intake air may cause it to freeze up. Check the instructions for your model before you set up the ducts this way.

Ventilating Dehumidifier

Another way to use a whole-house, ducted dehumidifier is to run your whole-house ventilation air through it. On the intake side, you connect two ducts. One of them brings in air from the house to dehumidify and distribute. The other duct brings in outdoor air to dehumidify and distribute.

To set up a ventilating dehumidifier, you need to make sure the model you're using can work with the entering air conditions of your mixed house and outdoor air. You also need a dehumidifier that can run the fan at times when the compressor isn't running. Not every model can do that.

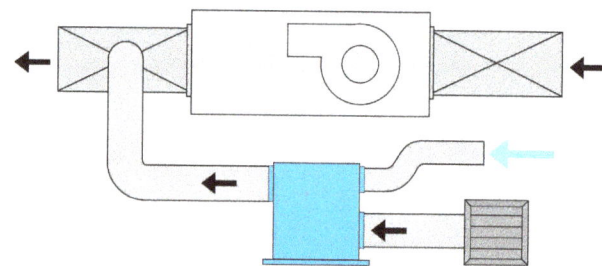

Figure 16.7. *The ventilating dehumidifier setup can work with any of the methods. The one shown here has an independent intake, and the dry, ventilated air is sent into the supply duct.*

Don't Send Dehumidified Air into the Return Duct

In the second method of ducting a dehumidifier, I showed the dry air going into the supply side of the heating and cooling ducts. That's the best way to do it. Why? Because you want the air conditioner to do as much of the dehumidification as it can. Unfortunately, many dehumidifier installation manuals show diagrams with the dry air ducted into the return. Don't do that!

When you install a whole-house dehumidifier, you do so for supplemental dehumidification. If you send dehumidified air into the return duct, you're using the dehumidifier as a replacement dehumidifier. It replaces some of the dehumidification capacity of the air conditioner because it dehumidifies air that would otherwise have been dehumidified by the air conditioner. That means the dehumidifier will run more, and you'll use more energy.

If you're worried about the air coming out of the air conditioner vents not being cool enough, keep these things in mind. First, whether you send the dry air into your duct system or directly into the house, it gets tempered by mixing with the rest of the air. Second, yes, that tempered air will be warmer than regular supply air straight from the ducts, but if the ducts are designed properly, you should never notice. Remember that rule about not blowing air on people? Third, the dehumidifier will run mostly at night and on cooler days, when the air conditioner isn't running enough to keep the indoor air dry. On hot sunny days, the air coming out of the supply vents should be nice and cold most of the time.

Chapter Takeaways

- Dehumidifiers are basically air conditioners tuned to remove a lot of moisture from the air.
- As homes become better insulated and more airtight, the need for supplemental dehumidification increases.
- Dehumidifiers come in room or whole-house configurations.
- When choosing a dehumidifier of either type, the two specifications to look at are capacity and energy efficiency.
- A whole-house dehumidifier can have its own, independent ducts, or it can be connected to the heating and cooling ducts.

CHAPTER 17

Ventilation

The imagery of wearing someone else's dirty underwear may shock you, but we essentially do something that could be worse whenever we take a breath in a room full of other people. It's not just air recently expelled from other people's lungs we should worry about, though. Indoor air is often more polluted than outdoor air. It's a soup of particulate matter of various sizes, volatile organic compounds, skin flakes, dust mite carcasses, mold spores, and more. We suck all that nasty stuff into our lungs with every breath.

Good indoor air quality is a team effort. Filtration (Chapter 15) can take care of the particles when done properly. To handle gases like volatile organic compounds and carbon monoxide, source control and ventilation are the best options. Source control means keeping the bad stuff out (Chapter 2). Yes, electronic air cleaners promise to zap all the bad stuff in the air, making a home's indoor air as pure as a hospital operating room. However, the available independent research mostly shows their effectiveness is dodgy. (See the sidebar "Two Reasons to Avoid Most Electronic Air Cleaners"

> *"Most civilized men and women are unwilling to put on underclothing that has just been taken off by another person or to put into their mouths articles of food or drink that have recently been in other people's mouths, but they take without hesitation into their lungs air that has just come from other people's mouths and lungs or from close contact with their soiled clothing or bodies."*
>
> *—John Shaw Billings, 1893*

on page 258.) Stick with the big three—source control, filtration, and ventilation—and your indoor air quality will be excellent.

Here, I'll start by explaining the three types of ventilation used in homes: local, buffer-space, and whole-house ventilation. Then I'll further divide whole-house ventilation into three types—exhaust-only, supply-only, and balanced—and give you the pros and cons of each.

Three Types of Ventilation Used in Homes

Local ventilation: This is basically exhausting air from the kitchen and bathrooms. It's source control for places where we put stuff into the indoor air that we'd rather not breathe or, in the case of moisture, stuff that might create other problems. In the kitchen, the big culprit is cooking. In bathrooms, it's moisture. We'll talk more about this type of ventilation in the next section.

Buffer-space ventilation: The great outdoors is unconditioned space. The living space inside our homes is conditioned. And then there are the buffer spaces. Attics, crawl spaces beneath the

house, some basements, and garages are neither indoors nor outdoors. Do you need to do anything about the air in those spaces?

Whole-house ventilation: Here's the main attraction of the ventilation chapter. Local ventilation and buffer-space ventilation are critical to managing moisture and eliminating pollutants at the source. But carbon dioxide from breathing, $PM_{2.5}$ from cooking, volatile organic compounds from furniture and carpets, and other pollutants floating around in a house need to be removed from the home or diluted with outdoor air using a whole-house ventilation system.

> **Filtration can catch a lot of the particles, but we need whole-house ventilation to dilute the concentration of gases.**

Filtration can catch a lot of the particles, but we need whole-house ventilation to dilute the concentration of gases.

In the old days, we ventilated the whole house passively. In 1893, John Shaw Billings wrote, "In ordinary dwellings . . . it is unnecessary to provide special apparatus for forcing or increasing the movement of the air." This method, if you can call it that, used a combination of open windows and random leaks in the building enclosure as pathways. Basically, we relied on infiltration for "fresh" air.

Today, windows don't get opened much, and houses are more airtight. But as we've seen with the COVID-19 pandemic, even leaky homes can benefit from whole-house ventilation. Ventilation and filtration can help dilute and remove airborne infectious particles to reduce the risk of transmission of illnesses like colds, flu, and COVID-19.

Hence, we do need a "special apparatus" to increase air exchange. But how much mechanical ventilation should we provide?

Local Ventilation: Kitchens

When you turn on the cooktop or oven in the kitchen, you put pollutants into the air. When you cook there, you add more pollutants. Gas cooktops produce carbon dioxide and water vapor when the combustion is complete. Incomplete combustion results in nitrogen oxides and perhaps carbon monoxide. Gas ovens can produce high concentrations of carbon monoxide when you first turn them on. Electric elements on a cooktop or in an oven produce ultrafine particles. Cooking produces fine particles ($PM_{2.5}$). Don't believe me? Get an indoor air quality monitor and watch what happens when you start cooking. Or look at Figure 17.1.

Because cooking is such a significant source of indoor air pollutants, you have to make important decisions regarding how you ventilate the kitchen. These include:

- Type of range hood
- Capacity of range hood ventilation
- Makeup air to replace air exhausted from the kitchen
- Whether to vent the hood to the outdoors or to recirculate
- Manual or automatic controls

Figure 17.1. *Note how dirty the walls and ceiling are above the gas range with no exhaust hood above. [Credit: The Energy Smart Academy]*

Figure 17.2. *Exhaust hood over a gas range [Credit: LG, CC 2.0]*

capture efficiency of their hoods to help you make a good selection, but for now you've got to use your best judgment to find one you think will do a good job of capturing that plume and exhausting it from the kitchen.

Figure 17.3. *A range hood with poor capture efficiency: The bottom is flat, and the hood isn't big enough to cover the whole cooktop.*

It can be exhausting to study everything we know about this topic, so let me give you my take on these choices before you.

Type of Range Hood

The big issue here is what's called capture efficiency. When you're sautéing food on the stove and the heat causes a plume of gases and particles to rise, you want a hood that will capture as much as possible of that plume. One thing to look for is a hood that extends over the whole cooktop. Most people use the front burners almost exclusively, so when the plume rises, you want the hood right above it (Figure 17.2). Another feature that helps is a downward-facing extension around the edge of the horizontal bottom surface of the hood. That helps to capture the plume when it rises. Flat-bottomed hoods let a lot of the plume escape (Figure 17.3). Another thing that helps a hood capture more pollutants is to have the cooktop against a wall. When it's on an island, the pollutants can escape on any side of the hood. A wall and cabinets on the sides of the hood make capturing pollutants easier.

Someday manufacturers will provide the

Capacity of Range Hood Ventilation

If you've been told you need to put in a range hood that can exhaust air from the kitchen at the rate of 500, 800, or 1,000+ cubic feet per minute (cfm), you may not need it. When you choose a hood with good capture efficiency, a high air flow rate is less important. For most cooktops and ovens, you can do a good job clearing the kitchen of cooking-related pollutants with less than 400 cfm (a significant number, as you'll see soon). The primary goal of a range hood is to remove pollutants. If you can do that with a lower capacity range hood, you save energy by not sucking as much conditioned air out of your home. That also improves comfort because you don't suck in as much unconditioned air. And it means you may not need to install a makeup air system.

Not everyone can use a low-capacity range hood, though. If you're putting in a commercial-style gas range, you should follow the manufacturer's guidance on range hood capacity. And plan on having a makeup air system tied into the range hood that will run whenever you're cooking.

Makeup Air to Replace Exhausted Air

Makeup air prevents the range hood from creating a large negative pressure in the house. A good makeup air system matches the amount of air exhausted through the hood with outdoor air to balance the outgoing and incoming air flows. Negative pressure can cause backdrafting of combustion appliances, which is why the building code says you need to provide makeup air for range hoods with a capacity of more than 400 cfm if there's an atmospheric combustion appliance in the house. If you can't reduce the capacity of the range hood, putting in a makeup air system may be necessary. Once you're committed to makeup air, you've got to decide whether to go with a passive system or one that has a fan.

A passive makeup air system is a duct connecting the kitchen to the outdoors. It has a damper that opens when the range hood comes on, allowing air from outdoors to come through the duct. A powered system is similar in that it has a duct and a damper, but it also has a fan. In Energy Vanguard's HVAC design work, we specify powered makeup air systems—if we fail to talk the client out of a high-capacity range hood. Passive air inlets often don't provide enough air, and infiltration in other parts of the house will increase.

But even if you don't have atmospheric combustion and your range hood has a capacity less than 400 cfm, you can still get a lot of negative pressure in a house by turning on a range hood. In an older home with a lot of air leakage, turning on a bath fan or a typical range hood may have no noticeable effect on the house pressure. That's because it's easy to replace the air being exhausted through the fan when there are so many pathways for air to come inside. However, in a super-airtight house (e.g., a Passive House), it takes only a little unbalanced air flow to create a large pressure difference. That pressure difference won't

make your ears pop, but it may reduce the air flow through your fan, make your fan use more energy, or suck bad air into your house. And that brings us to the next issue.

> **In a super-airtight house (e.g., a Passive House), it takes only a little unbalanced air flow to create a large pressure difference.**

Exhaust to Outdoors vs. Recirculating

Passive House designers often specify recirculating range hoods (sometimes called ductless hoods). The main reasons for this choice are to save energy by not exhausting conditioned air and to reduce the number of penetrations through the building enclosure, which helps achieve greater airtightness. A recirculating range hood also gets around the negative pressure and makeup air problems.

The recirculating range hood has a standard grease filter plus an activated carbon filter to catch pollutants generated by cooking. But hoods don't catch everything, so this method of kitchen ventilation pairs the recirculating hood with an exhaust vent connected to the energy recovery ventilator (ERV), which we'll cover later in this chapter. The hood filters out most of the pollutants, and the ERV exhaust helps keep other cooking pollutants from getting out to the rest of the house. In addition, the ERV operates at a higher rate—boost mode—during cooking to provide more exhaust.

Recirculating hoods, however, don't have a lot of support from the indoor air quality community because exhausting pollutants directly to the outdoors is seen as more effective. Several years ago, John Straube, PhD, PEng, a building scientist at the University of Waterloo and principal at RDH Building Science, said that recirculating range hoods are as effective as recirculating toilets. That's an exaggeration, of course, because there's no such thing as a recirculating toilet, but his point was that you should have your kitchen ventilation exhaust directly to the outdoors.

Several years ago, I visited a certified Passive House and spoke with the proud owners. It's a super-efficient house with the recirculating range hood setup, but they did tell me that after they cook bacon, it takes a day or two for the smell to clear out.

However, the technology is evolving, and I'm not ready to write off recirculating range hoods completely. Recently I previewed a prototype that could be a gamechanger. It's got five levels of filtration plus an air curtain to push the capture efficiency to near 100 percent. For now, I'm going to keep my hood that exhausts to the outdoors and recommend the same for you.

Manual vs. Automatic Controls

The function I'm talking about here is the activation of the range hood. Most hoods operate manually, meaning that you have to turn on the hood separately when you start cooking. Other options exist now that automate the process. One way to do this is to wire the range to the hood. When you turn on a burner of the oven, that also turns on the hood. Another way is to put a pressure sensor in the hood, triggering the fan to come on when the sensor determines that cooking must be happening below. You can do the same thing also with a temperature sensor in the hood.

Setting up the hood to come on automatically as soon as you start cooking can make a big difference in your indoor air quality. The biggest problem with kitchen ventilation in most homes is that the hood doesn't get turned on when people are cooking. Hardwire it, and you can breathe easier.

> *The biggest problem with kitchen ventilation in most homes is that it doesn't get turned on when people are cooking.*

Myth: An ERV Dehumidifies the Air

People sometimes get confused about what ERVs do with moisture, thinking that by using an ERV, your indoor air will be drier. Yes, that's true, but it's not the whole truth. The follow-up question to ask is, "Drier than what?"

An ERV will bring humidity into your house in summer if you're in a humid climate. It just brings in less humidity than if you were blowing air straight into the house. Some of the humidity in the incoming air stream gets transferred to the outgoing air stream, so the ventilation air comes in drier than the outdoor air. But how does it compare to the indoor air?

The heat and moisture exchange that occurs in an ERV is not 100 percent efficient. The best ones can exchange moisture at about 50 to 60 percent efficiency. That means the summer ventilation air coming into a house in a humid climate will be more humid than the air already in the house. That's the opposite of what a dehumidifier does, so no, an ERV does not dehumidify the indoor air.

Local Ventilation: Bathrooms

The kitchen is often the biggest polluter of indoor air. Bathrooms are not far behind. Showering and bathing make them a source of moisture, which is an issue for every home. Personal grooming products, pesticides, and cleaning products are common in bathrooms, and many put toxic chemicals into the indoor air. And then we have a nice academic euphemism to describe those things that come out of the human body and add to the pollutant load of indoor air: bioeffluents.

Thus, model building codes require bathroom ventilation. Unfortunately, those same codes give builders an out if a bathroom has an operable window at least 3 square feet in area, but that really isn't an acceptable substitute for mechanical ventilation. Aside from building codes, organizations like the Home Ventilating Institute (HVI) put out guidelines for bathroom ventilation, ASHRAE has created a standard for residential ventilation that covers bathrooms as well as kitchen and whole-house ventilation, and there's even a really good book called *Residential Ventilation Handbook* by Paul Raymer that covers bathrooms as well as other aspects of ventilating a home.

As with kitchen ventilation, you have choices to make.

- What air flow rate should the fan have?
- What kind of fan should you use?
- How should you duct the fan?
- Should you operate the fan continuously as part of the whole-house ventilation system?
- Can you ventilate the bathroom with an ERV or HRV?
- What should you do about noise?

Air Flow Rate

The model building code requires 50 cfm minimum for bathrooms (unless you take the window exception). Choosing the air flow rate isn't hard. For a fan that operates when needed, HVI recommends either eight air changes per hour or 1 cfm per square foot of bathroom floor area for bathrooms less than 100 square feet. They both come out about the same, somewhere in the 40- to 100-cfm range.

For larger bathrooms, HVI recommends sizing the fan by the number and type of fixtures: 50 cfm each for toilet, bathtub, and shower and 100 cfm for a jetted tub.

Fan Type

You have an array of options here. For bathroom-only ventilation, you can go with a ceiling-mounted fan, wall-mounted fan, or a remote inline fan. Most bathrooms have ceiling-mounted fans because that's the best place to catch the moist air rising from the shower or bath. Wall-mounted fans are less ideal for that reason. The advantage of inline remote fans is that they're quieter and you can use a single fan to ventilate multiple bathrooms. Just make sure it has properly installed dampers to prevent sending the exhaust from one bathroom into another bathroom.

Ducting

Bath fans should always be exhausted to the outdoors. Not to the attic. Not to the crawl space. And definitely not to another bathroom. However, in many existing houses, that's not the case. The fan in Figure 17.4 has no duct attached and was blowing moist air into the attic of this house for many years. The ducts attached to bath fans are often poorly installed. That's one reason most bath fans in older homes move about only half the air they're rated to move.

Figure 17.4. *A bath fan with no duct attached*

Figure 17.5. *A well-installed bath fan: The duct is short, straight, and mostly larger than it needs to be.*

To get good air flow, it's important to keep the duct as short and straight as possible. If you have to turn the air, use as large a turning radius as possible. And use a larger duct. Most bath fan ducts are 4 inches in diameter. Increase that to 6 inches, and the air flow will improve. Figure 17.5 shows a short, straight, oversized duct attached to a bath fan. This one's not perfect, but that kind of installation will result in a bath that exhausts as much air as it's supposed to.

Here are a few more bath fan ducting tips. Rigid metal duct is better than flex duct for this purpose, but if you do use flex, follow the guidance I laid out in Chapter 14. Insulating the duct is a good idea, too. In a cold climate, it should be required. Otherwise, the moist air can condense inside the duct. And to prevent water from draining back into

the bathroom and onto your head, slope the duct down and away from the fan.

Finally, bath fans spend the majority of their time turned off. That has the potential to turn the duct into a source of infiltration. Bath fans come with built-in backdraft dampers, but as you can see from Figure 17.6, they may not do a good job of stopping air from coming in. We had a client once who had mold growing on his ceiling because of humid outdoor air coming in through the duct when the fan was turned off. (The powered attic ventilators created the negative pressure.) On our recommendation, he installed a much better backdraft damper (the Cape Backdraft Damper from Tamarack), and the problem went away.

Figure 17.6. *The backdraft damper that comes built into many bath fans isn't capable of stopping many backdrafts.*

Continuous Operation

As we'll see later in this chapter, homes need whole-house ventilation. The least expensive way to do that is to use fans already installed and run them more. Controls are available for bath fans that allow them to run continuously or intermittently on a regular schedule to help meet the required whole-house ventilation. Some fans can operate at multiple air flow rates so they can run continuously at a lower rate and then go to a higher rate when you need more ventilation in the bathroom. Just because it's possible to do something, however, doesn't mean it's a good idea. (I'll just toss this idea out there and then maybe shoot it down in the whole-house ventilation section.)

Exhausting with ERV or HRV

If you want to make your bathroom ventilation part of the whole-house ventilation, another option is to do so with an energy recovery ventilator (ERV) or heat recovery ventilator (HRV). We'll cover them in more detail later, but what's important to know here is that you can exhaust air at the right ventilation rate with an ERV or HRV. You also get to recover the heat from the air being exhausted by an ERV or an HRV, and you also recover the moisture being exhausted by an ERV. Yeah, that latter bit is tricky with bathrooms.

Noise

In the old days, home builders didn't care much about how well a bath fan exhausted air from the bathroom. As long as it made noise, it passed muster. Noise was seen as a benefit because it covered up the . . . uhhhh . . . other noise that accompanies . . . uhhhh . . . the release of bioeffluents.

But the noise is a deterrent for using a bath fan to remove humidity, which is a more important job than covering up the sounds that people make in the bathroom. Also, a noisier fan is a less efficient fan. The most efficient fans are barely noticeable when running. So, get a good fan and let it do its job. If you really need to mask the noises generated in a bathroom, try soundproofing. If you need more, get a white noise generator or put a radio in the bathroom.

Laundry rooms sometimes have exhaust fans, and the advice above applies there, too.

Buffer Space Ventilation: Attics

Starting at the top, attics are described in various ways: encapsulated, semi-conditioned, conditioned, unvented, or vented. The first three in that list are variations of the same thing—attics that have been brought inside the building enclosure by putting the insulation and air barrier at the roofline. An unvented attic could be either inside or outside the building enclosure. A vented attic is—or should be—always outside the building enclosure.

Vented Attics

Venting attics was developed to help prevent ice dams in cold climates. It's often done in hot climates even though it's unnecessary. The ventilation can come from passive vents in the soffits, ridge, gable ends, or roof deck.

The attic ventilation could also come from powered attic ventilators, and in most cases, that's a stupid idea. Will it keep the attic cooler in summer? Likely. Will it do so by sucking conditioned air from the living space below through the leaks in the ceiling? Likely. Will you save money on your air-conditioning bill by keeping the attic cooler? Unlikely. Don't install powered attic ventilators. If you have them, turn them off. In addition to stealing cool air from the living space, they can depressurize the house. That in turn can suck moisture into the house, which can grow mold. A powered attic ventilator can even backdraft gas water heaters, which can pull carbon monoxide into the home.

> **A powered attic ventilator can backdraft gas water heaters, which can pull carbon monoxide into the home.**

If you have no gas combustion appliances and no air conditioning, these fans may help without causing problems. A whole-house fan would be a better idea, though. The best thing to do is air seal and insulate your ceiling better. If you're ambitious, you could put a "cool roof" on the house, which reflects heat.

Unvented Attics

If the attic is outside the building enclosure, the main reason for venting it is to prevent moisture problems in cold climates. You know what's better at preventing moisture problems in cold climates? Keeping moisture and heat from the house out of the attic. Air sealing and insulation do that. Still, venting an attic in cold climates does dilute the attic air with dry outdoor air and can be the difference between an attic that works well and a moisture disaster.

In a hot, humid climate, keeping outdoor air out of the attic can help because outdoor air has more moisture than house air. If ductwork is in the attic, venting with outdoor air may cause condensation, especially if the ducts are buried in insulation. The best thing to do here is air seal and insulate the attic floor and get the ducts into conditioned space. Then you don't have to worry about venting. Venting does keep the attic cooler, though.

Conditioned Attic

You can call the attic encapsulated if you like, but it needs to be conditioned in some way. Humid air rises in a home, so without any kind of conditioning, an encapsulated attic can have moisture problems. You can add conditioned air, use a dehumidifier, or include the attic in the whole-house ventilation plan. All of these can work.

Buffer Space Ventilation: Crawl Spaces and Basements

The best way to treat an enclosed crawl space or basement is to bring it inside the building enclosure and consider it conditioned space. Venting a crawl space or unconditioned basement to the outdoors may work in a dry climate, but it can lead to big moisture problems in humid climates.

The only way a vented crawl space can work in a humid climate is if the floor above the crawl space is air sealed and insulated really well. And that's a problem because it's usually easier to air seal and insulate the foundation walls.

Once you've brought a crawl space or basement inside the building enclosure, then you think about conditioning and ventilating it the way you would the other parts of the conditioned space. You may not need heating or cooling, especially for a crawl space, but you need a way to ventilate and possibly dehumidify. You can heat or cool by adding a small amount of supply air from ducts in the space, if there are any. The recommended rate is 1 cfm for each 50 square feet of floor area, or 20 cfm per 1,000 square feet. If you want to keep tighter control of the conditions, you could also add a dedicated heating and cooling system for the space. Ductless mini-splits may be a good option. (Yes, we've had some clients do that.)

To ventilate, you can use a small exhaust fan that sends crawl space air to the outdoors. For this to work, the crawl space needs to be air sealed tightly so the makeup air comes from the living space above. Transfer grilles between the crawl space and living space can provide pathways for the makeup air. As with supply air, the recommended rate is 1 cfm for each 50 square feet of floor area, or 20 cfm per 1,000 square feet.

Another option is to use a dehumidifier to control humidity. By running a small duct from the outdoors to the dehumidifier intake, you can provide fresh air to the crawl space as well.

Buffer Space Ventilation: Garages

A garage is a potpourri of stuff that emanates some nasty air pollutants: cars and the fumes that emanate from them, lawn mowers and other gasoline-powered equipment, gasoline for those machines, paint, fertilizers, pesticides, and carbon monoxide, a colorless, odorless deadly gas. Research shows that homes with attached garages have more carbon monoxide inside the living space than homes that don't have attached garages.

There's no requirement for garage ventilation in building codes. But adding ventilation to an attached garage can keep those nasties out of the air inside your home. Think of it this way: From an indoor air quality perspective, the difference

> **Homes with attached garages have more carbon monoxide inside the living space than homes that don't have attached garages.**

between an attached garage and a carport is essentially ventilation. A carport has a lot of it, an attached garage not so much.

Of course, the first line of defense should be a robust air barrier separating the garage air from the house air. Once you have that, the main

From Fan Scale to House Scale

The fans used in all three of the whole-house ventilation strategies discussed in this chapter are rated in units that make sense for the scale of air flow produced. In the United States, we use cubic feet per minute (cfm). Other countries use liters per second or cubic meters per hour. For ventilation purposes, a more meaningful unit is based on the size of the space being ventilated: air changes per hour (ACH). And that unit is the same for everyone the world over, whether your fans are rated in cfm, liters per second, or cubic meters per hour.

The way to go between your fan's air flow rate and air changes per hour is to factor in the volume of the house. Let's say your house has a volume of 10,000 cubic feet. When that volume of air moves through your ventilation system (either into or out of the house), you've had 1 air change. Doing 1 air change in 100 minutes (1.67 hours) equals 0.6 air changes per hour (1 ÷ 1.67).

Both units, cubic feet per minute and air changes per hour, measure the same thing: a volume of flow (cubic feet or air changes) per unit time (minutes or hours). So, going between the two is simply a change of units. Here's how to work it out once you know the air flow rate of the fan and the volume of the house.

To change cubic feet per minute to air changes per hour, we need two conversion factors: cubic feet per air change, which equals the volume of the house, and the number of minutes per hour (60). Let's use that 10,000-cubic-foot house and a ventilation rate of 100 cfm.

The minutes cancel out, leaving hours. The cubic feet cancel out, leaving air changes. So, all that's left in

$$Ventilation\ Rate = \frac{100\ cf}{min} \times \frac{60\ min}{hr} \times \frac{1\ AC}{10,000\ cf} = 0.6\ ACH$$

the units is air changes per hour, ACH, and the result of the arithmetic here is 0.6. Bob's your uncle!

We can simplify this process into one simple equation:

$$Rate_{ACH} = \frac{Rate_{cfm} \times 60}{volume}$$

weakness is the door connecting the garage to the house. As it turns out, that door can be the key to keeping polluted garage air out of the house. One device that can do that is GarageVent™. It's a controller that can turn on an exhaust fan in the garage every time any door in the garage is opened. Once turned on, the fan will run for a preset time. That keeps the garage at a negative pressure, making it harder for garage air to sneak into the house when the opportunity arises. To make this work, you need a bigger fan than most bathrooms have. Instead of 50 cfm, you need one that can exhaust 200 cfm or more from the garage.

But be careful! If the garage houses a gas water heater capable of being backdrafted, it's possible to create more carbon monoxide, some of which could find its way into the house. If the big garage door to the outdoors is closed when the exhaust fan comes on, it may pull some of its air down the water heater flue. If the water heater is firing at the time, it may be starved of oxygen,

burn the gas incompletely, and produce carbon monoxide. If you have a natural draft water heater in the garage, putting a 200-cfm exhaust fan there wouldn't be a good idea.

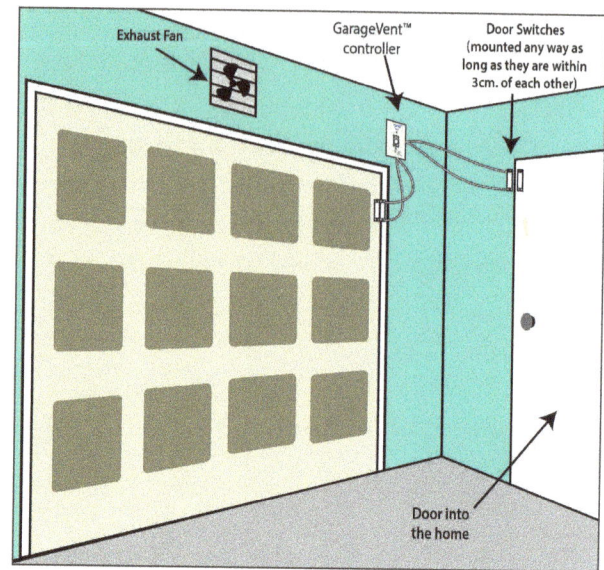

Figure 17.7. *An exhaust fan, a controller (e.g., the GarageVent), and door switches can keep polluted garage air out of the house. [Courtesy of AirCycler]*

Buffer Space Ventilation: Radon

Radon is another colorless, odorless gas that's bad for health. The National Cancer Institute lists radon as the second-leading cause of lung cancer, behind smoking. It's a radioactive decay product that comes out of the ground and seeps into houses through the foundation (slab, crawl space, or basement). In this case, the buffer space we're interested in is the soil beneath the house. Soil isn't a dense solid. It's a mixture of minerals, organic matter, and water with a network of interstitial spaces that contain soil gases, including radon.

Some areas of the country have more radon than others, and the US Environmental Protection Agency (EPA) has created a map of the United States showing the radon risk for each county (see Figure 17.10 on page 289). The EPA recommends keeping the radon level in homes below 4 picocuries per liter (pCi/L),

and the radon map is based on that threshold. Zone 1, the highest risk areas, includes counties where the indoor radon levels are predicted to be greater than 4 pCi/L. Zone 2 includes those counties where the predicted level is between 2 and 4 pCi/L. Zone 3 is for counties with less than 2 pCi/L. The predictions are based on other measurements in each county.

Figure 17.8. *A plastic pipe beneath a concrete slab is part of the sub-slab depressurization to keep radon out of the house.*

But guess what? You may live in a Zone 3 county and have Zone 1 levels of radon in your home. To find out, you need to measure it. You can do that by hiring a radon professional, buying a test kit and mailing it to a lab for analysis, or buying a radon monitor for the home.

After you've measured the radon in your home, the EPA recommends doing something to lower the radon level if it's higher than 2 pCi/L.

Radon is believed to get through the foundation due to pressure differences between the soil and the air in the crawl space, basement, or living space. The way to fix a house and lower radon levels is to depressurize the soil beneath the foundation. Figure 17.8 shows a plastic pipe installed in a foundation as a house is being built. This pipe will be beneath the concrete slab and connected to a vertical pipe that goes through the roof. The stack effect will draw soil gases up and out, depressurizing the soil so radon is less likely to enter the house. The radon vent can be passive at first. If the passive vent doesn't keep radon levels below 2 pCi/L, the radon vent can be made active with a powered fan.

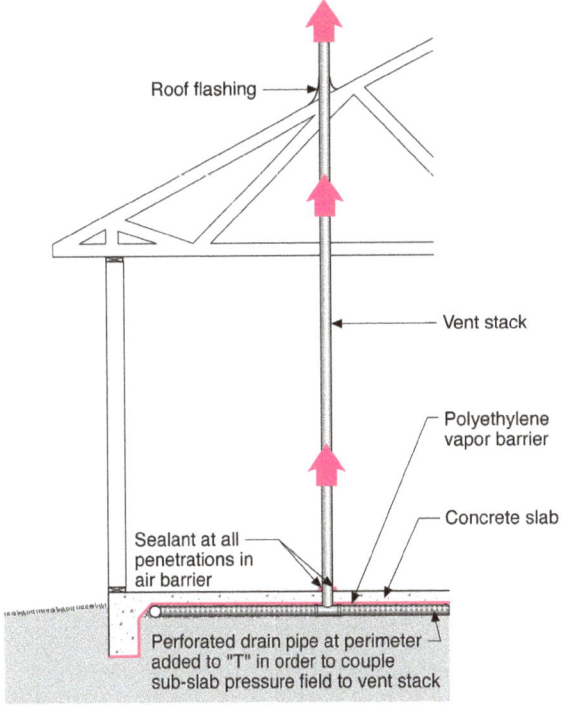

Figure 17.9. *Diagram of a radon venting system without a fan to create greater depressurization beneath the slab or crawl space vapor barrier [Credit: US EPA]*

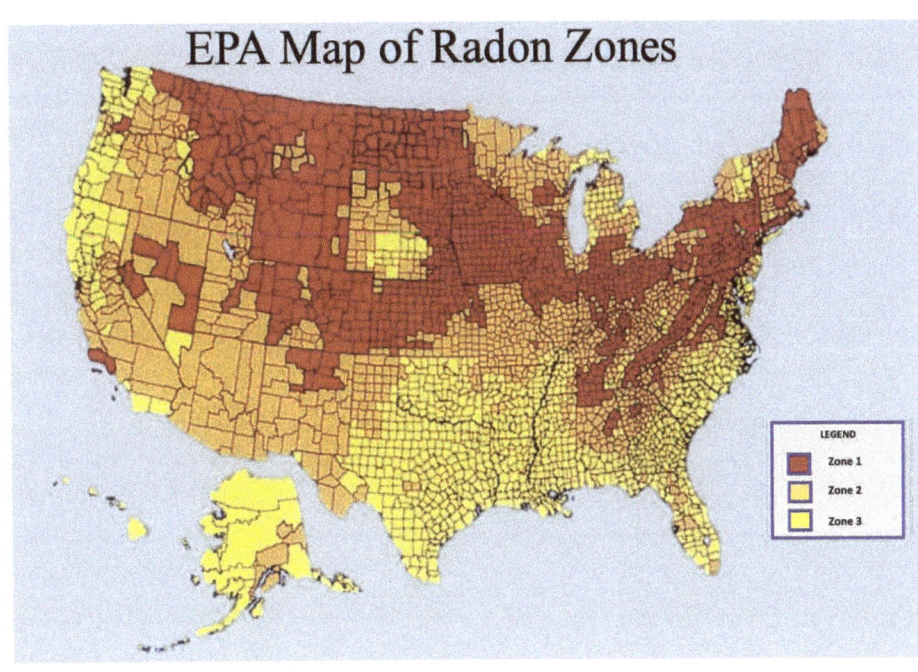

Figure 17.10. *Radon zone map of the United States [US EPA]*

How Much Whole-House Ventilation Do You Need?

How much ventilation you need is usually specified in one of three ways. We can put it in terms of the air flow rate of the fan providing the ventilation. We could also divide that rate by the number of people and specify ventilation in terms of air flow rate per person. Finally, we can put it in terms of the amount of air in the house using air changes per hour. Converting among the three is straightforward, so it doesn't really matter which we choose. (See the sidebar "From Fan Scale to House Scale" on page 287.) Often, the air flow rate is used to specify ventilation rates, but that's kind of abstract. The other two metrics make it conceptually easier to understand. Let's tackle the three in the order above.

Air Flow Rate Calculation

A natural starting point for deciding on the ventilation rate is to do what you're required to do. The International Residential Code (IRC) and the residential ventilation standard from ASHRAE (62.2) both use formulas based on the conditioned floor area of the house and the number of bedrooms to come up with a required minimum air flow rate. The IRC says you need 1 cfm for each 100 square feet of conditioned floor area plus 7.5 cfm per person, with the number of people defined as the number of bedrooms plus one. ASHRAE 62.2 is the same format with one change: It uses 3 cfm per 100 sf of floor area. ASHRAE 62.2 lets you take credit for infiltration and use a lower ventilation rate if the house gets a blower door test, but let's ignore that for now. (Note: This is a simplified discussion. See the actual documents for fuller explanations.)

Using those two formulas, we can calculate that a 3,000-square-foot house with three bedrooms would need 60 cfm under the IRC rule and 120 cfm using ASHRAE 62.2. If your eyes glazed over because of math and numbers, keep in mind that a typical house in the 2,000- to 3,000-square-foot range needs 50 to 150 cfm of ventilation.

> **A typical house in the 2,000- to 3,000-square-foot range needs 50 to 150 cfm of ventilation.**

Air Flow Rate per Person

Going to the second metric now, let's calculate the air flow rate per person. With the hypothetical four people in this three-bedroom house, that would be 15 cfm person (IRC) or 30 cfm per person (ASHRAE 62.2). If only two people actually live in the house, it's 30 cfm per person (IRC) or 60 cfm per person (ASHRAE 62.2). Ventilation rates for office buildings and schools are often given in terms of air flow rate per person, and the historical range is 4 to 60 cfm per person.

Air Changes per Hour

The third way to approach this problem is to think about replacing all the air in the house with outdoor air. When a ventilation system does that one time, it's called 1 air change. If it takes 1 hour, your ventilation rate is 1 air change per hour. It's the same concept used in describing blower door testing in units of air changes per hour at a specific pressure difference. Only now, we want the ventilation system to provide those air changes no matter the indoor/outdoor pressure difference.

The sidebar "From Fan Scale to House Scale" on page 287 shows how to convert the ventilation rates from cfm to air changes per hour. Let's assume our 3,000-square-foot house has 8-foot-high ceilings, making the volume 24,000 cubic feet. The results would be 0.15 ACH for the IRC rate of 60 cfm and 0.30 ACH for the ASHRAE 62.2 rate of 120 cfm. For context, ASHRAE's residential ventilation standard used to specify the required rate as 0.35 air changes per hour. In schools, hospitals, and office buildings, which have high densities of people, the required air changes per hour is higher. During the COVID-19 pandemic, indoor air quality experts have been recommending up to 6 air changes per hour, which could be met with a combination of ventilation and filtration.

For homes, ventilation rates of 0.15 to about 0.5 air change per hour are reasonable. Going lower will do little to help your indoor air quality. Going higher may use too much energy and create comfort problems.

Before we go further, I need to explain that the rates we talked about above are all for continuous ventilation. It's also possible to design a ventilation system to run intermittently. For example, if you need 100 cfm continuous and put in a 200-cfm fan, you'd run it for half the amount of time to get the same total amount of ventilation air. Ventilation controllers can adjust the runtime of a ventilation fan to however many minutes per hour you want. In this example, you'd set it to run 30 minutes out of each hour.

Now that we have this context, let's talk about making the choice of ventilation rate. For new homes, go by what your building department tells you to do. It's likely to be the IRC formula here in the United States, but you can always put in a system with a higher rate. If the house is going for certification in a program like ENERGY STAR, follow their rules. Most organizations see their requirements as minimums, so again, you can install more capacity.

If you're putting a ventilation system into an existing home and not bound by any codes or program requirements, you can size it however you see fit. However, it makes sense to size it so that it will be enough to make a difference but not so much that you lose control of the indoor temperature and humidity. You can use the guidance above and summarized below to make your choice.

- 50 to 150 cfm for a 2,000- to 3,000-square-foot house
- 15 to 60 cfm per person (number of people = number of bedrooms + 1)
- 0.15 to 1 air change per hour

How do you choose whether to stay toward the low end or go high? First, consider the needs of the people in the house. If anyone living in the home is chemically sensitive or has respiratory problems, a higher ventilation rate may be better. Of course, that depends on the quality of the outdoor air and the ability of the ventilation system to clean the air being brought in. Filtration and ventilation should go hand in hand. After looking at those issues, you need to understand the type of ventilation system you're installing, which happens to be the subject of the next section.

Three Whole-House Ventilation Strategies

The job of a whole-house mechanical ventilation system is to replace indoor air with outdoor air. Therefore, all mechanical ventilation systems need fans to move the air. We can use them in three distinct ways.

- **The exhaust-only ventilation strategy:** We can have fans that just blow air out of the house.
- **The supply-only ventilation strategy:** We can use fans that just blow air into the house.
- **The balanced ventilation strategy:** We can use a set of fans that exhaust and supply air in equal amounts.

Let's look at them in more detail now.

Exhaust-Only Ventilation

One way to ventilate a house is by using exhaust fans to take indoor air and move it outdoors. A house is not a vacuum chamber, so an exhaust fan will create a moment of nonequilibrium air flow, during which the house develops a negative pressure. Quickly, though, the outward air flow is balanced with air flowing in through any pathway it can find. If the ventilator exhausts 100 cfm from the house, 100 cfm of outdoor air comes in through the random leaks in the building enclosure.

Figure 17.11. The SmartExhaust exhaust fan controller replaces a regular switch and allows you to run the fan on a program. [Courtesy of AirCycler]

The way to do exhaust-only ventilation is to put controls on exhaust fans that provide the amount of ventilation you want. You can run them continuously at a lower rate or intermittently at a higher rate. The SmartExhaust™ from AirCycler is one controller you can use to do this with bath fans. Some fans and range hoods now come with these kinds of controls built in.

Exhaust-only whole-house ventilation has its advantages. It's the least expensive way to ventilate because you can use fans that are already in the house: the bath fans and range hood. This strategy is also the easiest to implement because it doesn't require additional ductwork or space. Another advantage is that it can reduce the likelihood of moisture problems in cold climates by keeping humid indoor air in winter from reaching the exterior sheathing in walls.

The disadvantages of exhaust-only whole-house ventilation are significant, however. First, you have no control over where the replacement air comes from when the fans run. If the house has an attached garage, guess where some of your ventilation air is coming from: the garage. It's the same with damp crawl spaces, dirty attics, or smelly storage rooms. Second, the air coming in does not get conditioned. Thus, it can make the indoor air too dry, humid, hot, or cold. Third, it can create moisture problems by pulling humid outdoor air into wall cavities, where it can collect in cool drywall and start unintentional biology experiments.

If exhaust-only ventilation is all you have, you may need to moderate how much you ventilate when outdoor conditions are bad. It works best on mild days when you have the windows open. Then it would enhance passive ventilation and make it less likely to pull bad air from the above-mentioned buffer spaces.

The disadvantages make this system a compromise favoring low cost over good ventilation. If you're in a place where this is the only ventilation you can do, use it but be aware of the risks. Monitor the temperature and humidity and get a low-level carbon monoxide monitor.

Supply-Only Ventilation

The supply-only strategy does the opposite of exhaust-only ventilation. It uses a fan to blow outdoor air into the house, and that ventilation air leaks out through the various pathways in the building enclosure. One of the major drawbacks of exhaust-only ventilation is not knowing exactly where your outdoor ventilation air is coming from. With supply-only, you do know where it's coming from and can choose the best location for the intake. Also, because this ventilation strategy only supplies air to the house, the pressure in the house can go positive. That can be good in a humid climate because it keeps the humid outdoor air from getting into the walls. And for the same reason, it's not so good for a cold climate because the humid air is indoors there. Pushing it into the walls can cause cold sheathing to get wet. (See Chapter 11.)

To implement the supply-only strategy, you have three options.

Option 1: Straight outdoor air: You can install a dedicated fan that blows outdoor air into the house through a very short duct system. Some fans have built-in sensors that limit the amount of ventilation when outdoor conditions are too hot, cold, or humid. The problem is that you may end up getting less ventilation when you need it most because the house is likely to be closed up tight on those really hot, cold, or humid days.

Where to put the ventilation air is an important decision, too. You don't want to dump into a space where it will have a noticeable impact on comfort. Instead of delivering all of the ventilation air through one vent, you could split it up and deliver smaller amounts to several rooms. It's still unconditioned air, but it's being distributed better. Similarly, you could put it in an unoccupied space where it will get tempered as it moves to where the people are, such as an open-to-below area or a closet. You need to make sure the air will move out of that area quickly enough not to cause moisture problems in a humid climate, though.

Another option is to put in a larger fan than is

needed for outdoor air and create a tempering plenum. The intake side of the fan would pull some air from outdoors and some from the house. Then it would mix them together before supplying the now tempered ventilation air to the living space.

Yet another distribution option is to send the outdoor air into the return side of the heating and cooling system ducts, causing it to be heated, cooled, and dehumidified when the system runs. Some designs dump the air in the living space near the return grille, and others put it directly into the return duct. Either way, this setup is similar to option 3 below.

Option 2: Ventilating dehumidifier: This is essentially the same as option 1 except that the ventilator also can dehumidify the air. A ventilating dehumidifier can run the fan that moves air separately from the compressor that dehumidifies. Thus, it can ventilate even when the air doesn't need to be dehumidified. If you're ventilating continuously, the compressor will cycle on and off based on the humidity. In summer in a humid climate, that may happen frequently throughout the day. In winter, cold air warmed up has a low relative humidity, and the compressor may not run at all.

Planning the delivery of the air into the living space is critical. In summer, the air from the dehumidifier will be warmer than conditioned air. In winter, the compressor probably won't run when bringing in outdoor air, so it will be delivering cold air to the house. By using the delivery techniques discussed in option 1—splitting up the air, delivering it to unoccupied space, using a tempering plenum, or putting it into heating and cooling system ducts—you can minimize the chance of comfort complaints.

Dehumidifiers are noisier than simple fans, so you'll need to consider where to locate the unit to keep the house quiet. Attics, basements, or crawl spaces are typical locations, but be careful about locating a dehumidifier right beneath or above a bedroom. If you can't keep the dehumidifier far enough away to eliminate unwanted noise, make sure to get as quiet a unit as possible. Look at the noise specifications, read reviews, and talk to owners, if possible.

Figure 17.12. *A ducted ventilating dehumidifier: The outdoor ventilation air comes in through the upper duct on the right side of unit. [Courtesy of Santa Fe Indoor Air Quality Solutions]*

Option 3: Using the air handler: This method uses the blower in an air handler, heating or cooling the ventilation air before distributing it. This method has a fancy name—central fan integrated supply—but the principle is straightforward. Whenever an air handler is running, it pulls air in through the return duct system. Most return ducts pull only from the conditioned space, but with this type of ventilation, there's an additional duct on the return side. Instead of the end of that duct pulling air from a room in the house, it pulls air from outdoors through an intake vent on the outside of the house.

However, if all you do is add a duct to the outdoors, you've simply created duct leakage. When the blower is off, this duct may allow outdoor air into the house, or it may be letting conditioned air escape to the outdoors. When the pressures on the house change, the direction of air flow through an air leakage pathway can change, too.

To make this supply-only system more than just duct leakage, you need to add two components: a motorized damper that can open and close the outdoor air duct and a controller to connect the motorized damper to the blower. When the blower comes on, the damper opens. When the blower turns off, the damper closes. That keeps the house from leaking when the blower is off.

This type of system can go one step further. The controller can turn the blower on when the house needs ventilation but not heating or cooling. At the same time, it opens the damper to allow that outdoor air in. It also can close the damper when the blower is running to provide heating or cooling without bringing in more ventilation air. And, as with the bathroom fan controller described earlier, you can set the controller to run the desired number of minutes per hour.

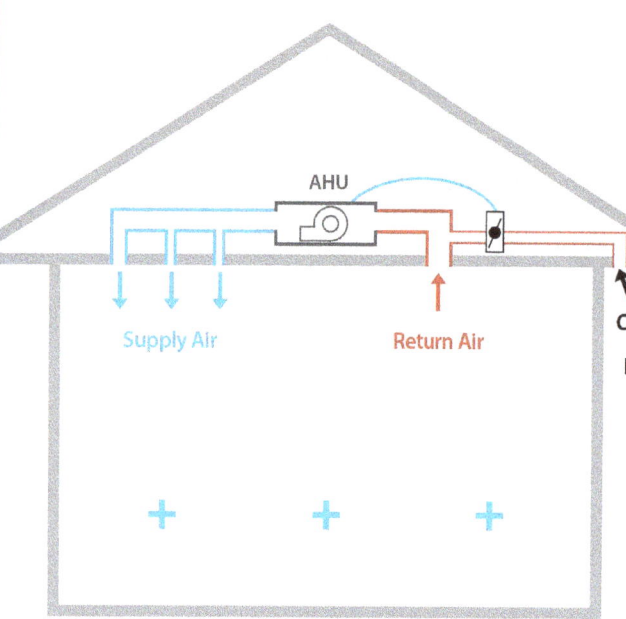

Figure 17.13. *A central fan integrated supply ventilation system uses the heating and cooling system blower to ventilate the house.*

Overall, the strategy of supplying outdoor air to the house by bringing it in through the heating and cooling system makes a lot of sense. It's a little more expensive than the exhaust-only strategy, but it's still in the hundreds of dollars, not thousands. This system also distributes the ventilation air around the house and keeps the house at a slight positive pressure. By running the outdoor air through the heating and cooling system, the ventilation air usually gets conditioned before reaching the people. It's possible that bringing outdoor air in without the system running may lead to comfort problems, but high humidity would usually be the issue there. Supplemental dehumidification can help with that.

Balanced Ventilation

Without recovery: One drawback of exhaust-only and supply-only ventilation is that both strategies induce pressure differences between inside and outside when the systems run. That can draw humid air into building cavities, causing materials to get wet and grow mold. With exhaust-only ventilation, the problem occurs in summer in humid climates. With supply-only, the problem occurs in winter in cold climates.

One way to eliminate the pressure difference is to combine an exhaust-only system with a supply-only system. If the exhaust and supply fans run continuously, connecting the controllers isn't necessary. If the fans operate intermittently, it's possible to connect the controls so the fans act in unison, but it's tricky.

This ventilation strategy is rare because you don't get a lot of benefit for the extra money you spend. Yes, it balances the pressures with equal air flow into and out of the house, but you don't recover any of the energy you put into heating, cooling, or dehumidifying the air you send to the outdoors. For that, you need a balanced ventilation system with heat recovery and, in most cases, moisture recovery, too.

Figure 17.14. *An energy recovery ventilator (ERV) or heat recovery ventilator (HRV) is the most energy efficient way to ventilate a home. This model by Zehnder is one of the most efficient on the market. [Courtesy of Albert Rooks, Small Planet Supply]*

With recovery: The whole-house ventilation systems described above all involve compromises. The big one that I haven't examined yet is the fact that they all result in outdoor air coming into the house and needing to be conditioned. And because every cubic foot of air coming in is matched by a cubic foot of air going out at the same time, you're losing expensive air—the air you've put money into conditioning.

What if we could exhaust air from the house but retain its heat in winter? Or what if we could bring in hot, humid summer air without all its heat and humidity? That's what an energy recovery ventilator (ERV) does.

In winter, you can think of an ERV as a bowling alley. Just as you're required to turn in your shoes before you leave, an ERV makes outgoing air turn in its heat and moisture in winter. In summer, an ERV is like a reputable saloon in the Wild West. People who want to drink and gamble there are required to check their guns upon entering. Similarly, the fresh air entering an ERV in summer deposits its heat and moisture into the outgoing air.

In summer, an ERV is like a reputable saloon in the Wild West. People who want to drink and gamble there are required to check their guns upon entering.

Let me explain that in terms of the air flow through the ERV, as shown in Figure 17.16. Number 1 is where the duct brings outdoor air into the ERV. It then travels through the core, following the path of the purple arrows. You can't see it in the photo, but there's a duct to send the outdoor air to the house when the air arrives at area number 2 in the photo. At the same time fresh outdoor air is being brought in, stale indoor air is being sent out. The duct exhausting air from the house brings indoor air to area number 3 in the photo. The indoor air travels through the ERV core and then leaves the house through the duct at area number 4.

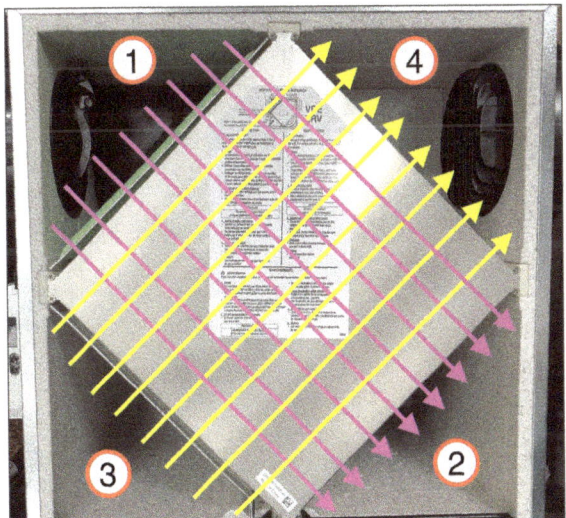

Figure 17.16. *Energy recovery ventilator air flow through the moisture and heat exchanger core. See text for explanation of numbers.*

The magic happens within the core. The two air streams pass through thin channels (Figure 17.15), separated only by a thin membrane. In a heat recovery ventilator, the membrane allows only heat to cross from one air stream to the other. In an energy recovery ventilator, the

Figure 17.15. *The core of an ERV or HRV has many thin channels, allowing the two air streams to pass by each other and efficiently exchange heat or heat and moisture*

membrane transfers both heat and water vapor. Because the air in each direction is split into many separate streams, there's a lot of surface area allowing good transfer of heat and humidity.

The heat and moisture recovery brings the temperature and relative humidity of the incoming ventilation air close to the temperature and relative humidity of the conditioned air already in the house. Those heat and moisture exchanges eliminate or reduce some of the costs you pay for ventilation. First, there's less conditioning of the ventilation air to do once that air is inside the house. Second, because the incoming ventilation air is close to indoor conditions, comfort problems are less likely. Third, the equal air flows of exhaust air and outdoor air reduce the likelihood of moisture causing trouble in the building enclosure.

In short, if you want more ventilation air in your house without having to suffer the ventilation penalty, an ERV can do that for you. Just make sure to get one that has a high efficiency of transferring heat and moisture, electronically commutated fan motors, and a MERV-13 filter on the incoming air side.

Strategy	Pros	Cons
Exhaust-only	• Inexpensive • Easy to set up	• Higher heating and cooling bills • Can bring pollutants in from buffer spaces • Can create moisture problems in humid climates
Supply-only	• Relatively inexpensive • Known source of ventilation air • Air can be conditioned before entering living space	• Higher heating and cooling bills • Can create moisture problems in cold climates
Balanced (with recovery)	• Balanced house pressure • Retains heat from conditioned air in winter • Keeps out heat from outdoors in summer • Helps maintain proper humidity	• Highest first cost • More difficult to install

Table 17.1. *Pros and cons of the three whole-house ventilation strategies*

Two Reasons to Oversize an ERV

For our example house, by looking at minimum requirements in codes and standards and what ERV capacities are available, we chose a continuous ventilation rate of 0.35 ACH, or 160 cfm. Once we have an ERV that can give us the continuous ventilation we want, we can always turn it down if we decide it's too much. The good thing about turning it down is that fans are more efficient when they run at lower speed.

And that's reason number one to oversize an ERV. If you want to be able to supply 200 cfm of ventilation to the house, get an ERV that can move 300 cfm or more. You don't want to get one rated at 200 cfm and run it at maximum capacity all the time. That's less efficient, and it interferes with reason number two.

Reason number two to choose an ERV larger than your continuous ventilation rate is so that you can boost it to a higher rate. If you're setting up the ERV to exhaust from bathrooms and the kitchen, you'll need one with a boost mode. Likewise, if you're having a party or have a sick person at home, boost gives you more fresh air when you need it. And that means you need an ERV with a capacity higher than your continuous ventilation rate. You can't boost something you're already running flat out on the highest speed.

Is it possible to over-ventilate a house? You certainly can cause humidity problems (too dry in winter, too humid in summer) with ventilation air. You can create comfort problems and high energy bills. You could even damage a house by sucking moisture into places where you don't want it, although the risk of this is drastically reduced with a balanced system that is neither negatively pressurizing or positively pressurizing the indoor space. That's why you get an ERV instead of using exhaust-only or supply-only ventilation. (Make sure to get one with high recovery efficiency and electronically commutated motors for the fans, too.) And more fresh air is better for health. It reduces the effects of hay fever and asthma and dilutes the concentrations of indoor pollutants. You don't want to skimp on indoor air quality, so don't skimp on the ventilation system.

Should You Get an ERV or an HRV?

In the section on balanced ventilation with recovery, I told you only about the energy recovery ventilator (ERV).[30] That's not your only option for this ventilation strategy, though. Let's look at the other type, which is a heat recovery ventilator (HRV).

The only difference between the two is the membrane in the heat exchanger. The membrane in an ERV allows both heat and moisture to move from one air stream to the other. On the other hand, in an HRV core, the membrane allows only heat to transfer. Another way of thinking about the two is that an ERV transfers both sensible and latent heat, and an HRV transfers only sensible heat.

Climate and Occupancy

The choice between an ERV and an HRV should land on ERV most of the time. In a warm, humid climate, an ERV brings in less outdoor humidity than an HRV. (Note: An ERV is not a dehumidifier. See the sidebar "Myth: An ERV Dehumidifies the Air" on page 282.) In a hot, dry climate, an HRV will make your already dry air even drier, sending your precious water vapor out into that desert air. In a cold climate, bringing in outdoor air without moisture exchange can result in extremely low humidity in winter because cold air is dry air. On the basis of climate, it's only in mild climates where it doesn't get too cold, humid, or dry where HRVs make sense—sometimes. That's why they're popular in the Pacific Northwest.

> *The choice between an ERV and an HRV should land on ERV most of the time.*

Occupancy, though, is another important factor to consider. The higher the density of people in a space, the more you might need to dry out the air with an HRV. For example, a small, airtight apartment or condo with two or three people in it may be too humid indoors with an ERV.

History, Efficiency, and Core Swapping

Some people think HRVs are the way to go because older ERVs didn't have good control over frost forming on the core. That's not the case anymore. ERVs work fine in really cold places now. Another reason people choose HRVs is that they're more efficient at transferring heat than are ERVs. What good is it to have high-efficiency ventilation, though, if you end up growing mold or going through 50 liters of skin lotion each year?

Another possibility is to do both. If you're in a humid climate and don't want to bring in a lot of water vapor with your summer ventilation, you need an ERV. But if your house is very airtight, you may get too humid indoors in winter with an ERV. In that case, you could have an ERV core

---

30. Here's a bit of building science trivia for you: The E in ERV doesn't really stand for energy. It stands for enthalpy, which is a type of energy that includes both heat and moisture.

for the summer and then swap it out with an HRV core for the winter. (Not every manufacturer makes models with swappable cores, so check the one you're buying if you think you may want to do this.)

The primary way to choose between an ERV and an HRV is to understand the moisture control needs of the space being ventilated. Look at the volume of air in the house compared to the number of people in the house. The more volume per person, the more likely you need an ERV. The less volume of air per person, the more likely you need an HRV. To put that into more realistic terms, two people living in a 2,000-square-foot house probably need an ERV, whereas three people in a 1,000-square-foot condo are probably better off with an HRV.

Advice for Buying an ERV

When you buy an ERV for a house, look for these features:
- A maximum rate about twice as high as you plan to run it continuously
- The capability of changing the rate so you can run it at a lower rate
- The capability to boost to a higher rate when you need more ventilation
- Fans run by electronically commutated motors (ECMs)
- A core with a high recovery efficiency for heat (ERV and HRV) and moisture (ERV) (The best units offer around 95 percent and 70 percent, respectively.)
- The capability of using a MERV-13 filter on the incoming air side

Make sure you look at the specifications of the models you're considering. There are plenty of low-cost, low-quality ERVs available. But there are also some high-quality, moderately priced ERVs. Do your homework.

Chapter Takeaways

- Ventilation is important for indoor air quality and humidity control.
- The three main types of ventilation are local, buffer space, and whole-house.
- The three main types of whole-house ventilation are exhaust-only, supply-only, or balanced.
- Balanced ventilation with recovery is done by an energy recovery ventilator (ERV) or a heat recovery ventilator (HRV).
- For most homes, an ERV is the better choice.

CHAPTER 18
Water Heating

Let's take a minute to appreciate hot water. You stand in front of the sink, turn a valve, and a continuous stream of water comes out. Even more wondrous, that water can vary in temperature from lukewarm to scalding, and we can deliver it to any part of the house. Just a few generations back, our ancestors would marvel at the convenience because hot water in buildings became a thing only in the late 19th century. As you read about the various problems associated with hot water in this chapter, don't forget to value simply having indoor plumbing and hot water. Now, let's put hot water in context and dive into the details.

Space heating and cooling get the most energy-saving attention because they have traditionally used the most energy in homes. That's because far too many homes have a lot of air leakage, not so much insulation, inefficient heating and cooling equipment, and leaky, inefficient ducts. Because the attention on space conditioning has led to big changes in energy codes, voluntary programs, materials, and products, space heating and cooling may not be the biggest energy user in a new home. Water heating has been the next largest energy consumer, and in new homes, it could be the largest. In many apartments, water heating has been the biggest energy user for a long time.

> *Space heating and cooling get the most energy-saving attention because they have traditionally used the most energy in homes.*

> *"A smart plumbing design starts with the location of the water heater."*
> *—Gary Klein*

In newer homes, the percentage of a home's total energy used for heating water is higher than in older homes because we've done so much to reduce heating and cooling energy consumption, while water heating has improved little overall. In condos, apartments, or super-efficient single-family homes, water heating can account for nearly half of the annual energy use. Despite that, home builders still install water heaters that are not much better than they were a few decades ago. However, new technology as well as the increasing prominence of water heating on the energy consumption pie chart is starting to bring about some needed change.

Even better, the improvements in hot water aren't all about saving energy. Some water heaters are downright dangerous because of the potential they present for putting carbon monoxide into your home's air. And some hot water systems are inconvenient and wasteful. If it takes 2 minutes for hot water to get to a faucet, the system wastes time, energy, and water. In this chapter, I'll provide some background for you on what kind of options you have when choosing a water heater, brief descriptions along with pros and cons for the main types of water heaters, and an explanation of the ugly duckling of hot water: the distribution system, which has so much room for improvement. But first, let's put the hot water in context by looking at the whole system.

Water Heating Is a System

What's the first image that pops into your head when you see the term "water heating"? It's probably a water heater tank. Depending on your interests or what you have in your home, perhaps you thought of a tankless or solar water heater. For most people, hot water is all about the device that heats water. Water heating, though, is a system, and the water heater is merely one component.

First, there's the water heater, which has two main inputs: water and energy. The hot water that comes out of the water heater then has to travel through a distribution system to reach the various fixtures—faucets, showers, dishwasher, etc. The fixtures have controls. And then you have the people, an important part of any water heating system.

On the input side, water varies from place to place. The mineral content or added water softening chemicals can affect the life span and maintenance of a water heater.

Water also varies from season to season, and the temperature of the water supply affects the energy use. In cold climates, the water coming into a water heater is colder than the water being heated in warm climates. The incoming water temperature is close to the average air temperature for a location, but it varies with location of the pipes and with the seasons. In winter, the water coming into a water heater is colder and needs more heating.

The type of energy input is an important choice. It could be electricity, natural gas, propane, wood, solar radiation, or some other type. The fuel you choose narrows your options for a type of water heater. Within types, though, you can choose low, medium, or high efficiency. You also may get to choose from models that store hot water in a tank or those that heat water on demand.

The output side of the water heater is the part that's gotten short shrift. When you choose combustion of a fuel to heat your water, there are two outputs: hot water and also exhaust gases. Removing the exhaust gases is a critical health and safety issue. Sealed combustion or direct vent water heaters are the safest, but the most common gas water heater uses a natural draft exhaust gas flue, making it the appliance most likely to put carbon monoxide into your home's air. Consider carefully when buying a water heater.

For electric and solar thermal water heaters, the main output is hot water. Heat pump water heaters have an additional output: cool, dry air. That can be nice in summer, but it may create problems in cold climates.

Sadly, the process of delivering the hot water to the rest of the house is greatly flawed in most homes. The hot water distribution systems still being installed today are based on out-of-date ideas and technology. Since the 1992 Energy Policy Act lowered the upper limits on water flow rates for different types of plumbing fixtures, hot and cold water lines have been oversized. The result is longer wait times for hot water, which wastes water and time. It also wastes energy because it strands more hot water in the pipes when the tap is turned off than would be stranded with right-sized pipes.

Also of great importance for the hot water distribution is the location of the water heater relative to the fixtures. The greater the distance between the water heater and the fixtures, the more water and energy are wasted. The most

> *Sadly, the process of delivering the hot water to the rest of the house is greatly flawed in most homes.*

efficient hot water distribution systems have the shortest runs and right-sized pipes.

The convenience problem can be solved with a recirculating system, which moves hot water through the pipes so you don't have to wait when you turn on the faucet. The most common type is a continuous recirculating pump. It keeps hot water close to every fixture 24/7, but it wastes a lot of energy, especially if the pipes are uninsulated. Putting it on a timer so it runs only during the high-use times can help. A demand-type recirculating system is much more efficient. Before you need hot water, you push a strategically located button, and your hot water will be ready in a minute or two without the need to run the water and waste water and energy.

But wait! There's more. The water heating system also includes the drains at each fixture. When you heat water, you use that heat only briefly while showering or washing dishes, and then you send it on its merry way down the drain. You're sending energy that you paid for down the drain, too. It's possible to recover some of that heat in a clever device called a drain water heat recovery system. It's simply a copper pipe wrapped around a drain, absorbing heat from the drain water. These devices are mainly used on showers. They run cold water through the copper pipe, preheating it on its way into the water heater or directly back to the shower or both.

There's your 10,000-meter overview of hot water, showing water heating as a system with many parts. Now, let's get into some of the details.

Water Heater Options

When it comes to heating water at home, you have options. The two main choices you have to make are the type of fuel and whether your water heater will store hot water in a tank or heat it on demand. Then those two choices lead to more choices. For example, you can get different kinds of water heaters with large differences in efficiency, both gas and electric.

A lot of factors can play into what type of water heater you choose: climate, location of the water heater, existing vs. new home, and your objectives. For example, if you live in a cold climate, you shouldn't put a heat pump water heater in the garage or a tankless water heater on the outside of the house. If your home has an electric water heater now, switching to gas will include additional costs because you'll have to find a way to bring in a gas line and vent the exhaust gases to the outdoors. And if your goal is to keep carbon monoxide out of your home's air, you'll avoid a natural draft gas water heater inside the home.

Now, we'll take a high-level look at the choices you have and then follow it up with a section on how water heater efficiency is rated before getting into the main types of water heaters used in homes.

Type of Fuel: Gas or Electric?

Although you can heat water with other fuels, the two most common—and realistic—fuel choices for homes are gas and electric. (I'm including propane with gas here.) When building a new home, you can go either direction. Electric water heating would be my choice. (See Chapter 4.) If it would cost a lot to get a gas line run to your house, that makes the decision easier. You'll definitely have electricity anyway, so if you install an electric water heater, the only impact may be the possible need for a larger electrical service.

In existing homes, switching the fuel used by your water heater can be difficult. Going from gas to electric may require a larger electrical service, especially in older homes that haven't had an electrical upgrade. Installing a heat pump water heater can reduce the need for electricity, but they still have backup electric resistance heating that will require as much power as going with straight electric resistance.

Similarly, changing your water heater from electric to gas can be difficult because you'll have to bring in a gas line and install an exhaust flue. Switching to a higher-efficiency gas water heater makes that easier because the flue can go straight out the side of the house instead of having to go up and out through the top.

Storage or Tankless?

The other big choice is whether to go with a water heater that stores hot water or makes it on demand. If you choose to heat your water with electricity, this choice is easy: Buy a storage model for whole-house water heating. The only way to heat water with an electric tankless water heater is to do so with electric resistance heating. (Heat pumps take too long.) The problem, though, is that it takes a lot of power to heat water quickly. To do this for a whole house, you almost certainly will need to upgrade your electrical service because it takes a lot of electrical current to deliver the power needed to heat water on demand. Tankless electric water heaters can work in some applications, but you should get a storage electric water heater for the whole house.

If you have natural gas, the storage and tankless options are both good, and each has its pros and cons. Tanks keep hot water on hand, but that comes with standby losses. Tankless water heaters make hot water on demand, but they are sometimes finicky. They also require electricity for the controls, so when the electricity goes out, you lose hot water just as if you had an electric water heater. With an electric storage water heater, you still have the hot water in the tank available for use even when the power goes out.

Once you've made the choice of a storage or tankless water heater, you need to decide on the capacity. For storage water heaters, that comes in two forms: the tank size and the first hour rating. Tank size, as with so many things, isn't just a simple number because there's the nominal capacity and the actual capacity. For example, my 80-gallon heat pump water heater has an actual capacity of 72 gallons. Fortunately, the yellow Energy Guide label on water heaters sold in the United States provides the actual capacity. It also tells you the first hour rating. My 80- (72-) gallon water heater is rated at 89 gallons of hot water in the first hour (but that includes some use of the heat strips, not heat pump only).

With tankless water heaters, the capacity is based on two factors: the flow rate and the amount of temperature rise needed. You can find the flow rate by using the flow rates of your hot water fixtures. The temperature rise depends on how cold the water supply is in your area. In hot climates, the water entering the water heater is warmer, so you don't need as much temperature rise. In cold climates, the entering water is colder and needs to be heated more. With those two factors, you can choose a tankless water heater that will meet your needs.

Efficiency

For the purposes of this section, I'm going to define water heater efficiency loosely. For example, a 90 percent efficient water heater is one that turns 90 percent of the input energy into heat that goes into your hot water. As you'll see in the section on the Uniform Energy Factor (UEF), the rated efficiency is a more carefully derived number.

If you go with an electric water heater, the most common type heats the water with electric resistance with an efficiency of about 90 percent. You could also install a more efficient heat pump water heater, which operates at roughly 300 percent efficiency. (Remember that a heat pump simply moves heat, so a 300 percent efficient heat pump water heater would put three times as much heat energy into the water as it uses in electrical energy.) Most electric water heaters store hot water in a tank, but it's also possible to get a tankless electric water heater (more on tankless electric below). A tankless electric water heater uses electric resistance, so it operates at about 90 percent efficiency.

Gas water heaters also come in different efficiency flavors. The three most common gas water heater efficiencies are roughly 60 percent, 80 percent, and 95 percent. My recommendation is to go with 80 percent or higher if you're getting a gas water heater. The standard water heater in the 60 percent range is the natural draft type. It uses air around the water heater for combustion and for draft in the exhaust flue, which makes it the most dangerous combustion appliance in most homes (as you'll see in the section on water heater types). The difference between the 80 percent and 95 percent gas water heaters is the same as the difference between the two main types of furnaces: The higher efficiency models condense water vapor in the exhaust and harvest the heat that otherwise would be lost through the exhaust flue.

Water Heater Efficiency

There are three types of water heater efficiencies to consider: firing efficiency, standby efficiency, and distribution efficiency. Here's what these terms mean.

Firing efficiency: When you convert one type of energy to heat for your hot water (as opposed to moving heat with a heat pump), your maximum efficiency is 100 percent. When you use electric resistance heat, that's what you get: 100 percent firing efficiency.[31] All of the electricity is turned into heat that goes into the water because the conversion happens in heating elements that are in the water. With gas, the standard firing efficiency is about 75 to 80 percent. With a condensing gas water heater, that efficiency goes to about 95 percent.

Standby efficiency: The second type of water heater efficiency is standby efficiency. Storage water heaters lose heat through the surface area of the tank. Consequently, a larger water heater will have greater standby losses than an equally insulated smaller model. You might think the losses would be the same no matter how the water in the tank gets heated, but there's a significant difference between gas and electric. Gas water heater tanks actually have more surface area than the same size electric water heater. Why? Because they have an exhaust flue running up through the middle of the tank. Some gas water heaters have another type of standby loss, too: a pilot light.

Distribution efficiency: This is the third type. This often-ignored part of the hot water system has started to get recognition in recent years. The obvious distribution loss is that hot water loses heat through the pipes when it leaves the tank and travels to the point of use. However, a bigger loss is the hot water that regularly gets stranded in the pipes. Two factors play a role in that loss: the length and the diameter of the pipes. I'll discuss both later in this chapter. A benefit of a hot water system with high distribution efficiency is that you don't spend as much time waiting for hot water to arrive.

Defining Water Heater Efficiency

The primary efficiency rating for residential water heaters in the United States is the uniform energy factor (UEF), an update of the older energy factor (EF). They both include only the firing and standby efficiency but not the

31. This is true when you use the site energy for the input electrical energy. For source energy, the maximum would be about 30 percent. See Chapter 4 for a discussion of site vs. source energy.

distribution efficiency. Before getting into the details, though, remember that efficiency is the output divided by the input, which is really just a measure of how much bang you get for your buck.

As discussed in Chapter 13, this equation is more complex than it looks because both the output and

$$Efficiency = \frac{Output}{Input} = \frac{Bang}{Buck}$$

the input depend on the operating conditions. With water heaters, the output is the volume of hot water that can be delivered at a specified temperature. The input depends on the energy source (e.g., combustion, electric resistance, heat pump, or solar), the inclusion of any other energy used (e.g., electricity for fan on power-vented water heater), and the temperature of the water supply. And for the same reason that the actual efficiency you get with a car isn't the same as the rated efficiency, your mileage may vary with water heaters, too.

> **For the same reason that the actual efficiency you get with a car isn't the same as the rated efficiency, your mileage may vary with water heaters, too.**

However, the primary utility of efficiency ratings isn't really to tell you how efficient your water heater will be. It's to give you a way to compare one water heater to another when you're making a purchase. Now, let's look at how water heater efficiency ratings might help with that.

Uniform Energy Factor

As stated above, in the United States and also in Canada, the current efficiency rating for water heaters is called the uniform energy factor (UEF). Without going too far into the details, we can say a little about how the output over input calculation is done. For UEF to be a good way to compare water heaters, it needs to be measured the same way by all manufacturers. The UEF test criteria include:

- Inlet water temperature
- Outlet water temperature
- Draw pattern, which differs for different size water heaters

The resulting UEF is a number that's less than 1 for most water heaters and in the 2 to 4 range for heat pump water heaters. UEF is basically a percent efficiency, so a water heater with a UEF of 0.96 can be said to be 96 percent efficient. One with a 0.59 UEF would be 59 percent efficient. A heat pump water heater with a 3.7 UEF would be 370 percent efficient. A heat pump water heater uses electricity to move heat rather than getting heat through an energy conversion, and this one moves 3.7 times as much heat energy as it uses in electrical energy. (More on that in the next section.)

The other thing to understand about UEF or any other efficiency rating for water heaters is that it's not the best way to compare water heaters that use different fuels. A gas water heater and an electric water heater may each have a UEF of 0.95, but that doesn't mean they're equivalent. One big difference stems from the site versus source issue (Chapter 4). Using gas at 95 percent efficiency on site is actually more efficient than using electricity at 95 percent efficiency when that electricity was generated by gas and coal combustion at a power plant. The net efficiency of generating the electricity that way and delivering it to the house is about 30 percent, so your actual efficiency is really in the 30 percent range when you use electricity that's generated off-site.

The best use for UEF or any other efficiency rating used for water heaters is to compare water heaters that use the same fuel. A 0.95 UEF gas water heater is definitely better than a 0.59 UEF gas water heater. But is a 0.95 UEF propane water heater better than a 0.90 UEF gas water heater? Maybe. What are your criteria for choosing one water heater or one fuel over another?

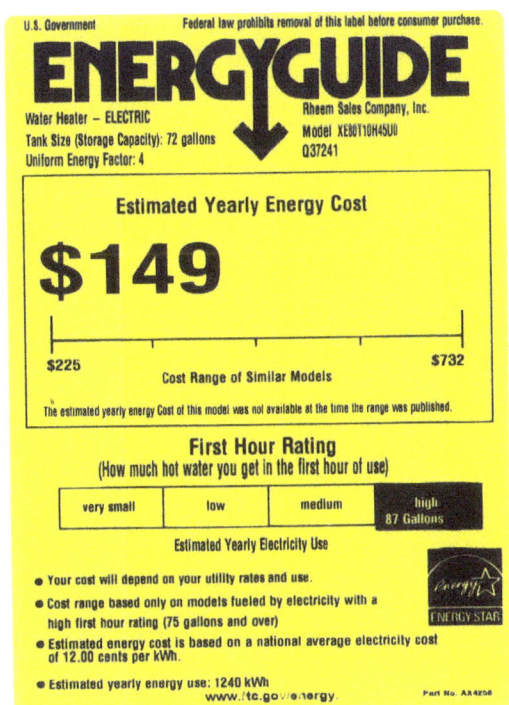

Figure 18.1. *The EnergyGuide for a heat pump water heater*

do it for you. Table 18.1 shows the results of my spreadsheet calculations for six different water heaters using three different fuels. (I assumed 44 gallons of hot water use per day and a temperature rise of 70 °F.)

Water Heater Type	UEF	Rate	Cost per year
Gas	0.6	$1.00/therm	$156
Gas	0.8	$1.00/therm	$117
Gas	0.95	$1.00/therm	$98
Propane	0.6	$1.50/gal	$254
Electric resistance	0.9	$0.15	$456
Heat Pump WH	3.7	$0.15	$111

Table 18.1. *Cost per year for six different water heater types and three different fuels*

If you're in the United States, you have another useful tool at your disposal to help you get a feel for the relative costs. Every water heater comes with a yellow label called the EnergyGuide, and it gives a lot of helpful information. On it, you can find the model number, the first hour rating, the UEF, and the estimated annual energy costs. It's a good way to compare water heaters without having to do the calculations yourself, although you might want to adjust the annual energy cost estimate using your local fuel rates. You also can use this information to find out when one type of water heater might have the same annual cost as another that uses a different fuel (e.g., gas versus heat pump water heater).

If it's cost, that's easy to determine. You can do a cost comparison using your local rates for the various fuels and a few other pieces of information. You'd need to know the efficiency of the water heater, the amount of hot water use, the entering water temperature, and some basic data like the specific heat of water and the energy content for the various fuels in your comparison. It's not hard to put together a spreadsheet that can do these calculations, but you can also find calculators online that will

Main Water Heater Types

Here's an overview of some of the main water heater types. There's a description of each, along with its benefits and drawbacks.

Electric Resistance Storage Water Heaters

The standard electric water heater uses electric resistance to heat water that gets stored in a tank. Electric resistance heating produces 1 unit of heat

for each unit of electrical energy, so we say it has a firing efficiency of 100 percent. But its overall efficiency rating will be less than 100 percent because of standby losses. The best water heaters of this type are about 95 percent efficient. If you go with this type of water heater, you may need a larger tank than if you were using a gas storage water heater. Electric water heaters add heat more slowly and thus have lower first-hour ratings than gas water heaters of the same size.

Figure 18.2. *Electric resistance water heater: Notice that there's no exhaust flue coming up through the middle, and there is an electrical conduit in the center of the top.*

The impact of this type of water heater on the environment depends on the source of the electricity. If the utility uses a majority of coal-fired electricity, it's not so good. Remember that the 100 percent firing efficiency is based on site energy. When you factor in the source energy in this case, it drops to about 30 percent. The good news is that electricity keeps getting cleaner because wind and solar are growing rapidly, and coal and gas are declining. Also, an electric resistance water heater makes a great companion for rooftop photovoltaics.

Electric Resistance Tankless Water Heaters

Here the heat source is the same as in electric resistance tank water heaters, but it doesn't store hot water. Consequently, this type of water heater uses a lot of power. You may need a larger electrical service if you try to use one for your whole house. They do make sense in some applications, though. With a low flow of hot water in a limited application, this type of electric water heater can be a good solution. For example, the Southface Energy Institute in Atlanta has a kitchenette with a small electric tankless water heater. The only hot water used there is for the sink and the dishwasher.

Because tankless electric water heaters use a lot of electrical power, you may think electrical utilities would like you to have a tankless electric water heater. They don't. First, that kind of power draw may coincide with times when their customers are using a lot of power. To cover all that use, they have to start up more expensive peaking plants. So, they try to limit their use by keeping their peaks down. Second, an electric resistance storage water heater also uses electric resistance, but it uses less power when it comes on, and it also can heat the water in the tank throughout the day. Some people even put their water heaters on timers to avoid the peak hours of the day, which can lower their electric bills if their utility offers time-of-use rates. And utilities like it when you use their nighttime electricity, which is often the cheapest kilowatt-hours they make.

Electric Heat Pump Storage Water Heater

Heat pump water heaters are ready for prime time. I have one in my house, and I love it! As you know from Chapter 13, heat pumps don't get heat through an energy conversion. They use electricity as the energy source (input) to move heat (output). In the case of an air-source heat pump water heater, the heat exchange process takes heat from the air and puts it into the water in the tank (Figure 18.3 on page 307). Choosing a location for the water heater and setting it up makes a difference in the capacity and efficiency of the heat pump, and it also makes a difference in the conditions of the air being used as a source of heat. Let's consider some scenarios.

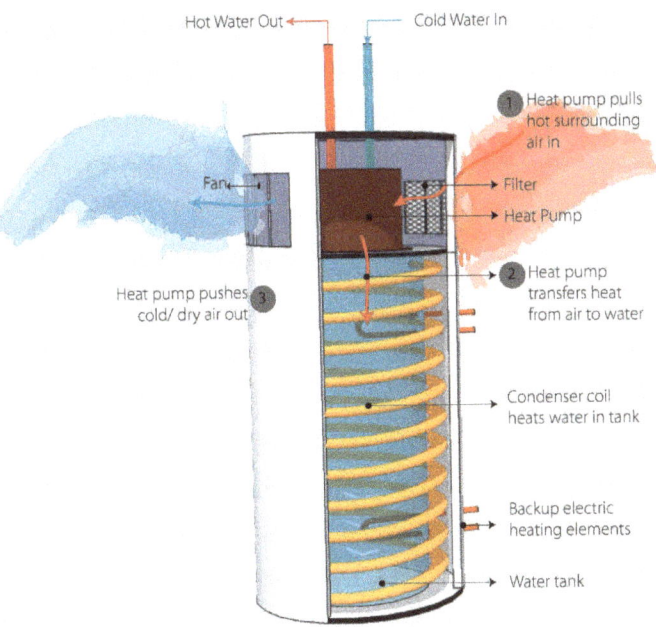

Figure 18.3. *Components of a heat pump water heater [Source: US Department of Energy, Building America Solution Center]*

Because we want to get heat from the air, a heat pump water heater works best when there's a lot of heat in that air. In a hot climate, putting the water heater in the garage might make sense. Garages get hot. And a heat pump water heater provides some cooling, too. It sucks heat out of the air and puts it into your hot water. A twofer! The amount of cooling you get depends on how much hot water you use, so a heat pump water heater by itself will help just a little bit in most cases. If you want to keep your garage comfortable in Phoenix or Orlando, you'll probably need more cooling. (Don't put that heat pump water heater in the garage just yet though. First, read the section on hot water distribution later in this chapter.)

Another good place to get warm air is from the attic. A conditioned attic usually runs warmer than the rest of the house, so it can be a great source of heat for your heat pump water heater. I'm not a fan of putting storage water heaters in attics because that's a lot of water over your head if it fails. But there's another way to use the heat from the attic. Some heat pump water heaters allow for ducting on the intake and exhaust side of the heat pump, so you can keep your water heater in the main part of the house or basement and still use the heat from the attic.

The output side of the water heater dumps cool, dry air into the space around the water heater or wherever the end of the duct is, if you use that capability. That may be a problem in winter, especially if the water heater is in the basement of a house in a cold climate. You can still use one in these situations; it just won't be as efficient as it would be in a warmer place. And you have to account for the extra cooling you'll get. Also, when you put a heat pump water heater in conditioned space, it's robbing Peter to pay Paul. The heat you pull out of the indoor air comes from whatever heating equipment is heating the space. Use high-efficiency space heating equipment to keep the overall efficiency high.

Figure 18.4. *A heat pump water heater is taller than a regular water heater because of the heat pump on top. You'll also see vents to move air through the top section.*

Those of you in cold climates, though, have another option. Just as you can use a heat pump to pull heat from the outdoor air for space heating, you can pull heat from the outdoor air to heat water, too. A split system heat pump water heater has an outdoor unit that collects heat, and that heat goes into water stored in a tank in the house. Even better, this type of heat pump often uses carbon dioxide as a refrigerant, not the typical refrigerants with high global warming potential.[32]

32. Yes, carbon dioxide is the main global warming gas, the one by which all others are judged. Its global warming potential (GWP) is 1. The refrigerant used in my heat pump water heater is R-134A, and its GWP is ~1,400, meaning 1 molecule of it is equivalent to 1,400 CO_2 molecules.

Heat pump water heaters are a great option for homes. When sized and located properly, they're no more obtrusive than any other water heater. Some models can be noisy, so check out the specifications and don't put it where you'll hear it. My Rheem model is in my basement mechanical room, and I barely hear it. Heat pump water heaters are still relatively expensive, but rebates and tax credits can make them affordable.

> **A split system heat pump water heater has an outdoor unit that collects heat, and that heat goes into water stored in a tank in the house.**

Natural Draft Gas Storage Water Heaters

This type of water heater is called natural draft because there's a gap between the top of the water heater and the bottom of the exhaust flue (Figure 18.5). The gap allows air from the room to be pulled in by the negative pressure in the flue, aiding the removal of exhaust gases. The burner is at the bottom of the flue, and it also pulls in room air to use for combustion. The combustion at the bottom heats the water in the tank, with the exhaust gases traveling up through a flue that goes through the middle of the tank. Some water heaters also have pilot lights, which burn gas continuously to ignite the burner when more heat is needed and are another standby loss. The efficiency of natural draft water heaters is about 60 percent.

I'm going to come right out and say it: Avoid natural draft water heaters. They are the least efficient and arguably the most dangerous water heater you can buy. They are dangerous because they pull air from the space around them to use for combustion and draft. If you put one in a small room, it may have trouble getting enough air for those two needs. Put it in a laundry room with a clothes dryer, and the dryer competes for air with

the water heater. Put an atmospheric combustion furnace in that laundry room, and now you've got more competition for air. Both the dryer and the furnace have fans, though, so guess who loses that battle: the water heater.

Figure 18.5. *A natural draft water heater has a gap between the flue carrying exhaust gases out of the house and the flue inside the water heater (arrow). It also has a metal flue.*

When the pressure in the space around a natural draft water heater is sufficiently negative (about 3 Pascals), air can come down the exhaust flue in a process called backdrafting. That means exhaust gases don't go up the flue, and instead they stay in the room where the water heater is and possibly are spread throughout the house. It also means the air flow through the burner changes, likely leading to incomplete combustion and the production of more carbon monoxide.

If you've already got this type of water heater, make sure you have a low-level carbon monoxide monitor in your home. (See sidebar on page 28.) Even if the water heater is in the garage, it can still backdraft. The exhaust gases, including carbon monoxide, can still get into your home. If you're considering buying a gas water heater, any other type will probably be safer.

Direct Vent Gas Storage Water Heaters

Direct vent gas water heaters are a step up from natural draft, but they share many of the same characteristics. The gas burner at the bottom heats the water. The exhaust gases travel up through a flue in the middle of the tank. The main difference is that instead of drawing air from the space around the water heater for combustion and draft, a direct vent water heater pulls in air from outdoors for these purposes. That makes this water heater safer than a natural draft model.

But that safety factor comes at a premium. You get little energy savings with this type of water heater compared to a natural draft model, but the price is significantly higher. Also, the venting may make it a safer gas water heater, but it's a less convenient one. This type of water heater works best near an exterior wall because the vent has to go out horizontally. The direct vent water heater comes either without a fan (Figure 18.6) or in a powered version that uses a fan to assist the air movement.

exhaust gases travel up through a flue in the middle of the tank. Unlike the direct vent type, the combustion air is still drawn from the space around the water heater. The other difference is that the gases don't draft naturally but are pulled up by a fan at the top of the tank. The exhaust venting is sealed, so the only way exhaust gases can get into the house is if the flue leaks.

The main benefit of a power-vented water heater is that it's safer than natural draft. But it costs 50 to 80 percent more than natural draft models, and it's only about 65 percent efficient (versus 60 percent for natural draft). So, you can forget about it paying for itself in savings. Also, you lose the benefit of having hot water when the electricity goes out because this water heater can't operate without the fan.

Figure 18.6. *Direct vent water heater with concentric intake and exhaust venting*

Figure 18.7. *Power-vented gas water heater*

Power-Vented Gas Storage Water Heaters

Power-vented water heaters (Figure 18.7) are a different kind of step up from natural draft. The gas burner at the bottom heats the water. The

Gas Tankless Water Heater

The tankless[33] gas water heater (Figure 18.8) has become popular in the past two decades. As with a furnace and other gas water heaters,

33. I'm going to refer to this type of water heater as tankless. If you're looking for a rabbit hole, you can look up the differences between tankless, instantaneous, and on-demand water heaters. Spoiler: They're all pretty much the same.

the combustion results in hot gases that must be exhausted to the outdoors. On their way out, the exhaust gases travel through a heat exchanger that transfers most of the heat of combustion to the water. The signal for the tankless water heater to turn on is someone turning on a hot water tap or the initiation of some other hot water demand. This water heater is usually installed inside the house, but it can be installed outside in places that don't freeze. It reduces the cycling losses because you don't have to keep a tank of hot water sitting around waiting for someone to turn on a faucet. You can go with an 80 to 85 percent efficient non-condensing model, but you may need expensive double-wall stainless steel vent pipes. Better would be to go with a higher efficiency condensing model that operates at about 95 percent efficiency and uses plastic vent pipes.

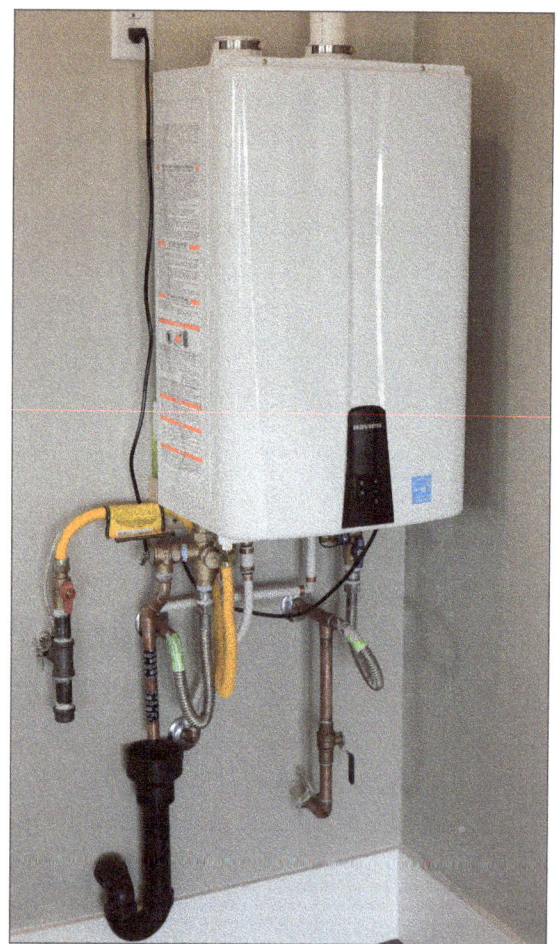

Figure 18.8. *Tankless gas water heater [Source: US Department of Energy, Building America Solution Center]*

As with the electric tankless water heater, a gas tankless water heater may require a larger gas service because it takes a high rate of combustion to create the heat needed to heat water quickly. They also can be finicky at times, and homeowners have had their nice warm showers suddenly turn cold in some cases. For some people, the biggest drawback of tankless gas water heaters is that they use gas to heat the water, but they also rely on electricity for the controls. That means that you won't have hot water when the electricity goes out. Worse, you won't even have the hot water in the tank like someone with an electric water heater would have.

	Natural Draft	Direct Vent	Powered Direct Vent	Power Vented	Tankless
UEF	0.6	0.6	0.65-0.70	0.65-0.70	0.8-0.95
Source of combustion air	Indoors	Outdoors	Outdoors	Indoors	Outdoors
Pilot light or electronic ignition	Either	Either	Either	Either	Either
Hot water available when electricity is out	Yes, what's in tank and more with pilot	Yes, what's in tank and more with pilot	Yes, what's in tank and more with pilot	Yes, what's in tank and more with pilot	No

Table 18.2. *Comparison of features of different types of gas water heaters*

Ground-Source Heat Pump Desuperheater

Yet another way to get hot water is to use the same process a heat pump water heater uses, but in a different way. A standalone heat pump water heater is dedicated just to heating the water. The cooling and dehumidification provided are a benefit or a drawback, depending on location and time of year. In contrast, a ground-source heat pump's main job is to heat and cool a home. In cooling mode, it takes heat from inside the house and moves it into the ground. In heating mode, it moves heat from the ground into the house.

In both modes, the heat pump puts a refrigerant through a thermodynamic cycle (see Chapter 13) that involves evaporation and condensation of the refrigerant. Heat added to the refrigerant after evaporation is called superheat, and some of that excess heat is available to be used in your hot water system. Naturally, to take superheat from a heat pump, you need a desuperheater. Now that name makes sense, right? This device is a heat exchanger that connects to your water heater. It's an option you can buy when you get a ground-source heat pump.

> **Naturally, to take superheat from a heat pump, you need a desuperheater.**

Using a desuperheater to make hot water does not replace your need for a primary water heater. The desuperheater is a preheater that heats the water as high as it can. Sometimes that's all you need. Other times the temperature needs a boost. So, preheat and boost are systems that are designed to make the most of the preheat function and minimize the boost energy. In summer, the desuperheater may provide 100 percent of your hot water. In the rest of the year, you'll get much less. If you're wondering how it heats water in the winter, the thermodynamic cycle in a heat pump generates superheat all year long. The heat pump still has the ability to heat the house sufficiently in winter even after removing some of the superheat. There's more heat available in summer, of course, so that's when it works best.

Is it cost effective? Maybe. Getting the desuperheater option will cost about as much as two electric resistance water heaters, so whether it ends up paying for itself or not depends on how much hot water you get from it, the efficiency of your booster water heater, and the cost of the two types of water heating energy. If you've already got a heat pump water heater, it won't make sense to get a desuperheater for a ground-source heat pump. If you're heating water with electric resistance or low-efficiency gas in an area with high fuel costs, it's probably cost effective.

Solar Water Heating

Solar thermal water heating has been around a long time. In some countries, it's popular, and even mandated. The concept is simple. Put water in a location that gets sunshine, and the water heats up. If you've ever gotten water from a garden hose that's been lying in the sun on a summer day, you know how easy it is to heat water with sunshine.

The devil, however, is in the details. You need a good backup source of hot water for cloudy days, and you need storage for nighttime. You have to keep the water from freezing in places where it gets cold enough for that to happen. And you've got to have a well-designed collector that gets the water hot enough but not too hot. Overheated water can turn into steam, and steam in confined places can explode. I won't go into the details of the various types of solar thermal water heaters here because I'm going to suggest a different way of using the sun to heat your water. And that's next.

Is Solar Thermal Water Heating Dead?

In 2012, longtime energy nerd Martin Holladay, author of the book *Musings of an Energy Nerd,* shocked a lot of people—and angered a few, too—when he published an article titled "Solar Thermal Is Dead." Then, two years later, he piled on with a follow-up article titled "Solar Thermal Is Really, Really Dead." His thesis was that solar thermal water heating, the darling of the 1970s and '80s solar movement, was significantly more expensive in first costs than using photovoltaics and a heat pump water heater. Worse for the solar thermal adherents, he showed that even photovoltaics paired with an electric resistance water heater beat solar thermal water heating.

Guess what? It's gotten even more lopsided in favor of photovoltaics plus electric water heating since then. Let's look at the numbers, and you can decide for yourself if you want to spend your money on a solar thermal water heater. The data we need to compare these three methods for using solar energy to make hot water are:

- Installed cost of the water heater tanks for the three systems
- The amount of electrical energy needed from the photovoltaics to heat water for two solar electric systems
- Size of the photovoltaic system needed for the electric water heaters
- Installed cost of solar equipment

Figure 18.9. *A solar thermal water system collects heat from the sun and puts it into hot water. [Source: US Department of Energy, Building America Solution Center]*

Once we have all those data, we can calculate the total cost of each system. Finding the costs of the water heater tanks is easy. A quick search of the Interwebs can turn up the numbers we need. All three systems use storage tanks for hot water. The solar thermal system typically uses a large electric resistance water heater for storage, and it also provides backup water heating for those times when the solar thermal system isn't up to the task. The photovoltaic plus electric resistance system uses a tank similar to the solar thermal system, and it's thus about the same cost. The heat pump water heater is a tank plus a heat pump, so it's more expensive. I paid $2,000 for my 80-gallon heat pump water heater plus $800 to install it. To reduce my cost, I could have waited until it was on sale, bought a smaller model, or both. The first row of Table 18.3 on page 313 shows the costs for the three tanks.

Next, we need to know how much electrical energy we need from the photovoltaics. This number stems from three things: the amount of hot water used, how much the water temperature must be increased, and the efficiency of the conversion process in turning photovoltaic electricity into heat. Hot water use varies by season, location, and household, but a family of four uses an average of about 44 gallons per day. Entering water temperature also varies by season and location, but I'll use 50 °F here. Heating the water to 120 °F results in a 70 °F temperature difference. The efficiency of the conversion process (in terms of uniform energy factor, UEF) is about 0.9 for electric resistance and 3 for heat pump water heaters. I'll leave the details of the calculation to interested readers and put them on the book website. The results are shown in the second row of Table 18.3.

Sizing the photovoltaic system takes a little effort, but the US National Renewable Energy Lab has a great website (pvwatts.nrel.gov) that can tell you how much electricity you can generate at your site. Using Atlanta, Georgia, for this example, I came up with a 2.15-kilowatt system needed for electric resistance water heating and a 0.65-kilowatt system needed for the heat pump water heater (third row of Table 18.3).

The cost for the solar thermal equipment varies by location and installer, but $8,000 to $10,000 seems to be a reasonable number. The costs of photovoltaic systems have dropped a lot in the past decade. When Holladay wrote his 2014 article, he used $3.74 per watt of installed capacity. In 2021, it's down to about $3.00 per watt. The fourth row shows the solar equipment costs.

And that brings us to the total costs for the three types of solar water heating systems. Solar thermal is the highest. Photovoltaics plus electric resistance is about three-fourths the cost of solar thermal. And the outright winner is photovoltaics plus a heat pump water heater, costing less than half the cost of a solar thermal system.

But wait! There's more. A solar thermal water heating system won't give you all the hot water you need in a year. Again, it varies by location and season, but you'll get between 60 and 80 percent of your hot water from a solar thermal system. However, the costs I showed for the two photovoltaic systems are to cover 100 percent of your hot water needs. To compare apples to apples, we need to scale those costs. If we assume the solar thermal system provides 75 percent of your hot water, we need to multiply the two photovoltaic system costs by 0.75. Those equivalent costs are shown in the bottom row.

	Solar Thermal	PV + Elec. Resistance	PV + HPWH
Elec. water heater cost, installed	$1,200	$1,200	$2,800
Electric energy needed	NA	3,000 kWh	900 kWh
Size of PV system required	NA	2.15 kW	0.65 kW
Cost of solar equipment, installed	$9,000	$6,450	$1,950
Total Cost	**$10,200**	**$7,650**	**$4,750**
Percent of hot water produced	~75%	100%	100%
Equivalent cost	**$10,200**	**$5,738**	**$3,563**

Table 18.3. *Comparison of costs for three methods of using solar energy to make hot water*

When you look at the numbers, it's clear that the best way to use solar energy to make hot water is with photovoltaics. Doing it with a heat pump water heater gives you the lowest overall cost. Using an electric resistance water heater might be more attractive, though, because you don't have to worry about it taking heat from inside your home or using a piece of equipment that may be more difficult to get repaired.

> **When you look at the numbers, it's clear that the best way to use solar energy to make hot water is with photovoltaics.**

If getting equipment repaired is a concern, that's another reason to stay away from solar thermal. If you happen to be a DIYer who loves tinkering, you certainly can make effective use of solar thermal water heating. For everyone else, just get an electric water heater (either type) and add enough photovoltaics to your rooftop or yard to cover its consumption.

Despite Holladay's dramatic declaration about solar thermal being "really, really dead," this analysis is not the final answer for everyone, everywhere. Some low-cost, do-it-yourself solar thermal systems are less expensive than photovoltaics plus electric water heaters. Also, this analysis doesn't include rebates, tax credits, or other incentives. Nor does it look at the life cycle costs of the three types of systems. The numbers in the table are first costs only. Still, the bottom line in that table doesn't signal a booming future for solar thermal water heating.

Hot Water Distribution: The Ugly Duckling of Energy Efficiency

I opened this chapter by having you imagine turning on the faucet and watching the water. Now imagine that you've just turned on the hot water and you've got your fingers in it as you wait for it to get hot. How long do you have to wait? As I write this in 2021, I have to wait an excruciating 2½ minutes for hot water to arrive at my kitchen sink. While I'm waiting, 3 gallons of water go down the drain. Then after I turn off the water, a pipe full of hot water is left stranded between the kitchen and the water heater. So, I waste water on the front end, energy on the back end, and time waiting that I'd rather use doing something else. Does it really have to be so bad?

The Primary Problem

When you think it through, it's easy to see that hot water distribution suffers because of one problem. When 3 gallons of water spill out of my kitchen faucet while I wait for hot water, that tells me something about the volume of water sitting in the hot water line between the water heater and the kitchen faucet. To waste less water and shorten my wait time, I need less water in that pipe. That's it.

> **To waste less water and shorten my wait time, I need less water in the pipe between my water heater and the kitchen. That's it.**

However, the amount of wasted water is often greater than the amount sitting in the pipes. The water that needs to be pushed out of the pipe to get hot water at the tap is called the structural waste. But when hot water flows through pipes that are too large, it doesn't just push everything in front of it until all of the structural waste is out of the pipe and the hot water arrives at the tap. No, the hot water mixes with the water already in the pipe and sometimes rides on top of the cold water that was in the pipe. That mixing increases the time to get hot water, and it increases the amount of wasted water, too. On average, roughly twice as much water comes out of the pipe before water that is 105 °F or hotter reaches the fixture.

The first part of the problem is excessive pipe lengths. That results from the design of a house and its plumbing system. The big reason is that the water heater and the wet rooms (i.e., the rooms where water is used) are too far apart. For example, when you put a water heater in the garage and a bathroom on the opposite end of the house, the hot water needs to traverse a whole lot of pipe on its way to the showerhead. The solution is shorter pipes through designing a floor plan that clusters the wet rooms in one part of the house—or at least a design that doesn't spread them out as far as possible.

Unfortunately, the actual hot water pipes are often much longer than the distance between the water heater and where the hot water is needed. Hot water pipes rarely take the shortest distance from the water heater to a fixture. In my house, a pipe going straight from the water heater to the kitchen faucet would be about 40 feet long. The actual hot water pipe is about 80 feet long.

The second part of the problem is that the pipes are too big in diameter. Why are they too big? Because our plumbing fixtures have gotten more efficient while hot water piping systems are still designed for higher flows. Flow rates of plumbing fixtures are far lower than they used to be, especially since the 1992 Energy Policy Act went into effect. For example, showerheads went from flow rates of about 4 gallons per minute (gpm) to 2.5 gpm, a drop of 38 percent or more. Dishwashers and washing machines cut their water use in half (Table 18.4). The International Association of Plumbing and Mechanical Officials (IAPMO) led the development of a water demand calculator first published in the *2017 Water Efficiency and Sanitation Standard for the Built Environment* (WEStand).[34] Its purpose is for right-sizing the branches and mains in residential applications. Consider using it for your upcoming projects.

Fixture	1992 and Earlier	After 1992	High-Efficiency
Bathroom lavatory faucet	3.5+ gpm	2.2 gpm	1.2 gpm
Kitchen faucet	3.5+ gpm	2.2 gpm	1.8 gpm
Showerhead	4+ gpm	2.5 gpm	1.5-1.8 gpm
Dishwasher	14 gal per cycle	6.5 gal per cycle	3.5 gal per cycle
Washing machine	51 gal per load	26 gal per load	12.6 gal per load

Table 18.4. *Flow rates for plumbing fixtures that use hot water*

A low-flow fixture certainly saves water. It even saves hot water, but only after the hot water arrives and you're actually using it. Without an efficient hot water distribution system, you still waste at least as much hot water as the high-flow fixtures while you're waiting for it to arrive at the tap. We wasted water faster in the old days because the water sitting in the pipes got pushed out faster with higher flow rates.

Installing a low-flow fixture doesn't change the volume of water in the line, the structural waste. It simply reduces the flow rate while leaving the same amount of water to push through before hot water can arrive. As mentioned earlier, though, the reduced flow rate may result in even more wasted water. With low flow, the hot water doesn't come rushing through the pipe, pushing everything in front of it all at once. That kind of displacement flow, or plug flow, doesn't happen with low flow rates in larger pipes. When the velocity is low, mixing occurs, which increases both the time it takes to get hot water and the amount of wasted water.

The key, then, is to decrease the amount of water sitting in the pipes by decreasing both the pipes' length and diameter.

The Hot Water System Rectangle

Gary Klein, a guru of hot water, has been pushing for change in this area for a long time. He and his colleagues developed a great tool for quantifying the efficiency of a hot water distribution system.[35] It's called the hot water system rectangle, and the concept is simple. You draw the smallest rectangle possible that includes the water heater and all the hot water fixtures in a house. Then you find the area of that rectangle, divide it by the conditioned floor area, and express it as a percentage. If the hot water rectangle is as big as the conditioned floor area in a one-story house, the ratio would be 100 percent. But guess what? It can be more than 100 percent in some cases. For example, if the hot water rectangle includes part of the garage because that's where the water heater lives, the number can be greater than 100 percent.

When you have a two-story house, you still draw a single hot water rectangle. It has to include the water heater and all the hot water fixtures for both floors. The hypothetical maximum would be 50 percent, but that's only if the rectangle doesn't cross the building enclosure to include the garage or other exterior space. For a three-story house, the hypothetical maximum would be 33 percent.

Even though we know the actual hot water rectangle can be larger than those numbers, they're useful guides as to how efficient a house is. You want the hot water rectangle to be as small as possible and the percentage as low as possible. If you're close to 100 percent for a single-story house, 50 percent for a two-story house, or 33 percent for a three-story house, that's not good. If

34. https://www.iapmo.org/water-demand-calculator

35. Klein, Gary, Jim Lutz, Yanda Zhang, John Koeller, 2020. *Final Report: Code Changes and Implications of Residential Low Flow Hot Water Fixtures.* California Energy Commission. Publication Number: CEC-500-2021-043

you're over those numbers, it's even worse.

The challenge is to reduce that ratio. If you're a home builder or architect looking to improve, this is easy to do. It's a lot cheaper to move rooms around on a computer screen than it is in a real building.

You want the hot water rectangle to be as small as possible and the percentage as low as possible.

Let's look at a simple example of a one-story house. Figure 18.10 shows the outline of a house, with the locations of the water heater and hot water fixtures indicated. The hot water rectangle ratio is often a high number when no one considers the efficiency of the hot water distribution system. In the first of the three layouts, the ratio is 93 percent. Without changing the floor plan much, we can reduce that number a lot. The second layout shows the kitchen rearranged to have the hot water fixtures near the center of the house and the two bathrooms also moved toward the center. The ratio for that configuration is 26 percent.

By making bigger changes to the floor plan, we can get an even bigger reduction in the hot water rectangle. In the third layout, the bathroom and kitchen hot water fixtures are even closer together, and the water heater and laundry room are also in the center of the house. The result is a ratio of 3 percent. And that's not the best we can do.

Klein worked with Habitat for Humanity builder George Koertzen in Stockton, California, and helped him make a dramatic improvement in the hot water rectangle ratio for the single-story houses he built. Before learning of the importance of clustering the wet rooms, Koertzen was building a floor plan with a 79 percent ratio. Then he saw the potential and got that down to 15 percent on his first attempt. Then 4 percent . . . and 2.5 percent . . . and finally, an astounding

0.8 percent! The way he got down to less than 1 percent was by first putting the two bathrooms on opposite sides of the same wall. Then he put the kitchen sink and dishwasher at one end and the washing machine at the other end of that wall. He installed the tankless gas water heater over the toilet in one bathroom and the home run manifold over the toilet in the other bathroom. The total length of pipe from the water heater to the farthest fixture is less than 10 feet.

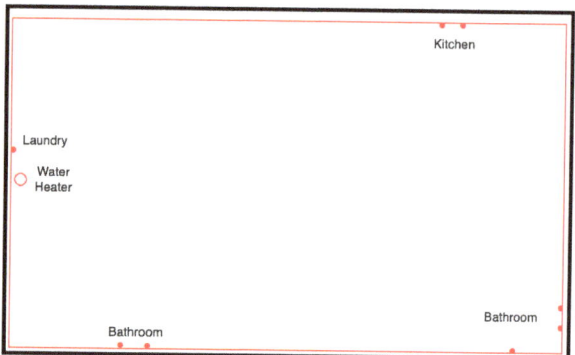

Hot Water Rectangle: 93%

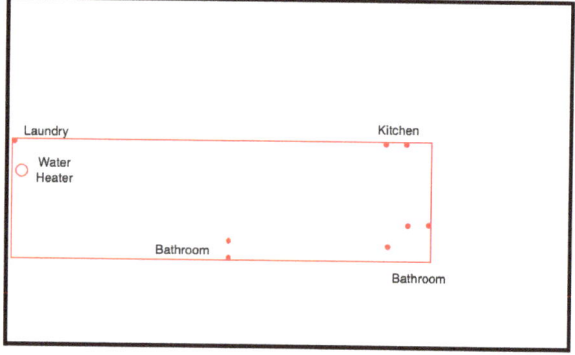

Hot Water Rectangle: 26%

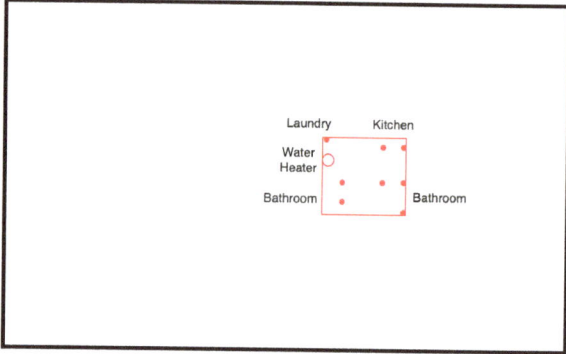

Hot Water Rectangle: 3%

Figure 18.10. *Example of reducing the size of a hot water rectangle by bringing the water heater and hot water fixtures closer together*

If you're a remodeler or homeowner trying to figure out how to improve the efficiency of the hot water distribution system in an existing home, you face more challenges. One of the less expensive options is to replace the hot water pipes (assuming they're accessible), reducing the length as much as you can and also right-sizing the diameters. Another option is to move the water heater to a more central location, if that's possible, and rerouting and rightsizing the piping at the same time. Or you could replace one large water heater with two or more smaller ones, closer to the hot water fixtures. The massively expensive option, of course, would be to gut the house and completely redesign the floor plan, clustering all the wet rooms in the same part of the house.

In each of those options, your goal is to reduce the size of the hot water rectangle and right-size the pipes. However, in most existing homes the least expensive option is to install a demand-activated circulation pump under a sink that is at the end of one or more of the trunk lines in the house. Klein has a good method for finding these locations.[36]

Trunks, Branches, Twigs, and Manifolds

The most common type of plumbing distribution design is trunk and branch. It has one or more trunk lines coming from the water heater with branches that split water off to serve different areas. Continuing with the tree metaphor, a twig is a pipe that serves only one fixture. Designing an effective and efficient trunk-and-branch plumbing distribution system is like designing an air distribution system for heating and cooling. It requires looking at multiple ways you could serve each fixture and finding a layout that optimizes the overall flow of hot water.

The best place to start is by studying the floor plan. With the locations of all fixtures and the water heater marked on the plan, look for a good path to run a trunk line. On the other hand, if your hot water rectangle is really small, the trunk line may be a short section of larger pipe with only twigs leaving the trunk. Who needs branches when everything is close? However, figuring out an optimal design requires more work when the wet rooms are spread throughout the house.

The next section is about recirculation systems, but let me say here that if you're going to use a recirculation system, having a single trunk line will help. That way, when your recirculation system gets hot water to the fixture farthest from the water heater, the whole trunk line is charged with hot water. However, sometimes it's best to design the system, with or without recirculation, in zones because of the locations of the wet rooms.

Let's look now at how to get the hot water from the trunk to the fixtures. Klein favors using twigs attached directly to the trunk. With a well-designed trunk, the twigs can be short and contain almost no structural waste. In such a system, once the trunk is charged with hot water, the fixtures will get hot water almost immediately.

Sizing the pipes comes after laying out the system. The place to start is the twigs because they're easy. You need to match the flow rate of the fixture with the correct size pipes and also meet the building code. In the United States, codes require a minimum of either ⅜ inch or ½ inch. (It's possible to make low-flow fixtures work with ¼-inch pipes for twigs, too, but only in homes where you have an engineer approve the use of smaller pipe diameters.) Most fixtures will work fine with the minimum size allowed.

If you can cluster your wet rooms and run only short twigs off a short trunk, you've created a manifold system (Figure 18.11). In that case, the short trunk acts as a manifold, and the twigs are all homerun lines. A manifold is a hub for all the pipes, which in this photo is made up of two vertical copper pipes. Homeruns in

36. https://www.garykleinassociates.com/PDFs/Protocol%20for%20Evaluating%20a%20HWDS%202014-10-10.pdf

plumbing or electrical design are pipes or wires that go directly from the source (water heater or electrical panel) to the end use. In a house with a large hot water rectangle, a manifold-homerun design won't be the most efficient because each use of a hot water tap charges a different line. If the pipes are uninsulated and not bundled, the hot water runs can lose a lot of heat. The synergy of getting hot water in the kitchen more quickly after you've used hot water in the bathroom disappears because each fixture's pipe is independent of the others, except where you have a bundle of pipes, as you see going through the top plate in Figure 18.11.

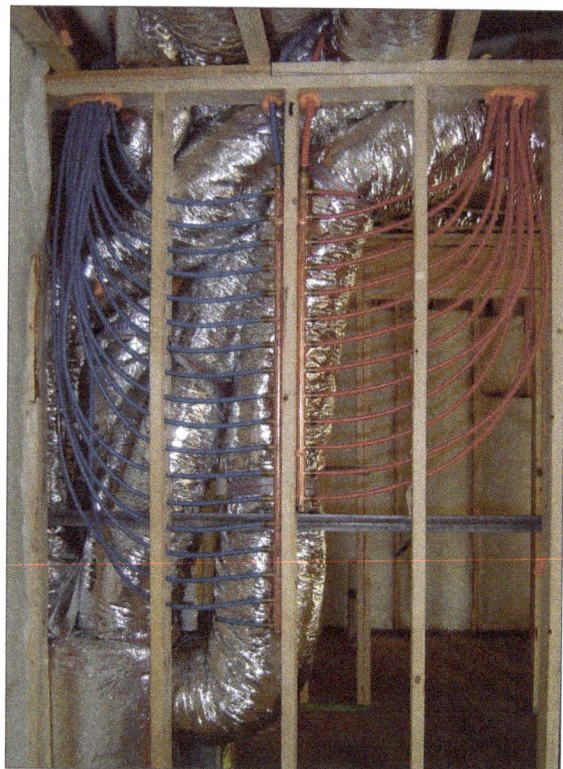

Figure 18.11. *A manifold and homerun water distribution system: The vertical copper pipes are the cold and hot water manifolds, and the blue (cold) and red (hot) pipes are the homeruns. The long, sweeping turns minimize pressure drops.*

Recirculating Pumps

Rather than fixing the real problem, sometimes people resort to a shortcut solution. If all you care about is getting hot water from the tap as soon as you open it, a continuous recirculating pump would be a great solution. As with so many solutions, though, this one comes with unintended consequences. You pay for that convenience up front and on your energy bills. The first cost of installing the recirculation system includes the pump and an additional pipe to return water to the water heater. Keeping that hot water circulating continuously through the pipes takes energy to run the circulator.

This system uses more energy to keep reheating the water to make up for all the heat lost as the pipes conduct and radiate heat away to the surroundings. Assuming the recirculating pump is used as a Band-Aid because the pipes are too long and too big, the extra surface area makes the heat loss worse. Then there's the extra pipe for the return hot water, adding to the surface area and the heat loss. And if you want to make it even worse, leave the pipes uninsulated.

A less expensive (but still not the best way) to get hot water quickly is to put that recirculation system on a timer. By setting the pump to come on before the peak water use periods each day, you get hot water quickly without paying for the continuous pump runtime and the constant heat loss. If you have a regular schedule and set the system to operate only for a short period a couple times a day, it can make your hot water system more convenient without an enormous energy hit, especially if the pipes are insulated.

A better way to take advantage of recirculation is by using what's called a demand recirculation system. You activate it by pushing a button, which could be located next to a bed, near an often-used fixture, or in some other convenient location. That gets the hot water moving into the pipes so it's ready when you go to turn on a faucet or shower. Rather than sending the not-yet-hot water down the drain, though, it puts that water into the cold water line or into a dedicated return line. It's a bit less convenient than the continuous or timed recirculation system because you have to push a button and wait. But it uses far less energy and doesn't waste water. A demand recirculation system like this reduces the pump runtime by 98 percent and the heat loss by 90 percent, compared to a continuous recirculation system.

Another option is to have the demand recirculation system triggered by a motion sensor. That kind of control strategy would prime the hot water pipes anytime someone is moving near the sensor, whether they need hot water or not.

It doesn't save as much energy as the push-button control, but it still reduces runtime by 90 percent and heat loss by 75 percent, compared to continuous recirculation.

> *A demand recirculation system like this reduces the pump runtime by 98 percent and the heat loss by 90 percent, compared to a continuous recirculation system.*

A Hot Water Retrofit for an Old Home

David Wasserman is an engineer who lives in an old house in Decatur, Georgia. When he got tired of waiting for a minute or longer to get hot water in his kitchen, he designed a retrofit for his hot water lines. He installed a short homemade manifold made of copper pipe, tees, and fittings to connect the copper pipe to his new ¼-inch PEX[37] hot water lines. When he ran his three new ¼-inch pipes to the kitchen and two bathrooms, he created parallel paths for the hot water to flow to the fixtures. But he didn't want the water taking both paths, so he also installed valves. Now, the larger copper pipes are closed off, and hot water travels through the smaller PEX pipes.

Figure 18.13. *One of Wasserman's new ¼-inch hot water lines: He installed a valve in the old ½-inch copper pipe and keeps it closed so water flows only through the new, smaller line.*

By changing to a smaller pipe, Wasserman appreciably cut the volume of water in the pipe between the water heater and the fixture. A ½-inch copper pipe holds nearly five times the amount of water as a ¼-inch PEX pipe of the same length. Also, a smaller pipe is better at pushing the water ahead of it instead of mixing along the way. Thus, the time for the hot water to reach the tap is reduced by more than a factor of five. Wasserman went from waiting more than 1 minute to get hot water at his kitchen sink to about 8 seconds.

This is a great outcome, but don't rush out to do this unless you do your homework. First, this will work only if the hot water flow rate is about 1.5 gallons per minute or less. Second, the length of the pipe should be 25 feet or less. Third, it's probably best to remove the unused sections of hot water pipe to eliminate stagnant water in the pipes.

---

37. PEX is an acronym for cross-linked polyethylene. The PE stands for polyethylene, the X for cross-linked. You may occasionally see it abbreviated as XPE or XLPE.

The ideal distribution system gets hot water to the tap in just a few seconds solely by having a minimal volume of water between the water heater and the tap. It's not hard to design new homes to accomplish that goal. However, with existing homes you can't always get the wait time low enough. In those cases, using a demand recirculation pump can solve the problem of excess waits and wasted water for just a bit more energy use.

Odds and Ends

Let me wrap up here with a few miscellaneous hot water topics.

Pipe insulation: I mentioned pipe insulation briefly, but it's an important energy-saving tool. Hot water draws occur at different times of the day. When one comes within an hour, say, of the previous draw, the water in the pipe may have cooled to room temperature already in an uninsulated pipe. With insulation on the pipe, the water will retain some heat, saving energy and water. Building codes are now requiring pipe insulation on the hot water lines.

Drain water heat recovery: The word "recovery" here means the same thing it does in a heat recovery ventilator. When you use hot water and send it down the drain, it still has a lot of thermal energy. A drain water heat recovery unit is a copper heat exchanger that wraps around the drainpipe. It's mainly used on shower drains, where the hot water will drain for several minutes or more. The efficiency of heat transfer can be higher than 50 percent, and the US Department of Energy says that the payback for these devices ranges from 2.5 to 7 years.

Anode rods and tank flushing: The typical storage water heater lasts about 10 years. Here's a little secret, though. They actually can last several decades. The reason they fail early is that the glass-lined tank gets corroded and starts leaking. At that point, they cannot be repaired. But water heaters come with a device to prevent tank corrosion: a sacrificial anode rod. It sticks down into the tank and gradually corrodes as it attracts minerals in the water. These rods may sacrifice themselves completely in as little as one year. If you don't replace it then, the minerals start attacking the tank. So, change the rod and keep your water heater going for several decades. This is especially important if you spring for a heat pump water heater. As expensive as that type of water heater is, you don't want to have to replace it just because you failed to change the anode rod when there's still lots of life left in the heat pump. Along with checking and changing the anode rod regularly, draining the crud from the bottom of your tank every year is a good idea, too.

Figure 18.12. *Drain water heat recovery installed on the shower drainpipe*

Faucet controls: The California Energy Commission published the results of a study on low-flow water fixtures in 2021 and said this was one of the surprising things they found: "A very large percentage of hot water draws are too short in duration and too small in volume for hot water to reach the fixtures."[38] The faucets may be at least partially to blame. When you have one valve that mixes the hot and cold for you, it's easy to open the valve with it set for a mix of hot and cold water. In fact, you have to pay close attention in order not to be calling for some hot water. And to make it worse, many of the faucet controls available make it difficult to know which side is hot and which is cold. Good people are working on this issue, but in the meantime, pay attention. Next time you reach to turn on the faucet, make sure you have it set for only cold water if you don't need hot water (or aren't going to run it long enough for hot water to arrive).

Chapter Takeaways

- Water heating is a system with inputs, outputs, water heater, distribution system, and end uses.
- Three choices you have to make when choosing a water heater are the fuel, whether to go with storage or tankless, and the efficiency.
- There are many types of gas, electric, and solar water heaters.
- Using photovoltaic modules and an electric water heater is probably the most trouble-free and least expensive way to do solar water heating.
- The hot water distribution system deserves much more attention.
- Shortening the hot water runs, using smaller diameter pipes, and insulating the hot water lines can provide huge benefits in efficiency and convenience.
- If you can't replace the distribution system, an on-demand recirculation pump can save water and energy.

38. Klein, Gary, Jim Lutz, Yanda Zhang, John Koeller, 2020. *Final Report: Code Changes and Implications of Residential Low Flow Hot Water Fixtures.* California Energy Commission. Publication Number: CEC-500-2021-043

CHAPTER 19

The Future of Homes

Throughout this book, I've focused on the building science underlying the various components of houses and pushed for a broader view of a house as a system. Of course, that building science is focused on the homes we live in now as well as those currently being built. Although the physics, chemistry, and other sciences aren't changing much, the materials, products, and methods we use in homes do change over time. Energy costs and availability, pandemics, and design preferences also force change on us. So, how will our homes evolve from here?

As the quote from Niels Bohr indicates, it's hard to know. I don't have a crystal ball to show me the future, and I'm generally not good at

> **"It is difficult to predict, especially the future."**
> –Niels Bohr

predicting where things will go. Several years ago, I attended a panel discussion where a speaker who called herself a futurist said something that stuck with me. She said what futurists do is to identify weak signals in the present world and try to figure out which ones will grow into strong signals. It could go the other direction as well. We can ask which present-day trends might fade out. I'll start with the latter.

The Disruption Isn't Coming . . .

In 1995, Harvard business professor Clayton M. Christensen coined the term "disruptive innovation," and people use it to describe all kinds of things now. In many cases, that term or its shortened version, disruption, is used incorrectly. For example, Christensen said the ride-hailing company Uber is not a disruptive innovator, although many people think of it as such. Without getting into the weeds on disruption theory, let's see what we can say about the companies involved in homes.

First of all, who is going to be disrupted? A huge number of different kinds of companies are involved in building, maintaining, and remodeling homes. We have designers, home builders, and trade contractors (HVAC, insulation, drywall, flooring, etc.). There are also manufacturers, suppliers, and specifiers. Can you disrupt just one part of the supply and labor chain to improve homes?

Consider the way houses are built. The majority are built onsite, one step at a time, with a lot of different companies and workers involved. Is the answer to be found in factory-built housing—manufactured, modular, or panelized?

What about vertical integration, where a construction company does the whole thing from design to commissioning? That's what the company Katerra was trying to do. If you haven't heard of them, just do an online search for "Katerra disruption." They had tons of money and a better chance of changing the housing industry than any other company. In the end, they failed. Their investors lost a whole lot of money. And Katerra actually did not meet the precise requirements for disruptive innovation, according to at least one of Professor Christensen's colleagues at Harvard Business School.

Xerox was ripe for disruption as technology advanced in the 1970s. Their product was high-end copy machines, and their market was large businesses. When personal copiers became available, Xerox faded into obscurity. IBM faced a similar fate when personal computers hit the market. Can you see anything like that happening in the new home construction market? How about remodeling? How about the HVAC industry? I don't see it.

. . . And Neither Is the Silver Bullet

Let's look at a different aspect of bringing transformation to the new and existing home markets. Is there a product or technology that can radically change how homes are built, maintained, and remodeled? Here are a few that have gotten silver bullet attention:

- Structural insulated panels
- Insulated concrete forms
- Factory-built housing
- Ductless mini-split heat pumps
- Kit homes (Sears sold a lot of them in the early 20th century!)
- 3-D printed homes
- Smart homes
- Tiny homes

All of these—and more—have been around long enough that if they were going to lead the revolution, they would have done so by now. No single product, component, sub-system, or technology is going to be the silver bullet that will magically transform how homes are built,

maintained, or remodeled. It's certainly not for lack of trying, though.

> *No single product, component, sub-system, or technology is going to be the silver bullet that will magically transform how homes are built, maintained, or remodeled.*

With the tech industry attracting massive amounts of investment capital, some companies are scouring the economy for industries to "disrupt" or silver bullets to create. The construction and HVAC industries have not been immune to their attempts. Some good companies and products have resulted from their efforts, and more will come in the future. But no silver bullet is going to magically transform the housing industry, making everything better, cheaper, and faster.

The Gap between Stupid and Hurt

New homes being built now are superior in many ways to homes of the past. We have better materials and products. We understand the building science that makes a home perform properly . . . or fail. And we have better building codes and programs that support high-performance homes. But because we've made homes so much more airtight and insulated, we've pushed building enclosures to the limit. As Joseph Lstiburek, PhD, PE, put it, "The gap

between stupid and hurt is narrowing."

For example, airtightness is a good thing. We know that houses don't need to breathe. They do need fresh air for the people inside, though. When you put people inside an airtight house with no mechanical ventilation, the indoor air quality is poor, and people can get sick. Another way airtightness can accelerate the gap between stupid and hurt is with combustion appliances. A natural draft water heater inside an airtight house can backdraft more easily and poison people with carbon monoxide.

Vapor retarders in the wrong place, botched flashing details, bad spray foam installations . . . There are many ways the hurt can show up quickly when someone does something stupid. The good thing about a narrowing gap between stupid and hurt is that it puts more pressure on the people who work on homes not to do stupid things.

Existing homes far outnumber new homes, and the gap between stupid and hurt is narrowing there, too. When a homeowner calls a spray foam insulation contractor to encapsulate their attic with spray foam, they may get a house that's more comfortable and energy efficient. Or they could end up with a mold outbreak in the encapsulated attic and the living space as well.

That happened to my father-in-law. Within two years of getting a shoddy spray foam job in his attic, he had mold growing in the attic, on the hallway ceiling, and other places. Why? Because the installers didn't know what they were doing. They didn't get the attic sealed well to the outside, so humid air could infiltrate the attic. They also didn't do anything about the bathroom exhaust fans that were venting to the attic. It's never a good idea to vent bath fans to the attic, but doing so doesn't affect the inside of the house as much when it's done in a vented attic.

Or take the case of the homeowner who got a new air conditioner and suddenly found water spots on the ceiling. Why? The HVAC contractor put in a larger air conditioner than had been there before. They kept the existing ducts, but they sealed them to reduce the amount of air that leaked from them. The result was a duct system that limited the air flow, which caused the air conditioner to run colder. That made the ducts cold enough to collect condensation when that hadn't been a problem before.

We know a lot of building science now that we didn't know before, and that should be a good thing. The problem, however, is that the gap between stupid and hurt is narrower now.

Complexity Breeds Incompetence

We ask a lot of our homes. Whether it's a single-family detached home, townhouse, or apartment, a home is a complex system made up of complex subsystems, with a lot of interactions among the various parts. The typical homeowner or renter can't know everything about how a house and all of its subsystems work. They are by definition incompetent in that arena. That's not a criticism. It's simply a fact.

Zen and the Art of Motorcycle Maintenance by Robert Pirsig influenced me profoundly when I was young. In one part of the book, he discusses his friends' irritation about a dripping faucet and discovers that they—and many others—have a deep fear and distrust of technology. (And that was before personal computers!) But that fear is counterproductive. Rather than addressing whatever technological issue we're dealing with, we try to ignore it, hoping it will just go away.

Pirsig has some good advice here: "If you run from technology, it will chase you." We don't all need to become experts in building science, able to distinguish vapor-permeable from vapor-impermeable membranes or hold forth on the pros and cons of the various airtightness metrics. But we need to know enough to find the right companies to design, build, maintain, and remodel our homes.

What I said about complexity breeding incompetence applies to professionals as much as to homeowners. For example, the spray foam contractor who worked on my father-in-law's house knew enough to be able to operate the equipment but not enough to encapsulate an attic properly. If you've ever had anyone work on your home, did they get it right? The first time? If you've never had a bad contractor, count yourself among the lucky few.

Contractors face the same complexity as homeowners, but on a deeper level. An HVAC technician has to know about furnaces, air conditioners, duct work, thermostats, and more. It takes years of experience and study to understand everything they need to know. And they don't all get there. It's easy to reach a level of competence that's good enough and then stop there. Maybe the boss doesn't expect more. Certainly, most homeowners don't expect more. If they do raise questions, many are easily fooled with jargon or things that sound like common sense but really aren't. "A house needs to breathe," they might say, in defense of doing a poor job with air sealing.

Complexity breeds incompetence. But that doesn't mean we have to accept it.

> **We don't all need to become experts in building science. But we need to know enough to find the right companies to design, build, maintain, and remodel our homes.**

The Revolution Starts with You

The way homes are designed, built, maintained, and remodeled is full of problems. In this book, I've explained the building science underlying good building practices. I've also shown how it's applied incorrectly because of contractors who don't understand or don't care. When you take shortcuts by using rules of thumb or conventional wisdom instead of building science, the result is often a compromised system that reduces indoor environmental quality, durability, energy efficiency, or some combination of them. How do we fix this?

Sam Rashkin, who led the ENERGY STAR new homes program at the US Environmental Protection Agency for 17 years, wrote a book titled *Retooling the US Housing Industry*. Retooling is a better word than disrupting because it doesn't have the association with the tech industry in Silicon Valley. His book is full of good advice about how the new home construction industry is broken and how to make new homes better. He correctly calls out the lack of building science education for architects and people who go through technical training programs. He also put his finger on one of the big reasons the HVAC industry is broken: They're sometimes blamed for problems they didn't create. For example, they oversize heating and cooling systems because houses, even new ones sometimes, are poorly insulated and not airtight.

The way out of this mess isn't as simple as saying architects, builders, trade contractors, and remodelers need to commit to high-performance homes and make sure they know building science. Some will do that because they want to do it right. Plenty, though, will do as little as they can. Building codes tell designers and contractors what they can and cannot do. In the 21st century, codes have improved and now do a better job of addressing the building science.[39] But the codes are no match for contractors who want to do the minimum—or less. Plus, the codes

---

39. I say "better" because building codes are the result of a sausage-making process, with building science advocates, manufacturers, and contractors battling for their ideas, products, and preferences. So, the building science in the codes isn't perfect.

are only as good as the enforcement. That statement about complexity and incompetence applies here, too.

I believe the way to fix the broken industry that designs, builds, maintains, and remodels homes is education. Building codes aren't going to force it to happen. Simply asking builders to do better won't work. Putting in quality control and quality assurance helps but won't get us all the way there. All of those things are part of the answer, but the complete solution needs to involve the home buyers, homeowners, and renters—the people who actually live in the houses. When they demand a better product, change will come.

Voluntary green building and energy efficiency programs can help, too. And better ways of financing or subsidizing the work that needs to be done will help push things along. It's going to take change from every part of the industry to revolutionize homes. Are you ready to do your part?

Putting It All Together

The best way to deal with complex systems like homes is by following that old advice about how to eat an elephant. Take it one bite at a time. And plan on it taking a while. The information in this book is an elephant. If you're new to this field, don't worry about learning it all at once. It will take a lot of reading, watching, doing, and discussing to understand building science on a deep level. But there's at least one thing you should feel confident about.

A house does *not* need to breathe. But people do.

Resources

This list is far from complete, but it will give you a lot of supplementary material to deepen your learning of building science.

Books

Builder's Guide to Hot-Humid Climates, Joseph Lstiburek, Building Science Press (2005)

Builder's Guide to Mixed-Humid Climates, Joseph Lstiburek, Building Science Press (2009)

Builder's Guide to Cold Climates, Joseph Lstiburek, Building Science Press (2006)

Builder's Guide to Hot-Dry and Mixed-Dry Climates, Joseph Lstiburek, Building Science Press (2004)

Buildings Don't Lie, Henry Gifford, Energy Saving Press (2017)

Electrify, Saul Griffith, The MIT Press (2021)

The Green New Deal, Jeremy Rifkin, St. Martin's Press (2019)

Handbook of Fundamentals, ASHRAE (2021)

Healthy Buildings, Joseph G. Allen and John D. Macomber, Harvard University Press (2020)

The Home Comfort Book, Nate Adams, CreateSpace Independent Publishing Platform (2017)

How Buildings Learn, Stewart Brand, Penguin Books (1995)

Healthy Housing Principles Reference Guide, Building Performance Institute

Insulate and Weatherize, Bruce Harley, Taunton Press (2012)

Living the 1.5 Degree Lifestyle, Lloyd Alter, New Society Publishers (2021)

Moisture Control for Residential Buildings, Joseph Lstiburek, Building Science Press (2021)

Musings of an Energy Nerd, Martin Holladay, Taunton Press (2017)

Residential Ventilation Handbook, Paul Raymer (2017)

Retooling the US Housing Industry, Sam Rashkin, Delmar Cengage Learning (2010)

Ventilation Guide, Armin Rudd, Building Science Press (2011)

Water in Buildings, Bill Rose, Wiley (2005)

Building Science for a Cold Climate, N. B. Hutcheon and Gustav O. P. Handegord, Wiley (1983)

Understanding Psychrometrics, Donald P. Gatley, ASHRAE (2013)

Ventilation and Heating, John Shaw Billings (1893) reprinted by Hardpress Publishing

Websites

Green Building Advisor, greenbuildingadvisor.com

Journal of Light Construction, jlconline.com

Building Science Corporation, buildingscience.com

Building America Solution Center, basc.pnnl.gov

Healthy Heating, healthyheating.com

Six Classes, sixclasses.org

US EPA, epa.gov

BizEE Degree Days, degreedays.net

PVWatts Calculator, National Renewable Energy Lab, pvwatts.nrel.gov

Database of State Incentives for Renewables & Efficiency,® dsireusa.org

Florida Solar Energy Center, fsec.ucf.edu

Efficient Windows Collaborative, efficientwindows.org

Cold Climate Housing Research Center, http://cchrc.org

Building Green, buildinggreen.com

Architecture 2030, architecture2030.org

RMI, rmi.org

Pro Trade Craft, protradecraft.com

University of Illinois Urbana-Champaign Building Science, appliedresearch.illinois.edu/impact-areas/building-science

Oak Ridge National Lab calculators, web.ornl.gov/sci/buildings/tools

Phius passive building info, phius.org

Carbon Switch, carbonswitch.co

Advanced Energy's crawl space site, advancedenergy.org/crawlspaces

Building Performance Institute, bpi.org

Documents, Papers & Other Resources

Indoor Air Quality Guide, a 718-page pdf available as a free download from ASHRAE. National Healthy Housing Standard, National Center for Healthy Housing, iaq.ashrae.org

ASHRAE Coronavirus (COVID-19) Response Resources, ashrae.org/technical-resources/resources

ASHRAE Standard 55: *Thermal Environmental Conditions for Human Occupancy*

ASHRAE Standard 62.2: *Ventilation and Acceptable Indoor Air Quality in Residential Buildings*

Thermal Comfort Principles and Practical Applications for Residential Buildings, by Robert Bean, healthyheating.com/Thermal_Comfort_Book.htm (2020)

A Common Definition for Zero Energy Buildings, US Dept. of Energy (2015)

Moisture Control Guidance for Building Design, Construction and Maintenance, EPA (2013)

International Energy Conservation Code (IECC), updated every three years (2021)

Hammer & Hand's Best Practices Manual, hammerandhand.com/best-practices/manual (2016)

BSD-013: Rain Control in Buildings, buildingscience.com/documents/digests/bsd-013-rain-control-in-buildings (2011)

Survey of Building Envelope Failures in the Coastal Climate of British Columbia, Morrison Hershfield Limited (1996)

Unplanned Airflows and Moisture Problems, Terry Brennan, James B. Cummings, and Joseph Lstiburek, PhD, Peng., ASHRAE Journal (2002)

The International Temperature Scale of 1990 (ITS-90), www.nist.gov/system/files/documents/pml/div685/grp01/ITS-90_metrologia.pdf (1990)

Thermal Metric Project, Building Science Corporation, buildingscience.com/project/thermal-metric-project(2015)

Cladding Attachment Over Thick Exterior Insulating Sheathing,Peter Baker, PEng, R. Lepage,BuildingAmerica, BSC, nrel.gov/docs/fy14osti/57825.pdf(2014)

Guide to Attic Air Sealing,Joseph Lstiburek, PhD, PEng,Building Science Corporation,buildingscience.com/documents/guides-and-manuals/gm-attic-air-sealing-guide/view

Air Cleaners and Air Filters in the Home, epa.gov/indoor-air-quality-iaq/air-cleaners-and-air-filters-home

Appendix A: A Few Special Numbers

-50	the pressure at which most single-point blower door tests are done, in Pascals
-40	the temperature at which the Celsius and Fahrenheit scales are equal
0	the freezing point of water on the Celsius temperature scale, equal to 32 °F
3.14159 . . .	pi, an irrationally interesting number
4	the EPA threshold for recommending radon mitigation, in picoCuries per liter (pCi/L). (But they also say you should consider mitigation if the level is between 2 and 4.)
5	the number of Celsius degrees equal to 9 Fahrenheit degrees
5.678	the IP equivalent to a metric (SI) insulation R-value of 1 (ie., R_{SI} x 5.677 $=R_{IP}$)
29.3	to convert the cost of electricity from dollars per kWh to dollars per therm (100,000 BTUs / 3,412)
50	The Fahrenheit temperature that equals 10 °C, a good reference point for converting between the two scales using 5s and 9s
55	the dew point temperature in Fahrenheit of conditioned air in summer at the recommended indoor design condition of 75° F and 50% RH
55	the number given to ASHRAE's thermal comfort standard
62.2	the number given to ASHRAE's residential ventilation standard
400	nominal air flow rate per ton of cooling capacity, in cfm
1,000	minimum floor area that you should be able to cool with one ton of cooling capacity, in square feet
3,412	the number of BTUs equal to 1 kilowatt-hour
7,000	the number of grains (a weird unit still in use in the dehumidification industry) in one pound of water
12,000	the number of BTUs in one ton of cooling capacity
67,890	the Guinness World Record for the number of digits of pi memorized and correctly recited
100,000	the number of BTUs in one therm

Appendix B: Units and Conversion Factors

Prefixes

Greek

Name	Symbol	Power	Decimal		English
exa	E	10^{18}	1,000,000,000,000,000,000		quintillion
peta	P	10^{15}	1,000,000,000,000,000		quadrillion
tera	T	10^{12}	1,000,000,000,000		trillion
giga	G	10^{9}	1,000,000,000		billion
mega	M	10^{6}	1,000,000		million
kilo	k	10^{3}	1,000		thousand
hecto	h	10^{2}	100		hundred
deca	da	10^{1}	10		ten
deci	d	10^{-1}	0.1		tenth
centi	c	10^{-2}	0.01		hundredth
milli	m	10^{-3}	0.001		thousandth
micro	μ	10^{-6}	0.000001		millionth
nano	n	10^{-9}	0.000000001		billionth
pico	p	10^{-12}	0.000000000001		trillionth

Roman Numeral

Symbol	Power	Decimal	English	Example
C	10^{2}	100	hundred	CCF, hundred cubic feet
M	10^{3}	1,000	thousand	MBTU, thousand BTU
MM	10^{6}	1,000,000	million	MMBTU, million BTU

How to convert units

To convert from one unit to another, you need a conversion factor. But how do you know whether to multiply or divide? It's simple. Just set up the conversion as a multiplication of the original number by the conversion factor in the form of a fraction. Then make sure to enter the conversion factor in a way that the original unit gets canceled out.

Here's an example. Let's say you want to know what the metric unit for a ton of air conditioning capacity is.

$$1 \text{ ton} = 12,000 \, \frac{BTU}{hr} \times \frac{1 \, kW}{3,412 \, \frac{BTU}{hr}}$$

$$= \frac{12,000}{3,412} \, kW$$

$$= 3.52 kW$$

The conversion factor is 1 kW = 3,412 BTU/hr. The 3,412 BTU/hr goes in the denominator so that it will cancel the BTU/hr in the original number.

This method also works for applying prefixes. If, for example, you wanted to convert 0.293 Wh to kWh, here's how you would do it:

$$0.293 \, Wh \times \frac{1 \, kWh}{1,000 \, Wh} = 0.000293 \, kWh$$

You also can just move the decimal the correct number of places if you know whether the number you're looking for should be bigger or smaller than the number you have. Going from Wh to kWh makes the number smaller, so we could have just moved the decimal three places to the left in the example above.

Energy

Abbreviations

BTU = British Thermal Unit

J = Joule

Wh = Watt-hour

kWh = kilowatt-hour

cal = calorie

Conversion Factors

1 BTU = 1,055 J = 0.293 Wh = 0.000293 kWh = 252 cal

1 Wh = 0.001 kWh = 860 cal = 3.412 BTU = 3,600 J

1 J = 0.000278 Wh = 0.0000000278 kWh = 0.239 cal = 0.000948 BTU

1 cal = 0.00397 BTU = 4.19 J = 0.00116 Wh = 0.00000116 kWh

Power

Abbreviations

BTU/hr = British Thermal Unit per hour

W = Watt

kW = kilowatt

ton = ton of cooling capacity, 12,000 BTU/hr

Conversion Factors

1 W = 1 J/s, by definition

1 BTU/hr = 0.293 W = 0.000293 kW = 0.0000833 ton

1 W = 0.001 kW = 0.000284 ton = 3.412 BTU/hr

1 kW = 0.284 ton = 3,412 BTU/hr = 1,000 W

1 ton = 12,000 BTU/hr = 3,516 W = 3.516 kW

Pressure

Abbreviations

Pa = Pascals

psi = pounds per square inch

iwc = inches of water column (same as iwg for inches of water gauge)

mm Hg = millimeters of mercury (same as Torr)

atm = atmosphere

Conversion Factors

1 Pa = 0.000145 psi = 0.00402 iwc = 0.0075 mm Hg = atm

1 psi = 27.7 iwc = 51.7 mm Hg = 0.068 atm = 6,895 Pa

1 iwc = 1.87 mm Hg = 0.00246 atm = 249 Pa = 0.0361 psi

1 mm Hg = 0.00132 atm = 133 Pa = 0.0193 psi = 0.536 iwc

1 atm = 101,325 Pa = 14.7 psi = 407 iwc = 760 mm Hg

Flow Rate

Abbreviations

cfm = cubic feet per minute
l/s = liters per second
m3/s = cubic meters per second
m3/hr = cubic meters per hour

Conversion Factors

1 cfm = 0.472 l/s = 0.000472 m3/s = 1.70 m3/hr
1 l/s = 0.0010 m3/s = 3.6 m3/hr = 2.12 cfm
1 m3/s = 3,600 m3/hr = 2,119 cfm = 1,000 l/s
1 m3/hr = 0.589 cfm = 0.279 l/s = 0.000279 m3/s

Appendix C: Celsius-Fahrenheit Conversions

Converting between temperatures on the Celsius and Fahrenheit scales is easy. You could install an app on your phone that would do the conversion for you, but it's much faster to do it in your head. All you need to know are two pieces of information. Forget about trying to remember that equation you learned in school. That's the hard way. The easy way is to learn the principles captured in Table C.1.

Fahrenheit to Celsius Conversion Table

°C	°F
-20	-4
-15	5
-10	14
-5	23
0	32
5	41
10	50
15	59
20	68
25	77
30	86
35	95
40	104

Table C.1. Equivalent Celsius and Fahrenheit temperatures, with every 5-degree change in the Celsius temperature corresponding to a 9-degree change in the Fahrenheit temperature.

Notice the two lines highlighted in yellow. Those are my two main reference points. I can figure out any temperature I want by skipping along in 5 °C increments, each time adding or subtracting 9 °F.

Another thing that makes this easy, at least for those of us in warmer climates, is the upward progression from 10 °C. As you go up in 5 °C increments (10, 15, 20, 25, 30, 35, 40), the last digit of the Fahrenheit temperature keeps dropping by 1: 50, 59, 68, 77, 86, 95, 104.

When a temperature is between the numbers in the table, I look at which line it's closest to and add or subtract multiples of 1.8 °F for each degree C. Actually, I usually think in 2-degree increments for this conversion. For example, if the temperature is 46 °F, that's 50 °F minus 4 °F. That makes the answer 10 °C minus 2 °C, or 8 °C.

It takes some practice, but once you get used to it, you should have a fairly easy time figuring out conversions for the range of temperatures we spend most of our time in: 0 to 100 °F (-18 to 38 °C).

And there's one special temperature where you don't have to convert at all. At negative 40 degrees, you can leave off the name of the scale because -40 °F equals -40 °C.

Appendix D: Acronyms, Initials, and Abbreviations

Acronym or Initials	What it stands for
AAC	autoclaved aerated concrete
ABAA	Air Barrier Association of America
AC	air conditioner
ACCA	Air Conditioning Contractors of America
ACH_{50}	air changes per hour at 50 Pascals
ACH_{nat}	air changes per hour Natural
ADA	another damn acronym (although this would really be initials)
ADA	Americans with Disabilities Act
ADC	Air Duct Council
AFUE	annualized fuel utilization efficiency
AGW	above-grade wall
AHJ	authority having jurisdiction
AHRI	Air Conditioning, Heating, and Refrigeration Institute
AH or AHU	air handler or air handler unit
AMY	actual metrological year (See TMY)
ANSI	American National Standards Institute
APHN	American Passive House Network (a.k.a. NAPHN)
ASHP	air-source heat pump
ASHRAE	formerly American Society of Heating Refrigerating & Air conditioning Engineers; just a name now
ASK	asphalt-saturated kraft (building paper)

Acronym or Initials	What it stands for
ASTM	American Society for Testing and Materials
BA	Building America
BAS	building airflow standard
BCAP	Building Codes Assistance Project
BPI	Building Performance Institute
BPM	brushless permanent magnet motor (same as ECM)
BS	building science
BSC	Building Science Corporation
BTL	building tightness limit
BTU	British Thermal Unit
CADR	clean air delivery rate
CAR damper	constant airflow regulator
CAZ	combustion appliance zone
CCF	hundred cubic feet
ccSPF	closed-cell spray polyurethane foam
CDD	cooling degree days
CFA	conditioned floor area
CFIS	central fan integrated supply (ventilation type)
CFL	compact fluorescent light
cfm	cubic feet per minute
cfm50	cubic feet per minute at 50 Pascals
CHP	combined heat & power
CMU	concrete masonry unit
CO	carbon monoxide
CO	certificate of occupancy
CO_2	carbon dioxide
COP	coefficient of performance

Acronym or Initials	What it stands for
COVID	coronavirus disease
CYA	cover your ass
CZ	climate zone
DB	dry bulb (temperature)
DER	deep energy retrofit
DHW	domestic hot water
DIY	do it yourself
DOE	US Department of Energy
DP	dew point
DX	direct expansion (cooling system based on refrigeration cycle)
ECM	electronically commutated motor (same as BPM motor)
EEM	energy efficient mortgage
EER	energy efficiency ratio
EEV	electronic expansion valve
EF	energy factor
EFL	Environments for Living
EIA	Energy Information Administration
EIM	energy improvement mortgage
ELA	envelope/enclosure leakage area
ELR	envelope/enclosure leakage ratio
EPA	US Environmental Protection Agency
EPS	expanded polystyrene
EqLA	equivalent leakage area
ERV	energy recovery ventilator (technically enthalpy recovery ventilator)
ES or ESTAR	ENERGY STAR
ES V3	ENERGY STAR Version 3
EUI	energy use intensity (kWh/sf or BTU/sf)
FC or FCU	fan coil or fan coil unit
FHA	US Federal Housing Authority

Acronym or Initials	What it stands for
FLA	four-letter acronym or five-letter acronym
FPR	filter performance rating
FROG	finished room over garage
FTC	US Federal Trade Commission
GBA	Green Building Advisor
GC	general contractor
GIGO	garbage in, garbage out
GSHP	ground-source heat pump
GWP	global warming potential
HDD	heating degree days
HEPA	high efficiency particulate air
HOA	homeowners association
HOT2000	Canadian energy code compliance software
HP	home performance
HPwES	Home Performance with ENERGY STAR
HRV	heat recovery ventilator
HSPF	heating season performance factor
HUD	U.S. Department of Housing and Urban Development
HVAC	heating, ventilating, and air conditioning
IAPMO	International Association of Plumbing and Mechanical Officials
IAQ	indoor air quality
ICAT	insulation contact, air tight (designation for recessed can lights)
ICC	International Code Council
ICF	insulated concrete form
IEA	International Energy Agency
IECC	International Energy Conservation Code
IEQ	indoor environmental quality
IR	infrared

Acronym or Initials	What it stands for
IRC	International Residential Code
IREC	Interstate Renewable Energy Council
LVL	laminated veneer lumber
iwc	inches of water column (pressure unit)
iwg	inches of water gauge (pressure unit, same as iwc)
KISS	Keep it simple, stupid
kWh	kilowatt-hour
LBL	Lawrence Berkeley Laboratory (old name, still used by some)
LBNL	Lawrence Berkeley National Laboratory
LCA	life cycle analysis
LED	light emitting diode
LEED	Leadership in Energy & Environmental Design (USGBC program)
LEED AP	LEED Accredited Professional
LEL	lower explosive limit
LLNL	Lawrence Livermore National Laboratory
LTO	leakage to outdoors (duct leakage)
MEC	Model Energy Code
MERV	minimum efficiency reporting value
MJ	megajoule
MPR	microparticle performance rating
MSDS	material safety data sheet
NAHB	National Association of Home Builders
NAPHN	Passive House Network
NASEO	National Association of State Energy Offices
NATE	North American Technician Excellence

Acronym or Initials	What it stands for
NCI	National Comfort Institute (not to be confused with Comfort Institute)
NFPA	National Fire Protection Association
NFRC	National Fenestration Rating Council
NIST	National Institute of Standards and Technology
NPP	neutral pressure plane
NPV	net present value
NREL	National Renewable Energy Laboratory
NZE	net zero energy
OCEAN	Online Code Environment and Advocacy Network
ocSPF	open-cell spray polyurethane foam
OEM	original equipment manufacturer
ORNL	Oak Ridge National Laboratory
OSB	oriented strand board
OVE	optimal value engineering (includes advanced framing)
pCi/L	picocuries per liter (a measure of radioactive decay)
PCO	photocatalytic oxidation
PDW	pre-drywall
PE	professional engineer
PHIUS	Passive House Institute US (rebranded as Phius, just a name)
PHPP	Passive House Planning Package
PM	project manager
$PM_{2.5}$	particulate matter 2.5 microns or smaller
PM_{10}	particulate matter 10 microns or smaller
PPE	personal protective equipment

Acronym or Initials	What it stands for
PSC	permanent split capacitor
PTAC	packaged terminal air conditioner
PTHP	packaged terminal heat pump
PV	photovoltaic
PV	present value
QA	quality assurance
REC	renewable energy certificate
RECS	residential energy consumption survey (from the US EIA)
RH	relative humidity
RTFM	Read the Friendly Manual
SARS-COV-2	severe acute respiratory syndrome coronavirus 2
SDO	Standards Development Organization (ANSI designation)
SEER	seasonal energy efficiency ratio
sfbe	square footage of building enclosure
SHF or SHR	sensible heat fraction or sensible heat ratio
SHGC	solar heat gain coefficient
SIP	structural insulated panel
SIPA	Structural Insulated Panel Association
SIR	savings investment ratio
SMACNA	Sheet Metal and Air Conditioning Contractors' National Association
SPF	spray polyurethane foam
SPFA	Spray Polyurethane Foam Association
SVOC	semi-volatile organic compound

Acronym or Initials	What it stands for
SWAG	scientific wild-ass guess
TAB	test and balance
TESP	total external static pressure
TLA	three-letter acronym (although this is just initials, not an acronym)
TMY	typical metrological year
TOD	transit-oriented development
TXV	thermal expansion valve
UEF	uniform energy factor
USGBC	US Green Building Council
UVGI	ultraviolet germicidal radiation
VOC	volatile organic compound
VRF	variable refrigerant flow
VRV	variable refrigerant volume
WB	wet bulb (temperature)
WCD	worst-case depressurization
WEStand	Water Efficiency and Sanitation Standard
WH	water heater
WRB	weather-resistive barrier, water-resistant barrier
wrt	with respect to
WUFI	Wärme-Und Feuchtetransport Instationär (hygrothermal modeling tool)
XPS	extruded polystyrene
ZEB	zero energy building
ZPD	zonal pressure diagnostics
ZNE	zero net energy (same as NZE)
ZIP	brand of roof and wall sheathing

Appendix E: Construction Terminology

This is not a complete list of all the terms used in construction. It includes some of the main terms used in wood-frame construction in North America. Some definitions in this list are specific to building science. "Kneewall," for example, may mean something different than the definition here when you hear a framer or builder say it.

Figure 1. *Framing in the bottom part of an above-grade wall*

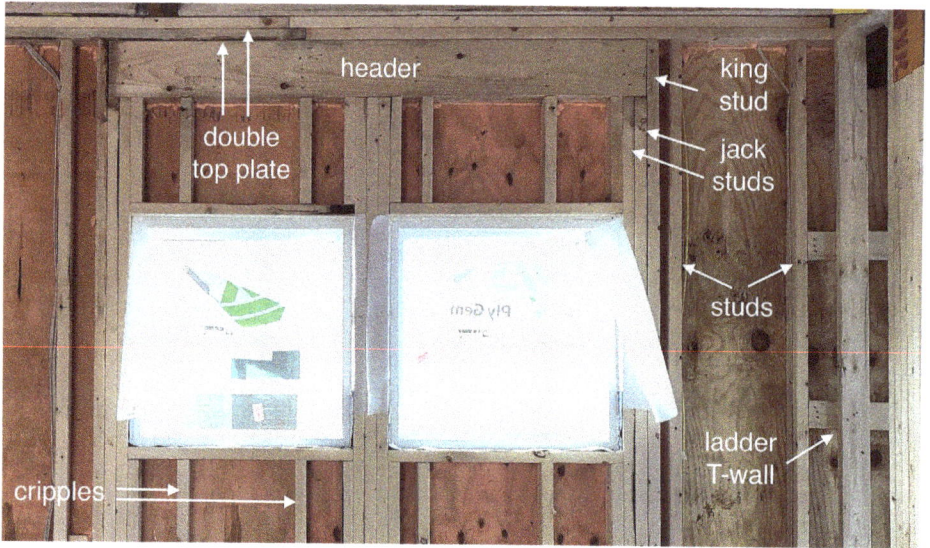

Figure 2. *Framing in the top part of an above-grade wall*

Advanced framing	Framing methods that result in less use of wood without compromising structural integrity
Attic kneewall	Vertical wall that separates conditioned space from unconditioned attic space
Balloon framing	A type of framing that uses 2-story studs for a 2-story house. The 2nd floor joists are nailed to the studs, leaving an open stud cavity. Has been mostly replaced by platform framing.
Beam	Horizontal structural member supporting the weight of the building above. Can

Figure 3. *Open-web floor trusses, the pieces of wood held together with metal plates here, make it easy to run pipes, wires, ducts, and other services through a framed floor.*

	be made of dimensional lumber, engineered lumber, steel, or other mterials. Sometimes called a girder.
Blocking	Pieces of wood between framing members for purposes of stiffening or reducing air flow in the cavity
Bottom plate	the horizontal wood framing member at the bottom of the wall. When it's on a concrete slab or foundation wall, it may be called a sill plate or mudsill (Figure 1)
Bridging	Small pieces of wood or metal inserted diagonally between joists or rafters for bracing and load-spreading
California corner	A type of three-stud corner that leaves a gap for insulation
Cantilever	Structural part of a building that projects beyond its support
Concrete masonry unit	Hollow concrete masonry unit made from cement and aggregates
Cricket	A wood-framed triangular structure installed over top of an existing flat or pitched roof to channel water away from areas susceptible to water damage, like chimneys or dead valleys
Cripple	A short stud, usually above or below a window (Figure 2)
Deadwood	Extra wood added to the structure to provide places to attach drywall, cabinets, or other parts of a building
Dormer	Structural element protruding from a roof to add more space beneath the roof as well as windows for light and ventilation
Eaves	Horizontal roof overhang
Elevation drawing	Drawings of the front, sides, or back of a house
Engineered wood	Wood products made up of smaller pieces of wood. Common types used in houses are oriented strand board (OSB), laminated veneer lumber (LVL), I-joists, and plywood.
Fascia	The board that runs along the eave and to which gutters are attached
Footing	The concrete on which foundation walls sit, transferring the load from the house to the ground
Furring strip	Thin strips of wood attached to a wall or ceiling for various purposes, such as a rain screen or to level or straighten a surface
Gable	Triangular section of wall at the end of a pitched roof
Header	a larger framing member that spans openings for windows and doors. It provides the support needed for the structural load from the weight above. (Figure 2)

I-joist	An engineered wood framing member used in floors and ceilings. Made with smaller pieces of wood, an I-joist can be stronger than dimensional lumber relative to its weight
Jack stud	a less-than-full-length stud on which a window or door header rests. How many jack studs do you see in Figure 2?[39]
Jamb	The side of a window or door opening
Joist	Horizontal framing members that provide structural support in floors and ceilings
King stud	a full length stud on each side of a header. It goes all the way up to the top plate. Each header typically has two king studs, one on each end. (Figure 2)
Ladder T-wall	An advanced framing method to build T-walls that can be insulated at the intersection (Figure 1 and Figure 2)
Ledger board	A horizontal board nailed to a beam and used to support joists that attach to the beam
Nail plate	metal plates nailed into studs to protect electrical wiring or refrigerant lines behind the nail plate (Figure 1)
Open-web truss	framing members for floors and ceilings made with long pieces of wood that form the bottom and top of the truss (the flanges) and shorter pieces of wood in the middle (the web). Metal gusset plates hold them together. These trusses are engineered and should not be cut. (Figure 3)
Partition wall	Non-load bearing wall that separates parts of the interior space
Party wall	Wall separating adjacent dwellings in a multi-family building or attached housing. Also called a demising wall.
Pier	Vertical load-bearing structural support, often as part of a foundation
Platform framing	A framing system in which the floor joists of each story sit on the top plates of the walls for the story below
Punch list	The list of items that remain to be finished to close out a construction project
Purlin	Boards in a roof that run perpendicular to the rafters to spread out the load
Rafter	Framing member that follows the roof's slope and supports the load of the roof deck, roofing materials, and any other loads (e.g., snow or photovoltaic modules)
Raised-heel truss	Engineered roof framing members with extra height at the eaves to allow for more insulation of the exterior walls
Ridge	The horizontal line at the intersection of two sloped roof surfaces
Roof truss	Engineered roof framing members with cross-bracing to carry the roof loads with smaller pieces of lumber than a framed roof
Rough opening	the opening for a window or door created by the framing around it
Sheathing	A layer of boards, engineered wood (plywood or OSB), or other materials that cover floors, walls, and roofs. May be structural or non-structural (foam board)
Sill	Horizontal framing member at the bottom of a building or window
Soffit	The horizontal material beneath the eave of a roof or used in interior structures. A dropped "soffit" is sometimes used to hide ductwork.
Stem wall	Short walls that are part of the foundation
Stepped foundation	A concrete or masonry foundation wall that steps down in height as the exterior grade drops. This reduces the cost of the foundation as framed walls on top of the stepped parts are less expensive to build.

39 There are 7 jack studs – 2 on each end and 3 in the middle.

Stick building	A construction method that uses smaller pieces of wood than traditional timber framing. It also usually implies the house is built on site rather than in a factory.
Stud	A vertical framing member. Most are regular studs. At a rough opening, jack and king studs support the header. (Figure 2)
Subflooring	The sheathing used on top of the floor joists. It supports the finished floor.
T-wall	The intersection of two walls. It's mainly of importance when one of the two walls is part of the building enclosure. The one shown here uses an advanced framing technique that allows insulation behind the intersection. (Figure 2)
Top plate	The horizontal wood framing member at the top of a wall. Most top plates are doubled, with two stacked horizontal boards. The joints in the two top plates are offset for extra strength. Also, a double top plate allows you to overlap the upper top plate in a T-wall to provide extra strength. Some advanced framing uses a single top plate, but that technique requires careful planning. (Figure 2)
Valley	Part of a roof where two sloped sections intersect in a V shape. Because two sections of roof drain to it, valleys collect a lot of water and their drainage must be carefully detailed
Window buck	Wood frame set into a window rough opening. These take on extra significance in houses with exterior insulation as the window buck will protrude beyond the wall sheathing

Figure 4. *This cantilever has open-web floor trusses and blocking to close up the air barrier above the exterior wall.*

Appendix F: Series and Parallel Heat Flow

Chapter 10 touched on series and parallel heat flow. The five kinds of R-value discussion showed that when you factor the effect of framing and windows into the calculation, the R-value decreases. Here, we'll look at the calculations behind those changes.

Calculating with R-values

A house has an enclosure, which separates the conditioned space from the various types of unconditioned spaces (ground, garage, attic, etc.). The enclosure is made up of assemblies. The assemblies are made up of materials. And we start with the materials because that's where the first level of R-value originates. So, let's say we have a wall with insulation between the wood studs, drywall on the inside, and sheathing and cladding on the outside. What's the R-value of the wall? That's where things get tricky because it's not just the R-value of the insulation. I'll outline the important parts here and then get into the details in the sections below.

The insulation in the building cavities typically provides the greatest part of the R-value. In a wall with R-19 insulation, for example, the clear-wall or whole-wall R-value is probably R-19 plus or minus R-2. (See pages 148-9 for definitions of those terms.) That R-value comes from combining the R-values of the materials in two different ways. Some materials are in series, meaning any heat going through the wall has to flow through each layer on its way through. For that type of heat flow, you simply add the R-values.

The other way heat flows is through parallel pathways. For example, some of the heat moving through a wall will go through the cavities, where the insulation is. Another part of the heat flow goes through the framing, where the wood is. To find the combined R-value there, you have to calculate an average. But there's more to it than just averaging the separate R-values. That won't work, as you'll see below.

The key to finding these combined R-values when you have parallel pathways is the relationship between R-value and U-factor.

$R = 1/U$ (F-1)

and

$U = 1/R$ (F-2)

Let's jump in and see how this works.

Layers in series

One way heat flows is layer-by-layer through a building assembly made of multiple materials stacked together. Figure F.1. shows two layers (A and B) separating the warm side from the cool side.

This method of heat flow is pretty simple. All the heat has to flow through each layer. Starting from the warm side (because of the Second Law of Thermodynamics), the heat flows through the pink layer (A), then the grey layer (B). With the caveat about one-dimensional heat flow below, the same amount of heat flows through any section of the assembly.

Series Only

Warm

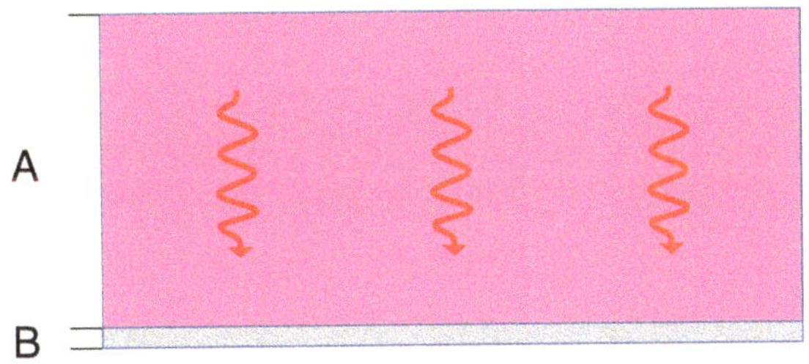

Cool

Figure F.1. *When heat has to flow through a series of different materials, we just add the R-values.*

Now here's that caveat. Heat flow isn't really as simple as I'm making it out to be. To understand complex phenomena, we always start with simplified cases and then add complexity. In reality, heat flows in three dimensions, and we have to consider what happens at the boundaries. For this analysis, though, we're considering heat flow in only one dimension. That means a red arrow represents the same amount of heat flow no matter where it enters the assembly.

If all our assemblies were like this, we'd have an easy time with the math for R-values: All we have to do is add them all together.

Here's the rule:

Series Heat Flow: Add the R-values

And here's the equation:

$R_{total} = R_A + R_B$ (F.3.)

If you've put R-5 foamboard on an R-2 concrete wall, for example, the R-value of the combination is 7. Got more than two layers? Just add them all together: $R_A + R_B + R_C + \ldots$

Parallel pathways

The standard wall, ceiling, or floor assembly, however, isn't just a series of continuous layers. The cavities and the wood framing are two parallel pathways in the main part of the wall. Windows and doors represent more pathways. A header above a window is yet another pathway, different from the studs and plates. (Headers must be treated separately because they're not solid wood. They're often made of two pieces of wood separated by a gap, which is filled sometimes either with insulation or partially with wood spacers.)

Figure F.2. shows the heat flow through two different pathways: the framing of a wall (#1) and an insulated cavity (#2). (We're ignoring the other layers, like drywall and sheathing, for now.) The heat that goes through the insulated cavity (#2) has a harder go of it because insulation is more resistive to heat flow than wood is. The short red arrows in the insulation path indicate the lower rate of heat flow. The rate of heat flow through pathway #1 is higher because the R-value of wood is about three times less than the R-value of typical wall insulation. (The R-value of wood is about 1.1 per inch of depth, whereas fiberglass, cellulose, and open-cell spray foam insulation are about 3.7 per inch.)

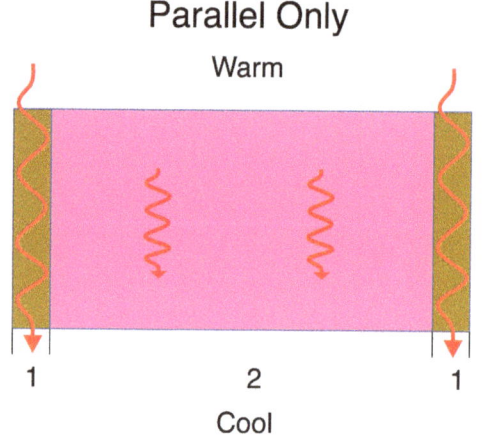

Parallel Only

Warm

1 2 1

Cool

Figure F.2. *When heat flows through parallel pathways, the combined R-value comes from averaging U-factors.*

How do you find the combined R-value of an assembly like this? You can't just average the two R-values. The first problem with that method is that it doesn't consider the different areas of the pathways. In a wall with studs spaced every 16" apart, you've got 1.5" of wood and 14.5" of insulation in each cavity, so there's a lot more area with insulation than with wood. When you add the wood in the bottom plate, top plates, and other framing members, a standard wall has about 23% wood and 77% cavity.

But we can't just do a weighted average of the R-values either. We actually have to go back to the heat flow equation (Q = U x A x ΔT) to figure out how to do it, and it turns out that we have to do a weighted average of the U-values, not the R-values. Once we find the average U-value, we can convert to R-value to find the average resistance to heat flow, using the equation R = 1/U.

Here's the rule:

Parallel Heat Flow: Do an area-weighted average of the U-values

And here's the equation:

$$U_{avg} = \frac{(U_1 \times A_1) + (U_2 \times A_2)}{A_{total}} = \frac{(\frac{1}{R_1} \times A_1) + (\frac{1}{R_2} \times A_2)}{A_{total}} \quad (F.4.)$$

If you've got three or more pathways, you add more terms to the numerator: . . . + (U_3 x A_3) + (U_4 x A_4) + . . . You can add as many terms as you need to include all the parallel pathways. After you've got your average U-value, you can then take the reciprocal (1/U_{avg}) to find the average R-value.

The series and parallel combo

Most building assemblies are a combination of layers in series and pathways in parallel. In a wall, for example, you've got the framing (or insulation) in one layer, then drywall on the inside and sheathing (usually OSB) and cladding on the outside. There are also air films, drainage planes, and sometimes other stuff to add in there, too, but I'll keep it simple here. Once you know this part, you can add in the other layers or more pathways without a problem.

Figure F.3 shows a simple example of a series-and-parallel combination. It could be a ceiling with 2x10 joists, insulation between the joists, and drywall below. (I've ignored air films and other stuff here.)

To solve this, you start by identifying the two parallel pathways, 1 and 2. Then you notice that each pathway is a series of layers, A and B. You add the R-values for each layer and then do a weighted average of the resulting total R-values for the two pathways. Table 1 lays it out.

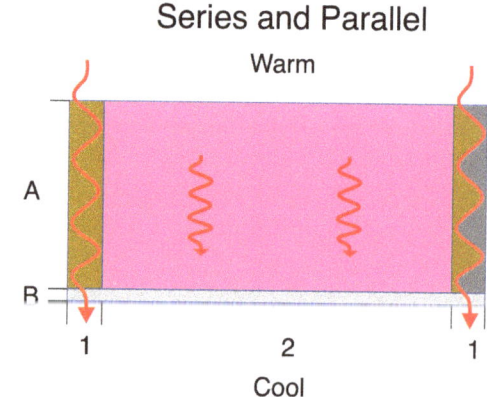

Series and Parallel

Warm

A

B

1 2 1

Cool

Figure F.3. *An example of heat flow through two parallel pathways (1 and 2) and two layers (A and B).*

	Path 1	Path 2
Joists	11.5	—
Insulation	—	30.0
Drywall	0.5	0.5
R_{total}	12.0	30.5
Area (sf)	94	906

Table F.1. *The R-values for the different layers in the two pathways of this example.*

The total R-values are 12.0 for pathway #1 and 30.5 for pathway #2. The areas are 94 and 906 square feet, so to find the average U-value, you'd set up the equation as follows

$$U_{avg} = \frac{(\frac{1}{12} \times 94) + (\frac{1}{30.5} \times 906)}{1,000} = 0.038$$

That gets us most of the way to the answer. We want the average R-value in the end, so we do the reciprocal:

$$R_{avg} = \frac{1}{U_{avg}} = \frac{1}{0.038} = 26.6$$

And that's our answer. We don't have an R-30 ceiling just because that's the R-value of the insulation we installed. We have an R-27 (rounded) ceiling after we consider the heat flow through the different layers and pathways. The wood, with its lower R-value, represents a thermal bridge and reduces the average R-value.

Why windows are rated by U-value

If you've ever wondered why insulation is rated by its R-value and windows are rated by U-value, the difference is materials versus assemblies. Generally speaking, insulation materials are rated by R-value and assemblies are rated by U-value. The reason is that we have to use U-factors to find the combined thermal performance of an assembly, as we've done above.

Assemblies are combinations of layers in series and parallel pathways, so to find a number that characterizes their thermal performance, you do the calculation for average U-value. Rather than taking the next step and calculating the average R-value, manufacturers just report U-value. Not a big deal, especially since we can go between R and U so easily by taking the reciprocal.

The real world is complex

As I pointed out in my caveat above, the real world is more complex than we're making it out to be here. Also, the examples I used in this article are simpler than the analysis usually done to find U-values for assemblies since I've ignored air films, the complexities of framing, and the other layers that are often present.

Knowing the information provided above, you can set up a spreadsheet that allows you to put in the R-values for the various layers in each pathway and see the resultant average U-value and average R-value. If you want to get into more accurate modeling of heat flow, you can use a software tool like THERM or WUFI.

Now that you know the fundamentals, you can start calculating average R-values for building assemblies. Then you'll see how important a little bit of uninsulated area (like the attic pulldown stairs) can be or why it's important to keep your insulation flat, not lumpy. And if you really want to understand thermal bridging, you've got to understand layers and pathways.

Appendix G: More About Heat Pumps

Chapter 13 covered heating and cooling equipment but more needs to be said about heat pumps. In this appendix I'll cover some concepts that are essential to understand if you work with heat pumps. Even if you just use them, you need to understand when to use the emergency heat setting on the thermostat . . . and when not to use it.

The Balance Point for Heating

With furnaces, boilers, and electric resistance heat, the capacity of the heating system isn't affected by the outdoor conditions. In air source heat pumps, however, the source of heat is the outdoor air. And as the outdoor air gets colder, there's less heat available to bring indoors. That means the heating capacity of a heat pump is dependent on the outdoor conditions. In fact, the capacity goes in the opposite direction from the load. Figure G.1 shows the story.

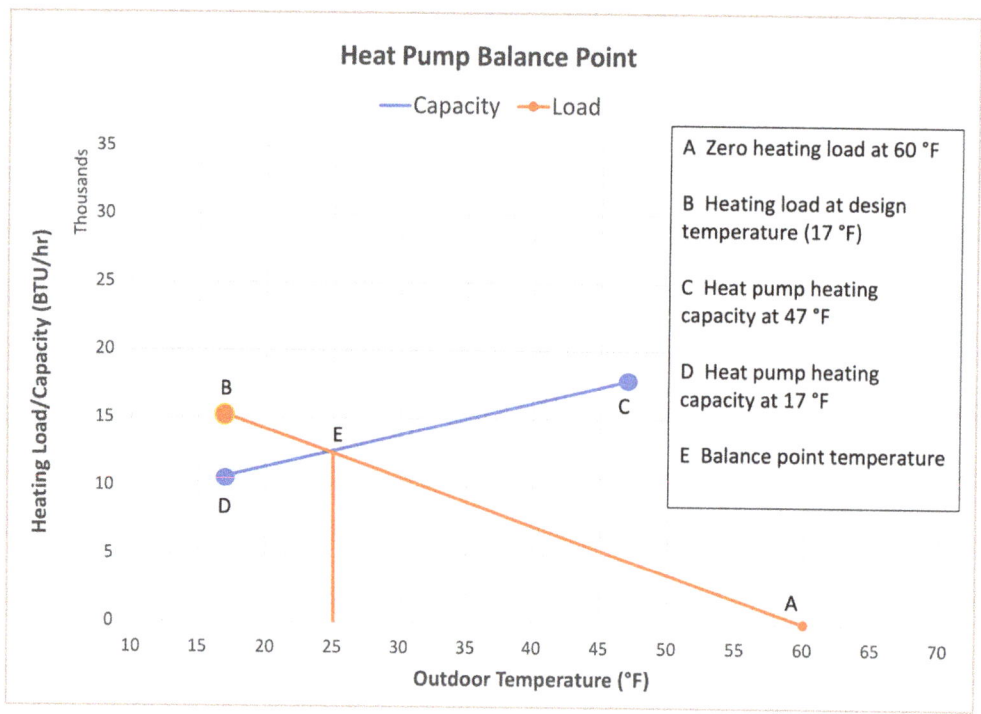

Figure G.1. A graph of a home's heating load combined with the heating capacity of a heat pump shows at what temperature the balance point occurs.

The graph here is a simplification. I drew the home's heating load as a straight line between zero heating load at 65 °F and the result of the load calculation at the home's outdoor design temperature, 17 °F in this case. Then I added the heating capacity of the heat pump, based on the manufacturer's data for the outdoor temperatures of 17 °F and 47 °F. Again, I assumed a linear change in the capacity as the outdoor temperature changes. Neither the load nor the capacity will change in that way, but this simplification is adequate to illustrate the concept of the balance point temperature.

The important points to note about the relationship between heat pump heating capacity and a home's heating load are:

- As the outdoor temperature goes down, the load increases and the capacity decreases.
- At a certain temperature–the balance point–the capacity is equal to the load.
- For outdoor temperatures below the balance point, the home may need supplemental heat.

You can see all of these points illustrated in Fig. G.1. Starting at 65 °F on the horizontal axis and moving to the left (lower temperatures), you can see that the heating load goes from zero (point A) to about 15 kBTU/hr at 17 °F (point B), the outdoor design temperature for this home. Makes total sense. As the temperature drops, the house needs more heat.

At the same time, the capacity of the heat pump goes from 18 kBTU/hr at 47 °F (point C) to about 11 kBTU/hr at 17 °F (point D). Again, it makes sense. As it gets colder outdoors, there's less heat available in the outdoor air.

Those two lines meet at point E, the balance point. That's where the home's heating load is equal to the capacity of the heat pump. For outdoor temperatures above the balance point, the heat pump can provide more than enough heat for the home. For temperatures below the balance point, the heat pump can't keep up with the heating needs for the home (at least on paper). I'll come back to the issue of the capacity being below the load in the next section.

Changing the Balance Point

For conventional heat pumps, the balance point is often in the mid-30s Fahrenheit. That's not a given, though. The balance for a home can be significantly lower than that or even up in the 40s or 50s Fahrenheit. Why? Because the balance point depends on the efficiency of the house (heating load) and on the size of the heat pump (heating capacity).

One way to get a lower balance point is to make the house more energy efficient. That moves the load curve down and the balance point to the left. The other would be to increase the equipment size. Of course, if you do either of these, it benefits your heating efficiency, but you may end up with an oversized cooling system.

Let's say you want a heat pump that can provide all the heat you need at the outdoor design temperature. In the home shown in Fig. G.1, for example, a heat pump rated at 30 kBTU/hr instead 18 kBTU/hr would do that. The blue line would move up, and point D would be higher than point B.

Similarly, we could move the orange line down by insulating, air-sealing, or making other improvements to the house that would reduce the heating load. And as with a bigger heat pump, a more efficient house would move the balance point to the left on the graph.

Lowering the balance point is great for heating. If that were the only consideration, we could make the house as efficient as possible and then put in a heat pump big enough to ensure the balance point is below the design temperature. The problem, however, is that oversizing can have a deleterious effect on cooling, especially in humid climates. You need equipment sized close to the cooling load to get good dehumidification. Even in a dry climate, oversizing affects comfort negatively because the system comes on and goes off more frequently (short-cycling).

The good news is that many inverter-driven mini-split heat pumps can get you a lower balance point without the negative effect on cooling. Some of them provide the same heating capacity at 5 °F—or even lower—as they do at 47 °F.

Supplemental, Auxiliary, and Emergency Heat

The balance point discussion above raised an important issue. If your heat pump can't provide as much heat as your load calculation says you need, what do you do? In Fig. G.1, the difference between point B and point D (when B is higher than D) is the deficit in heating capacity. The house needs about 4 kBTU/hr more heat than the heat pump can provide. That's the amount of heat you need to supplement to the heat pump to meet the heating load at design conditions.

Let me define three related terms here to help clarify this topic:

> **Supplemental heat** – the amount of additional heating capacity needed to make up the difference between the heating load and the heating capacity at design conditions
> **Auxiliary heat** – the amount of additional heating installed with the heat pump
> **Emergency heat** – the amount of additional heating installed to heat the house when the heat pump stops working

One of these definitions is not like the others. The auxiliary heat is what's actually installed. Supplemental and emergency heat are uses for the auxiliary heat.

In most heat pumps, electric resistance heating serves as the auxiliary heat. It's easy to install but it also is the source of a great many high-bills complaints received by electric utilities. If the thermostat isn't wired properly, it can run when it's not supposed to. I've heard of cases where it was even running in summer, making it really hard for the heat pump to cool the house.

And there's the bad advice given out by people who don't understand heat pumps (even some in the HVAC industry). Because the balance point is usually in the 30s Fahrenheit, some people advise homeowners to turn the thermostat to the emergency heat setting whenever it's cold outside. And cold could mean below 40 °F. (Yes, I've run into that.) When you set the thermostat to emergency heat, you're turning off the more efficient heat pump and using only expensive strip heat to heat the whole house. Don't do that! Let the heat pump do as much heating as it can and then use the auxiliary heat only to supplement the heat pump.

Electric resistance heat isn't the only source of auxiliary heat, though. A hydronic coil connected to the water heat is another way to get that extra heat. (See the hydronic air handler section in chapter 13.) With inverter-driven heat pumps that provide full capacity at really low temperatures, you may not need any auxiliary heat. By having multiple zones each served by separate heat pumps, you have built-in redundancy and may not need a separate emergency heat system. If one heat pump goes out, you can use the ones that still work.

Do Heat Pumps Work in Cold Climates?

I won't keep you in suspense. Of course heat pumps work in cold climates. Thousands of homes in Canada, New England, and elsewhere are testament to their ability to keep a house warm. Let me give you an example.

Gary Nelson, shown in Fig. G.2, cofounded The Energy Conservatory and has played a huge role in infiltration and duct leakage testing. He has lived in the same Minneapolis home for several decades, making many improvements to it over the years. After a large renovation in 2017, he installed a ducted mini-split heat pump. The conditioned floor area is about 2,500 square feet, is extremely airtight and insulated. He also put in super-duper windows (triple-pane, argon-filled, 3 low-e coatings).

The result of those improvements is that his heating load is a mere 18 kBTU/hr. In square feet per ton (see chapter 12), that would be about 1,700. That's a low-load home in a really cold climate. How has it done?

In their first winter with the heat pump, they had a low temperature of -15 °F, which is 5 degrees below their design temperature of -10 °F. The heat pump had no trouble keeping the house at their setpoint of 72 °F. In the second winter, the outdoor low was -27 °F. The indoor temperature dropped to 62 °F, but that's because they were away. If they had been home, he told me, the additional heat from the internal loads would have raised the temperature. And if that hadn't gotten it warm enough, they would have baked some cookies! Nelson's home is just one of many successful stories of heat pumps in cold climates.

The keys to successful incorporation of heat pumps in cold climates are enclosure improvements, an accurate load calculation, cold-

Fig. G.2. Gary Nelson heats his Minneapolis home with a heat pump and no auxiliary heat.

climate heat pumps, and good contractors. You can heat a leaky, poorly insulated house with heat pumps, but it's harder. Make the house more airtight, add insulation, and perhaps improve the windows, and you'll be happier with the lower-temperature heat provided by a heat pump. Once you've done that, find out how much heat the house needs with a load calculation done by a professional.

The next steps involve choosing the right kind of heat pump and a good contractor to install it. Make sure to choose models designed for cold climates. Ideally, that means choosing a heat pump that can provide its full heating capacity down to very low temperatures. Finding a good contractor is also important. Look for those who are certified by the manufacturer, recommended by others, and have a lot of experience with heat pumps. Ask prospective contractors about their attitudes toward heat pumps. Quite a few don't like them and don't understand them, so you want to find that out before hiring them.

Index

Note: Page numbers followed by f indicate figures; those followed by t indicate tables; those followed by n indicate footnotes.

Acknowledgments

In the "without whom this book could not have been written" category, there's only one possible person to name. (Okay, there are two, but it would be in poor taste to acknowledge myself here.) The person who, above all else, made this book possible is Jeffrey Sauls. He's my right-hand man at Energy Vanguard and has done a masterful job keeping the company running during the two years I've focused on writing this book. And that's no small feat in a time when we had the COVID-19 pandemic, too. He's also the person I most frequently ask questions, bounce ideas off of, and seek feedback from.

Mike Barcik has been a friend, mentor, and co-worker since I took a home energy rater class with him in 2003. I later had the good fortune to be able to teach a great many of those weeklong training classes with him from 2008 to 2010. Getting to listen to him in those classes was when I really started understanding building science. He also was the inspiration for one of my most popular blog articles: "Naked People Need Building Science."

Joseph Lstiburek, PhD, PE, has been a mentor, supporter, and friend for more than a decade now. He has been generous with his time and his intellectual property, letting me use a bunch of his classic images in this book. He also has generously made one of the most valuable collections of building science knowledge available for free at the Building Science Corporation website (buildingscience.com). After a memorable evening in Denver, though, I will never again try to keep up with him in drinking Scotch whisky.

Liz Seiberling deserves a big mention here, too. She was my thesis advisor in graduate school, but the reason I'm acknowledging her here is that while I was working on my doctoral research with her, she was designing and building an off-the-grid home in central Florida. It was completely solar-powered, and she had a well, greywater system, and composting toilet, too. Oh! And she and her husband bought a sawmill and cut the lumber for the house themselves. (You can find info about the house by searching her name and "solar cracker.") She was the inspiration behind my building a house in Georgia, which launched me into my career in building science.

I owe a tremendous debt of gratitude to the folks who gave me feedback on the manuscript of this book: JR Babineau, Mike Barcik, Roy Collver, Lorraine Conard, Roy Crawford, Aaron Grin, Lew Harriman, Kevin Hart, Gary Klein, Gary Nelson, Elaine Roberts, David Treleven, Kohta Ueno, and Larry Weingarten. Their insights helped make this book better.

Many, many others helped me in one way or another over the past two decades, and there are too many to thank here. A few that come to mind, though, are Kristof Irwin, Marcus Bianchi, Amanda Hatherly, John Semmelhack, Mike MacFarland, Martin Holladay, Marc Rosenbaum, Gavin Healy, Dan Perunko, Katrin Klingenberg, John Straube, Lloyd Alter, Sam Rashkin, David Butler, Nikki Krueger, Kohta Ueno, David Hill, Danko Davidovic, Kimberly Llewellyn, Foster Lyons, David Wasserman, Arlan Burdick, Gary Nelson, Gary Klein, Larry Weingarten, Claudette Reichel, Mac Sheldon, John Rockwell, Skylar Swinford, Alexander "Andy" Bell, Peter Troast, Bryan Orr, Sydney Roberts, Carl Seville, Michael Anschel, Dick Kornbluth, and Chris Van Rite.

A bunch of people helped by allowing me to use their excellent images in this book: 475 High Performance Building Supply, Todd Abercrombie, AirCycler, the Air Duct Council, Robert Bean, Jim Breitenbach, BuildRight/Malco, Erik Daugherty, David Goulding, Erik Henson, Home Innovation Research Labs, Luis Imery, Dan Kolbert, Joseph Lstiburek, Mike MacFarland, Danny Orlando, ROCKWOOL, Albert Rooks, John Semmelhack,

Southface, Bill Spohn, Taunton Press, The Energy Conservatory, and Chris Timusk.

For the second printing, the following studious readers sent me several good suggestions that are now incorporated into this book. Those people are: Martin Holladay, Greg Goodman, Robert Jordan, Dan Levy, Donald Brodsky, Paul Little, Mike Wiese, Mike Murphy, and Conrad Maillet.

I kicked off this project in March 2020 by doing a crowdfunding campaign through Publishizer. The result was 1,002 pre-orders from 505 different people. The top investors were:

Champion: Passive House Alliance Austin (100 copies)

Boosters: Bryan Orr, Dan Goss, Jarrett Davis (50 copies each)

Advocates: Rickie Sims, Skylar Swinford, Keith Graff, Eileen O'Hara, Dustin Cole, Kevin McNeely, Reuben Saltzman, Mark Garrity, Jeffrey Flaherty, Brian Rauch, Dennis Celsor, Francisco Navarro, Steve Saunders (10 copies each)

Supporters: David James, Griffin Hagle, Alex Williams, Marcus Bianchi, David Leopold, Phil Brown, Doug Hunt, John Holahan, William Spohn, Jeffrey Sadler, John Semmelhack, Walter Pappas (6 copies each)

On the mechanics of publishing this book, my publisher and editor, Jennifer Bright, has been stellar. Her quick responses and excellent suggestions have been a tremendous benefit.

Finally, my wife, Elaine Roberts, has supported me through thick and thin with this project (and more), even though it meant that the basement of our house remained a mess until the book was done. And she also read through the whole manuscript with her poet's eyes, helping to make it more readable to lay people and professionals alike.

About the Author

Allison A. Bailes III, PhD, has been called "a well-known troublemaker and a general pain in the ass" by his friend Joseph Lstiburek, PhD, PE. He writes the widely read Energy Vanguard Blog, where he has been stirring up trouble since 2010. After earning a doctorate in physics from the University of Florida and doing time in academia, Dr. Bailes found his calling in the field of building science. Since 2001, he has done everything from building a high-performance home to serving as regional manager for the EarthCraft House green building program to spending countless hours in crawl spaces and attics, analyzing and fixing homes. His company, Energy Vanguard, does consulting, training, and HVAC design for residential buildings.

www.ingramcontent.com/pod-product-compliance
Lightning Source LLC
Chambersburg PA
CBHW041109120626
46547CB00019B/2645